THE OXFORD HISTORY
OF ENGLAND

Edited by SIR GEORGE CLARK

FROM
DOMESDAY BOOK
TO
MAGNA CARTA
1087–1216

BY

AUSTIN LANE POOLE, D.Litt.

SECOND EDITION

Oxford   New York

OXFORD UNIVERSITY PRESS

Oxford University Press, Walton Street, Oxford OX2 6DP

Oxford New York
Athens Auckland Bangkok Bombay
Calcutta Cape Town Dar es Salaam Delhi
Florence Hong Kong Istanbul Karachi
Kuala Lumpur Madras Madrid Melbourne
Mexico City Nairobi Paris Singapore
Taipei Tokyo Toronto

and associated companies in
Berlin Ibadan

Oxford is a trade mark of Oxford University Press

© Oxford University Press 1951

First published 1951 as volume three of The Oxford History of England
Second edition 1955
First paperback edition 1993

British Library Cataloguing in Publication Data
Data available

Library of Congress Cataloging in Publication Data
Poole, Austin Lane, 1889-1963.
Domesday book to Magna Carta, 1087-1216 / by Austin Lane Poole.—
1st pbk. ed.
p. cm.
'First published 1951 as volume three of The Oxford history of
England'—T.p. verso.
Includes bibliographical references and index.
ISBN 0-19-285287-6 (alk. paper) : £10.95
1. Great Britain—History—Norman period, 1066-1154. 2. Great
Britain—History—Angevin period, 1154-1216. 3. Domesday book.
4. Magna Carta. I. Title.
942.02—dc20   DA195.P66 1993   92-32686 CIP
ISBN 0-19-285287-6

5 7 9 10 8 6 4

Printed in Great Britain by
Biddles Ltd
Guildford and King's Lynn

PREFACE TO SECOND EDITION

IN this edition, beyond the correction of obvious mistakes, there has been little change of substance except in Chapter V where the discovery by Professor R. A. B. Mynors of the lost ending of the *Gesta Stephani*, the most important narrative source for the history of the Anarchy, has necessitated important alterations. References in the footnotes have been given to new editions, especially to the valuable series of *Medieval Texts* in the course of publication by Messrs. Nelson, and the more important books published in recent years have been included in the Bibliography. The maps which in some cases were unsatisfactory have been improved.

I should like to take this opportunity to thank Mr. Howard Colvin, Mr. J. O. Prestwich, and other friends who have kindly drawn my attention to some mistakes in the previous edition.

A. L. P.

ST. JOHN'S COLLEGE
OXFORD
12 *August* 1954

PREFACE TO FIRST EDITION

THIS book has occupied the leisure hours of some twenty years of my life which has been principally engaged in teaching and administration. This prolonged period of gestation may be reflected by some unevenness in the treatment of the several chapters and perhaps also by some change of emphasis developed in the course of my studies. I have already set out in my *Obligations of Society in the XII and XIII Centuries* (published in 1946) evidence and illustrations of certain matters discussed in chapters 1, 2, and 12. While this has enabled me to reduce the bulk of the present volume, a small amount of overlapping in the two books has been unavoidable.

I have had the great benefit of the advice of the authors of the preceding and succeeding volumes in this series, Sir Frank Stenton and Sir Maurice Powicke, and of the general editor; and many other friends have given me help in the preparation of this book. To all these I wish to convey my deep sense of gratitude. More particularly I am under very great obligations to Professor V. H. Galbraith, who read much of the book in manuscript, and to Lady Stenton, who read the whole of it in proof. It would be impossible adequately to express how much I owe to these two scholars. I can only offer them my most sincere thanks for their help and for placing their great knowledge so generously at my disposal.

A. L. P.

ST. JOHN'S COLLEGE
OXFORD
24 *February* 1951

CONTENTS

I. GOVERNMENT AND SOCIETY

III. TOWNS AND TRADE

IV. THE CONQUEST OF NORMANDY
(1087–1135)

V. THE ANARCHY
(1135–1154)

VI. CHURCH AND STATE: ANSELM

VII. CHURCH AND STATE: BECKET

VIII. LEARNING, LITERATURE, AND ART

IX. THE CELTIC FRINGE

(a) SCOTLAND

(b) WALES

X. THE ANGEVIN EMPIRE
(1154–1189)

XI. THE LOSS OF NORMANDY
(1189–1204)

XII. JUSTICE AND FINANCE

xiv CONTENTS

XIII. KING JOHN AND THE INTERDICT
(1204–1213)

XIV. KING JOHN AND THE CHARTER
(1213–1216)

LIST OF MAPS

I
GOVERNMENT AND SOCIETY

W E are concerned in this book with the history of England during the reigns of the six kings who followed William the Conqueror—his two sons, William Rufus and Henry I, his grandson Stephen, and the early Plantagenets, Henry II and his two sons Richard I and John. The period also covers the years between two of the most famous documents of English history, we might say of all medieval history for they are unique, unparalleled in Europe—Domesday Book and Magna Carta. The accession of one bad king in 1087 and the death of another in 1216 are purely incidental and of little or no historical importance; the documents mark epochs. Widely as they differ in character (and perhaps they have nothing else in common than their fame) they are alike in this: succeeding generations appealed to them as monuments only a little less authoritative than the Bible.[1]

The hundred and thirty years which separate Domesday Book and Magna Carta witness the growth of a nation. William the Conqueror was king of the Anglo-Normans (*Rex Norm-Anglorum* as a writer of the early twelfth century describes him);[2] John was king of England (*rex Angliae*). The 'description' of England (*descriptio* was the official title of the great survey which we know as Domesday Book) relates to a country inhabited by two peoples, a small dominant Norman aristocracy and the English natives. The kings of the twelfth century in their writs address their subjects as 'French and English'. The Great Charter has nothing to say of French or Normans; the English alone are the recipients of John's concessions. Gradually during the twelfth century the dividing barriers are broken down. Henry I, who married a Scottish princess, Matilda, English by upbringing,

---

[1] The first known occasion on which Domesday Book was used as legal evidence is in a suit of the abbot of Abingdon concerning Lewknor (Oxon.) where the matter is determined at a court held at Winchester by reference to the *Liber de Thesauro* (*Chron. Mon. de Abingdon*, ii. 116) quoted by Round, *Feudal England*, pp. 142–4. It may be dated either between 1108 and 1109 or between 1111 and 1113. For a later instance cf. *Curia Regis Rolls*, i. 263 (1200), where a certain Robert 'ponit se super rotulum Wintonie'. For the use made of Domesday in the years immediately following its compilation see V. H. Galbraith, *Herefordshire Domesday* (Pipe Roll Society, New Series, vol. xxv), Introduction.

[2] *Chronica* in *Liber Mon. de Hyda* (Rolls Series), p. 297.

encouraged the process of blending: 'by intermarriage and by every means in his power', says Walter Map, 'he bound the two peoples into a firm union'.[1] Although the process was slow, and in 1157 the justiciar, Richard de Lucy, can still speak of 'us Normans' and of protection 'against the wiles of the English', nevertheless in the later part of the century we are told that among the free population it was well nigh impossible to tell whether a man was Norman or English.[2]

But at first, as William of Malmesbury deplores,[3] the Normans had it all their own way; they were the governing class, the feudal society, and at their head there was an all but absolute king. The position is brought out with striking force by an analysis of the distribution of land as revealed by Domesday Book. The total annual value (exclusive of the towns and of course of the four northern shires which were not included in the survey) has been estimated in round numbers at £73,000, the great bulk of which came from the southern and eastern parts of the country. Of this sum the king and his family received £17,650; his servants and officials, the king's sergeants, £1,800; the church £19,200; and some few trusted Englishmen £4,000. The remainder, amounting to a sum of £30,350, was apportioned out into some 170 baronies as rewards for the Normans who had shared in the enterprise of conquest.[4] From these figures it is obvious that wealth and power (which was then the same thing) were in the hands of the few—the king, his barons, and perhaps we should add, the church.

The king, as we have said, was almost absolute; not as the early Stuart kings claimed to be absolute by virtue of a theory of divine hereditary right, for no such theory was recognized in the eleventh or twelfth centuries. The principle of primogeniture, for which Henry II strove, was only established in the thirteenth century. Before this, succession to the throne was governed by no one rule, but was influenced by a number of considerations: kinship with the royal house (which was deemed essential), popular election (which often merely confirmed an accomplished fact), designation by the late king, and personal

[1] *De Nugis Curialium*, v, c. 5.
[2] *Chron. de Bello*, pp. 88–9; *Dialogus de Scaccario*, I. x.
[3] *Gesta Regum*, i. 278 (§ 227).
[4] The figures are those of W. J. Corbett in *Camb. Med. Hist.* v. 507–8.

fitness all played their part. Although the theory of inheritance was gaining ground under the influence of feudal ideas and the practical example of France, in fact of the six kings who followed the Conqueror, Richard I alone succeeded in accordance with the strict rule of hereditary succession, and the title of four of them was challenged by a rival. Until the chosen successor was crowned he was merely *dominus*, the territorial lord and head of the feudal state; after his coronation he became *rex* with all the attributes of regality.[1] From his coronation he began to reign; his regnal years (until the time of Edward I) were reckoned from the day of coronation; and from the coronation rites, and especially from the anointing, he derived divine authority.[2] The anointed king ceased to be merely a layman, but took on a sacerdotal character; he was king *dei gratia*,[3] he was God's vicar, *rex et sacerdos*. The divine source of temporal as well as spiritual power was admitted everywhere in Christian Europe although various interpretations might be placed on how that power should be exercised. The most extreme and outspoken advocate of royal supremacy, a twelfth-century author commonly known as the 'Anonymous of York', who wrote in defence of Henry I in his conflict with Anselm, regarded the king as on a higher plane than the priest, and so argued that he had a right to interfere in ecclesiastical matters.[4] But even John of Salisbury, who belonged to the party of the church reformers, was equally convinced that the king derived his authority from God, and elaborated his doctrine in the most coherent treatise on political philosophy produced in the middle ages, the *Policraticus*, the statesman's book.[5] The lawyers took the same attitude. Both

[1] The Empress Matilda (who was never crowned) usually adopted the style *Anglorum domina*. Both Richard I and John in the interval between their election and coronation use the title *dominus Angliae*. Cf. Round, *Geoffrey de Mandeville*, pp. 70 ff.; *Ancient Charters* (Pipe Roll Soc., vol. x), no. 55. *Curia Regis Rolls*, i. 255, 384.

[2] For the significance of the coronation see P. E. Schramm, *A History of the English Coronation* (1937), *passim*.

[3] This was used by Stephen and Henry II in their charters of Liberties (*Statutes of the Realm*, pp. 3–4) and was adopted as a regular part of the royal style in charters issued after May 1172. Cf. R. L. Poole, *Studies in Chronology and History*, pp. 302–7, where the arguments of Léopold Delisle, who first marked this change of style, are summarized and discussed.

[4] In his treatise 'De consecratione Pontificum et Regum' (*Mon. Germ. Hist.*, *Libelli de Lite*, iii. 667) the following passage occurs: 'Potestas enim regis potestas Dei est, Dei quidem est per naturam, regis per gratiam. Unde et rex Deus et Christus est, sed per gratiam, et quicquid facit non homo simpliciter, sed Deus factus et Christus per gratiam facit.'

[5] It was completed in 1159, that is to say, before the *Politics* of Aristotle was known

Glanvill and Bracton believed that the king represented God, although the latter, writing in the thirteenth century after the subjects' right of resistance to a tyrant had been vindicated in the reign of John, was careful to explain how in fact this power should be restrained.

This sacrosanct position of royalty the Norman and Angevin kings did all they could to exploit. The idea of ruler-worship, expressed in liturgical *laudes* before the crowned king, travelled from Byzantium to the west, and with the Normans was adopted in England.[1] A celebrated passage in the Peterborough chronicle[2] recalls how

'thrice he [William I] wore his crown every year, as often as he was in England; at Easter he wore it at Winchester; at Whitsuntide at Westminster; at Midwinter at Gloucester; and then were with him all the rich men over all England, archbishops and suffragan bishops, abbots and earls, thegns and knights'.

Convenience of business and pleasure made it impossible to adhere rigidly to the practice of holding the feasts at the regular places named by the chronicler. But they were strictly observed by kings wherever they happened to be. Henry I, it is recorded, thrice wore his crown in a wooden chapel at Brampton in Huntingdonshire, where he intended, it appears, to establish a royal seat.[3] These occasions were bound up with ritual and pageantry; feasting and frivolity. The litany *Christus vincit, Christus regnat, Christus imperat* was chanted before the king,[4] and a group of sergeants had special duties to perform in connexion with the ceremonies.[5] At these great crown-wearings the king exhibited himself in all his glory, and impressed on the minds of his subjects the dignity of the crowned monarch.[6] Henry I

in western Europe. It represents, therefore, the purely medieval point of view. For a discussion of his views on kingship see J. Dickinson, *Speculum*, i (1926), 308.

[1] For the liturgical importance and ritual of the crown-wearing see E. H. Kantorowicz, *Laudes Regiae* (1946), especially pp. 93-101 and pp. 171-9.

[2] Anglo-Saxon Chronicle, *sub anno* 1187.

[3] *Curia Regis Rolls*, vii. 349-50. He planned to build the chapel of stone and also to provide lodgings for his barons (*hospitia baronum*), ibid. He spent Christmas 1120 at Brampton (Henry of Huntingdon, p. 243) and a number of charters are dated from there. See Farrer, *An Outline Itinerary of Henry I*, Index, under Brampton.

[4] The payment of 25s. to the royal chaplains who sang the *Christus vincit* on the great feasts is frequently entered on the accounts of the exchequer. The earliest entry is on the Pipe Roll of 34 Henry II (p. 19). The entries are collected by Kantorowicz, op. cit., p. 174.

[5] Cf. A. L. Poole, *Obligations of Society*, pp. 65-6.

[6] The statement of Stubbs (*Const. Hist.* i. 562) followed by Round (*King's*

claimed and exercised the supposed power to heal the scrofula. The widespread belief in the thaumaturgical power of kings seems to have developed from traditions of the time of Edward the Confessor who is said to have learnt and practised the art in Normandy; and popular faith in the healing art became in the twelfth century so firmly rooted that it was transmitted as an attribute of royalty down to the days of Queen Anne who touched Samuel Johnson for the scrofula.[1] Henry II persuaded the pope, Alexander III, in 1161 to canonize the most venerable of his ancestors, Edward the Confessor, and so exalted the English king in this respect above his continental contemporaries, none of whom could claim descent from a saint.[2] The cult of St. Edward, whose life was rewritten by the most eminent hagiographers of the twelfth century, gave solidity and prestige to the Anglo-Norman monarchy.

But just as it was at his coronation that the king acquired divine authority, so too it was at his coronation that he imposed upon himself limitations to his power. By the oath taken at his coronation he bound himself by obligations to his subjects. He promised that the church and the people should keep true peace; that he would forbid rapacity and iniquity; and that he would show equity and mercy in all his judgements. We have seen, however, that the succession to the throne was often uncertain, often disputed. In these circumstances the bishops and barons were able to require in return for their support more explicit promises than those contained in the vague phrases of the coronation oath. The oath was expanded into a 'charter of liberties'. These charters, issued in turn by Henry I, Stephen,

Sergeants, p. 202) and Schramm (*English Coronation*, p. 58) that Henry II gave up the solemn crown-wearings after 1158 rests on insufficient evidence. The chanting of *Christus vincit* on Whit-Sunday, 1188, referred to in note 4 above, implies a crown-wearing, and there is good evidence for the practice under John and Henry III.

[1] On this subject see the elaborate monograph by Marc Bloch, *Les Rois thaumaturges: Étude sur le caractère surnaturel attribué à la puissance royale particulièrement en France et en Angleterre* (1924). Owing, however, to a mistaken belief that the *Vita Edwardi* (ed. Luard, Rolls Series) on which he relies, was not written before 1103, Bloch argued that the idea of the royal power of healing was first introduced into England under the influence of Henry I. See R. W. Southern, *Eng. Hist. Rev.* lviii (1943), 385 ff., where he gives good reasons for supposing the life to have been written by Goscelin within a very few years of the Confessor's death. Cf. also Eleanor K. Heningham in *Speculum*, xxi (1946), 438, n. 76, and 451, n. 134.

[2] The canonization of Charles the Great which Frederick Barbarossa obtained in 1165 failed in effect, for it was the work of an anti-pope. France had to wait for its sainted monarch till after the death of Louis IX.

and Henry II, are of fundamental importance in English constitutional history; they placed the king under the law. The king pledged himself to abolish 'evil customs' and to restore the 'law of King Edward', the good law of the past. Reciprocally his subjects took the oath of allegiance. Both king and people were thus bound by mutual obligations.[1]

How far these restraints were effective in limiting the royal power depended largely on the character of the king. Monarchy in the twelfth century was essentially personal, even patriarchal. 'The prince', wrote John of Salisbury,[2] 'is controlled by the judgement of his mind alone', and the lawyers were fond of quoting the familiar text from Roman law 'quod principi placet legis habet vigorem'.[3] Such expressions seem to reflect the real nature of the Anglo-Norman kingship. The little writ— a legacy from the Anglo-Saxon chancery—by which the king issued his instructions, is framed in a very personal and peremptory form and bears the stamp of the autocrat:

'William king of the English to N. the sheriff, greeting. I command you that you cause bishop Remigius and his canons to have their church of Kirton with the tithes which belong to it and of Hibaldstow likewise, as they better held it in the time of my father. And see that for want of justice I shall hear no further complaint about the matter. Witness the bishop of Durham; by William Warelwast'.[4]

The king does not merely reign, he governs. Political and constitutional development depended therefore to a great extent on the vigour and personality of the king himself. He appointed his own officers in church and state; he conducted his own foreign policy, declared war, generally led his own army, and made his own peace. He had his own independent income on which he was expected to live and to carry on the affairs of state. It was a feudal income derived chiefly from the crown lands, the recognized feudal dues, and certain arbitrary taxes known as tallages, which could be imposed on the towns in the royal demesne, on his unfree tenants, and on the Jews. There were

---

[1] Cf. Glanvill, ix. 4: 'Mutua quidem debet esse dominii et homagii fidelitatis connexio, ita quod quantum homo debet domino ex homagio, tantum illi debet dominus ex dominio praeter solam reverentiam.'

[2] *Policraticus*, v. 6.

[3] So Glanvill, Prologue.

[4] Writ of William Rufus (1087–8). *Registrum Antiquissimum of the Cathedral Church of Lincoln* (ed. C. W. Foster), i. 15; Davis, *Regesta Anglo-Normannorum*, no. 305.

also the profits of justice. These were substantial, for the king's court was not merely a court for his own immediate tenants and for suitors who failed to obtain justice in a lower court, but it took cognizance of an ever-increasing number of cases in which he, as head of the state, was interested—the pleas of the Crown. The peace is the king's peace, and he must take cognizance of any matter that can be regarded as a breach of the peace. The kings of this period were slowly training a bench of judges, but the court held before the king himself remained the supreme court of justice. In the famous Battle abbey suits, which are fully reported,[1] we hear of Henry II constantly intervening, rebuking one or other of the parties and calling them to order; and he was said to be so just in his judgements that whoever had a good case was anxious to have it tried before him, whereas whoever had a bad one would not come before him unless he was dragged.[2] King John took a lively interest in the administration of justice; rolls of pleas heard before him survive and the rolls of his justices frequently record that a case must be postponed until he can be present in person or be spoken to about it.

There is no capital, no permanent seat of government, such as London and Westminster afterwards became. The king moves ceaselessly from place to place about England or his continental dominions, seldom staying anywhere for more than a few days or a week, and holding his court at some royal castle, an abbey, or a hunting-box, at Rockingham, Bury St. Edmunds, or Clarendon; and with him moved also all the paraphernalia of government—his treasure, his business documents, his chancellor and clerks with their writing materials, and the multifarious staff of his household. This ambulatory court, living on the country through which it passed, was a cause of serious grievance. In the time of Rufus it was undisciplined and licentious; and such was the terror that its coming inspired that the inhabitants, we are told, would hide themselves in the woods and other places until the danger had passed. Henry I did something to improve this state of affairs, and besides imposing severe punishments on offenders, assigned definite subsistence allowances to each member of the court.[3]

[1] *Chron. de Bello*, pp. 84 ff.
[2] Walter Map, *De Nugis*, v, c. 7.
[3] Eadmer, *Hist. Nov.* 192. Walter Map, *De Nugis*, v, c. 5. Haskins (*Norman Institutions*, p. 115) points out that some of the allowances are earlier than Henry I's edict and 'written customs'.

The close association of the ordinary work of government with the domestic life of the king is strikingly illustrated by the organization (which can be traced to a Frankish origin) of the royal household. Its composition in the time of the Norman kings is known from a curious record, drawn up shortly after Henry I's death, the *Constitutio Domus Regis*, the establishment of the king's household.[1] Here official business and finance, provision for the chapel and the secretarial work, cooking and eating, fighting and hunting are strangely intermixed. There are great officers of state like the steward and the constable; there are menials like scullions, a laundress, and a hearth-boy. To each were allotted allowances of bread, wine, and candles, and also wages which were adjusted according to whether they lived in or went home for their meals. Some of these officials either in addition or instead of wages were tenants in sergeanty, holding lands in virtue of their offices. At the head of the list is the chancellor, the chief of the royal chaplains, with a stipend of 5s. a day and an allowance of one lord's simnel cake, two salted simnels, a measure of clear and a measure of ordinary wine, one thick wax candle and forty bits of candle. At the lower end of the scale we have the watchmen who have double rations and 1½d. a day for their men and four candles; in addition they have in the morning a couple of loaves, one dish, and a gallon of beer. Like the chancellor the other heads of departments, the steward, the chamberlain, the butler, and the constable[2] had the maximum stipend, but only if they ate *extra domum*; if *intra domum* they had 3s. 6d. The steward (*dapifer*) had charge of the hall (*aula*) and all that pertained to it including the kitchen, pantry, and larder, each of which had a master dispenser at its head, while the chamberlain (*camerarius*) presided over the chamber (*camera*) with his staff which included the bearer of the king's bed, the king's tailor, and the ewerer (*aquarius*) who dried the king's clothes and prepared his bath. These two divisions, the hall and the chamber, with the chapel, were the component parts of the king's house roughly corresponding to the state apartments and the private apartments of the modern palace. Next to the chamberlain came the treasurer which recalls the fact that the

---

[1] The text is in the *Black Book of the Exchequer* (ed. Hearne), pp. 341–59 and in the *Red Book of the Exchequer* (ed. Hall), pp. 807–13 . See also G. H. White, *Trans. R. Hist. Soc.*, 4th ser., xxx (1948), 127–55 and *Antiquaries Journal*, xxx (1950), 52.

[2] Until the end of the twelfth century there were several stewards and constables who served in turn in the household.

royal treasure in primitive times was kept in a chest in his bed-room. The wine and dessert were under the care of the chief butler (*pincerna*) with a staff of cellarers, cupbearers, and fruiterers. The constable had general supervision of the outdoor staff especially, as his name implies, the stables; and with him was associated the marshal, an official at this time of a lower rank, to whom was entrusted the duty of maintaining order and discipline at court. In their department were ranged all the servants connected with the royal sport, the keepers of hounds, keepers of the king's mews (breeding-pens for hawks), and the various hunt servants, stag-hunters, wolf-hunters, cat-hunters (*catatores*). They also controlled the king's bodyguard of archers. And yet, somewhat incongruously, both the constable and the marshal had seats and special duties at the exchequer, the former was supposed to witness writs, the latter to supply receipts (*tallies*) for gifts and liveries made from the treasury and the chamber. The itinerant character of the twelfth-century court is indicated by the provision of carters and packhorses for each department.

This medley of ministers and menials recorded in the *Constitutio Domus Regis* is not of mere antiquarian interest. The king's household, his *familia*, was the nursery-school of states-men; within it promotion was easy to the man of administrative ability.[1] Many who came into prominence in the government of church and state started life as royal chaplains; at least one bishop reached his exalted position from the king's larder.[2] Further, it was the centre of administration and the source from which all government departments developed.[3] Out of the household was slowly born the Civil Service. The descent of English bureaucracy from the chamber in which the king slept and the adjacent closet, the wardrobe, where he hung his clothes, is one of the curiosities of history. Even when, early in the eleventh century, as a result of the growth of centralized government and a more elaborate system of finance, the treasury came to be located at Winchester and, later still, when the

[1] Owing to the good prospects a career in the household offered, men would pay large sums to get their sons placed there. Thus Hugh de Verli gave Henry II 500 marks that his son might be 'in protectione Regis ut clericus suus'. *Pipe Roll 28 Hen. II*, p. 46.

[2] William of Malmesbury, *Gesta Pontificum*, p. 303.

[3] For what follows see Tout, *Chapters in Medieval Administrative History*, vol. i, *passim*.

exchequer broke away from the household establishment to become a separate department, the chamber continued to be a place where the king kept a current account into which moneys were directly paid without passing through the hands of the exchequer officials. It was also a secretarial office where letters were received, issued, and authenticated by the king's private seal.[1] Hence after the exchequer and the chancery had become departments of state, the chamber, and later the wardrobe, were retained as a domestic exchequer and a domestic chancery. Through these household institutions a strong king might in many directions control government independently of the great ministers of the Crown.

Nevertheless, if there were few or no constitutional limits to the exercise of royal power, there were at least restraining influences. A king might do this or that of his own will; but if he did something that conflicted with the interests of the great barons and leading churchmen, he would find obstacles in his path which it would be difficult to override. Although not obligatory, it was customary and a matter of common prudence to take the magnates of the kingdom, on whose support he was really dependent, into his confidence, and to consult with them and gain their consent on questions of policy and public interest. Henry I acknowledged their right to be consulted when, immediately after his coronation, he wrote to Archbishop Anselm, who was then in exile, 'I commit myself and the people of the whole kingdom of England to your counsel and to the counsel of those who with you ought to advise me';[2] and he claimed that he was crowned by the 'common counsel of the barons'.[3] In Henry II's time the abbot of Battle in a celebrated case argued that a king could not make a permanent change in the laws of the country without the common consent of the barons.[4] The 'counsel and consent' of the barons to the public acts of the king becomes in process of time increasingly frequent and less a matter of form; questions are debated and occasionally opposed.

Those whose counsel and consent the king was accustomed to seek were the members of the *curia regis* or, as it might be termed to emphasize its consultative as opposed to its judicial aspect,

---

[1] The small or privy seal was already in use in the reign of John. Tout, *Administrative History*, i. 153.

[2] *S. Anselmi Opera Omnia*, ed. F. S. Schmitt, iv. 109, *ep.* 212.

[3] *Charter of Liberties.*

[4] *Chron. de Bello*, p. 66.

the *magnum concilium*, the great council of the realm. It was a court essentially feudal in character comprising the tenants-in-chief or barons, including the bishops (who sat as barons),[1] with the principal officers of the Crown like the justiciar, the chancellor, the treasurer, and the steward. It might be a large gathering as at the great courts at which the king wore his crown, or it might consist merely of the few barons and counsellors who formed the normal entourage of the king. But when a question of importance was under discussion the court must be sufficiently representative, and we hear of adjournments until more barons could be present.[2] Nevertheless, large or small, it was the same court, the *curia regis*, and it exercised the same functions, judicial, deliberative, financial, and administrative. It was only very gradually that the court became departmentalized; even the exchequer, the first to break off from the parent stem, was still the *curia regis ad scaccarium*.

The *curia regis*, then, was the effective organ of the centralized government of the Norman and early Angevin kings; and it was composed of men who as possessors of large estates or, to use a technical term, 'honors',[3] held an important stake in the country. Their advice could not be ignored, for without their material support the king could not carry out his policy. Magna Carta is the supreme, but not the only example in this period, of successful resistance by the barons to a king who ruled in defiance of custom and their wishes. The king's tenants-in-chief were not without the means of making their power felt; in the last resort they might renounce their homage and fealty, and rebel. They themselves had their courts and their households organized like the king's court in miniature; they also had barons—for so the more substantial mesne tenants were designated in the twelfth century[4]—who formed the court and

---

[1] 'Non sedemus hic episcopi, sed barones', the bishops said when asked to declare judgement on Becket. *Materials for History of Archbishop Thomas Becket* (Rolls Series), iii. 52.

[2] In 1204, for example, when the seisin of a certain manor was in dispute, the few barons who were present recommended an adjournment until the archbishop and other magnates and *sapientes* of the land could be there. *Curia Regis Rolls*, iii. 124.

[3] For the meaning attached to the word 'honor' and the whole subject of the honorial baronage, see Stenton, *The First Age of English Feudalism*, chs. ii and iii, and *Anglo-Saxon England*, pp. 619–26.

[4] As early as 1121 the knightly tenants of Bernard de Neufmarché are described as his *barones*. Round, *Ancient Charters* (Pipe Roll Soc., vol. x), no. 6.

council of the honor without whose consent they too hesitated to act; they had stewards who presided over the court in the absence of the lord and who acted as the chief executive officers. A great man, like William of Aumale, earl of York in Stephen's reign, could address his letters to 'his steward and his sheriff and all his barons and ministers, French and English' very much like the king himself.[1] Waleran of Meulan and others gave orders to their 'justices'.[2] Some few had a private exchequer: William, earl of Gloucester (1147–83), had one at Bristol, Robert, earl of Leicester (1118–68), also had one, and in the next century Roger Bigod had one at Carlow.[3] Only an organized chancery seems to be lacking to complete the parallel between the royal and baronial household; but the barons had their chaplains and clerks who at least imitated in their masters' letters the style of the royal chancery; while some of the very greatest like John, count of Mortain, William, earl of Warenne, and Rannulf, earl of Chester, even had their own chancellors.[4] They had, besides, a body of retainers who performed the military service due to the king.

It was essentially a military society which, if not actually engaged in war, had to be always prepared for it. The barons held their lands in return for undertaking military duties; they held by the sword and the coat of mail (*per loricam*). Far the greater part of the land of England was held in this way. All the barons, all the bishops (save the bishop of Rochester who was at this time directly dependent on Canterbury), and nearly all the older and greater abbeys held their estates by knight's service.[5] This system, introduced by William the Conqueror into England from Normandy,[6] was already well developed by the time that Domesday Book was compiled. The amount of the service due

---

[1] Farrer, *Early Yorkshire Charters*, iii. 34.

[2] Stenton, *English Feudalism*, pp. 67–8, 265.

[3] Ibid., pp. 68, 266; Round, *Ancient Charters*, no. 37, p. 60; Orpen, *American Hist. Rev.* xix (1914), 251. Hugh de Neville, the influential adviser of King John and chief justice of the forests, also seems to have had an exchequer. *Pipe Roll 4 Jo.*, p. 57.

[4] Round, *Cal. of Docs., France*, p. 16; *Early Yorkshire Charters*, ed. Clay, viii. 50; Stenton, op. cit., pp. 34, 259.

[5] The abbeys of Gloucester and Battle are notable exceptions. No religious house founded after 1070 held by military tenure. See H. M. Chew, *The English Ecclesiastical Tenants-in-Chief and Knight Service*, pp. 8, 10.

[6] This was established by J. H. Round in his essay on 'The Introduction of Knight Service into England', printed in *Feudal England*. See also Stenton, *Anglo-Saxon England*, pp. 625–7, 673–4.

from each of the tenants-in-chief was generally fixed arbitrarily in round numbers without any exact relationship to the size or value of the holding.[1] The king was not himself greatly concerned with how the knights were found provided that they were properly trained and equipped with a coat of mail, helmet, shield, and lance.[2] He might be given an estate or he might be retained in the lord's household.

The process of enfeoffment, which had begun before William Rufus ascended the throne, was necessarily slow. In the closing years of the eleventh century the employment of household knights was still common. It was, however, soon abandoned by the ecclesiastical tenants (who would find it troublesome and embarrassing to have a body of men-at-arms about their establishments) in favour of planting them on the land. Among the lay baronage, on the other hand, it persisted far into the twelfth century; in 1166, as the *cartae baronum* disclose, not a few barons, especially in the north and east of England, retained knights on the demesne. Richard de Haia, in Lincolnshire, had enfeoffed fifteen of his quota of twenty knights, and a Cambridgeshire vassal, Stephen de Scalers, only ten out of a total service of fifteen.[3] These famous *Cartae*, which answered questions put to the tenants-in-chief by Henry II in 1166 concerning the number and names of knights they had enfeoffed, afford the earliest comprehensive information we possess about the organization of military service. They show that the process of parcelling the baronial estates into knights' fees had been in the main completed before the death of Henry I, for the number created since that date (those of 'new enfeoffment' which form a separate item in the returns) add little to the total. They show too that the majority of the royal vassals had in fact enfeoffed more, some many more, knights than were required for the performance of their military obligations, their *servitium debitum*. The bishop of Lincoln, for example, who was charged with sixty knights, had enfeoffed 102, and the bishop of Exeter, who owed seventeen and a half, had created twice that number of fees. The purpose of Henry's inquiry was both political and financial.

---

[1] The value of an estate seems to be taken into account in later times. Cf. the grant of land made in 1200 to William Brewer which he shall hold in chief of the king 'per servitium quod illi terre imponet cum scierit valorem ipsius terre'. *Pipe Roll 2 Jo.*, p. 161.

[2] Assize of Arms, cl. 1 (*Gesta Henrici II*, i. 278).

[3] *Red Book of the Exchequer*, pp. 367–8, 390–1.

He was about to leave England for a prolonged visit to his continental dominions, a visit which actually occupied four whole years (March 1166 to March 1170). He wished to be assured of the loyalty of the English knighthood by seeing that all those who held by military tenure had done allegiance and had been duly enrolled.[1] And as events proved, during this stormy period, which included the Becket struggle and the conquest of Brittany, there were no symptoms of disturbance in England. The financial object was to raise the *servitia debita* of those tenants who had enfeoffed more than the requisite number of knights by adding on the surplus. An examination of the records, however, shows that the policy of establishing a new assessment based on the actual facts of enfeoffment met with the steady opposition of the tenants-in-chief. Like the similar attempt made by King John in the great inquest of service of 1212, it had little permanent success.[2]

The problem of knight's service in respect of the mesne tenants presents even greater difficulties than the obligations of the barons to the king. The relatively simple scheme of the eleventh century grew more elaborate and complex in the course of the twelfth. What is the size of a knight's fee? How much land would a knight expect to receive in return for the performance of the service required of him? There is evidence that in the west midlands on the highly organized lands of the see of Worcester, a knight's fee was usually 5 hides, a fact which suggests a connexion with the 5-hide unit of the Anglo-Saxon thegn.[3] Unfortunately the simple formula of the Worcester record 'Quatuor virgate terre faciunt unam hidam et quinque

[1] D. M. Stenton, *Camb. Med. Hist.* v. 590; F. M. Stenton, *English Feudalism*, p. 137, n. 3.

[2] See Chew, op. cit., p. 22, where she shows that Round (*Feudal England*, pp. 285–6, 289) was wrong in supposing that the *Cartae* of 1166 'superceded' the old *servitia debita*. The scutage of Ireland assessed in 1171 was paid by some tenants for fees of new enfeoffment, for example, by the abbot of Tavistock (*Pipe Roll 24 Hen. II*, p. 12) and Lambert de Scoteigni (ibid., p. 3; cf. the roll of 18 Hen. II, p. 94) after a delay of five years. On the other hand some of the lay tenants and nearly all the ecclesiastical did not recognize this obligation. So, for instance, on the roll of 18 Henry II, under Norfolk and Suffolk, Reginald de Warenne, the bishop of Norwich, and the abbot of Bury are entered as owing scutage of new enfeoffment; the debts continue to be recorded on the rolls for the next twenty-four years, till 1196, but nothing was ever paid into the treasury. For the inquest of 1212 see *Book of Fees*, pp. 52 ff.

[3] See M. Hollings, 'The survival of the Five Hide Unit in the Western Midlands', *Eng. Hist. Rev.* lxiii (1948), 453–87.

hide faciunt unum militem' cannot be used for general application. On the contrary, astonishing diversity prevails. Two of
the six fees of the abbey of St. Albans contained 5½ hides, the
remaining four, 6, 7, 7½, and 8½ hides.[1] In Dorset we find
a fee of only 2 hides,[2] and in Cambridgeshire one of 27.[3] In
the north of England they tended to be larger but even more
variable. Yorkshire, for example, reveals remarkable differences;
10 or 12 carucates to the fee seems to be usual, but there are
instances of fees composed of 7, 8, 14, 15, 17, and 20 carucates.[4]
Moreover, land measures, the hide or the carucate, except for
fiscal purposes when they were reckoned at 120 or 100 acres,[5]
were themselves not standardized. Obviously, then, we must
dismiss any idea of a knight's fee of normal or uniform size.
Land values in terms of the pound or the mark (two-thirds of
a pound) provide a more satisfactory conception of the knight's
fee; and it is certain that in the thirteenth century when distraint of knighthood was introduced, the possession of land
worth £20 a year was considered the proper holding of a knight.
But here too we are not on sure ground, for there is evidence
which points to a unit of half that value as being perhaps more
common.[6]

The feudal army was never large. Although the usually
accepted estimate of about 5,000 is almost certainly too low, it
can hardly have ever exceeded 7,000 knights; and it may but
rarely have been mustered at its full strength. Each knight was
required to serve for a period in the royal army at his own cost.
It is usually asserted that this period of service was forty days,
though the only definite contemporary evidence implies that
this relates only to times of peace, when perhaps a knight might
be required to spend such a time in training, and that in time of
war a knight should serve for two months.[7] However this may

[1] Chew, op. cit., pp. 124 f.
[2] *Red Book of the Exchequer*, p. 210.
[3] *Curia Regis Rolls*, ii. 53.
[4] Farrer, *Early Yorkshire Charters*, ii, nos. 808 (7 carucates); 789 (8 car.); 663, 692,
702, 723, 802, 830 (10 car.); 666, 718, 732, 822 (12 car.); 669 (14 car.); 786
(15 car.); 734 (17 car.); 807 (20 car.).
[5] The Domesday hide was 120 acres, the long hundred of six score. One hundred
acres were reckoned as a carucate for the assessment of the carucage of 1198
(Hoveden, iv. 47).
[6] Stenton, *English Feudalism*, pp. 166 f., 189.
[7] In a charter of the first half of the twelfth century John Fitz Gilbert, the father
of William Marshal, grants land at Nettlecombe in Somerset to Hugh of Ralegh
to be held for the service of one knight 'tali divisione quod si werra est inveniet

be, we may presume that if a campaign was not over in this short space of time, the knight must remain in the field, but at the king's expense. It seems to have been understood, at least in the thirteenth century, that the service could only be demanded if the king himself was present in the army.[1]

Difficulty in raising the feudal levy led very early to the commutation of the service by money payment. The practice of paying scutage (shield-money), levied at a fixed rate of a pound or two marks on the knight's fee, in lieu of actual service in the field crept in soon after the institution of knight-service itself. There is abundant evidence of it in the time of Henry I; and a charter of the very first year of that reign suggests that it was already an established usage by the year 1100.[2] At first we hear of it with reference to the ecclesiastical tenants—the levy of 1156, the earliest about which we have detailed information, was only paid on lands of the church. This must not, however, be attributed to any special privilege they possessed; they could, like any other military tenants, be required to provide the actual corporeal service.[3] But they were often in trouble in finding knights to carry out their obligations, and when they did, these might be, like the Canterbury contingent sent by Anselm to the Welsh campaign of 1097, unfit men, poorly trained and equipped.[4] Nevertheless, the practice of commutation was soon extended to the lay baronage who also experienced some difficulty in fulfilling their commitments.[5] The difficulty was increased when Richard I in his later years kept the army almost continuously in the field. Both barons and under-tenants showed reluctance to spend so long in campaigning abroad, even though by the gradual adoption of what is known as the 'quota' system[6] only a fraction of the feudal host was called upon to serve. Many barons both lay and clerical were glad enough to avail them-

mihi unum militem procuratum duobus mensibus et si pax est xl diebus ad tale servitium quale milites baronum terre facere debent rationabiliter'. It is printed in *Collectanea Topographica et Genealogica*, ed. Madden, Bandinel, and J. G. Nichols, ii (1835), 163.

[1] The service of the four and a half knights due from the abbey of Evesham was only required by Henry I *me presente*. See *Cal. of Charter Rolls*, i. 257, quoted Chew, op. cit., p. 99.

[2] W. A. Morris, *Eng. Hist. Rev.* xxxvi (1921), 45. The charter grants among other privileges quittance of scutage to the priory of Lewes.

[3] Chew, *Ecclesiastical Tenants-in-Chief*, pp. 38 f., 46.

[4] Eadmer, *Hist. Nov.*, p. 78.

[5] Stenton, op. cit., p. 178.   [6] Below, p. 370.

selves of a new alternative method of commutation, apparently first offered them in 1196, by which, on payment of a lump sum arbitrarily fixed and generally considerably in excess of the normal scutage assessment, they could rid themselves and their knights of the whole burden of service. On payment of such fines they received an authorization from the exchequer to recoup themselves by levying a scutage on their under-tenants,[1] not necessarily only the military or even the free tenants; we hear also of villeins contributing to their lord's scutage.[2]

There was another reason why commutation became in the twelfth century almost a necessity. Compact holdings had never been a normal feature in the rural organization of England, and in the twelfth century the disintegration of estates developed rapidly. It is with fractional rather than entire fees that charters of this period are chiefly concerned. Subinfeudation has played havoc with any neat arrangement of knight-service. We meet with a half, a quarter, a fifth, a sixth, a tenth, a twentieth, a fortieth, and even a hundredth part of a knight's fee.[3] On a well-organized estate the several tenants, who among them were responsible for the service of one knight, might arrange to perform the service in rotation or in some such manner, but it is impossible to conceive that the mass of holders of minute and scattered fractions could render their service in this way. As early as the reign of Henry I a charter records the grant of an estate in Warwickshire to be held 'by a third part of the service of one knight in such a way that he shall acquit his whole service by the yearly payment of twenty shillings'; at the end of the century (1197) we read that Robert Blundus shall render 'the service of a tenth part of a fee of one knight by money (*per denarios*)'. Knight-service in respect of these small tenantry must always have been a matter of cash; scutage from their point of view was merely an additional tax added on to the rent.[4]

---

[1] These are entered on the chancellor's roll of 1196 (Pipe Roll Soc., N.S., vol. vii) as fines *ne transfretent*, that they may not cross with the army. Thus the abbot of Evesham renders account for £10 (p. 16): 'ne transfretet in tercio exercitu et pro habendo scutagio suo de feodo iiii militum et dimidii militis.'

[2] *Curia Regis Rolls*, i. 16 (1196). They are said, however, to have done so voluntarily (*sponte sua*).

[3] See Stenton, *Danelaw Charters*, no. 539, where a grant of two-thirds of a half-bovate is made for the hundredth part of the service of a knight's fee. Cf. Introd., p. cxxxi.

[4] This is clearly brought out in a case when a jury in 1214 was called upon to decide whether a certain man owed 'scutagium, scilicet quintam partem tercie

The feudal host, the expeditionary force (*expeditio*), was not, even in the warlike days of chivalry, always in being. It was only mustered when need arose and when fighting had to be done. Castles, on the other hand, had always to be kept in a state of preparedness. Garrison duty in the Norman period was probably a more serious call on the time and energies of the knightly class than service in the field. A knight, under the conditions of his tenure, might be required to perform castle-guard at a royal or baronial castle or even both. The tenants of the great honor of Richmond (whose earls were connected with the ducal house and from the middle of the twelfth century themselves held the duchy of Brittany) had to furnish the guard at Richmond castle; approximately thirty knights were assigned for each period of two months throughout the year.[1] Similarly the forty knights of Bury St. Edmunds had the duty of garrisoning the royal castle of Norwich; they worked for three months in groups of ten in rotation.[2] Castle-guard was often required at some far-distant fortress; Northamptonshire knights, for instance, had to assist in the ward of Dover castle. It was no doubt because of the exacting nature of the service and the consequent difficulty of enforcing its performance that it was generally commuted at an early date for money rents, usually assessed at 6*d.* or 8*d.* for a day's service, that is at the normal daily wage of a hired knight in the reign of Henry II.[3] Such payments may be traced for centuries after the castle had ceased to be an essential feature of the defensive organization of the country. As late as the beginning of the eighteenth century or even later Wytham, Tubney, Hanney, and many other little places in Berkshire were paying a pound or a few shillings 'ward money', representing their ancient obligation to the abbey of Abingdon to furnish castle-guard at Windsor castle. In Richard I's reign the garrison of the royal castles was generally composed of a few knights and a larger number of sergeants, all of whom received fixed rates of pay.

The word sergeant (*serviens*) is used in the middle ages in a

partis i militis'. *Curia Regis Rolls*, vii. 156. For other evidence see A. L. Poole, op. cit., pp. 45–7.

[1] *Early Yorkshire Charters*, ed. C. Clay, v, Part II, pp. 11–12. Cf. also Round in *Archaeological Journal*, lix (1902), 144; and Stenton, *English Feudalism*, c. vi.

[2] Cf. A. L. Poole, op. cit., pp. 48–50.

[3] But by cl. 29 of Magna Carta knights were still permitted to discharge the duty in person if they wished.

non-technical sense to denote a common soldier and in a technical sense for a tenant in sergeanty, that is to say, one who holds land by some specialized form of service. This class comprised men of widely different social standing from high officers of the Crown to men who, as Magna Carta states,[1] merely provided the king with small knives, arrows, or the like. Often the services due from men of rank and dignity were purely menial in character and were only performed at the king's coronation, such as holding the basin and towel when the king washed his hands; many others were of a martial kind, providing so many horse or foot soldiers or bearing the king's standard; others again were concerned with the king's sport. Examples taken from thirteenth-century lists of Oxfordshire sergeanties will give some idea of the great variety of such services.[2] They include a dispenser, a larderer, a preparer of herbs, a naperer (who was required to provide one table-cloth a year) besides several ushers, falconers, and men charged with duties connected with the forest. Of some the service is more specifically defined: one must bring a dinner of roast pork for the king when he hunted in Wychwood forest; another carries the banner of the king within the four ports of England.[3] Henry de la Mare holds by usher service with the special duty of guarding the court strumpets, and Henry de la Wade of Stanton Harcourt must strew fodder for the king's beasts and mow and carry a meadow of hay in the park at Woodstock. Henry I fenced-in the park at Woodstock for his menagerie which is said to have included lions, leopards, lynxes, camels, and a favourite porcupine sent to him by William of Montpellier. It is possible that this sergeanty originated with the service of feeding Henry I's pet animals.[4] In

[1] Cl. 37.

[2] This is a conflation of several lists contained in the *Book of Fees*, but based on the original return made by the sheriff in response to the king's request for an inquiry concerning military tenures and sergeanties in 1212 (pp. 103–4). Cf. also pp. 252–3, 344, 588–9. For the details of these sergeanties see A. L. Poole, op. cit., pp. 66–74.

[3] This curious service is described in later lists as that of 'carrying the banner of all the infantry of the hundred of Wootton'. *Book of Fees*, pp. 253 (1219), 1172 (1250).

[4] There is a reference to the purchase of hay *ad nutrimentum ferarum* in Woodstock park in 1201, when the usual supply from Oxford was spoilt owing to floods (*Pipe Roll 3 Jo.*, p. 206). For Henry I's menagerie see William of Malmesbury, *Gesta Regum*, ii. 485. Henry of Huntingdon (ed. Arnold, p. 244, *sub anno* 1122) refers to Woodstock 'ubi rex cohabitationem hominum et ferarum fecerat'. Henry II kept a bear which he took about with him on his travels (*Pipe Roll 22 Hen. II*, p. 91).

later days, when perhaps there were no more beasts at Woodstock, Henry de la Wade's service became one of keeping falcons.
Sergeanty, like other tenures burdened with services, reflects a
time when land was plentiful and money was scarce. But with
the growth of a money economy it became out of date. Though
at the beginning of the thirteenth century some few sergeants
were still performing the duties on which their tenure depended,
the majority were doing them by deputy or not doing them at
all. In the middle of the century many sergeanties were commuted into money rents.

A tenant's obligation to his lord was not confined to the mere
rendering of the service due from his fief, the *servitium debitum*.
The lord required a 'relief', a succession duty, when an heir
entered into possession of his inheritance; he could take money
from his tenantry on special occasions (aids, *auxilia*); he could
enjoy the profits of an estate when the heir was a minor, and he
could control the marriages of the widows and daughters of his
tenantry. In fact, no woman could be lawfully married without
the consent of her lord, and in this the free were little better off
than the unfree with their payment of merchet. These irksome
claims, which applied to all military and sergeanty tenures and,
as far as reliefs and aids were concerned, to socage tenures as
well, were often shamefully abused. Many of the clauses in the
charters of liberties from Henry I's coronation charter to Magna
Carta, and those to which the barons attached greatest importance, were simply promises that these rights incidental to
feudal tenures should be exercised with proper discretion.
William Rufus had used the relief as a means of extortion;
Henry I, in order to win the barons to support him against his
brother Robert, said that it should be 'just and legitimate'.[1] By
Glanvill's time it was definitely recognized that a 'just and
legitimate' relief was 100s. for a knight's fee, a year's rent for a
socager;[2] and it seems clear on the evidence of the Pipe Rolls
that the king contented himself with these sums. But he was still

Otherwise no other king seems to have cared for animals till Henry III who had
three leopards and a camel sent to him by his brother-in-law, the emperor Frederick
II (Matthew Paris, *Chron. Maj.* iii. 324, 334). He also had an elephant, the gift
of Louis IX of France, which was kept in a house specially built for it in the Tower
of London where it died in 1258 (*Close Rolls, 1254–6*, pp. 34, 46, and *1256–9*, p. 256).
  [1] Coronation Charter, cl. 2.
  [2] Glanvill, ix. 4. The same amounts appear in the early twelfth-century compilation, the so-called *Leis Willelme* in the chapter (20) which deals with heriots.
Liebermann, *Die Gesetze der Angel-Sachsen*, i. 507.

at liberty to exact what he pleased from his barons, and in fact did so unscrupulously. The relief on a barony was supposed to be 'reasonable'; and it was generally understood that £100, the figure at which it was afterwards fixed in Magna Carta (cl. 2), was 'reasonable'. But this sum was often greatly exceeded or might only be acceptable to the king after the proffer of a substantial bribe.[1]

The practice of extorting heavy reliefs at the top of the feudal hierarchy had its repercussions all down the ladder. The baron, mulcted of a large fine when he entered into his inheritance, passed on the burden to his under-tenants by exacting from them an aid. The aid originated in the idea that it was the duty of a tenant to assist his lord with money in times of need. The occasions when a lord might properly be expected to be in financial straits came in course of time to be limited to three: the ransom of his body, the knighting of his eldest son, the marriage of his eldest daughter once. But the sums demanded must be 'reasonable', that is to say, they should be within the tenant's means to pay, and not so heavy that he could no longer maintain himself in his social position.[2] Nevertheless, neither the king nor other lords appear to have paid much attention to these salutary rules. They demanded aids for all kind of necessities, for discharging the relief, as we have seen (though this was recognized by Glanvill as correct), for paying their debts, or for stocking their farms. Similarly the bishops and abbots might take toll of their parochial clergy on certain occasions, for instance, when they had to make a journey to Rome.[3] Although the Great Charter insisted that aids should be 'reasonable', they still remained undefined. We have to wait till the reign of Edward I before we get aids limited in amount.[4]

If lords used reliefs and aids as means of extortion, they dealt even more unscrupulously in the matter of wardship and marriage. The promise of Henry I that he would take no money for the licence to marry, and would not refuse it unless the marriage

[1] Cf. A. L. Poole, op. cit., pp. 95–6.
[2] Glanvill, ix. 8.
[3] The occasions are recorded very precisely in a charter of Geoffrey of Anjou relating to the priory of Cunault of the year 1143: 'Decrevimus etiam propter paupertatem hominum, quod Priores de caetero ipsos non talliarent nisi in tribus casibus, videlicet quando Prior novus est, et quando aliquam emptionem faciet domui suae, et quando vocatur ad capitulum suum semel.' P. Juénin, *Nouvells Histoire de l'Abbaye . . . de Saint Filibert de Tournus* (Dijon, 1733), Preuves, p. 156.
[4] Statute of Westminster I (1275), cl. 36. Cf. Magna Carta, cls. 12, 15.

were to one of his enemies, went for nothing.[1] Widows and heiresses were freely sold in marriage to the highest bidder or to the king's friends, often of low degree, to their 'disparagement';[2] or the lady had to pay a substantial fine 'that she may remain a widow as long as she pleases' or 'that she be not constrained to marry herself' or 'that she may marry herself to whom she pleased'. As the century advanced the marriages of male as well as female heirs were controlled by the lord. The right of wardship was in itself natural if we consider the intimate relations which existed between a lord and his vassal; moreover, an heir who was under age was by reason of his youth incapable of performing the service by which he held his estates, and therefore, it was argued, the lord was entitled to the profits of these estates instead. It extended in the case of boys till the age of twenty-one and in that of girls till the presumed marriageable age of fourteen. It was not the principle, but the shameless profiteering which went on to the permanent detriment of the property which caused such bitter feeling. Wardships were often sold at a high price to individuals who made what they could out of them. Though it was a recognized rule that an estate should be handed back to the heir when he came of age in as good condition as when it was received, the custodians were frequently neglectful, sometimes dishonest. They were not even required to render an account of their stewardship. The sums demanded in respect of wardship and marriage, arbitrary as they seem, were not fixed altogether irrespective of the facts. The Crown took pains to discover through the itinerant justices[3] the relevant details: the age of the widows, the number and ages of the children, the size and value of the property. Chance has preserved the record of such information relating to twelve counties in the year 1185—the 'Rolls of ladies, boys, and girls in the king's gift'.[4] A typical entry from the returns of Cambridgeshire runs as follows:

'Eugenia Picot, who was the daughter of Ralph Picot of Kent,

[1] Coronation Charter, cl. 3.

[2] Cl. 6 of Magna Carta and other documents lay particular stress on the point that marriages should be 'without disparagement', i.e. should be between persons of equal social standing, between *pares*.

[3] Assize of Northampton, cl. 9 (1176), and Articles of the Eyre, cls. 5, 6 (1194). Hoveden, ii. 91, iii. 263.

[4] *Rotuli de Dominabus et Pueris et Puellis*, printed, with a valuable introduction by J. H. Round, by the Pipe Roll Society, vol. xxxv.

and the wife of Thomas Fitz Bernard, is of the gift of the lord king, and is thirty years old. She has in the hundred of Radfield a certain manor which is worth £25 per annum, and is of the fee of Gilbert Malet: William Malet gave the said manor to the said lady in dower. And she had three sons of Thomas Fitz Bernard and one daughter: the eldest son is ten years old, the middle one eight years, the third three years. The lord king gave the daughter to the son of John de Bidun.'[1]

A few years later this Eugenia offered the king £80 for the custody of her son John and his land.[2] All this information was important for determining the price which could be put on the widow and children in the marriage market. Often these entries include a statement of the amount of stock on the farm and a note is added whether by an increase in the number of cattle, sheep, and pigs, a larger return could be obtained; such knowledge was of value to prospective purchasers of wardships.

Although the Norman and early Angevin kings made heavy demands on their feudal tenantry by way of reliefs and fines, and from wards and widows, they were, nevertheless, astonishingly lenient in the matter of payment. They were in no hurry for a settlement. Walter Brito, for example, who succeeded to his father's estates in Somerset in 1165, was charged with a relief of £200. Year by year he paid a small sum into the treasury; some years he paid nothing. The balance, without any apparent concern, was carried over to the next account, and it was not until 1198, thirty-three years after he had entered into his inheritance, that the exchequer clerk was able to write him off as quit.[3] Such humane treatment, if it does not excuse, at least mitigates the harshness of these royal exactions. The lot of the twelfth-century debtor was on the whole lighter than that of those in similar plight in later ages.

It must not be supposed that all tenants holding by knight-service, the occupiers of a mere fraction of a knight's fee, ranked in the social sense as knights. The knights were a small and select body, the county aristocracy. To become one of them a man must be knighted with elaborate ceremonial; he was given by his lord rich and expensive clothes and equipment. King John ordered the sheriff of Hampshire, for example, to provide Thomas Esturmy, his valet, with a robe of scarlet with a hood

[1] Ibid, p. 87. [2] *Pipe Roll 34 Hen. II*, p. 38.
[3] *Pipe Rolls 11 Hen. II to 10 Ric. I.*

of doe skin and a robe of green or brown, a saddle and a pair of bridles, a rain cloak, and a mattress and a pair of sheets 'when he becomes a knight'.[1] He must only enter the ranks of chivalry with an appropriate outfit. He then might have an equestrian seal (a privilege grudged in early times to lesser men), to authenticate his documents.[2] Heraldry emerges in the first half of the twelfth century to give distinctiveness to men otherwise indistinguishable by reason of their enveloping armour which completely concealed the face. By the peculiar devices on his shield and his coat, on the trappings of his horse and the flag on his lance, a knight could be recognized on the field of battle. The royal arms, three lions *passant, gardant*, first displayed on the second seal of Richard I (which was first brought into use in 1198) may be traced back to 1127 when Henry I knighted his son-in-law Geoffrey of Anjou and hung round his neck a shield of golden lions.[3] Heraldry developed with the tournament, the warlike exercise in which knights delighted to indulge and in which the heralds had their particular functions.[4]

Like everything that is most characteristic of chivalry, the tournament was introduced from France. At the time of which we speak, towards the end of the twelfth and the early thirteenth centuries, it was not the formal, highly regulated jousting watched by courtiers and fair ladies, as it became in the later middle ages; it was a serious and often bloody affair, in which a concourse of knights charged about on the open plain without goal or boundaries; and it was attended by great personal danger. It was, as Walter Map punningly remarks, 'a sport which they call a tournament, but the better name would be torment'.[5] Repeated papal decrees had condemned those 'detestable fairs vulgarly called tournaments in which knights are wont to meet together to display their prowess and valour'. Nevertheless its popularity grew. It was made legal in England

---

[1] *Rot. Lit. Claus.* i. 3. *Pipe Roll 6 Jo.*, pp. 120, 213, and introd., p. xxxiv.

[2] 'Moris antiquitus non erat quemlibet militulum sigillum habere.' *Chron. Mon. de Bello*, p. 108. In a charter of Geoffrey de Mandeville, second earl of Essex (died 1166), the words occur: 'Istam cartam feci signari sigillo dapiferi mei ... donec sim miles et habeam sigillum, et tunc eam firmabo proprio sigillo'; quoted F. P. Barnard, *Mediaeval England*, ed. H. W. C. Davis, p. 204. By the end of the century it was usual for the small freemen to have seals on which they put distinguishing devices, sometimes a play on the surname.

[3] See Anthony R. Wagner, *Historic Heraldry of Britain*, p. 40, and the references there given.

[4] Ibid., p. 14.   [5] *De Nugis*, ii, c. 16.

by Richard I in 1194 under conditions: it must be licensed by the king, and each combatant must pay an entrance fee (payable in advance) according to his rank, ranging from 20 marks for an earl to 2 marks for a landless knight. It must also be held on one of the recognized tilting-grounds. These were five in number and distributed about the country: between Salisbury and Wilton, between Warwick and Kenilworth, between Stamford and Wansford, between Brackley and Mixbury, and between Blyth and Tickhill. These regulations served a military and a financial purpose: the tournament provided training for the knights and it brought much-needed money to the king's purse. But their primary object was probably to exercise a strict control over a sport which might easily result in a serious breach of the peace or even disguise preparations for a baronial revolt.[1]

This military aristocracy lived in castles. The castle was normally, though not always, the centre, the *caput*, of the honor.[2] It is the symbol of the feudal age, at once the home and defence of the feudal baron, the centre of his power. The word used for the lord's dwelling, dungeon (the French *donjon*), which only in later times acquired its sinister meaning, is derived from the Latin *dominium* and expresses lordship.[3] In the grassy mounds and crumbling stone towers dotted over the face of the country can best be visualized the social and military life of the medieval aristocracy. The outcome of wars and rebellions was generally determined not by battles in the open field but by the reduction of the enemy's strongholds. At first these were of a very rudimentary character, hastily built in

[1] The writ is printed in *Foedera*, i. 65. The tournament is fully treated by N. Denholm-Young in *Studies in Medieval History presented to F. M. Powicke*, see especially pp. 240–5. I am, however, unable to accept his location of the Stamford referred to in the text as 'Stamford in Suffolk not far from Thetford and Bury, *not* Stamford in Lincolnshire'. This view does not explain the *Warineforde* which appears to be Wansford Bridge a little south of Stamford on the Great North Road.

[2] Sometimes the advowson of a church is described as the *caput honoris*. So Hamelin de Andevill claimed the *advocatio* of the church of Knebworth (Herts.) as the *capud honoris sui* (*Curia Regis Rolls*, vii. 138). Similarly Roger de Camville claimed the advowson of the church of Pickwell (Leics.) as *capud hereditatis sue* (ibid., p. 139), and Michael of Stifford the advowson of the church of Stifford (Essex) as *capud honoris* (ibid., p. 324). These instances all occur in cases of the years 1214–15.

[3] Hamilton Thompson, *Military Architecture in England during the Middle Ages*, pp. 46–7. The dungeon was the tower or keep, while the word *castellum* originally signified a fortified enclosure or ward. See Round, *Geoffrey de Mandeville*, App, O (p. 328).

time of stress by unskilled labour with materials ready to hand. In its simplest form the eleventh-century castle consisted of an artificial mound of earth (the *motte*) surrounded by a moat and crowned by timber fortifications, a palisade, and a tower. The mound was placed sometimes in the centre, but more commonly on the circumference of a fenced enclosure (the bailey or ward) in which were ranged the domestic buildings. The period of peace and order which followed the Norman settlement provided the necessary leisure for the erection of the more permanent and solid structures which were required in order to keep abreast with the progress in the art of siege warfare. Wooden buildings were naturally very prone to destruction by fire, and they offered little resistance to the heavy battering-rams and stone-throwers employed against them. Masonry, therefore, came to replace timber. Where a castle was originally sited on natural ground, stone was used at an early date. Ludlow, one of the homes of the Lacys, perched on the crest of a hill rising steeply from the river, affords an example of early Norman castle building, elaborate in design and of solid construction; its stout walls flanked with towers at the angles, form an inner ward entered by a great tower gate-house of several stories providing living apartments; it has also a circular Norman chapel within for the use of its lord and his friends.[1] The artificial mound, on the other hand, was not sufficiently compacted to bear a heavy weight of masonry. The bailey could be enclosed by a curtain wall, its approach protected by a gate-tower, and the palisade on the mound replaced by a high stone wall to form what is known as a 'shell keep' as at Lincoln or Berkeley. But the square stone keep on the man-made hillock at Christchurch in Hampshire with its contemporaneous stone hall in the ward is a rare specimen of a simple conversion of a motte-and-bailey stronghold to meet the progressive needs of defence and domestic comfort. Generally the castle builders of the twelfth century started on fresh solid ground on which could be erected walls and towers of great height and thickness; and the central feature of fortresses of this kind was the massive rectangular keep. Though long in use in France, the White Tower at London, and the great keep at Colchester are the only examples of this form of military architecture which belong to

[1] See the detailed and well-illustrated description by W. H. St. John Hope in *Archaeologia*, lxi (1908), 257.

the age of the Conquest. Most of the square keeps are of the time of Henry II when, after the experience of the anarchy which prevailed under Stephen, the unlicensed private castle was being eliminated, and these impressive monuments of royal authority were raised and entrusted to constables who could be relied upon to maintain the peace. Licences to build private castles were granted sparingly during the early Angevin period. As, however, progress was made in the construction of fortresses, so too there were corresponding developments in methods of destruction. Experience in war soon found out the vulnerability of the rectangular tower; its corners could be easily undermined; its field of fire was severely limited. The polygonal or cylindrical keep, such as still stand at Orford or Conisbrough, was introduced to remedy these defects. But a more radical change in military architecture was already in process before our period ends; a change designed at once to give the defenders more freedom of movement and greater opportunity for offensive action. Emphasis was no longer given to the central keep, but to the outer fortifications which were protected by strong angle towers; a second and even a third ward was added. The transition had set in towards the idea of concentric lines of defences which reached its finest achievement in the great Edwardian castles that guarded the principality of Wales.

As the century advanced, this society, essentially military in character with its castles, its cavalry fighting, its tournament, was growing less warlike in outlook. The army was becoming professionalized, and those knights who still took part in campaigns or in garrison duties, did so for pay. The knights were already 'knights of the shire' and devoted their time and attention to the judicial and administrative work of their counties. Their services were constantly required on juries; often they had to bear the record of a suit which was transferred from the local court to Westminster; they might be employed as coroners or be 'assigned' to take the oath of the peace. In a multitude of ways these knights, who were released by commutation from service in the field, could usefully occupy themselves in the affairs of local government. They were already in training to undertake the important role which they were to play not only in the government of counties but also in the government of the country itself in the following centuries.

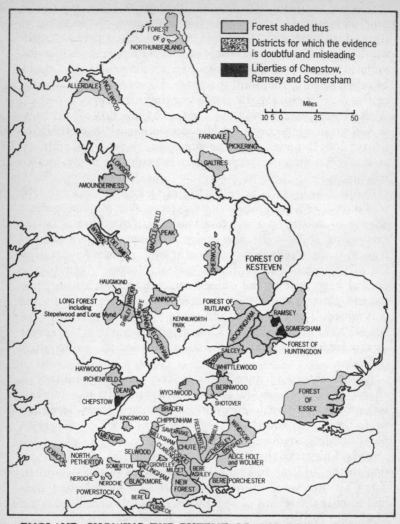

ENGLAND, SHOWING THE EXTENT OF THE ROYAL FOREST
ABOUT THE MIDDLE OF XIII CENTURY
(See p. 30, n. 1).

In the intervals between battle and business the feudal
aristocracy followed the hounds. The forest looms large on the
scene of medieval England. The forest clauses of Magna Carta
were deemed to be so important that in the reissue of 1217 they
were taken out of it, and augmented to form a separate charter,
the Charter of the Forest. The forest was, as Richard Fitz Neal
the author of the 'Dialogue of the Exchequer' describes it, 'the
sanctuary and special delight of kings, where, laying aside their
cares, they withdraw to refresh themselves with a little hunting;
there, away from the turmoils inherent in a court, they breathe
the pleasure of natural freedom'.[1] At convenient places near
the hunting-grounds lodges were built where the king could
conduct the business of state and take his exercise. That at
Clarendon near Salisbury, which has been partially excavated,
was commodious and elaborate in design; in Kinver forest in
Staffordshire Richard I built one of which the exchequer
accounts give a description. It stood within a fortified enclosure,
16 perches in length and 16 feet in height, and it contained a
hall with adjacent offices, a kitchen, a chamber, a jail (to keep
forest offenders), and a fishpond.[2]

For the indulgence of the royal sport great tracts of land were
set aside and subjected to a rigorously enforced code of law.
It is not easy to determine with accuracy the area of this vast
game-preserve which contained within its bounds numberless
villages and encircled great towns. It grew steadily under the
Norman kings, and probably reached its widest extent in the
reign of Henry II when it embraced perhaps not far short of a
third of the whole country. Stephen made some attempt to
redeem his promise made in his second charter of liberties to
disafforest the lands afforested by Henry I, and more forest
land was reclaimed owing to the king's weakness during the
anarchy. But with the restoration of order these, and more
besides, were reafforested by Henry II. Henceforth it began to
diminish. Though much new afforestation was in later times
attributed to King John, in fact this king, like his brother
Richard I, adopted the practice of selling his rights in certain
forests to relieve his financial necessities. All the forests, for

[1] *Dialogus de Scaccario*, i, c. 11.
[2] For Clarendon see the article by Tancred Borenius and J. Charlton in *Antiquaries Journal*, xvi (1936). Much of the work was evidently done in the years 1175–6 when substantial sums were spent on it. Cf. *Pipe Roll 22 Hen. II*, pp. 171–5. For the lodge at Kinver, see *Chancellor's Roll 8 Ric. I* (Pipe Roll Soc., N.S., vol. vii), p. 81.

example, in Devon and Cornwall (except Dartmoor and Exmoor) were disafforested in 1204 at the price of 5,000 marks from Devon and 2,200 marks and twenty palfreys from Cornwall.[1] The making of the New Forest and the injury it caused to the inhabitants is a familiar fact of history;[2] but it is less well known that at one time the entire county of Essex lay under forest law or that a broad belt of country stretching from the borders of Lincolnshire southward to the Thames, could be officially described as the forest between the bridges of Stamford and Oxford. Indeed, but three counties (Norfolk, Suffolk, and Kent) are certainly known to have contained no land subject to the forest law. It was not merely over the royal demesne that the king claimed the exclusive rights of the chase. In wooded country which provided good cover and pasturage, no matter whether it belonged to the king or his barons or the church, the beasts might range freely and unharmed, and the land was placed under the irksome restrictions which the special law imposed. It was 'the safe mansion of wild beasts'.[3]

The object of the forest law was the preservation of certain beasts, 'the beasts of the forest': the red and the fallow deer, the roe, and the wild boar (the venison); and of the growing timber and undergrowth which gave them shelter (the vert). The king would often grant to his tenants, especially to his ecclesiastical tenants, the right to take the smaller game 'within the forest and without'. So the monks of Chertsey might keep hounds and hunt foxes, hares, and cats in their Surrey woodlands;[4] the nuns of Wix might keep a small pack of harriers to take hares in the Essex forest for the benefit of their sick;[5] and the abbot of Abingdon might even hunt roebuck in the neighbouring woods of Cumnor and Bagley.[6] A particularly favoured subject might enjoy extensive hunting privileges. Thus William Brewer,

---

[1] *Pipe Roll 6 Jo.*, pp. 40, 85; for Devon see *Rot. Chart.*, p. 132; *Foedera* (under wrong date), p. 89. For other examples of disafforestation in 1204 see *Pipe Roll 6 Jo.*, pp. 32, 189. Cf. also M. L. Bazeley, *Trans. R. Hist. Soc.*, 4th ser., iv (1921), 146–8, and her excellent map showing the extent of the forest in the thirteenth century, reproduced here by her kind permission.

[2] F. H. M. Parker (*Eng. Hist. Rev.* xxvii (1912), 26) attempted to show that the making of the New Forest did not involve the depopulating of flourishing villages as implied in the contemporary chronicles. But see F. H. Baring (ibid. 513).

[3] *Dialogus de Scaccario*, i, c. 12.

[4] *Cartae Antiquae* (Pipe Roll Soc., N.S., vol. xvii), nos. 109, 112–13, 115, 117.

[5] Ibid., nos. 92–3.

[6] *Chron. de Mon. de Abingdon* (Rolls Series), ii. 114, 219, 220, 247.

by a charter of King John, was permitted to course the hare, the fox, the cat, and the wolf throughout the king's lands, and the roe in the chase of Devon outside the bounds of the forest, and on his own estates he might have the pheasants and partridges as well.[1] But the roe, the only beast of the forest included in these privileges, was not highly esteemed by sportsmen; he would drive away the other deer, and on this account was struck off the list of beasts of the forest in the reign of Edward III by a decision of the court of King's Bench.[2] But no one save the king and his foresters might touch the red or the fallow deer or the wild boar which was already rapidly becoming extinct. Wolves still lurked in English woods of the twelfth century; they were pests to be exterminated rather than preserved. Officers were appointed to clear the forests of them; the Northamptonshire family of Engaine from early times held lands at Pytchley by the service of chasing wolves from those famous coverts.[3] In Henry II's time only a few pence were paid for their capture, but so great was the nuisance they caused that King John was prepared to give 5s. for a wolf's head.[4] As the king had his forests, so the barons and country gentlemen had their deer parks which they protected against disturbance by what means they could. Besides, it became increasingly common during the twelfth century for the king to grant to manorial lords the right of 'free warren', that is to say, they were given an exclusive sporting licence to take the smaller game on their own estates. Over what was left—and it probably was not much—the general public might hunt and shoot at will.

They hunted in the middle ages with a mixed pack. There was one (liam hound), a heavily built hound, led on a leash for starting the quarry from its lair; there were a few couple of greyhounds (*leporarii*) which hunted by sight; and a larger number of ordinary hounds (*brachetti*) which followed the scent.

[1] *Cartae Antiquae*, no. 248.
[2] Turner, *Select Pleas of the Forest* (Selden Soc.), p. x.
[3] They also held land at Laxton (Northants.) and elsewhere. *Red Book of the Exchequer*, p. 533; *Book of Fees*, p. 9. In inquisitions of the time of Henry III we hear that their service comprised hunting the wolf in the four counties of Northampton, Huntingdon, Oxford, and Buckingham (*Cal. of Inq. Henry III*, nos. 166, 809). A running wolf with two pieces of broken spear above and the head of an axe below is the device on their seal. See *Sir Christopher Hatton's Book of Seals*, plate iii, no. 120.
[4] 10d. for three wolves in Hereford (*Pipe Roll 13 Hen. II*, p. 77). For payments in John's reign see *Rot. Misae 2 John* (ed .Hardy), p. 144; *Rot. Misae 14 John* (ed. Cole), pp. 233, 256.

An army of officials was employed for the management and organization of the royal sport; huntsmen and kennelmen, foresters and woodwards, verderers, who had the special duty of attending the forest courts, and regarders, who made periodical visitations of the forest. Above all were the justices, who at intervals of three, or in later days seven, years held the forest eyre to try offenders. We hear much about the private extortions of these forest officers, who were in a position to exercise a petty tyranny in their districts. Complaints were general and well founded against 'the evil customs of the forests and warrens and of foresters and warreners'.[1]

The lot of the forest dweller was a hard one.[2] He had, it is true, certain privileges: he might turn his pigs and cattle to graze in the woods except for a fortnight before and a fortnight after Midsummer day, the Fence Month as it was called, when the deer were fawning, on payment of a small fee to the agisters, the officers charged with the duty of collecting forest rents; he might have a limited right to take dead wood for fuel and for the repair of his cottage. But if he went beyond his rights, if he lopped a bough or felled an oak, he was guilty of 'waste'. He could not carry bow and arrows; if he kept a dog, it must be 'lawed' or mutilated by the cutting off of three claws from the fore paw, so that it could not run after game. At every turn he was subjected to harsh restrictions and petty annoyances. The Assize of Woodstock (1184), which embodies earlier legislation, is the first surviving written body of regulations enacted to preserve 'the peace of the king's venison' (pax venationis suae). From the early thirteenth century when a beast was found dead representatives of the four neighbouring townships were required to hold an inquest on the carcass. Circumstantial evidence was taken as proof; suspects were imprisoned to await the next session of the justices in eyre; sometimes they might languish for years before they came up for trial. The medieval poacher was hardly dealt with. The report of a Northamptonshire case taken at the Forest Eyre of 1209 will illustrate the tyrannical way in which the forest law was administered and

[1] Magna Carta, cl. 48.
[2] In some forests there were certain customary rights enjoyed by the inhabitants: in Malvern Chase they were free of murder fines, and there was a special 'law of Arden' which defined the right of the commoners in that famous resort of huntsmen. *Rolls of the Justices in Eyre for Lincolnshire 1218–19 and Worcestershire 1221*, ed. D. M. Stenton, Selden Society, vol. 53, p. lxvii,

will demonstrate the reality of the grievances which the Charter of the Forest of 1217 was designed to remedy, or at least to mitigate:

'Thomas Inkel, forester of Cliffe, found in the wood of Siberton a place wet with blood, and he traced the blood in the snow as far as the house of Ralph Red of Siberton; and forthwith he sent for the verderers and good men. They searched his house, and in it they found the flesh of a doe; and they took Ralph and put him in prison at Northampton, where he died. But before he died he accused two fellow evildoers of the forest, Robert Sturdy and Roger Tock of Siberton. And the foresters and verderers searched their houses, and in the one they found bones and in the other ears and bones of wild beasts; and both were taken and imprisoned. Robert Sturdy comes before the justices and says that the hounds of Walter of Preston used to be kennelled at his house. Walter's huntsmen ate venison whence came the bones. Walter comes and confirms his statement, saying that his hounds were kennelled in his house for fifteen days while he was hunting bucks. Roger Tock comes before the justices and denies everything. And the verderers and foresters witness that the ears and bones were those of beasts which the hunters of Walter of Preston took. And because Roger lay for a long time in prison, so that he is nearly dead it is adjudged that he go quit; and let him dwell outside the forest.'[1]

Thus he was not released on the ground of his proved innocence, but because owing to his long sojourn in prison he was 'nearly dead' and even then he must move his dwelling out of the forest area. If an offender escaped capture or if a charge could not be brought home to any individual, the whole township might be at the king's mercy: a hart is found dead in a wood and 'because nothing can be ascertained of that hart it is ordered that the whole of the village of Maidford be seized into the king's hand';[2] a fishpond is taken into the king's hand because a hart was drowned in it.[3] Savage penalties were often inflicted. Under the Norman kings it might be mutilation or even death, and it was not till 1217 that forest offenders were secured in life and limb.[4] The Angevin kings, however, probably from avaricious rather than humanitarian motives, normally contented themselves with imprisonment and the exaction of heavy fines. Above a hundred men were fined for forest offences

---

[1] *Select Pleas of the Forest*, ed. J. G. Turner. pp. 3–4. The record of the case is slightly abbreviated.   [3] Ibid., p. 4.

[2] Ibid., p. 9.   [4] Charter of the Forest (1217), cl. 10.

in Hampshire in the year 1176 in sums ranging from 500 to half a mark, and totalling £2,093. 10s.[1] Poachers in the New Forest may have been punished with particular severity. So at least may be inferred from the threat contained in a charter of Henry I granting Rannulf Flambard, bishop of Durham, protection in his forests. It concludes: 'I specially forbid you, Guy of Balliol, to hunt in his forests. If anyone presumes upon this, he shall pay me a heavy fine, as if he were hunting in my New Forest.'[2] Nevertheless, most counties could furnish substantial lists of fines *de misericordia pro foresta* in the same year or in any year that a forest eyre was held. Evidently the forest in the twelfth century was a fruitful source of revenue. Besides judicial fines there were considerable rents accruing from pasturage and from assarts or clearings made in the forest for agricultural purposes. There were also profits in kind. From the king's woods came timber for ships and for the building and repair of castles; the venison stocked the king's larder and fed the large court which followed him up and down the country. The economic value of the forest was not unimportant.

The picture of oppression, avarice, and selfish indulgence which charters and the records of forest eyres reflect, disregards a brighter and more human aspect of forest life. Not all foresters, verderers, and regarders were harsh and tyrannical. They were local men who might often sympathize with the trespasser; sometimes they were loath to enforce rigorously the law they were supposed to administer. They were themselves frequently in trouble, as the record puts it, 'because they did not do what they ought'.[3] There was a less sinister side of the forest. Sloth, the secular priest in *Piers Plowman*, who could 'nought perfectly' say his Paternoster, could yet rhyme of Robin Hood.[4] Little is known of this elusive and irresponsible sportsman; but it is certain that in 1230 the sheriff of Yorkshire was accountable for 32s. 6d. of the chattels of Robert (or Robin) Hood, *fugitivus*,[5]

---

[1] *Pipe Roll 22 Hen. II*, pp. 193 f.
[2] *Arch. Aeliana*, 4th ser., vii (1930), 52.
[3] *Select Pleas of the Forest*, pp. 6–7.
[4] v, ll. 401–2:

> I can nouȝte perfitly my pater-noster as þe prest it syngeth
> But I can rymes of Robyn hood and Randolf erle of Chestre.

[5] *Pipe Roll 14 Hen. III*, p. 274. See L. V. D. Owen, in the *Times Literary Supplement* of February 1936. Another view represents Robin Hood as a personage at Wakefield in the time of Edward II.

and that Rannulf, earl of Chester, with whom he is associated in the lines of *Piers Plowman*, flourished between 1181 and 1232. But whether an historical outlaw or, as is sometimes thought, merely a wood sprite of medieval folk-lore, Robin Hood, the hero of romance, of ballad writers, and of May Day festivities, represents the cheerful side of the life of the forest, where merry and carefree men consorted in defiance of the law.

II
RURAL CONDITIONS

IT is an idle task to attempt anything like an exact estimate of
the population of England during the middle ages. Domesday Book (1086) provides some basis for calculation, but
only a very unsatisfactory one. For, apart from the total omission of the four northern counties and part of Lancashire, of
London, Winchester, Bristol, and some other towns, whole
classes are either altogether excluded or only casually introduced. Thus few of the clergy, a negligible number of women,
and no children are recorded in the returns. If a census of the
population had been taken in any year of the twelfth century,
it would probably have ranged, at a rough guess, round the two
million mark. The natural tendency to grow was to some extent
counteracted by unsanitary conditions, by plague, pestilence,
and famine, and, though there are perceptible signs of increase
during the period, the population can scarcely ever have much
exceeded two and a half million souls.[1] Of these the town
dwellers still represented a relatively insignificant, though
increasing, proportion. The vast majority of the inhabitants of
the country lived in villages and were engaged in agriculture
and its attendant occupations.

The typical medieval estate was known as the manor. It might
embrace several villages or less than one, but in its simplest form
it was coincident with the village and was subject to a single
lord.[2] It was the unit of rural organization. The normal village
may then be conceived as a community composed of the lord of
the manor and a number of free and servile or villein tenants,
mutually co-operating in the cultivation of the village lands.
The lord reserved for his own use a portion of the estate, known
as the demesne, the home farm, which was cultivated for him by
his dependent tenants in return for their holdings, the villeins
working regularly two or three days in each week with additional
work in the busy seasons of the farming year, and the freemen,

[1] Maitland (*Domesday Book and Beyond*, p. 437) estimates the population in 1086
at 1,375,000. J. C. Russell, *British Medieval Population* (Univ. of New Mexico Press,
1948), puts the figure at just over 1,100,000. The number actually recorded in
Domesday Book is 283,242 (Ellis, *General Introduction to Domesday Book*, ii. 514).

[2] Pollock and Maitland, *Hist. Eng. Law*, i. 605. For the non-coincidence of manor
and vill, see E. A. Kosminsky, *Econ. Hist. Rev.* v (1935), 31.

who paid money rents, performing only relatively light, occasional, and specific tasks. That some such system of estate organization, which will be discussed more fully hereafter, obtained in many parts of the country is abundantly clear. We must, however, guard ourselves against the assumption that it was in any sense universal. Even the demesne was not essential to the manor. There were manors with no demesne just as there were manors with demesne but no villeins. The great estates of the Cistercians, for instance, which during the twelfth century spread widely over England, especially in the north, were generally worked by lay brothers (*conversi*).[1]

Over wide areas of England wholly different systems prevailed. The Danes had left an ineffaceable mark on the social structure of the north-eastern counties. There the 'unity of the village was independent of the organization of the manor'; the very word *manerium* rarely appears in documents relating to the northern Danelaw; the village is scarcely ever subjected to undivided lordship; and the mass of the peasantry of Anglo-Scandinavian origin enjoyed a measure of freedom quite unparalleled in the south and west of the country. They were almost entirely independent of manorial organization; they held their lands by the payment of rent with only occasional services; and were apparently themselves responsible for the payment of the geld charged on their tenements. They make grants of land under their own seals, they endow churches, they attest charters. Society in the Danish districts is singularly conservative; it reflects in every aspect the ancient and freer past.[2] Many of these features characteristic of the northern Danelaw and particularly of the land between the Humber and the Welland are also observable in East Anglia. There, too, there is a looseness in the organization of society and a striking independence among the peasantry.[3] Then in the extreme north, in the old kingdom of Northumbria, yet other tenurial systems obtained, with an archaic survival of thegns and drengs, whose

[1] See Kosminsky, op. cit., p. 33.

[2] F. M. Stenton, *Documents Illustrative of the Social and Economic History of the Danelaw* (cited hereafter as *Danelaw Charters*). Introd. p. lx and *passim*, and 'The Free Peasantry of the Northern Danelaw' in *Bulletin de la Société Royale des Lettres de Lund*, 1926, pp. 73 ff., where 302 grants of land made by peasants are calendared. The evidence is conveniently summarized by the same author in the *Proceedings of the British Academy*, xiii (1927).

[3] Cf. D. C. Douglas, *The Social Structure of Medieval East Anglia* (Oxford Studies in Social and Legal History, ed. Vinogradoff), pp. 205-19.

tenures are burdened with cornage rents[1] and with a strange mixture of knightly and servile services; they, for example, perform honourable military services, yet submit to the payment of 'merchet', elsewhere a mark of servitude, while the tenants in bondage paid rents in kind and rendered only trivial labour services.[2] Kent was always peculiar in its social arrangements. A record of customs drawn up in the time of Edward I declares that 'all the bodies of Kentishmen be free'.[3] This, of course, is a broad generalization. There was a substantial and important class of free peasants who held by a special form of tenure known as gavelkind, who owed rents and relatively light services of ploughing and reaping, and who were protected by a special custom. But it must not be inferred that the county of Kent was devoid of villeins.

An analysis of the Domesday figures bears out the general conclusion that in the shires which were most directly affected by Scandinavian influence there was more independence than elsewhere. In Lincolnshire, for example, there are almost as many free sokemen as there are villeins and their congeners, bordars and cottars; in many wapentakes the freemen were in the majority.[4] As we move westward across the map, however, the proportion of freemen to the servile classes diminishes until in the south-west the free tenants form a negligible element in society. In Oxfordshire, for instance, they represent no more than one-half per cent. of the entire inhabitants.[5] These facts are of even greater significance than the geographical area to which they relate would seem to indicate; for the eastern counties were at once the most densely populated and the most prosperous. Norfolk stands highest with a recorded working population in 1086 of 27,087; and it still kept its lead about a hundred years later when Jordan Fantosme enthusiastically wrote:

> Who can tell me or who can mention
> A country from here to Montpellier which is worth

[1] Apparently in origin a tax on the number of horned beasts kept, but now commuted into a fixed rent.

[2] Cf. on the whole subject of Northumbrian tenures Maitland, *Eng. Hist. Rev.* v (1890), 625, and J. E. A. Jolliffe, ibid. xli (1926), 1.

[3] *Statutes of the Realm*, i. 223.

[4] Cf. the tables setting out the percentage of sokemen to villeins and bordars in the wapentakes of the northern Danelaw in Stenton, *The Free Peasantry of the Northern Danelaw*, pp. 77–9.

[5] For the percentages of the free and servile classes see the map in Seebohm's *English Village Community*, p. 85.

That of Norfolk of which you hear me speak,
More honoured knights, nor more liberal,
Nor more merry dames to give freely,
Except in the city of London, whose peer no one knows.[1]

Lincolnshire comes next with a Domesday population of 25,301, and Suffolk with 20,491. The large county of Devon, which stands next in the list, had only 17,434.[2]

The legal position of the Domesday villein is not easy to determine.[3] The evidence on the whole suggests that he was still personally free in 1086. But in fact the question of status only became of real importance when the common law developed in the course of the twelfth century. It then became a serious matter to the peasant whether or no he could get the protection of the courts. The sharp distinction between freeman and villein begins to emerge with the growth of the system of royal writs; it became necessary to decide who should and who should not have the benefit of this royal boon. The lawyers were striving to reduce the whole population into the simple classification free or serf, *aut liberi aut servi*. The result of this sorting out seems to be a more even distribution of free and servile throughout the country by the end of the twelfth century. Some of the Lincolnshire freemen have become serfs,[4] and many of the Oxfordshire serfs have become free. Indeed a study of the legal records of the period leaves one with the impression that every county had an abundance of free peasants farming small properties of a few acres or a virgate or two, which they jealously defend by the possessory assizes in the king's courts. Villeins could not serve on juries,[5] yet there seems to be no lack of free and lawworthy men to undertake the endless public duties imposed by the Crown on the shires, hundreds, and vills. How this change came about we shall attempt to explain later; for the present we will consider the position of the villein, farm labourer and small-

[1] In *Chron. of Stephen, &c.*, ed. Howlett. iii, ll. 908–12.
[2] The county populations as recorded in Domesday have been conveniently tabulated by Henry Ellis, *General Introduction to Domesday Book* (1833), ii. 511 f.
[3] I have discussed this subject more fully in my *Obligations of Society in the XII and XIII Centuries*, chapter ii of which what follows is in part a summary.
[4] Stenton, *Danelaw Charters*, pp. lxxx–lxxxi.
[5] See, e.g., *Pipe Roll 33 Hen. II*, p. 5. Edward Leg is fined half a mark 'because he chose rustics for the assize'. Cf. *Curia Regis Rolls*, vii. 26, 288. But the representatives of the four vills who were associated with the twelve freemen in the presentment of criminals according to the Assize of Clarendon were no doubt often villeins. See Pollock and Maitland, *Hist. Eng. Law*, i. 421.

holder combined, whom we have come to regard as typical of the manorialized estate.

A Northamptonshire peasant defends his freedom in 1198, declaring that he is neither 'rusticus nec servus nec villanus, nec natus in villenagio', nor has he ever done servile works or customary services.[1] These are the legal terms to denote villeinage. The fine distinctions of the servile class which we meet with in Domesday, bordars and cottars, reappear in manorial records but they are unknown to the law of the twelfth century. The peasant is a villein, a member of the village community; he is a native, that is a villein by birth; he is a simple rustic; sometimes he may be termed a *consuetudinarius*, a man who performs customary services; he is sometimes described as *servus*, a serf, one who does servile work. But the serf of the middle ages is not a slave. Slaves in the ordinary sense of the word, male and female, *servi* and *ancillae*, form a substantial class in the Domesday survey. But after the Conquest attempts were made to suppress the traffic in slaves. Anselm at the London Council of 1102 issued a canon against the practice of selling Englishmen 'like brute beasts'; Wulfstan by his preaching checked the thriving slave-trade between Bristol and Ireland.[2] The new Norman lords themselves emancipated many of the slaves they found on their estates, and these joined the ranks of the lower class of the peasantry, the bordars and the cottagers. Within a century of the coming of the Normans there was little trace remaining of servitude. Nevertheless, many aspects of medieval serfdom were very like slavery. The serf was the lord's chattel with whom he could do as he pleased except slay him or maim him. The lord could tallage him at will, he could exact a degrading fine from him when he gave his daughter in marriage (*merchet*), he could seize his best beast when he died by way of a heriot, a death duty; he could compel him to grind his corn in his mill, and perhaps bake his bread in his oven at a price. The lord could even sell him and sometimes his family as well for a few shillings or a pound or two. There are occasional records of such transactions. The villein was not trusted to carry weapons; there is no hint before 1225 that he was sworn to arms.[3] On the

---

[1] *Curia Regis Rolls*, i. 67.

[2] Wilkins, *Concilia*, i. 383, cap. xxviii; *Vita Wulfstani* (Camden Soc., ed. Darlington), pp. 43, 91.

[3] Cf. *Curia Regis Rolls*, i. 45, 67, where a man claimed as a villein by the abbot of Evesham protests his freedom on the ground that 'in jurata domini regis fuit ipse

other hand he was not entirely without rights. The lord, as we have said, could not slay or maim his villein; he could not even thrash him without the risk of trouble; an Essex lord in Henry I's time was fined 40s. for this offence.[1] Then at the end of our period the lord was prevented from bringing his villein to ruin; by a clause of the Great Charter 'his wainage', that is his tillage, his means of livelihood, was protected from arbitrary amercement.[2] He was protected too by the custom of the manor which gradually hardened into a local law defining the extent of a peasant's obligations to his lord. Moreover, as against anyone else but his lord, he had the same rights as a freeman. He was a tenant at will so that he could be ejected at the lord's pleasure. In fact, however, the villein tenement normally passed undivided from father to son (very often to the youngest son according to the custom known as 'Borough English') by hereditary succession, so long as the services were duly performed.[3] He may pay small rents in money or in kind, a few pence, some hens, and a number of eggs, but he must perform labour services; this seems to be the essence of villeinage. He must work for his lord for so many days in each week in addition to 'boon works', special tasks, *precaria*, at certain seasons or on certain occasions. He holds by fork and flail, *ad furcam et flagellum*.[4] In theory, at least, he must do whatever he is appointed to do 'nor shall he know in the evening what he shall do on the morrow'.[5] This uncertainty of service and the payment of merchet were already applied in the end of the twelfth century as tests of villeinage in the courts. Two Northamptonshire peasants, for instance, declared that they were villeins and customary tenants of a certain lady 'by doing whatever work she should order and by giving merchet for their daughters'.[6] Nevertheless, the services required of a villein were in fact generally known, and often minutely specified. The Black Book of Peterbrough, drawn up between

---

juratus ut liber homo ad habendum arma'. The earliest evidence for the villein being included in the Assize of Arms is the writ for the collection of a fifteenth in 1225 printed in *Foedera*, i. 177.

[1] 'pro rustico verberato' (*Pipe Roll 31 Hen. I*, p. 55).
[2] Magna Carta, cl. 20.
[3] For the origin of the term 'Borough English' see Pollock and Maitland, *Hist. Eng. Law*, i. 647. Cf. *Curia Regis Rolls*, vi. 355 for a case where the land passed to the villein's wife who would not render the services, and hence it was taken back into the lord's hands.   [4] Ibid. i. 22 (Linc.), 313 (Bucks.), iii. 8 (Norfolk).
[5] Bracton, iv, c. 28.
[6] *Curia Regis Rolls*, i. 16. Cf. also Vinogradoff, *Collected Papers*, i. 112–28.

1125 and 1128, when the abbey was vacant and in the king's
hands, gives a detailed description of its manors. In the manor
of Kettering there were forty villeins each holding a virgate of
land. This is what was required of them:

'Those men plough for the lord for each virgate 4 acres for the
spring sowing. And besides this they shall find ploughs for the lord's
use thrice in winter, thrice in spring, and once in summer. And those
men have 22 ploughs among them with which they work. And all
those men work three days in each week. And also they render
yearly from each virgate by custom 2s. 1½d. And all the men render
50 hens and 640 eggs.'[1]

This was a fairly simple set of duties. Both the week work and
the boon work, which the peasants on the estate of the Templars
at Guiting in Gloucestershire had to perform for their virgate of
land in 1185, were far more elaborately set out:

'Each virgate of land which owes services must work with one
man for two days in each week from Martinmas (11 November) till
the time for haymaking, and then they will mow for four days a
week as long as there are meadows to be mown and hay to be carried.
If the meadows are mown and the hay carried before the feast of St.
Peter ad Vincula (1 August), they shall return to working two days
a week till St. Peter ad Vincula, and afterwards for four days a
week unless the corn crops are so forward that they can reap them;
and if they can reap them, then on Monday they must work with two
men, and on Tuesday with one man, and on Wednesday with two
men, and on Thursday with one man, until the corn is carried, and
when the corn is carried, four days a week till Martinmas. Besides
this, each virgate which renders work must plough as a boon work
(de bene) an acre and three quarters, and thrash the seed corn, and
sow the land and harrow it for the winter sowing; and, if the master
wishes it, carry loads to Gloucester or wherever he wills. Each team
must also plough two acres of pasture. All the labourers must also
against Christmas make one load of malt and similarly against Easter,
and for drying the malt, they must get one load of wood; the said
labourers must also move the sheep-fold twice in the year, at the
master's bidding, and they must spend two days at the washing and
shearing of the sheep to see that they are properly tended.'[2]

This is a very comprehensive list of services and covers most of
the operations of a farming year. Onerous as they seem, it should

[1] Chronicon Petroburgense, ed. Stapleton (Camden Soc.), p. 157.
[2] For the Latin text see Records of the Templars in England in the Twelfth Century, ed.
Beatrice A. Lees, pp. 50 f.

be remembered that it was in fact the tenement, the virgate, and not the individual tenant on which the burdens were imposed. The villein tenant was responsible that the work was performed; but he might well have a wife and grown-up sons, perhaps also brothers, who would take their share in the performance of these tasks and also in the cultivation of the family holding.

The virgate, like all medieval measurements, varied in size; it might be as small as 15 or as large as 80 acres, but it may be regarded as generally approximating to 30 acres.[1] Our examples refer to the superior villeins, holders of a normal virgate of about this area. There were, however, different grades of villeins. On the Peterborough manors, for instance, there were semi-villeins with half a virgate and proportionately lighter services. The class of *bordarii* which bulks so largely among the Domesday population is not very commonly found on twelfth-century manors; and where they do appear they seem to be indistinguishable from the much more frequent class of cottars.[2] These with their 'toft and croft', their cottage homestead and small adjacent enclosure, eked out a meagre livelihood on the lands of the lord and on those of the more prosperous villeins. Their principal function was to provide a reserve of labour which could be called upon in times of stress. The cottar might hold a few acres in the village fields—five is the commonest number; he might be required to do a day's work a week for his lord, perhaps two at the busy seasons; he might have to perform relatively light boon works; but he evidently had plenty of time on his hands to hire himself out as a wage-earner or to engage in some specific occupation or trade. The manorial cowman (*vaccarius*), the shepherd (*bercarius*), the swineherd (*porcarius*) ranked among the cottagers, and so too the village smith, wheelwright, or carpenter.

Two classes of villeins were in an exceptional position: those on the demesne manors of the Crown and those who, though personally free, held in villeinage. The former included the villeins not only on the manors actually in the hands of the Crown, but also on those which had at any time since the Conquest been royal manors. In later times, in the second half of

[1] Vinogradoff, *Villeinage*, p. 239. Likewise the bovate, the typical peasant holding in the north-east, was variable in size, but was commonly about 20 acres. See Stenton, *Danelaw Charters*, p. xxviii.

[2] The two terms are actually used for the same set of tenants on the Peterborough manor of Pytchley (*Liber Niger*, p. 161).

the thirteenth century, this land was known as 'ancient demesne' and the proof came to be whether or not it was recorded in Domesday Book as *terra Regis*. The villein tenants on these estates, villein sokemen, as Bracton called them, enjoyed many immunities and privileges: they were relieved of many of the burdens attached to ordinary villeinage; they could leave their tenements when they wished, and though they were denied the benefit of the assizes, they were protected by the royal courts both against ejectment from their holdings and against increase in their services. This privileged form of tenure was not, as was once thought, a survival from earlier times when peasants enjoyed a greater measure of freedom than was normally allowed to them in the feudal age, but it grew out of the administrative and judicial changes of Henry II's reign. The king had the right to tallage the villeins on his demesne; it was therefore in his own interest that they should be prosperous and able to pay their tallage.[1] The freeman who held in villeinage presents another anomaly. He was a villein of his own accord, *villanus sponte sua*.[2] The unprovided sons of small freemen, in order to acquire some land to give them a livelihood, might voluntarily assume the burdens and disabilities incidental to villeinage; but by doing so they seriously jeopardized the position of their descendants, who, their free status forgotten, might not unnaturally come to be regarded by their fellow peasants as ordinary villeins.

In the course of the twelfth century villein services were often commuted for money payments. There is a large and growing class of tenants who render no services or only insignificant services, but instead pay rents. One of the questions put to the jurors at the inquisition on the Glastonbury estates of 1189 was, 'if any land which ought to render work had been made free in the time of Bishop Henry [Henry of Blois, Bishop of Winchester, who was abbot of Glastonbury 1126–1171] or since', whether, that is to say, the servile *opera* have been commuted for money rents.[3] In fact on these Glastonbury manors there had been much commutation. Nor was this merely a local peculiarity. The evidence of the dozen or so other surveys, which relate to conditions of the twelfth century and which range over a wide

[1] See the important article by R. S. Hoyt, *Eng. Hist. Rev.* lxv (1950), 145–74.
[2] *Curia Regis Rolls*, iv. 234.
[3] *Liber Henrici de Soliaco Abbatis Glaston. An Inquisition of the Manors of Glastonbury Abbey* (Roxburghe Club), p. 21.

geographical area, points in the same direction—to a commutation of villein services for money rents. From the two surveys of the manors of Burton abbey (Staffs.), both belonging to the time of Henry I, it is evident that many peasants who according to the earlier record had performed services were, when the second was taken some years later, paying 2s. or 3s. for their couple of bovates.[1] Perhaps the clearest evidence of change from a real to a money economy comes from the documents relating to the English estates of the abbey of the Holy Trinity at Caen. These were surveyed at three periods in the twelfth century: in the early years of the reign of Henry I, and twice within a few years of each other in the reign of Henry II. At Minchinhampton (Glos.), a manor of this house, in the first survey approximately 17 virgates were held by services and 9 by the payment of rent; in the second 8 were held by services, 8 were wholly commuted and 10 partially commuted (with the option of work or rent); in the last all those with the option of work were paying rent.[2] No doubt many of the tenements charged with rents in the twelfth century had always been so held and represent the ancient *gafol*, the rented land of Anglo-Saxon times; but equally plainly many had become rent-paying as a result of a lively movement towards commutation in this period. The amount of villein services demanded depended on the requirements of demesne agriculture. On the Peterborough manors, for instance, the demesne lands were extensively farmed, and the labour services of the villeins were generally exploited to the full. On other estates, however, a portion, sometimes even the whole of the demesne, was leased out to tenants, and the erstwhile villeins became rent-payers, variously termed *censuarii, molmen, firmarii*. It was obviously more convenient for an absentee landlord, like the nuns of Holy Trinity at Caen, to collect rents rather than to be burdened with the business of farming; and so, too, for the Templars, whose lands were largely managed on a monetary basis, since their concern was the crusade, and their manors were chiefly of value to them as providing financial support for their work in the east.[3] Why

[1] *The Burton Abbey Twelfth Century Surveys*, ed. C. G. O. Bridgeman, The William Salt Archaeological Society, 1916.

[2] These figures, kindly supplied to me by T. H. Aston differ slightly from those given by Postan, *Trans. R. Hist. Soc.*, 4th ser., xx (1937), 183.

[3] Cf. B. A. Lees, *Records of the Templars in England in the Twelfth Century*, pp. xxvii, xxxvii.

monastic houses, like Burton or Glastonbury, adopted this new method of estate management is not so clear; but even to them it might seem less troublesome and scarcely less profitable to take rents rather than to submit to the perpetual worries and anxieties of a farming landlord, just as they found it easier to take a scutage from their knightly tenants than to have the trouble of providing a trained warrior for the king's expeditions.

How far this change in the method of holding involved also a change in personal status is difficult to determine. It is a question that admits of no decisive answer. The evidence points both ways. In the surveys the two classes are generally sharply distinguished, *sive villanus sive censuarius*. We have seen that in the Glastonbury inquest the phrase is used 'if land which ought to render work has been made free and to what extent is it free', and in the same document we find the statement that a certain peasant 'holds more freely than his predecessors were accustomed to hold'.[1] Nevertheless that the lord could and often did revive the labour services of tenants who had been accustomed to pay rents implies that this measure of freedom was limited. In fact the next century, perhaps owing to greater agricultural prosperity and to an increased demand for produce in the markets owing to the growth of the urban population, witnessed a reaction. There was more intensive cultivation of the demesne with a corresponding increase in or recovery of labour services.[2]

The line between the free and the unfree was always in this period very indistinctly drawn. Mixed marriages added to the confusion. Freemen married bondwomen and free women married villeins. Such matrimonial intercourse shows that there were no insuperable social barriers dividing the free from the unfree. But what was the status of the progeny of such alliances? Usually the courts adopted the rule that the child follows the condition of the father. Peasants are constantly in the royal courts pleading their free status. Time after time local juries are called upon to give a verdict whether a man be a villein or no, *utrum sit villanus necne*. The kin are produced; pedigrees are closely investigated; the tests of services and merchet are applied. But the intermarriage of free and serf, the practice of freemen holding in villeinage, commutation of services, changes in terminology, had all combined to make the matter so intricate

---

[1] pp. 21, 121.
[2] For evidence of the reaction see Postan, op. cit., pp. 185-9.

that the very neighbours are often at a loss to determine the condition of their fellow tenants.

Although commutation of services did not give a villein his freedom, there were several ways by which this could be acquired. The lord could give him his freedom by charter, sometimes in return for a small quit-rent,[1] or the villein might purchase it; but technically at least this must be done not with his own money (which was deemed to be the property of his lord) but through an intermediary. Thus in 1207 a woman claimed in the courts that she had been redeemed 'per alium et per alterius pecuniam'.[2] Though definite evidence of manumission is rare in this period, it is certain that what has survived represents much that has since perished, for private charters of small men had little chance of survival in the rough and tumble of medieval life. The manumission was performed publicly in the presence of witnesses and ceremoniously. The lord taking the liberated serf by the right hand presented him to the sheriff in full county court, claimed him quit of his servitude, and furnished him with the arms of a freeman.[3] There were also less conventional methods of enfranchisement. A peasant could gain his freedom by assuming holy orders; but after 1164 he might only do so with the consent of his lord.[4] He might also escape to a town where, if he remained unreclaimed for a year and a day, he became free. The German proverb 'Stadtluft macht frei' ('town air enfranchises') applies to England no less than to the continent. It may be assumed that the nascent towns welcomed recruitment from the country, for the admission of escaped rustics is often specially recorded among the privileges of a chartered borough.[5] Nevertheless it is no less evident that the lords made efforts to recapture them; if, however, they failed to do so within four days, they could only recover their fugitive villeins by an appeal to the courts. Sometimes these emancipated villeins rose to positions of importance. The surname Villanus, Villain, le Vilein is occasionally attached to persons who took a prominent part in local affairs and to some even who reached the dignity of knighthood. Sir Robert Thorpe, the

[1] Cf. A. L. Poole, op. cit., pp. 30–4.   [2] *Curia Regis Rolls*, v. 77.
[3] *Willelmi Articuli Londoniis Retractati*, 15, Liebermann, *Die Gesetze der Angel-Sachsen*, i. 491.
[4] Constitutions of Clarendon, c xvi.
[5] For example Newcastle-upon-Tyne, Lincoln, and Nottingham (A. Ballard, *British Borough Charters, 1042–1216*, pp. 103–4). Cf. *Willelmi Articuli*, c. 16.

fourteenth-century chief justice and chancellor, was descended
from a Northamptonshire villein who was enfranchised in the
first years of the thirteenth century.[1]

The system of farming was of course largely affected by the
character of the ground. The downlands of Sussex and Wiltshire, the moorlands of Yorkshire, the marshes of Lincolnshire
were obviously more suitable for pastoral than for arable farming; and in such localities flocks of sheep and herds of cattle
rather than large arable fields were the conspicuous feature of
the rural scene. Where, however, the soil permitted, a crop was
grown. This is the essence of the open-field system, a system of
farming of great antiquity, which prevailed in the greater part
of England in the twelfth century, which persisted, despite its
defects, for many centuries, and which in one or two villages has
survived even to our own times.[2]

When, as in the twelfth century, the mass of the population
was engaged in agriculture, the bulk of the produce was
obviously consumed at home; the primary object of farming
was to supply the simple wants of the family. A virgate was supposed to be sufficient to sustain a peasant and his household;
at the manor of Christian Malford in Wiltshire where certain
virgates were too small to support a family, two were thrown
together to form one.[3] The principal business of the farm was,
therefore, the arable crops, the provision of bread, the vital need
of subsistence. The land was worked usually in two or three
large unenclosed fields on a system of strict rotation. If there
were two fields, as was the rule, for example, in Lincolnshire,
one was cultivated while the other lay fallow; if there were
three, two were under cultivation while the third was fallow.
But in either case a three-course husbandry was observed: one
portion was sown in the autumn with wheat or rye, another was
cultivated in the winter and seeded with a spring crop of wheat,
barley, or oats, with vetches, beans, or peas, while a third rested
fallow to recover its fertility in preparation for the autumn

[1] *Henry of Pytchley's Book of Fees*, ed. Mellows, p. 55.
[2] For a detailed examination of its working see C. S. and C. S. Orwin, *The Open
Fields* (Oxford, 1938). It is illustrated from the estate at Laxton (Notts.) where the
system is still practised. For an indication of its general prevalence, see the map,
ibid., p. 65.
[3] 'Pro duabus virgatis computata fuit terra illa, sed quia non potuerunt duo
homines ibi vivere, redacte ille due virgate ad unam.' *Inquest of the Manors of
Glastonbury Abbey, 1189* (Roxburghe Club) p. 113.

sowing of the next season.¹ In each of these fields the peasant farmer had so many strips, each of which roughly represented a day's ploughing and was separated by other strips belonging to his fellow tenants.² We are not here called upon to explain how this complex and inconvenient system of holding arose. It has recently been plausibly suggested that it naturally evolved from the action of the plough, from the co-aration of the villagers in the clearing of forest and waste in the distant past.³ But since then many changes had taken place; more land had been taken into cultivation by clearance of forest (*assarts*); and many plots had been reallocated. It seems that the principle of equity governed the later distribution of strips so that each peasant had his share of the good and the bad soil. So, when in the time of Henry II a certain Simon of Keyworth granted to Haverholme priory a bovate containing 17 acres of arable in Normanton on the Wolds, it was distributed as follows: 6 acres were to be in the better land, $5\frac{1}{2}$ in the mediocre land, and $5\frac{1}{2}$ in the worst land.⁴ The demesne lands of the lord of the manor might be held in a consolidated block or might be, and more frequently were, scattered and intermingled with those of his tenantry.⁵

The fields under cultivation were ploughed, sown, and harrowed by the villein tenants supplemented when necessary by the hired labour of cottagers. The productivity was not great. The average yield from a sowing of 2 or $2\frac{1}{2}$ bushels to the acre of winter wheat would not, even on a well-run farm, be above 10 bushels, whereas today a farmer would be ill-content with less than 30 from the same sowing.⁶ But the difference is more

---

¹ In the two-field system, the field under cultivation would be sown partly with an autumn partly with a spring-sown crop. The rotation was therefore the same. Cf. Orwin, op. cit., pp. 49 f.

² The holdings of the Kentish peasantry were apparently at one time in compact units known as *juga* or *dolae*. But gradually these had come to be split up as a result of the division of land among coheirs (the system of *gavelkind*) and the peasants held small parcels scattered in several contiguous or neighbouring *juga*. See Gray, *English Field Systems*, ch. vii. For East Anglia where the peasant holding tended to be consolidated in one part of the village area, see D. C. Douglas, *Social Structure of Medieval East Anglia*, p. 206.

³ Orwin, op. cit., p. 40.

⁴ Haverholme Priory Charters, ed. C. W. Foster (*Lincolnshire Notes and Queries*, xvii, 1922–3), no. 169. This neat example of equitable distribution is quoted by Stenton, *Danelaw Charters*, p. xxvii, n. 10.

⁵ For the compact demesne see Stenton, op. cit., pp. xxxiii, lviii.

⁶ Cf. *The Anonymous Treatise on Husbandry* (Walter of Henley, ed. E. Lamond), p. 71. For average corn yields taken from the account rolls of the manors of the bishop of Winchester, which have survived from the early years of the thirteenth

due to the advance in scientific methods than to the defects of the open field. There was no idea in the middle ages of selection of seed, which indeed had often to be found for the demesne lands by the villeins themselves; sowing broadcast is more wasteful than the seed-drill; dung and marl were the only known fertilizers, and there was no adaptation of manures to the special needs of the soil; more corn was left on the ground after the reaping-hook than after the modern reaper and binder. Nevertheless the method of open-field farming was in some respects convenient, for it spread the work evenly throughout the year; and it was, perhaps, not as wasteful as is generally said. It appears that every cultivable bit of the ground was brought under the plough in lands, headlands, and gore-acres (as the odd corners of the field were called), and nor is it necessary to believe that these narrow strips were generally divided by wasteful balks of unploughed turf.[1] The system had of course serious limitations: it allowed no place for individual enterprise or initiative. Every farmer must do as his fellow did; he must grow the same crops, he must perform the same farming operations, and perform them at the same time. He must farm, in short, according to rules, grown rigid through age and custom, over which he had little or no control. It may have been the natural system in the circumstances of the time, but it was wholly unprogressive.[2]

The livestock occupied a relatively secondary place in this system of farming. Apart from the small closes or crofts which adjoined the homestead and which supplied grazing for perhaps one or two milking cows and a few calves, the village farmer

century, see William Beveridge in *Economic History Supplement to the Economic Journal*, May 1927, pp. 155 ff., and January 1930, pp. 19 ff. R. V. Lennard has shown, however, that these statistics require modification, since they do not make allowance for tithe, for corn granted as a perquisite to reapers, and for rents paid in kind, all of which were normally taken from the crop in sheaves before thrashing, and were therefore not reckoned in the reeve's account of grain (ibid., February 1936, pp. 173 ff., and February 1937, pp. 325 ff.).

[1] The view expressed by the Orwins, op. cit., pp. 43 ff. against the theory of the unploughed balk has been challenged, and it is held that in some parts of the country, where the fields were ploughed flat without ridge and furrow, the turf balk divided and gave access to the strips. *Econ. Hist. Rev.* 2nd ser., i (1948), 34 ff. and iv (1951), 14 ff. But cf. the Orwins' reply in the second edition (1954), pp. 48–51.

[2] This is strikingly illustrated by the statistics brought together by Beveridge (op. cit. (1927), pp. 160–1): 'Broadly over the whole range of 250 years from the beginning of the thirteenth to the middle of the fifteenth century, the productivity of the soil under wheat shows no general change of level . . . the general impression is one of stability and stagnation.'

had largely to depend upon the wild grasses and rough herbage of the pastures, woodlands, and waste, which stretched away beyond the arable fields. But even his right of common was strictly limited; he could only turn out a number of sheep or cattle commensurate to the size of his holding. The lord of the manor himself was bound by the same rules and was stinted in the number of beasts he could put to graze on the commons which were in law his own. After the harvest the temporary fencing of the open arable fields was thrown down and laid open for the village stock to feed upon the stubble. Appurtenant to the manor was also some meadow land, reserved for the hay crop, which, like the arable fields, was divided among the tenants usually by annual allotment in strips or doles, and when the hay was carried it too became commonable pasture, and from Lammas to Candlemas (1 August to 2 February) the village cattle might feed on the lattermath. Pigs were driven into the woods to browse and to fatten on the acorns and beech-mast. Nevertheless it was generally only the free tenants that got these rights for nothing; the villeins were required to pay rents. Pannage was usually at the rate of a penny for a yearling pig, a halfpenny for a young pig;[1] occasionally it was charged not per head but at a fixed sum.[2] On some manors a rent (*herbagium*) was imposed for agisting sheep and cattle on the common pastures either for all or for those in excess of a specified number. The meagre accommodation for livestock on the average arable farm was, moreover, being continuously encroached upon by the practice of assarting or making clearings in the waste, which might be added to the common fields or enclosed for the use of the lord or one of his tenants.[3] Towards the close of the twelfth century, for example, a tract of 1,500 acres of pasture in Lincolnshire was converted into arable land.[4] In these circumstances it is not surprising that we hear of frequent complaints of cattle straying on to the growing crops. It must have been very difficult to carry even the necessary stock through the winter when there were no root crops to eke

---

[1] N. Neilson, *Customary Rents*, pp. 71 ff.

[2] At Aston Rowant (Oxfordshire), for example, it was 12*d*. a year. *Curia Regis Rolls*, iii. 143.

[3] Cf. T. A. M. Bishop, 'Assarting and the Growth of the Open Fields' in *Econ. Hist. Rev.* vi (1935), 13.

[4] *The Earliest Lincolnshire Assize Rolls*, ed. D. M. Stenton (Lincoln Record Society, vol. 22), no. 65.

out the small supplies of hay. Indeed the poverty of the cattle in winter is strikingly shown by the fact that it was reckoned that the average value of the milk-yield of a cow during the twenty-eight weeks from September to April was but 10d., while for the twenty-four weeks of summer it was as much as 3s. 6d.[1]

A specific example will best serve to indicate the amount of stock kept and the profits that were made on an average mixed farm. The manor of Great Tew in Oxfordshire was assessed in Domesday at sixteen hides, and was held by Odo, bishop of Bayeux. There were six plough-teams on the demesne; there were 288 acres of meadow and 101 of pasture; and it was worth £40. After the rebellion of Bishop Odo in 1088 the manor was escheated to the Crown; in 1130 the king's men of Tew rendered £36 of the farm of the manor, and not long after it was granted by Stephen to Rannulf, earl of Chester. When in 1165 it was again in the king's hands it was evidently in a very poor condition for the yearly farm had dropped to £16, and in 1167 it required to be completely re-stocked at a cost of £23. 19s. 0d. The animals purchased were 48 oxen, 5 farm horses, 20 cows and 2 bulls, 2 boars, 680 sheep, and 20 swarms of bees. The effect of this re-stocking was to raise the value from £16 to £30. Further improvements were then made. £9. 8s. 6d. was expended on seed-wheat and oats, the granary and the ox-stables were repaired for £1. 3s. 4d., and the ploughshares were put in order at the cost of 18s. This capital outlay again enhanced the annual value, bringing it up to £40, the Domesday figure.[2] It will be noticed that the Crown agent in purchasing the seed-corn adopted the precept later inculcated by Walter of Henley[3] that 'seed grown on other ground will bring more profit than that which is grown on your own'. As proof of this the author suggests a very modern form of test: 'Plough two selions at the same time', he writes, 'and sow one with seed which is bought and the other with corn which you have grown; in August you will see that I speak truly.' The ground under cultivation on the manor of Great Tew appears to have changed little since 1086, for the forty-eight oxen represent the six full plough-teams of eight oxen[4] recorded in the great survey; the

---

[1] *Treatise on Husbandry* (Walter of Henley), p. 77.
[2] For the early history of this manor see W. Farrer, *Honors and Knights' Fees*, ii. 240.   [3] p. 19.
[4] The team of eight oxen, conventional in Domesday Book, is also the most

cows and bulls form two dairy units (*vaccaria*) each composed of ten cows and a bull, which it was reckoned might bring in a profit of anything between 20*s*. and 30*s*. a year.[1] Pigs were a staple article of food, and all but the breeding sows and young litters were normally killed off in the autumn and salted down for winter consumption.

The sheep were the animals of the greatest utility. A hundred, it was calculated, would add £1 a year to the profits of the farm.[2] Their fleeces were always a safe commercial asset; their skins were in increasing demand as parchment for writing material; and in many parts of the country, especially on the rich pastures of the Kent, Essex, and Lincolnshire marshes, their milk produced an excellent cheese. Walter of Henley,[3] writing in the thirteenth century, reckons that twenty ewes fed in pasture of salt marsh can yield as much cheese and butter as two cows, i.e. a wey of cheese (about 256 lb.) and half a gallon of butter a week. It was seemingly only in the last resort that sheep were sent to the butcher; this at least is suggested by the blunt entry in the accounts of the manors of the bishopric of Lincoln when they were in the king's hands (1185): '63*s*. for sheep sold which could not live'.[4] Murrain, probably in the middle ages a generic term for any disease which attacked animals, must have been endemic when beasts, good, bad, and indifferent, and belonging to many owners, rich and poor, fed upon the same pastures. There can have been no shortage of carcasses of beasts put on the market 'because they could not live', or at best were in no condition to breed or produce good fleeces. On the ordinary arable farm the value of the relatively small flocks folded on the stubble after the harvest in treading and manuring the soil was scarcely less than the wool on their backs; but on the wide stretches of moor and downland it was for their fleeces that

common in other records, though we find teams of almost any size up to ten. Nevertheless this does not mean that eight oxen or horses (for the teams were often mixed, oxen and horses) were actually yoked to the plough. In practice the working team was usually four. The full team was perhaps divided into two working teams each under its own ox-herd. See H. G. Richardson, *History*, xxvi (1942), 287.

[1] *Pipe Roll 30 Hen. II*, p. xxxi. The *vaccaria* at Odiham brought in 20*s*.; that in Windsor Park, 25*s*.; and 10 *vaccariae* in the New Forest rendered 30*s*. each. *Pipe Roll 33 Hen. II*, p. 194; 2 Ric. I, p. 13?

[2] *Rotuli de Dominabus* (Pipe Roll Soc., vol. xxxv), p. xxxiv.   [3] p. 27.

[4] *Pipe Roll 31 Hen. II*, p. 125: 'lxiii s. de ovibus venditis que vivere non poterant.' Cf. Walter of Henley, pp. 29–31.

sheep were bred.[1] The large estates of an abbey or of a great
baron might carry very big flocks. The nuns of the Abbey of
Holy Trinity at Caen in the reign of Henry I kept a flock of
1,700 on their Cotswold estate on Minchinhampton Common,
and the bishop of Winchester in the early thirteenth century
had 1,764 on his Wiltshire manor of Downton. But it was not
only the great landowners who kept substantial flocks of sheep,
the peasants especially in districts where there were large
common pastures adjacent to the village, would often keep a
large number. From a return for the assessment of a fifteenth
on moveables in 1225 we learn that on the Glastonbury manor
of Damerham with its neighbouring hamlet of Martin some ten
miles south of Salisbury the 198 villagers kept as many as 3,760
sheep, while the abbey itself had no more than 570 pasturing on
the chalk downs.[2] With the increasing demand for wool more
attention was given to breeding. On the downs and moors only
the short, coarse-woolled sheep could thrive, but on the richer
pastures a fine curly-woolled sheep was bred. In 1196 on the
manor of Sulby in Northamptonshire 100 of these at 10d. each
replaced 100 coarse-woolled sheep at 6d. each. The capital
expenditure of 33s. 4d. had the effect of raising the annual
revenue from the estate by 17s. 8d., viz. from £9. 2s. 4d. to £10.[3]

The market value of stock shows a remarkable stability and
uniformity during the first twenty years for which prices have
been recorded (1163–83). In any county and in any of these
years an ox could be had for 3s. and sheep for 4d. apiece; cows
and bulls could sometimes be bought for 2s. 8d. or even 2s., but
3s. was the commonest price; breeding sows and boars, though
occasionally sold at 8d., stood with remarkable consistency at
1s. In the 1180s a period of agricultural prosperity set in, which
was accompanied by a sharp rise in prices. A farmer had now to
give 4s. or 5s. for his plough-beasts, and sheep rose 2d. to 6d.
apiece.[4] The prices which the king was prepared to give for
stock were fixed in 1194. Among the instructions given to the
itinerant justices, who visited most of the counties in September

[1] On the whole subject see Eileen Power, *Medieval English Wool Trade*, especially
Lecture II. Unfortunately, these valuable lectures based largely on unprinted
materials lack documentation.
[2] Power, op. cit., p. 30.   [3] *Chancellor's Roll 8 Ric. I*, p. 190.
[4] The figures are taken from the accounts for stocking the royal manors given in
the Pipe Rolls. See my note on 'Live Stock Prices in the Twelfth Century' in *Eng.
Hist. Rev.* lv (1940), 284, where the evidence from this source is printed in full.

of that year, was to see to the stocking of the royal manors, and the regulation prices are given:

'The price of an ox shall be four shillings, and of a cow the same, and of a farm horse the same; and of a fine woolled sheep 10*d*.; and of a coarse woolled sheep 6*d*.; and of a sow 12*d*. and of a boar 12*d*.'[1]

Landlords began to review the management of their estates with the object of seeing how they could increase their profits. The results of their investigations were set down in elaborate surveys or custumals, several of which date from the dawn of this era of prosperous agriculture.[2] A little later, in the thirteenth century, the practical and detailed treatises on husbandry, to which reference has been made, were compiled for the guidance of manorial lords. It was, however, chiefly the monastic houses that took advantage of the improved conditions. The laymen have a very poor record to show as landlords. From the evidence of a large number of manors in the wardship of the Crown in 1185, we may gather that they were habitually understocking their estates. We are told, for example, that Margaret of Munfichet's Cambridgeshire manor of Foulmire is worth £16 with its present stocking of two plough teams and 40 sheep; but if it were well stocked with three teams, 200 sheep, and 21 pigs, it would be worth £20. One manor, that of Rochford, Essex, was entirely devoid of stock when it came into the king's hands.[3] Shortage of capital seems to be the only adequate explanation for this slovenly farming.

In primitive times the bulk of farm-produce was consumed in the homes of the producers, and even in the eleventh century probably only a comparatively small proportion found its way to the local market. In the period under review, however, towns were developing rapidly, and townsmen were giving themselves up more exclusively to urban occupations. Correspondingly there was an increasing demand for articles of food, which was carried often over long distances along bad and hilly lanes to the market towns. Carting services were among the more irksome duties imposed upon servile tenants; the bordars on the estate of the Templars at Guiting were required to carry to Gloucester or Hereford (distances of some twenty and forty

---

[1] Roger of Hoveden, iii, 265.

[2] e.g. Glastonbury, 1189; Durham, *c.* 1183; Worcester, 1182; The Templars Inquest, 1185. Cf. Postan, op. cit., p. 175 n.

[3] *Rotuli de Dominabus* (Pipe Roll Soc., vol. xxxv), pp. 86, 73–4.

miles) or anywhere else the master ordered.[1] The needs of the neighbouring townsmen did not, however, exhaust the demand for agricultural produce. There was a growing export trade in some farm products. Then, castle garrisons had to be provisioned, armies had to be supplied with rations, the king's table had to be furnished when he travelled about the country. The sheriffs had to enter into large contracts to meet these requirements. More than 3,000 loads of corn, for example, were sent over to Ireland during the king's campaign there in 1171,[2] 1,900 chickens were purchased in Kent for the coronation feast in 1189,[3] and the carcasses of no less than 2,217 bacon pigs were shipped in 1203 to Rouen for the king's army in Normandy.[4]

When a lord was possessed of several manors he entrusted the general supervision to a steward who paid periodic visits to satisfy himself that his lord's interests were properly attended to and to preside over the manorial court. On the larger manors, and especially if the lord was an absentee, there would also be a bailiff to take charge of the work on the farm as the lord's representative. But the actual organization of the work from day to day, the direction and overseeing of labour, was the business of the reeve, or, as we should probably call him today, the foreman. He was always, it seems, a villein and was appointed by his fellow villagers. Among the duties usually assigned to the reeve was the keeping of the farm accounts. These for the manors of the bishop of Winchester have been preserved from 1208 in an almost unbroken series down to the fifteenth century, and illustrate with a wealth of detail every branch of rural economy. They set out the rents received from lands let on lease, customary rents such as pannage, the amount collected by way of tallage, the profits of the court, the buying and selling of stock, the yield and disposal of the crops, the expenditure on repairs and buildings, on ditching and hedging, and conclude with an elaborate statement of the stocktaking, showing the changes in the number of cattle, sheep, pigs, &c., which have taken place in the course of the year of account. That the unlettered reeve could record all this on notched

[1] *Records of the Templars*, &c., p. 51; above, p. 42.
[2] *Pipe Roll 18 Hen. II*, passim.
[3] *Pipe Roll 1 Ric. I*, p. 233.
[4] *Pipe Roll 5 Jo.*, p. xv.

sticks or tallies aided by his memory throws light on the intelligence of the better-class medieval peasant.[1]

The disputes and petty offences of the tenants were tried and punished by small amercements in the manor court or, as it was commonly called, the halimote. It was an ancient rule that 'every lord may summon his man that he may stand to right in his court'.[2] Here probably every fortnight[3] cases which merely concerned the manor were dealt with—cases of trespass in the woods or pastures, of sowing the lord's land badly, of the non-performance of boon works, or of brawling in the village street. Here too the tenants brought up their own grievances. But besides these purely manorial matters the lord was accustomed to try minor offences against the law of the country, against the king's peace. He had, in fact, assumed a jurisdiction which strictly belonged to the Crown. In spite of the prohibition contained in the Assize of Clarendon,[4] he claimed the right to take the 'view of frankpledge'. Twice a year, after the fashion of the hundred court at the sheriff's tourn, the manorial court became a police-court to deal, on the presentation of a jury of the chief pledges, with any offences short of felony. Hundreds of charters of the twelfth century make grants of land to important men with sake and soke, toll and team, and infangenetheof.[5] But none of these time-honoured words except the last (the right to hang a thief taken red-handed) had any particular application to criminal jurisdiction, certainly they were not held to comprise view of frankpledge. This was normally claimed as a prescriptive right; and was ultimately admitted as such by Edward I in 1290 if on an inquiry *quo warranto* it could be proved to be as old as the coronation of Richard I.[6] Very frequently the lord of the manor also claimed the right of enforcing the assize of ale, to see, that is, that the ale that was

---

[1] The accounts for the Winchester manors had been printed in full for the year 1208-9. *The Pipe Roll of the bishopric of Winchester*, ed. Hubert Hall. Those for the single manor of Crawley over a series of years have been printed by N. S. B. and E. C. Gras, *The Economic and Social History of an English Village*, pp. 186 ff.

[2] *Leges Henrici*, 55, 1. Liebermann, *Gesetze*, i. 575.

[3] Maitland, *Select Pleas in Manorial Courts* (Selden Soc.), p. xlix.

[4] c. 9. For the system of frankpledge see below, pp. 394-5.

[5] For the meaning of these terms and their significance see Stenton, *English Feudalism*, pp. 99-105. N. D. Hurnard in an elaborate article in *Eng. Hist. Rev.* lxiv (1949), 289-323 and 433-60, challenges the generally accepted view expounded by Maitland. She argues that this formula only conceded a very limited criminal jurisdiction.

[6] Pollock and Maitland, *Hist. Eng. Law*, i. 572.

brewed was good ale, and that it was sold at the standard tariff.
This was fixed in John's reign: when wheat was sold for 3s. a
quarter, barley for 20d. or 2s., and oats for 16d. or 18d., then
brewers may sell 2 gallons of ale for a penny, in boroughs
3 gallons, in country and market towns 4 gallons for a penny.[1]
At Chester in 1086 the penalty for making bad ale was the
cucking-stool (*cathedra stercoris*).[2] The lord in the thirteenth
century was still expected to possess this and the other necessary
instruments of justice (*judicialia*), the pillory, the stocks, and the
gallows. He defended these rights jealously. The manor of
Aldenham belonged to the abbot of Westminster, but the abbot
of St. Albans had ancient judicial rights which he still claimed
to exercise. A jury in 1201 found that if anyone has to undergo
the ordeal it shall be done in the pit (*fossa*) of St. Albans; if he
ought to be hanged, it must be done on the St. Albans' gallows;
if a duel is to be fought, it must be fought within the hundred of
St. Albans.[3] Nevertheless a lord seems to have preferred to
make a profit out of his court, and most offences of this kind
were punished by a small pecuniary fine of 6d. or 1s.

The manor, however, was not a legal unit; it was upon the
village, the township, the *villata*, that the multifarious public
duties and responsibilities were imposed. The reeve, the priest,
and four better men represented the village in the shire and
hundred courts;[4] the four lawful men of the village associated
with the representatives of the hundred in the presentment of
crime; representatives of four neighbouring villages were required to attend coroners' inquests. It was the duty of the village
when a crime had been committed to raise the hue and cry after
the criminal, to capture him if they could, and to keep him in
custody. If it fails in its duties, it is amerced. It is amerced for
all manner of sins of commission or omission: for failure to
pursue a felon, for concealment of crime, for hanging a thief
without view of the king's officer, for taking royal fish, for taking
toll illegally, for sending a man to the ordeal of water without
warrant, for ploughing up the king's highway, for receiving a

---

[1] *Reg. Malmesb.* (Rolls Ser.), i. 134; Maitland, *Select Pleas in Manorial Courts*,
p. xxxviii.

[2] *Domesday Book*, i. 262b. Few can have afforded the alternative of a heavy fine
of 4s.

[3] *Curia Regis Rolls*, ii. 56.

[4] *Leges Henrici*, 7.7. Liebermann, *Gesetze*, p. 553. The priest afterwards dropped
out. Pollock and Maitland, *Hist. Eng. Law*, i. 545, n. 1.

man who was not in tithing, for allowing Flemings to carry away their chattels.[1] In every case the liability rested not on individuals but on the village as a whole. So too it was with financial imposts: the village was assessed as a whole, and it was apportioned 'as the men of the village determined it'.[2] When the village and the manor were coincident, the manorial organization, the manor court naturally provided the necessary machinery for carrying out the legal responsibilities placed upon the community. There were, however, villages with no lord of the manor and there were villages with several. We hear of villages leased to the villagers to farm for themselves[3] and often, especially in the north and east of England, of villages where the lordship was divided among many lords.[4] There is little evidence to show how the men of such lordless or many-lorded villages managed their affairs. But it seems difficult to avoid the conclusion that from time to time they gathered in village meetings to discuss and regulate their joint interests in the cultivation of the fields and in rights of common; and that in the same meetings they decided on matters relating to their public duties.[5]

The lord with his manor house, his extensive demesne, and his court stood for power and authority in the village. But the parson with his church filled a no less essential place in the life of the peasants. The church, which often still stands as a monument of the twelfth-century community, was the nucleus of village activity. There the peasants gathered not only for religious observances on Sundays and Holy Days, but also for their merry-makings, their dancing, and their drinking-bouts; sometimes it served too for a market-place. Unseemly brawls and even the shedding of blood caused the bishops to prohibit such practices; but despite the denunciations they continued throughout the middle ages. The parish priest would not rank among the aristocracy of medieval county society. He was often of humble birth, poorly educated, and seldom rich. He had his

[1] See the list of amercements collected by Madox from the Pipe Rolls, *Exchequer* (ed. 1711), pp. 374-95.

[2] Cf. Vinogradoff, *Villeinage*, p. 357 and note 1.

[3] *Pipe Roll 30 Hen. II*, p. 135; *Rotuli de Dominabus*, p. 32.

[4] The lands of two lords at Willoughton (Lincs.) are so inextricably mixed up that the men of the village are unable to separate them. *Records of the Templars*, p. 101. Cf. Introd., p. xxxi.

[5] See Stenton, *Danelaw Charters*, pp. xliv, lxii, lxii n. 1. Maitland (*Hist. of Eng. Law*, i. 610 ff.) is inclined to minimize the communal side of village activity.

solemn duties to perform which no doubt enhanced his position:
he baptized, married, and buried the peasants, sometimes he
preached to them. But on week-days he was working, like any
other peasant, in the fields, on his glebe which might, like the
lord's demesne, lie in strips intermingled with those of his
parishioners. Sometimes he was scarcely distinguishable from
the villein tenants. The parson in a Staffordshire village even
did week-work for his lord in return for his croft.[1] Generally,
however, he had a double share in the holding, two instead of
the single virgate of the ordinary peasant. Besides cultivating
his land he had another important duty in the village farming:
he was expected to provide and maintain the entire animals of
the community—at least the parish bull and parish boar, sometimes the ram or stallion as well.[2] One thing, however, always
militated against an easy intimacy between parson and
parishioners: dues and rents either in money or in kind were
unceasingly demanded by the church and were a perpetual
source of friction. There were churchscots for the support of the
clergy and Romescot for the support of the pope (though only
a portion, if a substantial portion, of this tax was actually sent
to Rome); there were customary renders of Christmas hens and
Easter eggs. When on a peasant's death the lord of the manor
had seized his best beast as a heriot and the parson the second
best as a mortuary, there was little left for the widow. But unquestionably the most onerous of these dues was the tithe. The
church demanded a tenth not only of the crops of corn and hay
(the great tithe) but also of lambs and wool, of cheese and butter,
of fruit and honey, in fact of any produce of the farm. In fairness
to the parish priest it must be said that he did not always get
the whole tithe. Before the end of the twelfth century the
monastic houses had 'appropriated' a large number of churches,
and put in vicars at small, sometimes quite inadequate, salaries,
themselves taking the great tithes.

We may conclude this chapter with a few words on the lighter
side of the peasant's life. Rural merry-makings were usually
connected with pagan or Christian festivals, with Twelfth
Night or Candlemas, with May Day or Midsummer, with

[1] 'Ailwinus presbyter in Wismera (Wetmoor) 1 domum & 1 croftam de Inlanda
& operatur 1 die.' *Burton Cartulary*, ed. Bridgeman (William Salt Archaeological
Soc., 1916), p. 220.
[2] *Camb. Med. Hist.* vi. 531.

Lammas or Michaelmas; and the notion behind them was an invocation for a prosperous ploughing, sowing, or reaping, or a thanksgiving ceremony for a successful crop. The original purpose may often have been forgotten, but still on such occasions the villagers congregated to sport on the village green. We may assume, like the men of London in the twelfth century, they engaged in wrestling, cock-fighting, and bull-baiting.[1] In winter, again like the London youth, they slid and skated on the flooded and frozen meadows. Football (foteballe) is not specifically mentioned till much later (1409); but if we may believe that it originated in a fertility cult, a scramble or scrimmage for the possession of the head, the most prized part of the sacrificial beast, it must be exceedingly old.[2] Drink, however, was the principal solace of the village labourer. Festivals and celebrations of every kind were accompanied by an ale-drinking, a scotale, in which the highest credit was accorded to him who made the most of his fellows drunk and himself emptied the largest tankards.[3] Englishmen of all classes had a reputation for deep drinking. Drink then as now was a frequent cause of quarrels and village crime. The following story of two Wiltshire peasants told in the king's court in 1211 may be assumed to illustrate the rougher side of life in a medieval village.[4]

'Richard of Crudwell appeals John Scot and says that on the eve of Our Lady's birthday three years ago, the said John came from Ashley where he had been at a scotale and in the way as he came from Cirencester market made Richard get up behind him on his horse, and whereas Richard had thought that he would give him a lift in good faith, he struck out his hand backwards with a knife in it and struck Richard and wounded him in the right shoulder so that he fell off the horse, and John dismounted and again struck him with the knife and gave him another wound on the shoulder higher up (and the first wound was four and a half inches deep), and left him nearly dead, and besides this robbed him of forty-three shillings in coin from his purse and of a gold ring price fifteen pence; and when

---

[1] Fitz Stephen in *Materials for the Life of Beckett*, iii. 8–11. An excellent translation of this famous description of London by H. E. Butler is appended to Stenton's *Norman London* (Hist. Assoc. Leaflet nos. 93, 94, 1934).

[2] The suggestion is made by Sir Edmund Chambers, *Mediaeval Stage*, i. 149.

[3] See the constitutions of Richard Poore, bishop of Salisbury (dated between 1217 and 1223), *Sarum Charters* (Rolls Series), p. 134: 'ille . . . plus laudatur qui plures inebriat et calices fecundiores exhaurit.'

[4] *Curia Regis Rolls*, vi. 137. The English rendering is Maitland's *Select Pleas of the Crown* (Selden Soc., vol. i), pp. 58–9.

he had done this, Richard went home as best he might on all fours; and on the next day, the day of S. Mary's birth, he informed the king's serjeant, Robert of Hale, who came and saw the wounds and granted him the king's peace and went away; and five nights afterwards John came with his force to the house of Richard's mother in Crudwell and burgled her house and bound her and so treated her that never afterwards was she leal of body, but got her death thereby; and afterwards he robbed the house and carried off whatever was therein; and on the fourth or fifth day after the burglary Richard came to his mother and found her in the said condition, and she bade him, in case of her dying before him, to prosecute her death against the said John; and all this he offers to deraign against him as the court shall consider.

And John comes and defends all of it word by word, and offers two marks for an inquest by lawful men of the neighbourhood to find whether Richard makes this appeal out of hate and spite, or for good cause.'

But these wassailings must have been only occasional relaxations for the twelfth-century peasants. Even with ale at a half-penny a gallon he could not afford to indulge himself with great frequency.

III

TOWNS AND TRADE

A FOREIGNER visiting London in the last years of the eleventh century, though impressed by its spaciousness and the magnitude of its population, found the only thing that called for remark was the phenomenal number of savage dogs that lurked about St. Paul's at night-time to the terror of the passers-by.[1] This, however, scarcely does justice to the city which had long since attained to a position of pre-eminence in the kingdom. In 1135 it was described as the metropolis and queen of the whole kingdom; its citizens were, like those of the Cinque Ports, 'barons'. It had been surrounded by a wall since Roman times, and it was now approached by seven gates. Besides the White Tower, two other strongholds were already standing, both on the western side, the castle of Montfichet and Baynard's castle whose lords commanded the military forces of the city and controlled the Thames fishing as far as Staines bridge.[2] Still its pretensions were modest; its houses were unsubstantial structures, mostly of wood and thatched with straw. Fire and tempest wrought havoc in such conditions. William of Malmesbury gives a vivid description of a south-easterly gale in 1091 that destroyed 600 houses in London: churches were heaped upon houses; roofs, rafters, and beams hurtled through the air.[3] Another catastrophe occurred in the first year of Stephen's reign: a fire starting from London Bridge swept through the city, demolishing St. Paul's and most of the rickety dwellings as far as St. Clement Danes, some distance to the west and outside the wall. A new city arose upon the ashes, and the wealthier citizens took the precaution to build their houses of stone and tiles.[4] This was the London represented to us by William Fitz Stephen who wrote his famous description somewhere about 1180.[5] He was himself a Londoner, and extremely proud of the city of his birth. But allowing for pardonable exaggeration, it was evidently then a very fine and prosperous place with its

---

[1] Hugh of Flavigny, *Mon. Germ. Hist. Script.* viii. 495-6.
[2] *Eng. Hist. Rev.* xvii. 485-6.   [3] *Gesta Regum*, ii. 375 (§ 324).
[4] *Liber de Antiquis Legibus* (ed. Stapleton, Camden Soc.), pp. 197, 210.
[5] *Materials for the History of Thomas Becket*, iii. 2-13. Cf. above, p. 61, n. 1.

13 monasteries and 126 parish churches; with its schools and its
streets cleansed by sewers and conduits; with its lordly habita-
tions for the rich and its rows of orderly houses, backed by
spacious gardens planted with trees, for the less well-to-do
citizens. It had its markets and its tradesmen's stalls each in its
appropriate quarter. It had also its public cook-shop ready to
satisfy the needs of the most fastidious stomach. It was, moreover, already stretching out beyond the ancient walls. The palace
of Westminster, built by William Rufus, who held his first
court in the *Nova Aula* in 1099, was already linked up with the
city by a populous suburb; and a wooden bridge on the site
of the present London Bridge connected it with Southwark on
the south. This must have taken the traffic across the river
during most of this period, for, although a bridge of stone was
begun in 1176, it took over thirty-three years in building and
was not completed till towards the end of the reign of King
John.[1] Not long after Fitz Stephen's time, what we might call
a town-planning act was issued by Henry Fitz Ailwin, the first
mayor, with regulations regarding party-walls, which must be
built of stone, 16 feet in height and 3 feet in breadth, the construction and position of privies, protection of ancient lights,
and so forth. The ordinance was to be carried out by the mayor
and twelve specially elected persons who were to act as arbitrators in cases of dispute.[2] London was besides a city of pleasure
with its carnival and its horse-racing, with its opportunities
for sport of every kind—bull-baiting, bear-baiting, archery,
wrestling, and skating on the ice. The citizens also had an old
right of hunting in the Chiltern hills and in the adjacent
country both north and south of the Thames.

London, of course, soared far above all other towns in prosperity and importance, and it was fortunate in having escaped
by its timely submission to the Conqueror that ruthless ravaging
which was the fate of so many others, and which made them for
the time losers rather than gainers by the coming of the Normans. In Oxford, for instance, there were according to the
Domesday record only 243 houses capable of paying geld, the

[1] Its last stages may have been the work of Isenbert, master of the schools of
Saintes, who had built the bridges at Saintes and at La Rochelle. *Foedera*, i. 83.

[2] *Liber de Antiquis Legibus*, pp. 206–11; *Liber Albus* (ed. Riley, Rolls Series), p. 319:
cf. also introd., p. xxx. The assize is dated 1189, Fitz Ailwin being then mayor.
This presents a difficulty, for there is no evidence that he became mayor till the
setting up of the commune in 1191.

remaining 478, if not actually uninhabited and in ruins, were at least 'so devastated and destroyed that they could not render any tax'; and yet the Oxford farm—the fixed sum paid to the sheriff in lieu of the various dues, tolls, and rents owing to the Crown—had been almost doubled.[1] Chester, York, and Dorchester, to cite only a few, fared little better. Though doubtless this destruction of property was mainly the work of a conquering army, other causes contributed to it. The castle, which sprang up everywhere as a visible and threatening sign of Norman power, inevitably involved the wholesale demolition of houses,[2] and added to the discomfiture of the citizens by enhancing the authority of the sheriff, who was usually its custodian, alarmingly.

These, however, were temporary set-backs and were more than compensated for by the immense development of trade and commerce which followed after. The twelfth century is a flourishing period in the history of the English towns. Old ones grew, bulging this way and that beyond their ancient walls; new ones were founded both by the king and by private lords. In these newly created boroughs some system of town-planning seems to have been sometimes adopted; a prescribed frontage, a definite area for each house. At Stratford-on-Avon, for example, each burgage tenement was to be $3\frac{1}{2}$ perches in breadth and 12 in length. At Leek each burgess had half an acre for his dwelling and a plot of an acre in the fields. Some planning was even possible in the older towns which had grown up in a haphazard fashion; for the houses, other than those erected in stone by the more wealthy Jews, were slight wooden structures, even portable,[3] and a fire or a storm would, as we have seen in the case of London, almost certainly sooner or later demolish them, and thus provide an occasion for more orderly building. The description of a small building estate in East Street within the Gate, Gloucester, which King John gave to a citizen for development, has been preserved. The site was $32\frac{3}{4}$ rods in length and 12 rods in breadth, and the houses were made of boards and plaster and covered with tiles; they each contained a small hall,

[1] *Domesday Book*, i. 154.

[2] At Gloucester for instance, 'there were 16 houses where the castle stands which are now no more'. *Domesday Book*, i. 162.

[3] The house of a man who received heretics was to be carried outside the town and burnt ('domus . . . portetur extra villam et comburatur'). Assize of Clarendon, 1166, c. 21.

a chamber, and a kitchen, and were valued at a mark (13s. 4d.) a year, saving an annual ground rent (*longabulum*) of 13d. to the king.[1] Windows were screened at this time with linen curtains;[2] only in very important houses like the king's palace at Westminster were they glazed.[3]

In outward appearance, however, the borough may often have seemed to differ little from a large village with its open fields and its common pastures;[4] indeed in the course of the twelfth century not a few villages were in fact converted by a charter from the king or a lord into boroughs. The little town of Burford in Oxfordshire affords an apt illustration of this. In the Domesday survey it is described as an ordinary rural village with its 8 hides of land, its quota of villeins and bordars, its portion of meadow and pasture, and its two mills. It was even a decaying village, for whereas it had formerly been worth £16, in 1086 it was worth but £13. The lord, Odo of Bayeux, forfeited it with much other property in Gloucestershire and Oxfordshire in consequence of his rebellion in 1088, and it was granted to Robert Fitz Hamon, lord of the honor of Gloucester, who within twenty years created it a borough with all the free customs belonging to a borough—those of Oxford were adopted —including a market and even a gild merchant, the first in fact of which we have historical evidence. By a stroke of the pen, the villeins become townsmen with the free right to dispose of their property.[5]

At the time when Domesday Book was compiled the older borough had already acquired many of its essential features: it usually had its court, which in origin was the hundred court; it was as the later street names—such as Cornmarket or Horsemonger Street (the present Broad Street) in Oxford—indicate, pre-eminently a trading community; and while in most boroughs a certain amount of agriculture was practised, this had generally become an auxiliary and not the principal occupation of the burgesses. These held their houses and plots by a special form

---

[1] *Calendar of Inquisitions, Miscellaneous*, i, no. 170.
[2] 'linea tela ad fenestras'. *Pipe Roll 2 Ric. I* (1190), p. 156.
[3] 'ad reparandas fenestras vitreas domus Regis de Westmonasterio'. *Pipe Roll 25 Hen. II* (1179), p. 125.
[4] This aspect has been demonstrated by F. W. Maitland in his *Township and Borough*.
[5] Cf. R. H. Gretton, *Burford Records*, pp. 5–12. For the transition from villein to burgess cf. James Tait, *Medieval English Borough*, pp. 83 ff.

of socage tenure known later as burgage tenure; and lastly the rents and dues which comprised the 'farm' and which they owed to the king, were already compounded for a definite and fixed sum. The boroughs in the twelfth century also usually possessed a mass of archaic custom, some of which, like fixed rents—12*d.* was the most common rent for a burgage tenement —and the right freely to sell or devise property, were implied in burgage tenure; some, such as freedom from toll or the right to hear pleas, other than Crown pleas, arising within the borough in their own courts, were granted by charter; while some again, which regulated their trading and domestic concerns, might be sanctioned in by-laws made in the borough court or portmoot.[1] This body of custom was passed from one borough to another by the grant of a comprehensive charter. Thus the citizens of Oxford received the customs of London in a charter granted in 1155 by Henry II which declared that 'they and the citizens of London are of one and the same custom, law, and liberty'. In the case of doubt on a point of law the Oxford burgesses were to send to London for information, and the verdict of the Londoners was to be final;[2] consequently the king's court in 1203 upheld the claim of the prior of St. Frideswide that 'the citizens of Oxford ought not to plead except according to the custom and laws of the city of London'.[3] Then Oxford in its turn became a parent town, and passed its customs to Bedford, Lynn, and other places. The custom of the little Norman town of Breteuil was bestowed by its lord, William Fitz Osbern, earl of Hereford, upon his town of Hereford whence it spread to a large number of other rising boroughs, especially along the Welsh border.[4]

But at the opening of the twelfth century the boroughs had little independence of action. Their officers were royal officers; their courts lacked power of initiative and were ineffective; and they had no governing body of their own. They were, in fact, part and parcel of the shire organization. Their primary ambi-

[1] Such, for example, as the customs of Newcastle-upon-Tyne in the time of Henry I printed in *Acts of Parliament of Scotland*, i. 33–4.
[2] *Royal Letters addressed to Oxford*, ed. Ogle, p. 4.
[3] *Curia Regis Rolls*, ii. 143.
[4] A list of affiliated boroughs is given by Gross, *The Gild Merchant*, i, 241–81. A confusion between *Britolium* (Breteuil) and *Bristolium* (Bristol) led him, however, to attach a number of boroughs to the latter which really were affiliated with the former. For the customs of Breteuil see Bateson, *Eng. Hist. Rev.* xv. and xvi (1900–1).

tion therefore was to exclude the sheriff from meddling in their financial affairs and to be themselves responsible for the farm due to the king. That they were prepared to pay a high price, as much as 100, 200, or even 300 marks, for such a privilege shows the great value they set upon it. The natural corollary to the exclusion of the sheriff was the gradual evolution of municipal self-government. The policy of the Crown towards these aspirations varied from reign to reign. Henry I, perhaps realizing the value of the support of the towns, perhaps, too, thinking that timely concession might avoid the violent convulsions which so frequently characterized the communal movement on the Continent, showed a readiness to meet their more reasonable demands. It served the turn of Stephen and the empress, on the other hand, to use the boroughs as pawns in the game of bribe and counter-bribe to win the support of the nobility, and in this way not a few of them were mediatized in the hands of powerful barons. The urban policy of Henry II was strictly conservative; he shared the current idea that commune breathed revolution, and was chary of granting to the boroughs any considerable measure of independence. Their opportunity, however, came in the reigns of his sons. The pressing financial needs of Richard I and still more of John led these kings eagerly to accept the handsome proffers made by the towns in return for charters. John, indeed, through force of circumstances, was responsible for the great constitutional progress of the boroughs which marks the close of the twelfth and the opening of the thirteenth centuries. The general truth of this summary can be illustrated from the history of London which set the example for others to follow.[1]

London from early times had its courts. The folkmoot was summoned thrice yearly by the sounding of the great bell of St. Paul's; it was presided over by the sheriff and corresponded to the provincial shire court. The weekly husting was a meeting at the Guildhall at which the aldermen adjudicated on all kinds of civil business. These aldermen were also in charge of the wards into which by the time of Henry I the city was divided and which formed the basis of all local administration; their

---

[1] The clearest and most detailed account of the constitutional development of London is by M. Weinbaum, *Verfassungsgeschichte Londons 1066–1268* (Stuttgart, 1929). See also the admirable summary by F. M. Stenton, *Norman London* (Hist. Assoc. Leaflets nos. 93, 94, 1934).

wardmoots performed the work elsewhere done in the hundred courts. All the machinery was there for a strong and centralized municipal government. But such a development was seriously impeded by the existence of private jurisdictions or 'sokes' in the hands not only of prominent citizens, but also of bishops, monasteries, and magnates, who had often acquired these privileged estates in order to gain access to the London market. These immunities were confirmed in general terms in the charter granted by the Conqueror[1] and by that of Henry I.[2] This latter document, however, though on the whole conservative in character, forms a landmark in English municipal history,[3] for besides exempting the citizens from fiscal burdens such as the Danegeld and the murder fine, from tolls and customs-dues throughout England and at the sea ports, besides relieving them from the new procedure of trial by battle and limiting judicial amercements to the maximum figure of 100s., it gave them some measure of self-government. They acquired the right to render the farm of London and Middlesex, fixed at £300, direct to the exchequer,[4] and to appoint their own sheriff and their own justiciar to keep the pleas of the Crown. It was, no doubt, in defence of these privileges that in 1141 they formed some sort of sworn association, a commune on the continental model. It was, however, short-lived. Before the end of the same year Stephen, and a little later Matilda, granted to Geoffrey de Mandeville, the hereditary constable of the Tower and the bitter enemy of the Londoners,[5] the shrivalty 'as his grandfather held it' and united with it the justiciarship. Henry II, who, as we have said, was an opponent of civic independence, nominated the sheriffs himself and plundered the city by raising the farm to over £500. A half century passed after the loss of their liberties in 1141 before the Londoners again made a successful attempt to win self-government. The importance of Henry I's charter, therefore, lies not in its permanence—for it lasted no more than a decade—but in the fact that it was the first assertion of what came to be the common aspiration of all boroughs—emancipation from the financial and judicial organization of the shire.

[1] Liebermann, *Gesetze*, i. 486.
[2] Ibid., pp. 524–6. For an emended text see H. G. Richardson, *Eng. Hist. Rev.* xlii (1927), 80–7.
[3] Tait, op. cit., p. 157.
[4] Lincoln obtained the same privilege in 1130. Ibid.
[5] Cf. Round, *Geoffrey de Mandeville*, pp. 81, 174.

It was not, then, until after the death of Henry II, when political discord and heavy financial commitments provided favourable opportunities, that the movement towards municipal independence made rapid advances. In 1190 London acquired from the chancellor, William Longchamp, who was anxious to gain the support of the powerful interests in the city, the right to elect its own sheriffs and to render its old farm of £300 direct to the exchequer. But this lacked authority. Richard I, when he revisited England in the spring of 1194, took a fine of 1,500 marks from the citizens for the confirmation of their liberties which no doubt included the reduced farm;[1] it was, however, only in 1199 that they secured by charter from King John the fee farm and the right to elect the sheriffs, privileges which had been first granted them by Henry I nearly seventy years before. But they had to pay a high price for it: 'If they are willing to give those 3000 marks', the record states, 'they shall have their charter, but if not they shall not have their charter.'[2] In the meanwhile (in 1191) the citizens had conspired among themselves to wring from the party then in power, John, who was then count of Mortain, and Walter of Coutances, archbishop of Rouen, an organized form of government, a commune. There had been previous attempts, notably at York and at Gloucester, to imitate the continental scheme of town government, but they had been sternly repressed by Henry II.[3] This time it was a success, and two years later, in 1193, we hear something of its constitution: it had, like the communes of northern France, a mayor and échevins (*skivini*). Whether it was framed on the model of Rouen, as has been argued, or whether it merely attached foreign names to already existing aldermen, must remain a matter of uncertainty; but the foreign influence is unmistakable.[4] On the whole it is probable that the aldermen formed at least an authoritative element in this council, and apparently they did not manage the affairs entrusted to them

[1] In 1197 the farm of London and Middlesex is given as £300. *Pipe Roll 9 Ric. I,* p. 160.

[2] *Rot. de Oblatis et Finibus* (ed. Hardy), p. 11. The charter is contained in *Liber Custumarum (Munimenta Gildhallae Londoniensis,* ii, pt. 1, Rolls Series), p. 249. The citizens had also to give a good tonnel of wine and a good palfrey worth £5 to have a duplicate of their charter. *Pipe Roll 2 Jo.,* p. 153.

[3] Cf. Tait, op. cit., pp. 176 f. For the earlier attempt of London to set up a commune, above, p. 69.

[4] Tait, op. cit., pp. 251 f. and 266 f. Cf. J. H. Round, *Commune of London,* pp. 219 ff.

altogether in the best interests of the city. There was much popular discontent, and on more than one occasion (in 1201 and 1206) they had to be superseded by specially elected bodies.[1] They ultimately, however, appear to have won the confidence of the citizens, and the mayor and aldermen became the accepted governing body of London. The mayor set up by the commune of 1191, Henry Fitz Ailwin, held his office for life. Before the end of our period, however, a further stage was reached. King John, in the hope of winning the support of the Londoners in his struggle with the barons, a little more than a month before the agreement at Runnymede, granted them a charter which, besides confirming all their existing privileges, gave them the right to elect their mayor annually.[2]

The development of London was naturally in some respects different from that of other towns. It was immensely larger, and its administration was accordingly more complex; it dominated the small county in which it was situated and came practically to control it.[3] Elsewhere the position was reversed, and the county tended to dominate the town. Emancipation from this domination was therefore the first objective. In spite of his reluctance to encourage municipal independence, Henry II in a few cases permitted the burgesses the right to farm their town; but the right was always revocable at his pleasure; he never conceded a fee-farm, that is, a grant in perpetuity. For this they had to wait until the two succeeding reigns when such privileges were granted in profusion. The place of the sheriff came to be taken by town-reeves, who, though they were still royal officers for their appointment required the approval of the king's justiciar, were actually chosen by the burgesses themselves, and held their offices during good behaviour.[4]

Nevertheless, the borough with its elected reeves and its portmoot would still have been too weak to exercise an effective control over its affairs had it not been for its active and virile trade organization. A common feature of twelfth-century town charters was the concession of a merchant gild. The primary

---

[1] Tait, op. cit., pp. 267 f.   [2] *Rot. Chart.*, p. 207.

[3] The sheriffs were generally two in number; but they were both sheriffs of London and Middlesex, not one for London and the other for the county. See Round, *Geoffrey de Mandeville*, pp. 357-9.

[4] Cf. the charters printed in Ballard, *British Borough Charters*, pp. 242-6. The phrase in the charter to Northampton (1200) 'et non emoveatur quamdiu se in balliva illa bene gesserit' is significant.

object of this institution was, of course, the regulation of trade and commerce; but in fact it was provided with the means and power to do a great deal more. It had a revenue (arising from entrance fees) and an independent body of officials with an alderman at its head to carry out its business. Moreover, as the borough was first and foremost a trading community, membership of the borough and of the gild tended to be nearly, if not quite, identical. They were only 'two aspects of the same body'.[1] From the time of Domesday the Oxford freemen are indiscriminately termed 'citizens' or 'burgesses' or 'citizens of the commune of the city and of the gild merchant'.[2] The charters granted to Winchester are addressed sometimes to the 'citizens of Winchester' sometimes to the 'citizens of Winchester of the gild merchant'.[3] The common seal of the city of Gloucester, which was brought into use about 1200, bore the legend: *Sigillum Burgensium de Gilda Mercatorum Gloucestrie*,[4] and two years later (1202) the sheriff renders 2s. to the exchequer *de gilhalla burgensium Gloecestrie* that they may buy and sell *ad emendationem burgi*.[5] This is striking evidence of the identity of the borough community and the gild merchant at this time. Evidently in the twelfth century the gild organization was often employed for the transaction of purely urban affairs, in dealing with property, and in local government. This, however, was but a passing phase. The very facts that some of the most advanced towns, such as London and Norwich, had no merchant gild at all, and that in some towns there were burgesses who were not gildsmen, as at Ipswich, and gildsmen who were not burgesses, as at Lincoln, where the gild included not only Lincoln citizens but other merchants of the county,[6] preclude the possibility that the town constitution grew out of the gild. It was a makeshift to serve during the embryonic age of town life.

The impulse towards real self-government, towards something like corporate unity probably came from the Continent in the last decade of the twelfth and the first years of the thirteenth century.[7] The influence of the communal movement of northern

---

[1] Tait, op. cit., p. 229.
[2] Ibid., p. 226. Salter, *Medieval Oxford* (Oxford Hist. Soc., 1936), p. 35.
[3] *Foedera*, i. 50.   [4] Tait, op. cit., p. 230.
[5] *Pipe Roll 4 Jo.*, p. 173.   [6] See Gross, *Gild Merchant*, ii. 120, 146.
[7] Tait (op. cit., p. 291 and *passim*) emphasizes the determining influence of the continental commune on the growth of the borough constitution against the view

France and Flanders reveals itself in the office of mayor, which appeared in some dozen towns before the death of John, in councils of twelve or twenty-four elected members (*jurati, probi homines, skivini*, &c.) to aid and counsel him in the government of the town, and perhaps most clearly in the organization of the burgesses in sworn associations to maintain the new constitution and to abide by the rule of its officers. Besides self-government, the progressive town had or was aiming at financial independence. In 1201, for instance, we hear of the citizens of Lincoln raising money to be spent on the business of their town, and even claiming that they could not be tallaged except with their own consent.[1] The outward and visible sign of the emancipated borough was the common seal, the symbol of its corporate unity, which was to be used 'for the common honour and utility of the town and its burgesses'.[2]

In the boroughs we meet with a strange mixture of active progress and blind conservatism. They often clung tenaciously to outworn custom. Nowhere (except in the church courts where it hung on till the reign of Elizabeth) did the archaic mode of trial by compurgation so long survive; at London till the middle of the thirteenth century the testimony of a corpse was even admitted in a court of law,[3] while at Preston in the twelfth the primitive method of assessing damages for wounds at the fixed rate of 4*d*. an inch on the exposed parts of the body and 8*d*. on the covered parts was still in use. At Chester trial by jury was expressly prohibited by charter and at Bristol and Shrewsbury the assize of mort d'ancestor did not run. Notwithstanding all this, however, the townsman had come to represent the most progressive element in medieval society. They might still be regarded as socially inferior to the landed class, they might still be the objects of satire and derision in the literature of the period, but they could no longer be ignored. The inclusion of

of Maitland (Pollock and Maitland, *Hist. Eng. Law*, i. 659) and more recently of C. Stephenson (*Borough and Town*, 1933, pp. 171 f.) that it was of native growth. The former derived it from the borough court, the latter from the gild organization. For arguments against these views see Tait, op. cit., pp. 286 f., 296 f.

[1] *Curia Regis Rolls*, i. 418–19.

[2] The earliest examples of such seals appear at Oxford and York. In 1191 the *universitas civium* of Oxford authenticated an agreement *sigillo nostro communi* (*Cartulary of St. Frideswide's*, Oxford Hist. Soc. i. 36; cf. Tait, op. cit., p. 235).

[3] An oath taken on the grave of a dead witness by a living witness was regarded as the dead man's testimony. Bateson, *Borough Customs* (Selden Soc., vol. 21), ii, p. xxxiii.

the mayor of London among the twenty-five barons elected to carry out the terms of Magna Carta is an expression of the important position which the boroughs had reached by the beginning of the thirteenth century. Commercial prosperity had given them wealth and wealth had given them power. The strength of the towns lay in their economic organization as centres of trade.

The idea of association in clubs was a characteristic of medieval life. There had been gilds for social and religious purposes before the Conquest like the chapmen's gild at Canterbury or the *cnihtena* or knights' gild of London whose members in 1125 conveyed their property to the priory of Holy Trinity, Aldgate.[1] Soon the members of different crafts were forming associations for their mutual well-being; even the lepers tried to imitate their more fortunate contemporaries by forming themselves into a gild. We have spoken of the gild merchant in its connexion with the government of the borough in the twelfth century. We have yet, however, to discuss its essential function—the organization of the borough's trade. Although it only makes its first documentary appearance at earliest in the last decade of the eleventh century, it is recorded in some forty towns before the death of King John. In common with the gilds of the Anglo-Saxon period, the gild merchant had its social and convivial side; the members drank ceremoniously to the gild at their meetings or 'morning-speeches'; erring gildsmen were fined in beer; and like a modern friendly society, they looked after their sick brethren, buried their dead, and provided for the fatherless and widows. The gild was not, as has been sometimes said, a ring of the leading merchants, at least not in its early days. On the contrary, it cast its net astonishingly wide, and embraced traders and artisans, rich and poor, great and small. The gild rolls of Leicester, which date from 1196, include a remarkable variety of trades and professions such as weaver, dyer, wool-comber, shearman, tailor, hosier, tanner, leather-worker, shoe-maker, saddler, parchment-maker, soap-maker, leech, preacher, mercer, goldsmith, farrier, turner, cooper, potter, miller, baker, cook, butcher, waterman, mason, carpenter, plumber, porter, carter, and ostler.[2] It was obviously,

---

[1] Cf. Stenton, *Norman London*, pp. 13–14.

[2] Bateson, *Records of the Borough of Leicester*, p. xxix. Cf. also the rolls of the Shrewsbury gild which date from 1209 and have been printed by W. Cunningham in *Trans. R. Hist. Soc.*, N.S., ix (1895), 99.

therefore, not exclusive but popular in character, and admitted any honest tradesman (or woman, for that matter) who could pay the entrance fees and could find sureties to guarantee that he would perform his obligations. These involved the duty to be 'in scot and lot' with the burgesses, that is to say, to participate in the pecuniary burdens imposed on the borough, and to share bargains with fellow gildsmen, at least if one was present at the transaction and claimed to partake in it. To these men of diverse occupations was reserved the unrestricted right to trade within the borough. The gild, in short, exercised a trade monopoly in favour of its members, and was directed in the main against outsiders, strangers. These might buy and sell; but they were subjected to heavy tolls from which the gildsmen were free. In essence the gild merchant was a market gild.

Toll was the great restraint on the development of medieval trade. It was levied on sales and on purchases, in markets and in fairs, on highways and on bridges; nor could the merchant diverge from the straight way in order to avoid it. The occasional toll-gate or toll-bridge which even today impedes the free passage of the traveller illustrates the vexatious character of this form of local taxation. The amount taken varied from place to place. At the market of Yaxley in Northamptonshire 2d. was charged on a cart-load, 1d. on a horse-load, and ½d. on a man's load;[1] and these may be regarded as fairly representative. They were everywhere sufficiently high to be a serious hindrance to trade. To be quit of toll was therefore the most highly valued franchise which a town could acquire. Royal grants of this privilege generally embraced the whole of England, or the whole of England with the exception of London; some specially favoured boroughs like York enjoyed the privilege not only in England but in the king's overseas dominions; the townsmen of Wallingford obtained from Henry II a similar privilege as a reward for its loyalty to the Angevin cause in the civil war of Stephen's reign, or as the charter puts it 'for the service and great labour they sustained for me in the acquisition of my hereditary right in England'.[2] In their turn some continental towns such as Rouen and St. Omer were granted freedom of toll in England.[3] Private owners could of course only make restricted grants to their towns. But they did what they could to

---

[1] *Curia Regis Rolls*, i. 449. [2] *Cal. of Charter Rolls*, ii. 68.
[3] See Round, *Cal. of Docs. France*, nos. 109, 1322, 1352.

encourage trade. Thus the earls of Gloucester made the burgesses of Tewkesbury quit of toll 'within their demesne in the
honor of Gloucester and elsewhere in England according to
their ancient custom', Reginald, earl of Cornwall, quitted the
men of Truro of toll 'throughout the whole of Cornwall in fairs
and markets and wherever they might buy and sell'. Towns
were not the only recipients of such grants. Many religious
corporations enjoyed the same privilege. Indeed, so great was
the number of those exempted that the exclusive monopoly of
the gildsmen was severely curtailed. These grants of immunity
from toll in fact opened the way to a freer trading intercourse
throughout the country.[1]

In order to facilitate the collection of toll, it was convenient
to concentrate commercial transactions in definite places.
Henry I in his charter to Cambridge forbade any boat touching
at any hythe in Cambridgeshire except at the hythe of Cambridge, or any barges to be loaded except at Cambridge, or any
toll to be taken except at Cambridge.[2] This is perhaps an
extreme example, but the theory underlying the system of
markets and fairs was based on the same principle. The buying
and selling of everyday requirements were done at the local
markets which already in the twelfth century were held in most
well-populated centres. In early times Sunday had been the
normal market-day. Everyone was then free from his accustomed
labour, and at leisure to attend to his weekly shopping. But the
church reformers attempted with some success to put a stop to
this practical arrangement; in 1200 Pope Innocent III sent
Eustace, abbot of Flaye, to preach against it, and in consequence at Peterborough, Stamford, Barton-on-Humber, and
elsewhere, the Sunday gave place to a week-day market. But the
convenience of Sunday was so great that later in John's reign
there was a drift back. Thus in 1207 the earl of Clare obtained
permission from the king for a small payment to have his market
at Rothwell in Northamptonshire on Sunday 'as it used to be
before it was changed owing to the preaching of the abbot of
Flaye'.[3] It was only in the minority of Henry III under the

---

[1] Gras, *The Early English Customs System*, p. 26, concludes that by the end of the
twelfth century 'it was chiefly aliens, the poorer citizens of towns, and peasants, who
paid the town tolls'.   [2] Ballard, op. cit., p. 168.
[3] *Rot. de Obl. et Fin.* (ed. Hardy), p. 378; *Pipe Roll 9 Jo.*, pp. 136–7. For other
instances see ibid., Introd. p. xxvii. On the mission of Eustace see the paper by
J. L. Cate in *Études d'histoire dédiées à la mémoire de Henri Pirenne* (1937) and the same

influence of the papal legates Gualo and Pandulf and of Peter
des Roches, bishop of Winchester, that the change to week-days
was effectively carried out. Annual fairs were more important
events than weekly markets, and usually lasted for several days.
As the name implies (it is derived from the Latin *feriae*, holidays)
they were nearly always associated with festivals of the church,
often with the feast of the patron saint of the locality, and probably from the first business was combined with merry-making.
At these fairs not only the local inhabitants, but traders from
distant towns, and, at least at the big fairs like those of St. Ives
in Huntingdonshire, St. Giles at Winchester, St. Bartholomew
at Smithfields, or St. Botolph at Boston, merchants from foreign
parts also collected. It was at such great gatherings that large
wholesale transactions were carried out and that luxuries from
other countries were bartered and exchanged. In coming and
going, and during their stay merchants were protected from
molestation by the king's special peace. The fair had its own
special jurisdiction, its own court. The fair of St. Ives was
granted to the abbey of Ramsey in 1110 like any other privileged
property 'with sake and soke and tol and team and infangenetheoi
and with all customs just as any fair in England better has
them'.[1] It was from such jurisdictional rights that the well-
known court of Piepowder (dusty feet) developed in the next
century. While the fair was in progress all other business was set
aside, and on the occasion of the fairs of St. Giles and St.
Botolph even the sessions of the London husting court were
suspended.

Fairs and markets, on account of the tolls and dues arising
from them, were a source of considerable profit to their owners;
the proceeds of the fair of St. Giles, which belonged to the bishop
of Winchester, amounted in 1189 to as much as £146. 8s. 7d.[2]
They were therefore much in demand. The king's licence, however, was required before one could be established; and this was
only given if it was not injurious by causing loss of trade to
neighbouring markets.[3] This was often stipulated in the charter

author's 'Church and Market Reform in England during the reign of Henry III'
in *Medieval Essays in honor of J. Westfall Thompson* (Chicago, 1938).
  [1] *Cart. Mon. de Ramseseia* (Rolls Series), i. 240. For the development of the fair
jurisdiction cf. *Select Cases on the Law Merchant* (Selden Soc., vol. 23), Introd. p. xvi.
  [2] *Pipe Roll 1 Ric. I*, p. 5.
  [3] Cf. Salzman, 'The Legal Status of Markets' in *Camb. Hist. Journal*, ii (1928),
205.

of foundation. Thus the barons of Pevensey were granted in
1207 a fair on the nativity of St. John the Baptist, and three
days before and after, and a market on every Sunday, 'provided
that the aforesaid fair and market be not an injury to the neighbouring fairs and markets'.[1] In order to be innocuous it must
be at a reasonable distance from them. This distance Bracton
placed at 6⅔ miles, a third of a normal day's journey of 20 miles,
reckoning that a third of the day would be employed in going,
a third in returning, and a third in transacting business at the
market. Although later documentary evidence lends some support to this view, nothing so precise can be accepted as a definite
rule. The court adjudged the bishop of Ely's market at Laken-
heath to be injurious to the abbot's market at Bury St. Edmunds
though it was some 16 miles distant. But the abbot had to send
his bailiffs with nearly 600 armed men in the dead of night,
as Jocelin of Brakelond relates, who overturned the butchers'
shambles and the market stalls, in order to enforce his rights.[2]
A long and bitter dispute over market rights raged between the
abbot of Abingdon and the men of Oxford and Wallingford in
the early years of Henry II.[3] Competing markets were a fruitful
source of legal controversy and violent action in this age.

Free commercial intercourse, however, was rendered difficult
owing to the poorness of the means of communication. The
Roman roads had indeed been so well constructed that even in
spite of neglect they were still tolerably serviceable. The law-
books of the twelfth century distinguish three of these, Watling
Street, Ermine Street, and the Foss Way, together with the pre-
historic Icknield Way, as 'royal roads' (chimini regales); they
were under the king's protection, an assault committed upon
them was punished by a fine of 100s., and they should be wide
enough for two wagons to pass, for two oxherds to make their
goads touch across them, or for sixteen armed knights to ride
abreast.[4] The messengers of William the Lion in 1173 rode from
Scotland to the south coast in order to cross to Normandy 'by

[1] Ballard, op. cit., p. 175.

[2] Curia Regis Rolls, ii. 135, 136. Jocelin of Brakelond, Camden Soc., pp. 98–9.

[3] Chron. Mon. de Abingdon, ii. 227 f.; cf. L. F. Salzman, English Trade in the Middle
Ages, pp. 136–7.

[4] Leges Edwardi Confessoris, 12. 7; 13. Leges Henrici, 80. 2, 3. Liebermann, Die
Gesetze der Angel-Sachsen, i. 639–40, 596. Cf. Liebermann, Über die Leges Edwardi Confessoris (Halle, 1896), pp. 47–51, and F. M. Stenton, Economic History Review, vii
(1936), 3 ff.

the great metalled roads',[1] doubtless the Roman arterial roads connecting the wall with London and the coast. That the paving was to some extent maintained may be inferred from the duty of 'pavage' of which mention is made in charters of the period. Encroachment was prohibited, and the parson of Ebbesborne Wake and three of his parishioners got into serious trouble when in 1185 they dug up a bit of the Icknield Way.[2] Besides these great arterial roads, other roads connecting town and town, village and village 'by which men go to market or for other business' were said to be 'under the law of the county'.[3] But with the increase in trade and the concurrent increase in the volume of traffic passing over the roads, which developed in this age, the idea of 'the king's highway' was extended to cover all the principal thoroughfares of England. Some improvements were made; bridges, for instance, here and there replaced the less convenient ford or ferry-boat. But there is little to show that the roads were better or safer in consequence of the changes. We hear often of obstruction, of disputes over rights of way, and of assault. These of course are commonplaces of any century of our history. There is, however, evidence in plenty for the thirteenth century which is probably applicable to the twelfth of the evil state of the roads. In 1260, for example, the king took a drastic remedy: he ordered the master of the hospital at East-bridge to pull down his chapel at Blean between Canterbury and Whitstable and to throw the small stone and rubble into the highway 'for the safety of passengers and the improvement of the roads'.[4] The traveller might also be impeded by roads rendered impassable by flood or broken bridges. In 1212, for example, a boat had to be hired to carry the baggage of the king's wardrobe across the Thames because London Bridge was broken;[5] in the same year carts carrying wine from Southampton for the king in the north were delayed at Nottingham because they could not cross the Trent.[6] Movement cannot

---

[1] 'Par les granz chemins ferrez.' Jordan Fantosme, 'Chronique' in *Chronicles of Stephen, Henry II, and Richard I*, vol. iii (Rolls Series), l. 318. For the use of the word *ferré* for metalled cf. Roman de Renart, 'un chemin ferré'. Bartsch, *Chrestomathie* (6th edn. 1895), p. 214, l. 18.

[2] *Pipe Roll 31 Hen. II*, p. 191. Cf. also ibid., *12 Hen. II*, p. 49, a village is fined because it ploughed up the *viam Regiam*, and p. 89 a man is fined *pro Chemino Regio arato*.

[3] *Leges Edwardi*, 12, 9. Liebermann, *Die Gesetze*, i. 639.

[4] *Close Rolls, 1259–61*, p. 201.

[5] *Rot. Misae. 14 Jo.*, ed. Cole, p. 232.   [6] Ibid., p. 240.

have been easy in such conditions, especially in wintry weather and with loaded wagons.

Wherever available, therefore, waterways were used in preference to road transit, at least for heavy goods, it being, though slower, both easier and cheaper. The commercial importance of London and other towns such as Chester, Gloucester, or Norwich was largely due to their position on tidal rivers at points where they could be bridged. Goods could thus be carried far into the interior of the country and thence distributed over a wide area by a relatively short distance of road transport. The value of water-communications was well understood in the middle ages. Henry I in 1121, by converting the Fossedyke, which had originally been constructed by the Romans to drain the fens, into a navigable canal linking the Witham and the Trent, gave the city of Lincoln access both to the Humber and to the Wash, and so contributed to make it 'an emporium of men coming by land or sea'.[1] The monks of Sawtry (Hunts.) found it worth while to construct a canal to connect their abbey with the stone quarries at Barnack in Northamptonshire.[2] Free passage along rivers is sometimes specifically granted by the Crown. Thus the men of Gloucester by a charter of Henry II were permitted to traverse freely along the river Severn with timber, charcoal, and all other merchandise, and a somewhat similar privilege was given to the men of Nottingham on the waters of the Trent.[3] The existence at the end of the century of a body of Customs officials—three men with a small boat to keep the port of London—is another indication of the importance attached to river transport.[4] The use made of waterways may be illustrated by the building of Waltham Abbey which was carried out by Henry II (1177–83) as part of his penance for his connexion with the murder of Becket. Timber was brought from the Surrey woods by road to Weybridge and thence by the rivers Wey, Thames, and Lea to Essex; lead for the roof came from the Peak district of Derbyshire and was carried in 265 cart-loads to Boston in Lincolnshire and thence by sea and river to its destination. The frequent use of Caen stone, even in

[1] Will. Malmes., *Gesta Pontif.*, p. 312. For the cutting of the Fossedyke see Symeon of Durham, *Hist. Reg.* ii. 260; or perhaps Henry merely reopened the obstructed Fossedyke for navigation. See J. W. F. Hill, *Medieval Lincoln*, pp. 14, 173, 308.

[2] L. F. Salzman, *Medieval English Industries*, pp. 84–5.

[3] Ballard, op. cit., pp. 199–200.

[4] *Chancellor's Roll 8 Ric. I*, p. 18; *Pipe Roll 10 Ric. I*, p. 183.

districts where good stone could be quarried at no great distance, is another obvious example of the preference of water to road transport whenever possible. Yet even river navigation was not free from impediments. Barriers were often thrown across a river to facilitate the netting of fish, leaving only a narrow opening. These fish-weirs or kydells, as they were called, were forbidden on the Thames by Richard I in 1197,[1] and the prohibition was made general on all riverways throughout England by an article of the Great Charter (cl. 33). But it is evident from the frequency of complaints about fish-weirs in succeeding centuries that the interests of navigation and fishing continued to conflict.

Turning from distribution to production, we may first observe that England was well provided with the raw materials she needed. Her mineral wealth, coal, iron, and lead, had been exploited in the time of the Roman occupation, but had been sadly neglected by the Anglo-Saxons who did not take easily to industrial life. Indeed, the digging of coal was only again resumed in the thirteenth century; the terms *carbo* and *carbonarius*, which occur earlier, refer almost exclusively to charcoal, the only form of heating-fuel besides wood used in the twelfth century, and not to mineral or, as it was generally called, sea coal. The earliest definite reference to mineral coal is in a Bruges record where among exports from England to Flanders in the year 1200 there is mention of *charbon de roche*.[2] Iron-mining revived earlier, and Domesday Book affords evidence that it was operated in various parts of the country on the eve of the Conquest. The city of Gloucester in the time of Edward the Confessor rendered 36 dickers of iron[3] and 100 iron rods suitable for the manufacture of nails for the king's ships as part of its farm. The Forest of Dean was the centre of the industry; its forges were kept busy during the twelfth century turning out in large quantities bar iron and iron manufactured goods—picks and shovels, horseshoes, and nails for the king's use. For example, 100 axes, 1,000 picks, 2,000 shovels, and 60,000 nails were dis-

---

[1] *Foedera*, i. 67.

[2] 'Cartulaire de l'Estaple de Bruges', ed. Gilliodts, i. 19, cited by G. Dept, 'Les Marchands flamands et le roi d'Angleterre (1154–1216)', in *Revue du Nord*, xii (1926), 311, n. 1. Some passages in the Durham *Bolden Book* (1183) are said possibly to refer to mineral coal; but see Salzman, *Medieval English Industries*, p. 2.

[3] *Domesday Book*, i. 162. A *dicrum* was a lot of ten. Hence 36 *dicra* are equivalent to 360 bars.

patched to Ireland from Gloucestershire on the occasion of the expedition of 1172,[1] while 50,000 horseshoes with spare fastenings besides a large quantity of iron for the ships were provided for Richard I's crusade.[2] Iron was also worked in the north of England, but on a smaller scale, and the famous industry in the weald of Kent and Sussex only developed in the course of the thirteenth century. The forest forges, therefore, during this period held a position of unrivalled pre-eminence.

The lead and silver mines of Alston Moor on the borders of Cumberland and Northumberland or 'the mines of Carlisle' as they were called were a source of considerable wealth to the Crown. The progress of the industry can be judged by the rates at which the mines were leased. In 1130 the sum was £40; in 1159, £100; in 1164, £200; in 1165 it had reached 400 marks, and in the next year 500 (£332. 13s. 4d.), and at that figure it stood for a number of years. The output, however, was evidently falling. William Erenbald, the lessee, perhaps a German speculator, was unable to pay his rent;[3] arrears gradually accumulated until by 1178 they amounted to over £2,000. Accordingly in 1180 the rent was reduced to £200. But the mines continued to decline in value. In 1186 the rent was £100, ten years later only £50, and by 1230 they were worth no more than 10 marks (£6. 13s. 4d.). During the days of its prosperity, however, lead-mining was one of the more important of English industries. Nor was it confined to Cumberland; it was worked also in Derbyshire, especially in the Peak district, in Shropshire, and in the Mendips. It was used not only for home consumption on the great building operations which absorbed so much of Henry II's attention and money during the later years of his reign, but it was also exported in large quantities to France. In 1176 it was shipped from Newcastle to La Rochelle for the building of the abbey of Grandmont; in 1179 a hundred loads were sent from the same port to Rouen and thence to Paris for use on the church at Clairvaux, and a still larger consignment was dispatched for the same building two years later. In 1184, when work was in progress on the king's chamber at Gisors, twenty cart-loads of lead were shipped from Boston to Rouen and taken thence by road to the great castle of the Vexin.[4]

---

[1] *Pipe Roll 18 Hen. II*, pp. 119, 122.   [2] Ibid. *2 Ric. I*, p. 53.
[3] Cf. *Vict. County Hist., Cumberland*, ii. 338–9.
[4] *Pipe Rolls 22 Hen. II*, pp. 137, 141; *25 Hen. II*, pp. 27, 30; *27 Hen. II*, pp. 47, 65.

The ancient tin-mining industry in Devon and Cornwall also developed rapidly in the twelfth century. The output increased from approximately 133 thousand-weight[1] in the early years of the reign of Henry II to 901 at the end of the century; the quantity fluctuated considerably from year to year, but in 1214 it reached as high as 1,198 thousand-weight, an amount which was not greatly exceeded till the latter part of the seventeenth century.[2] The remarkable expansion of the industry was doubtless due to its systematic organization. In 1198 its control was taken out of the hands of the sheriff and placed under a special warden with a staff of government officials; and an elaborate system of weighing, checking, and stamping the tin before it was removed was introduced. The tinners themselves were protected by a charter granted by John in 1201[3] and were under the special jurisdiction of the warden and his court. Tin henceforward became a valuable source of revenue to the Crown. Besides an initial tax of 2s. 6d. in Devon and 5s. in Cornwall per thousand-weight collected after the first smelting which was compounded for a lump sum in the farm of the mines,[4] an additional tax of a mark per thousand-weight was levied after the second smelting. This yielded as much as £600 in 1199 and close on £800 in 1214.[5] The tin-mines of Germany were as yet not exploited; English tin was therefore in great request on the Continent, particularly at Cologne and in the centres of the Flemish metal-work industry—Huy and Dinant, Namur and Liége. A large quantity was also sent to France where, very possibly, it may have been used for the poor-quality coinage issued by Richard I for his continental dominions.[6]

In most parts of the country where suitable clay was available pottery was produced. The industry in north Staffordshire is generally regarded as rude and primitive until it was developed

Rot. Scac. Norman. (ed. Stapleton), i. 70. Pipe Roll 30 Hen. II, p. 29, and Rot. Scac. Norman., p. 111.

[1] A thousand-weight (miliare) was 1,200 lb. or half a long ton of 2,400 lb.

[2] Cf. the tables printed by G. R. Lewis, The Stannaries (Harvard Economic Studies, 1908), App. J.

[3] Cal. Charter Rolls, i. 380. For the reorganization of the industry cf. the account rendered by William of Wrotham, the first warden, on the Pipe Roll 1 Jo., p. 242.

[4] These at the turn of the century were £100 for Devon and 100 marks for Cornwall.

[5] Lewis, op. cit., p. 135.

[6] See the introduction to Chancellor's Roll, 8 Ric. I (Pipe Roll Soc., n.s.. vol vii), p. xix.

by Josiah Wedgwood in the eighteenth century.[1] But evidently
the output was considerable in the early thirteenth century and
it was manufactured not merely to meet the local demand, for
an entry on the Pipe Roll records under Staffordshire the purchase and dispatch of 4,000 plates and 500 cups for the king's
Christmas feast held at Tewkesbury in 1204.[2]

Nevertheless, important as these mining and industrial activities undoubtedly were, in the twelfth century the production of
wool was already beginning to surpass all other industries as the
chief source of England's wealth. Every farm had its flock of
sheep, many very large ones, and they were kept primarily not
for their carcasses but for their fleece. The labour of the early
Cistercians, who settled on remote and hitherto unproductive
sites in the Yorkshire wolds or the Welsh hills, contributed very
largely to the expansion of the sheep-farming industry. The
wool of the Cistercian and Gilbertine monasteries and of the
Premonstratensian houses figures as a special item in the sums
raised to provide for the ransom of Richard I, and the abbey
of Meaux in the East Riding of Yorkshire alone furnished 300
marks in wool, plate, and money.[3] A large part of the supply of
wool was certainly exported to Flanders where it was worked
into cloth; the Flemings readily joined in the rebellion against
Henry II in 1173–4 'to have his wool',[4] and the English records
abound with incidental references to Flemish merchants and
the 'wool of the Flemings'.[5] There was also, however, at the
same period a thriving weaving industry in England which
clearly absorbed a not inconsiderable quantity of the home-
grown wool.

In the later middle ages most of the important crafts formed
themselves into associations or gilds which supervised the training of apprentices, insured to the consumer articles of good
quality, and to the producer a fair price for his labour. But in

---

[1] *Victoria County History, Staffordshire*, i. 289.

[2] 'pro iiii milia scutellarum et pro quingentis ciffis.' *Pipe Roll 7 Jo.*, p. 160.

[3] Hoveden, iii. 210–11: *Chron. de Melsa*, i. 233. The importance attached to the wool of abbeys is shown by the order in 1204 that no merchant might remove wool from an abbey without licence and a certificate stating the number of sacks and the price of the wool. *Rot. Lit. Pat.* 42 b. Cf. also R. J. Whitwell, 'English Monasteries and the Wool Trade in the 13th Century', in *Vierteljahrschrift für Sozial- und Wirtschaftsgeschichte*, ii (1904), 1 ff.

[4] Jordan Fantosme, *Chronique*, l. 1001. Cf. also Gervase of Canterbury, i. 246.

[5] Gaston Dept, 'Les Marchands flamands et le roi d'Angleterre (1154–1216)', in *Rev. du Nord*, xii (1926), and G. T. Lapsley, *Eng. Hist. Rev.* xxi (1906), 509.

the twelfth century, except in the weaving industry, such associations were unusual. The London bakers had their gild early in the reign of Henry II, and at Oxford there was in 1130 and probably before a gild of tanners (*corvesarii*) who later amalgamated with leather-workers or shoemakers (*corduanarii*) in a cordwainers gild which had a continuous and flourishing history down to the middle of the nineteenth century.[1] Goldsmiths figure prominently among London craftsmen in the twelfth century, and evidently there was some association among members of the craft.[2] Indeed they actually formed a gild, but either because they failed or because they omitted to get it authorized by the king, it was swept away with eighteen other 'adulterine' gilds, among them gilds of pepperers, clothworkers, and butchers, in 1180.[3]

In respect of organization, however, the cloth industry was far ahead of any other. Already in the reign of Henry I the weavers of London, Lincoln, Winchester, Oxford, and Huntingdon, and the fullers of Winchester had obtained royal sanction to set up gilds in return for an annual rent. They held a monopoly of working cloth within a certain radius. For Oxford it was five leagues, for Lincoln twelve miles. The sum usually paid for this privilege was a mark of gold (£6), but London, through most of the century, paid twice this sum and Huntingdon paid only £2. Henry II licensed gilds for the weavers of Nottingham (1155) and of York (1163); and he further stimulated the rising industry in these two towns by giving to the former the monopoly of working dyed cloth within a radius of ten leagues and to the latter, with certain other named towns, the exclusive right of manufacturing cloths, tunics, or rays (striped material) in Yorkshire.[4] These, however, were not the only places where the industry had taken root. It was distributed widely over the country; we hear of weavers at Gloucester and a cloth fair at

[1] H. E. Salter, *Medieval Oxford* (Oxf. Hist. Soc., 1936), pp. 60–1. Henry II's charter (*Cal. Charter Rolls*, ii. 34) carefully distinguishes between the *corvesarii* and the *corduanarii*.

[2] F. M. Stenton, *Norman London*, pp. 21–2.

[3] *Pipe Roll 26 Hen. II*, pp. 153–4. They were amerced in sums varying from 45 marks to ½ mark. The names of the aldermen at the head of each gild, some of them prominent city men, are also given. Cf. G. Unwin, *The Gilds and Companies of London*, pp. 48 ff. Bodmin and Launceston, Barnstaple and Axbridge, and other places were similarly fined for gilds *sine waranto*.

[4] The charters are printed in Stevenson, *Records of Nottingham*, i, 1 and in Farrer, *Early Yorkshire Charters*, i. 263.

Worcester;[1] Stamford in Lincolnshire became famous at an
early date for its cloth, and the particular quality produced
there was sold under the trade name *stanfort* and was imitated
at Ypres and Arras; it was also evidently in greater demand
than any other variety of English cloth in Italy whither it was
carried through the medium of the great fairs of Champagne.[2]
Lincolnshire was indeed an important centre of the cloth trade.
It was manufactured in many varieties and in many colours;[3]
in 1182 large purchases of scarlet, the most expensive cloth,
were made for the king at 6s. 8s. an ell, of green say (cloth of
fine texture), at 3s., and grey say, at 1s. 8d. an ell. The Lincolnshire workshops also turned out 'blanchet' suitable for making
the white habit worn by the Carthusians established in England
a few years before at Witham in Somerset.[4] Linen was also
woven in England especially in Wiltshire where 2,000 ells of it
were purchased for the coronation of King John.[5] Weaving
more than other industries was subject to state control. The
Assize of Measures (1196), the substance of which was repeated
in the 35th article of Magna Carta, prescribed that woollen
cloth should only be woven in a uniform width of two ells within
the selvedges, and must be of even quality both in the middle
and sides. A standard ell, which, according to a tradition preserved by William of Malmesbury,[6] was the length of King
Henry I's own right arm, was to be used throughout the country
and four or six men were to be appointed in each town to see
that the regulations were enforced.[7] In fact, however, the assize
was little heeded, the merchants preferring to pay large fines
'that they might buy and sell dyed cloth as they used to do in

[1] *Cal. Chart. Rolls*, iii. 378; *Rot. Lit. Claus*. ii. 136b.
[2] According to the records of a Genoese notary in 1197, 214 pounds worth of
stanfort were sold in Genoa as compared with 44 pounds worth of other English
cloth. Cf. R. L. Reynolds, 'The Market for Northern Textiles in Genoa', *Revue
belge de philol. et d'hist.* (1929), p. 846. In 1203 four pieces *de stanforti de Ingeterra*
were sent to Sicily. Ibid., p. 841, n. 1.
[3] The industry was almost entirely dependent on imported dyes. See E. M.
Carus-Wilson, *Econ. Hist. Rev.* xiv (1944), 35–40.
[4] *Pipe Roll 28 Hen. II*, p. 50. This is apparently the earliest example of the use of
the word 'blanket'.
[5] *Pipe Roll 1 Jo.*, p. 169.
[6] *Gesta Reg.* ii. 487 (§ 411).
[7] Hoveden, iv. 34. For the date of the Assize of Measures see D. M. Stenton,
Pipe Roll 9 Ric. I, Introd., p. xxi. To implement the Assize standard 'measures and
gallons and iron rods and beams and weights' were made and sent to all counties.
Ibid., p. 160.

King Henry's time'.[1] The weavers, perhaps owing to their independent position, perhaps, too, to the alien element in their
ranks, were unpopular with the municipal authorities. They
were excluded from the gild merchant.[2] The towns which, in
the latter part of the twelfth century, were fast developing in
prosperity and self-government, not unnaturally resented any
organization in their midst which was outside their own control.
The stronger they grew the greater became the animosity against
them. In 1202 'at the petition of the mayor and citizens' the
king agreed to suppress the London gild of weavers; but only
on the understanding that the civic authorities would pay into
the treasury more than the equivalent of the sum which the
weavers had paid for their gild.[3] This they failed to do, and the
gild went on, paying the enhanced rent of 20 marks of silver.
Elsewhere there is similar evidence of intense hostility towards
the weavers. In 1200 the municipal authorities at Lincoln
asserted that 'fullers had no law or community with the free
citizens'.[4] The most striking evidence, however, of the unpopularity of the cloth industry comes from the 'law of the weavers
and fullers' which dates from the last years of the twelfth century. This relates to the towns of Winchester, Marlborough,
Oxford, and Beverley, and in the case of the first and last of
these towns it is expressly stated that this law they have 'from
the franchise and custom of London'.[5] Briefly summarized the
most remarkable disabilities were those which forbade the
weavers from selling cloth except to merchants of their city,
which prevented them from becoming freemen of their city
unless they first renounced their craft, and which made it unlaw-
ful for them to attaint or bear witness against a freeman. Such
harsh treatment was enough to cripple a rising industry. The
municipal authorities abandoned their hostility when it was too
late. The manufacture of cloth declined rapidly. There were
said to be more than 200 weavers at Lincoln in the time of
Henry II; by 1321 there was not one in the city or its suburbs.

[1] See the list of such fines collected in the introduction to the *Pipe Roll 4 Jo.*, p.
xx, and cf. the proceedings of the royal justices at Boston Fair in Hoveden, iv. 172.
[2] E. M. Carus-Wilson, op. cit.
[3] Cf. *Pipe Roll 4 Jo.*, p. 288: 'Cives Lond' debent lx. m. pro gilda teleria delenda
ita ut de cetero non suscitetur et pro carta R. inde habenda.' Cf. p. 285. For details
of the dispute see F. Consitt, *The London Weavers' Company*, i. 3–5.
[4] *Curia Regis Rolls*, i. 260; cf. Salzman, *Med. Eng. Industries*, p. 196.
[5] The best text of these laws is printed by A. F. Leach in *Beverley Town Documents* (Selden Soc., vol. 14), pp. 134–5. Cf. also Introd., pp. xliv–xlvi.

At Oxford there were sixty and more in King John's reign; by 1323 there was not one left. Yet while the industry was fast declining in the towns, stimulated by the introduction of the fulling mill, it developed steadily in the country districts of the north and west.[1]

English foreign trade may be conveniently considered under four heads: trade with Scandinavia, with the Rhineland and the Low Countries, with France, and with countries bordering on the Mediterranean. Economic and social relations, it should be observed, were not severed when England ceased politically to be a member of the group of northern countries. The Norse and Danish settlements in the north and east naturally enough continued to maintain a lively intercourse with their kinsmen across the North Sea.[2] In many places the Norse tongue was a second language. The evidence, fragmentary though it is, is sufficient to prove that commercial intercourse flourished: when in 1095 Robert de Mowbray seized and plundered four Norwegian trading vessels, William Rufus deemed it worth while to compensate the injured merchants from his own treasury.[3] Traders from Norway and Iceland, from Scotland and the Hebrides, frequented the port of Grimsby in the time of Henry I;[4] corn was exported to Norway whence in return came a regular supply of gerfalcons for the king's sport and also probably the coniferous timber which we hear of in use in the buildings at Clarendon, Ludgershall, Marlborough, and Woodstock.[5] Evidently there was a strong Norse colony in London; no less than six churches of the late eleventh and early twelfth centuries were dedicated to their national saint King Olaf (St. Olave). Both Danes and Norwegians might stay in the city for a year, while other foreign

[1] E. M. Carus-Wilson, *Econ. Hist. Rev.* xi (1941), 39 ff.

[2] The evidence is assembled by A. Bugge, 'The Norse Settlements in the British Islands', *Trans. R. Hist. Soc.*, 4th ser., iv (1921), 173, and F. M. Stenton, 'The Danes in England', *Proceedings of Brit. Acad.* xiii (1927).

[3] Ordericus Vitalis, iii. 407.

[4] *Icelandic Sagas* (Rolls Series), iii. 97. Cf. also the writ addressed to the Norwegians 'who come to the port of Grimsby' and other ports of Lincolnshire, quoted by Stenton, op. cit., p. 33, n. 1.

[5] *Pipe Roll 32 Hen. II*, p. 116; cf. Introd., p. xxi. The archbishop of Trondhjem, by a privilege which went back to the time of Henry II, was permitted to buy corn and other victuals even in time of scarcity. (*Cal. of Pat. Rolls 1232-47*, 259, cited Salzman, *English Trade*, p. 365.) For corn export see also *Pipe Roll 32 Hen. II*, p. 68, where licence to export corn is granted to a Norwegian merchant in return for two gerfalcons. Norway was the regular source of supply of these birds of which great numbers were required for the king's sport. Cf. also *Pipe Rolls 1 Jo.*, p. 289, and *4 Jo.*, pp. 104, 131.

merchants had to be gone within forty days, and the Danes had the further privilege of being allowed to go anywhere in England to fairs and markets.[1] Nevertheless, the Scandinavian trade with London was declining. No doubt the merchants preferred the shorter route to the east-coast ports. In the course of the twelfth century the Danes sold to the merchants of Cologne their hall which continued to be known as 'the hall of the Danes' (la saille des Deneis). Even commerce with north-eastern Europe and Russia (especially important for furs) was passing from the Swedes into the hands of the Germans who already in the twelfth century had factories at Novgorod and at Wisby on the island of Gotland; and Lübeck (founded in 1143) rapidly grew to a position of unrivalled supremacy in the Baltic trade.

William of Malmesbury, writing about 1125, speaks of the London wharves 'packed with the goods of merchants coming from all countries, and especially from Germany'; and he adds that when there is a shortage of supplies owing to a bad harvest, the deficiency is made up from Germany.[2] The great trade route from Constantinople along the Danube and the Rhine was controlled on its northern extremity by the men of Lower Lorraine, 'men of the Emperor' as they are called, who shipped to London gold and silver work, precious stones and cloth from Constantinople and Regensburg, or linen and coats of mail from Mainz.[3] In all this traffic the merchants of Cologne took the lead. They and their goods and their *hansa* at Dowgate a little above London Bridge were given special protection by Henry II in 1157 and again in 1175. Later, political expediency on the one side and economic interests on the other drew the relations between England and the great Rhenish city still closer, and in a charter granted by Richard I in 1194 and confirmed by John in 1213 the privileges which the traders of Cologne enjoyed in England were substantially increased.[4] The career of Arnold Fitzthedmar, who was born of German parents at London in 1201, and rose to be 'alderman of the German merchants coming to England', who played an important part in city politics in

[1] Bateson, *Eng. Hist. Rev.* xvii (1902), 499, 502. Bugge, op. cit., p. 194.
[2] *Gesta Pontif.*, p. 140.
[3] *Eng. Hist. Rev.* xvii (1902), 496, 499. The date of this text is presumed to be earlier than the time of Henry II, and perhaps as early as 1130. Ibid., p. 495.
[4] The documents are conveniently collected by B. Kuske, *Quellen zur Geschichte des Kölner Handels und Verkehrs im Mittelalter*, i. Cf. also M. Weinbaum, 'Stalhof und Deutsche Gildhalle zu London', *Hansische Geschichtsblätter*, xxxiii (1928), 45.

the time of Henry III, and wrote a chronicle of the mayors and sheriffs, illustrates remarkably the position of the colony of foreign merchants settled in London.[1] But German trade was not confined to London and Cologne. Though Fitzthedmar's mother came from Cologne, his father was a native of Bremen. We hear of German merchants at York early in the twelfth century,[2] and later at Chester.[3] The intimate relations established between England and the north of Germany by the marriage of Henry II's daughter Matilda with Henry the Lion led to a general widening of commercial connexions.[4]

About the middle of the twelfth century a road was constructed running westward from Cologne through Maastricht and Ghent to Bruges. In this way the great nodal point of German trade was linked directly with Flanders, which itself had been rapidly developing into an important centre of commercial intercourse, a meeting-place of merchants from Italy, France, and the north.[5] Essentially a land of urban industry rather than agriculture, Flanders was almost entirely dependent on her neighbours for her food-supplies and raw materials. The cutting off of the supplies of corn from England, if it did not threaten the country with actual starvation, must at least have caused grave distress; for, judging by the very heavy fines imposed in 1197 on English merchants trading with the enemy—an individual merchant was fined as much as 300 marks, while the port of Dunwich and that of King's Lynn had to pay a thousand marks or more—a very large quantity of grain was exported.[6] The stoppage of the export of wool caused an even more acute situation. For her thriving weaving industry the raw wool came very largely from England, and was so essential to her pros-

[1] See Dict. Nat. Biog., art. Fitzthedmar, Arnold.

[2] Will. Malmes., Gesta Pontif., p. 208.

[3] Liber Luciani de Laude Cestrie, ed. M. V. Taylor (Lancs. and Cheshire Rec. Soc. lxiv [1912], 46).

[4] See, for example, the trading privilege in favour of Hildebrand of Saxony in 1206, Rot. Lit. Pat. (ed. Hardy), p. 57b; and for the close connexion between England and Germany at the close of the twelfth century, A. L. Poole, 'Die Welfen in der Verbannung', Deutsches Archiv für Geschichte des Mittelalters, ii (1938), 129.

[5] Cf. H. Pirenne, 'The Place of the Netherlands in the Economic History of Medieval Europe' in Econ. Hist. Rev. ii (1929), 20, and Hist. de Belgique (3rd ed. 1909), i. 180. The importance of the road from Cologne to Bruges is shown by F. Rousseau in Ann. de la Soc. Archéol. de Namur, xxxix (1930), 210.

[6] See the lists of amercements imposed 'on those who sent corn to the king's enemies in Flanders' in Pipe Roll 10 Ric. I, pp. 92 f., 137 f., 209 f.; cf. also Introd., p. xiv, where the lists are analysed.

perity that friendship with England became an economic necessity. Early in the reign of Henry II (1154–8) there was a trade
agreement with the town of St. Omer and before the end of it
the merchants of fifteen Flemish towns under the leadership of
Bruges had formed themselves into an association—the *hansa* of
London—to regulate the wool-trade with England.[1] Politically
the interests of Flanders were naturally opposed to the great
Anglo-Norman power. But she had received a sharp lesson from
her active participation in the revolt of 1173–4; the goods of the
Flemish merchants in England were confiscated, and the same
punishment was inflicted on them in 1194.[2] The closing of the
English ports to Flemish merchants crippled the economic life
of the country. Without the king's safe-conduct, without his
licence to export wool, these Flemish traders were threatened
with ruin. The English kings were quick to realize the strength
of the economic pressure which they could exert. At the first
sign of friendly overtures towards France, King John would
immediately order the seizure of Flemish merchandise and in
this way effectually brought the count of Flanders to heel. The
great cloth towns, Ypres, Ghent, Arras, St. Omer, and the rest
for their part courted the friendship of the English kings, lent
them large sums of money, and made themselves generally useful; and they had grown sufficiently powerful to be able to
exercise a decisive influence on the foreign policy of Flanders.
To the political influence of the Flemish towns more than to any
other cause was due the Anglo-Flemish treaty of 1197, which
was renewed by John in 1199, and the prevention of a rupture
in that *entente* in the critical year of Bouvines.[3]

Trade with Rouen, which had been active in the late Anglo-
Saxon period, must, we may suppose, have increased when
England and Normandy were under the same ruler. But there
is a note of conservatism about the Rouen trade; her merchants
were still bringing in the middle of the twelfth century wine and
porpoises as they had done in the time of Æthelred the Unready;

[1] Round, *Cal. of Documents, France*, no. 1352. Pirenne, 'La Hanse flamande de
Londres', in *Bulletin de l'Acad. Royale de Belgique, Classe des Lettres*, 3rd ser., xxxvii
(1899), 65.
[2] For the seizure of the chattels of Flemings in 1194 see *Pipe Roll 6 Ric. I*, Introd.,
p. xxxiii.
[3] For Anglo-Flemish relations see particularly G. Dept, 'Les Marchands
flamands et le roi d'Angleterre (1154–1216)', in *Revue du Nord*, xii (1926), 303 ff.,
and *Les Influences anglaise et française dans le Comté de Flandre* (1928), where the material
is collected.

their wharf was still at Dowgate as it had been under Edward the Confessor.[1] The porpoise (crassus piscis) was, like the sturgeon and the whale, a 'royal' fish and reserved for the king. Sometimes the right to take them was granted away. Thus Henry I granted to Richard de Belmeis, bishop of London, by charter the right to take porpoises 'except the tongue which I reserve to myself'.[2] Wine, however, was certainly the principal export of France into this country. Rhenish wine was brought from Cologne, and by a privilege of Henry II (1157) was to be sold at the same price as the French. A large quantity of 'home brew' was also consumed even in the best houses; the archbishops of York had their vineyard at Askham near York, the earls of Gloucester at Tewkesbury, and even the king bought a quantity of cheap English wine at 10s. a barrel in Bedford. But the better-class wines, both red and white, the expensive wine (vinum expensibile) and sacramental wine (vinum dominicum), came from abroad, and the bulk of it, at least from the time of Henry II, from Poitou, Gascony, and Auxerre,[3] at prices ranging (in 1184) from about 26s. to as much as 34s. a cask. It was shipped by merchants of La Rochelle, Bordeaux, and Bayonne, who no doubt returned with cargoes of English commodities.

The prices of foreign wines were high, and at least as early as 1176 attempts were made to regulate them; that the regulations were little observed may be assumed from the record of fines[4] imposed year by year by the justices on vintners for selling wine contra assisam. Of this assize nothing is known, but a summary of an assize of wines issued by King John in 1199 has been preserved: wines of Poitou were to be sold at 20s. and those of Anjou at 24s. per tun or cask. Only the very special vintages could be put on the market at 2 marks at most. The prices were fixed too low and had to be raised; but the assize increased for a time the volume of wine imported and, as Hoveden records, 'the whole land was filled with drink and drinkers'.[5] However, in practice it had little lasting success. The vintners found it

[1] Cf. the charter granted by Henry II when he was duke of Normandy (1150–1) in Delisle-Berger, Recueil des Actes de Henri II, i. 18–21, and Æthelred's laws, iv. 2, 5 (Liebermann, Gesetze, i. 232).

[2] Cal. of Chart. Rolls, iii. 292, cited by Salzman, Med. Eng. Ind., p. 264.

[3] The varieties of wines obtainable are well represented on the Pipe Roll of 30 Hen. II. Cf. Introd., pp. xxv–xxvi. Much information on the early wine trade has been collected by A. L. Simon, History of the Wine Trade in England, vol. i (1906).

[4] Cf. Pipe Roll 22 Hen. II, p. 126, and later rolls.

[5] Hoveden, iv. 99–100.

more profitable to pay the moderate fines exacted for selling wines 'contrary to the assize' than to obey the regulations.

It is in the wine trade that the early indications of a system of customs comes before us most clearly.[1] From about the middle of the twelfth century a customs-duty paid in money (in the early thirteenth century it was 4*d*. a tun) was imposed on imported wines. This was in addition to the wine prise, which first appears about the same time, or the king's right of pre-emption at a little below market price of two casks in twenty of every ship's cargo, one from 'before the mast' where the inferior wine was stored, one from 'behind the mast' where the better was placed to protect it from the sea. In the time of John the price which the king paid was fixed at 20*s*. in all ports except Bristol where the price was 15*s*.; the duty therefore was the difference between these sums and the price of the wine in the open market on the casks seized. From these and two somewhat obscure taxes, lastage and scavage, the one an export, the other an import duty, arose a system of national customs. But they were modelled on local imposts and had the same defects; they were subject to many exemptions, and languished accordingly. When on 4 June 1204 John issued at Winchester his 'Assize of Customs'[2] he made a real advance towards the system which matured under Edward I. He imposed a duty of a fifteenth on all imports and exports of sea-borne trade, coastal trade alone excepted. The fifteenth, however, did not long survive; whether because of the opposition of the now powerful mercantile interest or because it was merely intended to be an emergency measure, it was quietly dropped a few years after it had been introduced.[3] But the sums collected during the period when it was enforced added substantially to the national revenue. Over a period of some sixteen months (20 July 1203 to 30 November 1204) they amounted to about £5,000, representing a volume of foreign trade of about £75,000 from the east- and south-coast ports alone. The figures (printed below) provide us with an instructive index to the relative importance of the business done at the

[1] For the question of the origin of the Customs and for what follows cf. N. S. B. Gras, *The Early English Customs System* (Harvard Economic Studies, 1918), pp. 21–53, 217–22. Cf. also J. H. Round, *Family Origins and Other Studies*, pp. 237–51.

[2] *Rot. Lit. Pat.*, pp. 42–3; Gras, op. cit., pp. 217–21.

[3] The 'fifteenth' may have been the evil tolls (*mala tolta*) from which merchants were relieved by article 41 of Magna Carta. Cf. McKechnie, *Magna Carta*, p. 402.

different ports at the opening of the thirteenth century.[1] Many of them, doubtless, were little more than fishing villages. The fasts imposed by the church and the difficulty of obtaining fresh meat in the winter months made fish a staple article of diet. Yarmouth owed its prosperity even in the twelfth century to its herring fishery and its herring fair; similarly the more northerly harbours like Scarborough and Grimsby flourished on the cod fish. From a Rye document we get some idea of the size of the fishing craft at this time; some were propelled by as many as twenty-six rowers, others by less than ten.[2]

It would appear that the overseas trade was largely in the hands of foreign merchants. English shipping was chiefly confined in the earlier middle ages to the coastal trade. We hear little of distant ventures. But what we do hear is significant. Saewulf, who cruised in the eastern Mediterranean in 1102-3, though by profession a merchant, made his voyage as a pilgrim. Godric again, saint and founder of Finchale, was for sixteen years a merchant seaman before he settled down to the life of a hermit; but like Saewulf, his two journeys to Jerusalem were really pilgrimages. He seems, however, to have combined business with duty, for, if the common identification is correct, he was that 'Gudric the pirate from England' who assisted King Baldwin (himself married to an English wife) after his disastrous defeat at Ramlah (1102). That on the return from the first of his pilgrimages he visited the shrine of St. James at Compostella makes it at least certain that he made the journey by sea. Wulfric, a citizen of Lincoln, was at Constantinople early in the century and was dispatched by the Emperor Alexius Comnenus with letters and gifts to Henry I and his queen.[3] English mariners, a mixture of pilgrim, pirate, and honest trader, participated in the early crusading enterprises to a greater extent than has usually been recognized. An English fleet of some thirty vessels captured Laodicea from the Turks in 1097, and materially assisted the land-forces engaged in the siege of Antioch by keeping open the communications with Cyprus.[4] The men from the east- and south-

---

[1] See Appendix at the end of this chapter. The figures are entered on the *Pipe Roll 6 Jo.*, p. 218. If the sums collected at the western ports, especially Bristol and Chester, were included the total would be very considerably increased. The tax had evidently been levied for some months before the regulations were issued on 4 June 1204.   [2] Ballard, *British Borough Charters 1042-1216*, p. 234.

[3] *Chron. Mon. de Abingdon*, ii. 46-7. J. W. F. Hill, *Medieval Lincoln*, p. 177.

[4] C. W. David, *Robert Curthose*, App. E (pp. 230-44).

coast ports of England who stormed and captured Lisbon in 1147 were on their way to the Holy Land, and they were rewarded by Alfonso I with trading privileges in Portugal.[1] Benjamin of Tudela, a great traveller in Europe and the east (c. 1165–70), mentions Englishmen at Montpellier 'where men come for business from all quarters', and also at Alexandria.[2] In the later years of the twelfth century there was a small colony of London business men resident at Genoa.[3] This evidence, fragmentary and disconnected as it is, has a considerable cumulative effect and enables us to draw the conclusion that intercourse between England and the Mediterranean through the Straits of Gibraltar was at least not negligible. It could not have been from a country inexperienced in seafaring that Richard I mobilized and equipped a large fleet for the third crusade. This expedition gave a fresh stimulus to commercial relations with the east. In the thirteenth century the English even had their own quarter at Acre (vicus Anglicorum).[4] It may be that the effects of the crusades have often been exaggerated; it may be that the only tangible results were the introduction into the west of the windmill and the black rat. Yet it is equally dangerous to minimize their importance. The great movement provided the stimulus for a closer intercourse with the near east which had directly and indirectly significant consequences on the development of western Europe.

[1] See C. W. David's introduction to his edition of the De Expugnatione Lyxbonensi (1936), pp. 12–26, and below, p. 150.
[2] The Itinerary of Benjamin of Tudela, ed. with translation, &c., by M. N. Adler, pp. 3, 76.
[3] R. L. Reynolds, 'Some English Settlers in Genoa', Econ. Hist. Rev. iv (1932–4), 317.
[4] Röhricht, Regesta Regni Hierosolymitani, pp. 285, 321, 325.

APPENDIX

Table showing the amount paid for the duty of a fifteenth and the volume of trade at the east- and south-coast ports from 20 July 1203 to 29 November 1204 as recorded on the Pipe Roll (see p. 94, n. 1 above).

	£	s.	d.	£	s.	d.
Newcastle	158	5	11	2,374	8	9
Yarm	42	17	10	643	7	6
Coatham		11	11	8	18	9
Whitby		4	0	3	0	0
Scarborough	22	0	4½	330	5	7½
Hedon	60	8	4	906	5	0
Hull	344	14	4½	5,170	15	7½
York	175	8	10	2,631	12	6
Selby	17	11	8	263	15	0
Lincoln	656	12	2	9,849	2	6
Barton-on-Humber	33	11	9	503	19	3
Immingham	18	15	10½	281	18	1½
Grimsby	91	15	0½	1,376	5	7½
Boston	780	15	3	11,711	8	9
King's Lynn	651	11	11	9,773	18	9
Yarmouth	54	15	6	821	12	6
Norwich	6	19	10	104	17	6
Dunwich	5	4	9	78	11	3
Orford	11	7	0	170	5	0
Ipswich	7	11	7½	113	14	4½
Colchester	16	12	8	249	10	0
Sandwich	16	0	0	240	0	0
Dover	32	6	1	484	11	3
Rye	10	13	5½	160	1	10½
Winchelsea	62	2	4½	931	15	7½
Pevensey	1	1	11½	16	9	4½
Seaford	12	12	2	189	2	6
Shoreham	20	4	9	303	11	3
Chichester	23	6	7	349	18	9
Southampton	712	3	7½	10,682	14	4½
Exmouth	14	6	3	214	13	9
Dartmouth	3	0	0	45	0	0
Saltash	7	4	8	108	10	0
Fowey	48	15	11	731	18	9
London	836	12	10	12,549	12	6

£4,958 7 3½ × 15 = £74,375 9 4½
volume
of trade.

IV

THE CONQUEST OF NORMANDY
1087–1135

THE Norman rulers of England were disagreeable men, masterful, stern, and cruel. The characteristic genius for political organization and administrative efficiency, which had crowned with success every Norman enterprise, in the duchy itself, in Italy, and in England, was inherited only by the youngest of the Conqueror's sons; but this and an aptitude for learning, usually greatly exaggerated, were the only features which redeemed the otherwise unpleasant character of Henry. Robert, the eldest of the family, who never ruled in England, Robert Curthose as his father called him because of his small size,[1] was different from his brothers. He was not harsh or cruel; he was in fact the reverse; he was too good-natured, too easy-going. He had perhaps the greatest faults of character; his life was self-indulgent and purposeless. But he also had far more attractive qualities than his brothers, qualities which make him almost likeable. His personal courage was conspicuous; he conducted himself with distinction on the first Crusade where, it was said, neither Christian nor pagan could unhorse him. He was affable, a good talker, and a good counseller to anyone but himself. His liberality was such that he could refuse nothing to anyone who asked, and so he dissipated his inheritance in a few weeks, granting away lands and castles to lawless barons and squandering his substance on worthless courtiers. As quite a young man, even before the conquest of England, Robert had been designated by his father as the future duke of Normandy and count of Maine; the designation had been more than once repeated; and the Norman barons had taken to him the oath of fealty. Moreover, primogeniture was the general rule in Normandy. William was not prepared to go back on his promise though he had no illusions as to Robert's character and in fact expressed on his deathbed his conviction that under Robert Curthose the country would be wretchedly governed. And wretchedly governed it was. As a ruler Robert proved despicable. He followed always the line of least resistance; powerful

[1] *Brevis ocrea* or short leggings. Ordericus Vitalis (ed. Le Prevost), iii. 262.

barons were allowed to do as they pleased; wrongdoers went unpunished; and Robert soon merited the universal contempt of his subjects.

The position in England was different from that in Normandy. There was no rule of primogeniture. It had been acquired by conquest and the kingship was elective. The Conqueror wished it for his second son, William, his favourite son, who had always been the most attached to himself and the most dutiful. He wrote therefore a letter to Lanfranc expressing his wish, and bade Rufus set off immediately to take possession of his kingdom. The latter was in fact already at the coast, preparing to cross the Channel, when he received the news of his father's death at Rouen. The influence which Archbishop Lanfranc exercised in England is remarkably shown by the absence of any sign of opposition to his carrying out the Conqueror's wish. 'No one', wrote Eadmer, 'without his consent could acquire the kingdom.'[1] Though it might well be argued that Henry, born in England and born of crowned parents, was the more fitting successor, or that Robert, the eldest son, had a better title, no one at the time raised a hand in either's behalf or so much as voiced their claim. There was not even the formality of an election. William I died on 9 September; on the 26th of the same month William II was crowned at Westminster. This short, thick-set, corpulent man with the ruddy complexion, which gave him in his own day the nickname of Rufus, was at the time of his accession about thirty years old. He had been carefully educated under the guidance of Lanfranc. But he had no taste for anything beyond hunting and military exercises and gained little benefit from the instruction of that great master. William of Malmesbury has drawn his character and makes what apology he can for him. But it amounts to very little: he was brave; he honoured his father's memory; he could at times act wisely and with decision, as, for example, when Le Mans was besieged in 1099, he left the hunting-field and, in spite of the protests of his companions, crossed the Channel in a gale and saved the situation. But these occasions were rare. In other respects he seems to have richly merited the evil reputation he has left behind. He was a cynical, vain, capricious, ill-tempered man. He was blasphemous and scoffed at religion. The money he extorted from his subjects he squandered on a mercenary

[1] *Hist. Nov.*, p. 25.

army and a licentious court. The effeminate character of his court, the absence of any mention of paramours or bastards, the horror and reticence of the chroniclers regarding his personal conduct make it tolerably certain that he indulged in unnatural vice.[1] From the moral standpoint he was probably the worst king that has occupied the throne of England.

Of the youngest son, Henry, the Conqueror made a rich but landless man. He bequeathed him 5,000 pounds of silver. That Henry was a good man of business is shown by the recorded fact that then and there, while his father lay dying, he weighed out his legacy to be sure that there was no deficiency. He was undoubtedly a very competent, a very capable man with a real gift for statesmanship. But he had most of the bad qualities of his brother Rufus as well. He was grasping, cruel, and lascivious. He was born after the Conquest (1068) and in England, and he subsequently married a half-English wife. These facts have led historians to regard Henry as almost an Englishman. But in truth his general bearing is that of any other Anglo-Norman baron. He could flatter the English when he had need of their help, but he really detested them, as Eadmer plainly tells us,[2] and carefully excluded them from any share in the government of the church or state. To contemporaries he appeared as an ideal king; to men who witnessed the utter wretchedness of the succeeding age, the reign of Henry with its peace, order, and justice must have indeed appeared wholly admirable.[3] In reality this stern, relentless man seems far removed from being the model of kingly virtues.

The dispositions made by William I, unimpeachable on the ground of equity, were, on other grounds, injudicious and un-workable. For the last quarter of a century the central feature in political history had been the Norman Conquest of England. Now it becomes the English Conquest of Normandy, a phase which lasts till the battle of Tinchebrai in 1106, and which is due to the dispositions of William the Conqueror. The barons, having estates in the duchy and in the kingdom owed allegiance

---

[1] This is indeed implied in the words of Eadmer, *Vita Anselmi*, pp. 359 f. There is a touch of irony when William in a solemn charter of 1090 bids the canons of Lincoln to lead chaste lives (*Registrum Antiquissimum*, ed. C. W. Foster, i. 7).

[2] p. 224.

[3] One writer of the time, Henry of Huntingdon, frankly admits that the idealization of Henry is due to a comparison with the misery of the period of anarchy (*Hist. Anglorum*, ed. Arnold, p. 256).

both to Robert and to William Rufus; so in the quarrels of the brothers they were bound to break faith with one or other of their lords. This awkward situation Ordericus Vitalis considers to be a primary motive for the support given by the Norman barons to the rebellion which broke out in the first year of Rufus's reign under the leadership of Bishop Odo of Bayeux and which had as its ostensible object the promotion of Duke Robert to the undivided rule of his father's dominions.

William on his deathbed, in a fit of remorse for his past severity, had released a group of important prisoners who had for some years languished in Norman dungeons: Earl Morcar, Wulfnoth and Ulf, the brother and son of King Harold, and Duncan, the son of Malcolm Canmore who had been retained as a hostage for the good faith of the Scottish king.[1] There was also Odo of Bayeux whose ambitious designs had led to his summary arrest in 1082. He now gained his liberty only at the repeated and urgent entreaty of his brother, the count of Mortain; for William rightly judged that the ambitious earl-bishop[2] could not be trusted farther than the gates of his prison. He was indeed no sooner at large and restored to his earldom of Kent (Christmas 1087) than he began to stir up trouble. His own motive for raising rebellion was probably that William of St. Calais, bishop of Durham, and not himself, had the first place in the councils of Rufus, and he disliked the influence of Lanfranc whom he regarded as largely responsible for his own imprisonment. But the separation of Normandy from England was no doubt the reason that it received as much support as it did. That 'nearly all the Normans' joined in the conspiracy is certainly an exaggeration.[3] There were not a few notable exceptions such as Hugh, earl of Chester, William de Warenne, and Robert Fitz Hamon. But even so it was sufficiently formidable to cause alarm. There were isolated and easily suppressed outbreaks in the east and midlands—at Norwich under Roger Bigod, in Leicestershire and Northamptonshire under Hugh de

---

[1] Morcar and Wulfnoth were brought to England by Rufus and there thrust again into prison at Winchester. Morcar ended his life in captivity, but his fellow prisoner was ultimately released and entered a monastery. The other two were more fortunate; they fell into the hands of Duke Robert who knighted them and set them at liberty.

[2] His seal portrays him as an earl on horseback on the obverse and as a tonsured bishop on the reverse. *Sir Christopher Hatton's Book of Seals*, Plate VIII.

[3] Will. Malmes., *Gesta Regum*, ii. 361 (§ 306).

Grentmesnil, the sheriff of Leicester. There was a more serious rising in the west, on the Welsh border where Roger de Montgomery, Roger de Lacy, and other powerful barons of the March pushed into Worcestershire where they were defeated by a force hastily got together by Bishop Wulfstan; from Bristol William of Eu swept through Gloucestershire and despoiled the royal manor of Berkeley, while the bishop of Coutances and his nephew, Robert de Mowbray, earl of Northumberland, made a plundering raid through Somerset and Wiltshire, burnt Bath, and were only checked when they reached Ilchester. But these were minor episodes of the rebellion. The serious danger was confined to the south-east—to Odo's earldom of Kent and to Sussex where his brother, Robert of Mortain, garrisoned the castle of Pevensey. Here Rufus himself took charge. He captured the castle of Tonbridge and, after a six weeks' siege, that of Pevensey together with the two brothers Odo and Robert. He then marched to Rochester, the centre of resistance, which, by agreement, Odo was to induce the garrison to deliver over to him. But instead, either by accident or more probably by design, Odo himself fell into the hands of the rebels who resolutely prepared to withstand the royal army. Although the great stone keep was not then standing—it was erected by William of Corbeil some forty or fifty years later—and even Gundulf's walled enclosure may not have been begun,[1] nevertheless the Rochester earthworks must have been an effective fortification against the methods of siege warfare of the eleventh century; for the garrison held out for some time and were only driven to surrender by the pestilential condition into which the place was reduced.

The collapse of the rebellion may be attributed to two main causes: first, the failure of Duke Robert to provide adequate support. He did not come over in person; he sent some troops under Eustace of Boulogne and Robert of Bellême who garrisoned Rochester; another party reached the coast during the siege of Pevensey, but was prevented from landing and almost annihilated at sea. But a more important cause of failure was the assistance given to the king by the church and the native English. All but one of the bishops of English dioceses—all but William of St. Calais of Durham—supported Rufus. The conduct of the English is perhaps the most interesting feature of the

[1] See Round, *Geoffrey de Mandeville*, pp. 337 f.

rebellion. William the Conqueror's government had been concerned with providing for the security of the throne against native risings. The position is now reversed: the danger comes from rebellious Norman barons, and their rebellions are suppressed by the English levies. The English had taken some part in putting down the risings which had occurred between 1068 and 1070; William of Malmesbury records that there were English soldiers in the army that William took with him in 1075 to suppress a revolt in Maine; and the fyrd of Worcestershire was certainly in part responsible for the speedy collapse of the rising of the earls in the same year. Nevertheless it was probably fear of the Conqueror's strong hand rather than any particular interest in his cause that impelled them to fight his battles. But the part played by the English in the rebellion of Odo of Bayeux was on a far larger scale than in any previous rising. They supported Rufus with enthusiasm. In 1088 William II enjoyed a popularity such as was never again accorded him. Proclamations were issued and the English came flocking to his standard. At Worcester and again at Rochester the success of the royal cause was due in the main to the English fyrd. In return for their help the king made handsome promises of good government, good laws, relief of taxation, and free hunting. The promises were, of course, forgotten when the danger was past; laws were then set aside, taxation became more oppressive, and the forest laws were made even more severe. Untrustworthiness in respect of his obligations was perhaps one of the traits in the king's character which was most resented. When rebuked by Lanfranc for his failure to keep his promise, he is reported to have answered in a rage, 'Who can be expected to keep all his promises?' Lanfranc died in May 1089, and with his death was removed the only restraint upon the conduct of Rufus.

William dealt leniently with the rebels. Odo alone was banished for ever from England. He retired to Normandy where he played a part in the politics of the duchy till he left with Duke Robert for the crusade. He never reached Syria, for he died on the way, at Palermo (February 1097). Some others suffered confiscation of their lands and a temporary exile. Among these was William of St. Calais, bishop of Durham, who at first had been the most trusted counsellor of Rufus, but whose conduct during the rebellion had been exceedingly dubious. While the Durham writers testify to his innocence and also give the fullest account of the business, all other contemporary authorities unanimously condemn him. That they were right seems clear; for in the long-drawn-out trial Archbishop Lanfranc took the chief part, and he would not accuse a fellow bishop without good reason. The case is interesting as the first state-trial of which we have a nearly contemporary report.[1] Bishop William was indicted for treason before the king's court. He demanded, not unreasonably, that his temporalities, of which he had been deprived, should be restored to him until he had been found guilty; he claimed the privilege of his order; he claimed to be dealt with according to the canons, and even at one stage of the proceedings produced a copy of that famous forgery, the Pseudo-Isidorian Decretals (at that time, of course, fully accredited) to strengthen his case.[2] Further, he obstinately refused to recognize the authority of the court composed, as it was, 'of the king sitting in judgement with his bishops and barons, his sheriffs and reeves, his huntsmen and other officers'. It was certainly a very secular court, but, as Lanfranc pointed out, it was not as a bishop but as a lord of a fief that he was undergoing his trial, and he reminded him of the judgement of the Conqueror on Odo who was sentenced not as bishop of Bayeux but as earl of Kent.[3] William of St. Calais, however, clung steadfastly to his position. He demanded to clear himself by compurgation, and, when this was refused, declared his intention of appealing to Rome. Rufus retorted by demanding the surrender of Durham castle, and only on that condition would he permit him to leave the country. In the end the castle was delivered up (14 November) and the bishop was granted a safe conduct to pass out of the kingdom. He went to Normandy, to the court of Duke Robert; but he did not pursue his threat of taking his case to Rome. We may indeed doubt the

---

[1] This is contained in a tract *De injusta vexatione Willelmi Episcopi Primi*, printed by Arnold in his edition of Symeon of Durham, *Opera* (Rolls Series), i. 170–95. For a criticism of this tract see H. F. Offler, *English Historical Review*, lxvi (1951), 321–41.

[2] This was probably the Durham book, the *Decreta Pontificum* which Bishop William presented to the cathedral and which is now in the library of Peterhouse. See Z. N. Brooke, *The English Church and the Papacy* (1931), p. 79.

[3] Even as late as 1194 this distinction was insisted upon. Cf. the case of Hugh of Nonant, bishop of Coventry, who had conspired with John in Richard I's absence on crusade. It was decided to subject him 'to the judgment of bishops in that he was a bishop and to the judgment of laymen in that he was the king's sheriff'. Hoveden, iii. 242.

sincerity of Bishop William's championship of the rights of his
order, for in the celebrated council of Rockingham not many
years later we find him stoutly supporting the king against the
just demands of Anselm. But in the meantime he had been
reconciled to William. On the third anniversary of his sentence
(14 November 1091) he had been restored to his see and to the
king's favour, and a few years later, perhaps at the Christmas
court at Gloucester in 1093, the point on which he had stood so
firmly at his trial was conceded. William Rufus granted him in
free alms all the lands which he had formerly held in fee. The
bishop could therefore no more be treated as a lay baron and
subjected to the jurisdiction of a feudal court.[1]

The rebellion of Odo of Bayeux was in reality a phase of the
great struggle between the sons of William the Conqueror for
the undivided dominions of their father. These dominions were
now still more divided; for Robert, in straits for money, had
parted with a large and valuable portion of his inheritance, the
Cotentin and the Avranchin, to his brother Henry for 3,000
pounds of silver. In the attempts of William Rufus to wrest the
duchy from Robert, Henry takes a not unimportant part, fighting now on one side, now on the other, and sometimes even
forced to play a lone hand against both brothers at once. But
there are other factors which affected the situation in these
Norman wars. Who should possess Normandy, the feckless,
inefficient Robert or the tyrannical Rufus, was obviously a
matter of serious concern to the king of France. The territory
under the control of the French Crown at this time comprised
hardly more than Paris and a few castles and estates in its
immediate neighbourhood; it was far weaker than Normandy
had been in the days of William I, smaller in extent, poorer in
its resources, less centralized in government. Clearly it was to the
advantage of the French monarchy that Rufus should be confined to his island kingdom, that Normandy should remain
under the ineffectual rule of Duke Robert. But unfortunately
for France, its king, Philip I, was too lazy, self-indulgent, and
unenterprising to play an effective role. His spasmodic appearances on the theatre of war did not seriously embarrass William

[1] H. H. E. Craster, 'A Contemporary Record of the Pontificate of Rannulf
Flambard', in *Arch. Aeliana*, 4th ser., vii (1930), 35-6. This, however, did not prevent Henry I from confiscating certain lands of the bishop who succeeded him
(Flambard) at St. Albans on 9 June 1101. This appears from a charter printed
ibid., p. 56, and from other charters of this series (pp. 45-50).

Rufus; he was easily bought off. In 1089 his aid was solicited by Robert, and, in the expressive phrase of William of Malmesbury,[1] 'belching from daily excess he came hiccupping to the war'; but he accepted money 'and returned to his feasting'. On another occasion he seems to have captured a castle or two. But his intervention did little to check the progress of the conquest.

The state of Normandy seemed to favour the projected invasion of William Rufus. It looked as though nothing was easier than to step in and take up the reins of government which Duke Robert was wholly incapable of holding. The condition of the country was deplorable; the ducal garrisons had been expelled from the castles which were then fortified by the barons and became centres of petty tyranny and violence; bands of freebooters roamed the country, plundering and robbing the churches and peasantry. Private war was the order of the day, and Robert made no attempt to restrain this lawlessness. The defenceless inhabitants would welcome a brutal tyrant like Rufus in preference to anarchy under Robert, and it is stated[2] that appeals from the oppressed churches supplied William with a motive for his first campaign. On the other hand, these lawless, freebooting barons, who were responsible for the desperate condition of affairs, preferred to have a merely nominal ruler, a ruler like Robert, to a man who might exercise an effective control over them. Typical of the Norman baron at his worst was Robert of Bellême, the eldest son of Roger de Montgomery and Mabel, the heiress of the ill-famed house of Talvas. He had already succeeded to the estates of his mother's family, large stretches of country and numerous castles lying on the borders of Normandy, Maine, and Perche; in course of years he was to add to his territorial strength by the acquisition of his father's lands in England[3] and the property of his wife (who spent a large part of her married life in the dungeons of Bellême), the heiress of Count Guy of Ponthieu. The most powerful and the

---

[1] *Gesta Regum*, ii. 363 (§ 307). The date is supplied in the *De Controversia Guillelmi Rotomagensis* printed in *Recueil des Hist. des Gaules*, xiv. 68. See David, *Robert Curthose*, p. 56.

[2] Orderic, iii. 316 f. The schedule of injuries and losses suffered by the nuns of Holy Trinity at Caen, printed by C. H. Haskins, *Norman Institutions*, pp. 63 f., provides a striking illustration of the desperate condition of the churches during the anarchy.

[3] Below, p. 117.

most dangerous of the Norman baronage, he was also the most repellent in character. In a society of ruffianly, bloodthirsty men, Robert of Bellême stands out as particularly atrocious; an evil, treacherous man with an insatiable ambition and a love of cruelty for cruelty's sake; a medieval sadist whose ingenious barbarities were proverbial among the people of that time.[1] Such men, and there were many like him on a lesser plane, did all they could to hinder a final settlement of the Norman question.

But the Norman barons had their vulnerable point. They were greedy of wealth, and Rufus was quick to see that his object would be more easily gained by corrupting the venal barons than by storming their castles. That money not men was the main instrument employed is illustrated by an incident in the campaign of 1094. The king ordered, we are told, 20,000 of the English militia to be mobilized for service in Normandy. When, however, they were assembled at Hastings ready to embark, he instructed his agent, Rannulf Flambard, to take from them the money provided for their subsistence (10s. each) and dispatch it to him abroad. The soldiers were sent home.[2] So the conquest of Normandy was achieved by no victory in the field, by the capture of no strategic position, but by an adroit use of the money wrung from the church and his English subjects. In this way, probably as early as 1089,[3] he secured St. Valery at the mouth of the Somme, a useful port and base of operations for the attack on eastern Normandy. So, too, by bribery and diplomacy he won over the strong frontier-fortresses of Aumale, Eu, and Gournai. One after another the Norman strongholds fell into his hands until he was master of the greater part of the duchy on the right bank of the Seine. Even in Rouen itself a popular rising in favour of Rufus, under the leadership of a wealthy citizen named Conan and inspired perhaps by the desire to retain the valuable trading connexion with England, was only suppressed after much street-fighting and bloodshed by the energy of Prince Henry and Robert of Bellême. All this happened in the course of the year 1090 while the king was still in England. He crossed the Channel about the end of January

[1] See on him in particular Henry of Huntingdon, *Epist. de contemptu mundi*, ed. Arnold (Rolls Ser.), p. 310.
[2] Florence of Worcester, ii. 35.
[3] See David, *Robert Curthose*, pp. 53 f.

1091[1] and his presence in the duchy was sufficiently alarming to rouse Robert to immediate action. But it was too late; even with the aid of his suzerain, the king of France, whose help he once more solicited, he could not retrieve the position. The barons deserted in large numbers to Rufus's court at Eu. There was nothing left for Robert but to accept such terms as he could get. These, which were arranged at Rouen and guaranteed by twelve prominent men from each side, were far from favourable. They amounted to a concession of the lands which Rufus had occupied, namely: the counties of Eu and Aumale, the lordships of Gournai and Conches (the one foothold he had won to the west of the Seine), and the abbey of Fécamp. The grant seems also to have included Cherbourg and Mont St. Michel which were not the duke's to give, for they formed part of the land which he had already sold to his brother Henry. On his side William Rufus bound himself to assist his brother in the recovery of the lands which had been held by William the Conqueror but which had, since his death, rebelled against their duke, and in particular the county of Maine.

The campaign for the recovery of Maine was not carried out; instead Robert and Rufus turned their arms against their youngest brother, Henry, who was preparing to resist the execution of the provision of the treaty which had assigned two of his possessions, Cherbourg and Mont St. Michel, to the king of England. He was attacked by the combined forces of his brothers, besieged at Mont St. Michel, and driven out of the Cotentin. Once more he was reduced to the position of a landless adventurer. During the summer of 1091 William and Robert acting together made some effort to restore order in the turbulent duchy. The *Consuetudines et Justicie*,[2] drawn up at Caen on 18 July 1091 as a result of an inquest concerning the rights and privileges of the duke, indicate a serious attempt to re-establish and enforce authority in Normandy. That it failed in its object was owing to the fact that affairs in England, disturbances on the Welsh and Scottish borders, urgently demanded the presence of the king on the other side of the Channel. But the brotherly concord, so surprisingly demonstrated by the events of

---

[1] On 27 January he granted a charter to John, bishop of Bath, at Dover. This was presumably just before he embarked for Normandy. Davis, *Regesta*, no. 315.

[2] The document is printed and discussed by C. H. Haskins, *Norman Institutions*, App. D.

the last months, was not destroyed by William's departure in August, for Robert and even the shamefully treated Henry accompanied him to England, and the whole family took part in the Scottish campaign made in the autumn of that year.[1]

Robert Curthose was back in his duchy by Christmas 1091; but Rufus made no suggestion of accompanying him to continue the good work of restoring order which had been so fruitfully begun before it was broken off by his sudden return to England. So the duke was left to fight his own battles in Maine and to intervene as ineffectively as ever in the feuds and rebellions of his turbulent subjects. This surly treatment was bitterly resented by Robert who made, through his envoys, a formal complaint at the Christmas court (1093) at Gloucester that William had not carried out his part of the treaty of Rouen. This reopened the Norman question and stimulated Rufus to renew his attempt to conquer the duchy. But the campaign of 1094 left things pretty much as they were. Conferences and attempts at arbitration failed;[2] and such success as William gained by his money and mercenaries was more than counteracted by victories of Robert and his ally, the king of France, in other parts of the duchy. At one moment William's firm position in eastern Normandy was threatened. But a substantial bribe induced King Philip to withdraw from the campaign and the situation was saved. In these later stages of the Norman war the youngest brother Henry had added to the embarrassments of Duke Robert. In 1092 he had become lord of Domfront at the invitation of the inhabitants who had suffered terribly from the brutal oppressions of Robert of Bellême. Using it as a base of operations he proceeded to reconquer the Cotentin, an enterprise in which he met with considerable success. This had been done with the encouragement of Rufus who in 1095, being detained in his own kingdom by more urgent affairs, entrusted him with the direction of his Norman interests.

[1] The three brothers appear as witnesses to a charter of William, bishop of Durham, who was restored to his see on 14 Nov. (Davis, *Regesta*, no. 318). W. Farrer (*Early Yorkshire Charters*, no. 928) dates it in December, on the return journey from Scotland.

[2] A. Fliche, *Le Règne de Philippe Ier, Roi de France* (1912), pp. 298 ff., argues ingeniously but unconvincingly that an unsuccessful arbitration by King Philip, which he supposes took place in the Vexin either at Pontoise or Chaumont, was the only event of Rufus's expedition of 1094, and that the events related by the English chroniclers really belong to the previous campaign of 1090-1. For a refutation of the hypothesis see C. W. David, op. cit., p. 86, n. 225.

The matter that occupied the king's attention in England in 1095 was a baronial revolt. Its leader was Robert de Mowbray, earl of Northumberland. He is described as a morose, taciturn man, strong and virile, swarthy and exceedingly hairy. He had rifled the cargoes of a few Norwegian trading vessels which had put into a Northumbrian port. On the complaint of the despoiled merchants, he was summoned before the king to answer for this act of lawlessness; but instead of appearing before the court he broke into rebellion. We cannot, however, believe that this trivial incident was the cause of a conspiracy the purpose of which was to deprive the king of his life and throne. Rather we may suppose it supplied the occasion for a revolt which had been long maturing against the despotic government of William Rufus. The conspirators belonged to the leading Norman families; they were, for the most part, the same men who had rebelled in 1088: Robert de Mowbray himself, Roger de Lacy, Gilbert of Clare, and William of Eu had all taken a prominent part in the earlier rising. It was a Norman rebellion and it is probable that these barons were in touch with the barons on the other side of the Channel, perhaps even with Duke Robert himself; but they proposed, we are informed, to set not Robert, but Stephen of Aumale, the son of William I's sister Adelaide and Odo of Champagne, lord of Holderness, upon the throne.[1] The danger was certainly serious, for Anselm in a letter to the papal legate, Walter of Albano, speaks of the daily expectation that the enemy from across the sea would invade England by the ports in the vicinity of Canterbury.[2]

The king acted with promptness and energy. He marched northward with a strong army drawn from all parts of the country and laid siege to the earl's castles of Tynemouth and Bamborough. Tynemouth fell after a siege of two months; Bamborough held out longer both because of the great strength of its position and because William was called off to deal with an incursion by the Welsh. In his absence the earl was enticed from his castle by a trick and captured; but his wife, Matilda de Laigle, still held out on the impregnable rock until, under the threat that her husband's eyes would be put out unless the castle was immediately surrendered, she was forced to yield. The fall of Bamborough ended the rebellion. William had

[1] Florence of Worcester, ii. 38.
[2] S. Anselmi Opera Omnia, ed. F. S. Schmitt, iv , ep. 191.

found by experience that his leniency after the revolt of 1088 had not been rewarded by subsequent loyalty. He therefore dealt severely with the rebels at his court at Salisbury in January 1096. Robert de Mowbray dragged out a long imprisonment until, according to one tradition, he was allowed to enter religion at St. Albans; his gallant wife, thus deprived of conjugal felicity, obtained a licence from Pope Paschal II to contract a second marriage with Nigel de Albini. Others received more or less harsh sentences: some were deprived of their English lands; some paid heavy fines. William of Eu appealed of treason, failed in the judicial combat, and was blinded and castrated; his kinsman and steward, William de Alderi, though he protested his innocence, was whipped at every church in Salisbury and then hanged. After this there were no more baronial revolts during the reign.

William Rufus, as we have seen, preferred paying out money to fighting battles. In this year, 1096, an unlooked-for opportunity presented itself of acquiring the duchy of Normandy by his favourite method of attack. Inspired by the enthusiasm which after the council of Clermont spread through western Europe and especially through France, Duke Robert took the cross. But crusading was expensive and Robert Curthose was inveterately impecunious. He must raise money on his duchy. So the bargain was struck. Through the mediation of Gerento, abbot of St. Benignus at Dijon, the brothers were once more reconciled, and Normandy was pledged to William for three years in return for a sum of 10,000 marks of silver. There were bitter complaints about the exorbitance of the taxation raised to meet this obligation. It is stated that the barons granted a geld of 4s. on the hide. If this was so, it seems that William here was acting in a perfectly regular manner. Though there is no other record of a levy of Danegeld in the reign, it was probably taken when occasion demanded. Nor for an emergency was the rate unduly high. Certainly the normal rate both before the Norman Conquest and in later times was 2s.; but William I, when a Scandinavian invasion was threatened in 1084, had levied it at the rate of 6s. on the hide. The rather pettish complaints of the ecclesiastical writers can be explained by the fact that the church was not, as heretofore, exempted. They seem indeed to have found some difficulty in raising the money; in some cases they seem to have had to sell their church plate, and

Anselm had to borrow his contribution from the monks of Canterbury on the security of his manor of Peckham.[1]

Under William Rufus Normandy, like England, was oppressed and downtrodden. But that it was efficiently governed is demonstrated by the few acts which have survived; they show 'the regular mechanism of Anglo-Norman administration at work'.[2] Moreover, we hear far less of those interminable private feuds which, in the years before 1096, fill the pages of Orderic's history with tedious monotony.[3] On the whole, therefore, it may be assumed that Normandy benefited by the change of masters. Secure of the duchy, William began to look farther afield; he is said by Suger, the minister and biographer of Louis VI, to have aspired to the throne of France, and there may be some truth in the statement. Just before his death he was, it seems, bargaining for Aquitaine whose duke was about to set off for the Holy Land. But his attention was first directed towards the extension of his immediate frontiers, to the conquest of the French Vexin and Maine, both of which had been the cause of unceasing trouble to the Conqueror. The first of these lay between Normandy and the Isle de France, the second between Normandy and Anjou. The attempt to conquer them would certainly therefore entail war with both the king of France and the count of Anjou. These campaigns occupy the last years of Rufus's reign and they are characterized by the same features as the wars for the conquest of Normandy: they begin with energy and determination, but flicker out, leaving behind no decisive result. In the attack on the Vexin in 1097 William Rufus had all the advantage on his side; he had men, money, and military experience, things in

[1] H. W. C. Davis, *England under the Normans and Angevins*, p. 108, argues that there were two distinct exactions imposed, an aid and a Danegeld. This, however, does not seem to be necessarily implied in the rather vague words of Florence of Worcester (ii. 40) and Eadmer (*Hist. Nov.*, p. 74), the texts on which he relies. All that they imply is that some gave voluntary contributions. The only coherent statement is that contained in the *Leges Edwardi Confessoris* in Liebermann's *Die Gesetze der Angelsachsen*, i. 636: 'Ipsi (barones) autem concesserunt ei quatuor solidos de unaquaque hyda, sanctam ecclesiam non excipientes.' It may have been on this occasion that the hoard of nearly 12,000 pennies, many of them newly minted, were buried in a leaden box at Beaworth, Hants, perhaps in order to escape the notice of the tax collectors. See J. H. Ramsay, *History of the Revenues of the Kings of England*, i. 7. But cf. G. C. Brooke, *Catalogue of English Coins in the British Museum. The Norman Kings*, i, pp. xxi–xxii.

[2] Haskins, *Norman Institutions*, p. 83.

[3] The fact that a number of the Norman barons accompanied Robert to Palestine may have also contributed to the absence of private war during these years. For a list of the crusading barons see David, *Robert Curthose*, App. D.

which his opponents were altogether deficient. Philip of France, always lacking in vigour, was now too fat to take the field; his son, Louis, to whom the task of defending the Vexin was entrusted, was still young, not sixteen years of age, and untrained. But in spite of his youth, his inexperience, and the meagreness of his resources, he did surprisingly well. He effectively prevented the English from making any real headway. Nor was Rufus any more successful when he resumed the campaign in the autumn of 1098; both Pontoise and Chaumont, the great castles that guard the Vexin and the approaches to France, resisted his attack, and even when he was joined by Duke William of Aquitaine he failed to accomplish anything beyond the devastation of the surrounding country. The castles south of the Seine, Montfort and Epernon, which he besieged, held out against him, and he was forced to come to terms. The only enduring monument of this inglorious war was the erection of the great fortress of Gisors, the work of the finest military architect of the day, Robert of Bellême. This stronghold on the right bank of the Epte, a few miles to the west of Chaumont, was destined to play an important part in the wars between England and France during the twelfth century.[1]

In Maine William met with better success, but rather by good fortune than anything else. After many vicissitudes Maine had passed under the rule of Count Helias of La Flèche, a young, energetic, and deservedly popular patriot, a grandson of the old count, Herbert Wake-Dog. Unluckily he fell into an ambush and was captured by Robert of Bellême who handed him over to Rufus. In this way Le Mans came under English control. But serious revolts supported by the Angevins required his presence there on more than one occasion (1098–9); and after his death it slipped away again from its allegiance to the English Crown. Helias was the last independent count of Maine, for his daughter and heiress married the younger Fulk, the heir of Anjou. In this way Maine became absorbed in Anjou, and with Anjou passed once more under the English Crown in the time of Henry II.[2]

---

[1] The castle was, however, largely rebuilt by Henry II between 1161 and 1181, and it was further strengthened by Philip Augustus when it came into his hands in 1193. Little therefore, if any, of the extant remains owe their origin to the genius of Robert of Bellême. See C. Enlart, *Manuel d'archéologie française*, Pt. 2 (1932), ii, 566, 575.

[2] [*For note see facing page.*]

The duchy of Normandy had been pawned, not granted in perpetuity, to Rufus. Robert was now on his way home from the Holy Land with a greatly enhanced reputation, for on the Crusade he had conducted himself with marked distinction. He became a great hero of romance round whom, after his death, legends grew.[1] On his homeward voyage he stopped in south Italy, and there married Sibyl, the daughter of a rich Apulian count, Geoffrey of Conversana, a nephew of Robert Guiscard. With his wife he obtained a handsome dowry, sufficient indeed to enable him to redeem his duchy from pledge. Rufus, however, had no intention of restoring Normandy and was probably preparing to contest his brother's return when he met with his fatal accident in the New Forest.

In the late afternoon of Thursday, 2 August, William Rufus was struck by an arrow while hunting near Brockenhurst. The body of the dead king was left deserted and unattended until some peasants thrust it on a rough farm cart and brought it to Winchester where it was unceremoniously buried beneath the tower. So much we definitely know. We can accept with tolerable certainty the fact upon which nearly all the authorities agree, namely, that Walter Tirel, lord of Poix in Ponthieu, discharged the fatal arrow.[2] But was it an accidental hit or was it deliberate shooting? This is a question that can never be determined. There are, however, some facts which look ugly, which seem to suggest a plot. Tirel fled immediately across the seas;

[1] Gaston Paris even believed him to be the hero of a whole poetic cycle now lost. See C. W. David, op. cit., ch. viii.

[2] It is true that he later asserted on oath that he was not in that part of the forest or even saw the king at all that day (Suger, *Vie de Louis le Gros* (ed. Molinier, *Collection de Textes*), p. 8). But it is difficult to understand how such a strongly established tradition could have grown up without foundation.

[*Note 2 from previous page.*]

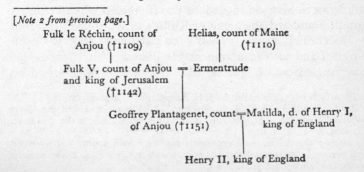

Fulk le Réchin, count of Anjou (†1109)
— Fulk V, count of Anjou and king of Jerusalem (†1142) = Ermentrude — Helias, count of Maine (†1110)

Geoffrey Plantagenet, count of Anjou (†1151) = Matilda, d. of Henry I, king of England

Henry II, king of England

his wife was of the family of Clare, and his father-in-law had enfeoffed him with lands in Essex; his two brothers-in-law, Gilbert and Roger of Clare, were members of the small party that hunted with the king that day.[1] Henry was also there, and he had most to gain by his brother's death. His actions seem to be premeditated: wholly disregarding his dead brother, he rode straight for Winchester, seized the treasury (always the first act of a usurping king), and the next day had himself elected. On 5 August, three days after the death of Rufus, he was crowned at Westminster. Finally, it may be added, when his position on the throne was assured, he treated the family of Clare with marked favour.[2] There is, at the least, enough evidence to arouse the suspicion that the sudden end of Rufus was the result of a conspiracy formed and organized among members of the house of Clare, a conspiracy of which Henry himself was cognizant.

In the first months Henry got through a tremendous quantity of work, work intended to impress on his subjects that the bad old ways of his brother had passed and that things were to be very differently conducted under the new régime. Never were Henry's qualities of efficiency and statesmanship displayed to better advantage than by these initial acts. In his coronation charter[3] he peremptorily disavowed the methods of Rufus: 'I abolish', he declared in the first clause, 'all the evil practices with which the realm of England was unjustly oppressed', and he then proceeds to outline the smooth and orderly justice which was to obtain for the future. In a tactful letter he announced his election to Anselm and urged his immediate return from his voluntary exile, and the archbishop complied with such good speed that he was back in England before Michaelmas. Confidence in his good intentions was increased when he thrust Rannulf Flambard, the agent of Rufus's worst oppressions, into the Tower. For a time he was even persuaded to give up his mistresses and to lead a respectable life with his virtuous and pious Anglo-Scottish queen, Matilda, whom he married on

[1] These facts were pointed out by J. H. Round, *Feudal England*, p. 472.
[2] Round, ibid. Cf. also F. H. M. Parker, 'The Forest Laws and the Death of William Rufus', in *Eng. Hist. Rev.* xxvii (1912), 26 ff., where the details are elaborated.
[3] Copies of the charter were apparently made for each county and were preserved as records in the cathedrals and principal abbeys. See R. L. Poole, *Studies in Chronology and History*, pp. 308 f.

11 November in the first year of his reign.[1] By these salutary measures and undertakings he sought to establish his position on the throne. His title was also recognized on the Continent in the most gratifying way; Louis, who during the last years of King Philip virtually ruled in France, came over in person to attend Henry's first Christmas court at Westminster. But there was still danger ahead. Duke Robert of Normandy was back in his duchy by September, and his claim to the throne of England had been voiced even before the election of Henry, on the very day of William's sudden death, by William of Breteuil, one of the hunting party, the brother of Roger, earl of Hereford, and Robert himself is said to have assumed the title when staying at Salerno to be cured of a wound on his return from Syria.[2]

In the history of the relations of England and Normandy the opening scene of the new reign is a repetition of the opening scene of the last: a rebellion in favour of Robert's claim to the English crown. Again it was supported by a significant body of Norman nobility both in England and in Normandy; again it was organized by a recently imprisoned bishop. The part of Odo is played by Rannulf Flambard who on 3 February 1101 escaped from the Tower and crossed to Normandy. Henry, who was genuinely alarmed, made extravagant promises of good government; he sent writs to all the counties reaffirming his coronation charter and bidding his subjects to bind themselves to defend his realm against all men and especially against his

[1] She changed her baptismal name Eadgyth or Edith to Matilda on her marriage. She was the great-granddaughter of Edmund Ironside:

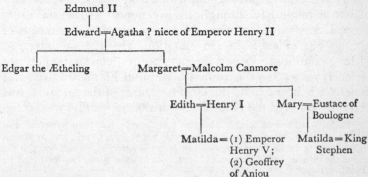

[2] The metrical treatise on hygiene, the *Regimen Sanitatis Salerni*, is thought to have been dedicated to him as king. It begins 'Anglorum regi scribit schola tota Salerni'. See Rashdall, *Medieval Universities*, ed. Powicke and Emden, i, p. 81.

brother Duke Robert of Normandy.[1] The country was thrown momentarily into chaos; there was consternation everywhere; only Anselm kept his head. He plays in 1101 the part that Lanfranc had played in 1088. But probably the danger was exaggerated, for the conspiracy ended very tamely. It was frustrated, as in the previous rebellion, by the alliance of the church and the native English. The shire-levies were wholly at Henry's disposal. William of Malmesbury gives us a description of the king personally supervising their training, going through the ranks, and instructing them how to meet cavalry. But there was no fighting to be done. Robert's army, a considerable force of cavalry, archers, and foot, was mobilized at Le Tréport. Through the treachery of some of Henry's sailors, this army was safely convoyed across the Channel and piloted into Portsmouth harbour where the king, whose troops were at Pevensey, was least expecting him (21 July). Passing by Winchester on the road to London, Robert came up with his brother at Alton. There a treaty was arranged and ratified by the oaths of twelve barons from each side, the terms of which seem to have amounted to a recognition by Robert of Henry's title to the English crown in return for an annuity of 3,000 marks. Henry further renounced all claims to lands in Normandy except the fortress of Domfront. Finally, an amnesty protected the duke's supporters from punishment.

Robert, it appears, was duped into surrendering a most favourable position, for, if his backing was anything like as strong as the narratives suggest, with a little more resolution and vigour he might have brought his invasion to a successful issue. From Henry's point of view the treaty was simply a means of getting out of an awkward situation. He had no intention of long continuing to pay the pension of 3,000 marks,[2] nor of seriously respecting the amnesty. Rannulf Flambard, who was generally believed to be the chief organizer of the invasion, was certainly restored to favour and to his bishopric; he was recon-

---

[1] The writ addressed to the shire court of Lincoln has been preserved and printed by W. H. Stevenson in *Eng. Hist. Rev.* xxi (1906), 505 ff., and by Canon C. W. Foster in the *Registrum Antiquissimum*, i. 47 (Lincoln Record Soc. 27). For the text of the reissue of the Coronation Charter see Ludwig Riess, *Eng. Hist. Rev.* xli (1926), 321-31.

[2] Cf. Will. Malmes., *Gesta Regum*, ii. 472 (§ 395): 'A promise of 3,000 marks deceived the easy credulity of the earl.' The payments ceased in 1103 when Robert, visiting England to intercede on behalf of the outlawed William de Warenne, was forced to give it up.

ciled to the king, absolved by both archbishops, and fully rein-
vested with his lands.[1] Rannulf's subsequent career, spent largely
in Normandy, probably supplies the motive for Henry's leniency
in 1101. The king no doubt thought that this dexterous intriguer
would be useful to him in connexion with his future designs on
the duchy.[2]

But the treatment of Rannulf Flambard was exceptional. Without openly violating the treaty, Henry found ways and means
of ridding himself of the more prominent Normans who had
opposed him. They were arraigned before the king's court for
some, often quite trivial, breach of the law and heavily fined or
deprived of their English lands. Among others dealt with in this
manner was Robert of Bellême who had played a leading part,
wholly unscrupulously, in almost every trouble that had arisen
during the previous reign. His activities had then been mainly
confined to Normandy. But in 1098, on the death of his brother
Hugh in Wales, he had by the payment of an enormous relief—
£3,000 is the sum named—acquired the English estates of the
house of Montgomery. These comprised, besides the great
earldom of Shrewsbury, the lordship of Arundel and a number
of castles and properties scattered through many counties. He
had thus become the most powerful of the barons in England
and no longer confined his activities to Normandy. As a supporter of Duke Robert in the recent invasion, Henry was determined to get rid of this dangerous man. He went to work warily
and judicially; for a whole year his spies were busy collecting
evidence on which to take proceedings. The result was that the
earl was summoned to answer at the king's court to an indictment of forty-five separate charges (1102). Robert of Bellême
did not wait to stand his trial where an adverse verdict would be
a foregone conclusion; instead he put his strongholds in a state
of defence. The king took the field in person, and one after
another the castles were surrendered—Arundel, Tickhill, Bridg-

[1] This fact, hitherto regarded as doubtful on account of the statement of Orderi-
cus Vitalis (iv. 273) that he was not reconciled to the king till after the battle of
Tinchebrai, 1106, has been definitely proved by charters published by H. H. E.
Craster, in *Arch. Aeliana*, 4th ser., vii (1930), 42 ff.

[2] In Normandy he obtained a dominating influence over the see of Lisieux
(1102), 'non ut praesul, sed ut praeses,' as Orderic says (iv. 117), for into the bishopric
itself he thrust first his brother, then his son, apparently a boy twelve years old.
Ultimately after Henry's victory in 1106 Rannulf handed over Lisieux to the king.
On Flambard's career see R. W. Southern, 'Rannulf Flambard and Early Anglo-
Norman Administration' in *Trans. R. Hist. Soc.*, 4th ser., xvi.

north, and finally Shrewsbury where Robert himself submitted. The enthusiasm with which the news of his capture and banishment was received is some indication of the terror which the earl inspired. The sentiment of joy and relief is reflected in a fragment of a popular ballad which Orderic has preserved:[1] 'Gaude, rex Henrice, Dominoque Deo gratias age, quia tu libere coepisti regnare, ex quo Rodbertum de Belismo vicisti et de finibus regni tui expulisti.'

Robert of Bellême worked off his rage and humiliation by perpetrating the most ruthless atrocities on the unhappy duchy, already torn and troubled by bloody private wars. Unoffending peasants, defenceless women, and churchmen were respected as little as the armed combatants. For a time a reign of terror prevailed in Normandy. Duke Robert offered some feeble resistance; but he was soon driven from the field by a crushing defeat and forced to conclude a discreditable peace with his powerful vassal.

Such being the state of affairs in Normandy, it is not surprising that we hear of refugees abandoning their country to seek the shelter of Henry's court and to beg him to take steps to end the anarchy. Ivo, bishop of Chartres, deeply impressed by the scandals that were allowed to go on—he was specially referring to the scandal in the diocese of Lisieux[2]—wrote to the king's chief adviser, Count Robert of Meulan, urging him to persuade his master to come to the help of the oppressed churches of Normandy. These appeals provided good moral grounds for a policy upon which Henry, there can be little doubt, was already decided, namely, the conquest of Normandy. He was drawing up his plans with care. Alliances were formed with all the powers that bordered on the duchy: the friendship of France had already been secured when, as we have seen, Louis had personally visited Henry immediately after his accession; in 1101 a treaty was concluded with Count Robert of Flanders according to the terms of which in return for an annual subsidy the count was to provide a force of a thousand knights for the king's service.[3] It

---

[1] iv. 177.   [2] Above, p. 117, n. 2.
[3] The original is preserved among the records of the exchequer and has been printed by Hearne, *Liber Niger*, pp. 7 f., and in the *Foedera* (Record Commission), I. 7 (wrongly dated 1103). It belongs to the year 1101 since it is attested by the chancellor William Giffard who resigned his office in April 1101 shortly after his appointment to the bishopric of Winchester. The amount of the subsidy is illegible; it is given by Hearne as 500 pounds, in the *Foedera* as 400 marks. The former is more likely to be correct for the document may well have been still legible when the *Liber Niger* was published in 1728.

was probably about this time, too, that Henry entered into agreements with the southern and western neighbours of Normandy, with Maine, Anjou, and Brittany, for all these countries sent contingents to his army in the decisive campaign of 1106. Robert Curthose was therefore effectively prevented from enlisting, as he had in his wars with William Rufus, aid from outside. Furthermore, by cautious intervention in the domestic quarrels of the Norman lords, Henry was forming a party in the duchy itself, and slowly undermining the ducal authority. Robert indeed could now only rely on the support of those men who on their own account had a grievance against King Henry, men, like Robert of Bellême and William of Mortain, who had been banished by him and deprived of their lands in England.

The stage was now set for the final scenes of the conquest of Normandy. It was accomplished in three expeditions: in 1104 Henry visited his stronghold of Domfront; he reinforced with his own troops the garrisons in the castles of those barons whose allegiance he had corrupted; and he forced his brother to hand over to him the county of Evreux.[1] This was more in the nature of a reconnaissance than a campaign. The serious work of conquest began when he landed in Holy Week 1105 at Barfleur in the Cotentin. In this district, Henry's first Norman possession,[2] his influence was already great, and it was quickly extended by the method, formerly so usefully employed by Rufus, of lavishly distributing money among the venal barons. Nearly all the more important men, we are told by Eadmer who was in Normandy at the time, were seduced in this way and rallied to Henry's side. But the tangible fruits of the campaign were Bayeux and Caen; the former was attacked and burnt to the ground, the latter was surrendered without a blow. However, the withdrawal at this point of his ally, the count of Maine, left his army too weak to push the campaign farther, and the last stage in the conquest was postponed for another year. In the interval there were conferences. A meeting of the brothers near Falaise led to no result. Nevertheless the situation must have been pretty desperate, for both Duke Robert himself and his ally, Robert of Bellême, visited England in the course of the winter 1105–6 with the hope of arranging a peace. But things

---

[1] This was as compensation for Robert's supposed breach of the treaty of Alton in concluding a peace with the rebel Robert of Bellême.

[2] Above, p. 104.

had gone too far, and Henry would have no peace. And in the summer, his preparations completed, he was again in Normandy.

The campaign opened with a siege of Tinchebrai, a castle belonging to William of Mortain, some thirty-five miles to the east of Avranches. While the operations were in progress, Duke Robert arrived and decided on an attempt to crush his enemy in a pitched battle. At Tinchebrai Robert never really had a chance owing to the immense numerical superiority of Henry's army. The opposing forces were drawn up apparently in successive divisions of both cavalry and infantry, but many of the knights, we are told, including the king and perhaps Duke Robert also, dismounted and fought on foot to give stability to the line. Indeed the interest of the battle from the point of view of military tactics is the unusual prominence given to the infantry.[1] The count of Mortain, leading the vanguard of the duke's army, opened with a fierce attack on the king's front line, which was composed of troops from Bayeux, Avranches, and the Cotentin, and drove it back. In the general confusion that followed the contingents from Maine and Brittany, who were drawn up at some distance on the flank, charged in and broke the ducal army to pieces. This ended the engagement which lasted scarcely an hour. Robert of Bellême, in command of the rearguard, fled from the field when he saw the way things were going; the rest of the duke's army was either taken or killed. On the king's side the losses were trifling.[2] The battle was fought on 28 September 1106, and it was decisive. The odd coincidence is noted by William of Malmesbury that the English conquest of Normandy was achieved on the fortieth anniversary of the Norman Conquest of England, for it was on 28 September 1066 that William the Conqueror landed at Pevensey. Duke Robert was among the prisoners and so, too, was the count of Mortain, and both dragged out the remainder of their wretched lives in prison. The latter was blinded to add to his miseries; but in-

---

[1] This was first emphasized by Sir Charles Oman in the first edition of his *Art of War in the Middle Ages*, against the view of most other writers on the subject. He has slightly modified his opinion in the light of fresh evidence (below, n. 2) in the second and enlarged edition of his work (1924), i. 381 ff.

[2] The formations and tactics of the battle have been much disputed. But much light was thrown on the controversial points by H. W. C. Davis who published (*Eng. Hist. Rev.* xxiv (1909), 728 ff., and with a correction ibid. xxv. 295 f.) a letter written by a priest of Fécamp very soon after the event describing the battle. The best recent commentaries are those by C. W. David, *Robert Curthose*, App. F, and by Sir Charles Oman, loc. cit.

fluenced perhaps by some sense of decency, Henry prescribed a more humane treatment for his brother, who in his successive prisons was adequately provided with food, clothing, and some of the comforts of life.[1] In his last days he was confined in the castle of Cardiff where he seems to have employed his abundant leisure in learning Welsh, for a pathetic little poem in that language is attributed to his authorship.[2] The line 'Woe to him that is not old enough to die' is a bitter reflection on the life tragedy of this misguided but rather attractive man. He survived his defeat at Tinchebrai for nearly twenty-eight years, and when he died in February 1134, an old man of eighty, he was buried in state beneath the high altar of the abbey church of St. Peter's at Gloucester where a fine effigy carved in wood still preserves his memory.

After his victory at Tinchebrai Henry set rapidly to work to enforce some semblance of authority in the distracted duchy. His father's system of government was once more established; his brother's alienations from the ducal domain were revoked; acts of violence were sternly punished; the unlicensed castles of the unruly barons were razed to the ground; and before he departed for England in the spring of 1107 order was so far restored that he could safely leave the administration in the hands of deputies, first among whom was John, archdeacon of Séez, now promoted to the see of Lisieux, a man of tried loyalty and long experience in governmental and judicial affairs.

It cannot be said, however, that the possession of Normandy was altogether a source of strength to the kings of England. Its conquest solved some problems: the allegiance of the barons was no longer divided between a king and a duke; the English Channel was really an English channel with both shores under one control. But it left other problems unsettled and added some fresh ones. Though Duke Robert was safely in prison, his son William, a boy of six years old, known as the Clito (ætheling, prince) or more aptly as 'the Exile',[3] was at large. He had fallen into Henry's hands when Falaise was captured in 1106, and the king would have been wise to have flouted public opinion and kept him like his father in close captivity. But he dared not do it. The child was therefore entrusted to the care of a kinsman and

---

[1] He was lodged in turn at Wareham, Devizes, Bristol, and finally Cardiff.

[2] See C. W. David, op. cit., p. 187, where it is printed with an English translation.

[3] Ordericus Vitalis, iv. 474.

for more than twenty years led a wandering life, always the centre of plots and intrigues, the ostensible object of which was to set him on the ducal throne of his father, but the real object to add to the difficulties and embarrassments of his uncle. Henry could never feel himself secure in Normandy while William Clito was alive and free. Then secondly, as duke of Normandy Henry was swept into the stream of continental politics which meant that he was frequently and often for long periods absent from his kingdom, a serious matter in an age when the conduct of government was so largely the personal business of the king. Normandy occupied an inordinate amount of his time; of the twenty-nine remaining years of his reign (1106–35) more than half were spent in the duchy.[1] It was a period of almost incessant war.

The Anglo-Norman power could not but be a serious menace to the neighbouring continental states, and particularly so to the French monarchy itself. In the time of Rufus France had not been an important factor in the situation; its king, Philip, was too weak and indolent to be effective. The position was very different when Louis VI succeeded to the throne in 1108 with the determined policy not only of making himself master in his own small domain—the Isle de France—but also of making the Capetian monarchy a power in western Europe. He inaugurated the policy of expansion which was to reach its goal a little more than a century later at the battle of Bouvines. But Louis had few resources and many enemies both within his domain and outside it; he had mistakenly looked on with approval while Henry had made himself master of Normandy, and now found himself faced with a strong hostile power on his northern frontier barring the way to the achievement of his ambition. With Normandy also stood the most persistent enemy of the kings of France, the house of Blois, to which it was attached by ties of kinship.[2] Henry's nephews, Theobald, the reigning count

[1] See C. H. Haskins, *Norman Institutions*, App. G, pp. 309 ff., for Henry's Norman Itinerary.

[2]

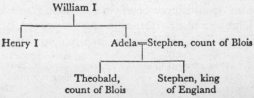

William I

Henry I   Adela⸺Stephen, count of Blois

Theobald,   Stephen, king
count of Blois   of England

of Blois, and Stephen, afterwards king of England, were generally to be found fighting in the Norman wars against France. Alone, therefore, Louis had little chance in any encounter with the Anglo-Norman power. He could, however, reckon on support in other quarters which made his aggressions if not actually dangerous at least a serious hindrance to Henry's government. Both the counts of Flanders and Anjou had reason to fear the strength of the king of England; the former, despite the Anglo-Flemish treaty of 1101 which had been renewed in 1110, was consistently on the side of France;[1] the latter had his own quarrel with Henry. Maine had become his by right of his wife on the death of Count Helias in 1110[2] and he refused the homage which the Norman dukes had regularly claimed in respect of that county since the time of William the Conqueror. Count Fulk always played a purely selfish game; but he often found that it served his interests best to aid his suzerain against his over-mighty neighbour. Lastly, on the side of Henry's enemies there was always a party of discontented Norman barons who found his firm rule little to their taste and were always ready to take advantage of his difficulties to further their own ends. Henry could have dealt quickly and decisively with any one of his opponents, but faced with attack from several quarters at once, he was prevented from concentrating his forces. The result was that the wars dragged on with short and intermittent pauses for the greater part of his reign.

In the first war (1111–13) fortune favoured Henry: Count Robert of Flanders was thrown from his horse on the bridge of Meaux and was killed (1111); Robert of Bellême, one of the leaders of the Norman rebels, fell into Henry's hands and was imprisoned for life (1112);[3] Alençon which lay within the borders of Maine was captured and Fulk had to sue for peace. He did homage for Maine[4] and betrothed his daughter Matilda

---

[1] Above, p. 118. Gaston Dept, *Les Influences anglaise et française dans le Comté de Flandre* (1928), pp. 17 ff., shows that it was the consistent policy of the counts of Flanders to try to separate England and Normandy, and that it was chiefly on economic grounds that they were obliged to depart from this policy. Cf. below, p. 376.   [2] Above, p. 112.

[3] He came to Henry's court as an envoy of Louis VI and was promptly thrown into prison first at Cherbourg and afterwards at Wareham where he spent the remainder of his life. The date of his death is not known, but he was still living in 1130 in which year the sheriff of Dorset accounts for his food and clothing (*Pipe Roll 31 Hen. I*, p. 12).

[4] Henry gives his own version of this transaction in a charter contained in the

to William, the only son and heir of the English king. Louis was again left isolated and it is possible that it was on this occasion that the two monarchs agreed to settle their differences by champions in single combat.[1] However this may be, in March 1113, near Gisors, Louis had perforce to accede to terms which enormously increased his enemy's strength. He recognized the English overlordship over Maine, Brittany, and the seigneurie of Bellême. This pacification was, however, short-lived. In 1116 the old alliance of France, Flanders, and Anjou was revived, and this time it was focused round the claim of William Clito to the dukedom of Normandy. Again it was supported by a group of discontented Norman barons, the most prominent of whom was Almaric de Montfort whose family was related both to the ruling houses of France and Anjou.[2] Although in the early stages the fighting went badly for Henry, he was ultimately once more successful in breaking up the combination: Flanders went out of the war when its count, Baldwin VII, was mortally wounded (1118); a separate truce was negotiated with Anjou and consummated by the marriage of William and Matilda at Lisieux in June 1119; again France was left isolated and compelled to face Henry unaided. The armies met casually at Brémule in the Vexin. The encounter that followed was little more than a skirmish; only a handful of men were engaged on each side; it was soon over, almost bloodless, but decisive. Disregarding the advice of his barons and without any plan of attack, Louis dashed impulsively against a well-ordered body of mostly dismounted knights. Those who escaped capture fled the field in disorder (August 1119). From war Louis turned to diplomacy. He was the equal of, perhaps even surpassed, Henry as a soldier, but as a diplomat he was altogether outmatched, and his essay in this field was a contemptible failure. He brought his supposed grievances and those of the Clito before the pope, Calixtus II, who in this year held a council at Rheims. The pope agreed to expostulate with Henry, but in a subsequent interview which he

cartulary of St. Evroul (printed by Le Provost in his edition of Ordericus Vitalis, v, p. 199): 'Hanc cartulam ego H. rex scribi feci anno quo comes Andegavensis mecum pacem fecit et Cenomannum de me, meus homo factus, recepit, &c.'

[1] The fact is known from an entry in the *Book of Fees*, p. 937, under the date 1242-3: 'The heirs of Nicholas Malemayns and Christiana Leddet hold in Burton (Latimer) of the barony of Alan Dynant who had that land of the gift of King Henry, grandfather of Richard I, who fought against the champion (*pugilem*) of the King of France between Gisors and Trie.'

[2] His sister Bertrade was the mother of Fulk of Anjou and stepmother of Louis VI.

had with him at Gisors he declared himself convinced of the justice of the king's actions—the conquest of Normandy, the imprisonment of Duke Robert, and all else of which he was charged. Through the pope's mediation a peace was once again patched up; Louis had to rest content with the homage of William the ætheling as heir to the duchy of Normandy and the wretched Clito returned to the life of a wandering exile.[1]

So matters stood in 1120. Henry's policy had everywhere triumphed: Louis's aggressions had signally miscarried; a peace-loving friendly count, Charles the Good, was reigning in Flanders; Fulk had set out for the Holy Land, leaving Maine under Henry's protection. Then everything was upset by a disaster at sea. On the night of 25 November the White Ship set out for England and foundered off Barfleur with all hands save one, said to have been a Rouen butcher, who lived to tell the story of the catastrophe. The vessel was the latest thing in marine transport, fitted with all the devices known to the ship-builder of the time. But the men were in no condition to put to sea; crew, marines, passengers were all, it seems, in an advanced state of intoxication; and when in their drunken excitement they attempted to overtake the fleet, which had preceded them, they struck a rock and sank. The loss of a ship must, of course, have been of common occurrence when troops and traders were continually passing between England and Normandy in not too seaworthy craft. The notoriety of this wreck is due to the very large number of distinguished persons on board; besides the king's son and heir, there were two royal bastards, several earls and barons, and most of the royal household. After four years in Normandy the court was returning to England, and many of the most prominent men had embarked on the ill-fated ship; its

[1] Henry's success may be partly attributed to his kinship with the pope which is noted by Orderic (iv. 398–9). They were second cousins:

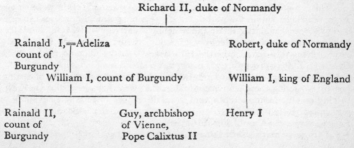

historical significance is that it left Henry without an obvious heir; the stability of the Norman dynasty, for which Henry had been sedulously working for the past twenty years, was seriously impaired; its immediate effect was to give a new and enhanced importance to William Clito, now the presumptive heir as the surviving male of the line of the Conqueror;[1] its ultimate result was the disputed succession and the period of anarchy which followed Henry's death.

When at the beginning of the year 1122 Count Fulk returned from Syria, he eagerly took up the cause of the Clito. He was already irritated by Henry who, indulging his natural avarice, returned his son's widow but retained the dowry. Fulk's first step was the marriage of the Clito to his second daughter, Sibyl, on whom he settled the county of Maine; this was parried by Henry who succeeded in inducing the pope to annul the marriage on the ground of consanguinity.[2] If this effectively prevented the Clito from acquiring Maine, it embittered still further the hostility of the count of Anjou who with Louis VI and Almaric de Montfort stirred up the insurrection in Normandy which brought Henry once more for a long sojourn in Normandy in 1123. It was Henry's masterly diplomacy, the creation of a diversion on the eastern frontier of France, which on this occasion shattered the machinations of his combined enemies.

A couple of months after the death of his son, Henry married his second wife. His object was definitely the hope of a male heir —a hope which did not materialize; but in choosing a German wife, Adeliza, the daughter of Godfrey of Louvain, duke of Lower Lorraine,[3] he was pursuing a policy which had been set on foot with the betrothal of his own daughter, Matilda, with the Emperor Henry V in 1109,[4] the policy of establishing a

---

[1] 'Jam solus regius esset haeres, et omnium expectatione dignus judicaretur.' Henry of Huntingdon, *Ep. de Cont. Mundi*, pp. 304-5.

[2] This is a good illustration of the unscrupulous use made of the pope's power to annul marriages within the prohibited degrees for political purposes. No question had been raised against William the Atheling's marriage with Matilda or later with his sister's marriage with Geoffrey of Anjou, though both stood in precisely the same relationship (cousins in the fifth degree) as the Clito to his bride. See J. Chartrou, *L'Anjou de 1109 à 1151*, p. 17, n. 4.

[3] This marriage established relations with Brabant which were of lasting importance. Among those who accompanied her were her chancellor Godfrey, who in 1123 became bishop of Bath, and her half-brother Joscelin of Louvain or, as he was called, Joscelin the Castellan, who was granted the honor of Petworth. See Farrer, *Honors and Knights' Fees*, iii. 17-18.

[4] They were married at Mainz on 7 January 1114.

political friendship between England and Germany. There are certain circumstances, in themselves of little significance, which, when taken together, indicate that relations of a more intimate character than heretofore were in fact established between the two countries in consequence of the marriage. In 1117 Ralph, archbishop of Canterbury, spent a week in the emperor's camp outside Rome; the presence of a nephew of the emperor[1] among the luckless passengers of the White Ship suggests that this young man had been with the English court in Normandy during the year 1120; at the end of his life, we are told, the emperor, acting on the advice of his father-in-law, attempted to raise a land-tax throughout Germany on the English model. The connexion between the two sovereigns was at any rate sufficiently close for them to plan in the summer of 1124 a concerted attack upon France. The threatened attack indeed came to nothing, for when the imperial army reached Metz, it turned back, partly because of the vast force which Louis had mobilized at Rheims in defence of his kingdom, partly because of an insurrection of the citizens at Worms.[2] It had, however, the effect of diverting Louis's attention for a time from Normandy; and there the rebellion was not revived after its virtual collapse with the capture of its leaders in the preceding spring in the skirmish at Bourgtheroulde, some fourteen miles south-east of Rouen.[3]

Nevertheless Louis, though repeatedly defeated in war and diplomacy, did not relax his efforts to injure Henry by means of William Clito. In 1127 he married him to Jeanne, a half-sister of his queen Adelaide, and conferred on him the whole of the Vexin including the three great border fortresses, Pontoise, Chaumont, and Mantes. But before William could make any serious attempt to possess himself of his dowry, a new field was found in which the unhappy man was required to employ his futile endeavours. On 1 March Charles the Good was treacherously murdered, leaving no direct or obvious heir but a host of pretenders to the county of Flanders. In these circumstances Louis VI took upon himself in his capacity of suzerain to foist

[1] Le Provost (Ordericus Vitalis, iv. 418, n. 1) supposes him to have been the son of Henry V's sister Agnes and Frederick of Swabia.

[2] The fullest account of Anglo-German relations is given by O. Rössler, *Kaiserin Mathilde*, ch. 2; cf. also G. Richter, *Annalen der Deutschen Geschichte*, Abt. III. ii, pp. 632 f.

[3] Ordericus Vitalis, iv. 456 ff.

his protégé into the vacant fief.[1] He was indeed accepted by a number of the Flemish nobles and maintained himself in an uneven struggle against his rival Thierry of Alsace for a year, until in July 1128 he received a mortal wound at the siege of Alost. Normandy had been a problem ever since it had been parted from England by the last disposition of William the Conqueror; it had absorbed the time, the money, and the anxious attention of both Rufus and Henry; Robert and his son William had had better claims to it and had always a party to support them. Now with the death of William Clito the duchy of Normandy was securely, incontestably welded with England.

The death of the Emperor Henry V in 1125 opened a way for the solution of some other difficulties, difficulties resultant on the death of King Henry's son and heir in the disaster of the White Ship. While the emperor lived Matilda could not be considered as heir to her father's dominions; it might lead to the absorption of England in the empire. She was now free both to inherit and to marry; she offered a solution to the question of succession and to the question of Norman-Angevin relations. In September 1126 she returned to England; on 1 January 1127 she was accepted by the barons as the successor to the throne. But they did so grudgingly, for the prospect of a female ruler was alike novel and distasteful. They feared also that this marriageable widow might entangle England with a foreign power and they tried to safeguard themselves against such a contingency by adding to their oath a proviso to the effect that she should not marry outside the kingdom without their consent. It failed in its purpose,[2] for within six months she was secretly betrothed to the son and heir of Fulk, count of Anjou, Geoffrey Martel; and he, when the marriage took place at Le Mans a year later (17 June 1128) was already virtually the ruler of Anjou, since his father, having taken the cross, had departed for Palestine.[3] The marriage was purely a political affair, its object being to detach Anjou from the French alliance.

[1] William Clito's claim was through his grandmother, Matilda, daughter of Baldwin V and wife of William the Conqueror. Henry I of England also put forward a claim on the ground of his descent from Matilda.

[2] It was, however, used with effect after Henry's death when it served as a pretext, so Roger of Salisbury argued, for releasing the barons from their oath and so enabling them to espouse the cause of Stephen.

[3] Count Fulk never returned to Anjou; he married Melisende, the heiress of Baldwin II, king of Jerusalem, to whose title he succeeded.

But they were an ill-assorted pair; the disparity of their ages was considerable, for she was twenty-five and he not much above fourteen; their temperaments, proud, quarrelsome, and autocratic, were incompatible; and hardly more than a year had passed before the boy husband practically repudiated his wife and packed her off, bag and baggage, to Rouen. He afterwards repented, summoned her back, and for a time lived with her in comparative amity.[1] It was in these years that she bore him children: Henry on 5 March 1133; Geoffrey (from whose birth the mother nearly died) 1134; and William 1136. The birth of Henry Plantagenet[2] seemed to put an end to any uncertainty about the succession. It brought the king once more to the Continent; he left England, never to return, in August 1133 for Rouen where, sunning himself in the pride and joys of a grandfather, he passed perhaps the happiest months of his life. By a masterful and adroit use of the means at his disposal he seemed to have won at every point. He was now an old man (in the middle sixties—a considerable age in medieval times) and having conquered or allied himself with his former enemies he might reasonably look forward to closing his reign in peace. But he had not reckoned with the unreliability of the Angevin or the turbulence of the Norman. His last days were embittered by domestic and political anxieties. He would have revisited England—he actually made three attempts to leave—in order to suppress disturbances in Wales, had not still more pressing difficulties detained him in Normandy where rebellion, instigated by his son-in-law and encouraged by his daughter, kept him busily engaged during the year 1135. Even his stout constitution was undermined by this ceaseless activity. On 25 November while staying for the hunting in the Forêt de Lyons,[3] which stretches eastward from the little river Andelle, he was

---

[1] She was restored to her husband on the advice of the barons at Northampton (8 September 1131) where, according to William of Malmesbury (*Hist. Nov.* ii. 534, § 455), the oath of fealty to Matilda was renewed. But, as J. H. Round points out (*Geoffrey de Mandeville*, p. 31, n. 2), in the subsequent contest of claims only the first oath is alluded to. There is still less ground for accepting the oath (mentioned by Roger of Hoveden) to Matilda's son Henry in 1133 for which there is no contemporary evidence.

[2] The name may have originated with Henry's father Geoffrey, who planted brooms (*genistas*) to improve his hunting covers. A. Cartellieri, *Historische Zeitschrift*, cxxxix (1928), 408.

[3] The actual place is Saint Denis near Gisors. This is evident from the charter quoted by T. Stapleton, *Rot. Scacc. Norm.* i, p. cxii.

seized with acute indigestion, brought on, it is said, by a meal of lampreys which always disagreed with him and from which his doctor had expressly ordered him to refrain. Fever set in and he died a week later on 1 December. His embalmed corpse was brought over to England and early in the new year was buried in the church of the monastery he had founded at Reading.

Henry I had ruled for nearly thirty-six years over England and twenty-nine over the duchy of Normandy. What in this long period of time had he achieved in the political sphere? He had certainly held his own, but he had done little more. By his energy and capacity, especially in diplomacy and statecraft, he had managed to outwit his numerous opponents and to suppress the rebellions of his subjects. Nevertheless, his enemies remained hostile and rebellions continued throughout his reign to harass his government of Normandy. He failed altogether to establish a durable peace. It was fear rather than love or even respect that he inspired in his subjects. He had by his exactions and by his arbitrary rule strained the obedience of his barons nearly to breaking-point. It may well be doubted whether a successor with a clear and undisputed title could have maintained Henry's system of government without modification. As things turned out, circumstances in a remarkable degree favoured a reaction, and the barons were not slow to take full advantage of the contested succession to emancipate themselves from the premature and over-rigid centralization set up by the last Norman king.[1]

[1] F. M. Stenton, *The First Century of English Feudalism*, pp. 216 f.

V

THE ANARCHY

1135-1154

ALTHOUGH Henry I was the father of at least twenty-one children, only two were born in lawful wedlock. Of these William had perished at sea in 1120, and Matilda alone survived to represent the direct and legitimate line of the dukes of Normandy.[1] Her father, anxious to secure for her the succession, had exacted an oath from the barons in 1127 to accept her as heir to England and Normandy. They had, however, sworn reluctantly, little relishing the idea of a female ruler. She had left England when she was eight years old; she had been brought up in Germany where alone she was appreciated and even regarded with affection. Her occasional visits after her first husband's death had neither familiarized nor endeared her to the English people; on the contrary, what they had learnt of her they did not like, for she was a disagreeable woman, haughty, tactless, and grasping. Her second marriage with Geoffrey of Anjou was little in her favour. It was an unpopular connexion, especially with the Norman barons, and, as the English chronicler says, 'all the French and English thought ill of it'. Indeed her anti-Norman intrigues so exasperated her father that he was said to have repudiated her on his death-bed.[2]

If we assume, as most of the leading men of the kingdom appear to have done, that despite the oath, despite the fact that she was the sole surviving lawful child of the late king, the empress was wholly unsuitable for the position, who were the alternatives? There were Henry's nephews, his sister Adela's sons, Theobald and Stephen of Blois. On the female side they were good Norman stock. The elder brother was a man of much consequence in his own country; he was count of Blois, Champagne, and Chartres, and the Norman barons instinctively turned to him; they were in fact actually engaged in electing him as their duke at Neubourg (Eure), when an emissary of the younger brother arrived to announce that he, Stephen, had

---

[1] The most complete and accurate list is that compiled by G. H. White in the *Complete Peerage*, vol. xi, App. D.

[2] Cf. Round, *Geoffrey de Mandeville*, p. 6.

stolen a march on them, had slipped across the Channel, and was indeed already crowned king. It was a *fait accompli*, and Theobald prudently, but not without some grumbling, accepted it. There were, however, good reasons why Stephen rather than his brother should have a better chance of success in this hazardous enterprise. He had been brought up by his uncle almost as an adopted child; he had been knighted by Henry's own hand, and had been endowed with rich estates both in England and on the Continent. He held the great honors of Lancaster and Eye, and in Normandy the county of Mortain; and by right of his wife he was also in possession of the county of Boulogne together with the English honor of Boulogne, for he had married Matilda, the daughter of Eustace of Boulogne and Mary, the sister of Henry I's queen.[1] His whole life had been spent either in England or in Normandy. In both countries he was well known and deservedly popular; for, in striking contrast to his two Norman predecessors, he was a man of an attractive personality. He was not, like them, hard and avaricious; he was a brave, generous, simple-minded man who in any other walk of life would probably have succeeded admirably; it is an exaggeration to say, as Walter Map, the twelfth-century satirist, said, that apart from his prowess in arms 'he was almost an imbecile'. His faults were lack of statesmanship and of decision and firmness. He had not the ability or the strength of character necessary to deal with the very difficult situation that confronted him.

But in these first days he had shown surprising sagacity and power of decision. By crossing to England as soon as Henry's death was known, he had forestalled his rivals; he was the only one of the possible candidates who was actually on the spot—a decided advantage. Though Dover and Canterbury refused to admit him, he was welcomed at London whose citizens flocked to meet him and elected him king by the special prerogative they claimed to possess.[2] Then, like William Rufus and Henry before him, he hastened to Winchester to secure the treasury. Here he was again in a position of advantage, for he could reckon on the powerful support of the bishop, his own

---

[1] It is estimated that the honor of Lancaster contained some 400 manors and that of Eye 260; the honor of Boulogne comprised about 120 knights' fees. Cf. Round, *Studies in Peerage and Family History*, pp. 167 f.

[2] *Gesta Stephani*, ed. K. R. Potter (Nelson's Medieval Texts), pp. 3-4.

younger brother, Henry of Blois. To his influence must be attributed much of Stephen's early success. Not only was he doubtless instrumental in persuading the treasurer, William de Pont de l'Arche, to deliver over the treasury and the castle of Winchester, but he also brought with him the weight of church support—the primate, Archbishop William, and, perhaps even more important still, Roger of Salisbury who, with his nephews, the bishops of Lincoln and Ely, controlled the administration. Thus strengthened, Stephen returned to London where he was crowned. Events had moved rapidly; it had all happened without any delay or struggle 'as in a twinkling of an eye'.[1] Henry I had died on 1 December; Stephen's coronation took place before Christmas, probably on 22 December. Early in the next year his election was confirmed by Pope Innocent II.[2] The importance of the papal recognition can hardly be over-estimated: it virtually acquitted the barons of the charge of perjury to which their action in accepting Stephen, after having sworn allegiance to the empress, laid them open. It removed the one really weak spot in Stephen's position.

The new king set out to rule in the approved manner. His first ceremonial court—the Easter court of 1136—was held at Westminster on 22 March with all the pomp and splendour which had graced the courts of the Conqueror and his son Rufus, but had been abandoned by the thrifty Henry. The son of King David of Scotland was there; so, too, were several of those who later became the leading supporters of the empress, Miles of Gloucester, the king's constable,[3] for example, and Brian Fitz Count. But the greatest of them all, the man whose adherence was all-important, Earl Robert of Gloucester, the empress's half-brother and afterwards the leader of her party, had not yet arrived in England. The council was therefore adjourned to Oxford where, early in April, Robert rendered a conditional homage and subscribed the charter of liberties in which the king recorded, in terms far more ample than the meagre charter issued at his coronation, his promise to observe the good laws and ancient customs of the kingdom. This act, witnessed by fourteen bishops and twenty-three of the most prominent men

---

[1] 'Sine mora, sine labore, quasi in ictu oculi'. Hen. Hunt., p. 256.
[2] Below, p. 192.
[3] That Miles was Henry I's constable and not merely constable of Gloucester castle has been proved by C. Johnson, *Eng. Hist. Rev.* xlix (1934), 83–4.

in England, marks the definite acceptance by the nation of Stephen as king.[1] Yet this result was not achieved without some sacrifice. Stephen's policy of winning support by concession, a policy which seriously weakened his authority and which, once begun, had perforce to be continued, was adopted at the very outset of his enterprise. He may perhaps have made some compact with the citizens of London who elected him; he certainly bound himself by sworn promises to the archbishop who crowned him.[2] The first charter he issued as king, at Reading, just after his coronation, was a *convention* in favour of a powerful baron, Miles, the constable; the first show of armed resistance (from David of Scotland) was settled by a substantial alienation of territory:[3] the support of Robert of Gloucester was secured by what can only be described as a treaty between equals. And all this in the first year of his reign. The last of these bargains was, however, probably wise; the winning over of the empress's natural champion to his side must have removed any lingering conscientious scruples which might still have been entertained. Indeed we are informed in so many words that after his (Robert's) submission almost the whole kingdom accepted him as king.[4]

His bold adventure had on the whole fared well. There were rebellions, notably in Norfolk and Devon,[5] but they were suppressed with promptitude and efficiency, and by 1137 the affairs of the kingdom were sufficiently ordered to permit Stephen to cross over to Normandy where the Empress Matilda had attempted to establish her claims. Some of the strongholds near the southern border—Domfront, Argentan, Alençon, and Séez—had indeed been handed over to her on her father's death. Such success, however, as she had won was more than counteracted by the outrages committed by her husband who entered the duchy and vented his anti-Norman hatred in an orgy of blood and plunder. His raiding, repeated after the lapse

---

[1] The lists of witnesses to the charters granted at the Easter court are printed by Round in App. C (p. 262) to his *Geoffrey de Mandeville*. They show that the attendance at London was even greater than at the adjourned court at Oxford. At the former there were nineteen prelates and thirty-two other magnates.

[2] Besides the coronation charter which merely recites in general terms his intention to preserve the laws of King Henry (*Statutes of the Realm*, i. 4) he took a verbal oath to the archbishop safeguarding the rights of the church. Round, *Geoffrey de Mandeville*, pp. 7-8.

[3] At Durham on 5 February. See below, p. 270.   [4] *Gesta Stephani*, pp. 8-9.

[5] For the protracted siege of Exeter castle see ibid., pp. 20-30.

of a six-months' truce negotiated by Count Theobald on his brother's behalf, only intensified the traditional animosity of the Normans towards their Angevin neighbours. When, therefore, Stephen landed at La Hogue in March 1137, he had a fine opportunity of gaining recognition in the duchy. The circumstances were all in his favour: the hostility of the Normans to Geoffrey, the friendship of the king of France and of Count Theobald; the loyal adherence of most of the bishops, five of whom, headed by the archbishop of Rouen, had even travelled to England in 1136 to acknowledge Stephen as their sovereign. But the opportunity was lost. The king's use of Flemish mercenaries aroused discontent and jealousy among the Norman barons and led to blows and desertions; an expedition planned against Geoffrey at Argentan broke down altogether from this cause, and Stephen in disgust concluded a truce with his rival (July). When at the end of the year he quitted the country he had lost the confidence of the Normans. He never again crossed the Channel.

In the course of the summer of 1138 two definite steps were taken by the Angevin party to promote the claim of Matilda to the throne of England. First, the empress appealed to the pope. The case was subsequently argued by representatives of both parties at the Lateran council held in the spring of 1139. It resulted in Innocent's reaffirming his previous recognition of Stephen's title.[1] The second move was more effective: Robert of Gloucester formally renounced his allegiance and prepared for war. The moment was well chosen.[2] Ever since his return from the Continent the king had been harassed by invasions from Scotland and rebellions in Wales; there were, too, sporadic insurrections in England. He was already seriously embarrassed by declared enemies and treacherous friends who, learning that the king was 'soft' (to use the adjective of the English chronicle), were ready to take advantage of his pliable nature and his reckless generosity. Robert's challenge met with an immediate response, especially among the leading families in the south and west country. Nevertheless, even in these districts the king's position was still far from hopeless. His answering campaign was not devoid of success, and several enemy strongholds,

[1] Below, pp. 193-4.
[2] William of Malmesbury (*Hist. Nov.* ii. 545, § 467) gives the time 'shortly after Whitsunday' (22 May).

including Shrewsbury and Hereford in the west and Dover and Wareham in the south, capitulated to his armies. He was received at Gloucester in 1138 and at Worcester in 1139 with every outward mark of goodwill. To the Worcester writer—admittedly an admirer—he was still (in 1139) the *rex magnificus* who, when he left the neighbourhood, had settled all things peacefully.[1] All might yet have been well with Stephen but for a fatal blunder: by an act of folly he lost the support of the church.

For many years past, from the early days of Henry I's reign, the administration of the country had been controlled by Roger, bishop of Salisbury. It was something of an accident, if we can believe the story told by William of Newburgh, that brought this priest of Avranches[2] out of obscurity into the king's service. Henry I, before he was king, came across him near Caen, and was struck by the rapidity with which he could say a mass. He was no time-waster. After his accession Henry made him his chancellor and in 1102 bishop of Salisbury, though owing to the investiture contest he was not consecrated till 1107. Soon afterwards he became justiciar, and in this capacity governed the country in the king's frequent absences abroad.[3] Such was his wealth, his power, and his influence that he was considered to be second only to the king;[4] indeed he coupled his own name with that of the king in the issue of royal commands.[5] Though he was now an elderly man he was still justiciar and he had trained and associated his family in the work of administration: his son Roger le Poer was chancellor, his nephew, Nigel, bishop of Ely, was treasurer, and another nephew, Alexander, was bishop of Lincoln and a man much in the court circle. These princely bishops had recently been building, strengthening, and garrisoning castles, and they moved about accompanied by large

---

[1] John of Worcester (ed. Weaver), p. 54.

[2] See R. R. Darlington, *Eng. Hist. Rev.* lxvii (1952), 565.

[3] In a document, which may probably be dated between 1123 and 1126, he styles himself 'Rogerius episcopus Saresburiensis sub domino nostro rege Henrico regni Anglie procurator'. *Eng. Hist. Rev.* xxxix (1924), 79. This is said to be the earliest extant document issued in the name of the justiciar.

[4] *Gesta Stephani*, p. 48.

[5] 'Praecipio tibi ex parte regis et mea', Round, *Ancient Charters*, Pipe Roll Soc. x. 38. For the date, probably 1137, see Pipe Roll Soc., N.S. xxi, p. lxxxiii. At the council of Winchester (August 1139) he is reported to have asserted that he had never held office under Stephen (Will. Malmes., *Hist. Nov.*, § 474). He may not have been formally appointed as justiciar by Stephen, but as the charter cited above shows he evidently acted as such.

retinues of armed men. Was this conduct, this castle-building, this multitude of retainers merely due to harmless vanity and a love of ostentation? The lay baronage, and especially the influential house of Beaumont,[1] whose jealousy such arrogance had aroused, thought otherwise. They suspected, not unreasonably, treacherous designs; for it was the common report, we are told, that these bishops were only awaiting the arrival of Robert of Gloucester to put their immense resources at the disposal of the king's rival. If they were really guilty of such treachery, it was only prudent to take measures against them. But nothing can excuse the manner in which it was done. The court was assembled at Oxford at midsummer for a council when a street brawl, in which the men of the bishop of Salisbury were involved, supplied the king with his opportunity. The supposed delinquents were seized, charged with breach of the peace, and, on their refusal to surrender the keys of their castles, placed under custody. Only the bishop of Ely escaped this treatment; he fled to his uncle's castle of Devizes. The king followed in pursuit, taking with him the two Rogers, father and son, whom he used with every indignity. After three days the castle was surrendered by Matilda of Ramsbury, the mistress of the bishop of Salisbury, who feared for the safety of her husband and son. There was no further resistance; the other castles were delivered up, and the royal resources, already much reduced, were satisfactorily replenished by the great stocks of money and munitions stored within them. But such trifling advantage was quite immaterial when compared with the disastrous effect the episode had upon the king's position in the country. The church was bitterly offended. There were, indeed, some, even among the clergy, who were prepared to justify Stephen's action; men who, like the archbishop of Rouen, took the view that it served the bishops right; that they could not canonically hold castles at all; that if

---

[1] The twin brothers, Waleran of Meulan and Robert, earl of Leicester, are said to have been the instigators; the former is implicated by the author of the *Gesta Stephani* (p. 51) and both by Orderic (ed. Le Prévost, v. 120). The earl of Leicester was afterwards excommunicated for holding the castle of Newark against the bishop of Lincoln, see *Registrum Antiquissimum*, i. 239 (Lincoln Record Soc., vol. 27). The Beaumonts and their connexions were an immensely powerful group. William de Warenne, earl of Surrey, was a step-brother, the earl of Warwick a cousin; Simon, earl of Northampton, married a daughter of Robert of Leicester, and Gilbert of Clare who became earl of Pembroke in 1138 married a sister. See G. H. White, *Trans. R. Hist. Soc.*, 4th ser. xiii. 51 ff. and xvii. 19 ff. and Stenton, *English Feudalism*, p. 239.

they behaved as laymen they should be treated as such; and the old plea, used so effectively in the trials of Odo of Bayeux and William of St. Calais, that the bishop was arrested not as a bishop but as a minister of the Crown, was once more brought into requisition. However much justification the king may have had in seizing the castles, he could not escape from the charge that he had laid violent hands on ecclesiastics, a deed which the church could not condone. His brother, Bishop Henry, was acutely resentful. The council which, by virtue of the legatine authority conferred upon him in the preceding March, he summoned to meet at Winchester on 29 August, deliberated on the matter for four days and then broke up without reaching a decision. But there was no reconciliation.[1] The defection of the church was the more serious as it came at (for Stephen) a most inopportune moment. A month later the Empress Matilda was herself in England. She landed (probably 30 September) with her brother Robert at Arundel where she took shelter with her step-mother, Adeliza, who had taken as her second husband William de Albini, lord of the honor of Arundel. Robert, for his part, made his way to Bristol which, till his death in 1147, continued to be the headquarters of his party.

During these critical days Stephen acted with deplorable indecision. It was the king's habit, as a contemporary wrote,[2] to begin many things vigorously and then to pursue them slothfully; so he would lay siege to one castle, throw it up, and pass on to another which at the moment seemed to him more threatening. Dunster, Corfe, Malmesbury, Marlborough, Wallingford, and Trowbridge were all besieged in turn in the course of the autumn, but only one of them, Malmesbury, fell into his hands. All his movements were utterly devoid of plan or policy. He had the empress in his power at Arundel, but with extraordinarily misplaced chivalry he sent her, under an escort provided by himself, to join her brother at Bristol.

The strength of her position in the west was much augmented by two men who now took up her cause. Miles of Gloucester, the constable, who was entrusted with the charge of the empress herself, was perhaps, after Earl Robert, the most powerful baron

[1] The fact that but one bishop, and he a foreigner, the bishop of Séez, attended the Whitsun court on 26 May 1140 is evidence of the complete and prolonged alienation of the church party.
[2] Hen. Hunt., p. 260.

of the west country, while the other, Brian Fitz Count, who is described as her inseparable companion, bound to her by mutual and undivided affection,[1] held the castle of Wallingford, the eastern outpost of the Angevin sphere of influence, and a persistent menace to the king's position at Oxford. Induced, apparently, to join the empress by the bishop of Winchester, he refused to change back when the latter, two years later, deemed it politic to revert once more to his brother's side. He was fighting, he explained in a letter to the bishop[2] in justification of his conduct, not for himself, not for reward, nor for what he could make out of it, but merely from personal loyalty to the late king who had befriended him; in this cause he had lost every acre he possessed, and therefore, he urged in self-defence, he was compelled to live by the plunder of his neighbours. This was indeed true, since for most of the period he was completely isolated in his Wallingford castle. Brian, a man of intelligence and education, was one of the better type of baron of the anarchy, a type more numerous perhaps than usually supposed, and whose honest purpose is lost sight of at a time when the majority of the class was making the very name of baron a byword for faithlessness, cruelty, and lawlessness.

We may pass over the details of the war which for the most part consisted of plundering raids, burning of towns, besieging of castles. An account of one of these everyday episodes by one who, in a simple narrative, relates what he himself witnessed, will illustrate the character of the warfare. The scene is at Worcester in the autumn of 1139, soon after the arrival of Earl Robert and his sister in England, an event which filled the citizens with alarm. They made due preparations and carried their goods and chattels into the cathedral which then looked 'like a furniture store'. Indeed it became 'a resort and place of gossip for the citizens' in which 'there was hardly room for the servants of God, so many were the sacks and chests. While the clerk intoned within, the child screamed outside; mingled with the sound of the psalms was the noise of mothers nursing or weeping over their children. At daybreak one morning in the beginning of winter (7 November) the city of Gloucester, in battle-array, supported with horse and foot beyond number,

[1] *Gesta Stephani*, p. 89. He was the son of Alan Fergant, count of Brittany, who had seen much service under Henry I.

[2] Printed by H. W. C. Davis in *Eng. Hist. Rev.* xxv (1910), 297 f.

advanced against the city of Worcester with intent to attack, plunder, and burn it to the ground.' Their first onslaught was beaten off manfully, but an entrance was made on the north side of the city where there was no fortification to block their path; then 'a vast mob of the enemy, infuriated and unrestrained, poured in and set alight to buildings in different parts of the city'. The greater part of the town, however, escaped the flames; but there was much plundering both within the wall and in the neighbouring country, and 'many were taken prisoner in the streets who leashed together like so many dogs were dragged away miserably; whatever their cruel victors demanded in ransom, whether they had the means or no, they were compelled to promise and forced to pay. These things happened on the first day of winter which will, doubtless, be very severe for the wretched victims.'[1]

This was the fate of numberless towns and villages; Worcester itself suffered twice in this way. But there were few engagements which merited the term of 'pitched' battles; such did not suit the purpose of most of the fighters, who, joining in the struggle from purely selfish motives, without any strong attachment to either side, did not want a decisive action. These ruthless marauders made war for profit, fighting intermittently and changing from one side to the other according to which was prepared to offer them the more attractive terms. There were some few loyal adherents of the empress who stood by her even when her cause was desperate and she had nothing to give. But even these regarded each other with latent suspicion and distrust as the treaty of friendship (*confederatio amoris*) which Robert, earl of Gloucester, made with Miles, earl of Hereford, shows. These two allies and companions in arms set down in writing the terms of their friendship and provided hostages for the keeping of faith.[2] As for Stephen, there were few on whom he could implicitly rely besides his Flemish mercenaries under William of Ypres.

As Matilda's strength lay in the western shires and particularly around Gloucester and Bristol, it was natural that most of the fighting should take place in this area. But in December

---

[1] John of Worcester (ed. Weaver), pp. 56-7. The passage has been abbreviated and in part paraphrased.
[2] Round, *Geoffrey de Mandeville*, p. 381; *Sir Christopher Hatton's Book of Seals*, no. 212.

1140 a diversion from this main field of operations was caused by the entrance of Rannulf, earl of Chester, into the dynastic struggle. This powerful baron ruled, in lordly independence, over a small kingdom; a contemporary[1] states that he controlled nearly a third of the country, which was almost true, if his family connexions are taken into account. His lands were by no means confined to the great palatine earldom of Chester; he had inherited large estates in Lincolnshire which it was his ambition to link by a chain of strongholds with his earldom. His half-brother, William de Roumare, was also a substantial Lincoln-shire landowner, and was about this time or shortly after created earl of that county. It was, besides, Rannulf's desire to recover the honor of Carlisle which his father had held, but had been forced to relinquish to Henry I, and which Stephen had granted away to the son of the king of Scotland. This was one motive which threw him on to the side of the empress; another was his relation-ship to Robert of Gloucester; he had married the earl's daughter.

Towards the close of the year 1140 Rannulf had seized and occupied the castle of Lincoln, but the matter had seemingly been condoned, for the king had visited the city shortly before Christmas, had rewarded the earl with extravagant concessions which included the castle and city of Lincoln besides a number of other castles, towns, and fiefs.[2] It was at the instance of the citizens, who complained of harsh treatment, that Stephen soon afterwards hurriedly returned.[3] Rannulf, entrusting to his wife and brother the defence of the castle, slipped away to collect reinforcements, and returned not only with his own Cheshire retainers and Welsh levies, but also with his father-in-law, Robert of Gloucester, accompanied by a substantial body of desperate men who, having forfeited their land for their adher-ence to the empress, had all to gain and little to lose by fighting against the royalists. This army made its way through the

---

[1] *Gesta Stephani*, p. 121.

[2] See the charter printed by W. Farrer, *Lancashire Pipe Rolls and Early Charters*, pp. 367-70, which seems to belong to this occasion though it has usually been assigned to the spring of 1149 following a conjecture by J. H. Round (*Eng. Hist. Rev.* x (1895), 87-91). Lincoln remained in the hands of Rannulf till it was sur-rendered to the king in 1146. Stephen was still in possession of it at least till the end of the year 1149 (*Gesta Stephani*, 145-6).

[3] The king's conduct in attacking Lincoln was, according to William of Malmes-bury (*Hist. Nov.*, § 487), criticized on the ground that he had been at peace with Rannulf and his brother and had not according to custom formally renounced his friendship, which they call defying—*quod 'Diffidiare' dicunt.*

sodden and marshy ground which bounds the city of Lincoln
on the south and west, and across the Fossdyke, swollen large
by the winter rains—for it was the 2nd of February (1141)—
sweeping aside, as they went, the few guards posted by the king
to impede their approach. Stephen, with his characteristic but
fatal sense of chivalry, threw away the advantage which his
position on the easily defensible heights gave him, and descended
into the plain for a fair fight. The battle was lost owing to the
pusillanimous conduct of Stephen's cavalry. It made no attempt
to withstand the wild and reckless charge of the disinherited
knights. The five earls,[1] who with their men composed the leading division on the king's right, turned and fled in disorder. The
earl of York and William of Ypres on the left, after scattering
the ill-armed Welshmen, were themselves in their turn routed,
leaving the king with his reserves of dismounted knights deserted
and alone to receive the full brunt of the combined attack of the
enemy horse and foot. He put up a great fight; he is depicted
'like a lion at bay' slashing with his sword till it snapped and
then hitting about him with a Danish axe till that broke too. At
last, felled by a stone, he surrendered to the earl of Gloucester.

The battle of Lincoln might well have ended the tragic reign
of Stephen for ever. That it was not decisive was largely due to
the empress herself who in the hour of her triumph conducted
herself with such high-handed arrogance, and with such utter
want of tact that before many months had passed she had lost
all and more than all the advantage which the victory had given
her. She never acquired popularity, nor aroused enthusiasm;
she never appears to have met with that universal recognition
'by the whole race of the English' of which the chroniclers
speak.[2] The story of her brief reign is soon told. She was still at
Gloucester when the news of the battle of Lincoln reached her

[1] The earls of Richmond, Norfolk, Northampton, Surrey, and Worcester.
Their idea of a fight was to begin with formal tilting: 'Temptavere primo regii
proludium pugnae facere quod Justam (*joust*) vocant, quia tali periti erant arte.'
Will. Malmes., *Hist. Nov.*, § 489.

[2] 'ab omni gente Anglorum suscipitur in dominam, exceptis Kentensibus', Hen.
Hunt., p. 275. Cf. *Gesta Stephani*, p. 76. An analysis of the signatories of her charters
reveals the fact that the number of her adherents was still, in spite of her victory,
not large, and that the area from which they were drawn was, as before, chiefly the
west country. It may have been at this time of uncertainty when no one knew who
was the rightful sovereign that the moneyers produced the coinage with the
strange, meaningless, but non-committal inscription PERERIC on the obverse in
place of the king's name. Cf. G. C. Brooke, *Catalogue of English Coins in the British
Museum, the Norman Kings*, i, pp. lxxxii–lxxxviii.

on 9 February. There she was joined by Robert of Gloucester with the captive king who was sent for safe custody to Bristol, while she herself made her way towards Winchester. Before, however, she could enter the city she had to make a bargain with the legate; she had to agree to leave all ecclesiastical matters in his hands. On this understanding she was admitted and received in state in the cathedral (3 March). A little more than a month later (8 April) she was formally elected.[1] On the motion of the legate, who managed the whole business, she was chosen *Domina Anglorum*, a style customarily used in the interval between election and coronation.[2] But Matilda was not destined to experience the latter ceremony which, following precedent, should have taken place at Westminster. The Londoners had from the first been favourable to Stephen; and when, at the summons of the legate, a deputation of the citizens came down to Winchester to associate themselves in the election, they merely interceded (ineffectually) on the king's behalf. It was more than two months later, shortly before midsummer, that at last they consented to admit the empress within their walls. Her stay was short and stormy. The city had recently been the scene of disorders; the citizens had formed some sort of sworn association for the defence of their liberties, a commune. Of the character of this movement we have no information, and it certainly did not long survive; but the independent spirit of the citizens was sufficiently aroused to refuse to tolerate the autocratic behaviour of the woman who imperiously claimed their allegiance and who, on entering the city, demanded from them a tallage. Amidst the clang of bells they flew to arms 'like a swarm of bees from a hive' and tumultuously expelled her from their gates. And as she fled, deserted by all but her brother Gloucester and her uncle, King David of Scotland, along the road to Oxford, the Londoners welcomed Stephen's queen and William of Ypres who, with a force raised in Kent, were pouring

---

[1] Presumably she did not herself attend this ceremony at Winchester, for her presence is not mentioned by any contemporary writer; and William of Malmesbury, who himself witnessed the scene and has left us a detailed account of it (*Hist. Nov.*, § 493) could scarcely have omitted to mention such a fact. She probably spent Easter (30 March) at Wilton, where Archbishop Theobald came to her, and thence travelled to Reading and Oxford, which was delivered up to her by Robert d'Oilli. For her movements see H. W. C. Davis (*Essays . . . presented to R. L. Poole*, pp. 180 ff.) who rejects the evidence of William of Malmesbury (followed by Round, *Geoffrey de Mandeville*, p. 66) that she spent Easter at Oxford.

[2] Round, op. cit., pp. 74 f., and above, p. 3 and n.

across the river and pillaging the southern parts of the city.
Queen Matilda, to whose fine and courageous qualities her
husband owed not a little of such success as he could claim, was
quick to take advantage of the trail of unpopularity and disgust
which her opponent had left behind. She pledged her own
Cambridgeshire estates as security for a loan from the justiciar
of London, Gervase of Cornhill; by the grant of enhanced concessions, she repurchased Geoffrey de Mandeville who from
siding with Stephen had transferred himself to the empress
during her ascendancy; then, at an interview at Guildford, she
won back that great intriguer, the legate, Henry of Blois, for his
brother's cause.

It was no doubt with the object of compelling the legate, if
necessary by force, to return to her allegiance that induced the
empress to leave Oxford, which, since her expulsion from London, had become her headquarters, for Winchester (31 July).
There almost the entire military strength of the opposing sides
met; even London sent a contingent reckoned by a contemporary
at nearly a thousand men-at-arms.[1] The empress opened by
besieging Wolvesey, the magnificent palace recently completed
by the bishop as a residence for himself. He retaliated by firing
the city, a large part of which, including the royal palace built
by the Conqueror,[2] was reduced to ashes. Then royalist reinforcements were brought up, and the besiegers found themselves
in the awkward predicament of being themselves closely besieged. At last, their position having become wholly untenable
through disease and lack of provisions, they decided (14 September) to retreat. The retreat became a flight, the flight a
rout—'the rout of Winchester'.[3] Matilda herself, more dead
than alive, managed to reach the welcome shelter of the walls of
Gloucester under the escort of her inseparable companion,
Brian Fitz Count. But her brother Robert, who brought up the
rear of the fleeing army, was less fortunate; he was surrounded
at Stockbridge and captured.[4] He only regained his liberty,

[1] *Gesta Stephani*, p. 85.
[2] 'totum palatium cum aula sua'. See Round, op. cit., pp. 126-7. Cf. *Curia
Regis Rolls*, iii. 119.   [3] *Gesta Stephani*, pp. 89, 91. *Wintoniensis dispersio.*
[4] S. Painter in *Speculum*, vii (1932), 70 f., attempts to harmonize the divergent
accounts of these events, and maintains (against Round, *Geoffrey de Mandeville*,
p. 130) the reliability of the story of the escape of the empress handed down in the
Histoire de Guillaume le Maréchal (ed. Meyer), ll. 183-276. It is, however, difficult
to attach great weight to an account which omits altogether any mention of the
capture of Earl Robert.

after much bargaining, in return for the release of the king (1 November 1141).

Stephen was now more popular and hence in a stronger position than he had been when nine months before he was defeated and made a prisoner at Lincoln. Not only had he won much sympathy by reason of the harsh treatment meted out to him in prison—for he appears to have been fettered in chains—but also the experiment of the rule of his rival was not one that many men wished to see repeated. In those few months of power the empress by her outrageous conduct had irretrievably damaged her own cause. The number of her supporters dwindled; and those that remained loyal to her were threatened with excommunication at the council which met under the auspices of the legate at Westminster on 7 December formally to recognize the king's restoration. At the Christmas festival, celebrated at Canterbury, Stephen submitted to a second coronation,[1] or at least wore his crown, as a token that he once again ruled over England. The affairs of the kingdom, a visit to York, and an illness, so serious that it was rumoured that he was dying, prevented the king from taking steps to complete the overthrow of his rival who remained unmolested at Oxford. It was not till June that he was sufficiently recovered to take the field. The time, however, was very opportune. Earl Robert at the end of that month crossed to Normandy to plead for assistance from Geoffrey of Anjou, and he was detained there till the autumn by the count who required his help in the conquest of the duchy. He then returned, with a body of some three or four hundred cavalry, only to learn that his sister's cause was in a more parlous state than ever. Stephen, after cutting the communications of the Angevin party with the Continent by the capture of Wareham,[2] and between Oxford and their western strongholds by seizing the fortified posts at Cirencester, Bampton, and Radcot, had broken into Oxford itself (26 September). He took the city by storm, burnt and sacked it, and drove the empress into the castle where for nearly three months she was closely besieged. Before Robert could get to her relief she had been forced by lack of provisions to make her courageous and romantic escape

[1] So Round (*Geoffrey de Mandeville*, p. 138) on the strength of a passage in Gervase of Canterbury.

[2] This, however, did not prevent Robert from landing there on his return from Normandy. He recaptured the harbour and town and, after a short siege, the castle (Will. Malmes., *Hist. Nov.*, § 522).

on a winter's night over ice and snow to her friends at Wallingford. The loss of Oxford—the castle capitulated immediately
after Matilda's flight—put an end to all hopes of Angevin success eastward of the upper Thames valley. The castle of Wallingford stood alone, a solitary and detached outpost in enemy
country, but for the rest Matilda's sphere of influence was again
confined to the west country. Here, after Stephen's defeat at
Wilton in 1143 and the subsequent surrender of Sherborne
castle, Earl Robert reigned supreme, and 'from sea to sea',
presumably from the Bristol Channel to the coast of Dorset, was
able to produce 'a shadow of peace'.[1]

But at this very time when we are told that in the west there
was 'a shadow of peace' scenes of unsurpassed savagery and
bloodshed were being enacted in the eastern counties. The
villain of the piece was the notorious Geoffrey de Mandeville.
At the opening of the reign Geoffrey had attached himself to
Stephen who rewarded him in 1140 with the earldom of Essex;
after the king's defeat at Lincoln he crossed over to the empress;
but on the latter's hurried flight from London he joined the
queen, and the concessions she granted him were confirmed
with interest by her liberated husband. By each tergiversation
he acquired fresh increments in offices, lands, and cash, until by
the period we have reached he had accumulated the posts of
sheriff and justiciar in three separate counties (Middlesex,
Essex, and Hertfordshire) and was constable of the Tower of
London;[2] it was this last office that gave him his chief importance in the eyes of the two combatants, for it virtually gave
him the control of the capital. That the Londoners resented this
control, and were in fact at bitter feud with the earl, is revealed
by the charter which signalized his next change of front, back
again to the empress; for in the hard bargain he drove he compelled his victim to make no peace with the burgesses of London
without his consent 'because they are his mortal foes'.[3] Although
this treaty, which was arranged at Oxford in the summer of
1142, was not made public, although Geoffrey continued osten-
sibly to be still the ally of the king and to frequent his court, it

[1] 'Et erat quidem illis in partibus umbra quaedam pacis, sed pax necdum per-
fecta' (*Gesta Stephani*, p. 99).
[2] He had inherited this from his father. The shrievalties of Essex and Hertfordshire were of course always combined during this period.
[3] The whole series of charters with an elaborate commentary are printed by
Round in his *Geoffrey de Mandeville, passim.*

was generally known that he was conspiring to set the empress again upon the throne. It was his suspected treachery and his domineering conduct—he is said to have practically usurped the royal authority[1]—that led to his sudden arrest at St. Albans in 1143. Charged with treason, he was given the choice of the gallows or the surrender of the Tower and of his Essex castles. He chose the latter alternative and went off to give vent to his violent rage on the innocent inhabitants of the Cambridgeshire fens. He occupied Ely and made it a fortress;[2] he seized the abbey of Ramsey, which, after driving out the monks, he converted into a military headquarters for his gang of ruffians and soldiers of fortune. From this unassailable stronghold in the midst of the fens he ravaged and plundered. Cambridge itself was ransacked and burnt; religious houses with their reputed wealth were the special quarry of these ruthless raiders. No profession, no sex, no age were spared. Every form of torture which the ingenuity of man could devise was employed to extort crippling ransoms from those who were unfortunate enough to fall into the hands of the terrible earl.[3] In these conditions all work was at a standstill; the fields were untilled; the crops uncut or destroyed. Over a stretch of twenty or thirty miles of country there was not an ox nor a plough to be seen. A serious famine, the inevitable result, added to the already enormous death-roll. It was in vain that Stephen tried to reach the perpetrator of all this suffering. Geoffrey merely withdrew into the very heart of his swampy fastness and defied attack. And so it might have gone on almost interminably had not a chance arrow struck him with a mortal wound while in August 1144 he was besieging a fortified post at Burwell. He died on 16 September.[4]

The career of Geoffrey de Mandeville, though not typical of the anarchy, was not without parallel; the earl of Chester's revolt two years later (1146) was precisely similar both in its inception and in its character. Suspected, not unreasonably, of treason, he was suddenly arrested by the king at Northampton,

---

[1] *Gesta Stephani*, p. 103. Some writers, following William of Newburgh (i, c. 11), connect Geoffrey's arrest with his detention in the Tower of Constance, the sister of Louis VII and the betrothed of Stephen's son Eustace. But as this occurred several years earlier, its connexion with the arrest in 1143 seems doubtful.

[2] Cf. the letter of protest by Pope Lucius II (1144) printed by W. Holtzmann, *Papsturkunden in England*, ii, no. 40 (p. 188).

[3] Cf. the fate of Godebold of Writtle, *Book of Fees*, p. 125.

[4] *Monasticon*, iv. 140.

and only liberated on the surrender of his castles; when released, like de Mandeville, he plunged into an orgy of the most ferocious brutality. But what these great magnates were doing on a prodigious scale, scores of lesser barons and free lances, up and down the country, were doing in a minor way, working riot and havoc from their castles and tyrannizing over their weaker neighbours, not with the purpose of benefiting either the king or the empress, but solely themselves.

Nevertheless, though the anarchy dragged on its wearisome course for some years yet, the fire had gone out of the Angevin party. Stephen's success at Faringdon in 1145, which cut the empress's communications between the Thames valley and her Gloucestershire strongholds, was regarded by contemporaries as a definite turning-point in the king's fortunes. Her supporters were losing heart; many, including Earl Robert's own son, Philip, deserted; and there was an attempt, unhappily fruitless, towards a reconciliation of the combatants. Geoffrey de Mandeville was now dead; Miles, earl of Hereford, one of the staunchest of her allies, had died from a hunting accident a year earlier (1143); and it was not long before Robert of Gloucester, the life and soul of his party, who, as William of Malmesbury justly says,[1] 'alone or almost alone was never swayed from his loyalty by the hope of gain or the fear of loss', followed them to the grave. He died at Bristol, 31 October 1147. Even the presence of the young Henry Plantagenet in England failed to revive the waning family fortunes. He was sent over by his father probably early in the year 1147. He came with a mere handful of men and, it seems, no money; he was easily routed at Cricklade and Bourton,[2] and, being reduced to great straits, only managed to get away through the generosity of Stephen himself who characteristically paid for his return to Normandy.[3] A few months later, in February 1148, Matilda herself gave up the fight and followed her son across the Channel.[4]

[1] *Hist. Nov.*, § 503.
[2] Probably Blackbourton near Bampton.
[3] J. H. Round, *Feudal England*, pp. 491 ff., rejected the story of this visit as a mere confusion in the *Gesta Stephani*. But cf. my article in *Eng. Hist. Rev.* xlvii (1932), 451.
[4] Gervase of Canterbury, i. 133. One charter of the empress is dated at Falaise on 10 June 1148 (*Sarum Charters*, p. 14). Dr. Salter, however, assigns one of her charters issued at Devizes to 1149 (*Oxford Charters*, no. 59). By this charter the empress confirmed to Oseney the church of St. George in the castle at Oxford. According to the Annals of Oseney the church was given in that year (*Ann. Mon.* iv. 26). But this entry may refer to the final confirmation made in 1149 by Stephen

There was another circumstance which helped to calm the troubled waters in England. The fall of Edessa in 1144 had given a fresh impulse to crusading. Stimulated by the preaching of St. Bernard, Louis VII of France and the emperor Conrad III took the cross in 1146, and their example was eagerly followed by great numbers all over western Europe and by not a few of the turbulent Anglo-Norman nobility. Among them were the two earls, Waleran of Meulan and William de Warenne; William of Dover, a typical soldier of the anarchy, who fought for the empress at Cricklade, threw up his command and set off for the Holy Land where he subsequently died; Philip, the son of Robert of Gloucester, a brutal and disloyal man, at last tired of his villainy and made the pilgrimage.

The only success which emerged from this otherwise disastrous crusade was an expedition in which the English played a prominent part. A force recruited from Germany, Flanders, and the English seaports embarked for Palestine in 164 vessels at Dartmouth on 23 May 1147; this army was composed not of great barons and knights, but chiefly of humble seafaring folk, hardened men, schooled, many of them, in the terrors of the Bay of Biscay, which was so familiar to them that the twelfth-century Arabic geographer Idrīsī speaks of it as the 'Sea of the English'.[1] They were ready for any adventure which came their way. On reaching Oporto they were engaged by Alfonso, the first king of Portugal, to help him drive the Moors from his newly-founded kingdom. The crusaders agreed to his terms, coasted round to the mouth of the Tagus, and closely invested Lisbon. After a siege of seventeen weeks the city was captured on 24 October. After this success an Englishman, Gilbert of Hastings, was made bishop of Lisbon, and introduced the Sarum missal which remained in use in Portugal till the sixteenth century.[2] In 1151, at the instigation of Bishop Gilbert, and again in 1189, at the time of the third crusade, English pirate-pilgrims took part in attacks against the Moors. These episodes are not without their importance in Anglo-Portuguese relations. Some of the adventurers, as names in contemporary documents prove, remained on the scene of their conquests and

and Archbishop Theobald (*Oxford Charters*, no. 61); and the empress's charter may, as Dr. Salter admits, be dated in 1147.

[1] H. A. R. Gibb, 'The English Crusaders in Portugal' in *Chapters in Anglo-Portuguese Relations*, ed. E. Prestage (1935), p. 9.

[2] W. J. Entwistle, *Eng. Hist. Rev.* li (1936), 695.

gradually developed commercial intercourse between the two countries.[1] In this way was inaugurated, at the very beginning of its history, a friendly relationship with Portugal which has lasted almost without a break to the present day.

Robert's death and the empress's departure suspended hostilities; the strain of the struggle was relaxed; the civil war, properly so-called, had lasted nine not nineteen winters. There were still many and some serious sporadic disorders, the work of individual barons and their retainers, but relatively during the years 1148 to 1153 the country was less disturbed.[2] In these years, and indeed in many localities during the anarchy itself, it may be doubted whether the state of England was very different from that which prevailed almost continuously in the twelfth century in many parts of Europe where the feud and the private castle were not prohibited.[3] It was just because England had been fortunate enough never to have known these instruments of oppression, these seeds of discord, that, when she at last experienced them, they appeared so particularly appalling. The English people had been 'spoilt', as we might say, by more than half a century of peace and strong rule for a state of things which on the Continent was almost a commonplace. We must allow, therefore, in attempting an estimate of the character and extent of the anarchy, for exaggeration and for impermissible generalization in the narrative accounts, of which several, and among them the best, were written in just those districts which we know to have been most seriously affected.[4] The famous passage in which the Peterborough monk vividly describes the horrors of the anarchy is almost certainly drawn from particular events which happened within a few miles of his own monastery, namely, that terrible orgy of wanton destruction and cruelty perpetrated by Geoffrey de Mandeville in the fen

[1] Gibb, l.c., p. 22 and note. A detailed account of the capture of Lisbon, written by Osbern, one of the crusaders, *De Expugnatione Lyxbonensi*, was printed by Stubbs in the introduction of his edition of the *Itinerarium Regis Ricardi* (Rolls Series), pp. cxlii ff. It has been re-edited with a very valuable introduction and notes, and an English translation by C. W. David (Columbia Univ. Press, 1936).

[2] That Stephen was never in control of the whole country he himself acknowledged when in the final settlement of 1153 he required 'the earls and barons of the duke (Henry of Anjou) who were never my men' to do him homage.

[3] See, for example, for the conditions in France, A. Luchaire, *Manuel des institutions françaises*, p. 228, and authorities there cited.

[4] The *Gesta Stephani* was possibly written by a clerk attached to the household of the bishop of Winchester; William of Malmesbury and John of Worcester were both writing in the midst of the theatre of war.

country in 1143-4 which we have already described. But it is
very questionable whether we are justified in regarding these
wild scenes as typifying the condition of England everywhere or
for the whole period of the reign.[1] It would probably be nearer
the truth to regard this and similar purple passages in the
chronicles as depicting extreme cases, which, just because they
were so exceptional and revolting, left an indelible impression
on the minds of those who witnessed them. It should be observed
that the official war, if we may use the term, the war, that is to
say, directed by the king on the one side and Earl Robert on the
other, was confined within fairly narrow limits. Robert, from his
strongholds at Gloucester and Bristol, was trying to extend
his power to the east, while Stephen, generally with Oxford as
his headquarters, spent his energy in an attempt to dislodge his
opponent from his position in the west. The bulk of the fighting,
therefore, took place in Wiltshire and Gloucestershire and in
the borders of the adjacent counties. Outside this area the war
was unofficial; conducted by some individual baron in the
name perhaps of the king or the empress, but with the object of
serving his own interests. How far this private war was general,
and how far it dislocated the life of the country, it is difficult to
determine; the evidence is insufficient and contradictory.

An attempt has been made to deduce from the amounts
written off on account of 'waste' in the assessments of Danegeld
in the second year of Henry II the extent of the damage inflicted
upon each particular county.[2] The results of investigation on
these lines are not very convincing, for we should have to conclude that Warwickshire (which heads the list of distressed areas)
suffered far more severely than any other county. The recorded
incidents hardly warrant this conclusion. There was the attack
on Coventry by the earl of Chester in 1147 and its defence by
the king which involved the plundering and wasting of the surrounding district. There is also a curious story of brigandage
mingled with romance told by the jurors on a grand assize some
seventy or eighty years later in the reign of Henry III (1221).[3]

---

[1] J. R. Green and G. M. Trevelyan dismiss the reign in a few paragraphs, con-
tenting themselves by quoting this celebrated text.

[2] The suggestion first made by Madox (*Exchequer* (1711), p. 479) has been elaborated by H. W. C. Davis, 'The Anarchy of Stephen's Reign', *Eng. Hist. Rev.* xviii
(1903), 630.

[3] *Rolls of the Justices in Eyre for Gloucestershire, Warwickshire, and Staffordshire,
1221-2* (Selden Soc., vol. 59), p. 167.

THE PRINCIPAL SCENE OF FIGHTING BETWEEN
STEPHEN AND MATILDA

They related how a certain Warin of Walcote 'an honest itinerant knight who fought in the war' passed through the dwelling of Robert of Shuckburgh, whose daughter he afterwards abducted. After the death of Stephen when peace was restored he fell into poverty because he could not rob as he used to do, but he could not refrain from robbery and he went everywhere and robbed as he used. The rest of the story, his capture in a reed-bed at Grandborough and his death in the pillory, does not concern us. All the places mentioned are neighbouring hamlets a few miles south of Rugby. Clearly his activities were confined to a very small area. Scraps of evidence like this are valuable as showing that men took advantage of the disturbed state of the country to live lawlessly. But is this sufficient to account for Warwickshire having suffered devastation to an extent more than twice that of Gloucestershire (which figures eighth on the list) and far more than twice that of Wiltshire (which comes fourteenth) both of which we know from unimpeachable evidence were rent by war and ruthless ravaging almost incessantly for nine or ten years? The towns provide an equally emphatic refutation of the argument. Rochester, which, as far as we know, was undisturbed by military actions, had a third of its *donum* remitted on the ground of waste, while Worcester, which was twice pillaged and burnt, in 1139 and again in 1150, paid its tax in full. It is beyond dispute that private war was fiercely waged in many parts of the country, and the ambitious policy of the earl of Chester caused widespread damage and misery. But it was not in the interest of the great barons to allow their lands to be wantonly plundered.[1] The midland shires, which, according to the Danegeld figures, suffered most from wasting, were under the control of a group of powerful earls—those of Leicester, Warwick, and Northampton —all anxious to keep the war out of their dominions, all capable of suppressing unruly castlemen. It is hard to believe that they permitted their lands to be so devastated that they could render no more than a fraction of their revenues.

Much damage was doubtless done to life and property by such irresponsible and undisciplined desperadoes as Robert Fitz Hubert from Devizes or William of Dover at Cricklade. Such men were a terror to their neighbours; but their careers of violence were usually short and the range of their activities

[1] Cf. Stenton, *English Feudalism*, pp. 244–5.

presumably very local, confined to the district immediately around the castle from which they operated. Moreover these castles were often weak and unsubstantial, probably wooden structures, quickly put up, but easily destroyed; of many, such as that at Cricklade itself, not a vestige remains to indicate their situation; the castle at Bampton, we are told, was of so slight a construction that it was perched upon the tower of the church. In the fighting itself the native inhabitants were little concerned; the cause of neither of the rivals stimulated any great effort among them such as that of Rufus or Henry I had evoked against the designs of Robert of Normandy half a century before. Occasionally we hear of the local men going into battle. A band of 'simple rustics' drove the king's son-in-law, a Breton count, from the castle of Devizes in 1141; their forced labour was probably fairly extensively used in castle building and similar work; but apart from the retinues of the great barons, the armies of the opposing sides were mainly composed of mercenaries. Robert of Gloucester recruited largely from Wales; Stephen relied principally on Flemish and Breton soldiers. The astonishing activity in ecclesiastical building in the middle years of the twelfth century, discussed below,[1] at least confutes the idea that civilian life and progress were altogether suspended in the days of the anarchy.

One of the most difficult problems of this difficult period is to discover how Stephen financed his wars. He began his reign, certainly, with a full treasury—the result of the hoarding and parsimony of his predecessor; he had occasional windfalls, such as when on the death of Roger of Salisbury in 1139, the immense wealth of that prelate fell into his hands. But we hear of no levy of Danegeld (though it may have been taken, as was customary, in the more orderly parts of the country) or of any exorbitant exactions. His opponents were often hard pressed for money, and are charged more than once with raising burdensome taxes; but no such complaint is made against the king. His expenses must have been great, yet he never seems to have been sorely in need of money. His coins, though indifferently struck, are of fairly pure metal and, in marked contrast to the

---

[1] Below, p. 189. Examples of large building operations in the districts particularly affected by the war are Malmesbury which was begun about 1145, the tower of Tewkesbury abbey c. 1140–50, and the choir of Peterborough which was finished between 1140 and 1143.

coins of the empress and her son, are generally only but slightly below the standard weight of 22½ grains. They compare very favourably with the mintages of Henry I.[1] This apparent absence of severe financial embarrassment may be partly accounted for by the fact that the wealthiest towns, with the exception of Bristol, lay in the east of England where Stephen's rule was not seriously contested and where trade and commerce were not, perhaps, unduly hindered. He seems to have borrowed extensively from the wealthy traders and repaid them in grants of land.[2] London, except for a few months in 1141, was always faithful to him; and the unwonted and persistent efforts he made to hold or recover Lincoln show the importance he attached to keeping in his own hands the most prosperous cities. If the great fair of St. Giles could be held as usual at Winchester within a year or two of its siege (1141), and if the fullers and weavers in the same city could each pay to the treasury the same sum (£6) for the privileges of their gild at the beginning of Henry II's reign as they had at the end of that of Henry I, it seems probable that industrial activity did not cease in consequence of the dynastic struggle.[3] The exchequer was undoubtedly sadly disorganized and thrown out of gear in the tumult of war; rents due to the treasury were appropriated by unscrupulous local magnates,[4] and the ravaged and impoverished land can hardly have rendered anything like its proper revenues; knowledge of the exchequer, wrote a witness who certainly had no love for Stephen, was almost obliterated.[5] Almost, but not quite. At the height of the anarchy (Christmas, 1141) Geoffrey de Mandeville was directed to account for the

[1] The evidence of surviving coins does not bear out the charges made by William of Malmesbury (*Hist. Nov.*, § 483) that Stephen grossly debased the coinage. See G. C. Brooke, *Catalogue of English Coins in the British Museum, The Norman Kings* (1916), p. cliii. The coins of Matilda and Henry Plantagenet are seldom above 16–17 grains. Ibid., p. cxviii f. Cf. also H. A. Grueber, *Handbook of the Coins of Great Britain and Ireland in the British Museum* (1899), p. 37.

[2] Cf. *The Chartulary of St. John of Pontefract*, ed. R. Holmes (Yorks. Arch. Soc. Record Series, 1902), ii. 395.

[3] The evidence for the holding of St. Giles's fair comes from a letter of the bishop of Winchester printed in *Eng. Hist. Rev.* xxv (1910), 301. For the craft gilds see *Pipe Roll 31 Hen. I*, p. 37; and *2 Hen. II*, p. 52. That Stephen raised irregular levies from towns appears from Henry II's charter to Winchester by which such exactions are quashed ('si aliquae consuetudines injuste levatae sunt in guerra, cassatae sint'. *Archaeologia*, xlix (1885), 214).

[4] The accusation is brought that the earl of Chester in 1146: 'regalium fiscorum redditus . . . reddere negligebat' (*Gesta Stephani*, p. 122).

[5] *Dialogus de Scaccario*, i. viii.

farms of the counties for which, as sheriff, he was responsible, 'at the exchequer';[1] and the Pipe Roll of the first year of Henry II, of which fragmentary excerpts have been preserved,[2] accounts for nearly the whole of the last month of the previous reign.[3] Evidently the financial system struggled along in some sort during this period of confusion and turmoil.

Likewise the course of justice must obviously have been seriously impeded by the wars, and where the confusion was most confounded it can hardly have been maintained at all. In this regard a scene in the shire-court held in the bishop's garden at Norwich soon after the year 1148 is illuminating. A controversy arose as to whether the jurisdiction in a particular case belonged to the shire or to the abbey of Bury St. Edmunds. It was decided (in favour of the abbey) on the testimony of an aged knight who had solid grounds for his claim to be an authority on precedent, for he vouched for the fact that fifty years had passed since he first began to attend the hundred and county courts with his father. He prefaced his evidence with these words: 'I am, as you see, a very old man, and I remember many things which happened in King Henry's time and even before that, when right and justice, peace and loyalty flourished in England. But because in the stress of war, justice has fled and laws are silenced, the liberties of churches, like other good things, have in many places perished.'[4] The old man speaks with a bluff honesty that rings true; but his words cut both ways. The laws might have been silenced and justice might have flown, but here a properly constituted court, presided over by a king's justice (William Martel), is seeking for precedents from the good old times and was making a gallant effort to get to the rights of the matter. Moreover the case does not stand alone; throughout this troubled epoch and in many different parts of the country we have record of writs and pleas, of king's courts and local courts, of suits heard and terminated.[5] There are even traces of legal development. It is indeed an odd circumstance

---

[1] 'ad scaccarium computabuntur' (Round, *Geoffrey de Mandeville*, p. 142).

[2] In the *Red Book of the Exchequer*, pp. 648-58.

[3] The exchequer year of 1 Hen. II extended from Michaelmas 1154 to Michaelmas 1155, and Stephen died on 25 October 1154. G. J. Turner, *Trans. R. Hist. Soc.*, N.S., xii. 127, supplies other evidence to show that Pipe Rolls were kept during the last years of the reign.

[4] The text is printed by H. M. Cam in *Eng. Hist. Rev.* xxxix (1924), 569 ff.

[5] Much evidence on this subject has been collected by R. Howlett in the preface to his edition of the *Gesta Stephani*, pp. xxxi-xxxix (Rolls Series).

that the earliest evidence for the procedure of recognition of novel disseisin and of the assize *utrum*, commonly attributed to the legal genius of Henry II, with many of its familiar formulae, appears in the reign of Stephen.[1]

The feature of the anarchy which has perhaps attracted most attention is the propensity of both combatants to increase the number of earldoms.[2] William the Conqueror had used the position of earl for a definite purpose, for he attached to it the duty of defence against Wales, Scotland, or the Channel; his earls were all palatine or semi-palatine. His sons did not adhere to this principle, but none the less they were sparing in their creations. Rufus made three, and Henry in the whole course of his long reign only two. There were but seven English earls in all at Stephen's accession.[3] In the four years between 1138 and 1142 this figure had been raised to twenty-two; the king had added nine and the empress six. This remarkable increase did not, however, as was once supposed, have the effect of lowering to any appreciable extent the standard of qualification. Both Stephen and Matilda seem to have been impressed with the idea that the dignity must be reserved for the highest in the land, for men whose personal distinction, territorial position, and signal services had earned for them a place in a very exclusive society. The new earls were therefore taken from the most aristocratic Anglo-Norman baronial houses.

In the administration of the shire the Norman earl had given place to the sheriff, a consequence of the centralizing policy of the Conqueror and his sons. He had sometimes, but not always the third penny, that is, a third of the profits of the pleas of his shire, which was soon commuted for a definite sum.[4] He had generally, but again not always, substantial landed interest in his shire;[5] beyond this, the earldom gave him little more than

[1] Below, pp. 406, 408.

[2] See particularly Round, *Geoffrey de Mandeville*, pp. 267–77; G. H. White, *Trans. R. Hist. Soc.*, 4th ser., xiii. 51–82; Stenton, *English Feudalism*, pp. 225 ff.

[3] This reckoning counts Huntingdon and Northampton as one, for they were both in the same hands.

[4] Already in 1130, the earl of Gloucester received £20 'pro parte sua comitatus' (*Pipe Roll 31 Hen. I*, p. 77), a figure at which it remained throughout the twelfth century. The Pipe Rolls record six other earls in regular receipt of sums 'pro tertio denario comitatus' from the early years of Henry II's reign, and these were all fixed: earl of Essex £40. 10s. 10d., earl of Hertford £33. 1s. 8d., earl of Devon £18. 6s. 8d., earl of Salisbury £22. 16s. 7d., earl of Arundel (or Sussex) 20 marks, earl of Norfolk £33. 6s. 8d.

[5] William de Warenne, earl of Surrey, is a notable exception. He held no lands

status. In the time of Stephen the rank of earl might help him in the pursuit of the ambition, which he shared with other great barons, of acquiring a control of the local administration, of obtaining the shrievalty or justiciarship in a county, or the custody of the castle which dominated the county town. This last was a favourite means of gaining local influence and many towns were thus 'mediatized' in the hands of a strong local magnate.[1] The fact, however, that the barons attached much importance to obtaining official recognition in charters of the powers they claimed to exercise seems to show that they were loath or perhaps regarded it as unsafe to act without the royal sanction. It is also true that often they had some hereditary claim to the positions they sought and occupied. Nevertheless, when once they were firmly entrenched and in the absence of a strong central government, they behaved with singular independence and disregard of the Crown. They took the law into their own hands and acted with almost regal authority; they issued writs in the royal manner; they dealt freely with the Crown prerogatives. Waleran of Meulan, who appears to have been made earl of Worcester about 1138, exempted the prior and monks of the church of Worcester from the Danegeld ('Gildum regis quod ad me pertinet') and from all customs, services, and forest rights ('quae prius regis erant et postea mea') in the vill of Tibberton in Worcestershire.[2] In one respect the sovereignty of the baron has probably been exaggerated. In a well-known passage William of Newburgh tells us that they one and all struck their own coins. Few puzzles have more sorely troubled the numismatist than that of the baronial issues; but it is at least a curious coincidence that of the four which can be surely identified two belong to barons who held estates within a few miles of William's abbey. It is a natural inference that he is generalizing rashly from the practice of his Yorkshire neighbours, whom Stephen left much to their own devices.[3] Had the

in Surrey at the time of his creation (between 1087 and 1089). See Stenton, op. cit., p. 231, n. 1, and (for other examples) p. 232.

[1] Stenton, op. cit., pp. 233 f.

[2] The charter is printed by H. W. C. Davis in *Essays . . . to R. L. Poole*, pp. 170-1.

[3] They were Eustace Fitz John and Robert de Stuteville; the latter in the next reign laid claim to lands at Coxwold which adjoins Newburgh Priory (Farrer, *Early Yorkshire Charters*, i. 272). A third issue is assigned to Henry, earl of Northumberland, son of the king of Scotland, also a north-countryman. Henry, bishop of Winchester, is the only southern magnate to whom a coinage can be assigned with tolerable certainty; the attribution of issues to Robert and William of Gloucester

custom been common we should expect to find more traces of it; but not a single coin bearing the inscription of any of the lordly earls of the south and midlands has come to light to prove that they used other than the king's money or at least money bearing the king's head and title.

It was, strangely enough, not in the period of the anarchy so much as after it, in the years 1148 to 1153, when the king was without a rival, but engaged in a struggle with the church, that these earls exhibit their power and independence most prominently. And among them all Rannulf, earl of Chester, stands out conspicuously. He had, as we have seen,[1] with total disregard of the interests of either party in the civil war, built up for himself a position of overwhelming strength in a stretch of country extending between Chester and Lincoln. The king had tried to appease him with lavish grants in 1140. But still unsatisfied, he remained violent, rebellious, and disloyal, and in 1146 he was compelled to surrender his castles. The remainder of his life was employed in an attempt to recover the lost ground which (except for Lincoln whose citizens were always hostile to him) he achieved by the concessions made to him by Henry, duke of Normandy, at Devizes in 1153.[2]

The earl's territorial power protruded into Leicestershire and Warwickshire, and he was thus brought face to face with another earl scarcely less influential than himself. This was Robert of Leicester who, if his family connexions are taken into account, controlled a large area in the south midlands; for his cousin was earl of Warwick, his son-in-law earl of Northampton, and his brother Waleran, earl of Worcester, who though an absentee landlord (since 1142) continued to keep a sharp eye on his English concerns. A clash of interests was almost inevitable. The way these two earls of Chester and Leicester handled this awkward situation illustrates better than anything the condition of the times. They made a treaty, an elaborate set of arrangements to govern their conduct towards each other: neither must attack the other unless a formal defiance has been given fifteen days previously; a belt of 'no-man's land', as it might be called, in which neither might erect castles, is drawn in a parabolic curve

and to Brian Fitz Count are at least questionable. Cf. G. C. Brooke, *Catalogue of English Coins in the British Museum*, pp. xcviii–cxxxiii, and C. W. C. Oman, *The Coinage of England*, pp. 117–23.

[1] Above, p. 141.

[2] Farrer, *Lancashire Pipe Rolls and Early Charters*, pp. 370–4.

round Leicester, springing from Rockingham and Coventry on
the east and west, and stretching northward to Gotham, some
sixteen miles from Leicester. Two bishops, those of Chester and
Lincoln, hold the stakes, two pledges, who shall be surrendered,
in the event of infringement of the agreement, to the injured
party. One of the most remarkable features of this treaty is that
the king is all but ignored; he is out of the picture; there is only
a grudging permission that if the king (the liege lord) makes
war on one of the earls the other may assist the king, but only
with twenty knights, and if he takes any plunder, it must be
returned in full. Nevertheless, although this convention emphasizes above all things a condition of feudal independence and its
corollary, a complete lack of effective central government, it
also reveals a desire on the part of the great feudatories to restore
some sort of order into the chaos. The feud could not be altogether abolished, but it could be regulated and restrained. It
was by means such as this adopted by the earls of Chester and
Leicester that the recovery of the country to a settled state
slowly advanced.[1]

In order to see how the reign ends we must notice the progress of the fortunes of the Angevins on the Continent. After
Stephen's brief visit to Normandy in 1137, such authority as he
had possessed rapidly waned; the leaders of his party, William
of Ypres, Richard de Lucy, the Beaumont brothers, and the
justiciar, William de Roumare, soon followed him across the
Channel; and the duchy was plunged, like England, into
anarchy. Then in 1141 Geoffrey of Anjou embarked seriously
on the task of conquest. He had learnt his lesson from his previous failures; he gave up raiding and plundering and went to
work systematically. With change of method came success. He
was already firmly established on the southern border; he had
control of Bayeux and Caen on the north; and in the course of
a few months, almost without bloodshed, he had won most of
the country between the Orne and the Seine. Then, with the
help of Robert of Gloucester, he advanced through the Bessin
and overran Stephen's own county of Mortain; he captured
Avranches, and, after some little resistance, Cherbourg which

---

[1] The document is printed and discussed by Stenton, who emphasizes its essentially feudal character (*English Feudalism*, pp. 249, 285). Its date cannot be accurately determined, but it must belong to the last years of the reign, between
1149 and 1153. Cf. also for its relation to similar agreements on the Continent,
H. Mitteis, *Lehnrecht und Staatsgewalt*, p. 585.

made him master of the Cotentin. The west of Normandy was his. In January 1144 he crossed the Seine and Rouen opened its gates. Its castle held out for three months; but when that too fell the conquest of Normandy was virtually completed.[1] He assumed the title of duke and was recognized as such by Louis VII of France.

For some five years Geoffrey ruled in Normandy; but he governed rather as regent for his son Henry than as duke by right of conquest. He was fully alive to the fact that it would take time before an Angevin count could become acceptable to the Normans, and he wisely associated his youthful heir, who had through his mother a legal title to the duchy, in the work of government; charters were issued with the counsel and consent of the boy or in the joint names of father and son.[2] Then, when the latter reached an age of discretion, Geoffrey transferred the duchy altogether to him. This was in 1150 when the young prince was seventeen years old.[3] He had been carefully educated for the responsible position he was destined to occupy. His schooling began under Peter of Saintes, a man noted for his skill in verse; it was continued during his first stay in England (1142–4) at Bristol where he came in contact with the famous scientist and traveller, Adelard of Bath; it was completed on his return to Normandy under the great grammarian William of Conches who compiled for his benefit a collection of ethical maxims. It is no matter for surprise, therefore, that Henry in later life became a patron of letters and that his court was frequented by literary men.

From the early days of the anarchy Henry claimed to be 'the rightful heir of England and Normandy'. He came with his uncle, Robert of Gloucester, to England at the close of 1142, and in this style confirmed a charter of the empress in favour of Aubrey de Vere when he was not yet ten years old.[4] Evidently he was brought up to the idea that the inheritance of England was properly, lawfully, and ultimately his. But the child had little better prospects of making good the Angevin claim than

[1] The castle of Arques near Dieppe was the last place to submit. It fell in the summer of 1145.
[2] Haskins, *Norman Institutions*, p. 131.
[3] For the date see *Eng. Hist. Rev.* lxi (1946), 81.
[4] 'rectus heres Angl. et Normann.' (Round, *Geoffrey de Mandeville*, p. 186). It seems more probable that the confirmation was executed after Henry's arrival in England than, as Round supposes, 'over sea'—between July and November 1142.

his mother, the empress. His second visit to England in 1147 was
pitiably ineffective.¹ When he came again to England in 1149 he
was a grown man and a more serious cause for alarm. He was
knighted at Carlisle by his great-uncle, the king of Scotland
(22 May) with whom and the earl of Chester he then prepared
to attack York. But Stephen in the meanwhile had hastened
northward with a large force, and his opponents dispersed.
Henry himself withdrew to the strongholds of Angevin influence
in Gloucestershire and Wiltshire where during the autumn he
was ceaselessly harrassed by the king's son Eustace. His only
success was a raid into Devon resulting in the capture of Brid-
port.² In January 1150 he was back in Normandy where he
remained till 1153.

In that interval much happened to alter the situation. On his
return he was plunged into a fierce war with his suzerain, Louis
VII, who was supported by his brother-in-law, Stephen's son
Eustace.³ It was only brought to an end in 1151 by Henry con-
senting to render homage for Normandy and to yield Gisors and
the Norman Vexin (the land between the Epte and the Andelle)
to the king of France.⁴ He was then making ready for a fresh
expedition to England when he was prevented by the sudden
death of his father on 7 September 1151 which made him count
of Anjou. Some months later by a splendid marriage he more than
doubled his continental dominion. Louis VII and his queen,
Eleanor of Aquitaine, had been married for some fourteen
years; but domestically the marriage was a failure. Louis was
too pious and rigid for his young, beautiful, and vivacious wife,
who declared that she had married a monk not a king.⁵ A
rumour of the queen's misconduct at Antioch while the two
were on the crusade got abroad, and there was talk of a separation. Pope Eugenius III, with whom they stayed on the homeward journey, did all he could to keep the ill-matched pair
together; he made them sleep in the same bed; he would hear
no word of divorce or consanguinity; and the king, answering
to the treatment, gave expression to his love 'in almost a puerile

¹ Above, p. 148.
² *Gesta Stephani*, pp. 142–8.
³ He had married Constance, daughter of Louis VI.
⁴ Gisors had already been ceded by Count Geoffrey in order to gain Louis VII's
recognition of his conquest of Normandy in 1144. *Hist. Gaufredi ducis*, ed. Halphen
and Poupardin in 'Chroniques des Comtes d'Anjou' (Collection de Textes, 1913),
p. 215. The terms of the treaty of 1151 appear to be those given in *Hist. Ludovici VII*,
ed. Molinier (Collection de Textes, 1887), p. 161.   ⁵ Will. Newb., lib. i, cap. 31.

fashion'.[1] The pope's well-intentioned efforts were attended with some success, for Eleanor arrived in France a pregnant woman, and had the longed-for son instead of another daughter resulted from this hallowed conception all might have been well. As it was, at Beaugency, they were separated by the convenient method provided by the church—they were declared to be related within the prohibited degrees, and Louis lost more than half his kingdom (21 March 1152). To avoid importunate suitors Eleanor immediately gave her hand and the duchy of Aquitaine to Henry of Anjou. They were married on 18 May of the same year.

It was not, however, until the following January that Henry was free from the wars with Louis VII in which this bold stroke, so devastating to the power of the French monarchy, involved him, and was able once more to cross the Channel to claim his English inheritance. Although in the intervening years there had been comparative peace in England; although Stephen had met with some success in his attempt to round up the strongholds which still remained loyal to the Angevin cause—it was indeed an appeal of despair from Wallingford that brought Henry to England in 1153; yet the king's position had been sensibly weakened by his quarrel with the church related elsewhere.[2] He was now opposed by a hostile archbishop and a hostile pope, and between them they had effectively thwarted his plan of establishing his family permanently on the throne, for Eugenius III forbade Archbishop Theobald to crown Eustace on the ground that 'Stephen appeared to have seized the kingdom contrary to his oath' (1152). In striking contrast to his previous expeditions, Henry's campaign of 1153 was an almost unqualified success. The king and the duke faced each other at Malmesbury, parted only by the river Avon, in normal times an insignificant stream, but now, in January, swollen by winter rains and all but impassable. A blizzard of driving torrential rain beat upon the royalist troops and sent them dripping and discomfited back to London, leaving the castle in the hands of the young prince. It would seem that after the capture of Malmesbury Henry secured his position in the west midlands.[3]

---

[1] These details are supplied by John of Salisbury who was living at the papal court at the time (*Hist. Pontif.*, cap. 29).   [2] Below, pp. 194 f.

[3] The chronology is very confused. It has usually been supposed that the campaign in the midlands took place after the truce made at Wallingford which must

He passed through Evesham, Gloucester, and Coventry; Warwick was surrendered to his men early in June,[1] and Leicester shortly before.[2] It was on the advice of the earl of Leicester that he successfully besieged Tutbury and won the earl of Derby to his side; Bedford was plundered and burnt. It was after 'he had captured a number of towns and very many castles' and subdued 'nearly half England' that he moved on to the relief of Wallingford. He was engaged in attacking the castle of Crowmarsh on the opposite bank of the Thames when Stephen and his son Eustace appeared on the scene. But the leaders of both sides now intervened to prevent a pitched battle; an interview took place between the king and the duke and a truce was arranged. The latter returned to the midlands where apparently the siege of Stamford was still proceeding; he was there on the 31 August.[3] Its capture was the last serious military operation.

The stage was laid for the closing act of this pitiable drama; many of the leading actors—Queen Matilda, King David of Scotland, the earls of Northampton, Warwick, and Chester—were either dead or died in the course of this year 1153. But what more than anything else eased the situation was the death in August 1153 of the king's eldest son, Eustace. This man, whose only merit was his soldiership, who, as a contemporary notes, 'wherever he was, did more evil than good', disgusted with the tame ending of the operations round Wallingford, had gone to vent his fury in East Anglia; he was plundering the lands of the abbey of Bury St. Edmunds when he met his end. Stephen was a tired, disillusioned, and disappointed man. He had no heart to continue the struggle for his second son William, who had taken no active part in the civil war. Moreover, he was already provided with a rich inheritance by his marriage with the heiress of the earl of Warenne (dead on crusade in 1148); and in the final settlement between Stephen and Henry he was

have been at the end of July or beginning of August (for Eustace died 17 August *infra paucos dies* after). Also it would be unreasonable for Henry to undertake a protracted and bloody campaign after the conclusion of the truce. The order of events followed in the text attempts to reconcile the narrative of the *Gesta Stephani* (pp. 154-9) with the evidence of charters (for which see Delisle–Berger, *Actes de Henri II*, i, pp. 52-71; *Reg. Antiq. of Lincoln Cathedral*, i, p. 97) and known dates. Cf. also Brooke, *Eng. Hist. Rev.* lxi (1946), 86, whose paper, however, was written before the concluding chapters of the *Gesta Stephani* were recovered.

[1] Before the death of the earl of Warwick on 12 June.
[2] 'ad Pentecosten (7 June) quo fui apud Legrecestriam', Delisle–Berger, i. 71.
[3] Ibid., i. 61.

secured not only in this inheritance, but also in the private estates, which Stephen had held before he ascended the throne, both in England and in Normandy (the honours of Lancaster, Eye, and Boulogne and the county of Mortain), with the addition of substantial estates in Sussex.[1] This generous treatment of Earl William reveals Stephen's concern for the future well-being of his son and Henry's anxiety to make sure of the English crown; but it also very materially smoothed the path of the peacemakers.

For some time the dignitaries of the church had directed their endeavours to the restoration of peace; for this object, at least, the old rivals, Archbishop Theobald and Bishop Henry of Winchester, could work in harmony; and now at last their efforts bore fruit. Duke Henry was admitted on 6 November into the city of Winchester where were arranged the terms of the treaty afterwards formally ratified in a charter granted at Westminster and witnessed by no less than fourteen bishops and eleven earls, besides a number of other prominent persons.[2] Stephen thereby declared Henry his successor on the throne *jure hereditario*, promised to maintain him 'as his son and heir', and to co-operate with him in the government of the kingdom; the duke for his part was to do homage to the king. The earls and barons were also brought into the agreement, for the adherents of either party were to do homage to the other. The bishops had negotiated the treaty, and they undertook to see that it was carried out by punishing anyone who infringed it.

At Oxford early in the new year the barons rendered their

---

[1] The right of Rannulf of Chester, who was alive when the settlement was made (he died 16 December 1153), to the honour of Lancaster recognized by Duke Henry this very year, was wholly ignored in this settlement. For the position of Stephen's son, William, see Round, *Peerage and Family History*, pp. 169 f.

[2] The ratification took place, as Henry of Huntingdon states (p. 289), before Christmas, for the copy in the *Red Book of the Exchequer* from which the *Foedera* text is printed (Rec. Com. ed. i. 18) bears the date 'Apud Westmonasterium anno ab incarnatione Domini nostri Jesu Christi M.C.LIII'. Berger's comment (Delisle-Berger, *Recueil des Actes de Henri II*, i. 62), 'Cette date n'a aucune valeur', on the ground that according to Gervase of Canterbury (i. 156) the treaty was concluded at Winchester, is groundless; the terms were agreed upon at Winchester in November, but the confirmation was made subsequently at Westminster by charter, as the marginal rubric of the document in the *Red Book* (f. 163) plainly states: 'Forma concordie inter Stephanum et Ducem Henricum cartis confirmata.' The statement, still often repeated, that the treaty was made at Wallingford is based on a confusion by the thirteenth-century chronicler, Roger of Wendover (ed. Coxe, ii. 255). The earliest text is among the Gurney MSS., *Hist. MSS. Com., Twelfth Report*, ix (No. 27), p. 119.

homage to the acknowledged heir. So far the treaty was satisfactorily obeyed. But there had, it appears, been some, perhaps
verbal, agreement that those outward and visible signs of
anarchy, the unlicensed or 'adulterine' castles, should be
destroyed. That the process of destruction was not proceeded
with sufficiently rapidly or thoroughly was a subject of complaint when the two princes met again at Dunstable. The matter
was then smoothed over. Nevertheless, before long Henry either
began to find that his position as Stephen's collaborator was too
difficult, or even that his life was not safe from royalist plots,[1] or
perhaps he considered that he could more usefully employ his
time in his continental dominions. However that may be, he
withdrew before Easter to Normandy where he remained till
the news of the king's death at Dover on 25 October 1154
brought him again to England to claim the throne which had
been awarded to him less than a year before by the treaty of
Winchester.

[1] Gervase of Canterbury (i. 158) has a story that when the two went to Dover
to receive the count of Flanders an attempt was made on the duke's life.

VI

CHURCH AND STATE: ANSELM

WILLIAM the Conqueror had done much to raise the condition, the character, and the reputation of the church in England. Though tenacious of control over the church, he had encouraged its reform. He had filled the sees and monasteries with bishops and abbots brought from Normandy or Lorraine, who were generally better educated and possessed of greater organizing ability than their Anglo-Saxon predecessors. These 'new brooms', if we may use the phrase, were, however, often arrogant, often tactless in their treatment of the native clergy. It was a needless insult to strike the names of Anglo-Saxon saints, venerated by the English, from the church calendars; the new abbot of Abingdon tried wholly to obliterate the memory of the great St. Æthelwold whom he contemptuously called merely 'an English rustic'; it was, as the abbey historians themselves admitted, inexcusable on the part of Abbot Paul, otherwise an excellent man and a kinsman of Lanfranc, to break up the tombs of the former abbots of St. Albans whom he liked to refer to as 'uncultured idiots'.[1] All this was gratuitously wounding the susceptibilities of the English clergy, and shows a far too wholesale condemnation of the customs of the old English church, which was not the hopelessly decadent church that it has sometimes been represented. Moreover, these imported ecclesiastics were themselves not always of unblemished character. Robert of Limesey, for example, who had been a royal chaplain and was raised to the bishopric of Coventry in 1085, had a shocking reputation, while the conduct of Thurstan, abbot of Glastonbury, was so scandalous that he had to be removed from his office.[2] Nevertheless, as a result of William's policy, a reform on the lines of the continental church had set in; and his death in 1087 was therefore a severe blow to

---

[1] Cf. *Chron. Monast. de Abingdon*, ii. 284; *Gesta Abbatum Monast. S. Albani*, i. 62. The subject is treated by Dom D. Knowles, *The Monastic Order in England*, p. 118. Lanfranc himself encouraged this attitude; the revived respect for Anglo-Saxon usages was due to Anselm and his English biographer Eadmer. Cf. R. W. Southern, 'St. Anselm and his Pupils', in *Medieval and Renaissance Studies* (Warburg Institute, i. 3 (1941)).

[1] See William of Malmesbury, *Gesta Regum*, ii. 388 (§ 341); *Gesta Pontif.*, pp. 310 and 197. Thurstan, in spite of his bad character, was afterwards restored by Rufus.

MEDIEVAL DIOCESES

the church both in the duchy and in England. In Normandy, owing to Robert's neglect and complete lack of governance, the church was exposed to plunder and every sort of abuse;[1] in England Rufus had a policy, but it was a policy of spoliation and no more. His recorded acts of piety are few: in accordance with his father's wishes he distributed gifts among the churches and monasteries at his accession; he endowed his father's foundation of Battle, the recently founded Cluniac house at Bermondsey, and, when seriously ill and in danger of death, the abbey of St. Peter's at Gloucester: occasionally he would enrich a church *pro anima patris*. But these are small benefits in comparison with the wholesale extortions which have made his reign notorious.

The means by which William II wrung money from the church was an ingenious adaptation of feudal principles to the special conditions pertaining to ecclesiastical fiefs. The vacant see or abbey was like a wardship: the services due could not be rendered, and the lord might justly take the revenues instead. The bishop-elect, like an heir entering upon his inheritance, should pay a substantial sum, an equivalent to the relief.[2] But if there was a theory to justify this last form of exaction, it could not in fact be distinguished from simony, the sin of paying a price for a spiritual office, the evil which it was especially the object of the Gregorian reform to eradicate. Herbert Losinga in 1091 bought the see of Thetford for a very large sum of money, a transaction which inspired a versifier to dilate on it and on the venal character of the whole church in fifty hexameters.[3] But it was the system rather than the man that was at fault, for by no other means could a clerk attain to a position worthy of his abilities. Losinga soon repented of his sin, went to Rome, resigned his bishopric, and received it back from the pope's hands. But this act of contrition only involved him in further difficulties: he had, contrary to the rule of William I, recognized a pope, Urban II, who had not been officially acknowledged in

[1] See the record of the injuries suffered by the nuns of Holy Trinity at Caen printed by Haskins (*Norman Institutions*, pp. 63 f.) from the Cartulary of the abbey.

[2] In the thirteenth century it was not unusual for abbeys to agree by charter to pay a relief on the death of an abbot. The abbot of Dorchester, for instance, in 1276 grants to Edmund, earl of Cornwall, 'quod in decessu sive amocione cuiusque abbatis domus nostre faciemus racionabile relevium' for certain lands in Warborough held of him. See H. Salter, *Eng. Hist. Rev.* xlv (1930), 282.

[3] They are printed in the *Monumenta Germaniae Historica, Libelli de Lite*, iii. 616 f. A shorter and slightly different form of the poem is given by William of Malmesbury, *Gesta Regum*, ii 386, § 338.

England. He was therefore for a time deprived of his see by the very king from whom he had purchased it. Herbert Losinga was a good bishop and a reputable scholar who himself contributed to the polemical literature of the Investiture contest a tract addressed to Anselm.[1] He was a man of energy and enterprise who moved his bishopric to the already flourishing trading city of Norwich where he built a fine cathedral. Both in character and attainments he was far superior to the majority of the bishops of his time who were generally taken from the ranks of the sycophantic clerks of the king's household. Abbeys were more difficult to dispose of, as the secular clerks were not eligible for such offices, and there were perhaps not many among the monastic clergy who could or would pay the large sums demanded of them. They therefore usually stood vacant for longer periods, while the king's officers entered upon their estates and managed them to the advantage of the Crown, appropriating the revenues and keeping the monks on a fixed and often narrow pittance of food and clothing.[2] At the time of Rufus's death there were eleven of the wealthiest abbeys and three bishoprics in the king's hands.[3]

The king's chief agent in this business was Rannulf Flambard, a Norman clerk of humble family, who had been for some years at the court of William I; he was a chaplain and keeper of the king's seal while Maurice, afterwards bishop of London, was chancellor (? 1083-6);[4] in Domesday he appears as a landowner with small properties in half a dozen counties. Under Rufus he rose to a position of the first importance in the administration. He was 'the king's chaplain', and in this capacity he was employed in every sort of executive and judicial work. As a justiciar we find him sometimes carrying on the government in England during the king's absence in Normandy. He was, in fact, as Eadmer describes him, 'the chief agent of the king's will'.[5] For these services he was rewarded by preferment in the church: in 1088 he was given the abbey of Hyde at Winchester,

---

[1] 'Ad Anselmum contra malos sacerdotes.' See Böhmer, *Kirche und Staat*, pp. 172 f.

[2] See Eadmer's description of the conditions at Canterbury during the vacancy which followed the death of Lanfranc (*Hist. Nov.*, p. 26).

[3] The list is given by Böhmer, op. cit., p. 155, n. 4.

[4] The assertion that he was treasurer is probably incorrect and due to a confusion with Rannulf the treasurer of York. See R. W. Southern in *Trans. Hist. Soc.*, 4th ser., xvi (1933), 101 f.

[5] *Hist. Nov.*, p. 41.

and just before the king's death he received the bishopric of Durham (1099), which he so shamefully abused that Henry I had to take it under his special protection.[1] No writer of the time has a good word for Rannulf, though they all admit his great ability: he was clever, competent, and astute; beyond this he was arrogant, ambitious, and wholly worldly. It is generally agreed that to him must be attached a large measure of the blame for the extortions which characterize the reign of Rufus. Even the mild Anselm uses strong expressions about him in a letter to Pope Paschal:[2] 'non solum publicanus, sed et publicanorum princeps infamissimus'. His name is expressly associated with some of the worst malpractices which no feudal theory could justify, such as when on the death of Bishop Wulfstan of Worcester he exacted reliefs from the under-tenants, or when in the last days of the aged Abbot Symeon of Ely he pensioned the monks and seized what was left over for the king. He it was who farmed the revenues of vacant churches and prolonged the vacancies so that the profits might continue to accrue to the royal treasury.

But in condemning Rufus and Flambard we should in fairness consider them in relation to the practice of the time. The attack on simony had been launched by the papacy not half a century before. It was still rife in Germany and in Italy; Philip of France was a flagrant abuser of the lay power over the church; in short, the Hildebrandine reform had not as yet been received either in England or on the Continent. William II has been universally condemned, and with justice; but it should not be forgotten that if he was the first, he certainly was not the last, to make the church a source of profit to the Crown. Henry I, notwithstanding the solemn protestation in his coronation charter, not only made free use of the revenues of vacant churches but frequently kept the sees void for long periods of time. If Canterbury was without an archbishop for four years after the death of Lanfranc, it was in similar case for five after the death of Anselm (1109–14). Moreover the Angevin kings were quite as unscrupulous in this matter as their Norman predecessors, and in 1161 Thomas Becket himself was rebuked by his friend John

---

[1] Henry's charter to the monks of Durham (*Cartae Antiquae*, no. 41) is granted 'on account of the injuries and violence which Rannulf the bishop did to them in his lifetime'.

[2] *S. Anselmi Opera Omnia*, ed. Schmitt, iv, *ep.* 214.

of Salisbury because there was a rumour abroad that he as chancellor was enjoying the fruits of three vacant sees.[1]

When Lanfranc died in 1089, Anselm, who had already attained a European reputation as a scholar, was generally regarded as the obvious successor to the primacy of Canterbury. Born at Aosta at the foot of the Great St. Bernard (*circa* 1034) of wealthy parents, he had early abandoned a life of easy comfort for that of a student. After some years of wandering through France he settled at Bec, attracted thither by the fame of Lanfranc as a teacher. There he became a monk and successively rose to be prior and abbot; there too he won for himself the position of being the first scholar, the leading theologian, of his age. He seemed to be eminently fitted to succeed his former master in the archbishopric. But Rufus had no wish to appoint a successor to Lanfranc or to forgo the rich addition to his financial resources which the Canterbury revenues provided. It was only some four years later, in 1093, when he lay ill at Gloucester, and seemingly dying, with the burden of his misdeeds heavy upon him, that he consented to an election. But Anselm, who happened to be conveniently at hand, in England, indeed even in the neighbourhood of Gloucester, exhibited the most unexpected reluctance to being elected; and in the end still violently resisting, still loudly protesting, he had forcibly to be invested with the office. In this way he was thrust into a position which he neither desired nor felt himself suited to fill. He was, as he said, a monk, and unfitted for secular affairs; for more than thirty years he had devoted himself to a life of learning and contemplation. Without skill or interest in the affairs of the world, entirely devoid of any business instinct, he was not unnaturally averse to assuming the many secular obligations and responsibilities which the position of primate, of first adviser of the Crown, of one of the greatest tenants-in-chief would entail. He was not, like Lanfranc, a statesman. Though by nature mild, he could at times be almost unreasonably obstinate, and on matters of principle no argument of expediency would move him. These qualities in Anselm and the cynical, bullying, violent character of his temporal lord made friction between them inevitable. It began indeed as soon as William had recovered from his illness and threw to the winds all the promises of better

[1] Exeter, Worcester, and Coventry. *Materials for the History of Thomas Becket*, v. 14.

living and better government which he had made under fear of death.

At a meeting with the king at Rochester in the summer Anselm put forward the conditions of his acceptance of the position to which he had so violently and unceremoniously been appointed. They were three in number: that the lands of the see be restored in full as they had been in the time of Lanfranc; that in all things spiritual the king would trust to his counsel; and lastly that he should be allowed to recognize Urban II as the rightful pope. Only the first of these was unequivocally conceded, and the third was the crucial one. It was opposed to the rule of the Conqueror that a pope should be recognized without royal authority. There were now two popes claiming to be apostolic—Urban II, the representative of the reforming party, and Clement III, promoted by the imperialist interest. In England opinion was divided, but on the whole, we are told, inclined towards Clement *pro metu regis*.[1] Even had he wished it Anselm could not do otherwise than acknowledge Urban, for he had already done so as abbot of Bec. He allowed, however, the matter to stand over for the present, and agreed, though still with reluctance, to accept the primacy. He did homage to the king for his temporalities at Winchester; he was enthroned at Canterbury on 25 September; and was finally on 4 December 1093 consecrated by the archbishop of York.

In the meanwhile other points of dispute had arisen—dispute over the lands belonging to the see; over the archbishop's contribution to the Norman campaign of 1094; and over the reform of morals. There were several interviews between the two, and their relations became more and more strained until they were no longer on speaking terms. In one of his fits of temper Rufus openly declared his loathing and contempt for the archbishop. This was on the eve of his embarkation for Normandy, and his attitude was not more conciliatory when he returned to England nearly a year later. Anselm once more raised the question of the recognition of Pope Urban by asking the king's leave to go to Rome for his pallium, without which he could not rightly perform the duties of his office; he could neither hold a council nor

---

[1] Support is given to this view of William of Malmesbury (*Gesta Pontif.*, p. 86) by the letters of Clement III to Lanfranc printed by Liebermann in the *Eng. Hist. Rev.* xvi (1901), 328 ff. Cf. also H. Tillmann, *Die päpstlichen Legaten in England* (1926), p. 18, n. 35; and Z. N. Brooke, *The English Church and the Papacy* (1931), p. 145.

consecrate a bishop. It was this demand that occasioned the famous meeting of the Council at Rockingham on 25 February 1095. The question which Anselm laid before the assembled bishops and barons was whether obedience to the pope was compatible with the faith he owed to the king. It was the old problem of the double allegiance required of a bishop. For his *temporalia* he owed fealty and homage to the king; but in respect of his *spiritualia* he was, as Lanfranc admitted, 'the vassal and servant of the pope'.[1] The Council of Rockingham settled nothing, although the matter was debated over a space of four days. The bishops, drilled into courtierly obedience by their apprenticeship in the royal chapel, recommended Anselm to submit himself in all things to the royal will; and one of them, William of Durham, even urged that he should be deprived of his see and driven from the country. The attitude of this bishop is particularly remarkable in view of the fact that a few years earlier, in 1089, he had himself denied the competence of a royal court to try a bishop on a purely secular charge and by making an appeal to Rome had committed precisely the same offence as Anselm—the recognition of Urban II before he had been officially acknowledged in England.[2] It was only the laymen who had the courage to resist, and refused to concur in any such unwarrantable measures, and the postponement of a decision was virtually a victory for Anselm.

The king, it seems, was now resolved to rid himself altogether of his intractable archbishop; but arbitrary as he was and ready to strain law and custom to the utmost extremity, he at least realized that this could only be authoritatively and effectively done by the pope, and by the pope whom all western Europe, outside the immediate sphere of imperial influence, recognized as apostolic—namely, Urban. This appears to have been the object of the secret mission of the two chancery clerks, Gerard, afterwards successively bishop of Hereford and archbishop of York, and William Warelwast, later bishop of Exeter, who had been dispatched to the curia: Urban was to be acknowledged in return for the deposition of Anselm. The envoys were also to bring back a pallium which Rufus proposed himself to bestow upon a more pliable metropolitan. From Anselm the

---

[1] *Lanfranci Opera*, i. 45 (ed. Giles), quoted by H. W. C. Davis, *A Selection of his Historical Papers*, ed. Weaver and Poole (1933), p. 109.

[2] Above, p. 103; cf. Jaffé-Wattenbach, *Reg. Pontif.*, no. 5397.

whole intrigue was of course carefully concealed. Things did not, however, fall out quite as Rufus had planned. The envoys returned early in May and with them a papal legate, Cardinal Walter of Albano. Landing at Dover, they proceeded straight to the king at Windsor where they arrived shortly before Whit-Sunday (13 May). Cardinal Walter opened the negotiations by granting a substantial privilege: the custom of the Conqueror's day that no legates or papal letters were to be sent to England except with the king's consent was confirmed by papal authority.[1] Confident of success in the main issue, the king now caused Urban to be publicly proclaimed as the canonical pope. But when he approached the question of the primacy, and demanded the summary deposition of Anselm, he met with an uncom--promising refusal.[2] The cardinal had got what he wanted; his master was authoritatively recognized throughout the dominions of the king of England; he had no further need to court the king's goodwill. Rufus had failed; his elaborately laid plan to degrade and humiliate Anselm had hopelessly miscarried; he could no longer even put forward the just defensible ground of complaint that the archbishop had acknowledged a pope without royal authority, for now he himself had ordered the same pope to be acknowledged. He failed again when he tried to induce Anselm to receive from his hands the pallium which the legate had brought from Rome. Anselm refused, and received it instead from the altar of his cathedral (27 May). Rufus had to submit to a reconciliation with the best grace he could.

Anselm was victorious. Already invested, consecrated, and enthroned, he was now in possession of the pallium, the symbol of the papal confirmation of his office.[3] But he was far from elated by his victory. Throughout the whole business he had been treated in the most humiliating manner, kept in ignorance

[1] Hugh of Flavigny, *Chron.* in *Mon. Germ. Hist. Script.* viii. 474–5. Hugh visited England a year later in the company of Gerento, abbot of St. Benignus at Dijon.

[2] Eadmer, *Hist. Nov.*, p. 69; Will. Malmes., *Gesta Pontif.*, p. 89 f. H. Tillmann, *Die päpstlichen Legaten in England*, p. 20, n. 44, supposes, on insufficient grounds, that Rufus intended not to depose Anselm but merely to humiliate him and make him bow to his will.

[3] According to Hugh of Flavigny (loc. cit., p. 475), the legate, in deference to Rufus, permitted the qualifying clause *salva fidelitate domini sui regis* to be inserted in the metropolitan oath of fealty to the pope. This is not so remarkable as it appears to Freeman (*William Rufus*, ii. 588) and J. M. Rigg (*St. Anselm*, p. 141). This oath was a recent innovation and much resisted. Even in the time of Paschal II (1099–1118) an archbishop regarded it as an unheard-of novelty. See J. P. Whitney, *Hilde-brandine Essays*, pp. 54 ff. and especially p. 56, n. 2.

of the legate's coming and of the negotiations that followed. The legate's own conduct was anything but satisfactory: he had taken and offered bribes; he had done nothing to check the misdoings of the king in ecclesiastical matters, far less had he attempted to reform the moral depravity of the king's court. Something in this direction might have been expected from the mission of Gerento, abbot of St. Benignus at Dijon, a member of the advanced Gregorian party, who visited England in the following year (1096). His main object, it is true, was to restore concord between the king and his brother Robert in order that the latter might be free to go on the Crusade—an object which he successfully accomplished—but he was also instructed to set on foot a reform of the abuses prevalent in the church under Rufus's governance. In this he failed. A messenger, perhaps a nephew of the pope, possibly in response to a bribe from the king, was sent from Rome to cancel his commission.[1]

Anselm was not long left in peace after his reconciliation. Two years later there was again friction. Rufus complained of the inefficiency of the Canterbury contingent sent to the Welsh war of 1097; they were poorly trained and badly equipped; and Anselm was summoned before the king's court to explain this remissness. He did not answer the summons. Instead he begged repeatedly for leave to go to Rome to discuss his difficulties with the pope. The request was always refused. In the end he went (November 1097) without the royal licence; but by doing so he forfeited his archbishopric, and the king once more enjoyed the revenues of the see of Canterbury.

His reception at Rome illustrates the high esteem in which he was held on the Continent. He was treated with every mark of respect; he was lodged at the Lateran, and welcomed by Urban as a man in a sense his equal, 'the pope and patriarch of another region'.[2] He was known as 'the holy man', and English visitors wished to kiss his feet like the pope's if he would let them. He divided his time between the papal court and the monastery of San Salvatore at Telese near Benevento, where, in tranquil content, he completed his famous treatise *Cur Deus Homo*. He was given the place of honour at the Council of Bari in October 1098 and at the Easter Council at Rome in 1099 at which strict

---

[1] Hugh of Flavigny (loc. cit.), who is the sole authority for this legation. Cf. Tillmann, op. cit., p. 21, n. 53.

[2] Eadmer, *Vita Sancti Anselmi*, p. 390.

decrees against lay investiture, simony, and clerical marriage were passed in his hearing. But with regard to his own affairs Anselm met with little satisfaction at Rome. Rufus was threatened with excommunication, but owing to the ingenuity of the king's agent, William Warelwast, the threat was never put into execution. Urban was before all else a diplomatist; he may have deemed it politic to make some sacrifice of justice in order to retain the goodwill of a powerful sovereign who had caused him to be recognized throughout his dominions. Anselm retired in vexation to Lyons, where he could reckon on finding welcome and sympathy from his lifelong friend Archbishop Hugh. And at Lyons and in the neighbouring country he spent the remainder of his first period of exile.

Nevertheless, the stay of Anselm in Rome is not without its importance, for when, at the opening of the new reign, he was invited back to England, he returned with the fixed resolve to enforce the Gregorian programme, and especially in the matter of investiture. He reached England, after an absence of nearly three years, on 23 September 1100, to be met immediately with a demand for homage in respect of the restitution of the temporalities of his see. This demand he peremptorily refused on the ground that such an act was opposed to the canons of the Council at Rome which he had himself attended. The practice in England with regard to investitures, as Eadmer states it, was that 'no one before Anselm became a bishop or abbot who did not first become the king's man and from his hand receive investiture by the gift of the pastoral staff',[1] and to this custom Anselm himself had submitted when Rufus had appointed him to the see of Canterbury. It was on the observance of this 'ancient custom', this 'custom of his ancestors',[2] that Henry now insisted; and it was not simply the insistence on a mere form or ceremony. The bishops and abbots of England were for the most part great feudatories, possessed of large estates owing services to the Crown, burdened with military and financial obligations. Clearly from the king's point of view it was essential that he should have some control over the appointment and the loyalty of these men of substance; but Anselm was not prepared to discuss the intrinsic merits of the case, to which indeed he seems to have attached little importance. To him it was a matter

[1] *Hist. Nov.*, p. 2.
[2] Will. Malmes., *Gesta Regum*, § 417: *antiqua consuetudo*; *mos antecessorum*.

of obedience to the authority of Rome; it was a question of
ecclesiastical discipline. When therefore Henry proposed that
an embassy be sent to Rome to ask the pope, Paschal II, to
relax the canons in favour of the ancient custom of the country,
Anselm was ready enough to comply. Paschal, however, less of
a diplomat and more of an intransigent than his predecessor
Urban, refused to make any such concession. A second and a
third embassy followed, each with no better success, and at last
under strong pressure Anselm himself was induced, in spite of
his age—for he was a man of near seventy years—to accompany
the king's envoys on a fourth journey to Rome. This was at
Easter 1103 and was alike fruitless. Neither pope nor king was
prepared at this stage to yield an inch from the position he had
taken up. Since therefore Anselm was prevented from performing effectively his duties as archbishop, he willingly enough took
the hint, imparted to him by the king's agent, to remain abroad
for the time being. Once more he took up his residence with the
archbishop of Lyons and once more the revenues of the see of
Canterbury were taken into the king's hands. Nevertheless, it
was not clear to men of the time that Anselm here was following
the right path. The investiture question was not a simple one.
It was not evident even to all good churchmen which was the
proper course, that consecrated by long custom or that directed
by recent papal legislation. To many thinking people it appeared wrong that Anselm should desert his flock for the sake of a
principle which had by no means met with general acceptance.
The gentle Abbot Gilbert Crispin of Westminster, the favourite
pupil and the intimate friend of Anselm, warns him in a set of
delightful verses of the grave responsibility he has incurred by
his absence from his post:[1]

> The tuneful pipe that loved to chant your praise
> Is hoarse and mournful now. Shepherd, it cries,
> Why is the Shepherd absent from the fold?
> The flock is wandering leaderless astray:
> None brings it back.

The contest was, however, essentially different in character
from that of the previous reign. It was carried on in a dignified
manner, without bitterness or apparent loss of temper; and the

[1] The text is printed by J. Armitage Robinson, *Gilbert Crispin, Abbot of Westminster*
(Notes and Documents relating to Westminster Abbey, no. 3), p. 83, and there is an
English rendering on p. 22, from which the opening lines are quoted above.

antagonists maintained throughout its course a not unfriendly correspondence. Anselm from his natural peace-loving disposition, Henry from his characteristic prudence, exercised remarkable forbearance. So the controversy dragged on until, in 1105, the pope took the step of excommunicating the king's chief adviser, the count of Meulan, and also the bishops who had received investiture from Henry's hands. Anselm followed by threatening the king himself with a like sentence. This brought the issue to a crisis. Henry was alarmed. Perhaps he did not fear ecclesiastical censure as such, but it would be a severe blow to his prestige, it would certainly injure his cause, to be excommunicated by so pious, so just, and so unworldly a man as Anselm. He sought an interview with the archbishop at Laigle in Normandy (22 July); he restored the revenues of Canterbury; he begged Anselm to return if he would only recognize the bishops whom he, the king, had invested with the ring and pastoral staff.[1] But Anselm was still firm on the point that he could not act without papal authority. The best part of a year passed before this was obtained; but at last Paschal seems to have realized that Henry was not the man to surrender that control over the church which his father had exercised; he must meet him half-way. So the road lay open for a compromise. In the negotiations and meetings which took place between Henry I and Anselm an important part was played by the king's sister, Adela, countess of Blois, who was on terms of intimate friendship with Ivo, bishop of Chartres, the famous canonist. Ivo had for some years been an advocate of compromise, recognizing that the lay power could not be reasonably excluded from all influence in ecclesiastical elections. Though kings must in no way presume to confer spiritual attributes upon a bishop, it was their proper right to invest him with his *regalia*, his temporalities. It was certainly largely the influence of Ivo of Chartres that brought the investiture contest in France to a peaceful and satisfactory conclusion in 1107. It is more than a mere probability that the settlement, which was finally reached in England and was sanctioned by a council at London in August of the same year, followed on lines suggested by him.[2]

[1] Those of Winchester, Hereford, and Salisbury.

[2] For the parallel course of the contest in England and France see A. Fliche in the *Revue Bénédictine*, xlvi (1934), 283 ff. The clearest expression of Ivo's views is in his letter to Archbishop Hugh of Lyons printed by E. Sackur in *Mon. Germ. Hist. Libelli de Lite*, ii. 642 ff. It is not without significance that Ivo's friend, Hugh of

No authoritative text has survived to inform us of the precise nature of the agreement of 1107. We have therefore to rely on the brief notice of Eadmer,[1] and on the relevant clause of the Constitutions of Clarendon (1164), which profess, and in this particular certainly seem, to be no more than a statement of the custom of Henry I's time. The king gave up the spiritual investiture with ring and pastoral staff, a ceremony in itself of little importance;[2] and its surrender by the lay power would hardly have contented Hildebrand. The original struggle, which is misleadingly called the 'Investiture struggle', was for the freedom of the church from secular interference, for free and canonical election without the taint of simony. Both in the settlement of the English controversy and in the Concordat of Worms which followed on similar lines, these objects were partially obscured. Henry may have admitted that the election should be free, but in fact it took place in the royal court and was conducted altogether under royal influence. Simony was not wholly eradicated; we hear sometimes of the right of free election being exercised after the payment of a sum of money. Anselm, we are told, conceded that a bishop-elect should not be denied consecration on the ground that he had done homage to the king. This may have been intended as a personal and temporary concession to Henry himself;[3] but the king took care that it became the custom that the elect should render homage before consecration, before, that is to say, he was empowered by consecration to exercise his episcopal functions.[4]

Fleury, who held somewhat similar views, dedicated his tract, written soon after 1102, *De regia potestate et sacerdotali dignitate* (ibid. ii. 466 ff.) to Henry I. The tract, however, seems not to have been written with any particular reference to the English controversy. The opinions of both writers are summarized by A. J. Carlyle, *Mediaeval Political Theory in the West*, iv. 97 ff. Cf. also H. Böhmer, *Kirche und Staat*, pp. 163 ff.   [1] *Hist. Nov.*, p. 186.

[2] Despite this concession, the Empress Matilda proposed to invest a bishop with the ring and the staff (below, p. 191), while King John in 1200 actually granted by charter to William Marshal, earl of Pembroke, *donacionem baculi pastoralis* of the abbey of Nutley (Bucks.), which was within his fee (*Foedera*, i. 81).

[3] This is the view of H. Böhmer, *Kirche und Staat*, p. 161. A similar view is taken by D. Schäfer regarding the Concordat of Worms: the concessions made by Calixtus II were personal to Henry V and not in perpetuity. (*Abhandlungen d. königl. Preuss. Akademie d. Wissenschaften*, 1905.)

[4] Cf. Constitutions of Clarendon, cap. xii (*Materials for the History of Becket*, v. 77), and Glanvill, ix, cap. 1: 'Episcopi vero consecrati homagium facere non solent domino regi etiam de baroniis suis sed fidelitatem cum juramentis interpositis ipsi praestare solent. Electi vero in episcopos ante consecrationem suam homagia sua facere solent.'

That Anselm regarded the appointment of a bishop or abbot as a royal appointment is manifest from his own letters. Writing to the pope the year after the settlement he says that Henry in making elections does not use his arbitrary will, but submits entirely to the advice of religious men, and again addressing Thomas, archbishop-elect of York, he writes, 'Since it has pleased the king, with the counsel of his barons and our consent, that you should be elected to the see of York'. Clearly the royal influence, however tactfully it may have been used, was decisive.[1] Moreover the character of the episcopate did not materially change by reason of the concordat. The same kind of men were chosen. Piety in matters of religion was seldom the primary qualification in the election of bishops; they continued to be normally men of affairs, administrators, chosen largely for their experience in conducting the king's business. Roger, who, though nominated by the king as early as 1102, was consecrated bishop of Salisbury by Anselm in 1107 immediately after the settlement, had served as chancellor. He proved himself a brilliant administrator and the founder of a family of episcopal administrators.[2] Richard of Belmeis, appointed bishop of London in 1108, had been sheriff of Shropshire, and, like Roger of Salisbury, founded an ecclesiastical dynasty.[3] The comment of Hugh the Chanter that by the surrender of the right of investiture the king had lost little or nothing, a little perhaps in royal dignity, nothing at all in power, seems to be a fair estimate of the result of the six years' contest.[4]

The movement for the reform of the church by the beginning of the twelfth century had aroused the interest of English scholars, who began to contribute to the polemical literature of the contest. The writer who is usually described as 'the Anonymous of York' makes a violent attack on what he regards as usurped powers of the pope; he vigorously defends lay investiture on the ground of the divine nature of kingship: the king represents the divinity of Christ, the priest but the manhood. The royal authority, therefore, in his conception towers above

---

[1] *Opera*, ed. Schmitt, v, *epp*. nos. 430, 443. Cf. Hen. Hunt., p. 245: 'dedit rex archiepiscopatum Cantuariae . . .'; 'dedit episcopatum Lincoliae'. This influence was also exercised in abbatial elections. See Dom David Knowles in *Downside Rev.* xlix (1931), 259, and the cases there cited. He notes only two instances of free election— at St. Albans in 1119, and at Gloucester in 1130.

[2] Above, p. 136.   [3] Cf. Stubbs's preface to Ralph of Diceto, i. xxi.

[4] *Historians of the Church of York*, ed. Raine, ii. 110.

the sacerdotal.[1] On the side of the reformers Gilbert Crispin, abbot of Westminster, contributed a tract on simony, Herbert Losinga, bishop of Norwich, one on the marriage of priests.[2] But in spite of this literary activity and in spite of the settlement of the investiture question in 1107, the reform movement made but slow progress. The king was at heart against it and clung tenaciously to the 'ancient custom'. After Anselm's death (1109) he relapsed into the ways that had made his brother's reign notorious. These malpractices he had renounced in his coronation charter in plain terms:

'First I make the holy church of God free so that I will neither sell it nor place it to farm, nor, on the death of an archbishop, bishop, or abbot, will I take anything from the domain of the church or from its tenants until a successor has been instituted to it.'[3]

These promises were made when his position on the throne was far from secure; now that he was firmly seated upon it, with his brother Robert closely imprisoned and the awe-inspiring Anselm dead, he could afford to forget his undertakings. The church was anything but free.[4] Henry practised simony; he kept bishoprics and monasteries vacant for long periods and purloined the revenues. Anselm's successor, as already mentioned, was not appointed until 1114, after a vacancy of five years; Ely remained vacant for two (1131-3), Coventry for three (1126-9), and Durham for five years (1128-33). Henry's exercise of the right to the personal belongings of a deceased bishop (*jus spolii*), a claim introduced into England apparently by William Rufus, evoked loud protests from Pope Honorius II.[5]

---

[1] *Tractatus Eboracenses*, ed. H. Böhmer in the *Mon. Germ. Hist. Libelli de Lite*, iii. 642 ff. The same editor has published portions of the treatises in his *Kirche und Staat*, pp. 436 ff., with an elaborate commentary (ibid. 177 ff.). For an English summary see A. J. Carlyle, *Political Theory in the West*, iv. 274 ff. Cf. also Z. N. Brooke, *The English Church and the Papacy*, pp. 157 ff.

[2] Losinga's tract has not survived. Gilbert Crispin's *de Simoniacis*, till recently only known from an entry in a Bec catalogue of the twelfth century, has been discovered by J. Armitage Robinson in a manuscript at St. John's College, Oxford (no. 149), and printed by him in his *Gilbert Crispin* (Cambridge, 1911), pp. 111 ff.; cf. also pp. 55 and 67 ff. W. Holtzmann, who has also published the tract in *Neues Archiv der Gesellschaft für ältere deutsche Geschichtskunde*, l (1933), 246 ff., thinks it was probably written between 1100 and 1103.

[3] *Statutes of the Realm*, i. 1.

[4] See the bitter complaint of the bishops at the beginning of the next reign of the oppression which the church suffered under Henry I. *Gesta Stephani*, p. 17.

[5] *Hist. MSS. Com.*, 5th Report (1876), p. 429, quoted by Böhmer, op. cit., p. 301. A specific instance of this is related by Henry of Huntingdon (*De contemptu mundi*,

In one respect Henry went even farther than his brother. The London council of 1102 had forbidden under heavy penalties the marriage of the clergy. During the war for the conquest of Normandy the king had discovered in this a means of increasing his financial resources; he had exacted fines from those who disobeyed the decrees, and was sternly rebuked by Anselm for doing so. The prohibition was repeated in subsequent councils; in 1128 the ecclesiastical authority was permitted to sell the unfortunate women into slavery (Canon 7 of the council of 1127). But the king continued to make a financial matter of it and 'received large sums from the priests for licence to live as before'.[1] One may, indeed, reasonably doubt the wisdom of these celibatic decrees. It was hardly to be expected that the lower clergy would pay much attention to such legislation when they saw men in high positions in the church openly disregarding it. The great Roger of Salisbury, who himself took a prominent part in these ecclesiastical councils, lived openly with his mistress, Matilda of Ramsbury, while his nephew, Bishop Nigel of Ely, was a married man, the father of Richard Fitz Neal, and scandalized the strict churchmen by putting in a married clerk as sacrist in his own cathedral; even the conduct of the papal legate who presided over the council of 1125 was not above suspicion.[2] It seems certain that a large number of the parish clergy and even the higher clergy[3] openly continued their intercourse with women. The legislation merely substituted an illicit for a legal relationship.

Henry's government of the church was, indeed, far from being acceptable at Rome. In 1115 Paschal II wrote a strong letter of protest: he complained that his letters were not received or his legates given a hearing without the royal permission; that no pleas, no appeals were brought before the papal court; that

p. 308) with reference to the death of Bishop Gilbert 'the Universal' of London. The bishop's boots, filled with gold and silver, were carried away to the royal treasury.

[1] Hen. Hunt., p. 251. Cf. *Anglo-Saxon Chronicle, sub anno* 1129. For similar measures taken by King John see the Annals of Waverley, *sub anno* 1208, *Ann. Mon.* ii. 261.

[2] '[Johannes Cremensis] cum igitur in concilio severissime de uxoribus sacerdotum tractasset . . . cum meretrice post vesperam interceptus est' (Hen. Hunt., p. 246). Gilbert Foliot, however, had a high opinion of the merits of John of Crema. See his letter to Becket in *Materials for the History of Becket*, v. 539.

[3] Ralph of Diceto (i. 305) referring to the promotion of Richard Peche in 1161 to the see of Coventry which his father had once held, quotes from Ivo of Chartres, the canonist, instances of marriage among the higher clergy. But it is doubtful whether the sons were born before or after the father was ordained subdeacon.

bishops were transferred from one see to another without any reference to the pope. This was all true and continued so until Henry's death. In 1119 when Calixtus II became pope he held a council at Rheims to which bishops from all the countries of western Europe were summoned. The English bishops were permitted to attend, but they were warned to air no grievances and to bring no innovations back with them. Nine legates were dispatched to England in the course of his reign, but one only— John of Crema in 1125—was permitted to preside over a church synod or to exercise any legatine authority. This indeed was the tradition in England, a tradition sanctioned by Paschal's predecessor and later admitted by Calixtus II. But it effectively prevented the pope from exercising any real control over the government of the church in England. In the English view, as Eadmer expresses it, none other than the archbishop of Canterbury should act as the pope's vicar. This was the happy solution of the difficulty which was ultimately reached when Honorius II granted a legatine commission to Archbishop William of Corbeil in 1126, a precedent frequently followed until in the thirteenth century it became the fixed rule that the archbishop of Canterbury should by virtue of his office be *legatus natus*.

The commission of Archbishop William as legate helped also to alleviate another source of discord. The seemingly interminable dispute between Canterbury and York reached an acute stage when Thurstan, the king's secretary,[1] was appointed (1114) to the see of York, and vigorously championed the independence of the northern province. The controversy further embittered the relations with Rome, for, while the king advocated the claim of Canterbury, successive popes supported that of York. The question was ultimately decided in 1126 in favour of York, for the evidence on which Canterbury based its case was palpably forged. The archbishop of Canterbury could, however, find consolation in his defeat from the fact that as legate he had an unimpeachable claim on the obedience of his brother primate.[2]

But the comings and goings of bishops to and from Rome, which the king could not altogether prevent, especially when a great cause like the dispute between Canterbury and York was

---

[1] Hugh the Chanter, in *Historians of the Church of York*, ii. 129.

[2] The whole dispute has been very thoroughly treated by M. Dueball, *Der Supremmatstreit zwischen den Erzdiözesen Canterbury und York, 1070–1126*, in Ebering's *Historische Studien*, Heft 184 (1929). Cf. also Brooke, op. cit., pp. 171 ff.

being investigated at the curia, necessarily brought the English church into closer contact with the papacy. Monasticism also promoted this gradual change; for the monastery, particularly the monastery of the newer orders, was the least insular of all institutions in England: it belonged to a cosmopolitan congregation, and often took its instructions from a religious house situated, like Cluny or Cîteaux, in a distant and foreign country. Even the older Benedictine houses resented the control of the diocesan bishop and desired to look direct to Rome for protection and guidance; only a few, however, succeeded in gaining this emancipation.[1]

Monastic reform had made rapid strides since the Norman Conquest. When a Norman abbot, Serlo, was appointed to the great abbey of St. Peter at Gloucester, he found there but two monks and eight small boys; on his death in 1104 there were more than a hundred inmates. This reform was largely effected by Cluny or by Norman abbeys which, like Jumièges or Fécamp, had themselves been reformed under Cluniac influences. Lanfranc's Constitutions, which he compiled for the guidance of the monks of Christ Church, Canterbury, and which were adopted in several of the older monasteries, were for the most part derived from the customs of Cluny.[2] The Norman kings themselves were interested in Cluny and were its liberal benefactors. The single monastery with whose foundation William Rufus was concerned, the abbey of Bermondsey, was Cluniac; when Henry I refounded the abbey at Reading he filled it with monks from the Cluniac priory of Lewes; similarly Stephen took the original complement of inmates (a prior and twelve monks) for his foundation at Faversham, where he, his wife, and eldest son were buried, from Bermondsey. Henry I completed the nave of the great church at Cluny itself which had been begun by Alfonso VI of Castile and was consecrated by Innocent II in 1132;[3] the same king made an annual contribution of 100 marks

[1] Only seven gained complete exemption during this period: Bury, St. Albans, Battle, Malmesbury, Evesham, Westminster, and St. Augustine's, Canterbury. See Dom David Knowles, *The Monastic Order in England*, pp. 579–91.

[2] R. Graham, *English Ecclesiastical Studies*, pp. 8 ff.; *The Monastic Constitutions of Lanfranc*, ed. Knowles (Nelson's Medieval Texts, 1951).

[3] See the paper on the monastery of Cluny by R. Graham and A. W. Clapham printed in *Archaeologia*, lxxx (1930). According to some authorities Alfonso of Castile was betrothed to a sister of Henry I, see Freeman, *Norman Conquest*, iv (2nd ed.), 852. Abbot Peter the Venerable praised Henry I in high terms: 'Magnus ille rex Henricus . . . qui sicut universo pene orbi terrarum notum est, cunctos sui

of silver, a liability which Stephen continued but commuted for the grant of the manor of Letcombe Regis; Henry's daughter, the Empress Matilda, enriched the abbey with numerous gifts including a great bell cast in an English foundry. His nephew, Henry of Blois, was still more intimately associated with Cluny. Brought up there from childhood, he became in course of time a monk and a close friend of Abbot Peter the Venerable; and at Cluny he remained until he was summoned to England by his uncle in 1126 to become abbot of Glastonbury. But his connexion with the monastery was not at an end: he paid frequent visits there especially in later life, and by his personal generosity and his ability for organization did much to re-establish the tottering financial position of the great abbey.[1]

But the number of Cluniac houses in England had never been great; it rose in the twelfth century to thirty or more, but of these some were quite insignificant little priories. Moreover, even before the close of the eleventh century the great work of Cluny had been done. In the monastic world there is a constant need of revivification; when an old order has grown rich and lax, another takes its place with youthful and ardent ideals of stern asceticism. So it was now. The reform movement had called into being new orders which set before themselves a standard of stricter and more disciplined life. The Austin canons were the first of these to be established in England, and their earliest foundations—the priories of St. Botolph at Colchester and St. Mary at Huntingdon and St. Gregory's at Canterbury can trace their origin to the last decade of the eleventh century[2]—were soon followed by a number of important houses scattered about England at Barnwell, Dunstable, Cirencester, Merton, Oseney, and very thickly in East Anglia and the south-eastern counties. The church of the priory at Carlisle became, on the creation of the see in 1133, the cathedral with a chapter of Austin canons, the only cathedral chapter so constituted.

A more powerful influence, however, on English monastic life was introduced by the Cistercians. The monastery of Cîteaux in the duchy of Burgundy was founded in 1098; but its

temporis Christianos principes prudentia transcendit, operibus evicit, largitate superavit.' *Bibliotheca Cluniacensis* (ed. Marrier and Quercetanus), col. 1309.

[1] See L. Voss, *Heinrich von Blois* (1932), pp. 108–19.

[2] For the difficult problem of the chronology of the earliest foundations see J. C. Dickinson, *Origins of the Augustinian Order and their Introduction into England*, pp. 98–106, and *Trans. R. Hist. Soc.*, 5th ser., i (1951), 71.

prosperity and rapid growth began only when St. Bernard with thirty companions joined the community in 1112. Yet, if the force of attraction which gave the new order its great popularity was due to St. Bernard, the real contribution of Cistercianism to the monastic world was the work of the Englishman, Stephen Harding, the third abbot (1109–33), and his *Carta Caritatis*.[1] This famous constitution, confirmed by Pope Calixtus II in 1119, bound the order together in one governmental system, providing for uniformity of observance, regular visitation, and the assembling of all the abbots in an annual general chapter to legislate for the growing needs of the order. Austerity and simplicity mark the early Cistercians, an aversion to splendour in dress or ornament in buildings; their rule prescribed that they should dwell far from the madding crowd.[2] The Cistercian system reflects the spirit of Puritanism, and it was this element (for Puritanism was always perhaps latent in the English character) which gave to the movement its special appeal in England. The first foundation was at Waverley in Surrey (1129); but the most famous abbeys of the order were in the north country, planted, as the rule prescribed, in the remote and sparsely populated dales of Yorkshire, at Rievaulx, Fountains, and Kirkstall. In spite of hard beginnings and rough times, the English Cistercians rapidly increased and prospered. By the end of Stephen's reign the number of their abbeys (if we include the thirteen houses of the order of Savigny which in 1147 was incorporated with the Cistercian) exceeded fifty.[3] This widespread monastic colonization was not in all respects to the advantage of the country. Their agriculture sometimes disturbed whole villages where the inhabitants were ejected and the houses deserted; there are even instances of parish churches being destroyed because their presence interfered with the solitude of the monks.[4]

---

[1] This is forcibly emphasized by Edmund Bishop (*Downside Rev.* lii. (1934), 221): 'As we look at St. Bernard's *Life* as he actually *lived* it, his activities as a whole and what they involved, I can conceive nothing (except secularity) more alien from the idea and spirit of Cistercianism; even his activity in writing and his correspondence first of all are not merely alien, but even *antagonistic*, to the conception of Cîteaux. . . .'

[2] 'In locis a frequentia populi semotis.'

[3] For a detailed account of the early Cistercian plantation see A. M. Cooke, *Eng. Hist. Rev.* viii. 625 ff., and Knowles, *Monastic Order*, chs. xiii, xiv, and App. XI and Table IV at the end of the volume.

[4] Knowles, op. cit., p. 350. Sometimes the consent of the disturbed peasants was

The Premonstratensian order of canons regular, founded by Norbert, afterwards archbishop of Magdeburg, the only other foreign order which took firm root in England at this time, owed much to the example of the Cistercians. Though the rule of St. Augustine was adopted, much was added from the *Carta Caritatis* and the customs of Cîteaux. After the date of their first settlement at Newhouse in Lincolnshire (1143), their progress was steady and rapid. To this period of monastic ebullition belongs also the foundation of the one purely English order. Gilbert of Sempringham started from small beginnings: about 1131 he provided for a few pious women a building attached to the parish church of Sempringham, in Lincolnshire, of which he was the incumbent. To minister to their wants first lay sisters, then lay brothers were added for domestic and agricultural work; and finally canons were introduced to serve the community as priests after the model of the order of Fontevrault. So was revived the double monastery for men and women. The Gilbertines flourished and increased; but in the majority of their twenty-eight houses the female element was eliminated. Eleven only were for both sexes.

This monastic revival began in the reign of Henry I; but it is a striking fact that its intensive development came during the nineteen years of anarchy which followed his death. It was the turbulent barons of the wars of Stephen and Matilda who endowed the movement, hoping to atone for their misdeeds by acts of piety. These munificent benefactions are made by barons conscious that their turbulence is a cause of annoyance and hardship to peace-loving people. They are acts of compensation, and the motive is sometimes openly expressed in the deed of gift. Roger of Hereford, for example, granted a manor to the abbey of Reading in order to make amends for the damage which he and his men had done to that house and its inmates *tempore werrae*; Gilbert, earl of Lincoln, pledged himself to pay

obtained. Cf. the charters printed by F. M. Stenton, *Eng. Hist. Rev.* xxxiii (1918), 344–7: 'hanc donacionem dedi concessione Oliveri filii mei et concessione sochamans predictarum villarum quorum predicta terra fuit.' Perhaps the most remarkable instance of the displacement of the local inhabitants is provided by the foundation by William de Roumare, earl of Lincoln, of the abbey of Revesby (Lincs.) in 1142. Three villages were involved, Revesby itself, Scithesbi, and Toresbi (the latter two have since disappeared from the map). The villagers were given the option of land elsewhere or 'to go and dwell where they will'. Only seven accepted the first alternative. The charter is printed by F. M. Stenton, *Facsimiles of Early Charters* (Northants. Record Soc. iv (1930), pp. 1–7).

a yearly rent to the priory of Pontefract in atonement for the harm done to that church in a private feud between himself and Henry de Lacy.[1] Stephen's great captain of mercenaries, William of Ypres, founded the Cistercian monastery of Boxley in Kent in 1143 at the very height of the civil war. William of Newburgh is not far from the truth when he comments that a far greater number of monasteries were founded in England during the short time that Stephen reigned than in the preceding hundred years.[2] The attitude of these rough and often brutal soldiers towards religion is not a little interesting. They plundered the land and endowed monasteries with the proceeds; they built castles and at the same time churches. A curious record informs us how, when war was violently raging, a certain Ralph of Worcester who had occupied nearly the whole county of Gloucester fortified a castle and built a church in the hamlet of Hailes near Winchcombe.[3] The castle has long since vanished, but the little parish church still stands today beside the ruins of the great abbey founded a century later by Richard, earl of Cornwall. In this great surge of pious foundations mention should be made of hospitals and leper houses. No fewer than twenty-four of these were already established before Henry I was dead, and during Stephen's reign men continued in this way to provide for the sick and aged poor.

The Knights Templars also owe their first possessions in England to Stephen, or rather to his wife, Matilda of Boulogne. She was naturally interested in the crusading order, being herself the niece of the first two rulers of Jerusalem, Godfrey of Bouillon and his brother Baldwin I. In 1137 she granted to the knights the manor of Cressing in Essex and two years later that of Cowley near Oxford. From these beginnings the Templars in England grew and flourished, and soon were the owners of

[1] I take these examples from F. M. Stenton's *First Century of English Feudalism*, p. 244.

[2] Will. Newburgh, i, c. 15. Cf. the statistics compiled by R. Howlett in the preface to his edition of this chronicle (vol. i, p. xiii): out of a total of about 698 dated foundations, 247 belong to the period before Stephen, 115 to the 19 years of Stephen's reign, 113 to the 35 years of Henry II, and 223 to later times. These figures must be regarded as no more than a mere approximation, particularly as V. H. Galbraith has demonstrated (*Camb. Hist. Journal*, iv (1934), 205 ff.) that the foundation charters were often drawn up several years after the founding of a monastery. The most reliable statistics and dates are those given by Dom David Knowles, *The Religious Houses of Medieval England* (1940).

[3] *Landboc . . . de Winchelcumba*, ed. D. Royce, i. 65.

large estates dispersed throughout the country. Similarly the other and earlier military order, that of the Knights of the Hospital of St. John of Jerusalem, whose first house at Clerkenwell dates from the beginning of Henry I's reign, developed its estates in England at this time.

But this monastic development was by no means the only way in which the reign of Stephen contributed to the advancement of the church. Stephen owed his crown mainly to the influence of the church and particularly to his brother, Henry of Blois, bishop of Winchester.[1] He was bound to make concessions to the church and he made them on an ample and generous scale. The charter of liberties,[2] issued at Oxford in the spring of 1136, was similar in character to the charter which Henry I had granted when he himself was insecure upon the throne; but it was more explicit and more far-reaching: the church was to be free—free, that is to say, from secular interference; elections were to be canonical and without simony, and during vacancies the sees were to be in the custody of the clergy or honourable men; the jurisdiction over ecclesiastics and their property was to be in the hands of the bishops; and all possessions of which the church had been deprived since the time of William I were to be restored; lastly, the clergy were given testamentary power to dispose of their personal effects, which could therefore no longer lawfully be purloined by the king under colour of the so-called *jus spolii*.[3]

It is not easy to determine how closely the king adhered to the promises contained in this charter. In the crucial matter of elections he seems at first to have acted correctly, and he co-operated with the legate, Alberic of Ostia, against the interests of his brother, Henry of Winchester, in the appointment of Theobald, who may rank with the two other products of the abbey of Bec, Lanfranc and Anselm, among the greatest archbishops of Canterbury. But he soon became less scrupulous; he

[1] The remarkable series of royal charters granted to the see of Winchester printed by V. H. Galbraith in *Eng. Hist. Rev.* xxxv (1920), 382 f., illustrate the value which the king attached to his brother's services.

[2] *Statutes of the Realm*, i. 3.

[3] The king, nevertheless, seems to have appropriated the enormous wealth of Roger of Salisbury in 1139 in order to replenish his fast-emptying treasury: *Gesta Stephani*, pp. 64–65. Henry II appropriated the personal property of Robert, abbot of Cirencester, on his death in 1187 (*Pipe Roll 33 Hen. II*, p. 27), and that of Archbishop Roger of York in 1181 (*Gesta Henrici*, i. 283, 289). Similarly Richard I despoiled Geoffrey Ridel, bishop of Ely, in 1189 (Hoveden, iii. 7).

would often require a large sum of money before he would grant *eligendi libertatem*,[1] and on other occasions he, acting with the bishop of Winchester, would use his direct influence to plant his own nominees, often relatives of his own, on the bishoprics and abbeys. It was an attempt of this kind which involved the king in one of the most remarkable and protracted episodes in the history of episcopal elections.[2] He caused his nephew, William Fitz Herbert, treasurer of York, to be appointed to the see of York in 1140. William, though indolent, was not altogether unsuitable for the post, and he died in an odour of sanctity (he was canonized by Pope Honorius III in 1226). He was charged with simony, unchastity, and intrusion; but simony and unchastity were not uncommon and royal intrusion was customary, and even had these charges been proved all might yet have been well with William (for he had the support of the majority of the chapter and of the cardinals at Rome) had it not been for the active opposition of a group of rigid, zealous, and indefatigable Cistercians backed by St. Bernard himself, who put forth against him all the violence and venom he so readily had at his command. The case was handled by no less than four popes before William was finally deposed by the Cistercian pope, Eugenius III, in 1147 in favour of his rival, Henry Murdac, abbot of Fountains. Stephen, however, held his ground, and for three years refused the new archbishop the enjoyment of the temporalities of his see. When his three leading opponents, Eugenius, Bernard, and Murdac, died in 1153, William was peaceably reinstated and had the satisfaction to live for one year the acknowledged archbishop of York before he himself died (perhaps by poison) on 8 June 1154. Stephen, however, never went so far in the exercise of his authority as his opponent, the Empress Matilda, who during her short ascendancy in the summer of 1141, in total disregard of her father's concordat with Anselm, agreed to bestow the ring and the staff upon William Cumin, a candidate for the bishopric of Durham.[3] Yet, in view of the examples we have quoted, it would be idle to

---

[1] Even in the later years of the reign. See the allegations of John of Salisbury with regard to the elections to St. Augustine's, Canterbury, and London in 1151: *Historia Pontificalis*, pp. 89, 91.

[2] See Knowles, 'The Case of Saint William of York', in *Cambridge Historical Journal*, v (1936), 162–77, and C. H. Talbot, ibid. x (1950), 1–15.

[3] 'Pactus erat Willelmus ab Imperatrice baculum et annulum recipere.' Wharton, *Anglia Sacra*, i. 711.

deny that Stephen, at least in his earlier years, made some attempt to continue the practice of his Norman predecessors in the matter of ecclesiastical appointments. It was only as troubles thickened around him and when the papacy had become definitely hostile that he seems to have left elections to take their own course. Gilbert Foliot was elected in 1148 to the see of Hereford without even a reference to Stephen, and he was consecrated at St. Omer by Archbishop Theobald *jubente domno papa*. Nevertheless the other English bishops present at the consecration refused to participate, on the ground that it was 'against the ancient customs that anyone should be consecrated outside the kingdom': further, despite an oath to the contrary, Foliot did fealty to Stephen on his return to England.[1]

Turning now to the relations with Rome, we have noticed that Stephen on his accession deemed it expedient to seek the pope's confirmation. This was granted apparently without hesitation or any serious investigation into his claims; and it was gracefully acknowledged by the king in the recitation of his title in the charter of 1136: he was not only 'elected by the assent of the clergy and people', and crowned by the archbishop of Canterbury, but also 'confirmed by Innocent, pope of the holy Roman see'. Innocent was no doubt guided in his decision by the overwhelming support which Stephen received in England in 1136, and by the fact that his petition was recommended by Innocent's firmest ally, King Louis VII of France. However that may be, he was not in a position to take full advantage of the powerful handle which Stephen's request had placed in his grasp. He, like Stephen himself, was faced with a rival, the anti-pope Anacletus II, who was, in fact, in possession of the city of Rome. He could not, like his great namesake Innocent III, in the German disputed election at the end of the century, use the golden occasion to wring concessions from the opposing parties. It was not till the anti-pope was dead (he died in January 1138) that he had leisure to turn his attention to English affairs. He then sent a legate, Alberic of Ostia, who (like John of Crema in the previous reign) was permitted to hold a legatine council, where seventeen canons were promulgated for the reform of the church. The next year the Empress Matilda brought her case before the pope, and the matter was argued by representatives of both parties at the Lateran Council of 1139. Innocent, how-

[1] *Hist. S. Petri Glouc.* (Rolls Series), i. 19; *Hist. Pontif.*, pp. 47–8.

ever, upheld his previous decision, and to this verdict he faithfully adhered throughout his pontificate.[1]

During this period Henry of Blois, bishop of Winchester, acted as the pope's representative; he received a commission as legate on 1 March 1139 and, henceforth until the death of Innocent II in 1143 he dominated alike over church and state, over king and archbishop.[2] This proud and pompous prelate was a man of great affluence, holding, besides his bishopric, the richest abbey in England, that of Glastonbury—both of which thrived under his rule owing to his capable administration of their property and to his generous benefactions. He was also a man of culture who appreciated the glories of ancient Rome, for when in 1151 he visited that city he bought up ancient statues, which he had sent back to Winchester.[3] Henry of Blois was a great bishop—a remarkable blend, as a contemporary observes,[4] of monk and warrior, being alike at ease whether presiding over a church council or fighting at the head of his armed retainers; he was a builder of churches, but also of castles, of which he is said to have possessed no less than six.[5] So long as he represented the pope he was naturally sympathetic with papal pretensions; and it was while he was legate that the practice of appeals to Rome became a normal and fairly frequent procedure.[6] But with the death of Innocent II everything was changed. A legateship was not a life appointment; it ended with the life of the grantor, and in the case of the bishop of Winchester it was not renewed. From a promoter he became almost an antagonist of papal claims; from a position of unquestioned leadership he was reduced to one of a mere suffragan bishop,[7] a subordinate

[1] See R. L. Poole, *Hist. Pontif.*, App. VI. Innocent wrote to the legate, Bishop Henry of Winchester, urging him to work for the release of the king in 1141. Will. Malmes., *Hist. Nov.*, § 501.

[2] He had had hopes of the primacy when Theobald was elected. But the legateship, granted him in compensation, gave him, of course, authority even over the archbishop.

[3] *Hist. Pontif.*, ch. 40. Edmund Bishop, *Liturgica Historica*, pp. 392–401, thinks it possible to identify two or three of the items in the list of Bishop Henry's benefactions to Winchester (which he there prints) with these Roman antiquities. His counter-seal, a small oval, shows a cameo with two busts (? of ancient Romans) face to face. *Sir Christopher Hatton's Book of Seals*, no. 466.

[4] *Monachus et miles.* Hen. Hunt., *De Cont. Mund.*, p. 315.

[5] Cf. Annals of Winchester, in *Annales Monastici*, ii. 51; below, p. 322.

[6] Henry of Huntingdon (p. 282) regards the practice of appeals as a novelty introduced by Bishop Henry, and notes that no less than three were preferred at the London council of 1151.

[7] Foreseeing this eventuality, he tried, without success, to prevail upon Innocent

of the archbishop of Canterbury, whom he now regarded with scarcely concealed hostility. There can be little doubt that he was behind the king when the latter forbade the primate and certain other bishops to obey the papal summons to the council of Rheims in 1148. This incident deserves notice, for it shows Stephen acting precisely as his predecessors had acted in matters of this sort. He did not approve of his bishops attending councils abroad; he had allowed but five to visit Rome for the Lateran Council of 1139; only three received his permission to be present at Eugenius III's council at Rheims. Archbishop Theobald, however, was resolved to go, and in fact went, crossing the Channel secretly in a small fishing-boat. But when he returned he was deprived of his temporalities and ordered out of the country. The pope threatened excommunication and interdict; but—and this is the most striking part of the story— neither did the king make the satisfaction demanded nor did the bishops carry out the pope's orders.[1] An exiled archbishop, deprived of his temporalities by a king supported by the majority of the bishops, reminds one forcibly of the trials suffered by Anselm at the hands of Rufus and Henry. A formal reconciliation was only arranged towards the end of the year when Theobald ventured to return to England.

Ever since the death of Innocent II in 1143 the papacy had shown a definite leaning towards the Angevin cause. Celestine II is spoken of as 'a disciple of the Angevins' who designed to strengthen their hands to the discomfiture of Stephen.[2] With the accession of Eugenius III, the Cistercian and friend of St. Bernard (a declared opponent of Stephen) in 1145, this antagonism became more pronounced. Now in 1148 it was undisguised, and was demonstrated by hostile acts of both king and pope: in 1150 Stephen refused a safe-conduct through England to the pope's legate proceeding to Ireland; in 1151 Eugenius granted a legatine commission to Theobald, whose leanings were now definitely to the Angevin side; in 1152 he forbade the archbishop to crown Eustace, Stephen's son and heir. However, it was not by acts such as these that the victory of the church was won. Popes and archbishops had opposed the Crown before, but

and his successors to raise the see of Winchester to a metropolitan see for the west of England.

[1] In consequence the bishops were for a time suspended, and Henry of Winchester had to make a journey to Rome before the sentence was removed.

[2] John of Hexham (Symeon of Durham, ii, p. 315).

the king's authority over the church had not been seriously shaken; and indeed the majority of the bishops seem still to have been behind the king, as was apparent when they refused to carry out the interdict in 1148. Stephen was politically weak, and ecclesiastics were losing confidence in the efficacy of his charters of protection.[1] Nevertheless he was struggling along, not wholly without success, in his predecessors' footsteps. That the power of the church increased so rapidly at this time was chiefly due to the fact that there were influential men both at Rome and in England ready and able to take every advantage which the king's political weakness gave them, who worked quietly and perhaps at the time almost imperceptibly to extend the sphere of ecclesiastical jurisdiction and of ecclesiastical authority generally.

At no period of history had English influence at Rome been so great. It was a notable band of Englishmen who had congregated there to assist in the work of the curia.[2] The senior of them, Robert Pullen, who had taught at Oxford before it was a university and who wrote an important volume of 'Sentences' before Peter the Lombard produced his standard work, was cardinal and chancellor of the Roman church from 1144 to 1146; Hilary, a canonist and afterwards bishop of Chichester, was employed in the chancery in 1146, and Boso, who later became a cardinal and chamberlain, was similarly engaged between 1149 and 1152. Nicholas Breakspear, who became pope as Adrian IV in 1154, was already a cardinal in 1149. There was also John of Salisbury, who entered the pope's service probably at Paris in 1147, became his clerk, and left a vivid narrative of what passed at the curia during these years in the *Historia Pontificalis*. Under the fostering care of this distinguished group the intimacy between England and Rome grew and ripened.

Correspondingly there was on the other side in England, at Canterbury, a no less remarkable set of men, forming the house-

[1] Monasteries were seeking papal protection and confirmation of their possessions. Cf. Z. N. Brooke, *Cambridge Historical Journal*, ii (1928), 215. The papal documents collected by W. Holtzmann, *Papsturkunden in England* (1931–6), reveal the fact that during the pontificate of Eugenius III (1145–53) English ecclesiastics were for the first time looking to the pope for help and judgement in their more ordinary concerns.

[2] See R. L. Poole, 'The Early Lives of Robert Pullen and Nicholas Breakspear', in *Studies in Chronology and History*, pp. 287 ff.

hold of Archbishop Theobald, working for the same ends. Most prominent of these were Roger of Pont l'Evêque, afterwards archbishop of York; John Belmeis, successively bishop of Poitiers and archbishop of Lyons; and Thomas Becket, or, as he was then known, Thomas of London. They were soon joined by John of Salisbury, who in 1154 left the service of the pope for that of the archbishop. Theobald was the first since Lanfranc seriously to promote legal studies in England; the litigation and the juris-diction of the church had increased and was rapidly increasing; nearly three-quarters of the letters written by John of Salisbury in his capacity of Theobald's clerk consist 'of directions, decisions, and mandates in cases brought before the arch-bishop'.[1] There was need for professional help in all this legal work, and it was necessary to provide instruction for the rising generation of clergy. To meet these requirements Vacarius, a Lombard jurist, was brought to England by 'the house' of Theobald about 1145. He proved so successful as a teacher of civil law that he was silenced in 1149 by Stephen, who, with the essentially feudal outlook of his age, regarded with suspicion the introduction of foreign law and jurisprudence.[2] The impor-tance attached to legal training is strikingly evident in the Canterbury schools. Becket himself a little later went abroad to study Roman and canon law, first at Bologna and afterwards at Auxerre; and when he succeeded Theobald as archbishop he carried on the tradition. The clerks of the archbishop's house-hold, these *Cantuarienses*, as Peter of Blois tells us, discussed and argued 'from prayers to meal-time' on points of law, on theo-logical problems, and on every topic of the day, 'in the manner of pleaders' (*causidicorum more*).[3] Here in the household of Arch-bishop Theobald are the leading actors of the great Becket contest; here unconsciously they were rehearsing their parts; without much straining of the imagination we can conceive of Becket himself passionately quoting the now famous words, 'Nec enim Deus judicat bis in idipsum', in this spirited Canterbury debating society.

[1] R. L. Poole, 'The Early Correspondence of John of Salisbury', in *Studies in Chronology and History*, p. 259.

[2] It was in this year that Vacarius produced his *Liber Pauperum* as a text-book for students. His suspension cannot have lasted long, for he was teaching again shortly after. Cf. F. de Zulueta, *The Liber Pauperum of Vacarius* (Selden Soc.), Introduction, ch. 1; Liebermann, *Eng. Hist. Rev.* xi (1896), 305.

[3] Peter of Blois, *ep.* 6, in Migne, *Pat. Lat.* ccvii; Liebermann, loc. cit., p. 308, n. 31.

VII

CHURCH AND STATE: BECKET

THE personality of Thomas Becket dominates the first sixteen years of the reign of Henry II, first as the energetic
chancellor and constant companion of the king, and later
as the stern unbending primate. Born at London on 21 December
1118 of middle-class Norman stock,[1] he received a sound education at Merton priory and afterwards at one of the city grammar
schools. But he never rose to be a great scholar; when he became
archbishop he kept an instructor to expound the scriptures for
him; and at the Council of Tours (1163) he dared not preach
because of his lack of skill in the Latin tongue.[2] He received a
business training in the office of a relative, Osbert Huitdeniers,
a rich city magnate who was justiciar of London in 1141, when
the Empress Matilda for a brief space occupied the capital;[3]
and from a family friend of good social standing, Richer de
Laigle, with whom after the death of his parents he used to stay
in his school holidays, he acquired his liking for field sports, for
hunting and hawking, which stood him in good stead when in
after years he joined the court circle. It was also through friends
of his family that he gained an introduction to Archbishop
Theobald, in whose household we have seen him a brilliant
member of a brilliant group.[4] At an early stage in his career he
was marked out for advancement; he was employed by Theobald on important missions to Rome,[5] and while still in minor
orders he was comfortably provided for in the church. He himself recalls, when he was upbraided by Gilbert Foliot for his
ingratitude to the king to whom he owed everything, that before
he entered the king's service he was already in possession of the
archdeaconry of Canterbury, the provostship of Beverley, many

[1] His father Gilbert was a merchant of Rouen settled in London, who at one time
held the office of sheriff; his mother was a native of Caen.
[2] Fitz Stephen, *Materials*, iii. 38; Draco Normannicus (*Chronicles of Stephen* &c., ii.
744; quoted F. Barlow, *Letters of Arnulf of Lisieux* (Camden Soc.), p. xli).
[3] Round, *Commune of London*, pp. 114–16.
[4] Above, p. 196.
[5] He accompanied Theobald to Rome in 1143, he attended the Council of
Rheims in 1148, and, according to John of Salisbury (*Materials*, ii. 303), he frequently visited the *limina apostolorum* on business of the church of Canterbury Cf.
C. C. J. Webb, *Eng. Hist. Rev.* xlvi (1931), 261.

churches, more than one prebend, and not a few other benefices.[1] As he ascended the ladder of promotion he took the appropriate order. Thus he was ordained deacon on his appointment as archdeacon (1154), and priest on his appointment as archbishop (1162). His exceptional talents and usefulness had carried him by the time that he was forty-five to the highest position in the church. Every detail of his life has been collected by a dozen or more contemporary biographers; but they were writing, for the most part, panegyrics in an uncritical spirit, when both friends and enemies joined together to revere his memory in the tragic circumstances of his death. He had certain virtues: he led a pure life in an age when chastity, especially at court, was rare, and he was of a generous disposition; looked at dispassionately, however, he appears as a vain, obstinate, and ambitious man who sought always to keep himself in the public eye; he was above all a man of extremes, a man who knew no half measures. He did everything with exemplary thoroughness, whether as chief of the king's secretarial department, or when fighting at the head of his 700 knights, or conducting a delicate diplomatic negotiation; whether in the hunting-field or at a game of chess; whether at a church council, at Mass, or in suffering martyrdom. In that rapid transition from the gay, splendidly dressed courtier who romped with the king to the proud and austere priest who mortified his flesh by abstinence and flagellation and excelled in ostentatious acts of charity and humility, one can see a great actor superbly living the parts he was called upon to play. He had an amazing versatility which enabled him to change easily from, as he once expressed it, being 'a patron of play-actors and a follower of hounds to become a shepherd of souls'.[2] It has been said in comparing him with Anselm that Becket 'had a theory of what a saint ought to do and tried to do it, while Anselm was a saint naturally, without thinking about it'.[3] This is true of Becket's whole career; there was an element of artificiality in it all.

His public career belongs to domestic and international rather than to ecclesiastical politics. For the first eight years of Henry II's reign, as chancellor, he was altogether a secular figure, only drawing a substantial portion of his income from

[1] *Materials*, v. 515.   [2] Herbert of Bosham, *Materials*, iii. 290.
[3] Freeman, in a letter to Dean Hook, *Life and Letters* (ed. W. R. W. Stephens), i. 326.

the revenues of the church. For nearly six out of the eight years he was primate he was in exile in France, where he divided Europe on the question of the justice of his cause. In the first quarrel and the last no ecclesiastical principle was at stake. He did not, like his famous predecessors Lanfranc, Anselm, or Theobald, hand down a great legacy to the church; if anything he perpetuated an abuse—the immunity of clerks from secular punishment for their crimes. It has been justly said that insistence on his fame as a great churchman, which was partly factitious, has robbed him of a fame which was truer and better deserved, as the great minister of a great king.[1]

In 1154 he was appointed archdeacon of Canterbury. This office was of a secular rather than an ecclesiastical character, involving the charge of the legal work of the diocese, and it was commonly bestowed by the bishops on their own sons, nephews, or friends, who found it an easy and lucrative form of livelihood and a stepping-stone to higher promotion.[2] The reputation of archdeacons in the twelfth century was none of the best, for they were given to extortion and injustice. The king on one occasion, when he heard a complaint against their malpractices at York, declared that the archdeacons and rural deans yearly extorted more money from the inhabitants of his kingdom than he himself received in revenue.[3] They were also accused of keeping churches vacant in order that they themselves might receive the income.[4] It does not appear that Becket was more scrupulous than his fellows in the performance of his work; there is evidence that he exacted aids for his personal benefit in the diocese of Canterbury, and more than once he was severely reprimanded by the archbishop for neglect of his duties through his long absences abroad, and was even threatened with anathema and the loss of the emoluments of his archdeaconry.[5]

Although preferred to the chancellorship by Theobald and Henry of Winchester with the object of promoting the interest

[1] Freeman, *Contemporary Review*, xxii. 132, quoted by L. B. Radford, *Thomas of London*, p. 239.

[2] Five archdeacons were promoted to bishoprics in 1173: Ralph of Diceto, i. 368. One of them, Reginald, archdeacon of Salisbury, who became bishop of Bath, was a son of Jocelin, bishop of Salisbury. Cf. also Stubbs's introduction to Ralph of Diceto, i, p. xxvii.

[3] Fitz Stephen, *Materials*, iii. 44.

[4] Cf. the letter of Alexander III (Jaffé-Loewenfeld, *Regesta*, no. 13909) quoted by Dom A. Morey, *Bartholomew of Exeter*, 1937, pp. 91–2.

[5] *Materials*, v. 10–13.

of the church, he at once became totally absorbed in the affairs of state as king's secretary, soldier, diplomat, or judge; and when there was a clash of interests between church and state he was usually to be found advocating the views of the court party. The heavy taxation imposed on the church for the Toulouse campaign of 1159 was laid to his charge, and in the violent dispute between the bishop of Chichester and the abbot of Battle regarding exemption of the abbey from episcopal control, he supported the royal prerogative against ecclesiastical authority (1157), although afterwards as archbishop he repudiated any responsibility in the matter. He had not rewarded the confidence of the bishops who furthered his promotion in the hope that he would faithfully serve the interests of the church.

In May 1162, a little more than a year after the death of Theobald, Becket was nominated archbishop. Foreseeing the inevitable rupture, he only yielded reluctantly to the pressure put upon him by the king and the legate, Henry of Pisa. He may therefore be wholly exonerated from the charge brought against him by his enemies that he had been anxiously awaiting this exalted position and leapt into it with indecent haste. Though there were some, perhaps many, who, like the Empress Matilda and Gilbert Foliot, thought that the life of the chancellor had been too worldly to fit him for such an office, though the monks of Christ Church, Canterbury, can scarcely have approved of the appointment of a man who was neither monk nor priest, yet in the end the election was made with unanimity; and Thomas Becket was consecrated by Bishop Henry of Winchester on the Sunday after Whit-Sunday (3 June), a day henceforth in commemoration of the great event to be held as a feast in honour of the Holy Trinity.[1]

There can be no doubt of Henry's motive in promoting Becket to the see of Canterbury. He thought that if the chancellorship and the primacy were in the same trusted hands he would be able to arrest the growth of the church's pretensions which through the weakness of Stephen's position, through the closer relations with Rome, and particularly through the development of the canon law studiously fostered by Archbishop Theobald, had advanced beyond all bounds. The church courts

[1] This, however, was not the origin of the feast as sometimes supposed. It had been observed in English monasteries since the time of Dunstan. See Knowles, *Eng. Hist. Rev.* lxix (1954), 318.

no longer confined their activities, as in the Conqueror's time, to 'causes touching the rule of souls'.[1] The definition was vague and left a wide margin of debatable ground between the clearly spiritual and the clearly temporal pleas. Marriage, incest, and testamentary causes belonged without dispute to the former category; but it was possible for the church lawyers to interpret almost any question of contract as a matter of breach of faith, and hence a spiritual cause. Henry II would not have laid stress on the point that questions affecting lay fees or pleas of debt belonged to the secular court, had not the church sought to bring them within its own purview.[2] Moreover, the archdeacons and rural deans, as we have seen, were not over-scrupulous in their exercise of all this jurisdiction; they accused laymen on insufficient evidence and often proceeded with little regard to law or equity. There was the celebrated case in the time of Archbishop Theobald described by Fitz Stephen, of the citizen of Scarborough blackmailed by a rural dean who threatened to accuse his wife of adultery though there was no evidence against her (*sine alio accusatore*).[3] The church courts further claimed the exclusive right to judge and to punish their own order. They could not, however, pronounce a sentence of blood; they could imprison, but seldom did so owing to the expense of maintaining prisons; more commonly they inflicted a penance or at most degradation. Such penalties might serve as a deterrent to the more respectable and beneficed clergy, but they had no terror for the disreputable multitude of persons who, without occupation or scruple, swelled the lower ranks of the profession, for the bishops seem to have demanded no standard of education or moral worth as necessary requirements for ordination. Scandals were frequent, crimes were committed almost with impunity, and it was said that since the king's accession above a hundred murders had been perpetrated by clerks.[4]

Henry had hoped, with Becket's assistance, to check such infringements, and to correct such abuses. He was quickly disillusioned. On his appointment as archbishop Becket at once

[1] Ordinance separating the Spiritual and Temporal Courts (Liebermann, *Gesetze*, i. 485).
[2] Constitutions of Clarendon, ix and xv. Cf. Pollock and Maitland, *Hist. of Eng. Law*, ii. 197 f.
[3] *Materials*, iii. 43-4. Clause vi of the Constitutions of Clarendon sought to remedy this state of things.
[4] William of Newburgh, ii, c. 16 (anno 1163).

resigned the chancellorship; and instead of devoting himself to the interests of the Crown worked exclusively for those of the church; instead of placing his great business capacity at the disposal of the king, he used it to administer the estates and to recover the alienated lands of the see of Canterbury. The two came to open quarrelling soon after Henry's return from Normandy in January 1163. It is unquestionable that Becket's conduct was gratuitously aggressive; he opposed the king at every turn, even on issues of purely temporal concern. At a council held at Woodstock in July Henry demanded that the sheriff's aid (*auxilium vicecomitis*), a payment customarily made by the counties to the sheriffs by way of reward for their official services, should in future be appropriated and accounted at the exchequer. The facts are obscure, but his object seems to have been as much to get a more direct control over these local officers as to bring financial profit to himself. Whatever the rights and wrongs of the matter, Becket resisted and resisted with success; for the demand had to be withdrawn.[1] He frustrated Henry's plans of aggrandizing his family by prohibiting the marriage of his brother William with the rich heiress, Isabella de Warenne, the widow of Stephen's son William who had died on the Toulouse campaign (1159); and, disregarding the well-established custom, he excommunicated without consulting the king a tenant-in-chief, William of Eynesford, in consequence of a dispute about an advowson.[2] Then a series of unpleasant incidents, crimes committed by clerks which went unpunished or were punished with undue leniency, provoked the king to action: there was a case of manslaughter in the diocese of Salisbury; a rape followed by the murder of the injured girl's father in Worcestershire; the theft of a chalice near London; and the murder of a knight at Dunstable by a canon of Bedford named Philip of Brois who, after having been acquitted in the bishop of Lincoln's court, was brought before the lay court where he not only refused to plead but insulted the royal justice, Simon Fitz

---

[1] See Round, *Feudal England*, pp. 497 ff, and Salzman, *Henry II*, p. 197. There appears to be no evidence for the statement by W. A. Morris, *The Medieval English Sheriff*, p. 114, that the aid was 'probably in 1163 appropriated to the treasury'.

[2] Cf. the rule of William I given by Eadmer (*Hist. Nov.* i. 10), and reiterated in the Constitutions of Clarendon, c. vii. Henry felt strongly on this point, and issued instructions to Bishop John of Poitiers in this year (1163) forbidding him to excommunicate any of his barons without first consulting him. See Bishop John's letter to Becket, *Materials*, v. 39. Henry II claimed advowsons for his courts in the Constitutions of Clarendon (c. 1).

Peter. The king, to whom the matter was referred, demanded that the clerk should be tried again on the charge of murder and also for his contempt of court. But Becket gave him little satisfaction; he dismissed the first count as already decided and imposed a sentence of flogging and a temporary suspension of his benefice for the second. William, canon of Newburgh, a contemporary and a sober critic, admits that the bishops brought upon themselves the great contest that ensued 'since they were more intent upon defending the liberties and rights of the clergy than on correcting and restraining their vices'.[1]

It was to remedy these grave abuses that Henry at a council held at Westminster on 1 October 1163 claimed the right to punish criminous clerks who had been duly tried and degraded in the episcopal court. The bishops, though at first inclined to yield, were ultimately persuaded by Becket's somewhat casuistical arguments to refuse their consent; nor was their answer to the king's next demand that they should swear obedience to the ancient customs of the kingdom more satisfactory. All but one— Bishop Hilary of Chichester—qualified their consent with the evasive 'saving our order'. Henry did not conceal his displeasure, and before he left the city next morning he deprived the archbishop of the honors of Eye and Berkhamsted, which he still retained from the days of his chancellorship, and he withdrew his son Henry from his guardianship. A meeting of the two former friends at Northampton shortly afterwards did nothing to amend the situation; both used bitter expressions which only tended to widen the breach.

Becket's position, however, was not a strong one. Many of the bishops when they dispersed after the stormy council of Westminster veered round to the king's side. Their leader, Gilbert Foliot, was destined to play a leading part in the ensuing struggle. Successively prior of Cluny and Abbeville, abbot of Gloucester and bishop of Hereford, he was now (1163) translated to London with the special object that he might be near at hand to advise the king.[2] His long experience, his great learning, and his exemplary life might well have entitled him to expect that he and not Becket should have been elevated to the primacy on the death of Archbishop Theobald, and doubtless there was a cer-

[1] ii, c. 16.
[2] Cf. Alexander III's letter authorizing the translation (Foliot's letters, ed. Giles, i, ep. cxlvi).

tain element of jealousy in the bitterness with which he opposed his rival.[1] But there was no pettiness in his character, and he adopted the line he did because he was convinced by experience and by his extensive knowledge of the canon and civil law[2] that it was the right one. That there were two sides to the question even Becket's most devoted admirers were forced to admit. It was, however, the attitude of the pope, to whom he appealed, that most disheartened Becket. The position of Alexander III was a difficult one: an exile from Rome and confronted by a rival, he could not afford to lose so powerful an adherent as the king of England who had supported him from the first, and had indeed on one occasion prevented the triumph of the anti-pope Paschal.[3] At all costs he had to avoid driving Henry into the imperial camp. John, bishop of Poitiers, was saying no more than the truth when in 1163 he wrote to Becket that he could 'expect no help from the curia in anything that might offend the king'.[4] On the other hand, the pope could not altogether disregard the appeals of Becket who genuinely, if mistakenly, thought that he was advancing the best interests of the church. The archbishop was a sore embarrassment to Pope Alexander, who accordingly from the outset of the quarrel exerted his efforts both by letters and by legates to attain a compromise. He failed, however, to realize that he had to deal with men who would have nothing to do with compromise. His halting, uncertain attitude is easily understandable, and was perhaps the only attitude he could in the circumstances adopt. But so far from assisting to bring about a settlement, it had the effect of prolonging the dispute. In the present crisis he instructed his agent, Philip, abbot of L'Aumône, to urge Becket to submit to the king.

Discouraged by the result of his application to the pope, deprived of the counsel and support of his closest friend, John of Salisbury,[5] who, having fallen under the king's displeasure, was

[1] Cf. the interesting remarks on Foliot by John of Salisbury in the *Policraticus* (vii. 24), written some years before the quarrel. Foliot habitually judged his superiors in position harshly.

[2] 'tam in divino quam in humano jure prudentior'. Alexander III's letter above.

[3] Cf. Luchaire (in Lavisse, *Hist. de France*, iii. 44): 'c'est surtout à Henri II que le pape Alexandre devait sa victoire.'

[4] *Materials*, v. 56.

[5] Peter of Blois (Migne, *Pat. Lat.* ccvii, *ep.* 22, col. 80) described him as 'the hand and eye of the archbishop'.

living in exile on the Continent, and deserted by his fellow bishops, Becket had, momentarily, to give way. At Oxford in December he promised unreservedly to observe the customs.

Henry would have been wiser had he been content to let the matter rest there; his mistake was to codify these 'customs of his ancestors',[1] and to force the bishops to commit themselves publicly to obey a concrete and authoritative body of constitutions. This was the object of the council which was summoned to meet at Clarendon, a favourite hunting-lodge near Salisbury, in January 1164. These famous constitutions recapitulated what professed to be the customs enforced by the Norman kings. They may be briefly summarized as follows: clause i asserted the right of the king's court to decide actions relating to advowson, and clause ix those relating to lay fee, and the question whether lands in dispute were held by frankalmoin or lay fee was to be determined before the king's justice on the recognition of a jury, a form of procedure which came to be known as the assize *utrum*; pleas of debt were likewise reserved for the king's court (cl. xv). Another clause (vi) protected laymen from being sued by archdeacons on untrustworthy or insufficient evidence; they were only to be arraigned by responsible and lawful accusers and witnesses. Provision was also made to deal with men whom, on account of their local influence, no one dared to bring to justice, by empowering the sheriff to empanel a jury of twelve men of the neighbourhood who on oath should declare the truth, a procedure similar to that formulated in the case of lay criminals by the assize of Clarendon two years later. Other clauses followed directly the rules laid down by William the Conqueror to govern the relations of church and state. So the clergy were forbidden to leave the country (cl. iv) or to carry appeals beyond the court of the archbishop, that is, to Rome, without the king's consent (cl. viii); the king's tenants-in-chief and ministers were not to be excommunicated nor their lands placed under interdict without his permission (cl. vii). Clause xii laid down the practice regarding vacant sees and abbacies—the right of the king to enjoy the revenues and the electoral procedure—which had become recognized in the reign of Henry I.

It was, however, on the famous third clause, which outlined Henry's plan for dealing with clerks charged with criminal

---

[1] Preamble to the Constitutions of Clarendon.

offences, that the great struggle turned.[1] The king was moderate in his demands. He was careful not to claim the right to try criminous clerks as appears to have been done before Becket intervened;[2] he did not even claim the handing over, the *traditio*, of the condemned or confessed criminal;[3] he simply required that after a clerk had been tried, convicted, and degraded in the bishop's court, the church should no longer afford him protection. The royal officer, who was to be present at the trial, could then carry him off to undergo such punishment as a layman in like case would suffer. It was against this 'double punishment' that Becket so violently protested, quoting repeatedly from Jerome's commentary on the prophet Nahum 'For God judges not twice for the same offence'.[4] But he was not on sure ground here. He was taking his stand, not on what was the law, but what should, in his view, be the law. Henry in this matter was relying on the advice of men learned in both the civil and the canon law.[5] Two canonists, who were writing at the very time of the great controversy, Rufinus and Stephen of Tournai, were of the opinion that a clerk should be degraded and then handed over for punishment by the secular court.[6] Henry's proposal was in accord both with general practice and with the law of the church; and it was only after Becket's murder and largely, no doubt, as a result of it that Alexander by the decretal *At si clerici* forbade the *traditio curiae* for the future.[7]

The Constitutions then represented not unfairly the practice

[1] For the interpretation of this clause and its relation to canon law see R. Génestal, *Le Privilegium Fori en France* (1924), ii, ch. v; Maitland, 'Henry II and the Criminous Clerks' in *Roman Canon Law in the Church of England* (1898); and Z. N. Brooke, *The English Church and the Papacy* (1931).

[2] Brooke, op. cit., p. 204.   [3] R. Génestal, op. cit. ii. 100.

[4] For this text in canon law see Brooke, op. cit., p. 205, n. 1. In 1163 Becket himself sentenced a clerk, whom he had degraded, to abjure the realm (Herbert of Bosham in *Materials*, iii. 267). But presumably as the degradation and the outlawry were inflicted by the same authority, he regarded them both as parts of one and the same punishment.

[5] Herbert of Bosham, *Materials*, iii. 266.

[6] Cf. Handley W. R. Lillie, S.J., in the *Clergy Review*, viii (1934), 274 f.

[7] c. 4. X. ii. 1. Cf. Génestal, op. cit., pp. 20 ff.; cf. also p. 94: 'Tout d'abord la règle appliquée est partout celle qui ressort du Décret de Gratien: dégradation et livraison . . . En Angleterre, puis en Normandie, c'est l'intransigeance de Thomas Becket qui fait disparaitre la vieille procédure franque et qui fait même interdire d'une manière générale par le pape toute livraison après dégradation.' Alexander's decretal was reversed by Innocent III's decretal *Novimus* (c. 27. X. v. 40) which sanctions this *traditio curiae seculari* very much in accordance with the procedure of cl. 3 of the Constitutions of Clarendon. Cf. Maitland, op. cit., p. 144; Lillie, op. cit., pp. 280-1.

of the past.[1] Yet it was one thing to promise obedience to vague customs, quite another to written law. The demand had the effect of reuniting the bishops in opposition to the Crown; they were standing 'motionless and unperturbed' in the face of the king's fury and the threat of armed force when to their astonishment their leader suddenly yielded and agreed, as he put it, to perjure himself.[2] Though he managed to evade setting his seal to the objectionable document, he gave his consent 'in good faith and without guile', and bade his fellow bishops do likewise. With this the opposition collapsed.

But the commission of the customs to writing had another injurious result: it drove the pope, to whom they were sent for ratification, on to Becket's side. However well disposed Alexander III might be towards the king, he could not give his written approval to usages which in some particulars were admittedly against the canons of the church. Six he could 'tolerate' but the rest he unequivocally condemned.[3] Becket for his part soon repented of the weakness he had exhibited at the council of Clarendon. He imposed upon himself exaggerated penances, even to the extent of abstaining from saying mass until he had obtained the pope's absolution for his perjury. Twice in his despair he tried to slip away from Romney across the Channel, but contrary winds or untrustworthy sailors frustrated his attempts to escape in this way from his difficulties.

Far greater troubles than Becket had already experienced were, however, yet to come. Hitherto the king had acted a little arbitrarily perhaps, but justly and certainly in the public interest. His conduct at the council of Northampton in October was both outrageous and undignified. This council had been summoned to hear an appeal of John the Marshal in a suit relating to a Sussex estate which had gone against him in the court of the archbishop. A hearing of the case had been previously arranged at Westminster, but Becket had excused himself from attending on the ground of sickness, whether real or feigned remains in doubt, and at the same time alleged a flaw in the Marshal's plea. When he presented himself at Northampton he was condemned unheard for contempt of court (for so

[1] See Brooke, op. cit., pp. 202–6.
[2] See Foliot's letter, *Materials*, v. 527–8.
[3] The Constitutions with the papal verdict on them are printed in *Materials*, v. 73.

the king regarded his previous non-appearance) and sentenced
to a substantial fine. Moreover, not content with this success,
the king proceeded to call upon the archbishop to account for
moneys which had passed through his hands during the period
of his chancellorship, the revenues of the honors of Eye and
Berkhamsted, a sum of £500 lent to him for the Toulouse campaign of 1159, another sum borrowed from a Jew on the king's
security, and finally for the revenues of vacant sees and monasteries, the whole amounting to an enormous sum. A composition
of 2,000 marks for all the claims was offered and declined, and
it became clear that Henry was now bent on nothing less than
the complete ruin of his former favourite. The bishops were
much perplexed and divided in their views, some pressing the
archbishop to submit, others even thinking that things had
come to such a pass that he had best resign his office to save the
church from ruin; only a few, like the aged Bishop Henry of
Winchester, took his part. In the last scene of this memorable
meeting, which lasted more than a week, Becket entered the
court bearing the cross in his own hands, signifying in this
spectacular fashion that he claimed the protection of the church
against the violence of the king. 'He was always a fool and
always will be'[1] was the comment of Gilbert Foliot when he was
asked by one of the clergy to remonstrate against such behaviour, and it is true that it only tended further to exasperate
the king. Throughout the proceedings Becket had pleaded in
vain that he had only been summoned to answer in the case of
John the Marshal, that he could not be expected to answer
concerning the financial details of his chancellorship without
due notice, that he had indeed spent all that he had then
received and more besides on the king's service, and that on
his elevation to the primacy he had been released from all
liabilities incurred in his former position. He had then appealed
to the pope and inhibited the bishops from again sitting in
judgement upon him. The bishops, thus restrained, with the
king's leave lodged a counter-appeal to the pope against
Becket's breach of the Constitutions of Clarendon which he had
sworn to observe, and the king called upon the earl of Leicester,
the justiciar, to pronounce the sentence upon him. But the
sentence was never heard; the archbishop refused to listen and
angrily left the council chamber amid shouts of 'Traitor'. That

[1] 'Bone homo, semper fuit stultus et semper erit.' Fitz Stephen in *Materials*, iii. 57.

night, disguised and by devious routes, he escaped from Northampton, and made his way to the coast and across the Channel to the safety of the Continent.

In England Becket's flight created little excitement. The usual measures were taken: an embassy of bishops and barons was dispatched to lay the king's case before the pope at Sens, and the revenues of the see of Canterbury were confiscated. Henry's vindictiveness in banishing from the country or thrusting into prison the archbishop's relatives and friends[1] was naturally condemned, but otherwise his actions at this time seem to have met with the general approval of both laymen and churchmen. William of Newburgh, a man of sound common sense, gives it as his personal opinion that the archbishop's conduct could not be regarded as praiseworthy, however much it might have proceeded from a laudable zeal, since it served no useful purpose and only tended further to incense the king.[2] Becket in fact found few sympathizers in England; and it is significant that his prolonged absence abroad seems to have made no difference in the working of the government. In spite of the position which he had occupied in previous years, he seems to have been little missed.[3]

Abroad the affair took on an international aspect. The leading powers sought to make political capital out of it. Louis VII, already the protector of Pope Alexander, became now the protector of Becket, for he had much to gain from the embarrassing position in which his formidable Angevin antagonist was placed in consequence of the archbishop's flight. But, while taking what political advantage he could from the situation, he at the same time made continual and genuine attempts to heal the quarrel. In the course of the six years 1165–70 he arranged with Henry no less than twelve interviews, ten of which actually took place, where reconciliation of the king and the archbishop was, if not the only, at least a prominent subject of discussion.[4] The

---

[1] Cf. an entry on the Pipe Roll of 1203 (5 John, p. 103): A certain Adam of Hales and his brothers owed '20 marks for having possession of their father's land in Shoreham of which their father who was with blessed Thomas in his persecution was by the will of King Henry and for no other reason disseised and imprisoned'.

[2] ii, c. 16.

[3] This is pointed out by Stubbs in his preface to the Pipe Roll of *12 Hen. II* (p. xii).

[4] See L. Halphen, 'Les Entrevues des rois Louis VII et Henri II durant l'exil de Thomas Becket en France', in *Mélanges d'histoire offerts à Charles Bémont* (1913), pp. 151 ff.

emperor for his part saw in the circumstances a possible opportunity of detaching Henry from the side of the legitimate pope.
It was dread of this happening that prevented Alexander from
adopting a more decisive policy; and even the king of France
admitted to John of Salisbury that for this reason he could not
undertake to urge the pope to stronger measures.[1] Their fears,
indeed, were far from groundless. More than once Henry was
on the brink of deserting the pope: at the diet of Würzburg
(June 1165), for example, his envoys—whether in obedience to
instructions is not clear and their action was afterwards repudiated—pledged their master's allegiance to the anti-pope,
Paschal III; and in the following spring Henry wrote in a
moment of irritation to the imperial chancellor that he had
been long seeking a good excuse for withdrawing his support
from Pope Alexander and his treacherous cardinals.[3] But it
never came quite to this, for Alexander wisely so tempered his
acts as to avoid giving unnecessary offence. Thus when he
authorized Becket to use ecclesiastical censures against those
who invaded the property of his church, he expressly exempted
the king, and when a little later (April 1166) he bestowed on
Becket a legatine commission throughout England, he excepted
the diocese of York.[3] Nevertheless, the situation was involved
and intricate, and much depended on the diplomatic tact with
which it was handled.

Although Henry was himself a good diplomat, he had in
former years entrusted delicate business of this sort to his
chancellor, Becket, who managed it with supreme success. Now
that Becket's services were no longer at his disposal, he had to
rely on men of less commanding personality. However, the men
who formed his *corps diplomatique* during the critical years from
1164 to 1170 were shrewd and able politicians, whose significance may be judged from the bitter invective levelled against
them by the archbishop and his partisans. John of Oxford,
afterwards bishop of Norwich, Richard of Ilchester, archdeacon
of Poitiers and later bishop of Winchester, both royal judges,
and John Cumin, who ended a strenuous life in the king's service
as archbishop of Dublin, were the most prominent among

---

[1] *Materials*, v. 162.
[2] Ibid. v. 428.
[3] Ibid. v. 317 and 328. The Pope was able in November 1165 to return to Rome
where he was in a stronger position to adopt a more definite line of policy. Cf. his
letter to Becket, ibid. v. 179.

Henry's ambassadors. It was they who were sent on diplomatic missions to Rome, to the imperial court, and to France, they that carried through the complicated intrigues to which Becket's exile on the Continent gave rise.[1]

We need not dwell on the tedious details of the long struggle. Becket in his refuge in the Cistercian abbey of Pontigny employed his time in study and in conducting a voluminous correspondence with his friends and enemies. While seeking to justify his own conduct, he dilated upon his supposed injuries. The tone of his letters became more and more querulous and acrimonious, rising in crescendo till it reached a climax with the famous missives in which he announced the sentences of excommunication delivered at Vezelay against his adversaries.[2] Richard de Lucy, the justiciar, and Jocelin of Balliol as the prime authors of the Constitutions of Clarendon, were especially singled out, but all who had observed or supported them were included in the condemnation; John of Oxford and Richard of Ilchester were excommunicated for having had dealings with the schismatic pope, and Rannulf de Broc and others for having 'usurped' the possessions of the see of Canterbury.[3] Even the king himself was threatened with similar treatment. The bishops remonstrated and appealed to the pope, while the king retaliated by bringing pressure to bear on the Cistercian order to obtain the archbishop's removal from Pontigny. But it was again the political situation which saved Henry from the effects of Becket's violence; for the pope, hard pressed in the autumn of 1166 by the emperor's invading armies, could ill afford to increase the number of his enemies. He therefore annulled the sentences passed by Becket, inhibited him for the time being from further molesting the king, and appointed legates, one of whom—William of Pavia—was prejudiced against Becket, even, in fact, his avowed enemy,[4] to arbitrate in the quarrel (December 1166). The cardinals proceeded with their task in the dilatory way commonly followed by papal legates, and the

[1] See for John Cumin, J. Armitage Robinson, *Somerset Historical Essays* (British Academy, 1921), pp. 90 ff.

[2] *Materials*, v. 392 ff.

[3] Rannulf de Broc farmed the Canterbury estates after their confiscation. Cf. *Pipe Roll 12 Hen. II*, p. 114.

[4] So Becket declared in a letter to his envoy at the papal court (*Materials*, vi. 151). In a letter to Cardinal Hyacinth he says he will not admit such arbitration (ibid. 215).

whole of the year 1167 was frittered away without anything being accomplished.[1] The archbishop was prepared to agree to any and every proposal, but with the exasperating evasive qualification *salvo honore Dei* and *salvo ordine suo*.[2] It was insistence on these formulae which wrecked the chances of a reconciliation when the two opponents met for the first time since their quarrel on 6 January 1169 at Montmirail in Maine. Becket's best friends, even the clerks who shared his exile, urged him to omit the offending words; but in vain, and a great opportunity for peace was lost. Another conference held in the autumn at Montmartre outside Paris miscarried on a point no less trivial: all was going smoothly, everything of importance had been conceded, but Henry refused to ratify the compact by giving Becket the kiss of peace.

So the dispute dragged on into its sixth and last year. The archbishop by his stubbornness, by his angry self-righteous letters, by his sentences of excommunication and his threats of interdict,[3] was trying the patience not only of his enemies but even of his intimate friends, when a fresh issue put new life into the struggle. This was the coronation of the king's son. The circumstances of his early life had doubtless made Henry particularly anxious to have the succession settled beyond all question. In the very first year of his reign (at Wallingford in April 1155) he had required the barons to swear allegiance to his son William, who was not yet two years old, and in the event of his death, to Henry, an infant of little more than a month. William, as had been expected, died, and the oath of fealty had been repeated to Henry in 1162.[4] It was in fact the last official act of Becket as chancellor. The king now desired to go a step further, to proceed to a crowning. Although without a precedent in England,[5] coronation of the heir in the lifetime of the father was a long-

---

[1] This was the first of several commissions appointed by the pope to arbitrate between Henry and Becket. But they all failed.

[2] Cf. *Materials*, vi. 517.

[3] Becket had excommunicated Gilbert Foliot and other supporters of the king in the previous spring; they were, however, absolved by the pope's instructions in February 1170.

[4] That some informal coronation took place on this occasion is implied by the fact that a crown of gold and regalia were prepared for the young prince. See *Pipe Roll 8 Hen. II*, p. 43, and Salzmann, *Henry II*, p. 52 n.

[5] It had been tried without success by Stephen, when he attempted to get Archbishop Theobald to crown his son Eustace in 1152, but the pope had intervened to prevent it.

established method of securing the succession on the Continent, and the plan was readily accepted by the barons; but there remained the very serious difficulty that the right of performing the ceremony was the undoubted prerogative of the archbishop of Canterbury, an exile and the king's sworn enemy. Henry pressed the pope to grant permission to the archbishop of York to act in his place; and once, in a moment of weakness, Alexander had indeed done so, though he revoked the licence before it was used.[1] The king, therefore, impatient of delay, proceeded without the requisite authority. At Westminster on 14 June 1170 the young Henry was duly crowned by Archbishop Roger of York in the presence of six assisting bishops. The event had damaging effects on the king's position: it united his enemies, all of whom for different reasons had cause to complain. The pope's prohibition had been ignored; the king of France's daughter had not been crowned with her husband, the young Henry; and Becket, of course, had suffered a fresh affront. Nothing was calculated so surely to arouse the angry passions of an archbishop of Canterbury as an attempt to infringe the prerogatives of his metropolitan see. There had been wild, ridiculous, and most undignified scenes produced by such attempted invasions. Thus at the coronation of Adeliza, the second wife of Henry I, in 1121, when Archbishop Ralph found the king already wearing his crown, he refused to proceed with the service until it was removed and replaced with his own hands, for he imagined that some other bishop had usurped his right. In 1176 a dispute over prerogative rights between the archbishops of Canterbury and York ended in blows 'fists, sticks, and clubs'.[2] Accordingly this last outrage, as he deemed it, superseded in Becket's mind all other points of difference between himself and the king.

England was lying under threat of interdict, when inconsequently, as it seems, with dramatic suddenness, within little more than a month of the coronation, the parties met at La Ferté Bernard near Fréteval some miles to the north of Vendôme, and went through a form of reconciliation. What motives induced these obstinate men, after six years of bitter enmity, without even discussing the issues for which they had originally

---

[1] The date of the letter granting the licence (*Materials*, vi. 206) is uncertain; the letter cancelling it (ibid. vii. 217) is definitely dated 26 February 1170; but there is some doubt whether it was in fact delivered before the coronation took place.

[2] Giraldus, *De Instr. Princ.* viii. 218. Cf. *Gesta Henrici*, i. 112; Diceto, i. 405; Gervase of Canterbury, i. 258.

fought (not a word was said about the Constitutions of Clarendon), to come together in friendship, it is not easy to understand.
Perhaps it was that Becket thought that once back in England
he could take more effective measures against the bishops who
had taken part in the coronation. Certain it is that his first acts
after the reconciliation were directed to this end. Having procured letters of authority from the pope, he served sentences of
suspension on the offending bishops, and on those who had
especially injured him, those of London and Salisbury, he added
excommunication as well. The next day (1 December) he
landed at Sandwich. He may have been warmly received by the
clergy and people at Canterbury, as the biographers emphasize,
but he was given anything but a welcome from those in authority:
Gervase of Cornhill, the sheriff of Kent, attempted to resist his
landing; Rannulf de Broc, who had administered the Canterbury
estates during his exile, met him with studied insults; and the
young king Henry, his former friend and pupil, refused to
receive him at his court at Woodstock. On Christmas Day the
archbishop retaliated by publicly denouncing and excommunicating his enemies from the pulpit of his cathedral. In the
meanwhile three of the suspended bishops, those of York,
London, and Salisbury, had proceeded to Normandy to lay
before the king their complaints of Becket's relentless conduct.
Their report, no doubt exaggerated, threw the king into a
paroxysm of rage and drew from him the rash words which led
to the martyrdom.[1] Four knights of his household, Reginald
Fitz Urse, William de Tracy, Hugh de Morville, and Richard le
Breton, without waiting till the king's anger had cooled,
hastened to England, and before the messenger sent by the
king to prevent any violence could arrive, Thomas Becket was
murdered in his cathedral.

No single event of this age so profoundly shook the Christian
world. Not only in England or in France, where he had spent the
last six years of his life, but everywhere throughout Christendom
he was venerated as a martyr. Within little more than two years
of his death he was, in response to popular demand, canonized
by Pope Alexander III (21 February 1173); in a short time an
order of knights of St. Thomas of Acre was instituted in the

[1] The shortness of time between Christmas and the murder (29 December)
almost precludes the hypothesis that it was the Christmas anathemas which gave
rise to the king's fury.

Holy Land. Nothing is more striking than the almost instanta-
neous birth of the cult of St. Thomas. And the cult grew and
prospered: antiphons were composed and sung in his honour;[1]
miracles in plenty were attributed to him;[2] churches were dedicated to him; and representations of him appear in every
medium, in every European country, in every age until the
Reformation, when the protestant iconoclasts, especially in
England, did what they could to obliterate his memory. In
stained glass and manuscript illuminations, in sculpture and
fresco, the details of his life and particularly the martyrdom are
elaborately portrayed. The cult was specially disseminated by
the daughters of Henry II in the dominions of their respective
husbands. Thus the earliest extant examples—a representation
of the martyr in enamel on a gospel cover in the cathedral of
Capua (? 1175–6) and a mosaic in the cathedral of Monreale
(? 1188–9)—come from the Norman kingdom of the south
whose king, William the Good, married in 1177 Henry's
daughter Joan; some fine wall-paintings at Brunswick may be
traced to the marriage of Henry the Lion with Henry's daughter
Matilda (1168); and the early Spanish examples to Eleanor's
marriage with Alfonso IX of Castile in 1170. There are also
portrayals of Becket at places closely connected with his life,
for instance, at Sens (a late-twelfth-century statue) and at
Rome (a fresco).[3] But in countries quite unconnected with the
Becket story there is a rich iconography: in Scandinavia, for
example, and especially in Iceland, which produced, besides, a
long saga of the life of the martyr.[4] In the later middle ages,
and very likely earlier, year by year the death-scene was re-
enacted in the cathedral; and men and women of every rank of
society eagerly performed the pilgrimage to Canterbury with
almost the same sense of satisfaction as if they had journeyed to
Jerusalem or Compostella.

When Henry recovered from the first stunning shock he
found himself in an awkward position. His continental lands

[1] See the early-thirteenth-century antiphon in English printed by Carleton
Brown, *English Lyrics of the Thirteenth Century*, pp. 67, 196 f.

[2] On this subject see E. A. Abbott, *St. Thomas of Canterbury, his Death and
Miracles*, 2 vols., 1898.

[3] See Tancred Borenius, 'The Iconography of St. Thomas Becket', in *Archaeologia*, lxxix (1929), and *St. Thomas Becket in Art* (1932). For the dating of the examples
at Capua and Monreale see Evelyn Jamison in *England and the Mediterranean
Tradition* (edited by the Warburg and Courtauld Institutes, 1945), pp. 25–9.

[4] *Thomas Saga Erkibyskups* has been edited by Magnusson for the Rolls Series.

had been placed under interdict; his envoys at Rome were refused an audience by the pope. And though these stern measures were subsequently relaxed, he deemed it prudent not to await the arrival of the legates who were dispatched to Normandy to dictate the conditions under which he might receive absolution for his supposed complicity in the murder. He therefore took the opportunity to carry into effect his long premeditated visit to Ireland. He was absent from October 1171 to April 1172. His plan was a good one. In the interval the angry passions of his opponents had somewhat abated, and he found on his return the cardinal legates prepared to negotiate on reasonable terms.

On 21 May 1172 Henry was formally reconciled with the church in the cathedral of Avranches; for though he declared on oath that he had neither ordered nor wished for the arch-bishop's death, he admitted that his unguarded words might have occasioned it. The terms on which he was granted forgive-ness had been already imparted to him by the legates a couple of days before. He was required to provide for the support of 200 knights during one year for the defence of Jerusalem and himself to take the cross for a period of three years unless excused by the pope (it was in fact excused, the king agreeing to found three monasteries instead);[1] he was to allow appeals to Rome;[2] and he must restore the possessions of Canterbury as they were one year before the archbishop's exile; he was also to make restitution to those who had suffered on account of their sup-port of the archbishop. In the official version[3] there was no specific mention of the Constitutions of Clarendon. All that was said on the subject was that Henry should renounce the customs which had been introduced into the kingdom in his time to the detriment of the church, which, Henry commented in a letter to Bishop Bartholomew of Exeter, 'I reckon to be few or none'. Indeed, he had always affirmed that the Constitutions were 'ancient customs', and he founded his whole case on this assump-tion. We may perhaps see in the ambiguous phraseology of this condition the hand of the ingenious Arnulf of Lisieux who, we

---

[1] Below, p. 229.
[2] Below, pp. 218-9.
[3] *Materials*, vii. 516-18. The absolution was repeated at Avranches on 27 Sep-tember after the pope had authorized the terms. The terms given in the pope's letter dated 2 September 1172, which is printed by Charles Johnson, *Eng. Hist. Rev.* lii (1937), 466-7, do not differ materially.

know, conferred with the legates to modify the terms as originally drafted in Henry's favour.

Unless, therefore, expressly revoked, the customs stood, and were in fact generally enforced. On questions of jurisdiction, the conflict of courts may easily be exaggerated. The same bishops and archdeacons often presided over the lay courts as they did over the spiritual; it might be more advantageous for a clergy-man to appear before a secular tribunal than before the court Christian. Alan, successively monk and prior of Christ Church, Canterbury, and abbot of Tewkesbury, a biographer of Becket and a great upholder of the privileges of the churches over which he ruled, became an itinerant justice and tried all manner of pleas of the Crown and assizes on the western circuit; nor did he find it against his conscience to appear before the king's court as plaintiff or defendant in pleas of advowson in strict accordance with the first clause of the Constitutions.[1] Indeed, if the bishops meddled with this matter they did so at a heavy risk. If it came to the notice of the secular authorities, they got into serious trouble; the bishop of Durham, for instance, was fined the large sum of 500 marks for venturing to hold a plea of advowson in the court Christian.[2] On one technical point Pope Alexander III even recognized an exception to the ordinary rules *secundum consuetudinem Anglicanam*.[3] It became the settled law that once the word advowson was mentioned in the church court the action was stopped.[4] Writs of Prohibition, which were probably instituted in the years immediately following, and with the object of implementing the Constitutions, stayed proceedings in the spiritual courts in pleas claimed by the Crown. Such writs had the effect of limiting the sphere of ecclesiastical jurisdiction and went far towards defining the faint line which divided spiritual and temporal jurisdiction.[5] The cognizance of disputes relating to lay fee, the subject of clause nine of the Constitutions, remained without question with the secular courts

---

[1] *Pipe Roll 1 Jo., passim; Curia Regis Rolls,* i. 280, 435.

[2] *Pipe Roll 30 Hen. II* (1184), p. 37.

[3] c. 19, X. iii. 38, quoted M. Cheney, *Eng. Hist. Rev.* lvi (1941), 193.

[4] *Curia Regis Rolls,* viii. 75 (1219): 'prohibitum est ei ne teneat aliquod placitum in quo fiat mentio de advocatione'. For the writs of prohibition on advowsons see Glanvill, iv. 13, 14. Cf. also J. W. Gray in *Eng. Hist. Rev.* lxvii (1952), 481.

[5] For the subject of Prohibitions see the important series of articles by G. B. Flahiff, C.S.B., in *Mediaeval Studies* of the Pontifical Institute of Mediaeval Studies of Toronto, vols. iii, vi, vii (1941–5). Many of those who obtained writs of prohibition were themselves clerics.

and was openly conceded by Pope Alexander III in a Bull of
the year 1178 which came to be incorporated in the canon law.[1]
The secular jurisdiction over the property of the church came
in course of time to be extended in this way to cover almost all the
land held in frankalmoign; the antithesis to lay fee became not
free alms but merely land consecrated to parish churches—the
parson's freehold. The Crown was equally successful in its claim
of jurisdiction in pleas of chattels and debts (Constitutions, cl.
14, 15) unless they arose from marriage or testamentary causes.
Already at the opening of the thirteenth century men were
being severely dealt with, amerced, or thrown into prison, if
they dared to plead on such matters in the court Christian.[2]

The most remarkable omission from the terms of Avranches
was the question of the criminous clerks. It was perhaps too
complicated a matter to be decided hurriedly, and required
further investigation. But it could not be ignored, for it had
been made the chief issue by the martyred archbishop. Ultimately, in 1176, a definite agreement was reached. In a letter to
the pope Henry undertook that in future clerks should not be
brought before a secular judge for any crime or misdemeanour
except for forest offences.[3] But it was not so simple a business
for a clerk accused of a felony to get the benefit of his order. He
came in course of time to be hedged about by elaborate for-
malities and procedure—the claiming by the bishop's officer,
the proving of his clergy, the preliminary hearing and the taking
of evidence in the lay court, the confiscation of his chattels, the
lingering in prison while all this was happening—before he
could arrive at the relatively comfortable security of the court
of Christianity; and in the process he might be surreptitiously
done to death, 'hanged privily by night or in the luncheon hour'
as the clergy complained in the next century.[4]

To the pope, however, a matter of far greater concern than
the treatment of criminous clerks was the freedom of appeal to

---

[1] c. 7, X. iv. 17. Ralph de Diceto (ed. Stubbs), i. 427. The Writ of Prohibition is
given by Glanvill, xii, cc. 21, 22. For fines imposed for pleading concerning lay fee
in court Christian see *Pipe Roll 29 Hen. II* (1183), pp. 12, 15.

[2] *Curia Regis Rolls*, i. 433; ii. 28.   [3] Ralph de Diceto, i. 410.

[4] For Benefit of Clergy see R. Génestal, *Le Privilegium Fori*, ii, particularly
chapter v; for the procedure in England see A. L. Poole in *Essays in Honour of James
Tait*, pp. 239 ff., and C. R. Cheney in *Eng. Hist. Rev.* li (1936), 215 ff. where a
rather different view is taken. The complaints of the clergy in 1237 and 1257 are
given in the Burton Annals (*Annales Monastici*, i), p. 255, and Matthew Paris,
Additamenta, Chron. Maj., vi. 356.

Rome; and here he won at Avranches a conspicuous success. Henry promised that henceforth he would not impede such appeals, provided that, if the appellant was held in suspicion, he would give an assurance that he intended no harm to the king or kingdom. The concession was probably inevitable. The practice of calling in the authority of Rome to settle ecclesiastical disputes had become common in the reign of Stephen. Causes great and small, dealing with all manner of different questions, were referred to the pope, who either dealt with them himself or more usually appointed men on the spot, judge-delegates, to hear and decide them with the full weight of papal authority. By 1164, when the king attempted to check it by the Constitutions of Clarendon, appeal to Rome had become an integral part of the ecclesiastical system. It was too firmly established to be lightly abandoned. When, therefore, by the settlement at Avranches the embargo was removed, the steady flow of suits to Rome was resumed once more without let or hindrance, and with ever-increasing frequency.[1]

In other respects the royal authority over the church was exercised in much the same way as before. John of Oxford, now bishop of Norwich, for example, received a sharp reprimand when, in contravention to the seventh clause of the Constitutions, he excommunicated the earl of Arundel without the king's approval.[2] Papal legates could not enter the kingdom without permission which might be withheld;[3] and bishops could not attend ecclesiastical councils abroad without the king's licence.[4]

Moreover, the king controlled elections to bishoprics and abbacies in accordance with the procedure laid down in the Constitutions of Clarendon (cl. 12). He had no objection to the

[1] Z. N. Brooke, 'The Effect of Becket's Murder on Papal Authority in England', in *Cambridge Historical Journal*, ii. 213 ff., argues that this concession opened a new era in the history of the church in England and that the canon law only now became really operative. He, however, neglects the earlier evidence and relies for his conclusions on the collections of decretals which were made at a later date with the express intention of bringing together for reference the letters of the great lawyer, Alexander III. See M. Cheney, 'The Compromise of Avranches of 1172 and the Spread of Canon Law in England', *Eng. Hist. Rev.* lvi (1941), 177 ff.

[2] Giraldus Cambrensis, *Opera*, vii. 70.

[3] John of Anagni, for example, who arrived at Dover in 1189, was forbidden to proceed farther *nisi per mandatum regis. Gesta Ricardi*, ii. 97; Hoveden, iii. 23.

[4] Hoveden, ii. 171 (Lateran Council of 1179). Cf. the letter of Alexander III in 1163 when he agreed that the attendance of English bishops at the Council of Tours should not establish a precedent prejudicial to the customs of the kingdom, *Materials*, v. 33.

election being 'free' so long as he was able to get his own nominee elected. His method is well illustrated by a writ which his irresponsible son, the young king, quoted in a memorandum sent to Pope Alexander in 1173. It refers to the vacancy at Winchester and runs as follows:[1]

'Henry, king of the English &c. to his faithful monks of the church of Winchester, greeting.

'I order you to hold a free election, but, nevertheless, I forbid you to elect anyone except Richard my clerk, the archdeacon of Poitiers.'

By this means the king availed himself of the opportunity presented by the large number of vacant sees at the time of Becket's death to bolster up the bench of bishops with his own supporters. The six who were appointed at a meeting in London in 1173 were drawn from the court party and included such men as Geoffrey Ridel and Richard of Ilchester, the archdeacon of Poitiers, both of whom had been conspicuous for their hostility to Becket throughout the long struggle. Henry's immediate object was no doubt to secure the support of the church against the rebellion of the young Henry which was already planned and known. The latter, from political rather than ecclesiastical motives, attempted to frustrate his father's policy by protests and appeals to Rome, and so far succeeded that the consecration of the new bishops was postponed for more than a year. Nevertheless, the desired result was achieved: during the rebellion and afterwards the church remained loyal and made no effort to interfere with the king's conduct of ecclesiastical affairs. Although as a result of negotiations with the legate Hugh Pierleone Henry promised in 1176 that he would not keep churches vacant beyond a year except when there was 'urgent and evident necessity', such urgent and evident necessity conveniently presented itself when it suited his purpose. Even William Rufus can scarcely have made a better income out of the revenues of the church than did Henry II. That seven English sees stood vacant in 1172 might be expected from the long absence of the archbishop from England; but that seven should be void in 1184 and, except for two, remained so for several years is justified by no such excuse, and can only be explained on the ground that the income accruing from them was too great a temptation to the avaricious king.

[1] Delisle-Berger, *Recueil des Actes de Henri II*, i. 587.

The net receipts arising from vacant churches in the former year amounted to over £4,000, in the latter to over £2,300, while York alone was bringing in a net annual profit of about £1,000 during the last eight years of Henry's reign.[1] That the church yielded tamely to the royal policy may be attributed in part, as has been noticed, to the docile disposition of the new bishops, in part to its lack of leaders. Richard, the prior of Dover, who in 1174 was elected to the primacy of Canterbury, was a feeble and ineffective person; his weakness was responsible, in the view of Richard of Ilchester, for the failure of the church to profit by the martyrdom of Becket.[2] He was followed in 1184 by the Cistercian Baldwin who, though a distinguished scholar and a deeply religious man, was injudicious and too austere to be a good leader, and he became involved in a long and bitter quarrel with the monks of Christ Church of whose easy and luxurious mode of living he could not approve.

Henry's successors continued the same policy of control. The four bishops appointed at the council of Pipewell in September 1189, Godfrey de Lucy to Winchester, Richard Fitz Neal, the treasurer, to London, William Longchamp, the chancellor, to Ely, and Hubert Walter to Salisbury, were all curial bishops. If we may judge by the expressions used by the chroniclers, these elections were made quite arbitrarily: John de Gray, for instance, received the bishopric of Norwich in 1200 'by the gift of King John' and the king 'gave to Giles de Braose the bishopric of Hereford'. Even the great quarrel with the papacy over the disputed election at Canterbury produced no change in the royal influence over elections. Innocent III, once the political victory was won, seemed to care little in what manner the church in England was governed. He instructed his legate Nicholas, cardinal bishop of Tusculum, to arrange that the numerous vacant sees should be filled by men not only distinguished by their good life and learning but also 'faithful to the king and useful to the kingdom'; and the legate accordingly quashed a canonical election made by the monks of Worcester in favour of a royal nominee, the chancellor Walter de Gray. It was only in the autumn of 1214 in the hope of winning the church to his side

---

[1] Cf. the tables compiled from the Pipe Rolls by J. H. Ramsay, *Revenues of the Kings of England*, i. 112, 163. The average receipts under this head during the reign are given ibid., p. 187.

[2] Giraldus Cambrensis, *Opera*, vii. 70.

in the impending struggle with the barons that John granted by charter the right of free election. But he still retained the right to the temporalities of vacant sees and monasteries; the churches had still to obtain the king's licence to elect; this, however, could no longer be withheld or deferred. The king could no longer make a steady income from vacant bishoprics.[1]

In spite of the immense efforts of the reformers, it is difficult to perceive any remarkable change in the character either of the higher or of the lower clergy in the twelfth or even in the early thirteenth century. There were at all ages men renowned for their religious and saintly lives in all ranks of the clergy, a St. Anselm or a St. Hugh of Lincoln; and there were men, like Bartholomew of Exeter and Roger of Worcester, who kept as much as possible out of secular politics, and used their learning and practical abilities whole-heartedly for the welfare of the church. But it would be wrong to regard such men as representative of their order. The bishops of Henry II's time, as in the time of his grandfather and his sons, were commonly good business men, men who were trained in the king's service and who continued to devote themselves chiefly to that service. Similarly a large proportion of the prebends or canonries were distributed as rewards among clerks in the royal household who seldom if ever visited the cathedral to which they were attached.[2] Bishops not only occupied the great offices of state, such as that of chancellor or treasurer, but even that of sheriff despite the fact that this was contrary to the canon law and expressly prohibited at a London council in 1175.[3] At the council of Windsor in 1179 three bishops, those of Winchester, Ely, and Norwich, were sent on circuit into the shires, though their appointment did not pass without protest.[4] In 1198 the monks of Canterbury protested to Innocent III that Hubert Walter was acting as

[1] *Foedera*, i. 126–7. It should be noted that sometimes during vacancies another bishop was sent to discharge the episcopal duties. So in 1207 the archbishop of Armagh visited the vacant see of Exeter (*Rot. Lit. Claus.* i. 88) and the bishop of Ferns that of Lincoln (*Pipe Roll 9 Jo.*, p. 14).

[2] Cf. A. Hamilton Thompson, *The Cathedral Churches of England*, p. 24. The canons of St. Paul's were exceptional. Owing to the proximity of their cathedral to the seat of government at Westminster, they could both serve as officials in the royal administration and reside. See M. Gibbs, *Early Charters of the Cathedral Church of St. Paul's, London* (Camden Ser.), p. xxvi.

[3] *Gesta Henrici*, i. 85. Hilary of Chichester was sheriff of Sussex in 1155, and Hugh of Nonant, bishop of Coventry, held the same office in the counties of Stafford, Warwick, and Leicester from 1190 to 1194.

[4] Cf. Ralph de Diceto, i. 434–6. Cf. *Eng. Hist. Rev.* xliii (1928), 171, n. 2.

justiciar, was giving judgements of blood, and was so involved in the affairs of state that he could not devote proper attention to the affairs of the church.[1] At the pope's request he accordingly resigned the justiciarship. But though he no longer took part in secular jurisdiction he can scarcely have given more time to his duties as primate, for in less than a year he had accepted the office of chancellor which involved him in ceaseless administrative work. Nor was this all. Bishops indulged their inclinations, whether it were in hunting or building or keeping open house for their friends, extravagantly. William of Newburgh, writing at the close of the twelfth century, complains that bishops in his day spent but little time in good works and grudged the moments when they were compelled to forsake their pleasures for more serious duties. The opulent splendour of Bishop Hugh de Puiset, the subject of these reflections (whose standard of magnificence may be judged by the still standing Norman doorway and the Norman gallery above in Durham castle), probably represents the position and the ambitions to which the average bishop of this period aspired.[2] He loved his purse better than his Bible, or as Nigel Wireker, precentor of Canterbury, put it in a couplet, using the common medieval play on the names of the Evangelists:[3]

> Praesul amat marcam plus quam distinguere Marcum,
>   plus et amat lucrum quam facit ipse Lucam.

When they did make a visitation of their dioceses, they made it with great parade, accompanied by a host of retainers who fed upon the parish or monastery to its great impoverishment. Longchamp, bishop of Ely, was a notorious offender; he would quarter himself on a monastery with such a crowd of men, horses, hounds, and hawks, that if he stayed but one night, the house could hardly recover within three years.[4] Pope Innocent III himself had to intervene to protect the churches of Bridlington priory on the complaint of the prior and canons that the archdeacon of Richmond made a visitation attended by

[1] Hoveden, iv. 47. He was a hostile critic and may have exaggerated Hubert's neglect. Cf. Richard I's letter announcing his resignation in *Foedera*, i. 71.

[2] William of Newburgh, v, ch. 10. Cf. also Stubbs, Introduction to Hoveden's Chronicle, iii, p. xxxv.

[3] *Satirical Poets* (ed. Wright), i. 106; Raby, *Secular Latin Poetry*, ii. 97. Cf. the satirical verses on Peter des Roches, bishop of Winchester, in *Political Songs* (ed. Wright, Camden Soc.), pp. 10–11.

[4] *Gesta Ricardi*, ii. 143.

97 horses, 21 hounds, and 3 hawks, and in short space consumed as much as would have sufficed for the whole household for a long time.[1] Hubert Walter attempted to curb the abuse by publishing a decree of the Third Lateran Council (1179) limiting the number of retainers: an archbishop might have 40–50 men and horses, a bishop 20–30; an archdeacon must be content with 5 or 7, and a rural dean with only 2; and there must be no hunting dogs or hawks.[2] Added to this there was the growing evil of plurality which extended to the hierarchy. Henry of Blois was both bishop of Winchester and abbot of Glastonbury for more than forty years, Godfrey of St. Asaph held the monastery of Abingdon *in commendam* between 1165 and 1175, while in 1214 the bishop of Ely enjoyed the regalia of the abbey of Thorney. The archdeacons, too, were often deeply engaged in other work; they were very commonly employed as itinerant justices,[3] and William of Wrotham, archdeacon of Taunton, was employed in high finance and practically controlled the navy and shipping in the time of King John. If we take all these circumstances into consideration, diocesan work must often have suffered from neglect or at least have been relegated to the group of officials who formed the bishop's household, their deputies[4] and the rural deans.

In his *Gemma Ecclesiastica* Giraldus Cambrensis has left us a picture of the life and manners of the clergy of his day. It has, like all his works, a strong flavour of satire; the follies and ignorance of the clergy are painted in exaggerated colours. Yet had there not been a substantial foundation of truth in his attack, the book would have been pointless; and Innocent III, when he was presented with a copy, could not be separated from it, and kept it always by his bedside for night reading.[5] The parish priest was often grossly illiterate, with scarcely enough Latin to repeat the church services correctly; he was shockingly ill-paid, and was driven to take money for masses and other spiritual offices to supplement his meagre income. He was usually married, or at least 'kept a hearth-girl (*focaria*) in his

---

[1] *Early Yorkshire Charters* (ed. Clay), v. 347.

[2] Canon of a provincial Council in 1200, Hoveden, iv. 130. For the extravagant diet of hawks see Poole, *Obligations of Society*, p. 68.

[3] Cf. *Fines 7 Ric. I ad 10 Johan.* (ed. Joseph Hunter), i, pp. lxii ff.

[4] A *vicearchidiaconus* of Cornwall witnesses a Tavistock charter (1175–84). *Eng. Hist. Rev.* lxii (1947), 366.

[5] Giraldus, *Opera*, i. 119.

house who kindled his fire but extinguished his virtue' and kept 'his miserable house cluttered up with small infants, cradles, midwives, and nurses'.[1] It was reported to Pope Clement III that the incumbent of the church of Whatton (Notts.), recently granted to the abbey of Welbeck, had not only acquired the church simoniacally (*mediante pecunia*), but that he had then married, and by his wife had *plures filios et filias*.[2] We hear of the archbishop of Canterbury making a special journey to Lincoln (1181) in order to prohibit the keeping of *focariae*, and one council after another legislated against the practice.[3] But canonical decrees and episcopal anathemas were alike ineffectual. Perhaps more serious than the breach of the rule of celibacy —for it may be argued that the church was setting an impossibly high moral standard for these uneducated priests to follow —was that benefices tended to become hereditary and descend from father to son. A Cambridge jury declared in court that:

'they knew well that a certain Langlinus, who held that church [St. Peter at Cambridge] and who was parson of that church, gave that church, according to what was then the custom of the city of Cambridge, to a certain kinsman of his, Segar by name, who held it for 60 years and more and was parson of that church; and he afterwards gave that church to his son Henry, who held it for 60 years.'[4]

The story told by these Cambridge jurymen was not (apart from the longevity of the incumbents)[5] extraordinary and the 'custom of the city of Cambridge' was evidently the custom elsewhere. Lucius III in 1183 wrote that he had heard that this was commonly done in some churches of which the abbot and monks of St. Benets of Holme, were the patrons. The father would accept a pension and pass the church on to the son, *quasi jure successionis*, and this had been done with the connivance not only of the patrons but of the Holy See itself. But that Lucius did not take a very serious view of this practice is suggested by a letter he wrote a year later to the abbot of St. Augustine's, Canterbury, on behalf of a poor scholar whose father was the parson at Willesborough (Kent). He proposed that it would be a satis-

---

[1] Giraldus, *Gemma Eccl.* (*Opera*, ii. 277).
[2] Holtzmann, *Papsturkunden in England*, i. 549.
[3] *Gesta Henrici*, i. 280; Hoveden, iv. 134.
[4] *Curia Regis Rolls*, v. 39.
[5] But incumbents were often appointed very young: a parson is said to have held the benefice of Sparsholt (Hants) for upwards of eighty years. *Curia Regis Rolls*, iii. 118.

factory arrangement if the father would retire and then the promising young son could be provided with the living, and pursue his studies unhampered by financial difficulties.[1] The system of hereditary succession might sometimes have happy results, as in the case of the scholarly son of the Kentish parson, but it certainly had its dangers and drawbacks.

In other ways, too, the lives of the parish clergy were far from exemplary. They would pass the evening at the village gild or drinking-house which, if we may believe Walter Map, every parish possessed—'bibitorias, *ghildhus* Anglice dictas'.[2] At Battle there were as many as three such places. The convivial meetings at these medieval night clubs led to drunkenness and licentiousness. Giraldus had studied at Paris and Oxford, had travelled far and seen much of the world, but when writing of the parish clergy he was naturally thinking chiefly of his own countrymen, who were notoriously easy and old-fashioned in their ways of life. Nevertheless, the laxity which he describes was not confined to Wales and could be paralleled in any English diocese. Indeed, the sober language of the church legislators tells the same story of a prevailing tendency to licentiousness, tavern-haunting, and brawling.[3]

The monasteries were passing out of the golden age. They provided a home for those who wished to devote their lives to religion or for those who, after an active life, wished in advanced years to retire from the turmoils of the world to end their days in repose.[4] But beyond giving hospitality to the traveller and some alleviation of the hardships of the poor, the monks of this period did not to any great extent influence the social or religious life of the masses of the people. Though the majority of the cathedrals, by a system peculiar to England, were governed by a monastic chapter, the monastery, which for its domestic concerns was ruled by a prior, had little or nothing to do with the affairs of the diocese.[5] Monks lived on their endowments, the

---

[1] Holtzmann, *Papsturkunden*, i. 486, 510.

[2] *De Nugis*, ii, c. 12.

[3] See, for example, the tenth canon issued by Hubert Walter in a provincial council at London in 1200. Hoveden, iv. 134.

[4] Cf. *Curia Regis Rolls*, viii. 389 (1220): 'Ipse reddidit se religioni, scilicet domui de Binedon in Dorset, ita quod mortuus est quantum ad seculum.'

[5] These were Canterbury, Winchester, Worcester, Durham, Norwich, Rochester, Ely, Coventry, Bath (Benedictine), and Carlisle (Augustinian). The only foreign example of a cathedral with a monastic chapter was at Monreale in Sicily, possibly copied from England.

revenues of their lands and parish churches, the gifts of lay benefactors. Hundreds of churches during the twelfth century came in this way to be 'appropriated' by monastic houses which became not only the patrons but also the rectors with the right to the tithes. They would usually institute a priest, removable at their pleasure and often at a stipend barely adequate to his needs, to perform the spiritual work of the parish. It was in connexion with an appropriated church that we first hear of the abuse of 'providing' foreign clerks with English benefices, an abuse which so gravely injured the spiritual life of England in the thirteenth century. On the presentation of the prior of Lewes, William Longchamp, bishop of Ely, gave the church of Caxton (Cambridgeshire) to a nephew of Pope Alexander III, the priory receiving a kind of quit-rent of three marks.[1] Even the regular canons seldom did parochial work but preferred the more leisured life of the cloister.[2] It was to remedy the irregularities and lack of diocesan control to which the system of appropriation gave rise that from the middle of the century bishops stipulated that the 'vicars' should be perpetual and properly instituted by themselves, and that a sufficient competence should be provided for them out of the property of the church.[3] The minimum that he should receive was later (in 1222) fixed at five marks a year. The possession of a parish church was, however, and continued to be a source of profit to the monastic house rather than a means of extending its spiritual activities.[4] Monks undertook no pastoral work; this was wholly the province of the secular church.

It was partly the fact that they had so little to do that led to the decline of monasticism. Monks, especially Cistercian monks,

[1] Holtzmann, *Papsturkunden*, i. 567–8 (1190–1).

[2] See W. H. Frere, 'The Early History of Canons Regular as illustrated by the Foundation of Barnwell Priory', in *Fasciculus Joanni Willis Clark dicatus*, pp. 203 ff.

[3] An early example of the establishment of a 'perpetual vicarage' is in a charter of Robert Warelwast, bishop of Exeter (1155–60), confirming the appropriation of the church of Milton Abbot to the abbey of Tavistock. He lays down the condition: 'ut perpetuus vicarius per manum episcopalem in eadem ecclesia Middeltone constituatur, et quod tantum ei de pertinentiis ecclesie assignetur unde se honeste exhibere et prelatis suis respondere sufficiat.' *Eng. Hist. Rev.* lxii (1947), 358.

[4] The church of Scarborough, for instance, was given to the abbey of Cîteaux by Richard I in 1189. According to the taxation of Pope Nicolas IV, about a century later, the value of the rectory was £106. 13s. 4d. and of the vicarage £5. 6s. 8d. *History of Scarborough*, ed. A. Rowntree, 1931. Cf. *Eng. Hist. Rev.* xlvii (1932), 725.

even more than the secular clergy fell under the whip of contemporary satirists. And the secular clergy themselves were no less bitter in their recriminations of the regulars. 'From the malice of monks, O Lord, deliver us', Giraldus would like to add to the Litany. These invectives, in which the vices of monks and nuns are often grotesquely exaggerated, pleased the reading public, who, no doubt, did not take them more seriously than they were meant. But there was enough truth in the charges to warrant censure. John of Salisbury, after praising the monastic orders in unmeasured terms, proceeds to dilate on the grave shortcomings of the few who brought discredit on the whole system.[1] By the end of the century things had grown worse. They now lived in more comfortable and commodious quarters and in place of their former frugality they now indulged in substantial if not luxurious diet. In a well-known passage in his autobiography Giraldus Cambrensis describes a dinner which he attended on Trinity Sunday at Christ Church, Canterbury. He was served with sixteen exquisitely cooked dishes and a variety of wines to match.[2] This, of course, was a great feast—especially at Canterbury, for it was on Trinity Sunday that St. Thomas was consecrated as archbishop—but even on ordinary days it is clear that with the extra 'pittances' which had become normal, the monks far exceeded the frugal diet prescribed by St. Benedict.[3]

Heavy outlay on buildings, extravagant living, expenses of litigation—for monastic houses were constantly engaged in long and costly legal disputes—crippled their finances. Not a few were in the tight grip of the Jews and moneylenders. Jocelin of Brakelond gives us a glimpse of the shocking state of the finances of Bury St. Edmunds in the last days of the aged and unbusinesslike abbot Hugh, who died in 1180. Jocelin himself saw the abbey's property dissipated as security for loans of £1,040, £400, and £880 to three creditors.[4] When the great financier Aaron of Lincoln died in 1185, a group of nine Cistercian houses were among his debtors, owing between them the great sum of 6,400 marks.[5]

---

[1] *Policraticus*, vii, c. 21. This was before 1159 when the work was completed.
[2] *Opera*, i. 51.
[3] Cf. Knowles, *The Monastic Order in England*, pp. 456 ff.
[4] *Chronica* (Camden Soc.), p. 2.
[5] *Memorials of Fountains Abbey* (Surtees Soc.), ii. 18; Jacobs, *The Jews of Angevin England*, p. 108.

Relatively few important abbeys date from the later years of the twelfth century, and those which do were chiefly houses of regular canons. The prohibition of new foundations by the general chapter at Cîteaux in 1152 put a virtual stop on the growth of the Cistercian plantation in England. Only some half-dozen houses came into being before King John's foundation of Beaulieu in 1204 put for a time new life into the fast-decaying system of the white monks.[1] Two of the three religious houses 'founded' by Henry II in expiation for his responsibility for the murder of Becket, though newly built on a lavish scale, were in fact no more than refoundations of existing ones; for he merely replaced secular by regular canons at Waltham, and disreputable nuns by others from Fontevrault at Amesbury. The only wholly new foundation was the Carthusian house at Witham in Somerset of which St. Hugh of Avalon, afterwards bishop of Lincoln, was the first prior.[2] Signs of decay were very evident. The injunctions of the legate, John of Ferentino, who attempted to set on foot a monastic reform in 1206, reveal the financial confusion and laxity of discipline that prevailed.[3] From the middle of the thirteenth century the number of inmates began steadily to decline;[4] sometimes a premium was expected from monks and nuns who wished to enter religion; and monasteries were becoming more and more a useful provision for superfluous friends and relatives. The judgement of Bishop Stubbs that 'their inhabitants were bachelor country gentlemen, more polished and charitable, but little more learned or more pure in life than their lay neighbours', if a little severe, is not perhaps far from the truth.[5] They were litigious capitalists

[1] Knowles, op. cit., pp. 252, 346.

[2] There is no reason to suppose that Henry adopted the plan of refounding existing houses out of a spirit of economy. The rebuilding cost a very considerable sum—above £1,400 at Waltham and £880 at Amesbury as appears from the *Pipe Rolls* of the years between 1177 and 1183; and he provided pensions, at least for the Amesbury nuns in addition. For the scandalous state of the nunnery when Bartholomew of Exeter and Roger of Worcester made a visitation in 1177, see *Gesta Henrici*, i. 135; *Rot. Chart.*, p. 13b.

[3] Printed by C. R. Cheney in *Eng. Hist. Rev.* xlvi (1931), 449. They are addressed to the abbey of St. Mary's, York.

[4] U. Berlière, 'Le Nombre des moines dans les anciens monastères', *Rev. Bénédictine*, xlii (1930), 29–31. Christ Church, Canterbury, had, for example, between 1066 and 1207 about 150 monks; in 1207 the number dropped to 77; in 1298 there were but 30.

[5] *Epistolae Cantuarienses*, Introd., p. cxix. Cf. the comments of Knowles, op. cit., p. 686.

who thought little of forging documents to protect their interests and property.

If, however, the discipline of the clergy was lax and their morals somewhat loose, their orthodoxy was beyond reproach. At a time when heretical sects were beginning to cause serious alarm to the ecclesiastical authorities in Italy, Germany, and France, England remained unshaken in her loyalty to the traditional faith. In 1165 some thirty Germans, men and women, apparently belonging to the Catharan sect, came to England. But their success was small; for they had converted only one woman (who afterwards recanted) before they were condemned in a provincial council held at Oxford in 1166, and handed over to the secular arm for punishment. They were whipped, branded, and exiled; by the express order of the king no one might receive them into his house, and they perished miserably in the wintry weather.[1] A solitary Albigensian appeared in London in 1210 and was promptly burnt. These are the only attested cases of heresy in the period under review; in fact the English church was practically unaffected by heretical creeds until the time of Wycliffe and the Lollards. And it carried the orthodox faith to other countries. English missionaries did valuable work in extending Christianity and in bringing order into the church in Scandinavia. Monastic colonies from Evesham and from the Cistercian houses of Fountains and Kirkstead were established in Denmark and Norway; the Englishman St. Henry, of whose early history nothing is known, was bishop of Upsala about the middle of the century and became the apostle and martyr of Finland after its conquest by the Swedish king, Eric IX. The English interest in the northern churches may have been stimulated by the legatine mission of the Englishman Nicholas Breakspear (afterwards Pope Adrian IV) who in 1152 organized the Scandinavian church. The English influence is reflected in the veneration of English saints, in the church architecture, and in the historical literature.

To the men of the twelfth century religion meant a very great deal. It is not without significance that men great and small invested their capital 'in pure and perpetual alms' for the safety

[1] The fullest account is given by William of Newburgh (ii, c. 13). Cf. also Walter Map, *De Nugis*, i, c. 30, where the number is given as 16. The law against receiving heretics is cl. 21 of the Assize of Clarendon (Hoveden, ii. 252). Cf. also Pollock and Maitland, *Hist. Eng. Law*, ii. 547.

of their souls; it was not merely for the love of adventure that
men in their thousands embarked on the hazardous pilgrimage
to the Holy Land; nor was it mere love of splendour that made
them build the most magnificent churches that architects of any
age could conceive. It was because religion to them was funda-
mentally the most important, the most real thing. It was the
vital force in their lives.

VIII

LEARNING, LITERATURE, AND ART

THE century which saw the recovery of the works of Aristotle, the real beginning of scholasticism, the rise of the universities, the age of Abailard and Gratian, may properly be termed a renaissance, an intellectual revolution which marks an era in the history of learning and education. Education in the middle ages was wholly the province of the church, and was primarily intended for the training of the clergy. It was controlled by the bishop or his deputy, the chancellor or *magister scholarum* without whose licence no one could teach or open a school. Unlicensed or 'adulterine' schools were ruthlessly suppressed by the bishops.[1] Although the canon law required a parish priest to provide instruction in singing and reading the psalter, we can scarcely credit the statement of Theobald of Étampes, who was teaching at Oxford in the early years of the twelfth century, that there were experienced schoolmasters (*peritissimi scholarum magistri*) not only in cities but even in villages (*in villulis*).[2] There were, however, attached to cathedrals, the larger monasteries, and collegiate churches, besides the elementary song schools (*scholae de cantu*), also grammar schools.[3] Grammar was the first and the most vital of the liberal arts, for it comprised not only the rules of grammar studied in the textbooks of Donatus and Priscian, but also classical literature or philology. Latin was the universal vehicle of speech and writing of the learned world, of the church, and of the law. It was the language of the lecture rooms and the text-books; the Bible was the Latin Vulgate, and Greek philosophy and Arabic science were known only in Latin translations. Latin was therefore the fundamental preliminary to the ordinary course of the *trivium* (grammar, rhetoric, and dialectic) and the *quadrivium* (music, arithmetic, geometry, and astronomy) as well as to the higher professions of divinity, law, and medicine. The standard and

[1] See the documents printed by M. Bateson, *Eng. Hist. Rev.* xviii (1903), 712–13, and J. H. Round, *Commune of London*, p. 117.
[2] The passage is printed by T. E. Holland, *Collectanea*, ii. 158 (Oxf. Hist. Soc. xvi, 1890).
[3] For the song school see A. Hamilton Thompson, *Church-Music Society, occasional Papers*, no. 14 (1942).

scope of the teaching in these grammar schools must obviously have varied from place to place. In the London schools the boys were instructed in all the branches of the *trivium*; they not only learnt Latin accidence and the rules of syntax, but were also taught rhetoric and logical disputation, 'a wrestling-bout of wit'.[1] There or at Canterbury, York, Winchester, or Lincoln, where a tradition of learning had lingered on from Saxon times, a decent education could no doubt be obtained; but generally it was necessary, or at any rate the fashion, for those who aspired to higher studies to proceed to the great schools of the Continent.

The intellectual reawakening of the twelfth century was marked and indeed greatly influenced by the transference of education from the regular to the secular clergy, from the monastery to the cathedral. The school of Bec under the inspired teaching of Lanfranc and Anselm had drawn students from all parts of western Europe. But Anselm was the last of the great monastic teachers; the monasteries were closing their doors to seculars. St. Bernard, who represents the new monastic ideals, so far from encouraging learning, spared no effort to stifle the growing enthusiasm for it. To him the Bible and the fathers were all the book-learning that was needful. This, however, did not content the men of the rising generation who naturally turned to the greater freedom enjoyed in the flourishing schools attached to the cathedrals of northern France or which gathered round a celebrated master.

The leading school at the opening of the twelfth century was that of Laon. Its master, who gave it its peculiar eminence, was Anselm of Laon, the *doctor doctorum*, as he was called. For many years past between Laon and England there had been close associations: Helinand, a clerk of Edward the Confessor, had been bishop there for nearly half a century (1052–98), and after a short interval another Englishman, Waldric, chancellor of Henry I, occupied the see; and Adelard of Bath, the famous scientist, taught there before 1109. When, in 1112, Waldric was murdered and his cathedral burnt in riots connected with the establishment of a commune, a party of canons came over to England in order to raise funds for the rebuilding of their church. They travelled through the greater part of southern England from Canterbury to Bodmin, visiting, among other places, Winchester, Salisbury, Exeter, Bath, and Bristol. Everywhere

---

[1] Fitz Stephen in *Materials for the History of Becket*, iii. 4–5.

they were received with a warm welcome, chiefly owing to the
respect in which the name of Anselm was held. This is a remarkable testimony of the wide reputation of the great teacher who
could number among his pupils William of Corbeil, archbishop
of Canterbury, and Alexander and Nigel, respectively bishops
of Lincoln and Ely, the nephews of Henry I's justiciar, Roger of
Salisbury.[1] But as the century advanced Paris took the place of
Laon as the popular resort of scholars; for Paris was now the
centre of the study of dialectic, and it was dialectic or logic
which chiefly stimulated the intellectual curiosity of the age
and so absorbed the world of learning that students, as John
of Salisbury complained,[2] hurried perfunctorily through the
courses of grammar and rhetoric in order to devote themselves
to philosophical disputation. We are not here concerned with
the growth of scholasticism, the battle of realism and nominalism,
of authority and reason, the application of philosophical method
to theological problems which horrified the old-fashioned
churchmen as much as it fascinated the new. Of this movement
Abailard, unquestionably the greatest intellect of the age, was
at once the most brilliant and original exponent. The Englishman John of Salisbury, perhaps, as has been said, the most
learned man of his time, is, however, more typically representative of the scholarship of the twelfth century. He moved,
as was the custom, from one school to another, whither his
studies or the reputation of a great master directed him, and
spent in all nearly twelve years over his education. He learnt
dialectic first from Abailard and afterwards from Abailard's
successors on the Mont Sainte-Geneviève. From Paris he proceeded to Chartres which was the centre of a humanistic movement 'anticipating, in its Platonism and in its love of ancient
literature generally, some of the characteristic tendencies of the
Renaissance'.[3] The study of Plato was revived there by the

---

[1] See Herman of Tournai, *De Miraculis S. Mariae Laudunensis*, ii. 6, in Migne, *Pat.
Lat.* clvi. 974 ff. Cf. R. L. Poole, *The Exchequer in the Twelfth Century* (1912),
pp. 53 ff., and also J. S. P. Tatlock, 'The English Journey of the Laon Canons' in
Speculum, viii (1933), 454 ff.

[2] *Metalogicon*, i, c. 24. 'Since then less time and less care have been bestowed on
grammar, and persons who profess all arts, liberal and mechanical, are ignorant
of the primary art, without which a man proceeds in vain to the rest.' Cf. R. L.
Poole, *Illustrations of Medieval Thought* (2nd ed. 1920), p. 104.

[3] C. C. J. Webb, *John of Salisbury* (1932), p. 6. On the importance of this
Platonic revival see R. Klibansky, *The Continuity of the Platonic Tradition*, published
by the Warburg Institute, 1939.

brothers Bernard and Thierry, and by William of Conches who wrote a Commentary on the *Timaeus*. The school of Chartres owed its pre-eminence to Bernard, whose method of teaching was still a living tradition when John came there, some eight years after the great master's death, to study grammar under William of Conches. Bernard of Chartres had little patience with the popular craze for logic-chopping. His insistence was on a thorough training in grammar, not merely in the rules of syntax and a knowledge of the illustrative extracts from classical authors contained in the current text-books, but in grammar in the wider sense, philology, a study of Latin literature. He set his pupils to daily exercises in prose and verse, instructing them to imitate the finest models, and encouraged a healthy rivalry by making them correct each other's exercises. They were required every day to commit something to memory, and to reproduce on the following day a part of what they had learnt, 'for with them the morrow was the disciple of yesterday'.[1] In this exacting school John of Salisbury was trained, and his work is a striking testimony to the success of the system. Though he returned to Paris to continue his education, it was at Chartres that he laid the foundations of his scholarship, that he learnt to write what is regarded by competent critics as the purest Latin of the middle ages. Although he knew no Greek, he was acquainted with what was available in translations, and was, indeed, in the pages of his *Metalogicon* the first medieval scholar to make use of the whole of Aristotle's *Organon*.[2] The breadth of his reading in the Latin classics is astonishing. He was familiar with all the greater poets with the exception of Lucretius, Plautus, Propertius, and Catullus. Of prose writers he chiefly admired Cicero whom he praises in the hexameter line:[3]

Orbis nil habuit maius Cicerone Latinus.

He had read, however, most of the authors that were known in his day, including Sallust, Suetonius, Valerius Maximus, Petronius, Seneca, the elder Pliny, and Apuleius; and his great work, the *Policraticus*, abounds in quotations culled from his wide

---

[1] *Metalogicon*, i, c. 24 (ed. Webb, p. 55). Cf. R. L. Poole, *Illustrations of Medieval Thought* (2nd ed., 1920), pp. 102 f.

[2] Manuscripts of the *Organon* existed at Canterbury and Rochester at the beginning of the twelfth century. See J. S. Beddie, 'Libraries in the Twelfth Century' in *Haskins Anniversary Essays*, p. 13.

[3] *Entheticus* (ed. Petersen, 1843), l. 1215.

reading in Latin literature.[1] But the study of the classics was a passing phase of the twelfth-century renaissance. Already in the middle of the century John of Salisbury could write that the more the young scholar learns the less he will read, he admires only Aristotle and despises Cicero;[2] and a generation later Alexander Neckham and Giraldus Cambrensis deplored the ignorance of this primary art of language among the students of their time who would plunge without the necessary training into the fashionable study of dialectic or the more lucrative study of the canon law, by that time a sure road to promotion in the church.[3]

In the meanwhile the prestige of the English schools was gradually developing. There was little perhaps in the middle of the twelfth century to mark out Oxford as the obvious and peculiar centre of academic study. There were other schools of equal or even surpassing importance. There was a flourishing one at Exeter and another at Northampton[4] where in the eighties Geoffrey of Vinsauf, an Englishman who wrote the standard text-book on the art of poetry, taught rhetoric and Daniel of Morley, the Arabic scholar, science; and as late as 1192 Gerald of Wales, when prevented on account of the wars from going to Paris, went not to Oxford but to Lincoln to pursue his theological studies. Oxford, however, was conveniently situated, easily accessible from London and the midlands, the west and the south. Politically it was a place of some importance; councils were sometimes held there, and the king had a residence in the city, Beaumont Palace,[5] besides a favourite seat near by

---

[1] For the extent of John's knowledge of the classics see C. C. J. Webb, *John of Salisbury* (1932), pp. 159 ff.; J. E. Sandys, *A History of Classical Scholarship* (3rd ed. 1921), i. 539 ff.

[2] *Entheticus* (ed. Petersen, 1843), ll. 110–14:

> Ut juvenis discat plurima, pauca legat,
> Laudat Aristotelem solum, spernit Ciceronem
> Et quicquid Latiis Graecia capta dedit,
> Conspuit in leges, vilescit physica, quaevis
> Litera sordescit, logica sola placet.

[3] Cf. the introduction of L. J. Paetow to his edition of *The Battle of the Seven Arts* (Memoirs of the University of California, vol. iv, 1914), pp. 22–3. This French poem by Henri d'Andeli, written in the first half of the thirteenth century, describes the triumph of the Paris logicians over the humanists of Orléans.

[4] On the importance of the Northampton school see H. G. Richardson, *Eng. Hist. Rev.* lvi (1941), 595. He suggests that when the school declined in the early years of Richard I's reign, a migration of Northampton students to Oxford may have taken place. Cf. also R. W. Hunt in *Trans. R. Hist. Soc.*, 4th ser., xix (1936), 27.

[5] Built by Henry I who spent Easter 1133 in the *nova aula*. Hen. Hunt., *Hist. Anglorum* (ed. Arnold), p. 253.

at Woodstock where he frequently came for the hunting. Early in the twelfth if not in the last years of the eleventh century a certain Theobald of Étampes, who had been a master at Caen, was giving instruction to 'sixty or a hundred' students, and subscribes himself in his letters as *Magister Oxenefordiae*.[1] Not much later (1133) Robert Pullen, afterwards a celebrated Paris master, was lecturing on theology there. Attached to the conventual churches in Oxford there were other men interested in learning. Walter, archdeacon of Oxford and provost of the chapel of St. George in the castle (1115-51), was the friend of Geoffrey of Monmouth, who himself was resident in Oxford about the same time;[2] it was indeed the archdeacon who provided Geoffrey with 'the ancient book in the British tongue' from which he is supposed to have worked up his fabulous history. Robert of Cricklade, who became prior of St. Frideswide about 1141, was certainly a man of considerable academic distinction; he wrote, besides theological works, an abridgement of Pliny; he had travelled in Italy and Sicily where he came in touch with some of the recovered Greek learning; and to him was dedicated by a Sicilian scholar, Aristippus, a translation of Plato's *Phaedo*.[3] He lived long enough to preach what by anticipation we might call university sermons. There was clearly about the place an intellectual atmosphere which required but a little stimulus to transform the Oxford schools into a *studium generale*, a general resort of students. Such a stimulus came when about 1167, in the heat of the Becket dispute, English scholars were recalled from Paris.[4] From about this time at any rate the

[1] The letters of Theobald and other documents relating to Oxford in the twelfth century have been conveniently collected by T. E. Holland, op. cit., pp. 151 ff. The period of Theobald's residence in Oxford is uncertain. He describes himself in a letter to Queen Margaret of Scotland (who died 1093) as *Doctor Cadumensis* (Caen); but in one addressed to Roscelin, the leader of the nominalists, the first master and later chief opponent of Abailard, he speaks of himself as *Magister Oxenefordiae*. Roscelin, according to a tradition accepted as a fact by Heinrich Boehmer (*Mon. Germ. Hist. Libelli de Lite*, iii. 604, and *Kirche und Staat*, p. 104, n. 1) but regarded with suspicion by H. Rashdall (*The Universities of Europe in the Middle Ages*, 2nd ed., iii. 16-17), came to England after his condemnation at the council of Soissons in 1092. If this were so it may have been the occasion on which the two scholars came into touch with each other.

[2] His name appears as a witness to several charters relating to Oseney and Godstow between 1129 and 1151. Cf. H. E. Salter, *Eng. Hist. Rev.* xxxiv (1919), 382-5, and *Oxford Charters* (1929), no. 60.

[3] Haskins, *Studies in the History of Mediaeval Science*, pp. 168 f.

[4] Rashdall's view that the origin of the university was due to a migration from Paris requires some modification; it allows 'too little room for the operation of

future of Oxford as a seat of learning was assured. When about
1187 Gerald of Wales read aloud his *Topography of Ireland* before
the assembled masters and scholars—an operation which occupied three whole days—he relates how he entertained among
others the doctors of the several faculties. The reputation of the
Oxford schools was even drawing scholars from the Continent;
Emo, an historian of Frisia, was there about 1190, and a Hun-
garian clerk was maintained at the public expense (he was
allowed 5s. a week) while he studied at Oxford between 1193
and 1196.[1] In the first year of the next century we hear of a
recognized head of the university, one J. Grim, who styles himself *magister scholarum Oxonie*. Facilities for study increased as the
university grew. Around St. Mary's church and Catte Street,
the nucleus of the original university, were clustered a group of
tradesmen to provide for the needs of scholars—a book-binder,
three illuminators, a writer, and two parchment-makers.[2] Perhaps for the benefit of students attending lectures an ingenious
Oxford doctor of theology, identified as John of Tilbury, one
of the *eruditi* who followed Thomas Becket into exile, had in-
vented a system of shorthand that enabled one to take down
words as rapidly as they were spoken.[3]

From the first there was trouble with the town. The citizens
looked upon the students as legitimate game to plunder. Indeed,
the masters and scholars joined together in a gild, a university—
for originally the word implied no more—in order to protect
each other against profiteering townsmen. In 1209 occurred the
first affray between the university and the city: a woman was
killed, accidentally it was said, by a clerk. By way of retaliation
several students were apprehended by the citizens, and two,

---

intellectual activities in England capable of developing contemporaneously along
lines similar to those which brought to birth the University of Paris'. *Medieval Universities*, Introd., 2nd ed. (1936), iii, p. xvii, and p. 29, n. 2. Cf. also H. E. Salter,
Medieval Oxford (Oxf. Hist. Soc., 1936), p. 91.

  [1] Rashdall, op. cit. iii. 32, n. 1; H. G. Richardson, *Eng. Hist. Rev.* lvi (1941), 603,
n. 3, seeks to discredit the suggestion that Nicholas the clerk *de Hungria* may have
been a poor scholar who came to England in the train of German agents engaged in
the business of the king's ransom and even doubts whether he came from Hungary
at all.
  [2] Rashdall, op. cit. iii. 27. The document (a transfer of property in 'Catte Street')
belonging probably to the first years of the thirteenth century is printed by Holland,
op. cit., pp. 178–9.
  [3] Cf. Valentin Rose, 'Ars Notoria, Tironische Noten und Stenographie im
12. Jahrhundert' in *Hermes*, viii (1874), 303–26; Herbert of Bosham in *Materials for
the History of Becket*, iii. 527.

with the king's consent, were hanged. The masters and scholars, some 3,000 in number according to the probably exaggerated report,[1] hurriedly dispersed, this way and that; some to Reading, others to Paris, and others to Cambridge where they formed the nucleus of the sister university.[2] For five years the life of the university of Oxford was suspended. It was the time of the great interdict when all ecclesiastical organization was in confusion; it was only, therefore, after John had made his submission to the pope that the scholars could have their revenge. The citizens were then compelled to accede to humiliating terms dictated by the papal legate. One of these is of paramount importance: it gave the jurisdiction over scholars to the bishop of Lincoln or his representative, the chancellor of the university; and in this way placed the university in that privileged position which it has enjoyed in a modified form to the present day.

Although there were distinguished teachers at Oxford in these early days, including such notable figures in their different ways as Alexander Neckam, Edmund of Abingdon or Edmund Rich as he is commonly called, Walter Map, and Robert Grosseteste, one of the earliest chancellors,[3] it was still the ambition of those who could afford it to go to the famous schools of the Continent; they would go to Paris, the pre-eminent home of learning, or, if they wished to specialize in the professions of law or medicine, to Bologna or Salerno. But the majority of scholars were not drawn from the well-to-do classes. Indeed, if we may believe the statement of Walter Map, the aristocracy cared little for serious education, they were 'too proud or too lazy to put their children to learning', and it was the rustics, he adds, who 'vie with each other in bringing up their ignoble and degenerate offspring to the liberal arts'.[4] More probably, however, it was neither the nobles, who, if they educated their sons at all, had private tutors for them, nor the rustics, but the middle class, relatives of the higher clergy, sons of knights and thriving tradesmen, who chiefly resorted to the schools and universities.[5] Facilities for a cheap education had immensely improved in the course of the twelfth century.

---

[1] Cf. Rashdall, op. cit. iii. 33, 328; 1,500 would probably be a truer estimate.

[2] That Cambridge owes its origin to a migration from Oxford is generally accepted; but its real beginning seems to date from some twenty years later. Ibid. iii. 278.

[3] On Grosseteste see the article by D. A. Callus in *Oxoniensia*, x (1945), 42 ff.

[4] *De Nugis*, i, c. 10.　　　　　　　　[5] Rashdall, op. cit. iii. 408.

Alexander, who was prior of Canons Ashby in the reign of John, tells us that in his youth 'there were scarcely any masters whose teaching was not mercenary, but now, by the grace of God, there are many who teach without a fee',[1] and as early as 1138 a London council had forbidden the practice of selling the permission to teach, the *licentia docendi*. Nevertheless, whether it was poverty or the extravagance consequent on a care-free life, the medieval student was, it appears, habitually short of money. Letters written home nearly always contain a request for supplies. A specimen from Oxford dating from the first quarter of the thirteenth century runs as follows:

'B. to his venerable master A., greeting. This is to inform you that I am studying at Oxford with the greatest diligence, but the matter of money stands greatly in the way of my promotion as it is now two months since I spent the last of what you sent me. The city is expensive and makes many demands; I have to rent lodgings, buy necessaries, and provide for many other things which I cannot now specify. Wherefore I respectfully beg your paternity that by the promptings of divine pity you may assist me, so that I may be able to complete what I have well begun. For you must know that without Ceres and Bacchus Apollo grows cold. . . .'[2]

Poverty and pleasure are recurrent themes of the student songs which vividly portray a certain type of student life.[3] They treat of love, wine, the flowers of spring, and whether composed in France or England, Italy or Germany, their application is common to all the *clerici vagantes*, the wandering scholars. The literary phantom, the personification of licentious lawlessness, known as Golias, appears to have been largely an English creation, and it is certain that in England Goliardic poetry attained a great popularity.[4] The following rhyming couplets, each followed by the refrain 'Tara tantara teino', are admirably descriptive.[5]

[1] Quoted by R. W. Hunt, 'English Learning in the late Twelfth Century' in *Trans. R. Hist. Soc.*, 4th ser., xix (1936), 20.

[2] Haskins, *Medieval Culture*, p. 10.

[3] The most famous collection of these is the *Carmina Burana* (ed. J. A. Schmeller). Some of the best have been collected and translated by Helen Waddell, *Mediaeval Latin Lyrics*, 1929; and John Addington Symonds made spirited English versions of many of them in *Wine, Women, and Song* (King's Classics, 1907).

[4] Cf. F. J. E. Raby, *A History of Secular Latin Poetry*, ii. 214–15, 223, 340.

[5] The full poem, which contains sixteen couplets, is printed by Wright and Halliwell, *Reliquiae Antiquae*, i. 237. The English rendering is by John Addington Symonds, op. cit., pp. 61–4.

Nos vagabunduli,	We in our wandering,
Laeti, jucunduli,	Blithesome and squandering,
Edimus libere,	Eat to satiety,
Canimus lepide,	Drink with propriety,
Risu dissolvimur,	Laugh till our sides we split,
Pannis obvolvimur,	Rags on our hides we fit,
Multum in joculis,	Jesting eternally,
Crebro in poculis, &c.	Quaffing infernally, &c.

There were doubtless many who lazed away their youth in this aimless and irresponsible mode of existence in taverns, at gaming, and in love-making, gaining little by way of education. It is the subject of the well-known satirical poem *Speculum stultorum* ('The Mirror of Fools') which Nigel Wireker, precentor of Canterbury, dedicated to William Longchamp.[1] It is the story of an ambitious ass, Burnellus (the 'Daun Burnel the Asse' of Chaucer's *Nun's Priest's Tale*), who, discontented with the length of his tail, goes into the world in search of a longer one. In the course of his wanderings he lost his tail, and finally reached Paris where he spent seven years in the schools, and, at the end of it all, he knew only how to bray, which he could do before. The English students, the satirist remarks, ate too much and drank too much, and were given to whoring, but 'apart from these vices there was nothing in them particularly reprehensible'. Everywhere the English seemed to have gained a notoriety for heavy drinking. Jacques de Vitry, who knew Paris at the end of the century, describes the distinctive characteristics of each nation: the French were proud and womanish; the Germans furious and obscene; the Lombards greedy, malicious, and cowardly; and the English were drunkards and had tails.[2] Even in Italy they had the same reputation. The Franciscan Salimbene noticed that it was the Englishman's habit always

---

[1] *Satirical Poets of the Twelfth Century* (ed. Wright, Rolls Series), i. 3 ff. Cf. F. J. E. Raby, op. cit. ii. 94 ff.

[2] *potatores et caudati.* The same sentiment appears in a line from an early-thirteenth-century poem quoted by F. Liebermann (*Mon. Germ. Hist. Script.* xxvii. 77, note):

'Angli caudati, qui sunt ad pocula nati'.

For the origin of the standing jest, especially common in France and Scotland, that the English had tails see G. Neilson, *Caudatus Anglicus* (Edinburgh, 1896). It seems to have arisen from the legend that St. Augustine punished the men of Dorset, who attacked him, by condemning them to have tails. Cf. Wace, *Roman de Brut* (ed. Le Roux de Lincy), ii. 251.

to drain off a beaker of wine, saying 'ge bi a vu' (I drink to you), implying by this that his friend must drink as much as he.[1]

We hear less of the serious, hard-working student in the contemporary songs and satires. His manner of life was less picturesque, more monotonous, and made less appeal. Edmund of Abingdon, afterwards archbishop of Canterbury and a saint, who was at Oxford university in its early days, was evidently an earnest scholar who regularly attended lectures in the stone-built school in the churchyard of St. Mary's. Yet he had his recreation, for we hear of him at Mass and stealing away after the elevation of the host to play games.[2] John de Hanville, however, who wrote satires in the manner of Juvenal, has left in a poem addressed to Walter of Coutances a very gloomy description of the hard conditions under which the poor scholar worked, with his shabby clothes, his squalid lodging, his sparse diet; his nights spent in toil, and his early rising to attend lectures.[3] Nevertheless, the moral drawn, as in many satirical pieces, that it was all vain labour, for the rewards went always to the undeserving, is not altogether justified. Means were, it seems, usually forthcoming for really serious scholars who, like Gerard la Pucelle, the friend of John of Salisbury, and later bishop of Coventry, or Stephen Langton, were provided with canonries or other resources to enable them to pursue their studies uninterrupted or to continue to teach in the schools.[4] Others again, like John of Salisbury himself, took private pupils while they were still completing their education. Walter Map, one of the best-known literary figures of the time, held office in the royal household; Walter of Châtillon, a poet of distinction, was employed in Henry II's chancery; and Roger of Hereford, a learned astronomer, acted as an itinerant justice.

Kings and nobles were patrons of literature: they liked to have literary men about them and to have books dedicated to them. Learning was encouraged in Norman and even more in

---

[1] *Mon. Germ. Hist. Script.* xxxii. 113, 220. This seems to correspond to the 'Wassail and dringail' of Nigel Wireker's *Speculum stultorum*, p. 63, and to the 'Wacht heil' which was answered by 'Drinc heil' in Geoffrey of Monmouth (vi, c. 12).

[2] A. B. Emden, *An Oxford Hall in Medieval Times*, p. 83.

[3] *Architrenius* (the Arch-mourner), Wright, *Satirical Poets*, i. 275; Introd., p. xxviii; Raby, op. cit. ii. 100.

[4] Cf. Powicke, *Stephen Langton*, pp. 32 f.; Stubbs, *Seventeen Lectures on the Study of Mediaeval and Modern History* (3rd edn.), p. 161. Also above, pp. 225–6.

early Angevin England.[1] The reputation of Henry I as a man of letters has been usually exaggerated.[2] But Henry II, and indeed all his family, had received a good education and were able to appreciate the work and the society of scholars. Count Geoffrey of Anjou was deservedly praised by the great schoolman William of Conches, to whom he entrusted his son Henry's education, for the care he took in bringing up his family.[3] Even his natural children were not neglected, for one of them, Mary, abbess of Shaftesbury, may with some probability be identified with Marie de France, the learned authoress who wrote lays and translated from English what she imagined to be Aesop's Fables.[4] Henry's mother, Matilda, too, must have had intellectual interests, since a pupil of Bernard of Chartres dedicated to her an edition of his celebrated master's works.[5] Eleanor, his wife, was also popular in literary circles, especially in her own land of Aquitaine. Her sons, Richard and John, inherited the literary instincts of the family. The former, like his mother, found his real home in the south of France, where he associated with troubadours, and probably himself indulged in verse compositions. His younger brother John, who was instructed in his youth by the great lawyer, Rannulf Glanvill, appears to have had some intellectual taste. He at least formed a small collection of theological books, the nucleus of a royal library, acquired from the abbey of Reading. This collection included Hugh of St. Victor on the sacraments, the *Sententiae* of Peter the Lombard, and St. Augustine's *De Civitate Dei*,[6] books which seem a little out of place in the hands of King John; he also had a copy of Pliny and he read history in the French vernacular (*Romancium de Historia Anglie*).[7] Kings in the twelfth century were expected to be literate; they 'must not plead ignorance of the law of God by reason of their military duties' wrote John of Salisbury. 'They should read and think about it every day, and this they

[1] V. H. Galbraith, 'The Literacy of the Medieval English Kings', *Proc. Brit. Acad.* xxi (1935).

[2] See C. W. David, 'The Claim of Henry I to be called learned', in *Haskins Anniversary Essays*, pp. 45 ff.

[3] Above, p. 161.

[4] See the articles of Sir John Fox in *Eng. Hist. Rev.* xxv. 303, xxvi. 317.

[5] I owe this information to Dr. R. Klibansky.

[6] *Rot. Lit. Claus.* i. 108. Cf. Powicke, *Stephen Langton*, p. 99.

[7] *Rot. Lit. Claus.* i. 29 b. Mr. A. Ewert, professor of Romance Languages at Oxford, has suggested to me that this probably refers to Wace's *Brut* or one of the 'Bruts' which began to be compiled about the beginning of the thirteenth century.

will not easily do unless they are literate.'[1] Working, therefore, in a country where learning was encouraged and appreciated, Englishmen were able to make a not inconsiderable contribution to the scholarship of the age.

The introduction of eastern science into the western world gives to the twelfth century its peculiar significance in the history of learning. Greek was still an unknown language to most scholars; the writings of the Greeks, therefore, had to be rendered into Latin before Hellenic culture became generally accessible. Some of this great legacy came direct by translation from the Greek: but more from the Arabs who had preserved, absorbed, and by their commentaries, especially in medicine and mathematics, developed classical learning. It was once thought that this influx of knowledge was an effect of the contacts made between eastern and western civilizations through the Crusades. It came, indeed, by many channels, by way of Spain, south Italy and Sicily, and Syria; but of these Syria is probably the least important, for the Crusaders went thither to fight, not in search of knowledge. In England the new learning found a receptive field. Already in the first years of the twelfth century there is evidence of an interest taken in mathematics and astronomy;[2] and in the diffusion of Arabic science English scholars played a significant part. Two of the pioneers were Englishmen, Adelard of Bath and his younger contemporary, Robert of Chester. Few facts of the life of Adelard are definitely known. Born at Bath in the latter part of the eleventh century, he studied at Tours and taught at Laon; he was a great traveller, visiting countries as far afield as Greece, Asia Minor, Sicily, south Italy, and probably Spain; he was living in England in 1130 and again between 1142 and 1144 when he dedicated his treatise on the astrolabe to the young Henry Plantagenet who was then at Bristol. It is not unlikely that he was employed in an official capacity at the exchequer. Some dozen or more original works or translations from the Arabic on philosophical, mathematical, and astronomical subjects, not to speak of a treatise on falconry, the earliest book of its kind known in western Europe, are attributed to him, the most important of which being perhaps his translation of the *Elements* of Euclid and, if it is really his work, of Ptolemy's *Almagest*, the authoritative source of

[1] *Policraticus*, iv, c. 6, quoted Galbraith, op. cit., p. 14.
[2] See C. H. Haskins, *Studies in Mediaeval Science* (1924), chap. vi.

ancient astronomy.[1] As a philosopher, he acclaimed Plato as *princeps philosophorum*, and his philosophical writings owe much to the *Timaeus*. Robert of Chester is a still more elusive person. Apart from his writings little is known of his life beyond the fact that he was archdeacon of Pamplona in 1143, and was in London in 1147 and 1150. He first appears in 1141 when Peter the Venerable, abbot of Cluny, engaged him and his friend and collaborator Herman of Carinthia, who were then together in Spain, to translate the Koran. His main interests, however, were not theological but mathematical and astronomical; and his chief contribution to learning is his translation, completed at Segovia in 1145, of the algebra of Al-Khowārizmī, which first introduced that mathematical system into western Europe. Possibly to him also, or to Adelard, is due the translation of another work of that famous Arabian mathematician on Indian arithmetic which had an important influence on the introduction of the Hindu-Arabic numerals into Europe.[2] In spite, however, of the obvious convenience in reckoning by this numerical system, medieval conservatism stood in the way of its general adoption. Occasionally arabic numerals appear outside scientific works, in the foliation of a manuscript or in a date,[3] but it was many years before they came into common use. They do not frequently occur in English records before the middle of the sixteenth century, nor were they in general use before the eighteenth.[4]

Scientific studies continued long to absorb the attention of some of the best English scholars. In the last quarter of the twelfth century Daniel of Morley, attracted by astrology, forsook the schools of Paris for Toledo where he studied under the great Arabic scholar, Gerard of Cremona, and returned to England 'with a precious multitude of books'; Alexander Neckham, the foster-brother of Richard I, who ended his life as

[1] The attribution is suggested by F. Bliemetzrieder, *Adelard von Bath* (Munich, 1935), and is accepted with reservation by E. Jamison, *Proc. Brit. Acad.* (1938), xxiv. 273.
[2] See D. E. Smith and L. C. Karpinski, *The Hindu-Arabic Numerals* (1911), p. 97; Haskins, op. cit., p. 33.
[3] Bodl. MS., Rawl. C. 317 (thirteenth century) is foliated in contemporary arabic numerals; so too the date, 1346, is endorsed on a twelfth-century Charter. 'Facsimiles of Early Charters', *Northampton Record Society*, iv. 124.
[4] This is the conclusion of Hilary Jenkinson, *Antiquaries Journal*, vi (1926), 264. The change from roman to arabic numerals in the accounts of St. John's College, Oxford, took place in 1736.

abbot of Cirencester, evinces in his *De Naturis Rerum* a wide if somewhat over-credulous knowledge of natural history; and before the century was out there was born, presumably in Scotland, Michael Scot, who worked at Toledo early in the next century, made the standard translation (from the Arabic) of Aristotle's treatises on animals, and became the famous astrologer at the court of the emperor Frederick II. In the same period the classical works of Hippocrates and Galen came to supplement, though not to supersede, the crude medicinal lore of old English leechcraft.

Fundamental in the intellectual development of the middle ages was the recovery of the works of Aristotle. Before the twelfth century only two works, the *Categories* and the *De Interpretatione*, were known in western Europe, and these in the translations of Boethius. By the middle of the century the hitherto unknown parts of the *Organon*, the *New Logic* as it came to be called, were recovered, and the whole work was first used, as we have already noticed, by John of Salisbury in his *Metalogicon*. By about the year 1200 the *Physics*, the *Metaphysics*, and the lesser works on natural philosophy were used by a certain Alfred the Englishman and to some extent also by Alexander Neckham. In the course of the next century nearly the whole corpus either in translation direct from the Greek or indirectly through the Arabic had become available to European scholars.[1]

'Of all the centuries', it has been said,[2] 'the twelfth is the most legal.' It was the age in which the canon law was codified and the civil law was glossed. The introduction and development of the canon law in England, and its immense importance in matters of church and state, have been discussed in another place.[3] If in England the civil (or Roman) law never became, as it did in many continental countries, the basis of the law of the land, its revival in the Italian schools during the twelfth century was not without influence. Although King Stephen tried to stifle the study of the civil law, although the church frowned on it,[4] although it led to no profitable profession, yet it prospered.

---

[1] The popularity of Aristotle is illustrated by the fact that by 1207 it has become a personal name. 'Magister Aristotiles' pays a fine to recover his land and chattels of which he was deprived for failing to pay a tax. *Rot. de oblatis et finibus*, p. 395; *Pipe Roll 9 Jo.*, p. 110.

[2] Pollock and Maitland, *Hist. Eng. Law*, i. 111.   [3] Above, p. 196.

[4] Pollock and Maitland, op. cit. i. 122. A bull of Pope Honorius III in 1219 forbade its being taught at Paris.

There was a thriving school at Oxford, where legal studies may have been first introduced by the Mantuan lawyer Vacarius, whose text-book for poor students, the *Liber Pauperum*, a volume of excerpts from the Digest and the Code of Justinian, was in general use towards the end of the century. About the year 1200 Thomas of Marlborough, who later studied under Azo at Bologna and became abbot of Evesham, was lecturing at Oxford seemingly on both canon and civil law.[1] The best intellects of the time, such as John of Salisbury or Peter of Blois, quote freely from Roman texts, and Richard I's chancellor, William Longchamp, is claimed as the author of a manual of legal procedure (*Practica legum et decretorum*). Nevertheless, beyond helping to mould the tangled mass of ancient custom and Anglo-Norman procedure into an ordered system, Roman law did not have a very considerable influence on the legal development in this country during the twelfth century. Glanvill shows some acquaintance with the *Institutes*, but his famous treatise, or the treatise which is usually attributed to him, the *Tractatus de Legibus et Consuetudinibus Regni Angliae*, is a book of English law little affected by foreign jurisprudence.[2]

The intellectual revival stimulated an interest in history. Everywhere in civilized Europe historical literature developed both in quantity and in quality. A broader, more philosophical, treatment of events begins to supersede the brief and arid notices of earlier times. Annals by their very nature had to be short, for originally they were restricted to what could be inserted in the margin of tables drawn up to find the date of Easter. The record of a year was confined to a single line of writing. Although most chroniclers had passed far beyond this primitive stage, annals in this form were still compiled in some places in England as late as the twelfth century, at Reading, Battle, Worcester, Chichester, and elsewhere.[3] But even where they were independent of an

[1] H. G. Richardson has used materials from a legal formulary contained in a manuscript in the university of Baltimore to show the existence of a vigorous law school at Oxford in the opening years of the thirteenth century, *Law Quarterly Review*, lvii (1941), 319–38. He has also printed some of the documents in *Oxford Formularies* (Oxford Hist. Soc., N.S., v), ii. 274–7.

[2] Pollock and Maitland, op. cit. i. 165. Cf. also Vinogradoff, *Roman Law in Mediaeval Europe*, pp. 86 ff., and Holdsworth, *Hist. Engl. Law*, ii. 176

[3] For the revival of this form at the abbey of Murbach in the Vosges, and its transmission to Normandy and thence to England, see R. L. Poole, *Chronicles and Annals*, pp. 58 f. The Annals mentioned above have been printed by F. Liebermann, *Anglo-Normannische Geschichtsquellen*.

Easter table, annals continued to be very jejune, recording little else than the deaths of kings, bishops, and abbots, the appointment of their successors, or perhaps an eclipse, an earthquake, or other significant portent; some, like those of Oseney, often merely state *nihil memoriale accidit* even for years which were crowded with matters of public interest.[1] Nevertheless, as the years go by these scanty annals blossom out, and by the next century they supply a full and useful record of events. The period marks the transition from the chronicle to the history. The scribes began to transcend the sharp limits prescribed to the annalists.[2] The best writers of this time, William of Malmesbury, Ordericus Vitalis, a native of England who lived and wrote in the Norman abbey of St. Évroul, or William of Newburgh, are historians in the proper sense of the term. They approach the history of their times with a fullness of detail, a spirit of criticism, and with a gift of narrative which makes their work not only valuable historical material but even worthy literary compositions. They interrupt the narrative with digressions on a variety of topics and with their own reflections; some of the more ambitious embellish it with a few stanzas of verse and strive after elegance of style.

Opportunities for hearing news were not lacking, for monasteries were far from being shut off from communication with the world outside. They held properties, they had dependent cells, often widely dispersed over the country. Their abbots were constantly moving about, visiting their estates or journeying to Rome on the business of their houses. Travellers would halt and spend a night in the abbey guest-house. No religious house could geographically be more isolated than that of Mont St. Michel 'in peril of the sea'. Yet it is astonishing how little of what was happening in the world escaped its abbot. Our knowledge of English affairs for the middle years of the twelfth century would be greatly the poorer but for the information sedulously collected and recorded by Robert of Torigni on that remote and sea-girt rock. Manuscripts passed freely from one monastery to another; the work of one historian was often copied and used as a starting-point by a writer in a different

---

[1] *Annales Monastici* (ed. Luard), iv, *passim*. The compiler found 'nothing memorable', for example, under the years 1165, 1166, 1169, and 1172.

[2] The distinction between chronicles and histories is well drawn by Gervase of Canterbury (*Opera Historica*, i. 87), though he himself offends against his own canons, for he writes a history and calls it a chronicle.

monastery who might add local details and continue the story with the events of his own time. Florence of Worcester, for example, based his chronicle on that of Marianus Scotus, an Irish monk who wrote at Mainz; Robert of Torigni's is a continuation of the chronicle of Sigebert of Gembloux near Liége. Facilities for writing were also improved: Paul of Caen, the first Norman abbot of St. Albans, equipped his house with a library and built a scriptorium, and his successor made provision for its upkeep. By the end of the twelfth century most of the greater Benedictine monasteries had substantial libraries, perhaps the largest being Christ Church, Canterbury, with not less than 600 volumes.[1] At Evesham certain revenues were appropriated for the purchase of parchment and for the payment of copyists.

Nevertheless the writing of history was not the sole prerogative of monks. Secular clerks, whose calling naturally brought them into touch with a wider or at least a different sphere of activities, also made their contribution to the historical literature of the twelfth century. Henry of Huntingdon was an archdeacon who had spent his early life in an episcopal household, Ralph de Diceto was dean of St. Paul's and had studied at Paris, while Roger of Hoveden was a clerk attached to the court of Henry II and was employed as an itinerant justice.[2] Each in his way was in a position to acquire exact knowledge of contemporary events. Cathedrals and the great abbeys, it should be borne in mind, were the safe repositories of public documents; the clergy, whether attached to a monastery or to a cathedral, would have ready access to these, and their inclusion in chronicles adds greatly to the importance of the latter as sources of history.

We have yet to mention that unique historical monument, the *Anglo-Saxon Chronicle*. No other country can boast of any vernacular history of so early a date; none, indeed, until about the time when the last annals of the English chronicle were being written. It had been kept up in the days of Edward the Confessor at some half-dozen monasteries; and in some of them it survived the coming of the Normans.[3] But Latin was rapidly gaining ground over the vernacular; one version was

---

[1] Knowles, *Monastic Order*, pp. 524–5.
[2] See F. Barlow, *Eng. Hist. Rev.* lxv (1950), 352.
[3] See Stenton, *Anglo-Saxon England*, pp. 679–81.

copied bilingually about the year 1100 at St. Augustine's, Canterbury;[1] another version written at Christ Church, Canterbury, with very meagre entries inscribed in the ancient form on the margin of an Easter table, retained the native language till 1110, when it breaks into Latin and only once returns again to English to record the dedication of Christ Church (1130).[2] Yet another version (now lost), compiled at the monastery of St. Augustine's, Canterbury, down to the year 1121, was copied at Peterborough, and was there continued until the accession of Henry II. This famous chronicle is of interest not merely for its vivid account of events in England under the Norman kings, but also for the evidence it affords of the survival of historical prose writing far into the twelfth century. Hereafter it dies, only to be revived more than two centuries later by John Trevisa. But about the time when the English chronicle was drawing to its close a new form of historical literature was coming into fashion. This was also in the vernacular, but it was in verse. So towards the middle of the twelfth century a clerk of Regensburg wrote the history of the empire in more than 17,000 verses, the *Kaiserchronik*; at the beginning of the thirteenth William le Breton in the *Philippide* related the deeds of Philip Augustus in French verse. Henry II engaged a Channel Islander, Wace, to compose an epic of the dukes of Normandy which was completed in the *Roman de Rou* down to the battle of Tinchebrai; Jordan Fantosme, who had been attached to the household of Bishop Henry of Winchester, wrote a long metrical account in Anglo-Norman dialect of the war with Scotland in 1173–4, in which he himself had taken part; and a trouvère of accomplished skill has left us a lively and realistic picture of chivalric society in a metrical life of William the Marshal.

Latin, as we have seen, was the language of the church and of scholars, of government and of the law in the twelfth century. It was a living language often undeservedly despised because it did not attempt (like the pedantic Latin of the renaissance) to be Ciceronian. At its best, as we meet it, for example, in the writings of John of Salisbury, it was pure and grammatical; at its worst, it was at least natural and unaffected, a language

---

[1] Cf. F. P. Magoun, jun., 'The Domitian Bilingual of the Old-English Annals: The Latin Preface' in *Speculum*, xx (1945), 65.

[2] Printed by Liebermann, *Ungedruckte Anglo-Normannische Geschichtsquellen*, pp. 3–8.

constantly enriched by borrowings from the vernacular and readily adapted to the needs of a progressive and changing society. When the classical vocabulary failed them, scribes would not hesitate to latinize an English or a French word. Thus *purkacia* (purchases), *drana* (drain), *cropum* (crop), *tierum* (halter), *pelfare* (to pilfer), *medlare cum* (to meddle with); sometimes they would insert a word in its natural form: *eschippre* (skipper), *blanchet* (blanket), *gingebred*; or a familiar phrase, such as *bi land et bi strand*, which could be understood by all.[1] This intermixture of languages became increasingly more common as time went on; but in the period of which we are speaking it was always restrained, and never reached such absurd lengths as it did in the later middle ages. The same mixing of languages is observable in the surnames or nicknames used to distinguish the numerous Johns, Geoffreys, and Roberts: *Galfridus Vis de Cat* (Geoffrey Catface), *Robertus Mangebien* (the hearty eater), *Joannes Wudecoc* (John Woodcock), or *Willelmus Surmelch* (William Sourmilk).[2]

The Latin tongue, however, was a prerogative enjoyed by the few, the men of letters, the clergy (or some of them), the officials. The Anglo-Norman court spoke French, and the peasants, the great bulk of the population, only English. With these the native language must be the medium of communication. Occasionally, indeed frequently in the years immediately following the Conquest, instructions were issued in English, sometimes in both English and Latin. A series of writs confirming to the archbishops of Canterbury the temporalities of their see was prepared bilingually down to the time of Henry II. Canterbury, however, was singularly conservative in this respect, and these texts seem to have been copied *mutatis mutandis* from ancient models, dating back to Edward the Confessor's grant to Archbishop Stigand (*c.* 1052) or perhaps even to a similar grant of Canute to Æthelnoth of the year 1020.[3] Although, therefore,

---

[1] These examples are taken at random from legal or exchequer records of the twelfth and early thirteenth centuries.

[2] *Pipe Rolls 32* and *33 Hen. II.*

[3] See J. Hall, *Early Middle English, 1130–1250*, Part II, p. 264. Henry I's confirmation to William of Corbeil (1123), which is in this form, is printed with facsimile and notes by Warner and Ellis, *Facsimiles of Royal and Other Charters in the British Museum*, p. 6. The persistence of the English tradition at Canterbury is again evinced by the interlinear insertion of an Anglo-Saxon version in the famous Canterbury Psalter copied by the monk Eadwine about 1150. This book has been reproduced in facsimile with introduction and notes by M. R. James in 1934. A further

these cannot be taken as illustrations of a general practice, they are not unique; a writ of Henry I confirming privileges in London to Archbishop Anselm, for example, is bilingual[1] and the boundaries of an estate were sometimes described in Anglo-Saxon even in the reign of Henry II.[2] Moreover, men were still pleading in English in the county court in 1116 and seemingly long after,[3] while magnates in the north of England addressed their vassals, their 'thegns and drengs', in Anglo-Saxon at least till the end of the eleventh century.[4] Occasionally in the period an official document was rendered in Anglo-Norman. A deed of the twelfth century was recently discovered among the Public Records,[5] and a correspondence between Stephen Langton and King John concerning the bishopric of Rochester in January 1215 was also conducted in this vernacular.[6]

To what extent the exotic aristocracy from Normandy became acquainted with the language of their adopted country it is impossible to ascertain. We may suppose that succeeding generations would pick it up in youth from nurses, servants, and rustics about their estates. The story of Hugh de Morville's mother has often been told on account of its terrible sequel and to show the evil stock from which the Becket murderer was descended. Overcome with an unrequited passion for a youth, she induced the latter to appear before her husband in play with a drawn sword. He is said to have been condemned and boiled to death. The chief interest of the tale lies, however, not so much in its lurid details as in the fact that the warning cry of the woman was in English: 'Huge de Morevile, ware, ware, ware, Lithulf heth his swerd adrage.'[7] English was therefore familiarly

interest is attached to this manuscript by the drawing and description of 'the star called comet . . . in English it is called "the hairy star" '. It has been identified as Halley's comet which appeared in 1145.

[1] F. M. Stenton, *Norman London*, p. 9, n. 1.

[2] Cf. the Tavistock Charter, *c.* 1174, printed in *Eng. Hist. Rev.* lxii (1947), 363. The increased use of the archaic letters ð and þ, evident in records of the last years of the century, is, however, an antiquarian revival rather than a survival. Cf. *Pipe Roll 9 Ric. I*, p. xxv.

[3] Ordericus Vitalis, quoted by Miss Dominica Legge in *History*, xxvi (1941), 165. Cf. Maitland, *Pleas of the Crown for the County of Gloucester*, p. xxvii.

[4] See F. Liebermann, 'Drei northumbrische Urkunden um 1100', in *Archiv für das Studium der Neueren Sprachen und Literaturen*, cxi. 276 ff.

[5] By H. Richardson, *Bulletin of the John Rylands Library*, xxiv (1940), 168.

[6] *Acta Stephani Langton*, ed. Kathleen Major (Canterbury and York Soc. 1950), pp. 19–21, 158; *Rot. Chart.*, p. 209.

[7] The story is related by William of Canterbury in his life of Becket, *Materials for the History of Becket*, i. 128.

spoken in at least some Anglo-Norman knightly households in the first part of the twelfth century. Unquestionably many of the higher clergy knew the native language and preached in it, like Odo, abbot of Battle (1175–1200), and Samson, abbot of Bury St. Edmunds (1182–1211), the latter in the local dialect (*lingua Norfolchie*). Indeed, as has been pointed out, 'the pulpit was the cradle of English prose'.[1] It was devotional literature in the vernacular which preserved the tradition of English prose writing through the period of its eclipse. At Worcester, owing to the influence of Bishop Wulfstan who held the see till 1095 and whose own life was written by a Worcester monk in Anglo-Saxon,[2] the persistence of the native language in religious works was particularly strong. Collections of sermons taken from those of the great homilist, Ælfric, and from other pre-Conquest sources, Anglo-Saxon versions of parts of the Bible, service books, and lives of saints, continued to be copied there in the twelfth century. The reputation of King Alfred was not forgotten; some of his translations from the Latin were still transcribed after the Conquest, and what were deemed to be his wise sayings, 'Proverbs of Alfred', were written down and form one of the more important texts of early middle-English literature. Their vogue is illustrated by the frequent quotation from them in the fine poem, 'The Owl and the Nightingale'. To the class of devotional literature also belongs the *Ancren Riwle*, admittedly the greatest vernacular prose work of this time, and perhaps the most interesting of the whole middle-English period. Written for the guidance of three noble anchoresses, much of it, indeed most of it, is devoted to the usual, somewhat pedantic, edifying instruction and biblical precepts suitable to religious communities but tedious to the modern reader. The concluding pages, however, contain some matter of more general interest, passages which throw light on domestic manners and social life. The unknown author writes with a fresh and simple style, with a natural gift for description and character-drawing. It enjoyed for three centuries an immense popularity; almost at once it became available in Latin and French translations; it became a classic. Unquestionably it fills a place of great importance in the

---

[1] A. G. Little in a review of *Literature and Pulpit in Medieval England*, by G. R. Owst, *Eng. Hist. Rev.* xlix (1934), 116.

[2] This has not survived, and it is only known through the Latin translation made by William of Malmesbury. See *Vita Wulfstani* (ed. R. R. Darlington, Camden Soc.), Introd., p. viii.

development of vernacular prose literature which, at this date, was unmatched on the Continent.

French, however, had gained rapidly over English since the coming of the Normans. It was *par excellence* the language of romance and of poetry. There is a crudity, a lack of refinement and grace about pre-Chaucerian English literature; and naturally so, for it was written for the entertainment of the humbler folk who were denied, by reason of their ignorance of the language, the finer compositions in Latin and French. Written, therefore, for an uncritical public, it displays, when compared with the literature of the Anglo-Saxon period, a certain loss of literary standard.

'*Beowulf* was composed for persons of quality, *Havelok* (an epic poem of the late thirteenth century) for the common people. Old English narrative poetry was, in its day, the best obtainable; English metrical romances were known by the authors, vendors, and consumers of them to be inferior to the best, i.e. to the French; and consequently there is a rustic, uncourtly air about them. Their demeanour is often lumbering, and they are sometimes conscious of it.'[1]

This hard criticism seems just. Moreover, even this rustic literature is borrowed or at least largely influenced by the French. An exception may be made in favour of 'The Owl and the Nightingale', a poem written in octosyllabic rhyming couplets in the southern dialect, retailing a debate between the two birds, the one representing solemn austerity, the other brightness and love, about the merits of their respective accomplishments. Though both the theme and the form are common in French models, yet it is original and, as one very competent judge has described it, 'the most miraculous piece of writing'.[2] The argument is pithy and it is alive; the author has an aptitude for effective simile (the Nightingale chatters 'like an Irish priest'); there is nothing of conventionality or the commonplace about the poem.

As in France romantic literature centred round the saga of Charlemagne and Roland, so in England the core of romance was the Arthurian legend. The fact that Charlemagne was not French and Arthur was not English was immaterial; they were

[1] W. P. Ker, *Cambridge History of English Literature*, i. 277.
[2] W. P. Ker, *English Literature: Mediaeval* (Home University Library), p. 181. The text with a translation has been edited by J. W. H. Atkins (Cambridge, 1922).

quickly adopted by these countries and became national heroes. Of Celtic origin, whether from Brittany, Wales, or Cornwall is very debatable and need not concern us here,[1] the story of Arthur was pieced together by Geoffrey of Monmouth (a man probably of Breton parentage, brought up on the south Welsh border, and closely connected with Oxford in its early days as a centre of learning) in the *Historia Regum Britanniae*. This famous and remarkable work, a strange medley of truth and fiction, of folk tradition and fantasy, thrown together into a twelfth-century setting of courts, tournaments, and love affairs, was completed about 1135 and dedicated to Robert of Gloucester, the natural son of King Henry I. Its popularity was immediate and widespread; some fifty manuscripts of the twelfth century alone are still extant; and it was almost universally accepted as genuine history.[2] Versions of the story were made in different languages and with fresh embellishments. Among the earliest of these 'Bruts' as they were called—the name is derived from Brutus of Troy, the legendary first king of Britain—is that of Wace, to whom we have already had occasion to refer as the author of a history of the dukes of Normandy. It was Wace's paraphrase of the story that, early in the thirteenth century, Layamon on the banks of the Severn turned into alliterative English verse. His work, however, is not a mere translation of Wace. He adds local colour, especially in his use of similes; he also develops the story, possibly from tales picked up from his Welsh neighbours. He tells, for example, of the passing of Arthur, and it is from him that the famous versions of Malory and Tennyson are ultimately derived. Layamon's poem, more-over, is English not only in language but also in spirit. It is patriotic, and the British Arthur becomes in his hands a national hero, the pattern of all that was best in English kingship. His work is even faintly reminiscent of the grand heroic poetry of the Anglo-Saxons. Many details essential to later Arthurian litera-ture are wanting in the *Historia* of Geoffrey of Monmouth:

---

[1] On this question and other problems of the Arthurian legend see E. K. Chambers, *Arthur of Britain* (1937).

[2] Ailred of Rievaulx in his *Speculum Caritatis* written in 1143 and William of Newburgh in his *Historia* written at the end of the century are almost alone among writers of the time to discern the real nature of Geoffrey's book. According to Newburgh he is weaving together *ridicula figmenta* (ed. Howlett, i. 11). For Ailred see Powicke, *Walter Daniel's Life of Ailred of Rievaulx* (Nelson's Medieval Classics, 1950) lxxxvii–ix.

Lancelot and Percival; Tristram and Iseult; the Round Table and the Holy Grail. Little by little these were added; gradually the full story was developed, chiefly indeed in France through the work of Chrétien de Troyes, Marie de France, and others; and by the end of our period the complete cycle is present in the literature of Europe.

Of early lyric poetry in the vernacular, little has survived. Some hymns in honour of the Virgin and St. Nicholas, attributed to Godric (1170), the far-travelled merchant who ended his days as a hermit at Finchale in the county of Durham, are extant with musical notation; some snatches of song, like that supposed to have been sung by the soldiers of Geoffrey de Mandeville when they laid waste the fens round St. Ives,[1] or the refrain 'Swete lamman dhin are' (Sweetheart, thy lover craves thy mercy) sung by dancers in a churchyard with which the Worcestershire parson, according to Giraldus Cambrensis,[2] accidentally greeted his congregation instead of with the customary 'Dominus vobiscum', have been casually inserted in chronicles. The carol—the word originally denoted a ring dance accompanied with song—was a popular form of amusement not only in the baronial hall but on the village green, and the singing of part-songs was a favourite pastime, especially in Wales and in the north country.[3] Songs, however, particularly secular songs, were often of a topical, transient character, and little likely to be written down or preserved. We may be sure that such fragments as have chanced to come down to us represent a substantial literature of this kind which was quickly forgotten and lost to succeeding generations.[4]

Looking back at the literary achievement of England in the twelfth century, we find, perhaps, disappointingly little of native inspiration. France provided the standard of taste in poetry and romance; France, or possibly we should say Provence, furnished the ideas. It was the Provençal poets who gave

---

[1] J. H. Round, *Geoffrey de Mandeville*, p. 213, quoting a manuscript of Matthew Paris's *Historia Anglorum*.   [2] 'Gemma Ecclesiastica', *Opera*, ii. 120.

[3] See the interesting chapter in Giraldus's 'Description of Wales' (book 1, ch. 13, *Opera*, vi. 189), where he speaks of the Welsh singers beginning in parts and ending in unison in B flat: 'in unam denique sub B mollis dulcedine blanda consonantiam, et organicam convenientia melodiam.' In Yorkshire, he tells us, they sang only in two parts, treble and bass. Cf. Gustave Reese, *Music in the Middle Ages* (1941), p. 387.

[4] Cf. R. M. Wilson, 'Lost Literature in Old and Middle English', in *Leeds Studies in English and Kindred Languages*, ii (1933), 14.

birth to the ideal of chivalry, of courtly love[1] which permeates the literature of this time and was handed on as a central theme of lyrical and even narrative poetry of later ages. In itself, of course, it is nothing new; the love-story, the worship of women, is age-old, and much the same whether it be the love of Aeneas for Dido or Tristram for Iseult, and doubtless the medieval writers learnt a great deal from Virgil and Ovid in their treatment of it. But the mode of thought, the atmosphere, is a fresh departure: it is chivalrous. This does not imply the mere trappings and display of chivalry which became rapidly debased, but what it really stood for, respect for and homage to women (a symptom of which was the increasing cult of the Virgin), courtesy, good manners, all that is properly understood by 'gentlemanly conduct', or what Sir Philip Sidney, imitating the Provençal sentiment, expressed in the line:

'Love of honour and honour of love.'[2]

It was this tradition of honour, which lies at the root of the chivalric ideal, that was passed on as a great legacy from the twelfth century to the present day.

Turning now to the stage, it should be first emphasized that the medieval drama, such as it was, owes almost nothing to the ancient world. William of Blois, brother of the more famous Peter, wrote a comedy called *Alda*, the plot of which he claims to have taken from Menander, probably the Ἀνδρόγυνος which he could have met with in a Latin translation during his residence in Sicily about 1167.[3] But it was only with the Renaissance that the west became acquainted with the Greek tragedians or with Plautus. Terence was known, but his works were not acted and they exercised little, if any, influence on the medieval playwright.[4] In the twelfth century, entertainment was provided by minstrels, jesters, or buffoons. The nobility had their own jesters, who were sometimes men of substance or became so by

---

[1] A. J. Denomy, C.S.B., in *Mediaeval Studies* (Pontifical Institute of Toronto), vi (1944), 175–260, derives Courtly Love from the Neo-Platonists, Plotinus—John Scotus Erigena—Albigenses, or by another channel Arabic Neo-Platonism—Arabic Mysticism. These he considers to be the influences that produced the early troubadours.

[2] Quoted by W. P. Ker, op. cit., p. 97.

[3] Raby, *Secular Latin Poetry*, ii. 61–3; Lynn White, jun., in *Eng. Hist. Rev.* 1 (1935), 487.

[4] Hrotsvitha, a tenth-century nun of the Saxon monastery of Gandersheim, wrote plays and imitated Terence; but she stands alone. Cf. Sandys, *Hist. of Classical Scholarship*, i. 506.

their professional attainments: William I's *joculator* appears in Domesday as an owner of considerable property in the city of Gloucester, and Henry I's *mimus* was sufficiently well-to-do to found the great priory of St. Bartholomew at Smithfield. Nevertheless, in general their reputation did not stand high; in Cheshire minstrels were classed with whores and placed under a special jurisdiction.[1] Indeed their performances were doubtless often far from edifying, obscene in language and gesture, and interspersed with ribald songs and coarse satire, such as the 'goliads' the roving students composed, sang, and disseminated about the world as they moved from one tavern to another. The clergy had their own form of buffoonery in the 'Feast of Fools' and similar farces held on the days following Christmas, while a primitive folk drama is also manifested in the popular observances, survivals of pagan ritual, on village festivals, particularly the May-day celebrations. All these *ludibria*, however, were frowned upon by the ecclesiastical authorities, and were prohibited by stern though ineffective decrees.

A more significant influence on the evolution of the drama was, however, contributed by the church itself in scenes with action and dialogue incorporated in its liturgy on the important Christian festivals. 'Representations' of the shepherds on Christmas night and of scenes of the resurrection in Easter week are provided for in the statutes of Lichfield cathedral made by Hugh of Nonant (1188–98); a *ludus* of St. Catherine was staged at Dunstable early in the twelfth century by the schoolmaster with copes borrowed (and unhappily destroyed by fire) from the abbey of St. Albans; and three plays, having as their subjects a miracle of St. Nicholas, the raising of Lazarus, and the story of Daniel, by an author whose name was Hilary and who very possibly was an Englishman, have been preserved. Although the evidence for England is scanty, it is sufficient to justify the opinion that such plays were performed in most great churches. The rapid growth of this form of drama took place when it became secularized; when it emerged from the nave of the church to the graveyard or the market-place. The increasing elaboration of the staging aided by the more frequent use of the

---

[1] Rannulf, earl of Chester (1181–1232), bestowed the 'magistratum omnium leccatorum et meretricum totius Cestriae' upon Roger de Lacy. His son John gave it in turn to his steward, Hugh of Dutton. In the time of Edward I the service is defined as the 'advocaria omnium menestrallorum (minstrels) et meretricium'. *Cal. of Inq.* iii. 145. Cf. Chambers, *Medieval Stage*, ii. 259.

vernacular made such a process inevitable. It had already begun before the end of the twelfth century, but its development belongs to a later age.

It has long been recognized that the Byzantine tradition has had a deep-rooted influence on the art of western Europe. It was inherent in the art forms of the Anglo-Saxon period when the school of Dunstan and Æthelwold in manuscript illumination was unsurpassed. This great school suffered something of an eclipse at the time of the Conquest.[1] The bishops and abbots imported from Normandy had little interest and little skill in the craft, and they had nothing to contribute to the great tradition they found established. But in the twelfth century it received fresh inspiration both from contact with the Norman kingdom of Sicily with its rich Greek heritage and from southern France. Sometimes a foreign craftsman might be employed in England or an English craftsman might perhaps have travelled on the Continent and seen at first hand the art treasures of Europe; but it was chiefly through the medium of illuminated books, which could be readily moved about, given away or borrowed, that the style of one country was transmitted to another. In the history of medieval art, therefore, manuscript illumination was of fundamental importance; it was commonly the prototype of mural painting and sculpture. At the time when the form of handwriting, the firm, neat, rounded script, known as the Carolingian minuscle, reached its perfection before it slowly gave way to the angular, untidy, but time-saving cursive, the art of illumination in England was also at its best. During the second half of the twelfth century the monastic scriptoria in many parts of England were producing volumes of unrivalled quality and elegance. Most remarkable of these are the great Bibles, the earliest of which was produced at Bury St. Edmunds (now among the manuscripts at Corpus Christi College, Cambridge) and the finest and most famous at Winchester. The Winchester Bible was begun when Henry of Blois, himself a patron of art, was bishop, and is the work of at least six artists of genius.[2] This splendid manuscript in three

---

[1] But for the essential continuation of the Anglo-Saxon tradition despite the dislocation caused by the Conquest see F. Wormald in *Proceedings of the British Academy*, xxx (1944), 127. The manuscripts connected with William of St. Calais, bishop of Durham, 1081–96, form an important link. See O. Pächt, *Bodleian Library Record*, iii (1950), 96–103.

[2] Cf. Walter Oakeshott, *The Artists of the Winchester Bible*.

volumes measuring $23 \times 15\frac{3}{4}$ inches is illustrated by two full-page outline drawings and very numerous initial letters into which are woven finely drawn and deeply coloured miniatures of biblical or allegorical subjects. It was in the twelfth century also that the bestiary enjoyed its greatest popularity. The text of these was usually based on the collection of moralizing tales of the Physiologus which belong to the early centuries of the Christian era; they are richly illustrated by highly coloured drawings of real or fabulous animals like the phoenix or the unicorn, and which became the exemplars for many of the grotesque carvings which may be seen on Romanesque churches.

This was a great age of ecclesiastical architecture. Within a century of the Conquest almost all the cathedral churches and the churches of the great Benedictine abbeys were rebuilt in a style which drew its inspiration from Normandy. But the architecture of this period is not a mere copy from the Norman. In England it developed and, in the opinion of a leading authority, the Anglo-Norman school became 'perhaps the most advanced and progressive of all branches of northern Romanesque'.[1] This impressive achievement is often attributed to the bishops and abbots of the Norman period. These, no doubt, initiated the work and raised the funds for carrying it out; a bishop was always anxious that his *cathedra*, his throne, should be in a building of dignity and splendour. Some, such as Gundulf, bishop of Rochester, who is said to have been very skilful and efficient in the work of a mason (*coementarius*)[2] or Rannulf Flambard, who was responsible for fine building work at each of the three churches with which he was connected (St. Martin's, Dover, Christ Church in Hampshire, and Durham), may well have had more than a mere amateur's knowledge of architecture. But they were not the architects in the technical sense. The expert work, the plan, and the construction were entrusted to a trained engineer (*ingeniator*) or a master-mason (*coementarius*) and the decorative work to other skilled craftsmen.[3] The names of some of these craftsmen are known:

---

[1] A. W. Clapham, *Romanesque Architecture in Western Europe*, p. 138, and for the whole subject the same author's *English Romanesque Architecture after the Conquest*.

[2] *Textus Roffensis* (ed. Hearne), p. 146, quoted R. A. L. Smith, *Eng. Hist. Rev.* lviii (1943), 268.

[3] Cf. A. Hamilton Thompson in *History*, x (1925), 139. Similarly, secular works, castles, &c., were built by professional engineers. Ailnoth *ingeniator* was in charge of most of the royal building operations during the reign of Henry II. Roger of Clare,

the rebuilding of the choir at Canterbury after the disastrous fire in 1174 was entrusted to William of Sens, a Burgundian, who took full charge of the work until he fell from the scaffolding and was so disabled that he had to relinquish his task and was replaced by William the Englishman; Geoffrey de Noiers, described as *fabricae constructor*, was employed by St. Hugh (who himself is said to have worked as a labourer, carrying hods of stone and mortar) in the rebuilding of Lincoln cathedral in 1192.

Without the aid of illustration and diagram it is arid and unprofitable to discuss in detail architectural development. The most striking feature about English Romanesque is the massiveness of its structure: the massive columns carrying heavy rounded arches, the massive central tower over the crossing, and the great length of nave, extending at Norwich to as many as fourteen bays. It was usual to build from east to west, so that when the choir was completed and dedicated the work of prayer could proceed, while the masons continued at leisure the building of the nave. The early Norman choirs, which often had a crypt beneath, followed one of two plans: either they ended with three apses as at Durham or St. Albans, or with a single apse and an ambulatory from which protruded three radiating chapels as at Norwich or Gloucester. But they built them too small and perhaps too austere to please succeeding generations, nor was there sufficient space for the number of altars required to meet the growing demand for Masses. So they were rebuilt, fire or collapse often providing the opportunity, extended, generally with a square instead of an apsidal east end, and enriched with Gothic embellishment. Little, therefore, of early English Romanesque remains standing to-day in the choirs of the cathedral churches. It is in the great naves that the massiveness and fine proportions of the building of the Anglo-Norman architects can best be appreciated. The most original and important feature is the treatment of the roof. Durham, begun in 1093 and finished in 1133, at once the finest and most perfect

earl of Hertford (*c.* 1153–73), retained a certain Roger *artifex* or *le Enginnur* in his service and the post appears to have become hereditary in the family for at least three generations, Westminster Abbey MSS. 2384, 2385, 2590, 2595, 2602. I owe these references to the kindness of Mr. Arnold Taylor. The professional was not, however, always employed; the repairs to the houses in the important castle of Nottingham were supervised by the doctor (*medicus*) and the parson (*persona*), *Pipe Roll 30 Hen. II*, p. 95.

example of the architecture of this period, was, if not the first church, at least the first still standing, which was covered by a stone vault carried on cross-ribs. In this system clerestory lighting could be obtained, a thing impossible with a stone barrel-vault which required a solid wall to take the strain. The latter part of the twelfth century saw the gradual change to Gothic. The pointed arch, its most obvious feature, was first introduced from Burgundy by the early Cistercians. It had developed in France in the first half of the twelfth century, and when William of Sens was engaged to build the choir at Canterbury, he adopted the style with which he was familiar in his home-town. Henceforth it was followed in all the great churches, notably at Lincoln and Wells which were being rebuilt in the last decade of the century. In these there is scarcely a trace of Romanesque.

The earliest Romanesque buildings in England were almost devoid of decoration, and it would seem that the masons had little skill in stone carving. Nevertheless, they soon learnt the art. The chevron pattern, the most characteristic and probably a creation of the Anglo-Norman school,[1] appears very early in the twelfth century (1110–20), and by the middle of the century half a dozen or more decorative motives had been developed on the arches, mouldings, and capitals in the Norman churches. As the century advanced the richness and variety of the decoration increased. The ignorance of drawing and anatomy revealed in the crude and primitive figure-sculpture of the Normans makes it necessary to look elsewhere for the source of the best English work. It probably derives from the Anglo-Saxon tradition which was itself affected by German and Scandinavian influences; and later in the century the French school of sculpture evident at Cluny, St. Denis, and Chartres began to affect English taste, and perhaps first appears in the carved capitals of the Canterbury crypt. During the same period parish churches all over the country were built or rebuilt in stone in the Norman fashion. These varied enormously in plan and elaborateness from a simple single chamber to a cathedral in miniature with aisled naves, transepts, and chancel. A typical example of a twelfth-century village church is that of Iffley near Oxford (1175–82) with nave, central tower, and chancel (later extended) and with the characteristic chevron decoration on the mouldings of the doors and windows. Some of the finest examples are very small churches such as Kilpeck in Herefordshire (*c.* 1145), one of a group of churches in that locality, all possibly the design of one architect. It has a nave, chancel, and apse, and is remarkable for the wealth of ornament particularly on the south doorway and for the curious series of grotesque birds, animals, and signs of the zodiac on the corbels which surround the exterior. Another fine specimen of a tiny (its overall length is under 50 feet) but highly decorated church is Barfreystone in Kent which also has a superbly carved doorway. It is on the tympana of these churches that Romanesque sculpture is displayed at its best. Usually the central figure is Christ in Glory as at Barfreystone or over the west doorway at Ely where it is supported by angels. On the tympanum over the south door at Malmesbury there is a somewhat similar design; but the finest and most important of the Malmesbury sculptures are the almost life-sized figures of the twelve apostles in the south porch. Monumental sculpture was still in a primitive stage and the figure lies awkwardly as if it were standing and not in a natural pose. Sculptors also exercised their skill very often on fonts. The figure carving of the virtues and vices on the late-twelfth-century font at Southrop in Gloucestershire is fine work, and the lead font at Dorchester abbey has good reliefs of the apostles. The richly decorated fonts set on five shafts and made of the blue-black marble of Tournai form an interesting group. Besides the well-known examples at Winchester and Lincoln cathedrals, the former presenting scenes from the life of St. Nicholas, the latter fabulous beasts, there are three others in Hampshire, one in Lincolnshire, and another at Ipswich. The entry on the Pipe Roll of 1194 that the merchants of Tournai render account of 100*s.* for the collection of their debts in the city of Winchester may be an indication of the date of these fonts.[1]

By modern standards the medieval church must have appeared a little garish. The whole building was animated by colour. Wherever there was a surface which could take paint, paint, it seems, was applied. Roofs, walls, arches, and the splays of windows were painted with biblical or allegorical subjects, with scenes from the lives of saints or with floral or geometric designs; the sculpture and carved decoration not only within the church, but even on its exterior were adorned with paint. From time to time these paintings were renewed, perhaps with a different and more fashionable subject on a fresh surface of lime-wash; and finally they were obliterated by the white-washing of the puritans. In recent times these coats of lime and over-paint have been skilfully removed revealing enough to enable the restorer to reproduce something of the original.[1] The series which is best preserved, however, is in the apse of the chapel of St. Gabriel in the crypt at Canterbury, which chanced to be walled up in 1199. The paintings thus escaped the repainting and lime-washing which was the common fate of other twelfth-century work of this kind. They depict round a central figure of Christ the nativity and naming of St. John the Baptist and the Annunciation. A remarkably complete scheme of mural decoration can also be seen in the chancel of the small church at Kempley in Gloucestershire. Though entirely different in style, the paintings in the nave of the church at Claverley (Salop) are of great interest. They represent a body of mounted knights in combat and are strikingly reminiscent of the Bayeux tapestry of a hundred years earlier. This famous stitch-work, unique both as a work of art and as an historical document, was probably made for Odo, bishop of Bayeux, who himself figures prominently on the 'tapestry'; he is, for example, depicted encouraging the boys with the aid of a heavy stick or mace ('Hic Odo episcopus baculum tenens confortat pueros') in the feigned or real flight of the Norman knights at Hastings. In the opinion of many recognized authorities it is of English workmanship (the English school of embroidery was held in high repute) and was completed in the last quarter of the eleventh century.[2] Windows in the twelfth century were of clear glass and therefore added nothing to the galaxy of colour. Stained glass was only introduced into England at the close of the twelfth century and only adorned the greatest churches. The glass in the choir at Canterbury and a fragment or two elsewhere is all that has survived. English stained glass belongs to the Gothic period.

[1] For the whole subject see E. W. Tristram, *English Medieval Wall Painting*, which is illustrated with numerous plates. In the opinion of some experts Dr. Tristram's restoration has been too thorough.

[2] See the introduction by Eric Maclagan to *The Bayeux Tapestry* (King Penguin, 1943).

IX

THE CELTIC FRINGE

(a) SCOTLAND

IN 1087 the boundary between the kingdoms of England and
Scotland was still undetermined. Circumstances might well
have fixed it either at the Forth, the northern extremity of
the old Anglian kingdom of Bernicia,[1] or at the Tyne or even
the Tees where indeed it actually rested in the reign of David I
(1124–53). On the west the Scottish kings had a valid claim to
Cumbria, the district described as situated *inter Angliam et
Scotiam*,[2] which comprised Cumberland and the northern half of
Westmorland, with its southern boundary on the river Duddon;
a land with racial affinities to Scotland, for there, as in the west
of Scotland, a strong Norse element, introduced from Ireland
or the Hebrides, was superimposed on a population predominantly Celtic.[3] Furthermore, at one time, again under
King David, in whose reign Scotland reached to the height of
its power, the Scottish dominion stretched into Lancashire, and
controlled the district between the Duddon and the Ribble
which formerly had been a part of the ancient kingdom of
Northumbria.[4] Lothian, the land between the Forth and Tweed,
was already at least partially anglicized when it was annexed to
the Scottish Crown by Malcolm II in 1018; it had political
associations with England; and the English chronicler regarded
it as different from Scotland when he wrote that Malcolm III
marched 'out of Scotland into Lothian in England'.[5] It was
therefore a natural asylum for the Northumbrians hustled away
by the attacks of William the Conqueror and the harrying of
the north. Among the fugitives was Edgar the Ætheling, the
grandson of Edmund Ironside, and his two sisters, one of whom,

---

[1] Scotland was actually divided at this line in the time of Alexander I (1107–24).
Had this arrangement persisted, says Hume Brown (*Hist. of Scotland*, i. 72), 'Lothian
and Cumbria must inevitably have gone to England'.

[2] Inquisition of Earl David as to the extent of the lands of the church of Glasgow,
c. 1124, printed by A. C. Lawrie, *Early Scottish Charters*, p. 44.

[3] See Alexander Bugge, 'The Norse Settlements in the British Islands', *Trans.
R. Hist. Soc.*, 4th ser., iv. 197 ff. (1921).

[4] See particularly W. Farrer, 'The Domesday Survey of North Lancashire, &c.'
in the *Transactions of the Lancashire and Cheshire Antiquarian Society*, xviii (1900), 88 ff.

[5] *Anglo-Saxon Chronicle*, sub anno 1091.

Margaret, married the Scottish king, Malcolm Canmore (or Bighead), who had come to the throne by his victory over Macbeth in 1057 and was still reigning when our period opens with the accession of William Rufus. This marriage profoundly affected the history of both countries. It led, in the first place, through the influence of Margaret and her sons to the complete anglicization of the Lowlands; secondly it provided the Scottish king with a pretext for his aggressive raids into England which he could allege were made to redress the wrongs of his brother-in-law.

The ejection of Edgar the Ætheling from Normandy and his Norman lands was declared to be the motive for a plundering foray in 1091 when William Rufus was absent on the Continent. It was checked, and, as soon as he could get back to England, Rufus retaliated by an invasion of Scotland by land and sea. His fleet, however, was broken up in a storm and his army was delayed by a more urgent danger on the Welsh border; consequently it was already late in the campaigning season—the latter part of November—when he, accompanied by his two brothers, reached the Forth. He therefore adopted the prudent course of allowing his brother, Duke Robert, and Edgar the Ætheling to negotiate a treaty which followed the lines of that made by his father at Abernethy on the banks of the Tay in 1073: in return for confirmation in his twelve English vills and the promise of an annual payment of twelve marks of gold, Malcolm became Rufus's man 'with all such obedience as he had rendered to his father'. For William Rufus this was mere temporizing. He had no intention of leaving Malcolm unmolested. In the next year (1092) he drove Dolfin, son of the Northumbrian Earl Gospatric, from Cumbria, capturing Carlisle, the western doorway into Scotland, which he rebuilt and fortified with a castle, and where he planted a colony of rustics imported, it is said, from the southern parts of England. The English frontier was, as a result, advanced to the Tweed-Cheviot line. Malcolm came in person to the court at Gloucester in August to protest against this outrageous breach of the treaty of 1091. But Rufus refused even to see him and intimated that he could bring his complaint before his court like any other of his vassals. The king of Scotland was not, however, prepared so to interpret his act of homage; returning to Scotland he collected an army for another, a fifth, invasion of England. But he had scarcely crossed the border when he and his son Edward were treacherously slain near Alnwick by Morel of Bamborough, an intimate friend of his own, the steward and kinsman of Robert de Mowbray, earl of Northumberland (13 November).

The great changes that were initiated in the reign of Malcolm Canmore were largely the work of his wife who survived him but a few days. Queen Margaret seems to have exercised a remarkable influence over her rough and ferocious husband who acted as her Gaelic interpreter, who indulged her whims, and took it in good part when she rifled his money chest to perform an act of charity. From her biography, probably written by her confessor Turgot, no flaw in the saintly character of the queen can be discerned: she devoted her time and strength to pious works; finding the Scottish church sadly in need of reform and wholly out of touch with Rome, she herself with the help of three monks, whom Lanfranc had sent at her request from Canterbury, undertook the task of reforming it; and procured the abolition of its peculiar usages and the establishment of the observances of the continental church in their place. Her innovations were not, however, generally welcomed by the clergy and people of Scotland, and perhaps for that reason she left the organization of the church with its married monks and its hereditary benefices (her own son Æthelred was hereditary lay abbot of Dunkeld) unchanged. It was only gradually, under the direction of the English priests who entered Scotland during the twelfth century, that the Celtic church fell into line with the rest of western Christendom. But there are traits in the character of Queen Margaret that are less commonly associated with sanctity. She was a domineering woman with a strong will of her own; she was conventional and almost ostentatious in her love of splendour in dress and in the things about her. She introduced a high standard of luxury and good living into the cold and comfortless court of the Scottish kings. This had more than a social importance. The delicate food, the French wines, the rich silks and hangings could not be procured in the country; their use stimulated commercial dealings with the foreigner and brought Scotland into economic relations with the outside world.

A Celtic reaction followed the death of Malcolm and Margaret. The English immigrants were driven from the court and for a few years Donald Bane, the late king's brother, sat uncertainly on the throne of Scotland. His title was contested by Duncan, a son of Malcolm by his first marriage, who had spent a large part of his life in England or Normandy, having been handed over as a hostage to William I in 1072. But he was killed in 1094. After that (1094–7) Donald Bane governed the country in conjunction with Edmund, one of Margaret's sons who did not share the anglophil outlook of the rest of the family. But in 1097 the English interest prevailed. The veteran Edgar Atheling at the instance and with the aid of William Rufus marched into Scotland, defeated Donald Bane, and established Edgar, the eldest of his sister's surviving children, on the throne. Under him and his two brothers who reigned successively over Scotland for more than half a century, the changes inaugurated by Margaret were further developed. They had been carefully educated to English ways; they had all, at one time or another, visited England; two had married English wives. Their sisters, Edith (Matilda) and Mary had been brought up in England under the care of their aunt Christina at the abbey of Romsey,[1] and in England they made splendid marriages, the one with King Henry I, the other with Count Eustace of Boulogne. These intimate connexions with England and the English court facilitated and made natural the anglicization of the Scottish lowlands. The English language during these years became the common speech of the people of the south of Scotland.

The reign of Edgar, a quiet unassuming man whom Ailred of Rievaulx, who knew the family,[2] likens in all things to his ancestor Edward the Confessor, was a period of peaceful development interrupted only by the Norwegian conquest of the western Isles. His brother Alexander lived and ruled chiefly in the country north of the Firth of Forth leaving, according to a plan arranged by Edgar, the more anglicized districts of Lothian and Cumbria to his brother David. He had therefore to respect the Celtic traditions deeply rooted among the rebellious highland Scots who abhorred and resisted the English innovations. Nevertheless he contributed something towards the progress of the country especially in the reform of the church; for he, like

[1] They did not become professed nuns as was alleged against Edith. She convinced Anselm, who made a careful investigation of the case, that she only wore the veil in order to keep off importunate and undesirable suitors. Eadmer, *Hist. Nov.*, pp. 121 f.

[2] He was dispenser of David I till about 1134. Cf. F. M. Powicke, *Scottish Hist. Rev.* xxiii (1925), 34 ff.

the rest of his family, was noted for his piety. When, for example, he gained a victory over the rebels of the north, he commemorated the event by founding the monastery of Scone which he filled with Austin canons from the Yorkshire priory of Nostell. If his attempt to bring order into the diocese of St. Andrews was not altogether successful,[1] its failure was due to no lack of effort on his part, but to the indecent rivalry of Canterbury and York for the obedience of the church of Scotland,[2] a repercussion of the great contest between the metropolitan sees that was being fought out at the same time in England.[3]

Of the reign of David I it has been said that 'at no period of its history has Scotland ever stood so high in the scale of nations'.[4] It is certainly true that the Scotland that defied Edward I was largely his creation. He came to the throne in 1124, in the prime of life and with a ripe experience, for he had, during the reign of his predecessor, governed the lowland districts. He had lived much in England, where in the refinement and culture of English society he had, as William of Malmesbury remarks, 'rubbed off all the tarnish of Scottish barbarism'.[5] He had mixed with the Anglo-Norman aristocracy of the court of Henry I. He was, in fact, himself an English earl, since, by his marriage with the daughter of Waltheof, he had inherited the honor of Huntingdon.[6] With his wife, too, he succeeded to a claim on the much coveted earldom of Northumberland, for her grandfather was Siward, the last of the great Northumbrian earls. It was in furtherance of this claim more than anything else that involved him and his successors in wars with the kings of England.

King David's name stands first among the laymen who on 1 January 1127 bound themselves to recognize Henry I's daughter, the Empress Matilda, as the successor to the throne of England, and to her cause he, more or less steadfastly, adhered through the nineteen years of the anarchy. He was her uncle;

[1] Alexander appointed first Turgot, the author of the life of St. Margaret, and secondly Eadmer, the biographer of St. Anselm. But both these hagiographers found the position impossible and withdrew to England.

[2] The papacy strongly supported, as it did in the English issue, the claim of York. The Scots desired complete ecclesiastical independence which they ultimately got by a bull of Pope Clement III in 1188. Below, p. 278.

[3] Above, p. 184.   [4] Hume Brown, History of Scotland, i. 74.

[5] Gesta Regum, ed. Stubbs, ii. 477 (§ 400).

[6] For the vast extent of this honor see W. Farrer, Honors and Knights' Fees, ii. 294 ff. It contained more than seventy sub-fiefs distributed over eleven counties.

but there was nothing in this, since he stood in the same relation to Stephen's queen, also named Matilda, the daughter of his sister Mary and Count Eustace of Boulogne. But it suited his policy in 1135 to abide by his oath of 1127: it provided a motive for invasions across the border, the ostensible object of which was support of the empress's cause, the real object to secure Northumberland which he claimed in right of his wife. The narratives of these attacks are very good and very full, and they make it abundantly clear that on David's part it was a war of ambition and aggression. In the terms of treaties which interrupted a campaign or finished the war the empress, the alleged cause of the whole affair, was altogether forgotten. It must be conceded that David's conduct during the period 1136 to 1139 was exceedingly discreditable.

Stephen had not long been crowned (26 December 1135) before David was over the Tweed and had captured all the border castles except Bamborough. He was not, however, strong enough to risk a pitched battle; so, when Stephen advanced to Durham, he withdrew his army and obtained very favourable terms of peace: his son Henry was granted Carlisle, Doncaster, and the honor of Huntingdon. For these he became Stephen's vassal and for a time lived at his court till a trivial incident of etiquette gave David the desired excuse to renew his hostility. He recalled his son and was only deterred from again invading England during Stephen's absence in Normandy by a formidable army which assembled at Newcastle to resist him. On the king's return, however, he threw out a challenge: he would break the truce unless the earldom of Northumberland was granted to his son. The demand was refused, and David once more marched into England.

This invasion of the northern counties in 1138 was perhaps the most revolting and appalling episode of the whole civil war of Stephen's reign, hardly surpassed even by the fiendish atrocities committed by Geoffrey de Mandeville and his men in the fen country in 1144. Ailred of Rievaulx, the friend and devoted admirer of King David, cannot excuse the lack of control which permitted such wild and fearful excesses. Richard of Hexham, who witnessed the ruthless savagery from the walls of his monastery, records the lurid details of the murder of women and children, of girls and matrons, stripped and roped together, driven into slavery at the point of the spear. No doubt all the motley host of Scots and English, of Norwegians from Orkney and the Isles, of Normans and even Germans and Danes[1] contributed to this orgy of cruelty, but all accounts agree that the Picts of Galloway, 'those bestial men',[2] were the perpetrators of the worst and most unspeakable horrors of this grim campaign. In February Stephen made an attempt to put an end to it; but David merely withdrew, and the king, already beset with difficulties in the south, had to return whence he came, leaving the Scottish army unimpaired to pour once again into England. This time the invasion penetrated into Lancashire where some troops under David's nephew, William Fitz Duncan, defeated an English force at Clitheroe.[3] In the meanwhile, the main body to the east under David himself had reached the Tees.

The campaign organized by Archbishop Thurstan of York and some barons of the north country was in the nature of a holy war to stop the inhuman atrocities of this army 'more barbarous than any race of pagans'.[4] The soldiers were prepared for the fight by fasts and prayers; crosses and sacred banners accompanied them on to the field of battle; and the battle itself was fought round a great ship's mast set up on a wagon to which was attached a pyx containing the consecrated host and the banners of St. Peter of York, St. John of Beverley, and St. Wilfred of Ripon. It was this erection which gave the familiar name of the battle 'of the Standard'. But first they made an attempt to settle the matter by arbitration. Robert Bruce and Bernard of Balliol, both landowners in Scotland, friends and vassals of King David who had refused to associate themselves with his war of devastation, pleaded the unreasonableness of his action and offered even to procure the earldom of

---

[1] See J. Steenstrup, 'Kong David', in *Dansk Hist. Tidskr.* (1932), p. 290. The strange passage of the continuator of Sigebert of Gembloux (*Mon. Germ. Hist. Script.* vi. 386) of a Danish invasion against England in 1138 must refer to the Danes who assisted in David's invasion. That it was led by the Danish king who claimed the throne of England for himself has no foundation in fact.

[2] Richard of Hexham, *Chronicles of Stephen, Henry II, and Richard I* (ed Howlett, Rolls Series), iii. 152, 157. 'de Pictis qui vulgo Galleweienses dicuntur'.

[3] This raid penetrated into Coupland where Calder abbey was plundered. If William Fitz Duncan had already acquired this district and Skipton in Craven by his marriage with Alice, one of the co-heiresses of William Meschin, the brother of Rannulf, earl of Chester (Farrer, *Early Yorkshire Charters*, iii. 468, 470), it seems likely that he made the attack because he was being forcibly kept out of his inheritance. See *Victoria County History, Cumberland*, ii. 243, n. 4. He may also have had a private feud with his neighbour, Ilbert de Lacy, lord of the honor of Clitheroe, who held lands in Craven.   [4] Richard of Hexham (*Chron. of Stephen*, &c.), iii. 151.

Northumberland for his son Henry. But David was deaf to all argument. So at six o'clock on a misty morning (22 August) the armies met on Cowton moor, some miles northward from North-allerton. The men of Galloway, lightly armed with sword, pike, and leather shield, and still more lightly clad in the shortest of kilts,[1] at their own insistent demand and against the better judgement of David, were in the front line of attack. In spite of their fierce rush and reckless courage, they were helpless against the dismounted mailed knights interspersed with archers who formed the English vanguard. They broke against the 'iron wall'[2] of soldiery and the rain of arrows. 'Like a hedgehog with its quills', wrote Ailred,[3] 'so might you see a Galwegian bristling with arrows yet still brandishing his sword.' They broke and fled. In spite of the gallant attempts of David and his son to save the situation, the rout became general. By nine in the morning the remnant of the Scottish army was fleeing away to the north. Completely as he had been defeated, King David, who had made good his escape to Carlisle, was not yet prepared to retire to his own kingdom. He continued to devastate Northumber-land for another month until the united efforts of his niece, Queen Matilda, and the papal legate, Alberic, bishop of Ostia, induced him to make peace. The terms, which were finally agreed upon at Durham on 9 April 1139, were remarkably favourable. Stephen's position was becoming daily more critical and it was worth his while to make some sacrifices to rid himself of his northern opponent. He granted the earldom of Northum-berland, reserving only Bamborough and Newcastle, to David's son Henry, and both father and son for their part swore to live loyally at peace with Stephen and gave hostages as security for their good intentions. The king of Scotland took little further part in the civil war. In spite, however, of the terms of the treaty by which he had pledged his loyalty to Stephen, he did not hesitate to co-operate with the empress in the short period of her ascendancy in 1141 after the king's capture at Lincoln; he was with her at London and shared in the rout of Winchester later in the same year from which he only made his escape with difficulty. In 1149 the empress's son, Henry of Anjou, whilst on

---

[1] 'leaving their buttocks half-naked' (*seminudis natibus*). Ailred, *Relatio de Stan-dardo*, in *Chronicles of Stephen*, &c. iii. 186.

[2] Hen. Hunt., p. 263. Cf. Ailred, p. 192, *scutis scuta junguntur*.

[3] Ibid., p. 196.

a short visit in England, met his uncle David at Carlisle and received from him the honour of knighthood. The two then planned a campaign against Stephen and were joined by the earl of Chester who settled by a compromise the territorial disputes he had with the king of Scotland, an agreement which was to be sealed with a marriage alliance.[1] But Stephen getting news of these events hurried to York with a large army, and the expedition was abandoned.[2]

David, in fact, devoted his later years almost exclusively and far more profitably to the consolidation and development of Scotland. In this his reign marks a new stage. Hitherto the prevailing influence had been English, represented by Edgar the Ætheling and his sister Margaret. The influence under David, owing to his upbringing, was predominantly Norman or Anglo-Norman.[3] It was now that the Norman families famous in Scottish history settled: Bruce, lord of Annandale, Moreville, constable and founder of Dryburgh abbey, and Walter Fitz Alan, the steward of Scotland (descended not from Banquo but from a family at Dol in Brittany)[4] the ancestor of the Royal Stewarts. Moreover, the Norman colonists were not confined to the district of Lothian; we find them in Fife and all along the coast from the Tay to Moray Firth. After the rebellion of 1130 lands in Moray itself were distributed among David's Norman followers from the northern counties of England. David's court was a Norman court and in his reign Scotland became a feudal country. The Celtic tribal system of land tenure gave place to a feudal system in which the king became the source of all landed property. The titles of earl and thane were substituted for the old Celtic ranks of mormaer and toisech; the sheriff, as the representative of the Crown in fiscal and judicial matters, now made his appearance in Scotland,[5] and the Norman mode

---

[1] Below, p. 275.

[2] John of Hexham, ii. 323. According to this author the expedition was abandoned because the earl of Chester failed to keep his engagement. But cf. *Gesta Stephani*, ed. Potter, pp. 142–3, and above, p. 162.

[3] He addresses his charters (which are in the form of the English chancery) to his men 'Francis, Anglicis, Scottis' (*c.* 1130), Lawrie, *Early Scottish Charters*, p. 76, or sometimes merely 'Francis et Anglicis' (*c.* 1127), ibid., p. 59.

[4] The Breton origin has been proved by J. H. Round who finally disposed of the mythical descent from Banquo. *Peerage and Family History*, pp. 115 ff., and the *Genealogist*, New Series xviii (1901), 1–4, 1901.

[5] The earliest reference to a sheriff is in the foundation charter of Selkirk abbey in 1120. See C. A. Malcolm, 'The Office of Sheriff in Scotland', *Scottish Hist. Rev.* xx (1923), 129.

of trial by the judgement of neighbours began to supersede the systems of compurgation and ordeal. David also encouraged the development of the Scottish burghs where Scots and English, Norman and Fleming mixed together in the pursuit of trade and commerce.

In the ecclesiastical sphere his reign also shows a notable advance. The connexion with Rome became close and intimate. Bulls dealing with the concerns of the Scottish church issued in large numbers from the papal chancery, and the country was included in the commission of the legates John of Crema (1124–5) and Alberic of Ostia (1138–9), both of whom made a journey to the north. The organization and development of the parochial system and the proprietary church largely belongs to this period.[1] David's charters supply evidence of an almost prodigal endowment of churches and monasteries. The impressive list of the king's own foundations, which included Kelso, Melrose, Newbattle, Jedburgh, and Holyrood, shows that Scotland shared in the great monastic revival which spread through Europe in the first half of the twelfth century. The English and Norman priests and monks who were introduced into the country swept away the last vestiges of the Celtic church in the Lowlands of Scotland.[2] They brought with them their own mode of building and decoration; and though few specimens of their work have survived the iconoclasm of the Puritan Reformation, an occasional example, like the little twelfth-century church of Leuchars near St. Andrews,[3] may still be met with here and there.

David's kingdom stretched far into northern England. He acquired about this time the franchise of Tyndale which lay between the upper waters of the north and south Tyne with its *caput* at Wark. On the eastern side he had some control over the

[1] See M. Morgan, 'The Organization of the Scottish Church', *Trans. R. Hist. Soc.*, 4th ser., xxix (1947), 135–49.

[2] Except perhaps in Galloway where Ailred of Rievaulx witnessed at Kirkcudbright as late as 1164 an attempt to make a burnt offering of a bull to St. Cuthbert. But the thing ended in an unseemly exhibition of bull-baiting in which one of the clerics, the ringleader in fact, was gored to death by the bull. Reginald of Durham, *Libellus de admirandis beati Cuthberti virtutibus*, &c. (ed. J. Raine, Surtees Soc., vol. i, p. 179).

[3] Its date is between 1183 and 1187. The chancel and apse survive, and 'may be reckoned among the best of the few examples of Romanesque buildings in Scotland'. See *Royal Commission on the Ancient and Historical Monuments of Scotland, Counties of Fife*, &c. (1933), p. 190.

country as far as the Tees, as William of Newburgh says,[1] and
he spent much useless labour in an attempt to foist his chancellor,
William Cumin, into the see of Durham. On the west he held
Carlisle with Cumberland, and, for some years of his reign the
lordship of the whole honour of Lancaster as well.[2] But his claim
to the southern portion, to the land between the Ribble and the
Mersey, was contested by Rannulf, earl of Chester, who in his
turn had a title through his father to Carlisle. These rival claims
were ultimately settled when David, in pursuance of his plan
for a concerted attack upon Stephen in 1149, ceded his Lancashire estates to the earl of Chester, who in return resigned his
claim on Carlisle.[3]

But this great extension of the king of Scotland's dominions did
not long survive the death of David in 1153. His only son, Henry,
had died the previous year leaving (besides younger children)
two sons whose respective ages were eleven and ten years old.
The elder, Malcolm, was recognized as heir to the throne of
Scotland, while the younger, William, inherited the earldom
of Northumberland. David's success in gaining the northern
counties was due partly to his personal ability as a ruler;
but he had wrested them from a weak king whose kingdom
was distracted and mangled by a devastating civil war. To
win them from Stephen was an easier task than to hold them
under Stephen's successor. It was hardly to be expected that
these children should be equal to it. Henry of Anjou, when he
was knighted at Carlisle in 1149, had guaranteed, it was said,
not to disturb the Scot in the possession of his English lands.
However this may be, the promise did not stand in his way when
the opportunity of recovering them was afforded him. He had
no difficulty in compelling Malcolm, who in the years following
his accession was beset with troubles and native insurrections,
to surrender the northern counties in return for a re-grant of the
honor of Huntingdon. This was at Chester in July 1157. At the
same time Malcolm did homage 'as his grandfather had done'.
Whether this was for Scotland, for Lothian, or merely for
Huntingdon is debatable; the authorities are not sufficiently

---

[1] I, c. 22 (*sub anno* 1149). He adds that through David's efforts peace was maintained in the north country.

[2] Cf. the two charters printed by W. Farrer in *Lancashire Pipe Rolls and Early
Lancashire Charters*, pp. 274 f. They may be assigned to the year 1147, see H. A.
Cronne, *Eng. Hist. Rev.* l (1935), 670 ff.

[3] Above, p. 273.

precise to supply a definite answer.[1] But as the king's vassal, he
and his brother supported Henry II on the Toulouse campaign
in 1159, and he did homage to the heir to the throne at Woodstock in 1163.[2]

Malcolm IV, 'the Maiden' as he was called from his personal
appearance and the chastity of his life, 'a terrestrial angel' as
William of Newburgh thought,[3] was not a strong king and his
only noteworthy achievement was the subjection of Galloway,
which he brought about, after three campaigns, in 1160. He was
succeeded in 1165 by his brother William, a man of a very
different character.[4] He was more a man of the world and he
was ambitious. He came to the throne intent on the recovery of
Northumberland, to the loss of which he had never become
reconciled. There was, it seems, little love lost between him and
his overlord. On one occasion, indeed, when a courtier unwisely
spoke favourably of the king of Scotland, Henry flew into a
passion, tore off his clothes, stripped the coverings from his bed,
and began to gnaw the straw from the mattress in the fierceness
of his rage. Though William from time to time attended Henry's
court, he was quietly working against him. In 1168 he offered
his support to Louis VII of France; then in 1173 came the
rebellion of the young King Henry to whom William and his
brother David had done homage on the occasion of his coronation three years before. The young king held out substantial
allurements for Scottish aid: William was promised Northumberland, David the earldom of Huntingdon together with the
county of Cambridge. The offer, after some hesitation, after
consulting his council (*sun plenier parlement*),[5] was accepted; and

---

[1] Hugh the Chanter is the only authority who describes the nature of the vassalage where he relates that Archbishop Thurstan openly declared that the king of
Scotland did homage for Scotland: 'Sed archiepiscopus noster et secreto et palam
in curia ostendit Scotiam de regno Angliae esse, et regem Scottorum de Scotia
hominem esse regis Angliae.' *Historians of the Church of York* (ed. Raine), ii. 215.

[2] See Jordan Fantosme, 'Chronique de la Guerre entre les Anglois et les Ecossois'
in *Chronicles of Stephen, Henry II, and Richard I* (ed. Howlett, Rolls Series), iii, l. 1259.
The assistance given to Henry II was resented in Scotland and led to a small rebellion. Cf. *Chron. of Melrose, sub anno* 1160, 'irati contra regem quia perrexit Tolosam'.

[3] ii, c. 19. Evidently the chronicler was unacquainted with the charter of *c.* 1159
to Kelso which, if genuine, reveals the existence of an illegitimate child. See A. C.
Lawrie, *Scottish Hist. Rev.* xii (1915), 438.

[4] His surname 'the Lion' was not, as popularly supposed, due to his bearing the
lion rampant on his shield, which was first borne by his son Alexander II. Like
Henry I of England he was designated 'the Lion of Justice' (by Boece and Fordun).
See C. C. Harvey, *Scottish Hist. Rev.* xi (1914), 337–8.

[5] Jordan Fantosme, loc. cit., l. 288 (p. 226).

the Scottish army 'armed men and naked' poured across the border.

The invasion of 1173-4 was of the usual kind, devoid of any strategic plan; the border castles were in turn besieged, though few were taken; the land was devastated and plundered; grim atrocities were perpetrated. To the southern writers all Scottish invasions were much the same; so similar, indeed, did they appear to the author of the *Gesta Henrici Secundi* that he did not hesitate to embellish his account of the campaign of 1174 with picturesque details borrowed from Henry of Huntingdon's descriptions of King David's invasion thirty-five years before. On the whole the northern barons remained loyal; the castle-garrisons in most cases held out against the besiegers.[1] The justiciar, Richard de Lucy, and the constable, Humphrey de Bohun, organized the resistance and were even able to make a retaliatory raid into Lothian on which they burnt the town of Berwick. The rebellion collapsed unexpectedly with the capture of the Scottish king. The story is told by Jordan Fantosme who witnessed the scene.[2] Leaving the Scots plundering in the west, William the Lion with the rest of his army, his Norman knights and Flemish mercenaries, went to besiege Alnwick. There he was taken unawares. The English army had approached from Newcastle under cover of a thick mist. The king made a gallant attempt at resistance; but his horse was killed and fell on its rider; and thus pinned to the ground he was captured by Rannulf Glanvill. This ended the northern rebellion. King William was brought to Henry II at Northampton (31 July 1174) and thence taken to Normandy where he was imprisoned at Falaise until the terms of his release had been arranged. By this treaty William of Scotland became the vassal of the king of England. There was no longer a doubt as to what this vassalage signified; the language is unequivocal: 'for Scotland and all his other lands'. The Scottish church was to be subject to the church of England, and the Scottish bishops and abbots were to hold their temporalities from the king of England. Similarly the lay barons were to do homage to Henry for their lands. The five strongest castles of Scotland—those of Roxburgh, Berwick,

---

[1] Those in charge of the castles which capitulated were heavily fined. The constable of the castle of Appleby, one of those which was given up, was fined 500 marks and twenty-five others were amerced in sums varying from 40 to 2 marks for being involved in the surrender. *Pipe Roll 22 Hen. II*, pp. 119–20.

[2] pp. 348 ff.

Jedburgh, Edinburgh, and Stirling—were surrendered into the
king's hands,[1] and a number of distinguished Scottish lords were
given over as hostages. On these very humiliating terms King
William obtained his release. At York in the following August
he and the bishops and barons of Scotland duly took the oath of
allegiance to King Henry and to his son 'saving the fealty due
to his father'.

William could do nothing of consequence without Henry's
consent. The Galwegians were at the moment in revolt and 'the
king gave permission to the king of Scotland to advance an
army into Galloway'. After their subjection Henry received the
homage and a large fine from the conquered chief, Gilbert
the son of Fergus. This was the general character of their relations; William was required from time to time to attend the king's
court in England or in Normandy; his wars, his movements,
even his marriage were the concern of his overlord. The Scottish
barons also felt the effect of the treaty of Falaise. In 1185, for
example, a dispute over the succession in Galloway was decided
in Henry's court at Carlisle.[2] On the other hand, in the matter
of the Scottish church the treaty was ineffective. It resisted subjection to the primacy of York and finally was placed directly
under the protection of the papacy by a Bull of Pope Clement III
in 1188.[3] In elections to bishoprics and abbacies Henry II seems
to have taken no part at all; even in the long contest over the
see of St. Andrews, which lasted from 1180 to 1188 and in the
course of which King William was excommunicated and his
lands placed under interdict, he only intervened (unsuccessfully) at the request of the parties concerned. But the pope
recognized the power which Henry could exercise if he so
desired, and tried to get him to do so: 'induce him', Clement
wrote, 'and if need be compel him by the royal authority which

[1] These five are mentioned in the document (*Foedera*, i. 30). But only Roxburgh,
Berwick, and Edinburgh are mentioned as being afterwards restored. See D. W.
Hunter Marshall in *Scottish Hist. Rev.* xxv (1927), 20 f.

[2] Duncan, the son and heir of Gilbert, lord of Galloway (who died in January
1185), and a ward of Henry II, was disinherited by his cousin Roland. Henry
marched at the head of an army to Carlisle where Roland made his submission.
The army was chiefly light-armed troops from Wales. From his feudal tenants he
took a scutage of £1 on the fee—the 'Great Scutage of Galloway'. See J. H.
Round, Introductions to the *Pipe Rolls of 32 and 33 Hen. II.*

[3] On the question whether this Bull was issued by Clement III or by Celestine
III in 1192 see A. C. Anderson, *Scottish Hist. Rev.* xxv (1928), 335 ff., for the view
taken in the text. For the opposing opinion see R. K. Hannay, ibid. xxiii (1926),
171 ff.

you hold over him and the power which has been granted to your royal highness'.[1] In the later years, however, Henry relaxed somewhat his stern attitude. He tried to arrange a marriage for William with his own granddaughter Matilda, the child of Henry the Lion of Saxony (1184); and when this was forbidden by the pope on the ground of consanguinity he provided for him with a daughter of one of his great barons, Richard, vicomte of Beaumont. Edinburgh was restored to William that he might settle it on his wife as a dowry, and the marriage was celebrated with great splendour in the royal palace at Woodstock (1186). Another sign of Henry's grace was the re-grant of the earldom of Huntingdon in 1185 which William transferred to his brother David. Moreover, the king of Scotland himself took a more independent line. Whether he initiated or simply concurred in the refusal to grant a tithe for the Crusade in 1188, as Henry commanded, is not clear; but it was certainly refused, and Henry did not press the matter further.

The redemption of Scotland from her dependence on England was one of the many side-issues emanating from Richard I's need of money for his Crusade. The two kings met at Canterbury where the deed of surrender dated 5 December 1189 was drawn up and sealed in the presence of three archbishops, five bishops, the king's brother John, and a number of distinguished barons.[2] The castles of Berwick and Roxburgh were restored; William was made quit of all the agreements which King Henry 'by new charters or by reason of the king's capture had extorted'; and the relations between the two countries were in future to be as they had been in the time of King Malcolm IV. For this document King William paid 10,000 marks. Henceforth during Richard's reign the most cordial terms of friendship prevailed. All that we know tends to confirm the general truth of the intimate associations and intercourse described by Fordun a century and a half later: the kings were 'like David and Jonathan' and the two nations 'were deemed one and the same'; 'the English', he continues, 'could roam scatheless through Scotland as they pleased, on foot or on horseback, this side of the hills and beyond them; and the Scots could do so through England, though laden with gold or merchandise'.[3] The two kings met from time to time and Richard provided handsomely

[1] *Gesta Henrici* ed. Stubbs (Rolls Series), ii. 57.   [2] *Foedera*, i. 50.
[3] *Scotichronicon* (ed. Skene), i. 274.

for the escort and expenses of the king of Scotland on the occasion of his English visits. The bishop of Durham himself was to conduct him from the Tweed to the Tees; the archbishop of York through Yorkshire; and so onward he was to be accompanied by bishops and sheriffs till he reached the king's court. A liberal allowance was made to him both on his journey and during his stay.[1] William reciprocated in these marks of friendship. He refused to countenance the nefarious designs of John during Richard's captivity; he subscribed 2,000 marks to the king's ransom and another 2,000 marks for the wars in Normandy in 1198;[2] he carried a sword of state before the king at his second coronation on 17 April 1194. Nor was the serenity of their relations seriously disturbed by William's revival of the old Scottish claim to the northern counties, to the 'dignities and honors which his predecessors had had in England'. This, in his view, comprised Northumberland, Cumberland, Westmorland, and even Lancaster. Richard wisely refused; and his counter-proposal that he should have Northumberland without its castles for 15,000 marks was hardly an acceptable compromise. So there the matter ended. The close connexion between the English and Scottish courts is also reflected in the legislation of the two countries. Hubert Walter's edict of 1195 for the preservation of the peace finds its counterpart in an assize of William attributed to the year 1197, and affords an illustration of the influence of English upon Scottish law which continued until, in Edward I's time, it was superseded by the influence of France.[3]

William the Lion was in 1195 still without a male heir, a fact which caused him some uneasiness, especially when in that year he fell seriously ill at Clackmannan. It was in these circumstances that the idea of a marriage of his eldest daughter, Margaret, a child of some seven years of age, with Richard's favourite nephew, Otto of Saxony, was first ventilated. But the scheme which envisaged the succession of Otto to the Scottish

[1] This remarkable document is printed in the *Foedera*, i. 62 f. It seems to have been carried on even in John's reign, see the account of the escorts in 1200 (Hoveden, iv. 140) and in 1206 (*Rot. Lit. Pat.*, p. 56); the latter refers to the *antiquum conductum*.

[2] *Pipe Roll 1 Jo.*, p. 119.

[3] The relevant passages are printed by A. C. Lawrie, *Annals of the reigns of Malcolm and William, Kings of Scotland*, p. 311. The Assize of Clarendon (1166) was the model for Scottish police regulations supposed to be enacted by William the Lion in 1175. See ibid., pp. 204-5, and R. S. Rait in *Eng. Hist. Rev.* xxvii (1912), 144.

throne met with energetic resistance in Scotland where, it was said, female succession or the rule of royal consorts was against the custom of the kingdom, at least if there was a brother or nephew of the reigning house available. Moreover, the young prince was unpopular in the north country; the Yorkshiremen had refused to have him as their earl in 1190. Although the negotiations dragged on for some time, the affair was finally settled by the birth in 1198 of a male heir, Alexander, who succeeded his father on the throne in 1214. Through him the line descended till the death in 1290 of Margaret, the Maid of Norway. After that it passed to the younger branch, to the family of William the Lion's brother David, earl of Huntingdon, from whom the three most-favoured candidates to the throne—Balliol, Bruce, and Hastings—all claimed descent.[1]

On the death of Richard I in 1199 William the Lion adopted a high-handed attitude. His sympathies would naturally be in favour of the claims of his sister's grandson, Arthur of Brittany, had they been seriously put forward in England; he had many years before, in 1191, actually entered into a secret agreement with the chancellor, William Longchamp, to recognize his great-nephew as heir to the throne, an arrangement which was probably in accord with Richard's own views for the succession.[2] He was obviously a potential enemy of King John, and one who might expect to have a price paid for his allegiance. He therefore at once demanded Northumberland and Cumberland. John prevaricated; William became importunate and threatening. For some time he refused to meet the king, and was only in the autumn of 1200 at last induced to come to Lincoln to render his homage. But in his own demands he met with no satisfaction:

[1] David was confirmed in the honor of Huntingdon by Richard in 1190. He married the same year the sister of Rannulf, earl of Chester. For the pedigree showing the descent of the pretenders to the throne in 1290 see R. S. Rait, *Relations between England and Scotland*, p. 214.

[2] The conspiracy is mentioned by William of Newburgh, lib. iv, c. 14. The relationship between William and Arthur was as under:

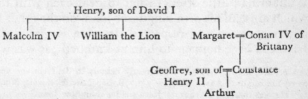

Henry, son of David I

Malcolm IV   William the Lion   Margaret⹋Conan IV of Brittany

Geoffrey, son of⹋Constance Henry II

Arthur

John contrived to put him off. For the next eight years there was perpetual friction. There were meetings which settled nothing; messages friendly and unfriendly were interchanged. There were acts, too, of friendship and hostility: wine for the king of Scotland was freed from the maletolt; but in the same year, 1204, we hear of two Scottish ships seized off the coast near Sandwich. William complained that the bishop of Durham had raised a castle at the mouth of the Tweed over against his own fortress of Berwick, an act which deprived him of the sole control of the frontier river; he therefore demolished it. John in his turn charged William with giving shelter to English fugitives. This was certainly true; the bishops of Salisbury and Rochester had been maintained at the time of the interdict in Scottish monasteries at the expense of the king of Scotland. The relations became more and more strained until in 1209 both countries prepared for war. But when John appeared in August at the head of a large army at Norham, William capitulated. How John managed to get him into his grips is difficult to understand. Yet rather than risk a battle he accepted the most humiliating terms: he paid 15,000 marks 'for having the king's goodwill' and he delivered over his two daughters into the custody of King John.[1] The only return he got for these sacrifices was that the castle at Tweedmouth was left demolished.

William was now an elderly and disappointed man. For more than fifty years his great ambition in life had been the recovery of Northumberland, with which his grandfather had invested him and of which Henry II had deprived him. After his ignominious submission in 1209 he was completely broken; all his impetuous energy had gone out of him; and the only care left him was his anxiety for the peaceful succession of his young son Alexander. To him he resigned his English estates in 1212; he sent him to King John to be disposed of in marriage,[2] and he and his son pledged their fealty to the king of England against all men. But this dependence on England was really necessary, for William had little strength left to deal even with the troubles which arose in his own kingdom. John, on the other hand, was, it seems, feared and respected. In 1212 Reginald, king of the Isles, did liege homage to him at Lambeth; it was with the aid

---

[1] *Foedera*, i. 103. William was already heavily in debt; in the year 1208-9 he owed the estate of Aaron the Jew £2,776. See Lawrie, *Annals*, &c., p. 358.

[2] He was married in 1221 to John's elder daughter Joan.

of an army of mercenaries which he sent into Scotland that a
native rebellion under Cuthred MacWilliam, a pretender to the
throne, was suppressed. Nevertheless this subservience had the
desired effect; for when William died in December 1214 his son
succeeded peacefully to the throne.

The civil disorders of the closing months of John's reign
revived in Alexander the hope of regaining the northern counties.
His support of the barons was rewarded by a small concession
in Magna Carta: his sisters and other Scottish hostages were to
be given up.[1] But his attack across the border in the autumn of
1215 only led to a counter-raid by John in which Berwick was
burnt and Lothian savagely plundered. When Louis of France
landed in the summer of 1216 Alexander joined him at Dover
and did homage for his English lands; but he only narrowly
escaped being cut off by John's army on his homeward march.
His intervention in English affairs had gained him nothing.
Carlisle, his one conquest, had to be surrendered in 1217; and
twenty years later (1237) the claim to the northern counties, the
aspiration of the kings of Scotland since the time of David I, was
once and for all abandoned in return for a grant of English lands
of the annual value of £200.[2] So closed the long contest. The
frontier between the two kingdoms along the Tweed–Cheviot
line which had been won by Rufus's conquest of Carlisle in
1092, lost in the troubles of the reign of Stephen, recovered by
Henry II in 1157, and bitterly contested during the long reign
of William the Lion, was now finally admitted by both nations.

(b) WALES[3]

Physical geography determined the character of the race and
the course of the history of Wales. It is a country broken by

[1] Clause 59. It was not carried into effect; for the two ladies remained in England
and eventually married into English baronial families, the elder, Margaret,
married Hubert de Burgh, the younger, Isabel, Roger Bigod, fifth earl of Norfolk.

[2] *Foedera*, i. 233. They were Wark and Grindon in Northumberland; and Pen-
rith, Scotby, Carlton, Langwathby, Salkeld, and Sowerby in Cumberland. See the
account rendered of the lands after the death of Alexander III from the Pipe Roll
19 Edw. I printed by J. Stevenson, *Documents illustrative of the History of Scotland*
(1870), i. 36 ff.

[3] Welsh nomenclature of persons and places presents something of a difficulty to
an Englishman. His eye, ear, and tongue can hardly cope with some of them. To
anglicize personal names might in some cases be justifiable, Griffith for Gruffydd,
for instance; but when carried to logical extremes names become almost unrecog-
nizable (who, for example, would recognize the grandfather of King Henry VII

high and rugged mountain ranges to which the inhabitants could withdraw with their belongings and defy their enemies; and even if the mountains failed them, they had a further retreat across the Irish Sea. It often happened that a chieftain, hunted from his hilly fastness, took refuge in Ireland, whence he would return in more favourable times, perhaps with Irish allies, to recover his fallen fortunes. For this reason Wales is a difficult land to conquer; but for the same reason it was difficult also to unite. The great mountain ranges, which gave the Welsh secure shelter and which did much to foster their spirit of independence, formed insurmountable barriers, breaking up the land into compartments, and providing no point, linked up by a good system of communications, which could act as a centre of administration. Even today there is no town in Wales connected by road or rail with all other parts of the country. It can be governed from London as easily or more easily than from any Welsh centre. So Wales never attained any permanent national unity or developed political institutions. Added to this, it was not in the nature of the people to combine; local rivalries and family jealousies were always more potent factors than any national sense. Even when a prince by force of character or force of arms succeeded, as Owain Gwynedd or the Lord Rhys succeeded, in establishing an unquestioned mastery over the country, on his death the work would be undone; his lands would be partitioned among his superabundant sons, and the old family feuds and the old rivalries would again revive, throwing the country once more into turmoil and disunion.

Owing to the character of the ground and the poorness of communications, conquest could not be successfully achieved by an army marching through the land. Although nearly all the kings of this period made expeditions into Wales, they effected little towards its subjugation. The work could only be done piecemeal, by the steady pressure of the Norman lords who had settled themselves along the whole length of the border. Against

under the name Eugene Theodore?). It has seemed best therefore to give the correct Welsh forms. In geographical names on the other hand there seems a case for anglicization. Many of the ancient divisions are represented by modern counties, and where this is the case the modern county name has been used, as, for instance, Brecknock for Brycheiniog.

The following sketch has been largely derived from the admirable *History of Wales from the Earliest Times to the Edwardian Conquest* by Sir John Lloyd (2 vols., London, 1911). To this and the authorities there cited the reader is referred for further study.

each of the three ancient divisions of Wales, Gwynedd, Powys, and Deheubarth, the Conqueror had set up an earl, entrusted with almost unlimited freedom of action not only for the purpose of defence, but also for the attack upon Welsh independence. The progress of the Norman advance was marked by castles erected and garrisoned with the object of controlling the land already won, and of acting as bases for further penetration. Wales, especially south Wales, bristles with castles. In this way the more fertile lowlands were soon occupied, leaving the natives to sustain themselves as best they might in the hills and moorlands or to become tenants of Norman masters. Sometimes a town grew up beside the castle, as at Hereford,[1] where William Fitz Osbern introduced the favourable customs of his Norman borough of Breteuil, which spread to many places up and down the border. The planting of boroughs was indeed an essential part of the Norman system of colonization bringing markets, trade, and Norman civilization into the newly won territory.[2]

By the end of the Conqueror's reign considerable progress had been made in the subjugation of the native Welsh princes. The earldom of Chester under Hugh of Avranches included the modern county of Flint and part of Denbigh. Farther west, between the rivers Clwyd and Conway, each of which was commanded by a strong fortress, the one at Rhuddlan, the other at Degannwy, Hugh's cousin, Robert of Rhuddlan, an intrepid soldier, was entrusted with the task of subjecting the whole of Gwynedd (or Snowdonia) to Norman rule. The prince of this district, Gruffydd ap Cynan, had been captured and was a prisoner at Chester in the hands of Earl Hugh. For a brief period this, the most impregnable part of the country, was under the domination of the Normans. Robert of Rhuddlan was, in fact, recognized by William the Conqueror as lord of 'Nort Wales' in return for an annual rent of £40. Nor was the advance checked when Robert was killed by the crews of some Welsh pirate ships at the Great Orme's Head in 1088; Earl Hugh succeeded to his position and even penetrated into Anglesey. By 1094 it seemed that a permanent conquest of north Wales was in process of achievement.

The wars which occupied the closing years of the eleventh century were, however, to show the hopeless insecurity of the

[1] Herefordshire is denoted in the Pipe Rolls of Henry II as *in Wallia*.
[2] Cf. Bateson, 'The Laws of Breteuil' in *Eng. Hist. Rev.* xvi (1901), 335.

Anglo-Norman position, and to reveal the fact that this region of Snowdonia was essentially the home and centre of resistance to the foreign intruders. In 1094, when Rufus was absent on the Continent, the Welsh broke out into sudden and fierce revolt. The leader was Cadwgan of the house of Powys, a man of weak and irresolute character; and it cannot be doubted that it was the native prince of Gwynedd, Gruffydd ap Cynan, now once more at liberty, who stimulated his countrymen to persevere in their striving for independence. The Normans were thrust back east of the Conway, into that district between the Conway and the Dee, later known as the 'Four Cantreds', which throughout the twelfth century was the scene of almost perpetual warfare. The revolt became so widespread and so successful that William Rufus, in genuine alarm, took action. But the campaign of the autumn of 1095 did little to check its progress: it was made too late in the year; the natives in their customary manner had withdrawn with their belongings to the mountains or across the straits to Anglesey; and the king and his army found themselves at the approach of winter stranded for lack of provisions and constantly harassed by enemy ambushes in the inhospitable valleys of Snowdonia. Retirement was inevitable. A second expedition, undertaken in the spring of 1097, was scarcely more effective.

A concerted attempt by the earls of Chester and Shrewsbury to recover the Welsh strongholds in 1098 had at first some success; they pursued the Welsh leaders, Cadwgan and Gruffydd, across the Menai straits into Anglesey, and beyond to Ireland. But the campaign closed with disaster brought about from an unexpected quarter. Magnus Barefoot, king of Norway, who happened to be cruising with his pirate fleet in the Irish Sea, made a sudden descent upon the island, attacked and defeated the Normans he found there, and then sailed quietly away without seeking to exploit his victory. But Earl Hugh of Shrewsbury was among the slain, and the dispirited survivors decided to abandon the attempt to hold Gwynedd. It was indeed a hazardous adventure. They had no fleet; the narrow passage between the mountains and the coast, which provided the only communication with their base at Chester, could be easily cut off, leaving them at the mercy of their remorseless enemies. Henceforth till the time of Edward I Snowdonia and Anglesey were not seriously disturbed by invaders. From time to time

POSITION IN SOUTH WALES

expeditions were made, but they had little result; and the English kings of this period were forced to content themselves with a more or less nominal recognition of overlordship from the princes of north Wales. This was all that was gained by Henry I's campaign of 1114. It was an exhibition of royal power on the grand scale: three armies bore down on Gwynedd from three different points. Earl Richard of Chester with King Alexander I of Scotland led one of these along the usual coastal road; another came from the barons of the southern marches; while Henry himself made his way between them across the Berwyn range. But the prudent Gruffydd, without risking a battle, satisfied the king with an oath of homage and a suitable fine, and he was left in peace to continue his patient work of consolidation. He lived on through the whole of Henry's reign, and when he died in 1137, very old, feeble, and blind, he had the satisfaction of having extended his eastern frontier far beyond the Conway to the Clwyd.

The story of south Wales is altogether different from that of the north. At first the Norman invasion had not fared so prosperously. After the premature death of William Fitz Osbern (1071) and the imprisonment of his son for complicity in the rebellion of the earls of 1075, there had been no earl of Hereford to organize the work of conquest. The border in 1087 was still substantially where William Fitz Osbern had left it, defined by a string of castles at Wigmore, Clifford, and Ewias Harold; only in Gwent, the country lying between the lower waters of the Wye and the Usk, had the Norman colonist, pushing forward from Monmouth and Chepstow, gained a firm foothold. In Domesday we find not a Norman lord but a formidable native prince, Rhys ap Tewdwr, recognized as the lord of south Wales, of the ancient kingdom of Deheubarth on the same terms— a payment of a yearly rent of £40—as Robert of Rhuddlan held Gwynedd from the Crown.[1] At the time, therefore, when the conquest of Gwynedd seemed almost achieved, the conquest of south Wales had scarcely begun. But on the death of Rhys in 1093 the Normans, aided by the incessant and murderous domestic feuds among the Welsh princes, found the opportunity to penetrate and establish themselves over a wide area of southern and central Wales.

Robert Fitz Hamon, one of the chief tenants of the Crown in

[1] Lloyd, *History of Wales*, ii. 394.

Gloucestershire, occupied Glamorgan, and built the castle of Cardiff which became the centre of a district administered like an English shire; Bernard of Neufmarché conquered Brecknock; and the family of Braose was planted at Radnor. In the centre of the march Earl Roger of Shrewsbury had already in the Conqueror's time advanced the frontier into Powys, where the castle, called Montgomery after the family lordship in Normandy, marked the limit of his conquest; now, pushing farther westward into the heart of the country, he made himself master of Cardigan, and even penetrated Pembroke, the south-western extremity of Wales, which he entrusted to his youngest son Arnulf.

The revolt of 1094, which had checked and indeed thrust back the Normans in Gwynedd, had also at least a partial and temporary success in the south. The foreign settlers were fiercely attacked; their newly built castles were captured and demolished; even the castle of Montgomery fell. Pembroke almost alone among the castles of Wales remained in Norman hands. Though at this time nothing more than a rough and primitive structure in the form of a stockade, thanks to its superb natural position on a promontory jutting into the sea, and to the resource of its constable, Gerald of Windsor, the founder of the house of Fitz Gerald, it successfully withstood a siege; and when the fire had gone out of the revolt it became the base for the reconquest of the surrounding country. In the border districts, in Brecknock, Gwent, and Glamorgan, the marcher lords had managed to hold their own; but between Pembroke and these eastern lordships lay a strong belt of land, corresponding roughly to the modern counties of Cardigan and Carmarthen, which as a result of the rising remained in the possession of the Welsh princes. This was the position at the close of the eleventh century and the death of William Rufus.

The event of the most outstanding importance in the early years of the reign of Henry I was the fall of the house of Montgomery, which, as we have seen, had exercised so large an influence in the affairs of Wales since the time of the Norman Conquest. Robert of Bellême, the owner of the vast continental estates of his family, had succeeded to the earldom of Shrewsbury on the death of his younger brother Hugh in Anglesey in 1098. He was the ablest and the most unscrupulous of the sons of Roger; he had used his skill as a military architect, for which he was famous, to good purpose on the Welsh march, both in the fortification of Shrewsbury itself and in the erection of the almost impregnable castle of Bridgnorth. But his oppression and ambition led in 1102 to his ruin in which his brother Arnulf in Pembroke was alike involved. The great earldom was not filled up; for a time the district was administered by a royal official, and in course of time the family of Mortimer, spreading out from its original centre at Wigmore, came to exercise the first place of authority among the lords of the middle march. But the absence of any great power here no doubt accounts for the prominence at this time of the princes of Powys who warred ruthlessly and incessantly against each other.

Cadwgan, the leader of the great revolt in Rufus's reign, was the chief gainer from this turn of events: he was confirmed in his position in Cardigan and in part of Powys, and he might have increased his power still further had it not been for his son Owain's fatal passion for Nest, the daughter of Rhys ap Tewdwr, the last great prince of Deheubarth. This Nest, sometimes not inappropriately called the Helen of Wales, had been the mistress of Henry I to whom she had borne one of his numerous bastard progeny; she had then married Gerald of Windsor, and by him became the mother of the first English conqueror of Ireland. The fame of her beauty led Owain to the mad escapade of abducting her. It was an act of defiance which the king could not overlook, and Owain and his father became outcasts. Cadwgan was given more than one chance of retrieving his old position; but his own weakness of character and the embarrassments to which he was exposed by the lawlessness of his son prevented him from taking advantage of these opportunities. He had recovered little of his former power when he was murdered by one of his nephews in 1111. The end of Owain's romantic and stormy career was as remarkable as its beginning: after years spent in plunder and murder or in exile in Ireland, he was established on the death of his father in a part of the family inheritance in Powys. In 1114 he made his peace with the king who received him into high favour and took him with him to Normandy; he was even honoured with knighthood. But two years later (1116) his original crime was avenged. While acting in the king's service he was set upon and slain by a body of Flemings under Gerald of Windsor. His death marks the close of the brief period in which Powys played a leading part in Welsh history.

In south Wales the reign of Henry I was a period of consolidation of the Anglo-Norman power, disturbed only by a single and
unsuccessful attempt by a native prince to recover the Welsh
independence. The fall of Arnulf de Montgomery was the occasion for a thorough colonization of the southern part of Pembroke
by a body of Flemings who about 1108 settled down as agricul-
turists and traders, almost wholly displacing the native inhabitants. So complete indeed was the displacement that Flemish
and later English became the spoken language; even the Welsh
place-names were superseded by names derived from the families
of the new settlers. It was organized, like Glamorgan, as an
English county with a sheriff who rendered his account to the
English exchequer. So it became known as 'Little England
beyond Wales'.

The family of Clare, destined to play so prominent a part in
Wales during the next century of its history, made its first
appearance in the country when Gilbert, son of the founder of
the house in England (Clare, Suffolk), replaced Cadwgan in
1110 in Cardigan; a little later his brother, Walter, best known
as the founder of Tintern abbey, was established between the
Wye and the Usk with the rock fortress of Chepstow as the
centre of his power. For the rest, the original conquerors or
their descendants strengthened their hold on the districts they
had already occupied: Brecknock came on the death of Bernard
of Neufmarché through his daughter into the hands of Miles
of Gloucester, the constable, the future earl of Hereford, while
Glamorgan, the conquest of Robert Fitz Hamon, after a period
in which it was administered as a wardship of the Crown,
passed with his daughter Mabel to the favourite natural son of
Henry I, Robert of Gloucester, the champion of his sister's
rights during the anarchy. In these years also Kidwelly and
Gower, districts into which foreign influences had hitherto
scarcely penetrated, were occupied and colonized by Norman
lords. By the end of Henry I's reign south Wales seemed almost
converted into an Anglo-Norman province. But this was on the
eve of the great insurrection which was again to give Wales back
for a time to the Welsh.

This great revolt was spontaneous in origin and was not
caused by the weakness of Henry I's successor whose claim to
the throne was as yet uncontested and whose inability to rule
was as yet unproved by experience. It was on 1 January 1136,

scarcely more than a week after Stephen's coronation, that the Welsh won their first success in a battle near Swansea in the vale of Gower, when some 500 of the Anglo-Norman colonists were slain. The death of Richard Fitz Gilbert, while riding through the forest in Gwent, followed by a decisive victory of the Welsh, led to the loss of Cardigan, save only the castle which, alone and isolated, held out for several years. The lords of the march failed to co-operate in the defence of their colonies; the plans of Stephen for the reconquest of Cardigan miscarried, like his other attempts to stem the tide of revolt. As the effort of the Welshmen to regain their freedom became increasingly more intense, so the inability of the government to cope with the situation became ever more manifest, until, with the out-break of civil war in 1139, it became altogether impossible for Stephen to make any further struggle. His position here was hopeless, for between him and the Welsh there were the lords of the march who, following the example of Robert of Gloucester, were almost without exception partisans of the empress. By the end of this calamitous period of anarchy and devastating war the whole of south Wales except the little Flemish colony in Pembroke had freed itself from its dependence on England.

The Welsh were fortunate in that when this opportunity came to them they had leaders both in the north and in the south who were capable of taking full advantage of it. These were Owain Gwynedd and Rhys ap Gruffydd. Rhys was the grandson of Rhys ap Tewdwr who at the opening of our period was virtually supreme in south Wales; he had taken the initiative in the recon-quest of the south during the anarchy, and had succeeded, like his grandfather, in establishing himself as the sole ruler in Deheubarth. Owain had already in the lifetime of his father, Gruffydd ap Cynan, proved himself an adept in the arts of administration and of war; he was one of those exceptional characters in Welsh history who combined the best qualities of his race with a prudence, moderation, and statesmanship rarely to be found among his impetuous, violent, and quarrelsome countrymen. While the attention of the English baronage was engaged in civil war, he was able to extend his frontiers: the castles of Mold and Rhuddlan fell into his hands, and the city of Chester itself seemed almost within his grasp.

Henry II, when he came to the throne in 1154, was thus faced with a serious situation, with these champions of Welsh

nationality ruling undisturbed by internal feuds or external invaders in the south and north of the country. But at first he was
too preoccupied with restoring order in England and in looking
after his continental interests to intervene in the affairs of Wales.
It was not till the summer of 1157 that he was free to give them
his attention. Giraldus Cambrensis in his 'Description of Wales',[1]
written at the end of the century, expounded the methods that
must be employed to subdue his country. The would-be conqueror must be prepared for a long campaign—at least a year—
for the natives will not risk defeat in a pitched battle but must
be gradually worn down; he must divide their strength by
fomenting quarrels among the native princes; he must cut off
their supplies, for which purpose the co-operation of a fleet will
be necessary; finally he must have light-armed troops capable of
following the enemy into their wooded and mountainous retreats.
The shrewdness of Gerald's observations is proved by the fact
that these were, in the main, the tactics adopted by Edward I
in his conquest of the country a century later. In some particulars they were used by Henry II in his expedition against Owain
Gwynedd in 1157. His plans were laid with elaborate care. As
the campaign might be protracted, might exceed the forty days
of feudal service, he adopted the system of engaging only a portion of the host ready to remain under arms for a longer period;
he had a body of archers from Shropshire who could penetrate
into the dense and hilly defiles; he had purchased the aid of
some of the neighbouring princes in north Wales; and, above
all, a fleet was brought from Pembroke to co-operate with the
army. But, in spite of the soundness of his preparations, the
campaign opened badly. While the main army advanced from
Chester along the coast, the king with the light-armed troops
made his way through the forest where he was entrapped and
nearly lost his life;[2] it was only with difficulty that he managed
to rejoin the main body; the men with the ships met with an
ignominious disaster when they landed for plunder in Anglesey.

[1] *Opera*, vi. 218 ff.
[2] This was the occasion when the constable, Henry of Essex, was said to have
thrown away the royal standard and fled in panic. He was accused of it six years
later, in 1163, by Robert de Montfort; and in a duel fought in the king's presence at
Reading the constable was defeated. Cf. Lloyd, ii. 498, n. 51. Salzman (*Henry II*,
pp. 31 f.) considers it probable that Robert de Montfort, having himself designs
on the constableship, trumped up the charge on the basis of a mere rumour, and
that Henry of Essex was really innocent.

Nevertheless both Henry and Owain realized that the con-
tinuance of hostilities could profit them little: Henry had
experienced reverses, Owain feared an open encounter with the
royal army which was still sufficiently formidable. Terms were
therefore arranged whereby the prince of Gwynedd rendered
homage and gave hostages; he was also required to withdraw
his frontier once more to Rhuddlan and the river Clwyd.

Rhys ap Gruffydd, the hero of the revolt in south Wales, presented a more difficult problem both because of his unreliability
and because of his violent, restless energy. He would often submit to King Henry and take the oath of fealty, but as often he
would break his oath, rebel, and cause the king to waste his time
in making or sending punitive expeditions against him. In 1163
Henry took him prisoner, and brought him back to England; he
was, however, soon released, and back in Wales he at once
began to repeat his old malpractices. He overran Cardigan, and
then joined in a general offensive movement against the Anglo-
Norman position in Wales. This revolt in 1165 was inspired by
Owain Gwynedd who since the treaty of 1157 had observed a
strictly correct attitude towards his overlord. It was no doubt
the king's occupation in other affairs, and in particular his
quarrel with Becket, that stimulated these princes to revive the
struggle for independence. To meet this menace Henry collected
a large army at Shrewsbury. The English feudal host was augmented by contingents from the king's overseas dominions;
mercenaries were hired from Flanders; and a substantial force
of light-armed troops capable of hunting the elusive Welshmen
from their mountain lairs was mobilized for service. A fleet from
the Danes of Dublin was also engaged to co-operate with the
land forces. Owain assembled his army, which was drawn from
all parts of Wales, at Corwen where he could bar the king's
advance into the interior of the country. But no action took
place. The inclement weather, the boggy state of the moorland
on the Berwyn slopes, and the shortage of supplies did their work,
and forced the English army to retire ignominiously whence it
came. This disaster was the end of Henry's attempt to subjugate
the country, the 'grave of his Welsh ambitions'.[1] The two
princes were left to continue undisturbed their triumphant progress. Owain succeeded in the north by the capture of the castles
of Basingwerk (1166) and Rhuddlan (1167) in carrying his

[1] Lloyd, ii. 518.

boundary to the estuary of the Dee. The independence of his position, which he maintained until his death in 1170, is illustrated by the fact that in 1168 he tendered his help to Louis VII of France in his war with Henry II. Rhys for his part completed the conquest of Cardigan by the capture of Cardigan castle, the stronghold of Roger of Clare, which had previously withstood many attacks, but which was now at last betrayed into his hands.

Till almost the end of the twelfth century the personality of Rhys ap Gruffydd dominates the history of Wales. Two factors contributed to enable him to maintain and increase his position of ascendency. These were, first, the difficulties which surrounded Henry II both at home and on the Continent, and, secondly, the conquest of Ireland, which in its initial stage was the achievement of the great Pembrokeshire families, Robert Fitz Stephen and his half-brother Maurice Fitz Gerald, and of course the earl of Pembroke himself, Richard of Clare, better known as 'Strongbow'. Their departure across the Irish Sea cleared the country of Rhys's most dangerous rivals; their success aroused the jealousy of the king, causing him to make a complete volte-face, and to take the native prince into his close favour and confidence. This was in 1171 when Henry was himself on his way to Ireland. Henceforth Rhys was the firm supporter, almost the representative of the king in Wales. He was secured in the possession of Cardigan and Carmarthen and other lands; in 1172 he was appointed 'Justice', a title which is taken to imply control over the lesser princes of south Wales; he came to be known as the Lord Rhys (*yr Arglwydd Rhys*). He was a great figure in his day, received with marked respect on his visits to England, and ruling at home with almost vice-regal splendour in his new-built castle of Cardigan. There at Christmas 1176 was celebrated the first Eisteddfod of which there is certain record. Two contests were arranged, one among bards, the other among musicians; the prize in each case was a chair and rich gifts. Then, as in later times, the pre-eminence of the north in poetry and the south in music was revealed; for the victor in the musical contest was a southern Welshman, in the bardic a native of Gwynedd.

Henry's confidence was not misplaced. Rhys proved his loyalty by signal services: he supported the king with a considerable force in the dangerous rebellion of 1173-4; he controlled the lesser chieftains, who, through his influence, were induced to present themselves at the English court at Gloucester in 1175 and at Oxford in 1177. These councils illustrate the working of the new policy which had been adopted in 1171 towards Wales. It was a policy of peace, not of war: of conciliation, not of destruction of Welsh independence. The king was content to leave the affairs of Wales in the hands of Welsh princes provided that they remained loyal and recognized his suzerainty. On the whole it was a success. The country was relatively quiet during these later years of Henry's reign; the Welsh were not fighting against the English and not much among themselves. On the contrary, not a few of them employed their military skill to their pecuniary advantage in the service of the Crown.

The church also played its part in the development of Anglo-Norman influence. It was a common practice of the invaders to grant a portion of the occupied land to a religious house in England or in Normandy, which would plant beside the castle wall a cell of its own with a prior and one or two lonely monks. Battle, for example, had its cell at Carmarthen, Sherborne at Kidwelly, and Tewkesbury at Cardiff. Sometimes they would found independent houses of the reformed pattern; nowhere outside Yorkshire was the Cistercian plantation so thorough as in Wales whose desolate moors and dales exactly suited the temperament of the early disciples of the movement and afforded them ample scope for their propensity for sheep-farming. Tintern was the earliest (1131) and perhaps the most well known, but it was Whitland built near the banks of the river Taf which became the mother-house of all the subsequent Cistercian foundations in Wales.

The consolidation of the power of the lords marchers was further assisted by the absorption of the Welsh church in the ecclesiastical organization of England. By the end of Henry I's reign the Welsh dioceses were all in the hands of bishops who had made their profession of obedience to the archbishop of Canterbury. As early as 1092 Hugh of Chester had forcibly intruded Hervé, a Breton, into the see of Bangor, where he enjoyed a brief and harassed existence before he was driven forth in the wake of his patron; and it was not till some twenty years later (1120), when a certain David, perhaps the chaplain of the king's son-in-law, the Emperor Henry V,[1] was elected to

[1] See Lloyd, p. 455.

the satisfaction of both parties, that the northern diocese finally became subject to the control of Canterbury. The southern sees of Llandaff and St. Davids presented less difficulty. The thoroughness of the colonization of south Wales made their absorption in the diocesan system of England both natural and inevitable: the former in 1107, the latter in 1115 came into the hands of bishops who not only professed obedience to Canterbury, but took an active part by their attendance at councils in the affairs of England.[1] The revival of the national spirit in Wales which manifested itself in the reign of Stephen had its repercussion in the ecclesiastical sphere in an attempt to restore the independence of the Welsh church. It took the form of claiming for St. Davids the position of a metropolitan see, cutting it adrift from Canterbury. The claim, entirely groundless, was quashed when the matter was argued at length between Archbishop Theobald and Bishop Bernard of St. Davids in the presence of the pope Eugenius III at Meaux in 1147. The triumph of Canterbury seemed to be assured when, on Bernard's death in the following year, David, son of Gerald of Windsor, was appointed as his successor. The new bishop not only subscribed obedience to the English primate, but bound himself on oath not again to raise the claim of St. Davids to metropolitan rank. Yet the question was twice again raised, each time unsuccessfully, first on the death of David himself and once more, twenty-two years later, in 1198 when it was fiercely fought out over a space of five years in Wales, in England, and at Rome. The protagonist of the native claim was the nephew of Bishop David, Giraldus Cambrensis, himself twice the unsuccessful aspirant to the bishopric. This usually vigorous, sprightly, and entertaining writer becomes almost tedious in the inordinate length of his narrative of this dreary cause and of his justification of his own supposed wrongs.[2] The Welsh church remained

---

[1] The fourth Welsh diocese, St. Asaph, was at this time in abeyance. It was not revived until the appointment of a bishop in 1143.

[2] The theme is dealt with in the *De rebus a se gestis*, the *De Invectionibus*, and the *De jure et statu Menevensis ecclesiae* (*Opera*, ed. Brewer, i, iii). From these sources a connected narrative has been rendered in translation by Professor H. E. Butler, *The Autobiography of Giraldus Cambrensis* (London, 1937). Giraldus accepted his defeats cheerfully; in 1188 he accompanied the archbishop of Canterbury on a tour through Wales with the object of inducing the Welsh to join the Crusade. See his lively description of the journey—'The Itinerary of Wales' (*Opera*, vi). After his second defeat he was reconciled with King John and his great enemy, Archbishop Hubert Walter, in 1204.

dependent on the primacy of Canterbury. The changes in ecclesiastical organization which resulted from the English influence inevitably broke up the national characteristics of the Welsh church; the 'clas' system by which a church was ruled by a community of secular canons gave place to a monastic or parochial organization so firmly established that it was able to withstand the shock of national revolts which caused the collapse of the Anglo-Norman power in the greater part of Wales.

The death of Henry II followed by the departure of his successor almost immediately after his coronation to the Holy Land was the signal for a return to the old strife and turmoil among the Welsh princes and between these and the Anglo-Norman settlers which Henry II's wise policy of moderation had done much to allay. The Lord Rhys, regarding his loyalty as personal to Henry rather than to the English Crown and indignant because King Richard refused to meet him when he came to Oxford after the coronation, broke into furious revolt, and carried on a ruthless and successful war with his neighbours till his death, at a ripe age, in 1197. He was the greatest of the princes of south Wales during our period, and the man who by his unceasing efforts and fine sense of patriotism kept alive the tradition of Welsh independence and nationality.[1] His task was certainly facilitated by the fact that the lords of the southern marches had in the later years of the twelfth century been very much weakened by failure of heirs and by the exodus to Ireland. Only the Mortimers of Wigmore and the family of Braose had steadily increased their power.[2] Heiresses brought great lordships to men who had little direct interest in the affairs of Wales: in this way Count John, by his marriage with Isabel of Gloucester, acquired Glamorgan, and William Marshal through the heiress of Richard, earl of Pembroke (Strongbow), became the possessor of the earldom and of the enormous, if scattered, estates of the family of Clare in England, Ireland, and south Wales. Both were generally absentee lords, and were primarily interested in English politics. To John, at any rate, the chief value of his Welsh inheritance (which he retained after his divorce from Isabel in 1200) was that it provided him with an

[1] For an estimate of his character and achievements see Lloyd, ii. 582.
[2] William of Braose was far and away the strongest of the barons of the march at the close of the twelfth century; he held authority over Brecknock, Builth, Radnor, and Upper Gwent.

almost inexhaustible supply of mercenary troops to aid him in his rebellions against his brother and in the troubles of his later years. That the justiciars left in charge of the kingdom during Richard's absence were not indifferent to the incursions of the Welsh is demonstratively proved by the vigorous efforts they made, both by land and sea, to relieve the castle of Swansea besieged by Rhys in the autumn of 1192, and by the expeditions made by Hubert Walter in 1196 and by Geoffrey Fitz Peter in 1198 against Gwenwynwyn, who, with some success, was attempting to revive the power of Powys. But they were too occupied by the critical state of English politics to be able to deal with the problem comprehensively and effectively.[1]

The period following the death of Henry II, which opens in this dark confusion, gradually clarifies and reveals the figure of Llywelyn ap Iorwerth, Llywelyn the Great as he came to be called, rising with rapid strides to a pre-eminent position in Wales, first with the friendship and help of King John and later joining with the barons to overthrow the king and to make what he can out of the civil war that ensued. Llywelyn, the grandson of the last great king of north Wales, Owain Gwynedd, was born in 1173, and he first made his name by the courage and resource he exhibited in the great battle fought at the mouth of the Conway in 1194 in which his uncle David was overthrown; in 1199 he captured the all-important border castle of Mold; and when John came to the throne he was already well on the way towards making himself master of the whole of Snowdonia. The new king, being himself a baron of the march, understood something of Welsh politics; he realized that the surest way of keeping the princes weak was to foment their local feuds, a policy which in his dexterous hands was partially successful. Thus he tried to play off Gwenwynwyn against Llywelyn. Llywelyn, however, was already too powerful and indeed too shrewd to be played with in this manner. Towards him, therefore, the king's attitude was conciliatory; and the treaty of 11 July 1201 was the result. By this agreement in return for recognition in the lands he had acquired, Llywelyn promised to render fealty to the king. Three years later, when John had returned from the Continent, the prince of Gwynedd did homage and was betrothed to the king's natural daughter, Joan (1204). He was thus able to continue on his path of success without

[1] Cf. D. M. Stenton, *Introduction to the Pipe Roll of 1193*, pp. xiii–xiv.

interference from England; in 1208 he overran and occupied
Powys which, on account of an act of aggression by Gwenwynwyn, had been taken into the custody of the Crown. But
even this bold stroke apparently did not disturb his relations
with John who continued to treat him with consideration. In
1209 Llywelyn gave evidence of his loyalty by taking part with a
following of Welshmen in the campaign against the king of the
Scots, and he repeated his homage, with other Welsh princes, at
Woodstock in the autumn of the same year.

Then came the rupture, sudden and unaccountable, in 1210.
It has been suggested[1] that Llywelyn had involved himself in
the attempt made by William de Braose to recover his lands, an
attempt which led to the latter's flight to France, where he died
shortly after, and to the gruesome murder of his wife and eldest
son at the king's hands.[2] John's determination to crush Llywelyn
and his confidence of being able to do so were no doubt
strengthened by his success in Ireland in the summer, and by
his triumphal marches through south Wales both going and
returning, which could not fail to impress the people of Wales
with a keen sense of the royal power. In 1211 an army, which
was joined by many Welsh princes of the north and Powys,
jealous of the power of the prince of Gwynedd, was mobilized at
Chester. Llywelyn employed the usual tactics: he and his men
withdrew with their goods and chattels to the impenetrable
mountains, leaving the royal army in imminent danger of
famine. John could do nothing but retire. But his purpose was
unshaken. Again he advanced, this time from Oswestry, and
this time with success; he burnt the city of Bangor and seized its
bishop who had defied the excommunicated king. Llywelyn was
hard pressed and obliged to submit to humiliating terms which
he only obtained through the intercession of his wife Joan, and
which deprived him of the Four Cantreds west of the Conway
besides imposing on him a heavy tribute in livestock and the
render of hostages. This success was followed by another in the
south. Falkes de Bréauté, who held Glamorgan for the Crown,
occupied the northern part of Cardigan, and built at Aberyst-
wyth a castle from which to control the new conquest. Clearly

[1] By Lloyd, ii. 631.
[2] William de Braose had first received great favour from John. Gower had been
added to his already extensive possessions in 1203. His sudden downfall in 1207,
like so many incidents of John's reign, is unaccountable.

John envisaged the subjugation of Wales, a return to the position of a hundred years before in the time of Henry I. But the Welsh princes, ready enough to assist the king in putting down Llywelyn of whose power they were not unnaturally jealous, were not prepared to stand idly by while the whole country was being brought under the despotic rule of the English Crown. The erection of the castle of Aberyswyth was a mistake; it gave the Welsh a clear insight into the king's real intentions; they broke into revolt; they seized and burnt the new stronghold; the upheaval spread and became general. Then Llywelyn joined and took his appropriate place as a leader of a Welsh national movement.[1] The elaborate plans for a campaign against the Welsh, which included the co-operation of the fleet,[2] in the summer of 1212 had to be suddenly cancelled, for John could no longer rely on the loyalty of his barons, and he was made aware of a conspiracy to betray him. He could not even prevent the two almost impregnable castles of Rhuddlan and Degannwy from falling into the hands of Llywelyn. In his impotent rage he set a price on the head of every Welshman delivered to him.[3] A respite, however, came later in the same year (1213) caused by John's submission to the pope.[4] It deprived the revolt of its character of a holy war against an excommunicated king; it resulted in a truce, negotiated by the legate Pandulf, which, with prolongations, lasted through the year 1214.

But during this interval John's position had become desperate. His plans for the recovery of his continental dominions had failed utterly at Bouvines (July 1214); his tyrannical government had driven a large section of the baronage to assume a threatening attitude; and his attempts to conciliate the Welsh in order to gain their help in the now inevitable struggle met with little, if any, success. Llywelyn captured Shrewsbury; the

[1] In spite of the national character of the insurrection, there is evidence that John had an abundant supply of Welsh soldiers in his employ. On 8 May 1213, for example, the payment of 1,200 Welshmen is recorded. *Rot. Misae, 14 John*, ed. Cole, *Documents illustrative of English History*, Record Commission, 1844, p. 263.

[2] In August orders were issued for eighteen galleys to be sent by Chester along the coasts of the lands of Llywelyn to destroy ships, galleys, and small boats belonging to the enemy, and to do them as much damage as possible. *Rot. Lit. Claus.*, pp. 121b–122.

[3] A payment of 6s. was made in 1212–13 to William, the man of Adam Crok, who brought six amputated heads of Welshmen who were in the service of Cadwallon to the king at Rochester. *Rot. Misae*, ed. Cole, p. 231.

[4] Innocent III had in 1212 released the Welsh insurgents from their allegiance to the king and freed their country from the interdict.

family of Braose, who had their own bitter quarrel with the king and were now bound to the prince of Gwynedd by a marriage tie,[1] took the opportunity to recover their lost lands on the southern march. They regained, among other strongholds, those of Abergavenny, Brecon, Radnor, and Builth. The one man who might have stayed the tide of the rebellion, William, the earl marshal, was too busily engaged in directing the critical affairs of the kingdom to give his attention to Wales. A pause in the triumphant progress of the national movement followed on the general settlement effected by the grant of the Great Charter; for by clause 56 it was provided that all lands and liberties of which the Welsh had been deprived during John's reign should be immediately restored; cases of dispute were to be determined by English, Welsh, or march law according to the location of the lands in question.[2] Nevertheless, as in England, it resulted in only a very temporary cessation of hostilities. John did not change his ways. Within a few months the struggle began again, and Louis of France had been invited by the barons to come over and take possession of the kingdom. The reopening of the English civil war provided Llywelyn with the opportunity for his great effort in south Wales. It was one of those rare occasions when the Welsh princes united in a common enterprise, and it was an overwhelming success. The great strategical centres, Carmarthen, Kidwelly, and Cardigan, capitulated; by the end of the year 1215 the district around Pembroke alone remained attached to the English Crown. At Aberdovey early in the next year, with a statesmanship only equalled by his soldiership, Llywelyn partitioned the conquered lands among the princes of the south, reserving for himself nothing. The soundness of a settlement of this kind can be best judged by its permanence. The settlement of Aberdovey lasted with but slight modifications through the lifetime of its creator (Llywelyn died in 1240), and it was not disturbed when Llywelyn made his peace with the English regency. He did homage to the infant king, Henry III, at a great council held at Worcester on 16 March 1218 in return for confirmation in the lands he had conquered.

---

[1] The family was represented by Giles, bishop of Hereford, and Reginald, sons of William who had died in exile in France (below, p. 315). Reginald married Gwladus, daughter of Llywelyn.

[2] Two other clauses also related to the affairs of Wales: 57, to the question of lands seized in the time of Henry II and Richard I, which was to stand over for the present; 58, to the return of Welsh hostages.

(c) IRELAND

A story is told of how William Rufus, standing on the shores of Pembrokeshire and discerning Ireland in the distance, boasted that he would span the sea with a bridge of boats and so make himself master of the island.[1] He was given to bragging and there may be some foundation for the tale. But however that may be, in fact he made no attempt to bring Ireland under English rule, nor did either of his two immediate successors. Yet the condition of the country rendered it an easy prey to the invader. The battle of Clontarf in 1014 had once and for all stemmed the tide of the Norse attack; the Ostmen, as the Scandinavian invaders of Ireland were called, settled down as traders and sailors in the coastal towns they had built—Dublin, Waterford, Wexford, Cork, and Limerick—and in the districts immediately surrounding them. But the battle had at the same time proved fatal for the prosperity of Ireland. Brian Boru, who by ruthless violence had established a supremacy the most complete Ireland had ever known—he is styled in an entry in the *Book of Armagh* as *imperator Scotorum*[2]—was killed in the fight. With his death all semblance of unity was destroyed, and a bewildering anarchy prevailed during which the provincial kings fought ceaselessly among themselves, rivalling each other for the once honoured but now almost meaningless title of high-king (*ard-ri*). These kings, 'kings with opposition' as they were appropriately named by Irish contemporaries, could no longer rely on the loyalty or military support of their subjects whose only real attachment was to one or another of the numberless tribal lords.

We need not dwell on this sordid chapter of Irish history in which battles and raids, murder and mutilation were of daily occurrence. One incident, however, in the struggle for power needs to be recorded on account of its sequel. Dermot McMurrough, king of Leinster, a ferocious, brutal man, with boundless energy and boldness, in 1152 abducted Dervorgil, the wife of Tiernan O'Rourke, a rival prince in Meath. Although the lady soon returned to her lawful husband, the insult was never forgotten; and revenge for the rape of Dervorgil was admittedly a primary cause of the expulsion of Dermot fourteen years later,

[1] Giraldus Cambrensis, *De Principis Instructione*, Dist. iii, c. 25 (*Opera*, viii. 290).
[2] G. H. Orpen, *Ireland under the Normans*, i. 30, n. 2.

an event which in its turn led to the intervention of the English in the affairs of distracted Ireland. In 1166 Rory O'Conor, who had thrust his way into the position of high-king, in alliance with O'Rourke made himself master of Dublin, and drove Dermot, now deserted both by the Ostmen and by his native subjects, from Leinster. On 1 August 1166 he set sail in search of English help. It was natural that he should make for Bristol, for between that city and the ports of south-eastern Ireland there had been for many years past a flourishing commercial intercourse. He was probably already known to the reeve, Robert Fitz Harding, who hospitably entertained him before he proceeded thence to France in quest of the court of Henry II.

The idea of an Irish conquest had been in Henry's mind since the very beginning of his reign. The project was considered at a council held at Winchester at Michaelmas 1155, and was only laid aside because the Empress Matilda, who had a great influence over her son especially in foreign policy, was opposed to it. Henry had, however, taken the important step of winning the pope's favour for his proposed enterprise. John of Salisbury had gone to Rome on the king's behalf, and obtained from Adrian IV a privilege—the famous Bull 'Laudabiliter' sanctioning the plan of conquest and also an emerald ring 'by which investiture of the right to rule over Ireland might be made'.[1] This sympathetic attitude of the papacy may be attributed to the grave concern with which she regarded the condition of the native Irish church. The isolation of Ireland from continental revolutions, which was in part responsible for her early culture, her intellectual eminence in the centuries preceding the Scandinavian invasions, had also been a cause of her undoing. For she had remained untouched by the advance of civilization which was in the eleventh and twelfth centuries affecting other European societies. While other countries were progressing, Ireland regressed. Religion, such as it was, was seated in the

[1] The original of the Bull 'Laudabiliter' and of its confirmation by Pope Alexander III have not survived, and are only known to us through their insertion by Giraldus Cambrensis in his *Expugnatio Hibernica* (*Opera*, v. 317). Although a great controversy has raged over these documents, there is no good reason to impugn their genuineness. For the whole subject see Orpen, op. cit. i, ch. ix. John of Salisbury refers to the emerald ring in *Metalogicon* (ed. Webb), iv, c. 42, and he alludes to the special interest of the papacy in the matter 'for all islands by ancient right by virtue of the Donation of Constantine are said to belong to the Church of Rome'. The date of the transaction was probably Michaelmas 1155. Cf. R. L. Poole, *Studies in Chronology and History*, p. 267.

monasteries without any central control. Organization and discipline were, it seems, wholly wanting; the morals of the clergy were little, if at all, better than those of the laity. The statement of St. Bernard in his life of Malachy, the saintly Irish reformer, that the see of Armagh in the eleventh and early twelfth century was held by 'hereditary succession' and that eight of the holders were married men and without orders seems to be substantially true.[1] The native marriage customs were strange and such as could scarcely be approved by orthodox churchmen. Some improvement had taken place when Lanfranc claimed for Canterbury primatial authority over the Irish church, a claim which was admitted by the Ostmen and even by some of the native princes.[2] Accordingly, bishops were appointed who, though of Irish birth, had been trained in English or Norman monasteries, and carried back with them to Ireland the prevalent ideas of the church reformers. Church synods were held and in the course of the first half of the twelfth century the church of Ireland came to be organized on an episcopal basis under the primacy of Armagh. There was, however, still much to be done, and Adrian IV no doubt saw in Henry II's projected conquest a way of bringing about a more drastic reform, and of attaching Ireland more closely to the Holy See. This connexion of the Irish church with England and Rome was not without its significance; for the reformed church nearly always favoured the Norman invaders rather than the native Irish princes.

Henry II received Dermot, when they met in Aquitaine, with favour; and though he was at the time too deeply engaged in continental affairs and with his dispute with Becket to give his personal attention to Ireland, he nevertheless secured Dermot's fealty, and sent him back to England armed with letters patent empowering his barons to engage themselves to assist him in the recovery of his lost possessions. The first to take advantage of this licence was Richard, earl of Striguil and Pembroke, commonly known as Strongbow. He entered into a compact by

---

[1] Ed. H. J. Lawlor in translation (S.P.C.K.), p. 45. In a note on p. 164 the editor has compiled a pedigree illustrating the hereditary succession of the bishops or, more properly, the coarbs of Patrick. This life and the editor's learned introduction provide an excellent description of the condition of the Irish church before the Norman invasion.

[2] In 1074 the Ostmen of Dublin requested Lanfranc to consecrate their bishop. Böhmer, *Kirche und Staat*, p. 115.

which, in return for his help, he was to marry Dermot's daughter Eva and succeed to his kingdom. Since, however, he was out of favour at court, he judged it prudent to defer the Irish adventure until he had first obtained the king's more definite permission. Actually, he did not set out until the summer of 1170. But in the interval Dermot had been able to recruit two Anglo-Norman lords, the half-brothers Robert Fitz Stephen and Maurice Fitz Gerald, who had played a prominent part in Welsh politics in Cardigan and Pembroke, and were well practised in fighting with light-armed troops in dense and hilly country, just the kind of warfare which would be required in Ireland. Satisfied with these promises and encouraged by a turn of events in his favour among his own people, Dermot returned to Ireland; but he was no sooner back than he was again attacked by his old enemies, and once more defeated. This time, however, he was not expelled, but, after giving hostages to Rory and making reparation to O'Rourke for the rape of Dervorgil, he was allowed to retain a portion of his tribal lands. Dermot accepted this settlement only to give himself a breathing space, for he had no intention of resting content with this shadow of his former power. He therefore sent urgent messages entreating his Norman friends to hasten to redeem their promises. Accordingly, on 1 May 1169, Fitz Stephen with a small mixed force of knights and light-armed Welshmen landed near Wexford. Not much was achieved by these first invaders; they captured Wexford which was handed over, as had been stipulated, to Fitz Stephen, and they made a couple of incursions into Ossory. But then they fell out among themselves, and one of their number, Maurice of Prendergast, with perhaps a third of the Anglo-Norman army, deserted to the enemy. The compromise, which ended this first phase of the invasion, left Leinster to Dermot who, in his turn, recognized the authority of Rory O'Conor as high-king. But peace had hardly been restored, when a fresh contingent under Maurice Fitz Gerald arrived at Wexford. With each addition of strength Dermot's ambitions grew. He now aspired to the conquest of Connaught, even to the position of high-king. He was, however, persuaded by his Norman allies that he could not hope to accomplish such aims without further reinforcements from across the seas. He wrote, therefore, to Strongbow, reminding him of his proffered help and begging him to hasten. The latter, taking some vague words uttered by Henry II as permission to seek his fortune by Irish conquest, responded to this appeal. He landed near Waterford on 23 August 1170 with a force more adequate to the task than had hitherto been brought to Ireland, composed, it is said, of 200 knights and 1,000 light-armed troops. He was also an abler man than any of the Norman leaders who had preceded him. In these circumstances, as might have been expected, his arrival was heralded by more decisive successes. Waterford was immediately captured by assault, and within a month Dublin, which, owing to its trading connexions and its archiepiscopal see, was already shaping as a capital city, fell into the hands of the invaders.

Dermot McMurrough did not long survive his restoration. He died at Ferns, the home of the Leinster kings, in May 1171, leaving as his successor Strongbow, who, according to the bargain, had married his daughter Eva. But the earl's position was fraught with difficulties. The Irish were not prepared to accept an alien lord as king of Leinster, and they united under the high-king, Rory O'Conor, to resist his pretensions. He was further embarrassed by the attitude which Henry II now adopted towards the Irish adventurers. He had become alarmed at their successes and ordered them to return home. Strongbow replied that he had gone to Ireland with the king's licence,[1] and tactfully added that what lands he had acquired there he would hold at the king's disposal. However, Henry's action effectively prevented further reinforcements from coming to aid him against the general rising which soon began to assume dangerous proportions. He himself and most of the English were besieged in Dublin through the summer months, while Fitz Stephen was shut up in a fortification he had constructed of turf and stakes at Carrick near Wexford. The situation became so desperate that the earl even offered to submit to the high-king, 'to become his man and hold Leinster of him'. But his terms were refused; Rory would only agree to allow him the three towns of Dublin, Wexford, and Waterford, and the negotiations were dropped. Dublin was saved owing to the fighting superiority of the trained and disciplined Normans and the superb courage of their leaders, in particular the constable, Miles of Cogan. An attempt made by the Ostmen to take the city by assault from the east was beaten

[1] The licence was, according to Giraldus and other authorities, actually given; it was afterwards revoked, but only on the eve of the earl's departure, when it was too late to draw back. Orpen, i. 181, 192 f.

off with heavy loss. Then a small band of the besieged, consisting
of only a few hundred men, sallied out and destroyed or dispersed the army of the high-king, amounting to many thousands,
in their encampment on the banks of the Liffey. The victory
was complete; but it came too late to save Robert Fitz Stephen
who was tricked into surrender and thrown into prison, where
he remained until, a month or so later, he was handed over to
Henry II and, shortly after, released.

Strongbow by his victory at Dublin was left master of the
important coastal towns and of a considerable region of the
interior, for some of the Leinster tribes had been induced to
submit to his rule. His security now depended not so much on
the hostility of the Irish chiefs as on the actions of the king of
England, against whose express command he had made the
expedition. News now reached him that the king had determined at a council of barons held at Argentan in July to come
himself to Ireland, that he had in fact returned to England and
had collected an army of 500 knights and many archers—perhaps 4,000 in all. A fleet of 400 ships was assembled at Milford
Haven to transport this formidable force and its necessary
equipment across the Irish sea. This was in September, not long
after the collapse of the siege of Dublin. In these circumstances
Strongbow deemed it prudent not to await his coming, but to
go to meet him. They met probably at Newnham on the banks
of the Severn where the army was mobilized, and there came to
terms: the earl was compelled to cede Dublin and the adjacent
country, Wexford, and Waterford, and all the fortresses. In
return he was later enfeoffed with the rest of Leinster by the
service of 100 knights. On the whole, therefore, he had come
well out of it; his rash enterprise had been by no means
unprofitable.

On 17 October 1171 Henry landed at Waterford with his
imposing army. It was provisioned and equipped as if for great
purposes. Corn and beans, cheese and bacon were brought in
abundant quantities; materials required in field engineering,
and even portable wooden towers for use in siege warfare, were
shipped across from Bristol. Everything was prepared as though
campaigning for a long period and on a prodigious scale was
contemplated. This, however, was not Henry's object. All this
show was intended to impress the natives with a sense of his
power. He professed to come not as their enemy but as their

protector, to control the activities of the high-handed Anglo-Norman adventurers, and to set things in order generally. He hoped that if he adopted this peaceable attitude the Irish chieftains would of their own accord submit to his overlordship; and he had not miscalculated. Almost immediately Dermot MacCarthy, king of Desmond, and O'Brien, king of Thomond, came to him, rendered their homage, and agreed to pay tribute. The example of these two provincial kings was soon followed by other princes of southern and central Ireland: only those of Connaught and of the extreme northern districts, Tyrone and Tyrconnel, held aloof.[1] But even these made no concerted attempt to check the spread of the English sovereignty.

At Dublin, which he made his headquarters during most of the winter of 1171–2, and which was already destined to be the capital of the Anglo-Irish settlement, the king built a royal palace in the native style. Here he held his court and entertained in sumptuous splendour the Irish princes who visited him. The city had been seriously depleted by the recent fighting; the relatively few remaining Ostmen were established in a quarter to the north of the river, while the city proper was granted by charter to the men of Bristol with the liberties and free customs which they had at Bristol. It was not, however, by any means exclusively occupied by Bristol men; a roll of the citizens made at the close of the twelfth century shows that the colonists who settled at Dublin came from towns widely scattered throughout England and Wales, and even from Scotland and France.[2]

The submission of the Irish princes was followed by the submission of the Irish church. The council of Cashel, presided over by Christian, bishop of Lismore and papal legate, and attended by the archbishops of Dublin, Cashel, and Tuam, besides many bishops, abbots, and other dignitaries of the church, met at Henry's instance in the course of the winter.[3] The canons which were then passed were designed to remove some of the more conspicuous irregularities of the native church and to bring it

[1] Giraldus (*Opera*, v. 279) says that Rory O'Conor of Connaught also submitted. But this is improbable. See Orpen, i. 264.

[2] See the list printed in *Historical and Municipal Documents of Ireland* (Rolls Series), pp. 3 ff. The document is summarized by Orpen, i. 270 f. Cork and Waterford also received the customs of Bristol during this period. Bateson, *Eng. Hist. Rev.* xv (1900), 74.

[3] The primate, Gelasius, archbishop of Armagh, although unable to appear on account of his great age—for he was nearly eighty-five—afterwards subscribed to the decrees of the council.

more into line with the church in England and with Rome. It may be assumed that the bishops took this occasion to swear their fealty to Henry and to recognize him by letters 'with pendent seal in the form of a charter' as lord of Ireland.[1] These letters were forthwith dispatched together with a request for papal confirmation to Alexander III, who not only confirmed his predecessor's privilege (the Bull 'Laudabiliter') but also on 20 September 1172 addressed three letters, one to the king himself, one to the bishops, and a third to the kings and princes of Ireland. They all, of course, animadvert on the 'enormity of vice', on the 'abominable foulness' of the Irish, and express the pope's rejoicing that a beginning has been made in the way of reform and his hope that still further effort will be made in the same direction. But more significant is the solemn admonition both to the bishops and to the native princes to maintain their loyalty to King Henry. These letters in the most authoritative fashion pronounce the pope's recognition of Henry's title to the lordship of Ireland.[2] The leaders of the Irish church acted wisely in supporting the newcomers, for these were generous in their benefactions. They built churches and cathedrals, and they founded monasteries in the lands which they conquered and settled. Under the Norman type of practical statesmen-bishops, of whom John Cumin, archbishop of Dublin (1182–1213), was the first, the church's wealth was enormously increased, its organization improved, and its association with the government drawn closer.

The winter of 1171–2 had been stormy, so stormy indeed that ships could not cross the Irish Sea. For many weeks Henry had been almost completely cut off from news of events outside; and when it came at last in March it was most disquieting. The papal legates were in Normandy, waiting to impose the conditions under which Henry might be absolved from the charge of guilt in the murder of Becket; they had been there all the winter, were now growing impatient, and even threatening the extreme rigour of ecclesiastical punishment if he delayed longer. In these circumstances the king hastened to complete his arrangements for the government of Ireland after his departure. Although he

---

[1] *Gesta Henrici*, i. 26; Orpen, i. 278.

[2] The letters, preserved in the Black Book of the Exchequer, are printed in Hearne's edition of the *Liber Niger*, i. 42, and in the *Foedera*, i. 45. They are summarized by Orpen, i. 301.

had treated Strongbow with fairness, even with generosity, he did not altogether trust him. It was for this reason, no doubt, that he set up a counterpoise to his influence by granting the kingdom of Meath as a fief to Hugh de Lacy; and it was Hugh, not Strongbow, whom he left as justiciar and his vice-gerent when he quitted the country on 17 April 1172.

Henry II might well be satisfied with the results of his six months' visit; he had won the recognition of nearly all the native princes without striking a blow. Nevertheless, ignorant of the Irish character, he did not realize that they could throw off their allegiance as lightly as they could give it; that an absentee 'high-king' left them even freer than before to indulge in their ceaseless domestic feuds and their lawless hostings. He failed also to see that the establishment of Anglo-Norman barons on a semi-independent footing there must inevitably lead to a conflict of interests. To confound Irish politics further there was soon to appear a third element in the Irish population. Besides the native Irish, besides the Anglo-Norman barons, there were those settlers who took Irish wives or adopted Irish customs and were regarded as 'English to the Irish and Irish to the English', and became in fact *Hibernis ipsis Hiberniores*. These Anglo-Irish were in time to prove an endless source of trouble to future governors of Ireland.[1] The Irish problem dates from 1172.

Strongbow and de Lacy were both soon recalled to help in the suppression of the great revolt which broke out in 1173. The earl's loyal service in Normandy was afterwards duly recognized by the king; and when he returned to Ireland in August 1173 he went back as governor, and with the town of Wexford and the castle of Wicklow added to his lordship of Leinster, where, owing to his statesmanlike qualities, he was able to maintain peace and some sort of order among his English and Irish subjects. Elsewhere his period of rule, which lasted till his death in the summer of 1176, was, like most of Irish history, turbulent. The native Irish were anxious to regain what they had lost, while the Anglo-Norman settlers were ambitious to acquire more. Treachery and murder were of common occurrence; savage attacks were answered by no less savage reprisals. The principal fighting was for the possession of Limerick which was captured, besieged, relieved, and at last abandoned by Raymond le Gros of the family of Carew, a general of some brilliance and great daring

[1] E. Curtis, *A History of Medieval Ireland* (1938), pp. 93, 95.

who inspired the complete confidence of his troops. It was not, however, till some twenty years later that Limerick finally succumbed to English conquest.

A new figure, destined to play a great part in Irish history, now appeared on the scene—John de Courcy. This adventurous soldier, a member of a Norman family settled in Somerset, came over with William Fitz Audelin who had been sent as governor to Ireland on the death of Strongbow. Discouraged by Fitz Audelin's aimless and obstructive policy, de Courcy determined to seek his fortune in a new field. The conquest of Ulster, achieved with almost incredible rapidity and success, is perhaps the most amazing episode in the history of the occupation. Contemporaries describe him as a hero of epic; tall and fair, brave and impetuous, he fought rather like a private soldier than as a commander, lopping off the heads and arms of the natives with the stroke of his sword. With a mere handful of men he set out from Dublin early in 1177; in February he captured the city of Downpatrick; and from this centre, after a series of battles generally fought against enormous odds, he gradually penetrated and became master of the whole eastern part of the province. In after years (1185) when he became justiciar he played a part in the general politics of Ireland, particularly in the feuds which incessantly rent the kingdom of Connaught; but it was as the conqueror of Ulster that he will always be remembered. Indeed, it has been said that the prosperity of eastern Ulster dates from his time.[1] He may have ruled it too independently; he may even, as has been said, have refused to do homage for it. Be that as it may, he incurred the displeasure of King John and the jealousy of his powerful neighbours, the de Lacys of Meath. Arrested, released, defeated and captured in battle by Hugh de Lacy the younger, he was finally (May 1205) supplanted by his captor in the lordship of Ulster. Although he was subsequently reconciled with the king and lived on till about 1219, he never regained his Irish lands or his influence in the affairs of Ireland.

In 1175, by the treaty of Windsor, Henry II had recognized Rory O'Conor as high-king on a tributary basis over those districts of Ireland where the Anglo-Norman rule did not as yet extend. But the plan was quite unworkable: Rory could scarcely exact obedience from his own subject-chieftains in Connaught,

<hr>

[1] Orpen, ii. 144.

let alone those of Ulster or Munster; and the pact was completely ignored when, at the council held at Oxford in May
1177, a new scheme for the administration of Ireland was devised. The king then determined that Ireland should be a provision for his youngest, his landless son John. For the present,
however, until he was of maturer years (he was now but ten),
he was to enjoy only the title of *dominus Hiberniae*, and the actual
work of government was entrusted to a viceroy in the person of
Hugh de Lacy. Hugh was a good administrator, and he soon
succeeded in establishing order out of chaos in his own lordship
of Meath. Following the example of Strongbow, he married in
1180 an Irishwoman, the daughter of Rory O'Conor. By his
marriage, by his moderation and justice, he won the sympathy
of the natives who submitted cheerfully to the change of rulers.
During his period of office as viceroy there was one notable
extension of English influence. In 1177 the kingdom of Cork
had been granted jointly to Robert Fitz Stephen and Miles
of Cogan for the service of sixty knights. These two experienced
campaigners proceeded forthwith to take possession of their
fief. They met with success and prospered; and although a
massacre of several of the leaders, including Miles himself,
and a general rising of the natives in 1182 threatened to
exterminate the English colony, relief came and the danger
passed. Henry II, however, always mistrusted de Lacy; after his
marriage with the daughter of the high-king he even suspected
him of aiming at the throne of Ireland. The suspicion was
groundless; nevertheless he was deprived of the custody of
Dublin in 1181, and though reinstated a year after he was
finally superseded in 1184. Two years later he met with the fate
which carried off so many Irish leaders: he was assassinated.

In 1185 John was deemed by his indulgent father to be
sufficiently mature to visit his Irish lordship. He set sail from
Milford Haven and landed at Waterford on 25 April. The eight
months which he spent in the island were disastrous alike to the
Anglo-Norman settlers and to the native Irish. He displayed at
once his inexperience as an administrator and as a soldier. Gerald
of Wales, who was in Ireland at the time, does not stint his
language in his general condemnation of the conduct of the
court of insolent and irresponsible youths, of John's reckless disregard of the counsel of men experienced in the affairs of Ireland, and of the dire consequences of such behaviour. From the

first moment of his arrival the prince aroused the hostility of the
Irish chiefs. He treated those who came to welcome him and
show him obedience with levity and contempt; his indis-
criminate grants to favourites caused jealousy and discontent;
his tactlessness almost had the effect of uniting the three native
kings, Donnell O'Brien of Thomond, Dermot McCarthy of
Desmond, and Rory O'Conor of Connaught, who were usually
at feud with each other, in a bond of amity to recover their
liberties; they at least withheld their homage. It was well for
Ireland that before the end of the year the king realized his
mistake, recalled John and his unruly companions, and entrusted the administration to John de Courcy, who was well
versed in all the difficult problems which the occupation of Ireland presented.

By a curious fatality many of the leading spirits in the Irish
venture were cut off in the prime of life, often leaving minors,
heiresses, or indirect descendants to succeed them. This circumstance tended to make for an unsettled condition, for the great
fiefs were taken into the hands of the Crown and administered
by royal agents who were perhaps ignorant of the ways of the
Irish. Thus Strongbow, Hugh de Lacy the elder, Robert Fitz
Stephen, Maurice Fitz Gerald, Miles of Cogan, Raymond le
Gros were all dead within twenty years of the first landing.
Their place was taken by a new generation, most of whom had
come over in the entourage of John; prominent among them
were Philip of Worcester, sent out in 1184 to supersede de Lacy
as governor and to prepare for John's visit in the following
year, Theobald Walter, John's butler (*pincerna*), brother of
Hubert Walter and head of the family of Butler of Ormond, and
William de Burgh, brother of Hubert de Burgh, and ancestor of
the Burkes of Ulster, Connaught, and Munster.

Death had also removed some of the native kings who had
played leading parts in the first years of the conquest. Rory
O'Conor, the last high-king of Ireland, had lost all semblance
of power before he died in 1198, and Donnell O'Brien, king of
Thomond, who by keeping on friendly terms with the Anglo-
Normans had managed to maintain his independence, died in
1195. Disputed successions and a fierce feud between the
O'Conors and the O'Briens seriously weakened the position of
the Irish in Connaught and Munster, and opened the way for a
further advance of the English conquerors. This advance was

chiefly due to the energy and enterprise of William de Burgh, who had married, shortly before, the daughter of Donnell O'Brien and now succeeded in bringing most of his land, representing the modern counties of Limerick and Tipperary, under English rule. He then intervened with success in the turbulent state of affairs which then prevailed in Connaught, and carried English influence north of the Shannon. But the capriciousness of King John and the jealousy of his justiciar, Meiler Fitz Henry, combined to work his ruin. Limerick had long before, in 1177, been granted to Philip de Braose who had failed to conquer it; the grant was renewed in 1201 at the price of 5,000 marks in favour of his nephew, William de Braose, who at this time enjoyed the special confidence and friendship of the king. Thus in Limerick de Burgh was reduced to the position of a sub-tenant; in Connaught he was superseded by a native prince (1204). Although he later recovered some of his lost lands, he never again exercised an influence in the affairs of Ireland.

The same jealous attitude, which King John adopted towards the great barons and which led to the downfall of de Burgh, also frustrated the activities of the greatest and most loyal of the men whose fortunes were linked with Ireland—William Marshal, earl of Pembroke. He had inherited the lordship of Leinster by his marriage with Isabel, the daughter and heiress of Strongbow, as early as 1189, but during Richard's reign he was too busily engaged in the Norman wars personally to take charge of his Irish interests. It was not, in fact, until after the loss of Normandy that he had the leisure to turn his attention to Ireland; and then he was thwarted at every point by the master he always served with chivalrous, almost quixotic, fidelity. Repeatedly the king forbade him to visit his inheritance. But at last, in spite of the king, he went, and from 1207 to 1213 he was the foremost figure in Ireland. Although hampered by the obstructiveness of the justiciar, Meiler Fitz Henry (who was removed from his office in 1208), and the suspicious jealousy of the king, by his organizing ability, his power of statecraft, and his remarkable integrity of character, he succeeded in establishing in Leinster a condition of law and order such as had never been previously known.

During the years 1209 to 1211 King John devoted his attention to the affairs of the Celtic fringe. In the former year he had brought William the Lion of Scotland triumphantly to submission; in 1211 he forced Llywelyn to come to terms; in the

interval, in 1210, he made his second visit to Ireland. The reason
he alleged for it was that William de Braose, a former favourite
but now a declared traitor, had fled there with his family and
had been sheltered by William Marshal and the de Lacys,
Walter and Hugh, respectively lords of Meath and Ulster. But
he no doubt welcomed the opportunity thus offered to increase
the power of the Crown and to diminish that of his too independent feudatories. On 20 June he landed near Waterford
with an imposing army, and in the course of the summer he
traversed the whole of eastern Ireland, receiving as he went, with
marked favour, the native princes. These in their turn readily
assisted him in rounding up his enemies in the great Ulster
fortress of Carrickfergus. Hugh de Lacy escaped and fled the
country, and so too did William de Braose; but the latter's wife
and son were captured, and their death from starvation at
Windsor Castle is one of the grimmest examples of the king's
merciless love of cruelty. His victory was followed by heavy
reprisals; the lands of many of the barons of Meath and Ulster
were confiscated, and either restored for ransom and hostages or
granted anew to his own adherents.

By the end of August John was back in England, having more
than achieved the objects he had set out to accomplish during
his nine weeks' stay: he had undermined the power of the great
Anglo-Norman barons and he had enormously enhanced the
royal authority. A strong stone castle arose in Dublin (it was
completed by 1215) as the seat and symbol of royal power. John
was 'lord of Ireland' in a very real sense at least in the parts east
and south of the rivers Bann and Shannon. The baronial
justiciars were replaced by churchmen who had no axe of their
own to grind: first by John de Gray, bishop of Norwich, and
then, in 1213, by Henry, archbishop of Dublin. The statement
of the English chronicler, Roger of Wendover, that John 'established there the laws and customs of England, appointing
sheriffs and other officers to administer justice to the people of
that kingdom according to English laws' although not a sudden
consequence of the expedition of 1210, as the writer implies,
seems to be substantially true of the settled districts. A beginning
had been made in the time of Henry II; then in 1204 the king
authorized the use of the writ of right and of the possessory
assizes of mort d'ancestor and novel disseisin; in 1207 an Irish
coinage was issued bearing the symbol of the harp. In 1210 John

extended these administrative developments and took measures
to ensure that they were enforced.

The conquest had been achieved by the superior discipline,
superior weapons, and superior tactics of the Anglo-Norman
armies. Even a small force of trained knights and archers could
usually get the better of a multitude of ill-armed and ill-disci-
plined Irishmen, however courageous they might be. To secure
the occupied territory, castles of a simple but effective pattern
sprang up in the trail of the conquerors. The 'motes' or im-
provised fortresses, like those which mark the footsteps of
William the Conqueror in England, consisted of a mound of
earth surrounded by a ditch and enclosure (bailey) and surmounted perhaps by wooden defences; they were admirably
suited to the purpose, being quickly erected by unskilled labour
with materials ready to hand and afforded protection to small
bodies of men against sudden assaults of the hostile inhabitants.[1]
The land thus gained was gradually feudalized on English lines,
parcelled out into fiefs of five, ten, or twenty knights, among
those who had taken part in the conquest.[2] There was, however,
no wholesale eviction of the Irish peasantry. The colonists were
not numerous; they required labour to cultivate their lands. So
the natives remained for the most part undisturbed to work the
fields under the improved methods of agriculture which the
new-comers introduced and without, as before, the ever-present
fear of cattle-stealing by their marauding neighbours. There
was, too, a marked advance in urban development. Not only
did the old coastal towns of the Ostmen receive a fresh stimulus
from royal charters and trading connexions which resulted from
the English conquest, but also in the interior of Ireland little
towns grew up under the shelter of castles, and came to share
in the new commercial prosperity.

When England was seething with rebellion, Ireland was at
peace. In part this may be attributed to the statesmanship and
organizing ability of the later viceroys and still more to the
sterling character and patient work of the greatest of the Irish
feudatories, William Marshal. But something is due to the king
himself who cared for Ireland and had a deliberate policy for

[1] Orpen, i. 340, 342, n. 1, and for the distribution of these castles see the map at
the end of vol. ii.

[2] A detailed and very interesting account of the subinfeudation of Leinster and
Meath is given in the *Song of Dermot and the Earl* (ed. Orpen), pp. 223–31.

governing it. The native princes acquiesced almost contentedly in the rule of foreigners; the Anglo-Norman barons, in spite of the capricious and arbitrary treatment they often had to put up with, were among the most loyal of the king's subjects during the last and most critical years of his reign. In 1212 twenty-seven of them headed by William Marshal declared in writing that they were 'prepared to live or die with the king and that till the last they would faithfully and inseparably adhere to him';[1] and when in the next year John held a muster of his forces against the threat of invasion from France at Barham Down near Canterbury, John de Gray, the justiciar, and the Marshal paraded with 500 knights (practically the whole knights' service due from Ireland) besides many other horse-men. Such unswerving, disinterested, and spontaneous loyalty is significant evidence of the general effectiveness of John's policy in his relations with his Irish lordship.[2] The two-thirds of Ireland over which the English rule extended was the 'land of peace'; what remained to the Irish was 'the land of war'. The Norman genius for administration left its mark on Ireland as it had on England; and the promising beginnings of a settled state did not die with John. It survived for a century until Edward Bruce with his army, flushed with his victory at Bannockburn, entered Ireland and began the process of disintegration which reduced most of the country once more to chaotic independence.

[1] The document is summarized in *Calendar of Documents: Ireland, 1171–1251*, no. 448.
[2] Cf. Curtis, pp. 117 f.; Orpen, ii. 319 f., takes a less favourable view of John's government of Ireland. He takes, however, a very favourable view of the general effects of the occupation. See particularly his article 'The Effects of Norman Rule in Ireland 1169–1333' in the *American Hist. Rev.* xix (1914), 245.

X
THE ANGEVIN EMPIRE
1154-1189

HENRY II was an international figure on the European stage; a ruler of a large composite state stretching from Scotland to the Pyrenees, a dominion comparable in extent, and indeed in the looseness of the bonds which united the component parts, only to the Holy Roman Empire. The continental lands of the 'Angevin Empire' as it is commonly, or the 'Norman Empire' as perhaps it should be more properly termed,[1] had been acquired by inheritance or marriage before Henry became king of England. Normandy he inherited from his mother; Anjou, Maine, and Touraine from his father; and Aquitaine, Poitou, and Auvergne came to him with his wife, Eleanor. Tours, which had been wrested from the house of Blois more than a century earlier by Geoffrey Martel, was of great strategic importance, the 'key to the Angevin Empire' as it has been described;[2] for it controlled the communications of northern and western France, and gave something of cohesion to the continental territories. But the real tie which bound them together was Henry II himself, to whom they all owed allegiance. Regarded from a modern standpoint, an oath of fealty seems but a slender bond of union; but in the middle ages government was still essentially personal, radiating from the king and his household wherever they might happen to be at any particular moment, whether in England or Normandy, Anjou or Aquitaine. And Henry was ubiquitous; his rapidity of movement astonished the king of France: 'now in Ireland, now in England, now in Normandy, he must fly rather than travel by horse or ship' he exclaimed on one of Henry's sudden appearances.[3]

He was certainly a remarkable character. When he was crowned king of England on 19 December 1154 he was in the prime of life (twenty-one years old) and already much experienced in the affairs of the world. From contemporaries who

---

[1] Haskins, *Normans in European History*, p. 85. Dermot McMurrough in addressing Henry II speaks of 'les baruns de tun Empire'. *Song of Dermot* (ed. Orpen), l. 285.

[2] Powicke, *Loss of Normandy*, p. 14; Haskins, op. cit., p. 88.

[3] Ralph de Diceto (ed. Stubbs), i. 351.

knew him well we are able to gather a tolerably clear idea of his personality.[1] Of medium height and stocky build, with a tendency to corpulence (which he kept in check by assiduous exercise) he gave the impression of a figure moulded for strength. He had, like many of his family, reddish hair, which he kept close cropped, a freckled face, and keen grey eyes which became fiery and bloodshot when he was seized, as he often was, by a fit of passionate and ungovernable rage. He neither courted nor acquired popularity. Indeed, many contemporaries gave him a very bad character, hardly better than was accorded to his youngest son who is often (though perhaps unwarrantably) regarded as the most evil king that ever sat upon the English throne. Gerald of Wales and Ralph Niger indulge in violent invectives on the subject of his oppression, his injustice, his immorality, his perfidy; the author of the 'Vision of the Monk of Eynsham' pictured him suffering the worst torments of hell as a punishment for his sins and vices. Such accusations were, of course, commonly levelled against men in high positions. A more convincing indication of his unpopularity is supplied by an incident recorded in one of Henry's own charters: he tells how at Bedford castle Ralph de Albini gratuitously hurled a stone at him.[2] It is said that he cared little for appearances or for the good things of life; that his clothes and food were of the plainest: he is even accused of parsimony. Nevertheless, judging by his bills for rich furs and silken robes, for plate and jewels, and for huge quantities of wine we may infer that he was not altogether averse to the enjoyment of regal splendour.[3] Essentially a man of action, he was never idle: his restless energy is perhaps his most marked characteristic. He was impatient of doing nothing; even in church he would while away the time drawing pictures or chattering in whispers to his courtiers. He never sat down, it was said, except when he was riding or eating, but would pass the day from dawn to dusk in the saddle, indulging his 'immoderate' fondness for hunting. Such statements, however, give an exaggerated idea of his addiction to an outdoor life. Certainly he preferred, if it could be arranged, to do

[1] Giraldus Cambrensis, *De Principis Instructione* (*Opera*, viii), pp. 213 ff. Walter Map, *De Nugis Curialium, passim*; Peter of Blois, *Ep.* lxvi, in Migne, *Pat. Lat.*, vol. 107.
[2] *Curia Regis Rolls*, iv. 270. For this offence Ralph forfeited the village of Didcot.
[3] See, for example. *Pipe Roll 23 Hen. II*, pp. 198, 201, where some £300 is accounted for clothes. (Cf. Round's Introduction, p. xxv.)

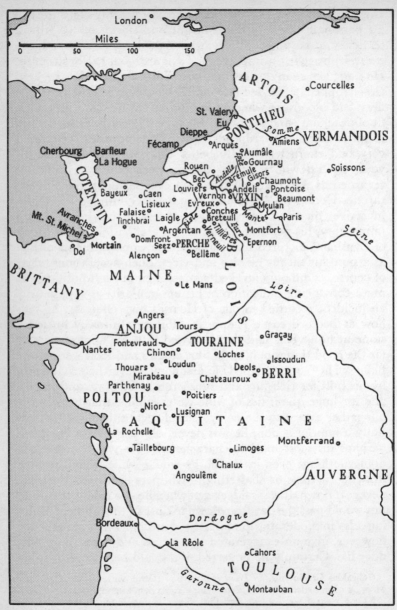

MAP OF THE ANGEVIN EMPIRE

his work in good hunting country, to hold his councils at his forest seats, such as Clarendon or Woodstock, and he took advantage of any opportunity that presented itself to exercise his favourite pastimes, 'hawking', for example, 'along every river and stream' as he proceeded on his way to attend the council of Northampton in 1164.[1] But he never neglected the business of state. Moreover, he had other ways than sport to employ his leisure: he had the taste for literature of a well-educated man, he was an accomplished linguist, and he enjoyed the society of wits and scholars. 'As often as he can get breathing-time amid his business cares', Peter of Blois wrote to his friend the archbishop of Palermo, 'he occupies himself with private reading, or takes pains in working out some knotty question among his clerks.'[2] Though a very competent soldier, he had no love of war for its own sake, and would never embark on it if he could reach his end by other means. His natural abilities, his immense capacity for work, his sound business instinct, his accessibility combined with an easy faculty for remembering facts and faces, all contributed to make him a statesman and diplomat of the first rank.

The problems raised by his continental dominions, their consolidation, their government and administration, were to absorb by far the greater part of Henry's reign. But before he could safely enter upon an active European policy, he had to make himself secure of England; for England had for him an importance quite incommensurate with its size, owing to the fact that it alone provided him with a crown which raised him equal in rank to the suzerain of his other lands, the king of France. To deliver the country from the tyranny of barons, and from the instruments of their tyranny, mercenary troops and unlicensed castles, was therefore the first object of his policy. The work was begun immediately after the coronation at the Christmas court at Bermondsey priory, where instructions were issued for the expulsion of the Flemings, for the destruction of such of the adulterine castles as still remained standing, and for the resumption of the royal castles and the alienated Crown lands. In carrying out these measures he was seldom vindictive. William of Ypres, Stephen's chief military commander, was permitted to retain his Kentish estates, which were worth more than £450 in

---

[1] Fitz Stephen, *Materials for History of Thomas Becket*, iii. 50.
[2] Quoted by Stubbs, *Lectures on Medieval and Modern History*, p. 137.

annual value, till 1157;[1] other Flemings were allowed to join their compatriots in their settlement in Pembrokeshire; but the remainder disappeared 'as phantoms vanish'. Further, in the selection of his ministers he did not confine his choice to men of his own party in the civil war. Nigel, bishop of Ely, who returned to his old office of treasurer, and Thomas Becket, who became chancellor in January 1155, had always supported the Angevin cause; but his two justiciars, Robert, earl of Leicester, and Richard de Lucy, had been loyal servants of Stephen, the one for most, the other for the whole of the reign. The process of recovery was also facilitated by the removal by death or other causes of several of the leading figures of the anarchy: no less than six of the earls created during that period died between 1153 and 1155;[2] Henry, bishop of Winchester, withdrew for a time to Cluny, and his numerous castles were demolished.[3] Most of the survivors, tired of war and plundering, willingly co-operated in the restoration of peace. Few resisted, but ineffectively: William of Aumale submitted at York and surrendered his stronghold of Scarborough; William Peverel fled when the king approached Nottingham, and spent the rest of his life in a monastery; Roger of Hereford yielded to the persuasions of Gilbert Foliot and made his peace by the surrender of his castles of Hereford and Gloucester. Only Hugh Mortimer on the Welsh march put up any fight; he fortified his castles at Bridgnorth, Wigmore, and Cleobury; but one after another they fell, and he too submitted (July 1155).

The task of re-establishing order had been so thoroughly done that the country remained undisturbed by wars and rebellions (except in Wales where disorders necessitated two campaigns in 1157 and 1165) until the great rising of 1173. Henry was therefore at liberty to give most of his attention to the affairs of the Continent. We have already noticed that the difficulty of governing these wide dominions was the lack of cohesion; there was no organized form of government, no common system of justice or finance; all depended on the skill and strength of the ruler. There was, however, an administrative link common to England and all the French possessions alike: the king's orders and instructions emanated from the same secretarial office.

---

[1] Round, *Geoffrey de Mandeville*, p. 275. [2] Stenton, *English Feudalism*, p. 226 n.
[3] Winchester, Mardon, Farnham, Waltham, Downton, and Taunton. *Ann. Mon.* ii. 51, iii. 17, iv. 380.

There was a single chancery for all the king's dominions controlled by a single chancellor who, with his staff of clerks, followed the court from place to place in its incessant perambulations. The clear, concise, businesslike writ of Henry II's chancery, drafted in the same formulae, could be understood everywhere, and gave some conformity to the mode of government. Moreover, if there was little to bind together this heterogeneous group of states which comprised the Angevin empire, there was, on the other hand, little or nothing to attach them more naturally to any other power. There was no French nation in the twelfth century; no feeling of patriotism or loyalty which impelled them to the king of France as to their natural ruler. It was, as has been said, 'little harder to rule these diverse lands from London or Rouen than from Paris'.[1] But the task would be easier if the frontiers were stronger. Consolidation was the first object of Henry's continental policy, the rounding off of his dominions by the acquisition of important neighbouring territories—the Vexin, Brittany, and Toulouse. By 1173 he was the overlord of all three.

When in 1144 Henry's father Geoffrey had gained possession of Normandy he had obtained the king of France's recognition of his conquest by the sacrifice of Gisors, the castle of which commanded the Norman Vexin; when in 1151 Louis put forward his brother-in-law, Eustace, Stephen's eldest son, as a rival to Henry in Normandy, peace was only obtained at the price of the whole Vexin. It was recovered not by war but by a marriage treaty; it formed the dowry of the infant princess Margaret, who was betrothed in 1158 to the king's eldest surviving son, Henry. The preliminary negotiations were conducted by the chancellor Becket who visited the French court at Paris in the summer. The state entry of Becket into the French capital (described in detail by his biographer)[2] with his army of flunkeys and squires, his trail of wagons and pack-horses richly caparisoned and mounted with monkeys, with his loads of beer and chests of gold to put the French in a good humour, presented a curious contrast with the later arrival of the unpretentious king, and must have caused some wonder in the minds of the inhabitants at the strangeness of a court where the normal

[1] Haskins, op. cit., p. 88. On the imperial character of Rouen see the verses quoted by Haskins, *Norman Institutions*, p. 144, n. 72.
[2] Fitz Stephen in *Materials*, iii. 29–31.

habits of master and servant seemed to have been reversed. The marriage treaty was duly agreed upon, and the princess was handed over to Henry's guardianship.[1] Since, however, she was but a few months old and the prince not yet four, there seemed to Louis to be no prospect of his being called upon for some years to come to yield up the Vexin, which, pending the marriage, was held in the custody of three Templars as trustees. But Henry regarded the tender ages of the pair as but a trifling inconvenience, by no means a serious obstacle to stand in the way of the object of his ambition. So, two years later, 2 November 1160, to the dismay and fury of Louis, the infants were married in the presence of two cardinal legates,[2] and the Vexin once more became a part of the dominions of the king of England.

Louis VII was too simple a character to treat successfully with so skilful a diplomat as Henry II.[3] He had allowed himself to be duped in the matter of the Vexin, and by another blunder he prepared the way for Henry's acquisition of Brittany. This question, which also came under discussion at the interviews between the two kings in the eventful year 1158, was, in its initial stages, bound up with the career of Henry's refractory brother, Geoffrey. The circumstances were these: Count Geoffrey, the father, considering his elder son sufficiently well provided for by his mother's inheritance of England and Normandy, bequeathed his own possessions, Anjou and Maine, to his younger son Geoffrey. Henry, as we should expect, objected to this partitioning, and, in 1156, defeated his brother, who attempted to carry out the will, and forced him to renounce his claim in return for a single castle—Loudun—and a money pension. At this moment, however, an opportunity presented itself of accommodating Geoffrey with land and of keeping him out of harm's way in Brittany. This province, since the death of Conan III in 1148, had been disputed by rival claimants. In 1156 the people of Nantes and lower Brittany, discarding both aspirants, chose Geoffrey as their count. On his death, two years

---

[1] There were two meetings, first on the Epte near Gisors, and afterwards at Paris. The conditions for the handing over of the Vexin, which was to take place in 1164 unless the pair were married earlier with the consent of the church, were contained in the peace made between Henry and Louis in May 1160. Delisle-Berger, *Recueil des Actes*, i. 251.

[2] The legates' sanction was Henry's reward for recognizing Alexander III as pope. Below, p. 328.

[3] Louis *vir nimis simplex* (Gervase of Canterbury, i. 166).

later, Henry quietly stepped in as his brother's heir. This arrangement, in which Louis willingly concurred, gave Henry a solid foothold in that county which the Norman dukes had always coveted, but where they had never succeeded in gaining more than a shadowy overlordship. It was, as Gervase of Canterbury noted, the first step in the conquest of Brittany.[1] It was also of particular value to the ruler of Anjou by reason of its geographical position: it gave him the command of the mouth of the Loire. The final subjection of Brittany was, like that of the Vexin, the result of a marriage. The heir of its duke, Conan IV, earl of Richmond, was a daughter, named Constance, whose hand was secured for the third of Henry's sons, Geoffrey. The Breton barons resisted; they clung tenaciously to their independence; they hated Norman domination. But their opposition was crushed in three campaigns (1166, 1167, 1168); and they were forced in 1169 to do homage to Geoffrey as the heir to the duchy. Two years later, on the death of Conan, the succession took effect.

The acquisition of the duchy of Aquitaine had brought Henry into contact with other powers than France: his territory on the south bordered on Navarre and Aragon; at its eastern extremity it approached the boundaries of the empire; and in between, on the south-east, lay the large and almost independent county of Toulouse, which Henry claimed, on rather slender grounds, as part of his wife's inheritance. To make good his claim, however, was a more serious undertaking than the subjection either of the Vexin or of Brittany; very elaborate preparations were accordingly made for its conquest. First he secured a useful ally in the district, Raymond Berengar, count of Barcelona, regent for his wife, the queen of Aragon, and arranged for the betrothal of the count's daughter with his second son Richard, whom he already designed—though the boy was not yet two years old—as the future duke of Aquitaine. He next raised a strong army. The lay baronage from all his dominions was summoned to serve in person; some brought with them their contingents of knights, others instead paid a scutage of two marks on the fee. From the church the king exacted not only the normal scutage payable by the under-tenants, but also very high arbitrary 'gifts' (*dona*) from the tenants-in-chief themselves, a grievance which they were not soon to forget. With the

[1] *Opera*, i. 166.

proceeds and with further taxation of the boroughs and the Jews,
a large mercenary force was hired.[1] But the campaign of the
summer of 1159 failed utterly, and chiefly through the intervention of Louis who, with unwonted energy, threw himself into
the town of Toulouse.[2] Henry scrupled to make a direct attack
upon his feudal superior (whose overlordship he had acknowledged on a visit to Paris in the previous autumn),[3] perhaps less
from chivalric motives than from a fear lest he might set a bad
example to his own vassals. So, after a useless siege and a good
deal of plundering, he withdrew, leaving Becket and the constable, Henry of Essex, to complete the operations. Cahors was
the only fruit of the expensive and carefully planned expedition.[4]
This rebuff combined with other events postponed for many
years the achievement of Henry's policy in this quarter.

While Henry was still encamped outside the walls of Toulouse
a schism occurred in the papacy. The death of Adrian IV on
1 September 1159 resulted in a double election; the majority
of the cardinals chose the chancellor Roland, who took the
name of Alexander III, while the imperialist minority set up
Cardinal Octavian, who assumed the title of Victor IV. By
the aid of bribery and physical force Victor soon gained an
ascendancy at Rome, and Alexander had to make a hasty
retreat to France. The attitude of the western powers and
especially of England at this crisis was obviously a matter of
decisive importance.

There can be no uncertainty about the grouping of the
powers in the early years of Henry II's reign: France was always
the actual or potential enemy, Germany, as in the time of
Henry I,[5] the natural ally of England. Political and economic
advantage, perhaps too the advice of his mother,[6] influenced
Henry to embrace alliance with the emperor. We get the first

[1] For the financing of the Toulouse campaign see Round, *Feudal England*,
pp. 275 ff.
[2] Louis, like Henry, anxious to strengthen his position in the Midi, had given his
sister Constance in marriage to Count Raymond of Toulouse (1154).
[3] Delisle-Berger, *Recueil des Actes de Henri II*, i. 194-5.
[4] A peace made between the two kings in May 1160 confirmed the results of the
wars of 1158-9. Ibid. i. 251-3.
[5] Above, pp. 126-7.
[6] The dowager Empress Matilda, since her withdrawal in 1148 from her contest
with Stephen, had settled down to a quiet and virtuous life near Rouen, and she is
said to have been her son's chief assistant in the management of his continental
affairs. Norgate, *Angevin Kings*, i. 442.

indication of this *entente* from Frederick who, in a letter dated 6 May 1157, addressed Henry as his 'most beloved brother and intimate and special friend'.[1] His ambassadors were in England that year;[2] and Henry's cordial response to these overtures is shown by the acts of the great council which met in July at Northampton. Here the merchants of Cologne were taken under the king's special protection,[3] and envoys were dispatched bearing magnificent gifts and a letter in which Henry with needless effusiveness and humility expressed his readiness to obey Frederick Barbarossa:[4]

'Our kingdom and whatever anywhere is subject to our rule we place at your disposal and commit to your power, that everything may be arranged at your nod, and that the will of your empire may be carried out in all respects. Let there be between us and our peoples an undivided unity of love and peace and safety of commerce, in such a way that to you, who are pre-eminent in dignity, be given the authority of command, and to us the will to obey shall not be lacking.'

Now the position was altogether changed. Neither Henry of England nor Louis of France was inclined to reject the obviously lawful pope; but, on the other hand, neither wished to break irrevocably with the emperor and so give an advantage to his opponent. Both accordingly sent their representatives to the council which Frederick summoned to meet at Pavia (February 1160) to decide between the rival popes; but they were instructed to take no part in the business, for the result—the recognition of Victor—was a foregone conclusion.[5] Then when the two kings made peace in May they agreed to take concerted action in the matter of the schism. In consequence of this decision the kings met at Beauvais and agreed between themselves to recognize

---

[1] Wibald of Corvey, *Epistolae* (*Monumenta Corbeiensia*, ed. Jaffé), p. 594.

[2] *Pipe Roll 4 Hen. II*, p. 112.

[3] B. Kuske, *Quellen zur Geschichte des Kölner Handels und Verkehrs* (1923), i. 1-2.

[4] Rahewin, *Gesta Friderici*, iii. 7 (ed. B. V. Simson, pp. 171-2). The letter is attested by Becket as chancellor at Northampton. It is possible, as H. W. C. Davis suggests (*Eng. Hist. Rev.* xxiv (1909), 772), that Henry II in his legislative work was influenced by Frederick's *Landfriede* edict of 1152 (*Mon. Germ. Hist., Const. et Acta Publica*, i. 194-8) which in some respects anticipates certain chapters in the Constitutions and Assize of Clarendon.

[5] The great importance which Frederick himself attached to gaining English support for his pope is shown by the fact that he sent on an embassy to the English court no less a person than his chancellor, Reinald of Dassel, archbishop elect of Cologne, together with Count Adolf of Holstein. Helmold, *Chronica Slavorum* (ed. Schmeidler, 1909), p. 170.

Alexander.[1] But Henry, alive to the importance to everybody concerned of the official pronouncement of this decision, only consented to make it when Alexander's legates gave their sanction to the marriage of his son with the infant French princess which gave him the actual possession of the dowry—the much coveted Vexin castles. The series of negotiations was brought to a conclusion when Henry, in the course of the year 1162, had an audience with the pope of his choice at Déols near Châteauroux on the banks of the river Indre.[2]

The decision did not in fact involve an actual break with Frederick. Burchard, the imperial notary, reviewing Frederick's position in December 1161, emphasizes the close relations which existed between his master and England;[3] during the year 1163-4 Henry's trusted ambassador, John Cumin, was watching events at the imperial court; and the vital importance which the emperor attached to the friendship of England is very clearly exhibited in the embassy dispatched in 1165 with the imperial chancellor, Reinald of Dassel, at its head to Henry II at Rouen. There two marriages were arranged, one between Henry's eldest daughter Matilda and the leading prince in Germany, Henry the Lion, duke of Saxony and Bavaria; the other between the next daughter Eleanor and the emperor's eldest son Frederick, a child not yet a year old.[4] The first of these betrothals matured in 1168 into a marriage which was destined to influence

[1] Acting on the king's instructions the English bishops at London in June, the Norman bishops at Neufmarché a little later, had given their decision in favour of Alexander before the meeting at Beauvais which took place on 22 July. See F. Barlow, *Eng. Hist. Rev.* li (1936), 264 ff.

[2] Not, as Robert of Torigni says (p. 215), at Cociacum, which has been identified as Choussy on the Loire; nor is there any evidence to support his statement that Louis VII was present at the interview. Alexander was at Déols from 9 to 24 September 1162. Jaffé-Loewenfeld, 10756-62; Bouquet, xv. 785. Cf. also B. A. Lees (*Eng. Hist. Rev.* xxi (1906), 92) who, however, ignores the difficulties introduced by the passage in Robert of Torigni.

[3] In a letter to Nicholas, abbot of Siegburg, 'Amplius rex Angliae cum domino imperatore intimi foederis firmabitur unione, ut illius cum domino nostro una sit voluntas de omni re. Nuntii illius sunt apud nos. Magnos etiam de suis ad illum in proximo mittet imperator.' H. Sudendorf, *Registrum*, ii. 138 (1849). I owe this reference to Professor F. Güterbock.

[4] Cf. Robert of Torigni, p. 224, and Henry's letter in *Materials for the History of Becket*, vi. 80. See also Ferdinand Güterbock, 'Barbarossas ältester Sohn und die Thronfolge des Zweitgeboren', *Hist. Vierteljahrschrift*, xxix (1935), 515, who shows that this was Frederick, the eldest son, not, as generally said, Henry the second son, who was not born till later in this year. Reinald afterwards crossed to England (*Pipe Roll 11 Hen. II*, p. 108) perhaps to visit the queen and the young princesses. Cf. Eyton, *Itinerary*, p. 78, n. 4.

profoundly the foreign relations of the Angevin kings; the second, however, failed to materialize. The interests of the two sovereigns gradually diverged and became antagonistic; and in 1170 Eleanor was married to Alfonso VIII of Castile. As regards the schism, Frederick's envoys had at least the satisfaction of having persuaded Henry to send representatives (John of Oxford and Richard of Ilchester) to the diet of Würzburg at Whitsuntide 1165 where the question at issue was the recognition of the new anti-pope, Paschal III; and the threat of recognizing the imperial pope was always held over the unhappy Alexander during the trying period of the Becket controversy in order to prevent him from taking extreme measures on behalf of the exiled archbishop.[1]

This quarrel broke out in 1164, but it was not, as one might suppose from the lengthy correspondence concerned with it, wholly absorbing. It was a hindrance, but it did not deflect Henry from pursuing the aims at home and abroad which he had set out to achieve. That his course did not always run smoothly, that his progress was slow, was only partially a consequence of the Becket question; it was as much due to the violent temperament, to the strong sense of independence of his continental subjects. It took three years to subdue Brittany (1166–9); Aquitaine, which had never submitted lightly to English rule, was continually in a state of revolt; trouble in Auvergne in 1167 led to a fresh rupture with King Louis, causing two years' intermittent warfare of the usual devastating but inconclusive character until at Montmirail in 1169 Louis received satisfaction by the renewed homage of the king of England and the homage of his two elder sons for the possessions they were designed to inherit. These had all been planned out: Henry would receive Normandy, Maine, and Anjou; Richard, who at the same time was betrothed to Alice, the second of Louis's daughters by Constance of Castile, Aquitaine; Geoffrey, the third brother, Brittany.[2] The arrangements foreshadowed in this treaty were carried farther step by step: Geoffrey received the homage of the Breton barons at Rennes in the summer of the same year; the young Henry was crowned in the summer of the next; and in 1172 Richard was solemnly enthroned in the church of St. Hilary at Poitiers as duke of Aquitaine. But, as Henry was soon

---

[1] Above, p. 210.

[2] Geoffrey was not present at the meeting; he was to hold Brittany, apparently, under his brother Henry who did homage for it. Cf. Eyton, *Itinerary*, p. 118.

to learn, these boys of his, like typical Angevins, were not content with mere titles: they wanted also the authority to govern. They had little sense of duty and no respect for their father whose ambitious policy they wrecked, and whose latter years they embittered by their disloyalty and their rebellions.

Nevertheless Henry's triumphs were not yet at an end. In 1170 the Castilian marriage of his second daughter, Eleanor, carried his influence across the Pyrenees; in 1173 at Montferrand in Auvergne[1] Raymond V of Toulouse admitted his suzerainty; he did homage to the two Henries, father and son, and to Richard as duke of Aquitaine. At the same meeting Henry seemed to have gained a still more momentous success—an entry into Italy. On the borders of Germany and Italy, not far distant from his Aquitainian frontier, lay the lands of Humbert III, count of Maurienne. These reached northward from the upper Rhone valley to the lake of Geneva, and eastward to the valley of Aosta and Turin; they comprised what came to be known as Savoy and Piedmont. Their strategic importance was immense for they commanded the whole group of the western passes through the Alps from the Great St. Bernard to the Mont Genèvre. The count was impecunious, in need of allies, and only had daughters to succeed him; he therefore in 1171 sent his envoy, Benedict, abbot of Chiusa, to the English court with marriage proposals: the infant John (born 1167) should have his eldest daughter Alice and inherit his entire possessions. The negotiations slowly matured and were completed early in 1173 at this assembly at Montferrand. Alice was then delivered over, as was the custom, to the custody of the intended father-in-law together with four strong castles; in return a portion of the stipulated sum was paid over to the count. Soon after the young Alice died and we hear no more of the project.[2]

The treaty with Count Humbert of Maurienne opened the way to the western passes of the Alps and to Italy; it is clear evidence that Henry II's ambitions did not stop short at the frontiers of France. Other circumstances point unmistakably in

---

[1] The meeting in the course of its proceedings adjourned to Limoges. Cf. Norgate, *Richard the Lion Heart*, p. 12, n. 1.

[2] The treaty is given in *Gesta Henrici* (ed. Stubbs), i. 35-41. The fulfilment of the provision that in the event of Alice's death her sister should take her place does not seem to have been demanded, and in 1176 it was arranged that John should marry the heiress of the earl of Gloucester. For the details see C. W. Previté-Orton, *The Early History of the House of Savoy* (Cambridge, 1912), pp. 337-41.

the same direction: in 1169 he was intriguing with the Lombard cities, with Milan and Cremona, Parma and Bologna, and with Rome, offering, if we may trust our informant, very large sums of money for their support.[1] It was also in the same year that negotiations were set on foot which resulted later (1177) in the marriage of Henry's third daughter Joan with William the Good, king of Sicily. This had the effect of drawing still closer the already well-established relations between the Normans of the north and south.[2] As illustrations of this connexion we may instance the fact that an Englishman, Robert of Selby, was at the head of the Sicilian chancery during the greater part of the reign of Roger (1101–54); that another Englishman Richard Palmer, successively bishop of Syracuse and archbishop of Messina, occupied an important position at the court of William I (1154–66); and that another, Walter of Offamil, who had been tutor of William I's children, became archbishop of Palermo and with his brother Bartholomew, bishop of Girgenti, belonged to the small circle which directed the government of Sicily under the second William (1166–89). On this side, Thomas Brown, who had spent his early days as chaplain to King Roger, was occupying a leading position at the English exchequer, and enjoyed for some twenty years the personal confidence of Henry II.[3] The Plantagenet influence stretched so wide that it need be no matter for surprise that contemporaries interpreted

[1] The information comes from a letter of John of Salisbury (*Materials*, vii. 30) and one of Becket's to the archbishop of Ostia (ibid. vii. 26). The offer to Milan was 3,000 marks and the repair of the walls, to Cremona 2,000, and to Parma and Bologna 1,000 marks each. Becket and his circle, who imputed every action of Henry as directed against themselves, took this to be a means of intimidating the pope to bring about their own destruction.

[2] Evelyn Jamison in her paper in *England and the Mediterranean Tradition* (edited by the Warburg and Courtauld Institutes, 1945), pp. 29, 32, attributes the alliance between England and Sicily wholly to the Becket affair. This is to ignore the close relations which already obtained and also the ambitious designs of Henry II.

[3] See Haskins, 'England and Sicily in the Twelfth Century' in *Eng. Hist. Rev.* xxvi (1911), 433, 641. Cf. also E. Jamison, 'The Sicilian Norman Kingdom in the Mind of Anglo-Norman Contemporaries', *Proceedings of the British Academy* (1938), xxiv. Thomas Brown, who was born in England, was at the Sicilian court in 1137 and his name appears in a document of 1143 as μάστρο θωμᾶ τοῦ βρούνου. In England he was king's almoner perhaps from 1159 and certainly from 1165 till 1175; he is described in the *Dialogue of the Exchequer* (i. 6) as 'in regiis secretis pene precipuus'. Hilary Jenkinson in his introduction to the *Catalogue of an Exhibition of Treaties at the Public Record Office* (1948), p. 13, throws out the very plausible suggestion that the office held by Thomas Brown was that of Protonotary, an official of the chancery who is mentioned in the constitution concerning fees of the Great Seal in 1199 (*Foedera*, i. 75–6).

Henry's aims as a design upon Italy if not upon the empire itself.[1] Such a conclusion is in line with the general trend of politics. These things were happening at the time when the Lombard League and the Normans of the south were preparing to resist to the death the aggressions of Frederick Barbarossa: Frederick was schismatic, the promoter, since 1160, of anti-popes. It is far from improbable that Henry, as Giraldus says, was 'invited by the whole of Italy and the city of Rome' to supplant the emperor in Italy.[2] Frederick was certainly apprehensive, and, had it not been for the question of the schism, would no doubt have formed an alliance with Louis of France to resist the growing pretensions of the king of England.[3]

But the triumph of Henry's policy at the Montferrand-Limoges conference was followed immediately by a serious check. We have seen that his sons had cause for discontent; in 1169 they had been given lands but no authority, and presumably not much in the way of an income. By the Savoy treaty three important castles (Chinon, Loudun, and Mirabeau) in response to a request of Count Humbert were to be settled upon the infant John, and as these were situated in Angevin territory, the younger Henry regarded the proposed transaction as derogatory to his own rights. The boys—for they were still only boys[4]—had their grievances and were filled with eagerness to rebel against their fond but masterful parent. Their sentiment was shared by their mother who had long since ceased to enjoy any conjugal felicity,[5] and had in fact for some years lived apart

[1] Giraldus Cambrensis (De Principis Instructione, Opera, viii, 157) connects the Maurienne plan and the Italian intrigues with a design to extend his sphere of power ad Romanum imperium. The Chronicon universale anonymi Laudunensis (ed. A. Cartellieri, p. 15) referring to the same event says that it was understood that the king aspired ad regnum Lumbardorum. Peter of Blois, who was at the Sicilian court between 1167 and 1169 (Ep. 113, Migne, vol. 207), says vaguely that he was present when the regnum Italiae was offered to Henry or to one of his sons. F. Hardegen, 'Imperialpolitik König Heinrichs II von England' (Heidelberger Abhandlungen, 1905), exaggerates the animosity of Henry towards Frederick Barbarossa. See the review of his article by H. W. C. Davis in Eng. Hist. Rev. xxi (1906), 363.

[2] Loc. cit.

[3] Frederick and Louis actually met in conference at Vaucouleur near Toul in 1171.

[4] In 1173 Henry was 18, Richard not yet 16, and Geoffrey a year younger.

[5] Giraldus (De Princ. Instr., p. 165) mentions that after the rebellion of 1173-4 and the imprisonment of Eleanor, the king, who had been a secret adulterer, began openly to live with Rosamund Clifford (Fair Rosamund). The expenses of a later mistress even appear on the Pipe Roll (30 Hen. II, p. 134): 'Pro pannis Regine et Bellebell' ad opus Regis' £55. 17s.

from her husband, ruling with her son Richard over her own inheritance in the south. There, holding her court at Poitiers, she was the presiding genius in a society of troubadours and knights who lived for chivalry and love, the tournament and war.[1] A little poem written in Middle High German and contained in a nearly contemporary collection of student songs, which can evidently only refer to her, testifies to her cosmopolitan fame:[2]

> Were the world all mine
> From the sea to the Rhine
> I'd give it all
> If so be the Queen of England
> Lay in my arms.

Queen Eleanor spared no effort to stimulate the discontent of her sons against her husband till she was captured, masquerading in male attire, before the actual outbreak of the rebellion. But in 1173 even Henry, the eldest of her sons, was too inexperienced to organize a movement of such magnitude. He never took the initiative; he was always in leading-strings. The rebellion was inspired and managed by Louis of France who saw in it an easy way to embarrass and weaken his dangerous rival. It was to Louis that the young king had gone on his return to France after his second coronation in 1172; and it was Louis who had advised him to demand a definite share in his father's dominions; and it was again to Louis that he escaped, eluding his father, after the conclusion of the Savoy treaty in March 1173. It was at the French court at Paris that Louis and the young king pledged themselves to mutual assistance, and that extravagant promises of lands and rents in England and Normandy were made to the foreign allies who were prepared to join in the enterprise.[3] Finally, it was at Louis's instigation that the very advantageous terms offered by Henry at Gisors in

---

[1] Cf. A. Kelly, *Speculum*, xii (1937), 3, and F. M. Chambers, ibid. xvi (1941), 465. The Courts of Love, however, at which Eleanor is supposed to have given judgements are probably nothing more than a literary conceit. M. V. Rosenberg's *Eleanor of Aquitaine* (1937), where this side of her life is enlarged upon, is of little historical value.

[2] For the German text see *Carmina Burana* (ed. Schmeller), no. 108a. The English rendering is that of Helen Waddell, *Wandering Scholars*, p. 216.

[3] The count of Flanders, for example, was to receive the whole of Kent with the castles of Rochester and Dover together with £1,000 in yearly revenue. *Gesta Henrici*, i. 44. The count was brought in *instigatione regis Francorum*, Ralph de Diceto, i. 373.

September were refused. The king of France was the director and he did his work clumsily. There was no objective, no plan of campaign, no co-operation between the different sections of the rebels. Under skilful control the revolt might have resulted in the ruin of the Angevin empire, for the majority of the leading barons on both sides of the Channel welcomed the opportunity of striking a blow at the king who had laid his hand on their castles and kept them strictly in subjection.[1] But the church remained loyal,[2] and so did the official class on whom Henry depended for the maintenance of order and the work of administration. It was, indeed, two of these, Richard de Lucy, the old justiciar, and Rannulf Glanvill, the future justiciar, who were almost entirely responsible for the failure of the rebellion in England. The smaller men in the country and the business men in the towns showed no symptoms of a desire to go against the government, for they, doubtless, had gained most by the reforms of Henry II. But it was the wide geographical area over which the revolt spread that made it dangerous. Normandy was the centre; but there were also risings in Brittany and Poitou; England was invaded and the king of Scotland crossed the border. It would have been all but impossible even for a man of Henry's outstanding abilities to cope with it had there been any sort of co-operation among the rebels. Fortunately there was none, and Henry, by his skilful handling, his cool decision, and the almost uncanny swiftness of his movements,[3] succeeded in breaking up one attack after another.

We need not dwell on the details of the warfare which continued with short breathing-spaces for a little more than a year and was of the character usual in those times: there were few engagements in the open; castles were besieged and sometimes taken; villages and the countryside were plundered and burnt.

---

[1] Cf. Stubbs, Introduction to the *Gesta Henrici*, ii, p. xlvii n., and Haskins, *Norman Institutions*, pp. 159–61.

[2] Hugh de Puiset, bishop of Durham, and Arnulf, bishop of Lisieux, a practised intriguer, alone joined the rebels. For the connexion of the church with the rebellion see above, p. 220.

[3] His flying visit to England in 1173, either in June (Norgate, *Angevins*, ii. 143) or in September (Ramsay, *Angevin Empire*, p. 174, n. 5), was so rapid and secret that no chronicler got to hear of it, and we know of it only from the record of his expenditure on the Pipe Roll. On another occasion he is said to have left Rouen on 22 July and reached Dol on the 23rd, covering a distance of some 140 miles in two days (*Gesta Henrici*, i. 57; cf. Ramsay, op. cit., p. 172). Peter of Blois says of the king that he frequently rode four or five times as far in a day as a normal day's journey. *Ep.* lxvi.

'Thus', said the count of Flanders, 'should war be begun: such is my advice. First destroy the land and then one's foe.'[1] It began in July with attacks on Normandy from the north-east by the count of Flanders and the young king, and through the Vexin by the king of France. The first was brought to an abrupt conclusion by the death of the count's brother, Matthew of Boulogne, near Arques; the other consisted of a long-drawn-out siege of Verneuil, part of which Louis captured during a truce before he was chased back to his own dominions by Henry. The Breton rising, led by Hugh, earl of Chester, and Ralph of Fougères, was quickly broken up by Henry's Brabançon mercenaries, and with the capture by Henry himself of all the leading rebels in the castle of Dol. There was now talk of peace, for the insurgents had been beaten at every point. But, though the terms which Henry offered to his sons were very generous, Louis, who still hoped to break the power of his rival, intervened; and the terms were refused.

The centre of action now shifted to England. The war here consisted, apart from isolated attacks on castles, of two distinct and almost uncorrelated invasions: the one from Scotland (related elsewhere),[2] the other from the Continent led by Robert, earl of Leicester, the son of the justiciar who had faithfully served the king during the first thirteen years of his reign and had died in 1168. At the outset of the rebellion he had crossed to France under pretence of going to the king's assistance; in fact he had joined not the king but the king's son. After the breakdown of the peace conference, he had sailed for England, landing at Walton in Suffolk at the head of a large body of Flemings on Michaelmas day.[3] After some minor local operations, he set out for his own castle of Leicester, which had been besieged in the early days of the rebellion. His Flemings, who were mostly weavers and had an eye on English wool,[4] advanced

---

[1] Jordan Fantosme (*Chronicles of Stephen*, &c., ed. Howlett, iii), ll. 450–1.
[2] Above, p. 277.
[3] Ralph de Diceto, i. 377; the chronology of the *Gesta Henrici* (p. 60) differs slightly and is also inconsistent.
[4] Jordan Fantosme, ll. 999–1003:

> 'We have not come to this country to sojourn
> But to destroy King Henry, the old warrior,
> And to have his wool, for which we have a desire.'
> Lords, that is the truth; they were mostly weavers.

Cf. Gervase of Canterbury, i. 246: *textoria arte dimissa.*

confidently, cheerfully dancing and singing in their native
tongue:

> Hop along, hop along, Billy boy, Billy boy,
> England is mine and thine.[1]

But they were doomed to disappointment. The constable,
Humphrey de Bohun, intercepted them at Fornham St. Gene-
vieve, a few miles to the north of Bury St. Edmunds, and cut
them ruthlessly to pieces with the help of the local peasantry
who made short work of them with forks and flails. The earl of
Leicester and his Amazon wife Petronilla were among the
captives and were sent to join the other distinguished persons
taken during the rebellion in the castle of Falaise. A truce concluded with Hugh Bigod, earl of Norfolk, the other leader of
revolt in the eastern counties, on the condition of his sending
home his Flemish mercenaries, ended this phase of the rebellion
or 'the Leicester war' as it is called in the records of the exchequer.[2]

Truces were arranged to cover the winter months, but in the
spring fighting began again on all the fronts. Henry returned
from a successful campaign in Anjou and Poitou to learn of a
serious situation in England: the king of the Scots had again
crossed the border; much of the north and midlands was in
revolt; and the count of Flanders with the young king was
preparing for an invasion, and had even sent forward an
advanced guard of Flemings who, after effecting a landing at
the mouth of the Orwell, had joined with the earl of Norfolk
and succeeded in capturing Norwich. Henry, genuinely alarmed
by the urgent messages he received, decided himself to go to
England. He seems to have regarded his present troubles as a
retribution for his indirect complicity in the murder of Becket.
When Richard of Ilchester, who visited him in Normandy un-
folded the tale of disaster, he is said to have avowed his guilt:

---

[1] 'Qui ... choreas ducentes patria lingua saltitando cantabant,

> Hoppe, hoppe, Wilekin, hoppe, Wilekin,
> Engelond is min ant tin.'

Matthew Paris, *Historia Minor* (ed. Madden, i. 381). Mr. K. Sisam informs me that
these lines are said to be the oldest Flemish verses that have been preserved.

[2] 'Guerra Leicestriae', *Red Book of the Exchequer* (ed. Hubert Hall), p. ccxiv;
Pipe Roll 21 Hen. II, p. 8. The Pipe Rolls of the following years supply evidence
that some of the Flemish mercenaries, who came over in 1173-4, did not in accordance with the treaty return to their country but settled in the north and eastern
counties and engaged in industry. Cf. G. T. Lapsley, *Eng. Hist. Rev.* xxi (1906), 509.

'St. Thomas, guard for me my kingdom! To you I declare myself guilty of that for which others bear the blame.'[1] And his first act on landing was the performance of a humble penance at the tomb of the Canterbury martyr. His piety was quickly rewarded. He had scarcely dragged himself on to London after his unwonted austerities of fasting, flagellation, and sleepless nights, and composed himself to much needed rest, when an insistent messenger thrust himself into his chamber to announce the news of the capture of the king of Scotland. Such was the king's relief that he rewarded the bringer of the joyful tidings, whose name was Abraham, with an estate in Norfolk.[2] This overwhelming catastrophe for the rebels really ended the business. It was followed almost immediately by the surrender of the chief centres of resistance: Huntingdon, which had been besieged for more than two months, capitulated; Hugh of Norfolk and the bishop of Durham made their peace and yielded up their castles. The threatened invasion by the count of Flanders was called off by Louis who now tried, as a last desperate venture, an attack on Rouen. But it was a forlorn hope. With characteristic energy, just a month after his coming to England, Henry was again crossing the Channel with his Brabançon mercenaries and a contingent of Welshmen. Within a week of his landing Louis was hurrying back to his own country. Richard alone was still defiant, but a short campaign in Poitou brought him to submission. In the final settlement, which was made on 30 September at Montlouis near Tours, the rebellious sons were treated with wise generosity: though they still had little or no independent power, they were given homes and good incomes,[3] and the young John, the question of whose endowment had been one of the immediate causes of the revolt, was now suitably provided for.

A general amnesty covered most of those who had taken part in the rebellion, and even those who, like the earls of Leicester

---

[1] Jordan Fantosme, ll. 1605–6.

[2] 'Ysac de Felmingham tenet quandam terram in Witton quam Henricus Rex, pater domini regis, dedit patri suo Habrahe pro rumore quem illi narravit de rege Scocie capto.' *Book of Fees*, p. 130. For the family see Blomefield, *Hist. of Norfolk*, xi. 33. Jordan Fantosme says the news was brought by one Brien, a man of Rannulf Glanvill, ll. 1981–2.

[3] Henry was granted an annual income of £15,000 Angevin (the equivalent of £3,750 English), Richard half the revenues of Poitou, Geoffrey half the revenues of the inheritance of his betrothed, Constance, with the prospect of the whole of it on his marriage. The text of the treaty is given in *Gesta Henrici*, i. 77 f.

and Chester, were excepted from it, were soon again received
into favour. Queen Eleanor alone remained unforgiven, she was
kept more or less under restraint during the remainder of her
husband's life. But if he dealt leniently with the barons, he dealt
ruthlessly with their castles. He was determined to remove from
them the power of resistance. A clause in the Assize of Northampton issued in 1176 instructs the justices to see that the
demolished castles are utterly demolished, and that those which
ought to be demolished are levelled to the ground,[1] and the
official records prove that the king's orders were carried out.[2]
The royal castles, on the other hand, were repaired and strengthened; work on these under the supervision of Ailnoth, the
engineer (*ingeniator*),[3] figures prominently in the accounts of
these years 1175-8. It was at this time that the great stone keep
at Newcastle upon Tyne was erected as a defence against the
Scots, and a little later (1180-9) that the castle of Dover, which
Matthew Paris aptly describes as 'the front door of England',
was rebuilt at the huge cost of between £5,000 and £6,000.

The king's victory was complete but expensive. Much damage
had been done in the country: we read that the abbey of
St. Benet's, Holme, was wasted and remained in 1176 still in a
state of partial devastation 'owing to the war of Earl Hugh';
that for three years part of the farms of the most affected counties
had to be respited owing to damage brought about by the
war; and that the weavers of Nottingham and Huntingdon
could not make their annual payment to the exchequer for their
gilds.[4] These examples are taken at random, but they indicate
considerable dislocation of industry and revenue in the country.
The expenses of the war were seemingly high, for Henry had
principally used mercenary troops who had to be paid well and
promptly. Something was got to meet this abnormal expenditure from fines of varying amount imposed on the rebels; more
from the tightening up of the judicial procedure by the Assize
of Northampton; but the largest contribution came from forest

---

[1] Clause 8 (*Gesta Henrici*, i. 110).

[2] Cf. *Pipe Roll 22 Hen. II*, pp. 60, 179. Lists of demolished castles are given in
Gesta Henrici, i. 126-7 and by Diceto, i. 404.

[3] He was also keeper of the king's houses at Westminster and of the Fleet prison.
Cf. C. T. Clay, *Eng. Hist. Rev.* lix (1944), 1 ff., and A. L. Poole, *Obligations of Society*,
pp. 64 f.

[4] *Pipe Roll 22 Hen. II*, p. 70; *20 Hen. II*, pp. 38, 140; *21 Hen. II*, pp. 89-90, 107;
22 Hen. II, pp. 60, 179; *22 Hen. II*, pp. 71, 91.

pleas. Under pressure of the crisis, in order to conciliate the people, the king appears to have given some instruction to the justiciar to relax the forest laws, and the people, great and small alike, had taken full advantage of the licence. Nevertheless, when the war was over, all who could be proved to have taken game or otherwise infringed the forest law were prosecuted and fined in exorbitant sums ranging from a half to 500 marks. In Oxfordshire alone the fines imposed in the year 1176 'de misericordia Regis pro foresta' amounted to £1,376, and in Hampshire the total sum exceeded £2,000.[1]

In the years following the rebellion (1175–82) the Angevin empire was at the summit of its strength. Henry II was now able to devote more of his time to the affairs of England, which, in consequence, enjoyed a period of peaceful and steady development. It was in these years that many of his judicial and administrative reforms were undertaken: the Assize of Northampton (1176) tightened up the procedure set up at Clarendon ten years earlier; a long overdue reform of the coinage was carried into effect in 1180–1; and a new system for national defence was organized in the Assize of Arms of 1181. Abroad English prestige stood very high. Embassies from foreign courts visited the country to solicit her friendship. Diplomatic courtesies were even interchanged with Manuel Comnenus, the eastern emperor, to whom Henry sent a pack of hounds as a present;[2] and the Spanish kings of Castile and Navarre submitted a territorial dispute to Henry's arbitration (1177). His old antagonist, Louis VII, was a disappointed man; he had no fight left in him and hardly an inclination to intrigue. The only serious cause of embarrassment between them was the position of Louis's daughter Alice who had been betrothed to Richard as long ago as 1169. Richard hung back, not unnaturally if we may believe the disgusting story related by Giraldus Cambrensis that Henry II was using his son's destined bride as his mistress.[3] The papal legate even threatened to place all Henry's lands

---

[1] *Pipe Roll 22 Hen. II*, pp. 30 f., 193 f. Another heavy crop of forest fines appears in the roll of the following year.

[2] *Pipe Roll 24 Hen. II*, p. 19. In the dispatch which Manuel sent to Henry he acknowledges the assistance given him by English nobles in his disastrous campaign against the sultan of Iconium (Hoveden, ii. 104). Besides the envoys of Manuel, there were also present at the court held at Westminster on 12 November 1176, ambassadors from the Emperor Frederick, the duke of Saxony, the count of Flanders, and the archbishop of Rheims. Ralph de Diceto, i. 416.

[3] *De Princ. Instr., Opera*, viii, 232.

under interdict unless the marriage was immediately fulfilled. But even this matter was not allowed to stand in the way of peace, and at a conference held at Ivry (21 September 1177) Louis was satisfied with a vague promise, and agreed to submit any outstanding differences between himself and Henry to the decision of arbitrators and to accompany Henry on a crusade. The crusade was in fact never made, but in 1178 the two kings co-operated in measures against the heretics of Toulouse, and in the same year Louis went so far as to take Henry's continental lands under his protection in order that Henry himself might be relieved of anxiety while he was engaged with the affairs of England. The next year they were again together at Dover when Louis came to England to visit the tomb of St. Thomas of Canterbury. It was the last active event of his long reign of more than forty years. On his return to Paris he was struck with such acute paralysis that he was unable to attend the coronation of his son which took place a few weeks later on 1 November. He died on 18 September 1180.

In Henry's continental dominions Louis's weakness and incapacity had on the whole a salutary effect. Normandy enjoyed a period of comparative quiet, and its administrative and financial system in the experienced hands of Richard of Ilchester, bishop of Winchester, who became the Norman justiciar in 1176, was set in order. It was only in Aquitaine that a state of wild confusion and unrest continued to prevail. The turbulent barons of the south were continually in revolt, incited, if incitement were necessary, by such restless spirits as the irresponsible troubadour, Bertrand de Born. Richard made ceaseless war on these disturbers of the peace with characteristic violence and impetuosity, and with astonishing success, reducing their castles as they rose in resistance; even Taillebourg, which was considered impregnable, capitulated before his attack (1179). Richard's genius for war enabled him to subdue even that 'hitherto untamed land'.[1] But his stern and relentless rule, his rigorous enforcement of justice and order, provoked the bitter enmity of his subjects and made them eagerly embrace the insidious treacheries of the elder brother, the young king. In character he was the very antithesis of Richard.[2] 'Rich, noble, lovable, eloquent, handsome, gallant, every way attractive, a

[1] Giraldus, op. cit., p. 247.
[2] The characters of the two are contrasted by Giraldus, op. cit., p. 248.

little lower than the angels—all these gifts he turned to the wrong side.' So a contemporary, who knew him well and wrote in the very year of his death, describes him, 'a prodigy of unfaith, a lovely palace of sin'.[1] In the Aquitanian wars he displayed his jealous and versatile nature to effect, and in his company was often to be found the third brother, Geoffrey, a worthless creature, who spent his life in aimless killing and plundering. The crisis came in 1183. The old king, who was then in France, made every effort to keep his unruly sons at peace among themselves, but in vain. The young Henry and Geoffrey joined a powerful combination of rebellious barons formed against their brother Richard. The rising threatened to spread and to develop into a dangerous attack on the Angevin power. The duke of Burgundy and the count of Toulouse declared for the rebels; and the king, in genuine alarm, called up the feudal levies of his continental dominions and sent instructions to England for the imprisonment of those who had participated in the previous rebellion of 1173–4.[2] The situation was saved, however, by the providential death of the young king from dysentery. He died on 11 June 1183, and the league almost instantaneously dissolved.

On the death of the young Henry, Richard naturally stepped into his position as the recognized heir to England, Normandy, and Anjou, which the king regarded as the essentially inseparable parts of the Angevin empire. Richard, however, was not prepared to accept the corollary of Henry's plan—the severance of Aquitaine as a portion for his youngest son. He had grown up in the southern duchy, had ruled it vigorously for more than ten years, and would not hear of giving it up. He successfully resisted the attacks of his brothers in 1184–5, and obliged his father to abandon this solution of providing for the landless John.

At the point we have now reached the young king of France entered upon his life-work—the break up of the Angevin empire and its incorporation in the royal domain. Philip, known to history by the surname 'Augustus' given him by his con-

---

[1] Walter Map, *De Nugis*, dist. iv, c. 1 (translation by M. R. James, p. 157).

[2] The lands of the leading rebel, the earl of Leicester, were taken into the king's hands, and he himself and his family were imprisoned, *Pipe Roll 29 Hen. II*, pp. 40, 75, 153. He was released the following year and his lands restored. There is evidence al o that there was communication between England and the rebels on the Continent. Ibid., p. 121.

temporary biographer,[1] was fifteen years old at his father's death. He was ambitious, full of energy, and possessed of great political sagacity, qualities which were conspicuously lacking in his father. Though not a great soldier, he was a shrewd and quite unscrupulous diplomat, and, like Louis XI with whom he has often been compared, gained far more by making skilful use of the mistakes of his opponents than by his own successes in the field. In his early years he was involved in fierce feuds with his maternal uncles of the house of Champagne and Blois, who controlled the court in the closing years of the reign of Louis VII, and with Philip of Alsace, count of Flanders, the uncle of his wife, Isabel of Hainault. From these difficulties he had been extricated partly through the good offices of Henry II, with whom at the outset of his reign (June 1180) he had renewed at Gisors the compact concluded at Ivry in 1177. In 1183 Henry did liege homage to his young suzerain for all his continental possessions.[2] Then in 1185 by the treaty of Boves Philip was freed from his embarrassments with the count of Flanders and left with a substantial portion of Vermandois, which included the city of Amiens, added to his domain. He could now safely turn his attention to his Angevin rival. There were pretexts in plenty for opening a quarrel: on the death of the young Henry the Norman Vexin, his wife's dowry, should have reverted to Philip; it had, however, been agreed in 1186 that it should form the dowry of the other sister, Alice, who had long since been betrothed to Richard.[3] Yet in 1187 she was still unmarried, and Philip demanded that both she and the Vexin should be restored to him forthwith. He claimed also as overlord the wardship of Arthur, the posthumous son of Geoffrey of Brittany who died, probably from an accident at a tournament, in 1186. Failing to get any satisfaction in these demands, Philip took to force,

---

[1] 'Sed forte miramini quod in prima fronte hujus operis voco regem Augustum.' Rigord, *Gesta Philippi Augusti* (ed. Delaborde), i. 6.

[2] But liege homage did not amount to unqualified obedience. Even this relationship was governed by custom. Local custom plays an important part in the politics of the Angevin kings; in 1194 Richard I refused to ratify a treaty with Philip Augustus 'because he was unwilling to violate the customs and laws of Poitou or his other territories', according to which the magnates should decide their disputes by the sword. Hoveden, iii. 255. Cf. also Powicke, *Loss of Normandy*, pp. 121 ff.

[3] *Gesta Henrici*, i. 343. The rights of the widow, Margaret, were at the same time bought out for £2,750 Angevin to be paid by king Henry. See the agreement, dated 11 March, in Delisle-Berger, *Recueil*, ii. 275; Landon, *Itinerary of Richard I* (Pipe Roll Soc., n.s., vol. xiii), p. 225.

marched into Berri, and laid siege to Châteauroux. Henry and Richard were quickly on the scene, and a truce brought to a speedy close the first encounter in the great conflict which was to end twenty-seven years later at Bouvines.

One of the more curious aspects of medieval warfare was the rapidity with which amicable relations were restored when the fighting was over. For the higher ranks, war was, in part at least, a game governed by the strict code of chivalry; it was only the unfortunate peasantry and other non-combatants who suffered from the savage plundering of the *routiers*. The leaders were one moment flying at each other's throats, the next eating at the same table, sleeping in the same chamber. Richard accompanied his recent adversary back to Paris where the intimacy, which had such unhappy consequences in the future, grew and ripened. For Philip it was a matter of policy; his plan was to bring about the ruin of the Angevins by fomenting the discord in Henry's family circle. Richard too had his reason: he already suspected that his father was playing him false, was promoting the interests of John at the expense of the elder son.

The disasters in Syria, the battle of Hattin (July 1187) followed in October by the fall of Jerusalem, might be expected to have resulted in the end of these domestic feuds, and to turn the energies of the western princes in a common endeavour to retrieve the fortunes of the Christians in the east. In part this happened. It was an obligation particularly incumbent on Henry, as the head of the house of Anjou, to go to the rescue of the younger branch of his family.[1] When in 1185 Baldwin IV, who for years had suffered from leprosy, was dying, Heraclius, the patriarch of Jerusalem accompanied by the grand masters of the Hospitallers and the Templars were sent to England on a

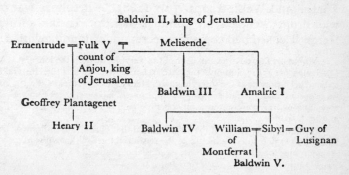

mission to Henry II.[1] They met the king at Reading in March 1185 and implored his assistance; they brought with them letters of Pope Lucius III in support of their appeal, and, according to some accounts, had even offered the kingdom of Jerusalem itself. The offer was prudently declined,[2] and, though many, including the archbishop of Canterbury and Rannulf Glanvill the justiciar, took the crusading vow, nothing was actually done to relieve the situation. But the news of Saladin's successes in 1187 shook Europe with a sense of catastrophe. It revived the flagging ardour for crusading, and nearly everyone of consequence, young and old, rich and poor, took the vow. Richard did so at once and enthusiastically; Henry and Philip tardily, and probably with little intention of carrying it out. But the crusade had the effect of bringing Henry's real design clearly into the light—his object was to supplant Richard in the succession by his favourite John. Anxious as Richard was to get off to the east as soon as possible, he would not do so until he had received a definite assurance of his rights as heir to the Angevin dominions; and this his father declined to give. More than this, he seems to have hindered the progress of his son's preparations at every turn.

Revolts broke out first in Aquitaine and then in Toulouse, which it was rumoured were instigated by Henry himself.[3] Richard put them down with characteristic vigour and success. He invaded the lands of Count Raymond, seizing one stronghold after another until he was within a few miles of the city of Toulouse itself which he would certainly have taken had not Philip Augustus, whose arbitration had been refused, created a diversion by again attacking Berri and capturing Châteauroux. In alarm, Henry left England for the last time with a force of English and Welsh troops (July 1188). A desultory war over a wide front occupied the summer months. In the autumn, it seems, Richard had come to a secret understanding with Philip;

[1] Arnold de Turre Rubea, master of the Temple, died on the journey at Verona (30 September 1184), and only the patriarch and the master of the Hospital appear to have been present at the interview with Henry II. Nevertheless, Terric, Arnold's successor as master of the Temple, appears to have reached England, for his travelling expenses are entered on the Pipe Roll of 1185 under Dover (*Pipe Roll 31 Hen. II*, p. 233).

[2] It was on the occasion of the king's refusal that Giraldus Cambrensis (*De Princ. Instr.*, p. 211) puts into the mouth of the patriarch the well-known words about the Angevin race 'de diabolo venerunt, et ad diabolum ibunt'.

[3] Giraldus Cambrensis, *De Princ. Instr.*, p. 244 f.

at any rate he appeared at a conference which had been arranged at Bonmoulins on 18 November in the company of the French king who himself seconded his demand to be recognized by Henry as his rightful heir. When this was refused, Richard turned to Philip, and, kneeling before him, did homage for all the continental lands saving only the fealty which he owed to his father. This dramatic scene was the occasion for the last rebellion which brought Henry, already a sick and weary man, miserably to his grave. Undutiful as Richard's conduct certainly was, he had great provocation. There can be little doubt that Henry's infatuation for John made him reluctant to grant a straightforward declaration of Richard's rights in the hope that he might by some means or other supplant him by his younger brother. He was carried away by his affection consciously and against his better judgement. The royal chamber in the palace at Winchester was adorned with paintings. Among them was one, executed at the king's command, which represented in allegory the tragedy of his life. A brood of four eaglets was depicted preying on the parent bird, and one, the fourth, was poised on the neck watching intently the moment to peck out the eyes. 'The four eaglets', the king explained, 'are my four sons who cease not to persecute me even unto death. The youngest of them, whom I now embrace with so much affection, will sometime in the end insult me more grievously and more dangerously than any of the others.'[1] John's name, in fact, appeared at the head of the list of those who had deserted him in the final struggle, and the knowledge added to the anguish and humiliation of his last hours.

The end was not long in coming. The actual outbreak of hostilities was delayed by the frantic efforts of the papal legate and the French bishops to bring about peace in the interests of the crusade, but when no settlement was reached at a conference at La Ferté-Bernard in May, Philip and Richard opened their attack. One stronghold fell after another and the old king, deserted by most of the barons of Maine, Touraine, and Anjou, was chased from Le Mans. Instead of retreating into Normandy, where he still might have found support, he clung to Angevin soil and made for Chinon, while the allies, continuing their triumphal advance, occupied most of Touraine, and on 3 July

---

[1] Giraldus Cambrensis, op. cit., p. 295. Cf. *Pipe Roll 28 Hen. II*, pp. 146, xxv, for the painted chamber at Winchester.

captured the city of Tours itself. The next day, at Colombières between Tours and Azay-le-Rideau,[1] they forced the dying king to submit to their humiliating terms: 'he resigned himself wholly to the counsel and will of Philip, king of France, in such a way that whatever the king of France should provide or adjudge, the king of England would carry out in every way and without contradiction.' Among other things it was stipulated that Richard should marry Alice and receive the fealty of the barons on both sides of the Channel. Henry was further required to pay an indemnity of 20,000 marks.[2] Two days later, 6 July 1189, Henry II was dead.

[1] The name of the place (which has since vanished from the map) is given by William le Breton (*Philippide*, iii. l. 737).
[2] *Gesta Henrici*, ii. 70.

XI

THE LOSS OF NORMANDY
1189–1204

THE crusade was Richard's dominating passion at the time
of his accession to the throne. He worked with a singleness
of purpose to remove every obstacle that might stand in the
way of its early and successful achievement. He acted quickly.
Immediately after the burial of his father at Fontevrault, he sent
instructions to England for the release of his mother, Queen
Eleanor, whom he authorized to act as his representative until
he should himself be able to cross the Channel; on 29 July he
was installed as duke of Normandy in the cathedral of Rouen
and received the homage of the clergy and people. Two days
later at Gisors he came to terms with Philip Augustus whom he
satisfied by surrendering his claims to Auvergne and part of
Berri and by adding 4,000 marks to the 20,000 which his father
had agreed to pay at Colombières. The two kings then arranged
to start for the east in the following spring. He made his peace
also with his recent opponents, those who had adhered to his
father. So far from showing himself vindictive, he actually
rewarded their fidelity, for he had a chivalrous respect for
loyalty and denounced as traitors his own companions in revolt.
It was in this spirit that he pardoned William Marshal who had
stood by the old king till the end and had unhorsed Richard and
nearly caused his death in the recent fighting. He did more than
this; for in accordance with his father's wish he gave him in
marriage one of the richest of the Crown heiresses, Isabel,
daughter of Richard of Clare, earl of Pembroke and Strigul,
better known as 'Strongbow'. From an impecunious knight
errant the Marshal became in a moment one of the most powerful of the English barons.

The same generous treatment he extended to his brothers.
Geoffrey, Henry's natural son, though quarrelsome and high-
spirited, had always been faithful. He had fought against the
insurgents in the north of England during the rebellion of
1173–4 and earned the praise of his father who met him, when
the rebels had been defeated, with the words: 'You alone have
proved yourself my lawful and true son, my other sons are really

the bastards.'[1] Since 1182 he had been chancellor, and he was
the only member of the family who attended his father at his
deathbed. His staunch loyalty was now rewarded by the archbishopric of York which had been vacant and in the king's
hands for the past eight years, rendering a solid net profit of
over £1,750 to the exchequer.[2] To his brother John, Richard
was liberal to the extent of folly. This, the most interesting and
in some ways most remarkable of Henry's sons, was born in
Beaumont palace at Oxford on Christmas eve 1167; he was
therefore now in his twenty-second year, and had long since
ceased to merit the nickname given him by his father at the
time of his birth of 'Lackland'.[3] In the settlement of 1174 he had
been given an income and several castles scattered about the
Angevin domain, including those of Nottingham and Marlborough. He was next given the estates of his great uncle,
Reginald, earl of Cornwall, who died in 1175; in 1177 he became
titular 'lord of Ireland'. Now, as his father had wished, he was
granted the county of Mortain and married to Isabel, the third
daughter of William, earl of Gloucester, who was made the
heiress of the whole of the valuable honor.[4] Besides these and
numerous castles, honors, and manors dotted about England,
among them the great honor of Lancaster, he was given six
entire counties—those of Nottingham and Derby, Dorset and
Somerset, Devon and Cornwall. Thenceforward till 1194 these
counties made no returns whatever to the exchequer. John not
only received the 'farm' of these shires, but also the profits of
justice.[5] He could rule them as arbitrarily as he chose. He had
his own exchequer, his own chancellor and justiciar. The only
check imposed on his freedom of action was the retention by
the government of certain castles, among them those of Nottingham, Tickhill, Gloucester, Exeter, and Launceston. He was also
'lord of Ireland' now in a far more real sense than he had been

---

[1] Giraldus Cambrensis, *De Vita Galfridi*, i, c. 4 (*Opera*, iv. 368). In 1173 he had
been appointed bishop of Lincoln, but difficulties of age and birth prevented his
consecration, and he resigned the see in 1182.

[2] This was the sum for the year 1183. See *Pipe Roll 29 Hen. II*, p. 59 and Introd.,
p. xxvi.

[3] For the name *Sine Terra*, see Norgate, *John Lackland*, p. 2, n. 2.

[4] Round computed the gross annual value of the honor of Gloucester at the
time of William's death (1183) at over £580. *Pipe Roll 30 Hen. II*, Introd., p. xxix.

[5] Stubbs, on the basis of the *Pipe Roll 1 Ric. I*, reckons the gross value of these
six counties at over £4,000. Preface to Hoveden, iii. p. xxv, n. 4. For John's
English estates cf. also the map in Norgate's *John Lackland*, p. 27.

in his father's time. Irish affairs had then been mainly directed
by the king himself, especially since John's blundering expedition in 1185; now they were placed wholly under his
authority. The imprudence of Richard's generosity towards his
brother was to be proved to his cost in the sequel. He tried to
rectify his mistake by causing John to swear to remain out of
England for a period of three years. But on the advice of the
queen mother he was released from his oath, and was indeed
in England almost as soon as Richard quitted it.

The king was received with enthusiasm when he landed in
England in the summer of 1189, for he had prepared the way by
an act which won him great popularity: he had thrown open the
prison doors and liberated all who had been arbitrarily or
unjustly imprisoned, especially for offences against the forest
law.[1] Though this measure may, as William of Newburgh tells
us,[2] have let loose upon the country a multitude of hardy jail-
birds, it may also be an indication that Henry in his latter years
had administered the criminal law with undue severity. On
3 September Richard was crowned at Westminster.[3]

Contemporaries held very varying opinions about the character of Richard I. To some he was thoroughly bad, 'bad to all,
worse to his friends, and worst of all to himself';[4] others credited
him with many fine qualities, and one, a clerk, called him in an
official document 'Richard the Good'.[5] He had, it seems, many
of the failings and some of the virtues of his race: he was hot-
tempered and irresponsible, generous and accomplished. He
was a lover of music and a patron of troubadours. Above all
he was a superb soldier. Though born in England, he had spent
his early life on the Continent, chiefly in Aquitaine. He was the
least English of all the kings of England; and the fact that he
was and continued to be almost a stranger to the country which
he was called upon to govern accounts for his initial mistakes.
He came to England on 13 August 1189, and left it, after four
months, on 12 December. He revisited it, when he was released

---

[1] *Gesta Ricardi*, ii. 74. Cf. *Magna Carta Commemoration Essays*, pp. 114–15.
[2] iv, c. i.
[3] The coronation of Richard I is the first of which we have a complete and probably official record. It is preserved in the *Gesta Ricardi* (ed. Stubbs), ii. 80; cf. P. E.
Schramm, *A History of the English Coronation* (1937), p. 69.
[4] 'Ipse malus erat omnibus, suis pejor, pessimus sibi.' *Gesta Henrici II*, i. 292.
[5] 'Anno Regni Regis Ricardi boni IX°.' *Feet of Fines 9 Ric. I* (Pipe Roll Soc., vol.
xxiii), p. 79.

from captivity, on 13 March 1194, and after a stay of two months returned to France where he spent the remainder of his life. These six months were all that he devoted to his kingdom in his ten years' reign. He used England as a bank on which to draw and overdraw in order to finance his ambitious exploits abroad. That the country stood and survived the strain is the highest proof of the soundness of Henry II's constructive work. Twice in the course of four years England was called upon to furnish money on a wholly unprecedented scale: first for the crusade, and secondly for the king's ransom when he fell into the hands of the emperor on his return.

Richard was determined to spare nothing to make a success of the crusade which he had undertaken with honest enthusiasm. In spite of the fact that load after load of money had been shipped to France in order to pay for the recent wars,[1] Henry II had left a substantial balance in the treasury, not less than 100,000 marks,[2] for the use of his successor. But Richard was already engaged to pay 24,000 marks to Philip Augustus; his coronation, unsurpassed in magnificence, must have been a costly affair; and his generosity to his brother had considerably reduced the sources of income. Exceptional needs could only be met by exceptional methods. There were many persons who, moved by the impulse of the moment, had taken the crusading vow, had then repented at leisure, and were willing to buy themselves out of their rash obligation at a high price. The pope had sanctioned this system of compounding, at any rate for those who, like Geoffrey Fitz Peter, William Brewer, and Hugh Bardolf, could plead the excuse of administrative duties at home. Public offices were profitable and readily saleable. A good example of both these methods of raising money is furnished by the case of Hugh de Puiset, the princely bishop of Durham, who gave 2,000 marks for the sheriffdom of Northumberland, and another 1,000 for the justiciarship and release from the crusade. The sheriffs were nearly all dismissed, and if they were allowed to regain their position, they did so only on payment of fines.[3]

[1] See, for example, the details of export of treasure in *Pipe Roll 33 Hen. II*, p. 203.
[2] Hoveden, iii. 8. Another authority puts it as high as 900,000. *Gesta Ricardi*, ii. 77.
[3] For the purchase of the sheriffdom of Northumberland see *Pipe Roll 2 Ric. I*, p. 21. The price in this case was exceptionally high; the king was often content with much more moderate sums. Robert de la Mare, for instance, paid no more than £100 for the shrievalties of Oxford and Berkshire. Ibid., p. 14.

Burgesses not infrequently purchased their right to have their cities at fee farm for relatively small sums, varying from £100 in the case of Northampton to 40 marks in the case of Shrewsbury. The largest single contribution to the crusade fund came from William the Lion, king of Scotland, who for 10,000 marks bought his release from the covenants of the treaty of Falaise. 'I would sell London', Richard is reported to have said, 'if I could find a suitable purchaser';[1] the generalization of a contemporary writer that 'everything was for sale—powers, lordships, earldoms, shrievalties, castles, towns, manors, and suchlike'—was indeed not far from the truth.[2]

In the arrangements which the king made for the government of the country during his absence, he showed little political wisdom or judgement of character. The post of highest importance was of course that of the justiciar, for it was he who acted as regent when the king was abroad. Richard seems to have regarded the old justiciar, Rannulf Glanvill, with suspicion, for he was removed from office and only allowed to recover the king's favour by a heavy fine. Shortly after, he set out for the crusade on which he died. His place was taken by Hugh de Puiset, bishop of Durham, who ruled almost supreme in the north country; for besides the palatine jurisdiction which he held by virtue of his bishopric and the recently purchased sheriffdom of Northumberland, he was connected through his wife, Adelaide, with the influential house of Percy. Richard, however, had not sufficient confidence in this northern magnate to trust him alone in the office of justiciar. He therefore appointed as his colleague William de Mandeville, earl of Essex, a trusted servant of his father's, and then, some months after the latter's death in November, William Longchamp, the chancellor and bishop of Ely.[3] The two justiciars, whose sphere of authority was divided by the river Humber, were as unlike as any two men could be. Ambition and ability were the only qualities they had in common. Hugh de Puiset was an aristocrat

---

[1] Newburgh, iv, c. 5; Richard of Devizes (ed. Howlett in *Chronicles of Stephen*, &c.), iii. 388.

[2] *Gesta Ricardi*, ii. 90.

[3] Longchamp was first employed as a clerk in the chancery under Geoffrey; he had then passed into the service of his brother Richard who made him his chancellor in Aquitaine. On Richard's succession to the throne, he became chancellor of the kingdom and bishop of Ely. His appointment as one of the justiciars was made at a council in Normandy in March 1190.

of the old school, connected by family ties with kings and counts, a man who lived and did everything in the grand manner. He was a man of culture and the possessor of a fine library.[1] He was also very experienced in the affairs of the world, for he had served his apprenticeship in arms in the wars of Stephen's reign and was already bishop of Durham before Henry II was king. Longchamp, on the other hand, was something of an upstart, one of those *novi homines*, whom the old baronial families would like if they dared to treat with contempt. Though not, as his enemies put about, the grandson of a runaway serf, he was certainly of relatively humble origin, and had won his promotion by his practical usefulness and by assiduous attention to his master's interests. His chief defects were those of over-confidence, inordinate love of power, aggrandisement of his family, lack of tact, and a complete failure to understand the English whom he openly professed to despise. It is not surprising, therefore, that he was little loved. In appearance too these men presented a curious contrast. Hugh looked his part, a fine handsome presence; while the short, ugly, deformed figure of Longchamp gave some colour to the exaggerated description of Gerald of Wales who likens him to an ape rather than a man.

Longchamp's first object as justiciar was to oust his colleague from any share in the government of the country. He had already found occasion to deprive him of the sheriffdom of Northumberland, perhaps because the stipulated sum had not been paid into the treasury,[2] and he had refused to admit him to the business of the exchequer. The next step was wholly unprovoked. The two met at Tickhill about Easter and the bishop of Durham was placed under arrest. He was taken to London where he was forced to surrender the castles of Windsor and Newcastle, and the rich manor of Sadberge which he had recently purchased from the king for the sum of 600 marks,[3] and to give hostages for his good behaviour. But Longchamp had not yet done with him. When the old bishop on his way home reached Howden in Yorkshire he was seized by Osbert, the chancellor's brother, who had been intruded into the office of sheriff, and kept there a virtual prisoner. His position in the north had

[1] For his books and treasure see *Wills and Inventories* (Surtees Soc. ii), pp. 3-4.
[2] The sum, 2,000 marks, was still owing at Michaelmas 1190. *Pipe Roll 2 Ric. I*, p. 21.
[3] Newcastle and Sadberge were subsequently restored to him by order of the king from Marseilles. *Gesta Ricardi*, ii. 110.

recently been seriously weakened by his rival who had visited York to punish the city for its savage attack upon the Jews in the preceding March. The chief instigators of the outrage were friends and connexions of the bishop of Durham, Richard Malebysse and William Percy, and on them the punishment fell most heavily; they were fined and their lands were confiscated. It was on this occasion also that the sheriff John Marshal was replaced by the chancellor's brother.

This manifestation of anti-Jewish hate which disfigured the first months of Richard's reign was unsurpassed in its ferocity. The Jews had settled in England at the time of the Norman Conquest, and for nearly a century they had been allowed to live in their quarters almost unmolested under the king's protection. In the course of time, however, this attitude of toleration was changed to one of antipathy. The ostentation which possession of great wealth enabled the Jews to display, and their unconcealed contempt for the practices of Christianity, made them an object of universal dislike; as usurers, moreover, they had gained a strangle-hold on the recently founded monastic houses whose splendid buildings they had financed, and on many of the smaller aristocratic families who sometimes took the initiative in these attacks with the hope of ridding themselves of their indebtedness by removing their creditors. This feeling of hatred was, in the second half of the twelfth century, intensified by the popular belief in the legendary 'ritual murders' or boy-martyrdoms, of which that of little St. William of Norwich in 1144 was the first and best known,[1] and by crusading enthusiasm which not infrequently found expression in a massacre of the infidels at home. An altercation with some Jews at the coronation festival gave rise to a general attack on the London Jewry, and massacring, burning, and plundering, despite the king's attempt to check it, continued into the small hours of the morning. From the capital the wave of fanaticism spread to the provinces, and the revolting scenes perpetrated at London were repeated at Lynn, Norwich, Lincoln, Stamford, and elsewhere. In the middle of March the infection reached York, where some 150 Jews, who had taken refuge in the castle,

[1] See Thomas of Monmouth's *Life and Miracles of St. William of Norwich*, edited with an introduction by A. Jessop and M. R. James, and the powerful refutation of the legend by Cardinal Lorenzo Ganganelli, afterwards Pope Clement XIV, in 1759, which has been translated by C. Roth under the title *The Ritual Murder Libel and the Jew* (London, 1935).

perished miserably, either at their own hands or at those of the infuriated populace. Although the Jewish communities survived the shock and plied their trade of usury for another hundred years under royal protection, the toll of blood taken in 1189-90 marks a definite stage in the decline of their prosperity.[1]

William Longchamp was now supreme in church and state; he was justiciar, chancellor, and papal legate—this last office having been conferred on him by Clement III at the king's request in June 1190—and he did not scruple to use his authority to the uttermost. 'The laity', writes William of Newburgh, 'found him more than a king, the clergy more than a pope, and both an intolerable tyrant.'[2] By his tactless and ill-judged acts he seems to have courted unpopularity. Even the exchequer clerks could not refrain from jeering at him: He owes £20 for the scutage of Wales; but there are many of his men serving in the army and 'therefore with angels and archangels he is quit'.[3] They ridiculed his brother Osbert by drawing a caricature of his face in the capital letter O of his name.[4] He made constant progresses through the country in the royal manner, accompanied by crowds of henchmen, quartering himself as he moved from place to place on the religious houses regardless of the heavy burden he thus imposed on them; he strengthened the strongholds under his control, especially the Tower of London; he brought mercenary soldiers from abroad; and he exacted immense sums of money both to meet his own extravagant expenditure and to satisfy the abnormal demands of his master on crusade, who was already entangled with debt to Italian merchants.[5]

The widespread dislike felt for Longchamp gave a wholly unmerited popularity to the king's brother John, who now became the centre of the opposition. Territorially, as we have seen, he was in a position of enormous power; he ruled a kingdom within a kingdom. He had a strong personal reason for desiring the overthrow of the chancellor, for the latter had

[1] The massacres are vividly described by the contemporary chroniclers, especially by William of Newburgh. See C. Roth, A History of the Jews in England, chap. ii, and 'A Hebrew Elegy on the York Martyrs' in Trans. of the Jewish Hist. Soc. xvi, 213-20.

[2] iv, c. 14.   [3] Pipe Roll 2 Ric. I, p. 116.   [4] Pipe Roll 9 Ric. I, p. xxvi.

[5] For his borrowings from Lombard merchants during his stay in Italy on his way to Messina, see Pipe Roll 3 & 4 Ric. I, p. 145. Eight hundred marks were borrowed from merchants of Rome for the expenses of Queen Eleanor who went to join her son in Sicily in 1191, and for the archbishop of Rouen. Ibid., p. 29.

accepted the king's arrangement of making not his brother John, but his nephew Arthur his heir in the event of his dying childless. Home politics, therefore, in the year 1191 resolved themselves into a duel between these two domineering men. A dispute over the custody of certain castles on 24 March at Winchester (the issue of which is unknown) was the first act of this drama; the second was concerned with Gerard de Camville, constable of Lincoln castle and sheriff of the county. This influential baron flouted the chancellor's authority; he was answerable, he maintained, only to John to whom he had given his allegiance. He was afterwards accused of permitting lawlessness and even of harbouring robbers who interfered with merchants attending the fair of Stamford. His act of defiance was followed by other incidents directed against Longchamp: John himself seized the castles of Tickhill and Nottingham, while Roger Mortimer raised the standard of revolt at his castle of Wigmore on the Welsh border. Longchamp acted at once: he reduced Wigmore and early in July laid siege to Lincoln castle. But at this stage a new figure, Walter of Coutances, archbishop of Rouen, intervened.

Despite the name by which he is usually known, Walter was of English not Norman birth; he was a native of Cornwall. An accomplished scholar and a capable rather than a brilliant statesman, he had occupied for some fifteen years a prominent place in the royal chancery.[1] He had served his apprenticeship in ecclesiastical affairs as archdeacon of Oxford (1175–82), and for a brief period before his translation to Rouen in 1184 he had been bishop of Lincoln. From 1191 to 1194 he was virtually ruler of England. Sent by Richard from Messina to mediate between the opposing parties he arrived in England on 27 June armed with commissions to use as circumstances might dictate: one authorized him to act as Longchamp's colleague in the government, the other, if the chancellor's conduct warranted such a drastic step, to supersede him altogether. The archbishop's task was, however, not easy. He was a careful man and anxious to act constitutionally. He 'would do nothing in the rule of the kingdom', we are told, 'except by the will and consent of his associates and by the counsel of the barons of the

---

[1] He was apparently keeper of the seal and is variously described as *sigillifer regis*, *archisigillarius*, and once *vicecancellarius*; see Delisle, *Recueil des Actes de Henri II*, Introd., p. 108.

exchequer'.[1] Longchamp, unpopular as he was, and possibly dangerous, had certainly the king's interests at heart as well as his own, while John was playing only for himself. But at last through his mediation an agreement, which was subsequently revised at Winchester on 28 July, was reached. Longchamp's position was less secure than it had once been. Not only was he faced with a large and growing body of relentless opponents, but his authority was now undermined by the king's special emissary, Walter of Coutances, and his commission as legate had lapsed on the death of Clement III at the end of March. He was therefore more easily persuaded to make concessions and (in the second treaty) a big concession: he agreed to throw over Arthur and to support John's claim to the throne if Richard should die on the Crusade, an event which, in the eyes of contemporaries, seemed highly probable.[2]

Order, however, had scarcely been restored before another and far more serious incident again kindled the flames of rebellion. Geoffrey, the natural son of the late king, after many vicissitudes had at last been confirmed by the pope in his appointment to the archbishopric of York and had been consecrated by the archbishop of Tours (18 August 1191). He prepared, therefore, to cross over to England in order to take up the duties of his see. The chancellor for many reasons wanted to keep him out of England and had attempted to forestall him both by instructing the sheriff of Sussex to prevent his landing and suborning the countess of Flanders to stop his embarkation.[3] In spite, however, of these precautions, Geoffrey succeeded in reaching Dover. But there he was met by Longchamp's sister, wife of the constable of Dover, who, failing to make him take an oath of fealty to the king and her brother, besieged him in the priory of St. Martin where he had taken refuge. Four days later he was dragged from the altar of the chapel and taken in custody to Dover castle (18 September). These outrageous proceedings, which brought to men's minds the martyrdom of

---

[1] Hoveden, iii. 141. Cf. B. Wilkinson, *Bulletin of the John Rylands Library*, xxviii (1944), 501, n. 4.

[2] For the confused chronology of these events see Landon, *Itinerary of Richard I*, p. 192; J. H. Round, *Commune of London*, pp. 207 ff., and the introduction to *Pipe Rolls 3 & 4 Ric. I*, pp. xv ff. On the expectation of Richard's death see Newburgh, iv, c. 16: 'Rege in Orientali expeditione posito, cum fere nullus reditum ejus speraret.'

[3] This fact does not rest merely on the gossip of Giraldus Cambrensis (*Opera*, iv. 387), but is confirmed by the *Pipe Roll* of 1191 (p. 141).

Becket, worked the ruin of the chancellor. In vain he protested that he had issued no order for the arrest of the archbishop; that he had merely required that he should take the oath of fealty to the king or return whence he came;[1] in vain he authorized the release of the prisoner. For a moment Geoffrey was almost a hero and a champion of the liberties of the church; his assailants were excommunicated by Hugh of Lincoln and he himself was received in solemn procession in London. The country was in a turmoil and the capital so hostile that the Michaelmas session of the exchequer had to be opened in Oxford.[2] John was not slow to take advantage of the chancellor's unpopularity and blunders. Guided by Hugh of Nonant, bishop of Coventry, a nephew of Arnulf of Lisieux, a dexterous and unprincipled politician who had inherited the diplomatic gifts of his uncle, he used the situation to good purpose. The malcontents collected at Marlborough where they were joined by the chancellor's fellow justices, William Marshal, Geoffrey Fitz Peter, and William Brewer. From Marlborough by way of Oxford the party moved to Reading where writs were issued for a council to assemble on 5 October, and an ultimatum was sent to the chancellor bidding him appear at the bridge over the Loddon some four miles from Reading in the direction of Windsor, where he had made his headquarters. Helpless and friendless, deserted by bishops, barons, and officials, he dared not appear before the council; instead he fled to London and sought refuge in the Tower. In the meanwhile the council met. One after another the members gave vent to their complaints against the chancellor. Besides the outrageous usage of Archbishop Geoffrey, he had treated his colleagues in the justiciarship with studied neglect; he had refused to co-operate with the archbishop of Rouen; he had acted shamefully towards Bishop Hugh de Puiset; he had put his relatives into important and lucrative offices. The proposal of the archbishop of Rouen to depose him from the office of justiciar was thereupon agreed to. Two days later, 7 October, John and his party reached London. Though the city at this moment was divided by domestic feuds, there

[1] So at least he wrote to the monks of Canterbury (*Epp. Cantuarienses*, p. 344), and when in April 1194 he was at last reconciled with the archbishop of York he took an oath supported by a hundred priests that 'he had neither ordered nor desired' the archbishop's arrest (Hoveden, iii. 250). The author of the *Gesta Ricardi* (ii. 211), however, says that Longchamp admitted having given the order for the arrest.

[2] See *Pipe Roll 3 & 4 Ric. I*, Introd., p. xviii.

were few who showed any enthusiasm for the cause of Long-champ. John and his friends met with a better reception. At a meeting held at St. Paul's, where the misdeeds of the chancellor were again rehearsed, the citizens, who were rewarded by the grant of their 'commune',[1] joined with the bishops and barons in his deposition. Longchamp, besieged in the Tower without hope of relief, could do nothing but submit. After surrendering the castles in his custody and giving up his brothers as hostages, he was released and allowed ignominiously to leave the country (29 October).

The downfall of Longchamp had been skilfully managed by unscrupulous men. That he was generally unpopular, domineer-ing, and often blundering may be at once conceded. Neverthe-less the fullest accounts of the events of this fateful year come from sources tainted with violent prejudice and animosity,[2] and it is beyond dispute that he was true to the king he served as his subsequent career shows. Moreover, there were those who did not share the general view of his character, Henry of Cornhill, sheriff of London, Peter of Blois (who spoke his mind plainly on the scandalous way by which he had been hounded out of office and out of the kingdom)[3] and the pope himself, who, we learn with no little surprise, confirmed Longchamp in the office of legate at the petition of 'all the English bishops'.[4] He was on friendly terms with the monks of Canterbury and was almost venerated at Winchester where he was known as *pater monachorum*.[5] At the lowest estimate it can be said that he served his country at least as well as, if not better than, the men that supplanted him.

At the council of St. Paul's Walter of Coutances became chief justiciar on the authority of the mandate which he had brought with him from the king in the preceding June. Whether this meeting, as one writer asserts,[6] constituted John *summus rector totius regni* is uncertain; if so it was wholly irregular, and justified the chancellor's accusation that he was aiming at

---

[1] Above, p. 70.

[2] Especially Giraldus Cambrensis, 'De vita Galfridi Archiepiscopi Eboracensis' (*Opera*, iv. 357).

[3] Hoveden, iii. 148.

[4] *Gesta Ricardi*, ii. 242. The date of Celestine's confirmation of Longchamp's legatine office is doubtful. The latter was still using the title on 13 May, six weeks after his commission had lapsed with the death of Clement III (Round, *Ancient Charters*, no. 58), and Celestine speaks of him as legate in a letter of 2 December (*Gesta Ricardi*, p. 221). Cf. also H. Tillmann, *Die päpstlichen Legaten in England*, p. 87.

[5] *Ann. Winton.*, p. 64.   [6] Richard of Devizes, p. 415.

the kingdom for himself. His plots and intrigues were unceasing. Early in 1192 Philip Augustus, having returned from the crusade, offered him all the English continental dominions if he would marry his sister Alice; and John was only prevented from crossing the Channel to discuss this tempting proposal by the timely arrival of his mother, Queen Eleanor, who alone could exercise any restraining influence over him. In the meanwhile he was endeavouring to get control of the royal castles, and was so far successful that he managed to persuade the castellans of two of the most important—Windsor and Wallingford—to deliver them into his hands. He was also negotiating with Longchamp who was prepared to offer him a substantial bribe if he would assist him to return; he did in fact return and landed at Dover in March. But the justiciars were firm; they bribed John to abandon the chancellor, who was ordered peremptorily to leave the country. England was in this state of political confusion, with a government incapable of coping with the scheming John, when the news came that the king returning from Palestine had fallen into the hands of his enemy the duke of Austria.

The crusade of Richard I belongs to world history, and is only indirectly connected with the trend of events in England. The well-known story may therefore be dismissed in the barest outline. Although Richard left England in December 1189, it was not until late in the next summer that he had sufficiently ordered the affairs of his continental dominions to enable him to set out on his voyage. He had collected a large fleet, and at Chinon, probably in March, issued ordinances for the maintenance of discipline on board.[1] At Tours he received the scrip and staff of a pilgrim, and at Vézelay in the first days of July he made his final arrangements with Philip Augustus, including an agreement to share equally the spoils of conquest. When he reached Marseilles he found that his fleet had not yet arrived; so, impatient of further delay, he embarked in hired vessels, leaving instructions for it to follow him, and coasted leisurely round the Italian seaboard to Messina. Arriving there towards the end of September, he found himself immediately involved in troubles, partly political, partly domestic, which engaged him the whole winter 1190-1. From the outset the inhabitants were hostile; they refused to admit his army within their wall,

[1] See below, p. 438.

denied him the necessary supplies, and caused so much vexation
to the crusaders that Richard was compelled to take the city by
storm. The Sicilian government was also hostile. Richard's
brother-in-law, William II, had died in the previous November,
and the crown should have passed to his aunt Constance and
her husband, the emperor Henry VI; but the idea of German
domination was repugnant to the islanders who chose instead
Tancred of Lecce, a descendant (by an illegitimate branch) of
Roger II. Tancred's first action was to thrust Richard's sister
Joan into prison and decline to deliver over her dowry and the
handsome legacy which William had bequeathed to Henry II
apparently as a contribution to the crusade. Though Joan was at
once released on Richard's demand, it was only after prolonged
negotiations that a satisfactory financial settlement was reached.
One of the terms of the agreement throws light on Richard's
intentions: his nephew Arthur was to be his heir if he should die
without issue, and he was to be betrothed to Tancred's daughter.
The part played by Philip Augustus in these proceedings was
always treacherous; while he secretly abetted Richard's enemies,
when there was spoil to be had he would claim his share
according to the agreement made at Vézelay—he even obtained
his dividend of the moneys paid by Tancred in respect of
William II's legacies. Richard's intended marriage with Berengaria, daughter of Sancho, king of Navarre—an alliance con-
tracted in order to strengthen his position on the southern
frontier of Aquitaine—accentuated the bitterness, for Richard
had been betrothed since his childhood to Philip's sister Alice.
It was not till March 1191 that these difficulties were smoothed
out at Messina. Richard freed himself of his obligations to Alice
by the payment of 10,000 marks and agreed to certain territorial
adjustments of the French possessions.[1] The whole winter had
thus slipped away in bickerings and discord, which the treaty
of Messina did little to allay, before the crusading kings again
set out on their voyage to the Holy Land.

Richard left Messina with a fleet of some two hundred vessels
on 10 April; but it was another two months before he reached
Palestine. The whole of May he was at Cyprus engaged in the
capture of the island from the Greek tyrant, Isaac Comnenus,
and in the celebration of his marriage with Berengaria who,
with his sister Joan, had accompanied the fleet; and it was only

[1] *Foedera*, i. 54. Cf. Powicke, *Loss of Normandy*, pp. 129, 131.

on 8 June that he joined the other crusading armies before the walls of Acre. This all important city, the great emporium of the eastern trade, had fallen into the hands of Saladin in 1187, and since the summer of 1189 had been ineffectively besieged by Guy of Lusignan, king of Jerusalem, a man whose leadership was discredited by his calamitous defeat at Hattin and whose throne was now disputed by a rival, Conrad, marquis of Montferrat. The recovery of Acre was the first and vital objective of the crusaders who poured in their thousands into Palestine during the years 1190–1. But the armies were disunited, exhausted, and demoralized; they were short of supplies and stricken with pestilence; and little progress was made until the arrival of Richard with large reinforcements, siege-engines, and stores. He at once assumed command of the operations, and within a little more than a month of his coming the siege, which had dragged on for two years, was brought to a triumphant close by the surrender of the city (12 July). Soon after this, Philip Augustus went home, excusing himself on the ground of ill health, but really anxious to secure his claim to Artois and eastern Vermandois (Peronne and St. Quentin) in consequence of the death of the count of Flanders during the siege of Acre, and to do what mischief he could in Richard's French possessions while he was safely out of the way. Richard himself stayed behind, and on 22 August began his march for the recovery of Jerusalem. But the advance over the sun-scorched country was a slow and arduous undertaking, hampered as it was by shortage of supplies and by sudden flank attacks from the Saracens who were moving parallel along the inland route. The victory at Arsuf (7 September) raised the prestige of the Christian armies and opened the way to Jaffa, which was occupied two days later. Before the end of the year Richard had led his host to within a dozen miles of Jerusalem. But disunity among the leaders was now more than ever pronounced; rivalries and divided counsels impeded decisive action, and the army, almost within sight of its goal, retreated back to the coast. In strange contrast to the discord which prevailed in the camp of the crusaders (which indeed was characteristic of the whole movement and one of the principal causes of its failure) was the remarkable understanding, we might almost call it cordiality, which existed between Richard and Saladin and still more his brother Safadin. They exchanged presents and courtesies; they held meetings and discussed in a friendly spirit possible ways of partitioning the Holy Land. Richard even offered his sister Joan in marriage to Safadin and actually conferred on the latter's son the honour of knighthood. The negotiations, however, came to nothing, and once more Richard marched towards Jerusalem, and once more came within a dozen miles of it; he himself even penetrated with an advanced party within sight of its walls. But, as on the former occasion, he found it necessary to withdraw his troops and to abandon for ever the hope of recovering the Holy City. A brilliant victory at Jaffa was the last event of this costly enterprise. News from England had long made Richard anxious to return; and a treaty, to last three years, was arranged which secured to the Christians a strip along the coast, including Jaffa and Acre, and the right of pilgrims to visit Jerusalem. On 9 October 1192 he sailed from Acre on his homeward voyage. After many adventures with pirates, storms, and shipwreck, Richard was thrown ashore with a few companions on the coast of Istria; thence, after more adventures, he reached the neighbourhood of Vienna where he fell into the hands of Duke Leopold of Austria (December) whom he had insulted and quarrelled with during the crusade.[1] In February 1193 it was arranged that he should be delivered over to the emperor Henry VI.

Richard's capture was an event of the first importance in the international situation. In the winter of 1192–3 the emperor's position was gravely critical; even his throne was in danger. He was encircled by bitter and determined enemies both within Germany and without; with the Welfs, who for years had opposed his family, the house of Hohenstaufen, and with a powerful group of Rhenish princes in the north; with the pope and with Tancred, the usurper of the crown of Sicily in the south. With all these England was closely associated. Henry the Lion, Richard's brother-in-law, was the head of the Welf family and had spent the years of his banishment from Germany at the

---

[1] Richard had overthrown the banner which the duke had set up in the captured city of Acre. This has usually been taken as the cause of the quarrel. But A. Schreiber (Hist. Vierteljahrschrift xxvi (1931), 268 ff.) considers that this episode did not originate the quarrel which was mainly owing to Richard's connexions with the Welfs. He also believes that the king did not come to Erdberg near Vienna accidentally, as generally thought, but intentionally, meaning to return through Hungary with whose king Bela III he had political relations. A project of marriage between Bela and Richard's niece was discussed in 1186. Cf. Gesta Henrici, i. 346; Pipe Roll 32 Hen. II, p. 178.

English court; with the district of the lower Rhine England was connected by mutual commercial interests; and with Tancred of Sicily Richard had entered into an alliance during his stay in the island on his outward voyage to Palestine. The king of England was therefore a trump card in the political game now placed in the hand of the emperor; and he played it with consummate skill.

What his opponents, and above all the English government, dreaded was that Philip Augustus would be allowed to exploit the situation for his own advantage; that he would succeed in preventing Richard's release, or, worse still, get him into his own power. He was prepared to bid very high for a prize which doubtless would result in the transfer of the French possessions of the king of England to himself without the necessity of fighting. Since his return from the crusade he had spared no effort to undermine Richard's position in France; but he had not met with the success he had expected: the French barons refused to attack the lands of an absent crusader, and the seneschal of Normandy had refused to surrender the castle of Gisors, the key to the Norman Vexin and indeed of Normandy itself, which Philip claimed on the basis of what was almost certainly a forged version of the treaty made at Messina in March 1191.[1] When Richard was a prisoner, however, he made headway: through the treachery of its castellan he won Gisors; he then overran the Vexin and laid siege to Rouen, which, however, under the command of Robert, earl of Leicester, successfully resisted and he was forced to withdraw. John was no less eager for the ruin of his brother. Immediately on hearing the news of his imprisonment he had hurried to Paris where he had done homage to Philip for the French possessions (perhaps for England too) and agreed to marry Philip's sister Alice. He then returned to England to stir up rebellion there. Preparations for an invasion were at the same time set on foot; a fleet was collected at Witsand for the transport of Flemish mercenaries, and the co-operation of Denmark was sought and won by a marriage-alliance between Philip and Ingeborg, the sister of Canute VI.

Though the situation appeared critical, Richard was not uneasy. 'My brother John', he said, 'is not the man to conquer a country if there is anyone to offer even the feeblest resistance.' The measures taken by the justiciars, guided by Queen Eleanor

---

[1] Cf. Powicke, *Loss of Normandy*, pp. 126 f.

who had a ripe experience (she was now over seventy years of age) both of Anglo-French politics and of the feuds of her sons, were prompt, thorough, and effective. The oath of allegiance to the king was again exacted; cities and castles were put into a state of defence, their walls repaired, their garrisons strengthened.[1] There was, we are told, a general muster of the people, rustics as well as knights, and the coasts over against Flanders were so carefully watched that the invading fleet failed to make a landing. Windsor, which had been occupied by John at the beginning of the war, was besieged by Walter of Coutances, and Tickhill, his northern stronghold, by the aged bishop of Durham; and both places were, it seems, on the point of surrender when Hubert Walter arrived direct from Richard in Germany (Easter 1193). The king was not yet liberated, the ransom had to be raised, the future was full of uncertainty; in these circumstances it was considered prudent to arrange a truce to last till the autumn. Before many weeks had elapsed, however, Richard and the emperor had come to terms; and John warned of the fact by Philip in the famous message, 'Look to yourself, the devil is loosed,' immediately fled to the French court.

The diplomacy of Philip Augustus had fared little better than John's attempt to supplant his brother in England. The alliance with Denmark had unfortunate consequences: his repudiation of his wife on the day after the marriage in August 1193 involved him in a long and serious quarrel with Innocent III, while his meddling in Danish politics alienated German opinion. Philip had miscalculated; he failed to realize that his aims for a strong and united France could not harmonize with Henry VI's known aspiration to universal sovereignty. The surrender of Richard to Philip was probably never seriously intended, but the threat of it served the useful purpose of a lever to exact better terms. These, when finally settled, were certainly hard, and included the crushing payment of 150,000 marks of silver by way of ransom.[2] But evidently the relations between the emperor and his captive had rapidly improved during these months. Richard was not kept in close confinement; he was allowed to hold his court at Spires or Worms or wherever he might be, and to transact the business of his kingdom; his friends, who visited

---

[1] Money was spent on over thirty castles during this year. The evidence is summarized in the introduction to *Pipe Roll 5 Ric. I*, pp. xvi–xvii.

[2] For the terms see Hoveden, iii. 215.

him in great numbers, were permitted to come and go un-molested; and he had his hawks sent to him to provide him with amusement. As early as 19 April he and the emperor both wrote letters to England in which they expressed the close mutual understanding, the indissoluble bond of friendship which existed between them; and this alliance, there can be little doubt, was directed against France. For the moment, however, it seemed politic to recognize the position which Philip Augustus had already won (a large slice of eastern Normandy); and a treaty to this effect was accordingly made by Richard's representatives at Mantes on 9 July 1193. But before Richard was actually set at liberty (4 February 1194) John had sacrificed to Philip much more territory in Normandy and Touraine.[1]

By the end of the year 1193 a substantial amount of the ran-som, at least enough to obtain his freedom, had been delivered to Germany. A great, an unprecedented, sum was needed, and the fact that the bulk of it was found is good evidence at once of the prosperity of England, the soundness of its financial posi-tion and of its administrative system.[2] How it was raised is not precisely known. The moneys collected were paid to specially appointed custodians of whom Hubert Walter and Richard Fitz Neal, the treasurer, were the chief, locked up in St. Paul's cathedral, and accounted for in a separate exchequer (*scaccarium redemptionis*); but evidently there were many arrears in payment and difficulties of accountancy.[3] Resort was made to various sources of supply: an aid or scutage (*scutagium ad redemptionem*) of 20s. on the knight's fee was taken, and a general tax of a fourth of revenues and chattels was levied from the whole population both clerk and lay; a concession was only made in favour of the parish clergy who were let off with a tenth.

[1] The agreement between John and Philip (printed in *Foedera* i. 57) is dated at Paris in January 1193; but evidently it belongs to January 1194. The practice of beginning the year at Easter was about this time becoming established in France. See Powicke, op. cit., p. 146, n. 3; Delisle, *Actes de Philippe Auguste*, no. 411; Cartellieri, *Philipp II August*, iii. 73; *Itinerary of Richard I*, p. 205, n. 6.

[2] A substantial portion was of course raised from the continental dominions. In the financial year 1194-5 Normandy alone sent £16,000 to Germany. Powicke, op. cit., p. 345.

[3] Owing to the use of a special exchequer the Pipe Rolls only furnish incidental information about the collection of the ransom. Valuable, though often obscure, evidence is provided by the fragment of the *Receipt Roll 7 Ric. I* (1195) published with the Pipe Roll of the same year (p. 259) and a *Curia Regis Roll* dealing with Wiltshire for the year 1194 published by Maitland for the Pipe Roll Society (vol. xiv).

The whole wool-crop of the Cistercians and Gilbertines was taken, and the plate of the churches was also requisitioned, although, much to their credit, many of the clergy preferred to pay more and keep their chalices.[1] In thanking the clergy for their generosity the king was careful to explain that he would on no account regard what they had given in this very special emergency as a precedent for future demands.[2] But even so the sum collected fell far short of the required amount, and other taxes had to be imposed—a carucage of 2s. demanded at the council of Nottingham in April 1194 and an exaction referred to as the 'ten shilling and upwards' tax (taillagium x solidorum et amplius) which baffles explanation.[3] Money was also raised by fines 'for having the king's pleasure' from those who had supported John in his rebellion or 'for joy at the king's return'[4] and by the now common method of selling offices at extortionate prices. The whole ransom, in fact, was never paid; in 1195 the emperor remitted 17,000 marks in order to prevent Richard from making peace with France, while the duke of Austria only received a pittance of the 25,000 marks due to him.[5]

Before obtaining his freedom Richard had been compelled to yield up his kingdom and to receive it back as a fief of the empire. Though this bondage was only of short duration—for Henry on his deathbed released Richard from his feudal obligations—it was not, while it lasted, without political significance. The emperor's plan, it seems, was to break the power of France, using Richard as the instrument.[6] He used his

---

[1] The bishop of Winchester, for example, paid £89. 18s. 'de calicibus episcopatus Wintoniensis ad redemptionem domini Regis', Receipt Roll, p. 263. Cf. also Hist. Mon. S. Petri Gloucestriae, i. 23. The king himself replaced some of the plate taken for his ransom. Hoveden, iii. 290.

[2] See Richard I's charter contained in a letter of Pope Celestine III to the archbishop of Canterbury printed by W. Holtzmann, Papsturkunden in England, ii, no. 275.

[3] Receipt Roll 7 Ric. I (Pipe Roll Soc., N.S., vol. 6), pp. 261–2. Cf. ibid., vol. xiv, pp. xxiii–xxiv.

[4] So Gerard de Camville was fined 2,000 marks 'pro habenda benevolentia domini Regis et pro terris suis habendis' (Pipe Roll 6 Ric. I, p. 118). The citizens of York paid 200 marks 'de dono suo pro gaudio adventus domini Regis ab Alemannia'. Ibid., p. 163.

[5] Cf. Landon, Itinerary of Richard I, pp. 78, 100–1.

[6] Hoveden (iii. 301) says it was known to the king of England that the emperor desired above everything to subject the kingdom of France to the empire. Innocent III, writing later to Philip Augustus, says this was the emperor's declared intention. Migne, ccxvi, Ep. 64, col. 1071.

authority as overlord energetically to promote the war with France, always urging Richard to greater efforts. The abortive scheme to make Richard the ruler of the kingdom of Burgundy or Arles, the land lying east of the Rhone, had the same object in view, the subjection of France to the empire.[1] A great advantage, even though at considerable cost, had been won; the dangerous alliance, which had been formed in the later years of the reign of Frederick Barbarossa between the Hohenstaufen and the Capetians had been, temporarily at least, broken. Philip Augustus could no longer rely on German support in his self-appointed task of destroying the Angevin empire.

On his way back to England Richard by the promise of annual pensions secured the alliance of many of the leading princes of Germany and the Low Countries, who did homage and fealty to him against the king of France. The list as recorded by a well-informed contemporary[2] is impressive: the archbishops of Mainz and Cologne, the bishop-elect of Liége, the dukes of Austria, Swabia, Brabant (or Louvain, as he is always called in English records) and Limburg, the marquis of Montferrat, the count palatine of the Rhine, the count of Holland, and Baldwin the son of the count of Hainault. Little immediately came of this vast confederacy. English finances were far too heavily strained by the raising of the king's ransom to embark at once on a policy of subsidizing foreign allies on so prodigious a scale, and only the archbishop of Cologne is known to have received a pension in 1194. But it marks the beginning of the great coalition which, in spite of set-backs due to the ambition and inconstancy of individual princes and to King John's temporary abandonment of the policy at the treaty of Le Goulet, was held together by economic interests and English gold, and gradually matured and grew in strength until it was finally broken by the great French victory at Bouvines in 1214.

By the time that Richard reached England (he landed at Sandwich on 13 March 1194) the rebellion which John had

[1] Cf. A. L. Poole on 'England and Burgundy in the last decade of the Twelfth Century' in *Essays in History presented to R. L. Poole* (1927), pp. 261 ff. It is noteworthy that Savaric, bishop of Bath, a kinsman and friend of the emperor, who took a prominent part in the negotiations for Richard's release, was shortly afterwards made chancellor of Burgundy. Ibid., p. 268.

[2] Hoveden, iii. 234; Gilbert of Mons, *Chronicon Hanoniense* (ed. Vanderkindere), pp. 284–5, gives a shorter list of princes. For the details of these alliances see A. L. Poole in *Studies in Medieval History presented to F. M. Powicke*, pp. 90–9, and below, pp. 452–5.

raised in his absence had been all but suppressed; the castles of
Marlborough, Lancaster, and St. Michael's Mount (whose
castellan died of fright on hearing the news of the king's
landing) had already been captured, and it was short work to
bring the two which still held out, Tickhill and Nottingham, to
submission. At a great council held at Nottingham after the
capture of the castle the fate of John and his chief conspirator,
Hugh of Nonant, bishop of Coventry, was decided upon. The
latter was to submit 'to the judgment of bishops in that he was
himself a bishop, and to the judgment of laymen in that he was
a sheriff of the king', an echo of the famous verdict of Archbishop
Lanfranc on Odo, bishop of Bayeux. In fact he had already lost
his sheriffdoms (the shires of Stafford, Leicester, and Warwick)
and he was allowed a year later to buy the king's pardon for
2,000 marks.[1] He however withdrew from public life to live in
Normandy where he died in 1198. John was cited to appear to
answer for his conduct within forty days on pain of complete
forfeiture. But he was already again 'Lackland', for the counties
he had controlled had been taken over by the government at the
outbreak of the rebellion, and his castles had been captured in
the course of it. Although the brothers were personally reconciled through the mediation of their mother at Lisieux in the
following May, it was not until sometime in the next year that
John was partially reinstated in his former possessions (the
county of Mortain and the honors of Gloucester and Eye but
without the castles).[2]

While he was punishing his enemies he did not forget his
friends. William Longchamp had served him faithfully during
the dark months of his imprisonment; no one had been more
active in the negotiations to obtain his release. He was now
reinstated in the full exercise of his office of chancellor which he

[1] *Pipe Roll 7 Ric. I*, p. 191. Hoveden (iii. 287) wrongly gives the sum as 5,000
marks. He was then restored to his bishopric of which he had been temporarily
deprived.

[2] Hoveden, iii. 286. He witnesses charters as count of Mortain on 10 June 1195
(*Itinerary of Richard I*, p. 102) and on 22 June (*Reg. Antiquissimum* (Lincoln Record
Soc., vol. 27), i. 123). According to Hoveden he also received a pension of 8,000
pounds in Angevin money or £2,000 sterling. The honor of Eye does not appear
to have been restored to him till Easter 1196 (*Pipe Roll 8 Ric. I*, p. 121). The account
of this honor in the *Book of Fees* (p. 138) contains no reference to John's tenure of
it. Evidently, however, he held it from the beginning of Richard's reign till Easter
1194 when he was deprived of it. His second tenure of it was of short duration,
for in 1198 it was granted to the duchess of Louvain. *Pipe Roll 10 Ric. I*, p. 94, and
below, p. 377.

retained, although he never revisited England after his departure with the king in May 1194, until his death at Poitiers in
1197. Walter of Coutances, who had played such a prominent
part during the critical years of Richard's crusade and captivity,
now too fades out of the arena of English politics. His later
career (he died in 1207) is wholly concerned with the affairs of
Normandy. The government of England was now left in the
capable hands of Hubert Walter. A student at Bologna[1] and
trained in the household of Rannulf Glanvill, with whom he had
family connexions, he had been usefully employed in judicial
and administrative work during the later years of Henry II's
reign. Though an indifferent and secular-minded ecclesiastic,
his promotion in the church had been rapid: he was appointed
dean of York in 1186, bishop of Salisbury in 1189, and, after his
return from the crusade, on which he had distinguished himself,
archbishop of Canterbury in May 1193. In 1195 his authority
over the church was strengthened by a legatine commission.
But it was in administration that his natural gifts, his clear-
sightedness, his attention to detail, his practical good sense, were
most effectively displayed. Before the end of 1193 he was made
justiciar and virtually ruler of England. To him fell the increasingly difficult task of finding money and armies for the wars in
France which during the next decade wholly absorbed the
energies of soldiers and administrators. Richard's last important
act before quitting England was to submit to a second coronation. Presumably it was considered necessary in order to re-establish his dignity after the humiliations he had suffered at the
hands of the emperor. The ceremony took place at Winchester
on 17 April 1194. On 12 May he set sail from Portsmouth,
never, as it happened, to return.

Richard realized that the struggle with Philip Augustus was
likely to be a long and a bitter one; he would require an army
almost continuously in the field. For such a purpose the existing military organization based on the national levy and the
feudal host was quite inadequate. The ancient fyrd had been
remodelled in 1181 by the Assize of Arms which required all
freemen (*tota communa liberorum hominum*) to furnish themselves
with arms according to their wealth. A similar ordinance had
also been issued earlier in the same year for the continental

---

[1] H. G. Richardson: Introduction to the *Memoranda Roll I John* (Pipe Roll Soc.,
N.S., vol. xxi), p. lxii, n. 7.

dominions.[1] But the object of the militia was primarily to provide for home defence; it was called out to suppress the rebellion
of John in 1193 and again when the country was threatened
with invasion in 1205. The general levy of Normandy, the
arrière-ban, and the military service due from the communes
might indeed be used to resist the aggression of Philip; but in
fact they played little part, and their service, such as it was, was
essentially local.[2]

The feudal levy was alike ill-adapted to a long war owing to
its short-term service, usually limited by custom to forty days.
Henry II had tried to remedy this defect when, for his invasion
of Wales in 1157, he called out a third of the knight-service which
would thus be available for a campaign lasting four months; and
the same plan was followed in 1194. In 1197 Richard demanded
300 knights for service all the year round, or, according to
another authority, a tenth of the knight-service; and John in the
critical year 1205 issued a writ requiring ten knights to equip
and maintain (at 2s. a day) one of their number for duty in
defence of the kingdom so long as should be necessary.[3] Such
expedients got round one difficulty. But there was another:
there was a growing reluctance on the part of the tenants to
undertake foreign service. The question was obscure and
became more so with the growth of the Angevin empire. Limits
must be set somewhere to the feudal obligations of these Anglo-
Norman barons. Whither were they bound to follow the king
into battle? Obviously no feudal contract could require their
service in Palestine, but what of Aquitaine where they likewise
had no direct interest? Richard himself seems to have admitted
some distinction between classes of tenants when in April 1196
he wrote to Hubert Walter instructing him to send immediately
to Normandy those whose *capita baroniarum* lay in Normandy;
those who owed knight-service in England (except the barons of

---

[1] The text of the Assize of Arms is given in *Gesta Henrici*, i. 278; for the Assize of
Le Mans see *Gesta Henrici*, i. 269. The example of Henry II was followed by Philip
Augustus and the count of Flanders for their dominions. Ibid. 270.

[2] Powicke, *Loss of Normandy*, pp. 311 ff. S. R. Packard (*Haskins Anniversary Essays*,
pp. 231 ff.) contests the generally accepted view that Richard and John created
communes in Normandy chiefly in order to gain their military service; a commune,
for example, was granted to the men of Fécamp in 1202 that they 'may be ready to
defend our land with arms' (*Rot. Lit. Pat.* 13b). He thinks that 'the communes of
Normandy were seldom, if ever, used upon the actual battlefield or for castle-guard
upon any considerable scale' (p. 237).

[3] Hoveden, iv. 40; Jocelin of Brakelond (Camden Soc.), p. 63; *Rot. Lit. Pat.* 55a.

the Welsh march) were to follow later with a few knights—not more than seven at most; and the ecclesiastical tenants should render such military service as would meet with his approval.[1] This vague phrase suggests that the king felt uneasy about exercising compulsion on the church tenants. However that may be, in the next year (1197) the knights of Bury St. Edmund in a conference with their abbot Samson and St. Hugh of Lincoln in a heated council held at Oxford,[2] vigorously asserted a claim (probably wholly without foundation)[3] that they were bound to serve only in England. They denied their liability to service overseas, but acknowledged their liability to scutage. The king's need was great, and for men even more than for money. These protests therefore met with little success, and the ecclesiastics could only escape the burden of service by a hard bargain; some of the monasteries paid an aid (*donum de militibus*) far in excess of the normal scutage rate.[4] Judging by the growing frequency of fines imposed 'quia non fuit ultra mare in servitio Regis' or 'ne transfretet in exercitu Normanniae', we must suppose that the lay barons were also showing some disinclination to serve abroad. It was not, however, until after the conquest of Normandy by Philip Augustus, when they no longer had any stake in that country, that they pressed their claim to exemption. The precise character of the document generally entitled 'the unknown Charter of Liberties' is not, and probably never will be, settled; but it formulates at the end of John's reign a practical compromise: foreign service should be confined to campaigns in Normandy and Brittany.[5]

In an age of chivalry, however, there can never have been any scarcity of knights who were wholly given over to the profession of arms and were ready to stay in the field or the castle so long as was necessary and so long as they were properly paid for it. The wage of a knight was relatively good, as wages went. The standard rate for most of the twelfth century was 8*d.* a day; but towards the close of Henry II's reign it had risen to 1*s.*[6] and he

---

[1] The importance of this letter (printed in the Rolls edition of Diceto, ii, pp. lxxix–lxxx) has been emphasized by Powicke, op. cit., pp. 314 f.

[2] *Vita Magna S. Hugonis* (Rolls Series), pp. 248–50; and Round, *Feudal England*, pp. 528 ff. The debate was occasioned by Richard's demand for 300 knights mentioned above.

[3] H. M. Chew, *Ecclesiastical Tenants-in-Chief*, pp. 38–41.

[4] See *Pipe Roll 10 Ric. I*, Introd., pp. xxi–xxiii.

[5] Below, pp. 471–2.

[6] Occasionally knights could still be hired at 8*d.* a day. Instances appear on the

seems often to have had advances of pay when serving abroad. Nevertheless these rates cannot be considered excessive if account is taken of his equipment which he had to provide himself. His charger (*dextrarius*) was an expensive animal; it could not be bought for less than 10 marks; and his elaborate armour of chain mail cannot have been cheap. No doubt he expected to make something from booty and the ransom of prisoners, for the rules of war, which were scrupulously observed, recognized his right to a share in whatever he captured. Nevertheless, he might well be out of pocket. The knight belonged to a small aristocratic class who no longer fought, as in the early days of feudalism, in divisions by themselves, but were employed either in the retinue of the king or a great baron or as commanders (constables or masters they are generally called) of units, approximately 500 strong, of paid men-at-arms.[1] Though the knights of the Norman wars of Richard and John might be required to serve for a longer term, fewer were required. Their reluctance to serve abroad was therefore a matter of less serious moment. The men-at-arms (sergeants, *servientes*), on the other hand, were professional soldiers (*solidarii*) who were recruited, largely from Wales, at fixed rates of pay. They received 4*d.* a day if they were mounted (with an additional 2*d.* a day for a second horse); 2*d.* a day if they were infantrymen. Besides these there were, of course, the foreign mercenaries who were used to an increasing extent during the wars of the twelfth century. They were of two kinds: there were those who, like the Genoese cross-bowmen or the Saracens brought by Richard I from the east, were employed because of their professional skill.[2] Wholly different were those bands of desperadoes, irresponsible adventurers, picked up by some captain, a Mercadier or a Gerard de Athée, in every corner of western Europe, who were known indiscriminately as routiers (*rutae*) or Brabançons. They lived for fighting and plunder; they spared neither sex nor age, neither the clergy nor the peace-loving traders; their ruthless cruelty and wanton destruction made them objects of universal detestation and fear.

Pipe Rolls of 1193 and 1199. It is difficult to account for the high rates paid in 1197 and 1205 (see the references above, p. 370) for in both these years the Pipe Rolls show 1*s.* to be the normal figure.

[1] Cf. A. L. Poole, *Obligations of Society*, &c., pp. 50–3.

[2] The Genoese bowmen seem to be first used in Anglo-Norman warfare in the 1180s. Cf. Powicke, op. cit., p. 333; for the Saracens in Normandy see ibid., p. 290, and *Scottish Hist. Rev.* viii (1911), 104.

Henry II and Richard wisely restricted their use to the Continent; but there, despite the prohibition of the church, they were employed with growing frequency.[1]

A force of paid knights and men-at-arms, of hired Welshmen and bands of foreign mercenaries, needed much money. Added to this there was the cost of building and upkeep of castles which, constantly stormed and battered by effective siege-engines, stone throwers, and Greek fire,[2] were always in need of repair. Times had changed since a French count half a century before had hopefully consulted the *Epitoma rei militaris* of Vegetius Renatus (who wrote in the fourth century) for guidance on a problem of siege warfare.[3] Everything had become more complex. Nearly £49,000 were spent on the defence of Andeli alone in the year 1197–8.[4] Load upon load of treasure was shipped across the sea to supplement the fast diminishing revenues of Normandy and Anjou. Scutages and aids were to become almost annual taxes in addition to tallages taken from the towns and the royal demesne. Hubert Walter declared in 1196 that in the past two years he had provided the immense sum of 1,100,000 marks of silver for the king's use.[5] Recourse was made to every kind of expedient to raise money, even to requiring charters to be re-sealed with the new Great Seal at appropriate fees.[6] War, even waged on the relatively small scale of the twelfth century, was becoming a costly business.

In the middle of May 1194 Richard crossed the Channel with a fleet of a hundred ships to engage in the long struggle which,

[1] The routiers were only twice used in England before the reign of John: in the suppression of the rebellion of 1173–4 (William of Newburgh, ii, c. 27; *Pipe Roll 20 Hen. II*, pp. 88, 135), and perhaps in the suppression of John's rebellion in 1193 (Hoveden, iii. 251). The fifth canon of the Third Lateran Council (1179) prohibited the use of the Brabançons, Navarese, &c., on pain of excommunication.

[2] Greek fire, a combustible mixture thought to be composed of sulphur, pitch, and naphtha, seems to have been introduced into western Europe after the Third Crusade. It was used at the siege of Nottingham in 1194 (*Pipe Roll 6 Ric. I*, p. 175) and at Dieppe in the following year (Hoveden, iii. 304).

[3] *Chroniques des Comtes d'Anjou et des Seigneurs d'Amboise*, ed. Halphen and Poupardin (Collection de Textes), p. 218.

[4] Powicke, op. cit., pp. 288, 303 f.   [5] Hoveden, iv. 13.

[6] The Great Seal of Richard I had an adventurous career. It was shipwrecked off Cyprus with the king's seal-bearer, Roger Malchiel, in April 1191, but was recovered when Roger's body was washed ashore; on the king's return from Palestine it fell into the hands of Leopold of Austria who possibly handed it over to the king's brother John, who may have used it for his own purposes. Richard regained possession of it in 1193, and shortly after a new seal was made, but it was not taken into use till the spring of 1198. See Lionel Landon, *Itinerary of Richard I*, pp. 173–83.

though interrupted by short truces and uneasy periods of peace, was to last until his death five years later. When he landed at Barfleur he was welcomed with a great show of popular rejoicing. The fame of the great crusader had not been dimmed by his captivity; his energy, his reckless bravery, his rapidity of action were not forgotten; nor had these qualities been appreciably impaired by advancing years and increasing corpulence. He could still move, as a contemporary (quoting Lucan) expressed it 'more swiftly than the twisted thong of a Balearic sling'.[1] Within a few weeks he had forced Philip to throw up the siege of Verneuil; had, by the capture of the important castle of Loches, recovered his position in Touraine; and had sent Philip himself and his army flying in disordered rout from Fréteval, leaving in his hands prisoners, treasure, and equipment. He then pushed southward to punish the rebellious barons of Aquitaine with such success that, as he wrote to the archbishop of Canterbury, he captured no less than 300 knights and 40,000 men-at-arms.[2] While he was thus triumphantly piling up victories in the south, his agents were arranging a truce at Tillières on the Norman frontier (23 July). It was largely manufactured by the church—a fact in itself sufficient to make it unpalatable to Richard who disliked ecclesiastical meddling in politics—and its terms, considering the recent English successes, were far too favourable to Philip. It was never strictly kept and merely provided an interval for further preparations. Moreover, had Richard needed any encouragement in his war-like intentions the emperor was always ready to supply it. In June 1195 the latter sent him a golden crown as a sign of his esteem and charged him 'by the fealty which he owed him' to invade the lands of the king of France, promising that he himself would assist him in the enterprise. He even forbade the king to make peace except with his counsel and consent, and remitted the balance of the redemption money, 17,000 marks, as a contribution towards the prosecution of the war.[3] Philip, alarmed at these negotiations, called off the truce, and the raids, the storming of castles, the plundering, began once more. Nevertheless, Richard was in desperate financial

---

[1] Hoveden, iii. 252. In November 1195 he made the three days' journey from Vaudreuil in Normandy to Issoudun in Berri in one day. Ibid. 305.

[2] Ibid. 257. The figures are no doubt exaggerated.

[3] Ibid. 300, 303-4.

straits, and had to resort to extraordinary expedients to find money to keep the war going. By the end of the year both parties were exhausted and ready to discuss terms such as might lead to a permanent settlement. If by the Treaty of Louviers Richard lost the Norman Vexin, at least Philip's other conquests east of the Seine were restored to him,[1] and he retained the much contested lordships of Issoudun and Graçay in Berri.

The peace, however, provided only a short respite. Already in the middle of April 1196 Richard regarded a fresh outbreak of war as imminent, and was requesting Hubert Walter to send more men and money to Normandy. He was also busy strengthening his strongholds and was beginning to crown the rock of Andeli with the most famous castle of the middle ages. Unfortunately Andeli did not belong to him; it was a manor of the archbishop of Rouen, who violently resisted Richard's action, laid Normandy under interdict, appealed to Rome, and was only ultimately appeased by a very advantageous exchange of lands which brought him in a net annual revenue of £1,405.[2] Nevertheless, from Richard's point of view, the bargain was probably a good one, for Château Gaillard, his 'beautiful castle of the rock' (*Bellum Castellum de Rupe*) strategically was magnificently placed in a commanding position on a bend of the river Seine. No better starting-point for the recovery of the Norman Vexin could have been chosen. It was built under Richard's personal supervision with all the ingenuity that his own practical experience in warfare and the engineering science of the day could devise. It became Richard's headquarters and his favourite residence during the remainder of his life. It was, however, a condition of the Treaty of Louviers that Andeli should not be fortified; the building of Château Gaillard, therefore, afforded a pretext, if one were needed, for the reopening of hostilities. The desultory warfare, which began with the siege and capture of Aumale by Philip in June 1198 and lasted with brief intervals till a few weeks before Richard's death, need not detain us. It went on the whole in favour of Richard, who reoccupied a large part of the Vexin.

In this his last war he was able to devote his attention entirely to the Norman problem, for by successful diplomacy he managed

---

[1] For the frontier now agreed upon see the map at the end of Powicke's *Loss of Normandy*.

[2] Powicke, op. cit., p. 174.

to secure his boundaries by a chain of friendly and allied powers. His frontier on the Pyrenees was protected by his brother-in-law, Sancho, king of Navarre; by the marriage of his sister Joan with Raymond VI in 1196 he converted the generally hostile county of Toulouse into a friendly neighbour. It was about this time also that his plan, inaugurated in 1194, of establishing a confederacy of princes in Germany and the Low Countries began to mature.[1] The fall from power of his brother-in-law, Henry the Lion, had resulted in a greater intimacy between England and the house of Welf, for this prince had spent the years of his exile from Germany (1182-5 and again in 1189) at the English court. He was now dead (1195), but his sons, who had been brought up in England, maintained close relations with Richard after their entry into public life and they had become men of consequence.[2] Henry, the eldest, had married the daughter and heiress of Conrad, count palatine of the Rhine, and himself became count palatine in 1195; a year later Otto, the second son, was made count of Poitou, and during the next two years was often in the camp of his uncle Richard or engaged in Poitevin affairs. In 1197 the counts of Flanders and Boulogne, both of whom had made treaties in 1196 with Philip of France, transferred their allegiance to Richard. Baldwin, who inherited Flanders on his mother's death in 1194 and Hainault on his father's a year later, was driven in the interests of his country to change his policy. The prosperity of the Flemish towns was being crippled by the economic pressure increasingly exerted by England during the years of hostility. Merchants had their goods confiscated and some were themselves imprisoned; an embargo was laid on the export of wool and heavy amercements were imposed on those who ventured to send grain and other commodities to Flanders. These counts not only protected Normandy from attack from the north, but also waged a harassing war with Philip in Artois.[3] In 1198, after prolonged negotiations, the duke of Brabant, and perhaps at the same time his neighbour, the duke of Limburg, were brought into the coalition.

---

[1] Above, p. 367.

[2] See A. L. Poole, 'Die Welfen in der Verbannung' in *Deutsches Archiv für Geschichte des Mittelalters*, ii (1938), 129-48. The third son, William of Winchester, as he was called (being born in that city in 1184), the ancestor of the future house of Brunswick, was also brought up in England.

[3] In these operations English troops appear to have taken part, for 280 sergeants were sent to Flanders in this year (1197). *Pipe Roll 9 Ric. I*, p. 164.

The former was rewarded by the grant of the valuable honor of Eye, to which his wife had an hereditary claim, and on suitable occasions would add *dominus honoris Eye* to his other dignified titles.[1] Even the north Italian magnate and future leader of the fourth crusade, Boniface of Montferrat, was receiving in this year a subsidy from the Norman exchequer. The final triumph of English diplomacy was reached when, on the death of Henry VI, Richard at the request of the German princes sent representatives to the electoral meeting and prevailed on the electors to choose his nephew Otto as king of the Romans and future emperor (June 1198). The only gap in this network of defensive alliances was the little county of Ponthieu round the mouth of the Somme; for its count had married Philip's sister, Alice, who had long been in English keeping, offered in marriage first to Richard and then to his brother John. But in the spring of 1197 Richard made a raid on the district, burnt the town of St. Valéry, and destroyed the shipping in the port, as a warning no doubt, of what might happen if hostile activities broke out in that quarter.

Richard's last fight with Philip Augustus was worthy of his career. When a truce conveniently arranged 'till the corn crops had been safely harvested' had expired, he with Mercadier and his Brabançons cut off the French near Vernon and drove the remnant across the Epte; he then, carrying the war into the enemy's country, captured the castle of Courcelles and intercepted Philip's army marching to its relief. In the rout that followed 'such was the crush at the gate of Gisors that the bridge broke under them, and the king of France himself, as we have heard, drank of the river, and other knights to the number of twenty were drowned. Thus we have defeated the king of France at Gisors,' Richard simply concludes his account of the battle in a letter to the bishop of Durham, 'but it is not we who have done it, but God and our right through us'[2] (September 1198).

The church now intervened in the interests of peace. The cardinal legate, Peter of Capua, had already negotiated the terms of a five years' truce to which the two kings finally agreed when they met on the Seine between Vernon and Andeli, Philip

---

[1] He styles himself in a charter 'Henricus dei gracia dux Lotharingie marchio Romani imperii et dominus honoris Eye'. Cf. *Pipe Roll 10 Ric. I,* p. xvii, and Poole, *Studies . . . presented to F. M. Powicke,* p. 95.

[2] Hoveden, iv. 58.

on horseback on the bank, Richard in a boat, on 13 January 1199. Each was to hold what he actually occupied at the moment when the peace was concluded.

The fighting in which Richard lost his life had nothing to do with the Norman wars. It was while besieging the castle of Châlus to punish a baron of the Limousin in a trivial dispute over treasure-trove that an arrow struck him in the shoulder. The wound proved fatal and he died on 6 April 1199.

The death of Richard was followed by a disputed succession. Although England and Normandy accepted John who had been designated by his brother as heir to the whole of his dominions, the barons of Aquitaine rendered their homage to Eleanor, the queen-mother,[1] while those of Anjou, Maine, and Touraine, in accordance with the custom of the country, swore allegiance to Arthur of Brittany, Richard's nephew. In adopting this policy they were actuated by no particular partiality to one side or the other; but they realized that their independence was more likely to be assured if they took as their lord a powerless boy (Arthur was no more than twelve years old) rather than a grown man, potentially dangerous, who was also king of England. Within a few weeks, chiefly through the agency of William des Roches, a powerful baron now made seneschal of Anjou and Maine, Arthur was recognized in Angers, Le Mans, and Tours. John acted at this critical time with remarkable decision and promptitude; having secured the royal treasure which was at Chinon, he went to Rouen where he was invested with the duchy of Normandy (25 April) and then to England where he was crowned at Westminster on Ascension Day (27 May). When, however, he returned to the Continent towards the end of June he found matters had changed for the worse. Constance of Brittany, acting in the interests of her son, had been prevailed upon to make common cause with the king of France, who received the homage of Arthur for all the Angevin lands and put garrisons of his own into the castles and towns which had acknowledged Arthur as their lord; and he sent the boy himself off to Paris for safe custody. Philip was playing the game at which he was so expert, of pitting one member of the family of Anjou against another. Neither party, however, was anxious to prolong the struggle. The country was impoverished by the

---

[1] Eleanor subsequently delivered the duchy to her son, retaining, however, a life-interest. *Rot. Chart.* 30b and *Foedera*, i. 77.

long wars, by the burning of towns, and the ruthless destruction practised by both armies, and especially by the mercenary troops employed by the English. Although John had renewed the old alliance with the count of Flanders in August, he did not, like Richard, inspire confidence as a leader. Baldwin showed little enthusiasm for his cause, and made his peace with Philip at Peronne a few months later (2 January 1200). John had also put himself in the wrong by taking up his Norman inheritance without the licence of his overlord, the king of France, who made the most of the legal standpoint. Philip, too, had his difficulties. William des Roches deserted him and got Arthur out of his hands. The matter of the divorce of Ingeborg had reached an acute stage, and France was placed under interdict (January 1200). So in the intervals of war there were truces and conferences which at last on 22 May resulted in a settlement at Le Goulet on the Seine below Vernon. The peace followed the lines of the treaty made at Louviers in 1196, but the frontier was modified in the interests of Philip. Besides the Norman Vexin (except Andeli with Château Gaillard which remained an English enclave in French territory) he gained the county of Evreux which he had occupied immediately after Richard's death. The long-disputed lordships of Issoudun and Graçay in Berri were to pass as dowry with John's niece, Blanche of Castile, who, it was agreed, should marry Louis, Philip's son and heir. In return for these concessions and an enormous relief of 20,000 marks, John was recognized as Richard's heir and did homage for all the French possessions. The feudal relationships which became increasingly important as the struggle went on were also clarified: Anjou and Brittany were assigned to him by the judgment of Philip's court, and Arthur was to hold Brittany, with certain safeguards, as John's vassal.

Among the turbulent barons of Aquitaine, perhaps none had given more unceasing trouble to their Plantagenet overlords than the counts of Angoulême. Besides the Angoumois, they laid claim against the powerful house of Lusignan to the county of La Marche. The importance of these lordships to the king of England became greatly enhanced when by the treaty of Le Goulet Berri was transferred to the king of France, for they provided his only access to Gascony. On Richard I's death Audemar, count of Angoulême, had allied himself with Philip, while Queen Eleanor, who had charge of John's interests in that

region, supported the Lusignan claim to La Marche. Shortly
after, however, by a sudden volte-face, the rivals were reconciled, and a marriage was arranged with Hugh the Brown of
Lusignan, and Isabel, the daughter and heiress of the count of
Angoulême, a girl fourteen years old. Such a union of the rival
houses was seriously menacing, and it was a triumph of Angevin
diplomacy when John succeeded in detaching the versatile
Audemar and bringing him over to his side. Whether it was
passion or policy that dictated the next move it is hard to say.
In 1199 John had been released from his childless marriage with
Isabel of Gloucester, and was in fact in the process of arranging
a new one with a Portuguese princess when the negotiations
were abruptly cut off, and he married, with her father's consent,
Isabel of Angoulême, the affianced bride of Hugh the Brown, on
30 August 1200.[1] It was a bold stroke, which secured to him a
valuable ally and the succession to the counties of La Marche
and Angoulême; and had he dealt more tactfully with the
injured parties by giving them proper compensation, it might
have proved successful. As it was, his arbitrary actions led to the
fatal quarrel which was his ultimate undoing. The house of
Lusignan was not one to be lightly played with; it had many
ramifications (among them Hugh's brother Ralph was count of
Eu in Normandy) and the disorders became correspondingly
widespread.

Philip Augustus must early have realized the immense capital
value to be made out of the dispute. But he bided his time, and
even entertained John at Paris with sumptuous splendour when,
after a stay of some months in England, he again revisited
France in the summer of 1201. By the autumn the moment for
his intervention had come. John had still further exasperated
the rebellious barons of Poitou; he had seized their lands,
charged them with treason, and proposed to settle the matter
by trial of battle, using himself professional champions. They
naturally refused to meet these gladiators, demanded to be tried
by their peers, and appealed to the king of France as their
supreme lord. In the following spring John was summoned to
appear before Philip's court at Paris on the complaints of the
Lusignans; he failed to answer the summons, was adjudged

---

[1] F. A. Cazel, jun., and S. Painter (*Eng. Hist. Rev.* lxiii (1948), 83-9) have shown
that H. G. Richardson's ingenious reconstruction of the generally accepted story
(ibid. lxi (1946), 289-314) conflicts with the available evidence.

contumacious, and sentenced to the loss of his French lands. Philip, in feudal terms, 'defied' his vassal as a traitor, and proceeded at once to carry out his judgment by force (30 April 1202).[1]

John was not well circumstanced for the reopening of the war. He had been at little pains to foster the cause of his nephew Otto and his other German allies. Although in May he issued a summons to the knights of Flanders, Hainault, and Brabant, and in fact many Flemish knights were in English pay and fought for John in the Norman campaigns, the close friendship between the two countries tended to cool after the departure of Count Baldwin on the crusade in 1202.[2] But between Flanders and Normandy was the territory of Boulogne, whose count, Renaud of Dammartin, a brilliant and indefatigable fighter, deserted in 1202 to Philip Augustus and took a prominent part in the fighting during the closing phase of the conquest of the duchy. Moreover, John was engaged on two fronts: it was not only Normandy, but the great English possessions in the south of France, the turbulent duchy of Aquitaine, that he had to defend. This gave an importance to the Peninsula. There too the position had sadly deteriorated. His two brothers-in-law, Raymond VI, count of Toulouse, and Alfonso IX, king of Castile, had at least temporarily seceded from the Angevin alliance, and the treaty which John in 1202 concluded with the king of Navarre scarcely compensated for these defections.[3]

In the spring of 1202, when hostilities began, Philip had no thought of annexing the whole of the Angevin dominions. Normandy alone he proposed to absorb into the royal demesne; he planned to replace John in the remaining provinces by Arthur of Brittany who in July was duly invested with Brittany, Anjou, Maine, Touraine, and Poitou. Then by a brilliant stroke John captured his supplanter. It happened at Mirabeau, a castle some miles to the north of Poitiers, where Arthur with the Lusignans was besieging Queen Eleanor in an attempt to conquer Poitou. John in one of those fits of violent energy of which he was sometimes capable, with almost incredible speed—he

---

[1] The clearest summary of the difficult and controversial question is that of Ch. Petit-Dutaillis in *L'Essor des États d'Occident* (*Histoire Générale*, ed. Glotz, iv, part 2, 1937), pp. 139 ff.

[2] In 1206 Philip of Namur, the regent in Flanders, concluded a treaty with Philip Augustus and was betrothed to his daughter. Cf. Gaston Dept, *Les Influences anglaise et française dans le comté de Flandre*, p. 48.

[3] The treaty was directed against Castile and Aragon. *Foedera*, i. 86.

covered the ground between Le Mans and Mirabeau, a distance
of well over eighty miles, in forty-eight hours—descended on
the castle, relieved it, and killed or captured the besiegers
(1 August). Arthur himself, Geoffrey of Lusignan and his
nephew Hugh the Brown, and 'all our Poitevin enemies' were
among the 200 and more captives who were led away, heavily
fettered, in carts destined for prisons in England and Normandy.[1]
This great success, the last on French soil before the triumphs
of Edward III, had it been used wisely might have postponed
the disruption of the Angevin empire for some years. Its immediate result was indeed most promising: Philip, who had broken
down the frontier defences of Normandy on the north-east from
Eu near the coast to Gournai on the river Epte, withdrew from
Arques which he was then besieging.[2] But by the cruel treatment meted out to his prisoners John aroused indignation
everywhere, and he lost any advantage which his victory had
given him. The Lusignans were soon ransomed, but twenty-two
of the captives imprisoned at Corfe castle are said by a usually
well-informed authority[3] to have died of starvation, and Arthur's
sister Eleanor was incarcerated for forty years in the castle of
Bristol.[4] The fate of Arthur himself remains a mystery. When or
how he died no man knew with certainty. That a crime had
been committed was soon suspected; but the secret was well
guarded, and it was only slowly that the truth leaked out. He
was thrown into prison at Falaise and afterwards moved to
Rouen, where, according to the best-authenticated story, on
3 April 1203 John, drunk and in one of his paroxysms of ungovernable rage, did him to death with his own hand and threw
the corpse into the Seine. It was once thought that in consequence of the murder John was again summoned to stand his
trial before the court of the king of France, and was sentenced
this time not only to the loss of his French fiefs, but of his kingdom as well. The weight of evidence, however, is opposed to
this view. The story of the second trial and condemnation was

[1] See John's account of the victory in a letter addressed to his barons preserved
in Coggeshall, pp. 137-8.

[2] On 21 July John had ordered the barons of the Cinque Ports to intercept
supplies destined for the French army at Arques (Rot. Lit. Pat., p. 15): shortage of
provisions may have expedited the retirement.

[3] Ann. of Margan (Ann. Monast. i. 26). As a concession to some prisoners 'ring-
chains' were substituted for 'fetters'. Rot. Lit. Pat., p. 17b.

[4] She was, however, liberally provided with clothes, and received 1 mark a day
for maintenance. Pipe Roll 6 Jo., pp. 92, 213, 219. She died in prison in 1241.

apparently trumped up in 1216, when Philip's son Louis invaded England, in order to justify his action before the world.[1] None the less, whether or no there was a trial and condemnation, the results were serious enough. Dissatisfaction spread rapidly among the baronage. With the desertion of William des Roches, the seneschal of Anjou and Touraine, resistance in the valley of the Loire soon collapsed. The garrison in the citadel at Tours held out till 1204, while Chinon under Hubert de Burgh and Loches under the mercenary captain Gerard of Athée managed to survive for another year; but these were isolated strongholds standing in occupied country. They could not become the starting points for the recovery of the lost ground.

The revolt of the Bretons in consequence of the imprisonment and suspected murder of their duke, Arthur, and the defection of the barons of Maine (Le Mans fell in the spring of 1203) widened the gap which severed Normandy from the still loyal Poitou; and Normandy was the prize which the king of France chiefly coveted. With his government at Paris, the control of the Seine and the northern seaboard were obviously of primary importance. But the conquest of Normandy presented a far more difficult problem than the conquest of the provinces around the Loire. Its sentiment was in favour of England; for a century and a half both countries had been ruled by the house of Rollo; many of the barons and churches of Normandy were great property-owners also in England; the towns and merchants of Normandy were bound to England by mutual commercial interests and privileges. Moreover, it was in a far better position to withstand attack. Its resources in men and money were considerable, and they could be easily reinforced from across the Channel; it was protected by a network of castles and defensive posts of which Château Gaillard was the last to be constructed and the strongest. In these circumstances, with good leadership and energy, it should have been possible to save it. Unfortunately John failed to display these qualities. He moved listlessly from place to place without plan or purpose. Once, in September, he made a raid into Brittany which intensified rather than suppressed the rebellious spirit of the Bretons. He

[1] Philip probably first heard the details from William de Braose, an eyewitness, who came to the French court as an exile in 1210. Powicke, op. cit., pp. 453 ff., and *Camb. Med. Hist.* vi. 315 and note. For the whole question cf. Petit–Dutaillis, *Le Déshéritement de Jean sans terre et le meurtre d'Arthur de Bretagne* (1925), and the same author's *L'Essor des États d'Occident*, pp. 142 f.

solicited the intervention of Innocent III; but Philip in the full flush of success merely retorted that feudal disputes were no business of the Holy See. Even before John's unaccountable retreat to England in December 1203 eastern Normandy had largely passed out of his control. As we have seen, Philip had forced the frontier posts on the north-east; he had driven wedges deep into other parts of the duchy. Alençon in the south and Vaudreuil, which guarded the river approach to Rouen, had been surrendered by treacherous castellans;[1] and the greater part of the country between the Eure and the Risle was also in his hands. Château Gaillard alone offered serious resistance. For six months, from September 1203 until March 1204, bravely defended by Roger de Lacy, the constable of Chester,[2] it held up the French advance. It fell on 8 March. There is a touch of irony in the fact that on the very day of its capitulation John was giving orders for his horses and hounds and falcons to be dispatched to Normandy in preparation for his coming. Once the great bastion on the Seine had fallen the progress of Philip Augustus was swift and sure. The Norman barons had no heart in fighting for a king who himself made so little effort to defend his dominions. They preferred to make bargains with the conqueror. So Falaise, Caen, Bayeux, Cherbourg, and Barfleur in turn capitulated without striking a blow; and while Philip pressed forward from the east, the Bretons attacked from the west, capturing as they advanced Mont St. Michel and Avranches. There was no need to invest Rouen, now completely cut off; Normandy was already lost before the capital (with the two fortresses Arques on the north and Verneuil on the south which were still in English hands) came to terms with the conqueror on Midsummer Day, 1204. The Channel Islands were all that were left of the Norman duchy in English hands.

[1] The surrender of Alençon by Robert, count of Séez, so infuriated the king that he recalls it in dating charters of this year: 'apud Beccum xx die Aprilis anno regni nostri quarto, quo comes Robertus Sagiensis fecit nobis proditionem apud Alenconem'. Round, *Cal. of Docs. France*, no. 391, p. 131.

[2] It is noteworthy that John recognized the loyal service of Roger de Lacy by contributing £1,000 to the heavy ransom which Philip Augustus demanded for him. *Pipe Roll 5 Jo.*, p. 214.

XII

JUSTICE AND FINANCE

IT has been rightly said[1] that in the last years of the twelfth century law becomes articulate. For certain legal purposes in the middle ages 3 September 1189, the date of the coronation of Richard I, was taken as the limit of legal memory. So by the statute of *Quo Warranto* of 1290 Edward I agreed that those who could prove that they had enjoyed their franchises continuously since that date had a prescriptive right to them. A few years earlier we have the first reasoned account of legal procedure in the treatise *De Legibus et Consuetudinibus Regni Angliae* attributed to Henry II's justiciar Rannulf Glanvill. A few years later, from 1194 to be more precise, we have legal records, plea rolls, notes taken down by clerks who were themselves present in the king's court.[2] In the early years of the thirteenth century these records become abundant. It will therefore be convenient at the point we have now reached, the year 1204, the year in which Normandy ceased to be a possession of the English Crown, to review the developments in the sphere of law which have set a significant and enduring mark on the judicial system of future centuries.

The Norman and early Angevin kings were not what we should call great legislators. They brought no code of law with them, and they did not, like their Anglo-Saxon predecessors, like Alfred, Edgar, or Canute, issue any. In the century and a half which elapsed between the Conquest and the concession of Magna Carta there are few legislative acts. Henry I made 'new statutes' concerning the coinage and theft,[3] and he modified the law relating to wreck. But this does not amount to very much. A hostile critic accused Henry II of being an innovator, abolishing old laws, and year by year introducing new laws which he called assizes.[4] Yet the Constitutions of Clarendon,

---

[1] Maitland, *Collected Papers*, i. 481.

[2] There is evidence that plea rolls were kept as early as the twenty-seventh year of Henry II (1181). See Maitland, *Select Pleas of the Crown* (Selden Soc., vol. i), p. xxvi, and *Curia Regis Rolls*, v. 76. But they have not survived.

[3] See the writ printed by Raine in *Historians of the Church of York* (Rolls Series), iii. 22.

[4] Ralph Niger, ed. Anstruther (Caxton Soc.), p. 168.

perhaps the most comprehensive act of Henry II, claimed to be no more than a record of the custom of his grandfather's time. The Norman kings professed to rule by the law of Edward the Confessor with some additions of their own. Private lawyers in the early years of the twelfth century compiled law-books which purported to be these laws or what they thought were these laws. The fullest and most interesting of these collections is the *Leges Henrici Primi*, so called because it opens with the charter of liberties issued by Henry I at his coronation. It is a rambling book, often obscure in language and meaning; it is a strange jumble of Anglo-Saxon dooms and the customary law of the time, supplemented by fragments collected from continental sources. Yet it is a serious attempt to establish what actually was the law in the first years of the twelfth century. The Normans were anxious not to emphasize the break with the past, and when they introduced some obvious innovation, such as trial by battle, they were careful not to enforce its use upon the conquered race. They retained the local system of administration through the hundred and shire; and Henry I issued an instruction requiring attendance at these courts at the same times and places as in the days of King Edward. The rivalry of seignorial jurisdictions, however, sapped the strength of these communal courts. Exemptions were freely granted from attendance at the hundred and in some cases from the shire also. Many hundreds were falling into the hands of ecclesiastical corporations and of private landlords.

Yet, notwithstanding the apparent lack of what may be properly called legislation, no period of English history has witnessed more far-reaching changes or marked a more steady growth in the sphere of administration of justice than the twelfth century. Even the most superficial comparison between the *Leges Henrici Primi* and Glanvill's treatise will reveal that nothing short of a revolution has taken place in the course of the century. The former describes a system essentially archaic, a system based on a fixed tariff of monetary payments as compensation for crime, on *weres* and *wites*; the latter is concerned wholly with the new procedure brought into being in the twelfth century based on writs and juries. This great change was due to the remarkable administrative capacity of Henry I and Henry II whose combined reigns occupied seventy years of the century, and it was achieved not by formal enactments, but by instructions given by these kings in writing or even by word of mouth to their ministers and judges. The king could offer his subjects a more rational method of settling their disputes than could be had by the ancient modes of trial by ordeal, compurgation, or battle; he could offer the jury, the sworn inquest of neighbours. The jury was a royal prerogative; the lord could not employ it in his private feudal court. By providing this better remedy, which he made readily accessible by sending his judges into the provinces, the king was able to tempt suitors, even though they had to pay a heavy price for the privilege, to bring their cases into the royal courts. The system of original writs provided the king with the opportunity to intervene in the cause of justice. A man, who claimed that he had failed to get justice from his lord, could obtain a writ from the king requiring his lord or the sheriff 'to do right' or he, the king, would do it for him. In consequence a mass of litigation which would have previously been dealt with in the local or feudal courts was now flowing into the royal courts. The judicial business of the country was becoming centralized in these courts where slowly but surely was being evolved a common law for the whole land.

The chief agent of the Crown in local government was the sheriff. After the Norman Conquest the earl, *comes*, had lost his administrative duties in the county and given place to his deputy, the *vicecomes*, who combined the functions of the Anglo-Saxon sheriff with those of the Norman *vicomte*. He was at the head of the fiscal, judicial, administrative, and military organization of the shire. He was responsible for the revenues due from the shire, for which he accounted twice a year at Easter and Michaelmas at the exchequer; to him were the king's writs addressed, and it was his duty to execute the king's instructions; he mobilized and commanded the local militia; he normally presided over the shire court.[1] At first these officials were almost invariably drawn from the ranks of the baronage; they were powerful territorial magnates with substantial local interests in the districts under their control. That they were often rapacious and oppressive was possibly of little concern to the king; but

---

[1] Under the Norman kings and even in the early years of Henry II we sometimes hear of a local royal justiciar for the shire who might or might not be the same person as the sheriff. A writ of Stephen (1153–4), for example, grants the king's justice in Lincoln and Lincolnshire to Bishop Robert Chesney as his predecessors had had it in the time of Henry I. *Registrum Antiquissimum* (Lincoln Record Soc.), i. 63 (no. 103). Cf. *Camb. Med. Hist.* v. 584.

that their interests were not always identical with those of the Crown, that they were unreliable, and even sometimes joined in rebellions were serious matters. It became expedient not only to restrict the powers of the sheriffs but also to select them from a less influential class of society. An important feature of Henry I's policy was the training of a ministerial class formed of men not necessarily 'of ignoble stock and raised, so to speak, from the dust', as the Anglo-Norman chronicler, Ordericus Vitalis, contemptuously puts it, but of relatively humble origin, who rose to influential positions by reason of their own abilities. Geoffrey de Clinton (Glympton, Oxon) and Ralph Basset, founders of famous families, who were sheriffs and held high places in the government of Henry I, or Hugh of Buckland, sheriff of no less than eight counties in the early years of the twelfth century, are typical examples of the new kind of official. These *novi homines*, these professional administrators, trained in the exchequer or the royal household, were more dependable and more closely in touch with the central government than the barons. They could be transferred from one county to another to prevent them gaining too much local influence; they could more easily be dismissed. It was only in times of political weakness that there was a reversion to baronial control in the shires. In the reign of Stephen the barons ruled in the provinces almost unrestrained, and even Henry II before he had fully established his authority to some extent was obliged to employ them. In his later years, however, local government was almost entirely in the hands of the official class.

The office of sheriff was evidently a lucrative one. Men were prepared to pay a high price to be appointed. Robert d'Oilli gave 400 marks for the shrievalty of Oxford in 1130, and in the time of Richard and John still larger sums were offered; William de Stuteville agreed to pay £1,000 for the county of York in 1201.[1] Obviously they expected to recoup themselves with interest at the expense of the local inhabitants. Besides the relatively small customary payment levied on the county and known as the sheriff's aid (*auxilium vicecomitis*), there were many other sources of profit both legitimate and illegitimate. The office provided tempting opportunities for peculation and extortion. Complaints about the misconduct of sheriffs were frequent during this period. Stephen in his second charter of liberties

---

[1] *Pipe Roll 31 Hen. I*, p. 2; *3 Jo.*, p. 158.

promised wholly to extirpate their exactions and injustices. In 1170, when Henry II had been absent from England for four years and the sheriffs had been left to do more or less what they pleased, the outcry against them was louder than ever. The king took swift and drastic action. He reached England in March; in April, in the middle of the financial year, he held a council at London where he suspended all sheriffs and instituted an exhaustive inquiry into their conduct. This inquiry, known as the Inquest of Sheriffs,[1] was not in fact confined to the royal officials. The commissioners were also required to take to task all landowners, lay and ecclesiastical, and their stewards, and all who held in custody any bishopric, abbey, or escheat. They were to discover what moneys had actually been received with or without authority since the king's departure from England in 1166; whether bribes had been given or taken to conceal favouritism or peculation; the precise value of the chattels of convicted felons; the sums contributed to the aid for the marriage of the king's daughter in 1168; the profits or abuses of the forest administration; whether the royal demesne was properly maintained and stocked. A few fragments of the answers to this comprehensive investigation have survived.[2] One of them, which refers to the city of Worcester, illustrates the kind of grievances felt by the public. The burgesses reported, for instance, that the sheriff, William de Beauchamp (he was one of those who were dismissed from office), had no less than a hundred properties held by burgage tenure on which he paid neither rates nor taxes; that the reeve of Gloucester took unauthorized customs from their ships plying to Bristol and Ireland; and that they were compelled to furnish a guard at Worcester castle which was not done in the time of Henry I and which cost them £24. 6s. 8d. The majority of the old sheriffs (among them the future justiciar, Rannulf Glanvill, who had been sheriff of York since 1164) were dismissed and replaced by men who were already employed at the exchequer. Henceforward Henry II

[1] Gervase of Canterbury, i. 217 ff.

[2] Those printed in the *Red Book of the Exchequer*, ii, pp. cclxvii–cclxxxi, were identified by Round (*Commune of London*, pp. 125 ff.) as returns to this inquest. A further fragment, from which the example used in the text is taken, was printed by J. Tait in *Eng. Hist. Rev.* xxxix (1924), 80–3. One other return has been discovered and printed by H. Suggett in the *Bulletin of the John Rylands Library*, xxvii (1942), 179. A particular interest attaches to this, as it is written in Anglo-Norman and appears to be the earliest surviving French document either in this country or on the Continent.

followed his grandfather's policy of using professional administrators rather than influential magnates as his agents in local
government.

While the reforms of Henry II increased the work, especially
the routine work, of the sheriff, they at the same time diminished
his power of independent action. The exchequer, as it became
more highly organized, kept a closer watch over his accounting;
the visitations of itinerant justices curtailed his judicial authority.
Nevertheless political disturbances might still afford him opportunities to assert his independence. Such a situation arose in
consequence of Richard I's prolonged absence abroad, his
brother John's rebellion, and the stormy government of William
Longchamp. In 1194 Hubert Walter, a brilliant administrator
trained in the tradition of Henry II's reform, became justiciar
and restored order. Among the instructions, the 'articles of the
eyre', which he issued to the justices who visited the counties in
the autumn of this year, were included two restrictions on the
sheriff's power. By one of these he was forbidden to act as
justice in his own county or indeed in any county where he had
held office since the beginning of the reign. The practice of
sending sheriffs on circuit was common. No fewer than eight of
the eighteen itinerant justices appointed at Northampton in
1176 were sheriffs of counties they visited. With their strong
local interests, however, they were unlikely to be unbiased. The
prohibition was a wise one, and was afterwards repeated in a
chapter of the Great Charter.[1] By the other three knights and
one clerk were appointed to keep the pleas of the Crown.
This order makes general for the whole country what certainly was in being in some parts many years before[2] and it
imposes the duty on the already heavily burdened class of

[1] c. 24, and no. 21 of the articles of the eyre of 1194 in Hoveden, iii. 264. Despite
this prohibition we find Reginald of Cornhill acting as a justice in Kent of which
county he was sheriff in 1206 and 1207. See *Pipe Roll 9 Jo.*, pp. 30, 35.

[2] Art. 20. Gross in his edition of *Select Coroners' Rolls* (Selden Soc., vol. 9) maintained against the prevailing opinion that the office of coroner was in existence at
least as early as the reign of Henry II. The correctness of this view is proved by a
letter addressed to Benedict, abbot of Peterborough, by William Basset, who was
sheriff of Lincolnshire from 1175 to 1185, contained in Henry of Pytchley's *Liber
Cartarum*, fol. x(*a*), and also in Robert of Swaffham's *Register*, fol. cxvi (*d*), both in the
possession of the Dean and Chapter of Peterborough (for a description of these
manuscripts see W. T. Mellows's edition of Henry of Pytchley's *Book of Fees*
(Northants. Rec. Soc., vol. ii), pp. xxvii, xxviii). This letter recites a writ of the
justices Thomas Fitz Bernard, Alan de Furnell, and Robert de Witefeld requiring
the attendance of Philip de Kyme *et custodes placitorum Corone* at a perambulation of

knights. These officials, soon to be known as coroners, were elected in the county court and took over certain duties for which the sheriff or his subordinates had previously been responsible. Their primary function then as now was to hold inquests on the bodies of those who died suddenly, accidentally, or by foul play. They acted with a jury usually composed of representatives of the four neighbouring townships, and collected and recorded on rolls the evidence while it was still fresh. This evidence was subsequently produced at the trial before the justices in eyre. The coroners also looked after the king's interests in certain other matters: they valued the chattels of a man suspected of murder; in a case of death by misadventure, if a man was killed by a fall from a horse or was drowned from a boat, they must set a price on the horse or the boat. This sum was devoted to charity, it is a gift to God, a *deodand*. They also took charge on the king's behalf of wreck and treasure trove.

Besides the sheriff and the coroners, a subordinate official, the sergeant, sometimes called the king's, sometimes the sheriff's, sergeant, sometimes the sergeant of the hundred, plays an important part in the routine business of local justice. He is identical with the bailiff of the hundred who is also mentioned in official documents of this period. He was employed in issuing summonses, in making arrests, in 'attaching' suspected persons by pledges to appear in court. If a man was assaulted or imprisoned, or if there was a village brawl, the sergeant would be called in. He had duties (of which he was probably relieved when coroners were instituted) in connexion with the presentment of suspected criminals, for we find him not infrequently amerced for concealing a plea of the Crown. In the districts where the system of frankpledge was not in force, that is to say, on the Welsh border, in Lancashire, and in the northern counties, the sergeants, here called sergeants of the peace, assume a more prominent and responsible role than elsewhere.[1]

boundaries of land at Fiskerton. The date must be 1182–3 when the judges named acted together and visited ten counties including Lincolnshire. Cf. *Pipe Roll 29 Hen. II*, p. 67 *et passim*. There is evidence to show that the office of coroner was already in existence in Normandy in 1171. See Powicke, *Eng. Hist. Rev.* xxv (1910), 710–11, and Haskins, ibid. xxvi (1911), 326–8.

[1] R. Stewart-Brown has made a careful study of the functions of the sergeants in these districts, *Sergeants of the Peace in Medieval England and Wales* (Manchester, 1936). He distinguishes them sharply from the hundred sergeants of other parts of England. It seems, however, that there is no essential difference in the two classes of officials. The independent position of the remote and border counties and the

Generally speaking the work of the twelfth-century sergeant of the hundred seems to have been somewhat similar to that of the later chief constable who, according to the writ enforcing watch and ward in 1242, were to do 'those things which pertain to the preservation of the peace'.[1]

The king at his coronation promised to keep good peace among his people and to repress wrongdoing. The maintenance of the peace is then a primary function of royalty. In an early age the king took upon himself a responsibility with regard to crime. A crime, at least a major crime, became a plea of the Crown; it ceased to be merely a personal matter affecting individuals. A list of these pleas has been preserved from the early years of the twelfth century.[2] A man, the formula runs, 'wickedly and in the king's peace' committed an assault, a murder, a robbery ('nequiter et in pace domini Regis'). The magic of these words brought before the king's justices even trivial offences such as blows and brawling and petty larceny, matters 'of the sheriff's peace' which should properly be heard in the county court.[3] The maintenance of the peace, however, without a professional police force was far from easy.[4] The want of such a force is strikingly evident in the twelfth century. The volume of crime is enormous. The plea rolls tell the story of a society where crime was frequent and brutal, much more frequent in proportion to the size of the population than it is today. The justices who visited Lincoln in 1202 had to deal with some 114 cases of homicide, 89 of robbery (generally with violence), 65 of wounding, 49 of rape, besides a number of less serious crimes.[5]

The criminal law has its roots in Anglo-Saxon England, but one innovation was introduced soon after the Conquest, the murder fine, the *murdrum*. This, according to the author of the

absence of the frankpledge and tithing organization sufficiently accounts for the additional burdens and responsibilities imposed on them.

[1] *Close Rolls 1237–42*, p. 482. A plan for instituting constables and chief constables to take over the military and police duties of the counties, hundreds and boroughs was drafted during the critical year 1205 when there was fear of invasion. See below, p. 439.   [2] *Leges Henrici*, 10. 1. Liebermann, *Gesetze*, i. 556.

[3] Glanvill, i. 2. Cf. the cases discussed in the introduction to *The Lincolnshire Assize Rolls 1202–1209* (Lincoln Record Soc., vol. 22), pp. l–li.

[4] An attempt to establish such a force is indicated in the payment charged against the county farm of Staffordshire in 1206 and 1207 for ten foot sergeants to guard the county against malefactors. *Pipe Roll 8 Jo.*, p. 112 and *9 Jo.*, p. 7.

[5] See the analysis of the criminal pleas of the Lincolnshire Assize by I. L. Langbein in *Columbia Law Rev.* xxxiii (1933), 1337.

Dialogue of the Exchequer,[1] was instituted by William I in order to protect the lives of his fellow countrymen newly settled in a strange land who were frequently attacked in lonely places by the natives. It was payable, if a murder had been committed and the murderer could not be produced, by the hundred, and it was assumed that the slain was a Norman unless his English nationality, his 'Englishry', could be proved by the testimony of his kinsmen.[2] There was no standard rate of payment for murders. The crushing figure of 46 marks (40 to the king and 6 to the relatives) mentioned in the earliest texts, seems never to have been exacted. In 1130, 10 to 20 marks was usual;[3] in 1175, 2, 3, or 4;[4] in the Lincoln record, already referred to, the sum varies from £10 to a mark. These are not great sums; but as the great franchises of privileged churches, abbeys, or barons were exempted from contribution, the burden tended to fall on those who were least able to pay. In the aggregate these fines produced a not insignificant revenue, and it seems probable that it was for what they brought in to the exchequer that they were retained long after the purpose for which they had been instituted had ceased to exist. It can only have been the temptation of financial gain that led to a wholly unjustifiable abuse of the system. It became the practice in some parts of the country to take the murder fine when no murder had been committed, but when death had occurred through accident or misfortune. There is evidence of it in Gloucestershire when the notorious Engelard de Cigogné was sheriff in the later years of John's reign. A boy, for example, was found drowned in the mill race at Colne Roger, and the village was mulcted in the sum of 18 marks.[5] It was not till half a century later when in the severe winter of 1257-8 large numbers died from starvation by the road-side that an end was made to this outrageous means of extortion.[6]

An important, though probably incidental, result of the

[1] i. 10. For the practice when first introduced see Stenton, *Anglo-Saxon England*, p. 676.   [2] Cf. A. L. Poole, *Obligations of Society*, pp. 84-6.
[3] *Pipe Roll 31 Hen. I*, for Wiltshire, p. 21, and Essex, p. 56. Smaller sums are occasionally recorded under other counties (e.g. 37s. under Oxfordshire); but we cannot be sure from an isolated roll whether this does not represent the unpaid balance of a fine imposed in a preceding year.
[4] A representative list is shown under Wiltshire in *Pipe Roll 21 Hen. II*, pp. 105-6.
[5] *Pleas of the Crown for the County of Gloucestor* (ed. Maitland), no. 92. For Norfolk cases in 1198 see *Linc. Ass. Rolls*, p. lv.
[6] Provisions of Westminster (1259), cl. 22. *Murdrum* was then limited to death by felony, and this in turn was in effect abolished by a statute of 14 Edw. III (1340).

murder fine was the incentive it provided for the detection of crime. It was clearly in the interest of the hundred to make every endeavour to seek out the murderer and bring him to justice in order to avoid the payment of the fine.[1] But the hundred was a relatively large territorial area; smaller and more personal organizations were likely to prove more effective in rounding up malefactors. So, to maintain some semblance of public order in the uncultured society of the twelfth century, a rudimentary police system was devised by which persons were made mutually responsible for each other's behaviour. This system, known as frankpledge, had grown out of the ancient arrangement of suretyship; it was a fusion of the Anglo-Saxon *borh* and tithing, a fusion which was probably not perfected till after the Norman Conquest. Being of native English origin the frankpledge system did not penetrate outside England or even to the whole of the country. It did not obtain in the northern counties or in the palatine or semi-palatine shires on the Welsh border, Cheshire, Shropshire, or Hereford; it was not carried into Ireland or into the king's dominions on the Continent. Further, certain persons or classes were not included. Barons and knights, freeholders[2] and clergy by reasons of their property or the respectability of their calling stood outside the system, as also did women. A lord himself was answerable for the good conduct of the men of his own household, men who were, as it was said, in his mainpast, who were fed by his hand; if one of these was accused of crime, it was the duty of the lord to bring him to justice.[3] All others over the age of twelve years whether free or servile were required to be in collective suretyship, in frankpledge and tithing.

They were formed into groups, usually of ten or twelve, under the direction of a tithing man or chief pledge, and became responsible for the conduct of their fellow associates. Sometimes the whole village formed a tithing. Should one of the group be suspected, it was the duty of the rest to produce him in court. If he fled, they must raise the hue and cry,[4] follow and capture

---

[1] N. D. Hurnard, *Eng. Hist. Rev.* lvi (1941), 386–8, regards the arrest and accusation of murderers as the essential object of the murder fine.

[2] 'Thomas non fuit in franco plegio quia liber homo fuit.' *Rolls of the Justices in Eyre for Worcestershire* (Selden Soc., vol. 53), no. 1207.

[3] See, for example, *Linc. Ass. Rolls*, no. 705.

[4] This was done by shouting and blowing horns. Cf. *Rolls of the Justices in Eyre for Yorkshire, 1218–19* (Selden Soc., vol. 56), no. 727: 'levavit clamorem et cornavit uthesium'.

him if they could, for should they fail to do so, they were 'at mercy' and liable to a fine. These fines were not heavy. In the early years of Henry II's reign they might be one or two marks or one or two pounds;[1] but later a standard rate of half a mark was generally adopted. Nevertheless, even 6s. 8d., shared out among ten or a dozen peasants who can have had little money to spare, was sufficiently burdensome. After a visitation of the itinerant justices the sheriff would usually account at the exchequer for a considerable sum arising from these fines.[2] We may suppose that the man who habitually broke the peace would find it hard to gain admission into a frankpledge group. He then became a liability on the township in which he was found; thus the village of Princes Risborough had to pay a fine of three marks in 1203 for receiving a man *extra francplegium*. Once the frankpledge had brought their member before a court their responsibility was at an end. If the suspicions proved to be well founded, he must be imprisoned or more often he was allowed to find men to go bail for his due appearance before the justices. These sureties, however, were not necessarily or even normally the frankpledge, but friends who voluntarily came forward to act on his behalf.[3] If they in turn failed in their duty, they were 'at mercy' and subjected to the half-mark fine.

This system was administered through the hundred court. Twice every year, at least from the time of Henry I, the sheriff presided at special sessions to see that the tithings were full, to see that all who should be, actually were in pledge, in other words to take what came to be known as 'the view of frank-pledge'. By the beginning of the next century these sessions came to be known as tourns (*turnus*); in the second reissue of Magna Carta (cl. 42) they were carefully regulated. By the Assize of Clarendon in 1166 the sheriff was authorized to enter any private court for the purpose of taking the view. Here, how-ever, Henry II was attempting more than he could hope to

[1] *Pipe Roll 12 Hen. II* (1166), pp. 87, 108.
[2] See, for example, the account of amercements rendered by the sheriff of Gloucestershire in 1176, *Pipe Roll 22 Hen. II*, pp. 125-6. They are mostly fines of half a mark imposed on tithings for failure to produce criminals and total £13. 6s. 8d. The roll of amercements of the Lincolnshire assize of 1202, which includes many murder fines, totals up to the large sum of £633. 15s. See A. L. Poole, op. cit., p. 84.
[3] This point has recently been elaborated by E. de Haas, *The Antiquities of Bail* (Columbia Univ. Press, 1940). Sometimes, however, the frankpledge did act as bail, see *Select Pleas of the Crown*, no. 24.

achieve. Lords of manors were already firmly entrenched in their franchises and they persisted in holding the view of frank-pledge (from which evolved their leet jurisdiction) themselves either with or without the sheriff.[1] It was, like all jurisdictions, a source of profit. The business there transacted had long since ceased to be confined to the mere inspection of the pledge groups. It was a police court for a number of trivial offences against public order such as the removal of landmarks, obstruction of the highways, brawling, and breaches of the assizes of bread and ale. These were reported by representatives of the township, the reeve and four men, in the presence of a jury of twelve freeholders of the hundred. Those found guilty were punished by fines. It was also at these 'tourns' or 'views' that the preliminary investigation of more serious crime was made. The record then taken was passed on to the justices at the next eyre.

A criminal could be brought to justice in one of two ways: by personal accusation or 'appeal' as it was called, or by public indictment. By the first of these methods the injured party or his near relation or his lord brought the charge and offered to prove it 'by his body', that is to say, by battle. Unless he was too old or unless he was maimed, he must be prepared to fight and fight to the death. It was often mortal, for one or other of the combatants was either slain in the battle or, if he survived his defeat, was hanged or at least severely punished. It was very violent; if they break their weapons, a late account of the duel relates, they must fight with their hands, fists, nails, teeth, feet, and legs.[2] Some consideration might be given to the combatant as a matter of grace. King John, for example, allowed Jordan of Bianney, a knight accused and afterwards convicted of felony, to leave Winchester jail, in which he was incarcerated, twice a day to practise fencing (*ad eskermiandum*).[3] Generally, however, the duels we hear of were fought not by upper-class litigants but by 'approvers', that is by men who had turned king's evidence and were released on condition that they would accuse and if

---

[1] Above, p. 57.

[2] *Collections of a London Citizen* (Camden Soc., 1876), p. 200, quoted H. W. C. Davis, *Eng. Hist. Rev.* xvi (1901), 730. Prefixed to the *Select Pleas of the Crown* (Selden Soc., vol. 1) is a reproduction of a drawing found on an assize roll of the reign of Henry III. It represents a judicial combat. In the background is a gallows showing the fate of the defeated party.

[3] *Rot. Lit. Claus.* i. 88b, 104b (where the name is given as Beunay).

necessary fight their accomplices.[1] This crude method of proof, introduced into England by the Normans, was not, however, the inevitable or even the normal issue of an appeal. We hear of many duels, but few were fought out. More frequently, as we shall see, the court required the accused to purge himself by one of the ordeals. The appeal was a troublesome and uncertain process. It seldom succeeded. Once it was started, it was necessary for the appellor to follow it up through the hundred and shire courts. Often he would seek the licence of the court to withdraw his suit at some stage of the proceedings and come to a compromise with the defendant; often his case would break down on some technical point: the hue and cry had not been raised; the wounds had not been exhibited to the proper authority; the evidence was contradictory; there was a flaw in the pleadings. If the appeal was withdrawn or dismissed or failed on any of these grounds the appellor rendered himself liable to a fine. Whether there was a conviction or an acquittal, the Crown profited. In the one case it would at least get the value of the condemned man's chattels; in the other it would collect up the fines for amercements from the plaintiff for bringing a false appeal, from the jurors for giving wrong evidence, or from the pledges because they had failed to produce their man.

It is remarkable that so many men, often men of small substance, were prepared to risk so many hazards to avenge a personal injury. There was an obvious need for an alternative method of prosecution. It was found by making the local community responsible for reporting and if possible prosecuting those suspected of crimes in its neighbourhood. Like so much else that was once attributed to the administrative genius of Henry II, the jury of presentment almost certainly has its roots in earlier custom, and may well go back to the well-known decree issued at Wantage by Æthelred about the end of the tenth century. This decree enacted that in every wapentake 'the twelve leading thegns together with the reeve shall go out and swear on the relics which are given into their hands, that they will not accuse any innocent man or shield any guilty one'.[2] It

---

[1] See, for example, *Curia Regis Rolls*, iii. 144, 145 and *Assize Rolls* (Northamptonshire Record Soc., vol. v), nos. 723–30. In the latter instance the same approver appealed eight accomplices; two cases involved duels. An approver while in the charge of the sheriff received payment of a 1*d.* or 2*d.* a day; they also appear to have been given instruction in duelling. Cf. *Pipe Roll 27 Hen. II*, p. 153.

[2] III Æthelred 3, 1 (Liebermann, *Gesetze*, i. 228).

is more than likely that the business of the reeve and the priest and the four men, who in certain circumstances represented the village at the hundred and county courts, was that of reporting suspected persons. The jurors (*juratores*) of Yorkshire, who in 1130 paid a large sum of money that they might be jurors no more, could only have been charged with the same duty.[1] A system of jury presentment was in use in the church courts in 1164. It is only, however, in 1166, in the Assize of Clarendon, that the system emerges from obscurity and that the procedure is for the first time clearly formulated.[2]

By this famous assize, issued 'with the consent of all his barons', Henry II instituted a comprehensive inquiry into crime committed since the beginning of his reign. Twelve of the more responsible men of the hundred and four of every township were required to declare upon oath before the sheriff in the county court, and before the justices when they visited the district, who were accused or suspected of being robbers, murderers, or thieves, or receivers of such (cl. 1). The sheriff, who was responsible for the carrying out of the assize, was given authority to enter any franchise for the purpose of making arrests (cl. 11), and he was directed to co-operate with the sheriffs of the neighbouring shires to secure the capture of criminals (cl. 17). To provide for the safe custody of his captives, jails were to be constructed in every county where they did not already exist (cl. 7). The Assize of Clarendon was issued immediately before a general eyre, and it contained the instructions on which the justices were expected to act. It was not, however, merely a temporary measure.[3] It was to remain in force, as the document expressly states, during the king's pleasure. When,

---

[1] *Leges Henrici*, vii. 7, 8 (Liebermann, op. cit. i. 553–4); *Pipe Roll 31 Hen. I*, p. 34.

[2] This view of the antiquity of the jury of presentment was tentatively suggested by M. M. Bigelow, *History of Procedure in England* (1880), pp. 134 n., 138. N. D. Hurnard in *Eng. Hist. Rev.* lvi (1941), 374, has collected some additional and impressive evidence to illustrate the practice of communal presentment in the period preceding the Assize of Clarendon. She seems, however, to underrate the importance of the latter document which she regards as novel only in its severity, and as only a temporary expedient to suppress brigandage. Her attempt to explain away the contrast between the new and the old customary procedure in clause 5 is not entirely convincing.

[3] Some clauses of a temporary character relating to questions of the moment were inserted. So, for example, clause 21 deals with a group of heretics condemned at an Oxford council in the same year. Similarly in the Assize of Northampton clause 8 refers to the destruction of castles made necessary by the recent rebellion.

moreover, it was reissued in a revised form at Northampton ten years later, in 1176, its permanence was again emphasized: 'this assize shall hold from the time the assize was made at Clarendon continuously until this time, and henceforth so long as it shall please the king'.[1] This Northampton ordinance, which also immediately preceded a visitation of the itinerant justices, added forgery and arson to the list of indictable crimes. A further stage was reached in the royal edict published by Hubert Walter in 1195.[2] This edict, while repeating in general terms the substance of the Assize of Clarendon relating to the arrest of criminals, emphasized the duty of all to follow the hue and cry, and to assist in the capture of malefactors. All above the age of fifteen were required to take, before knights assigned for this purpose, an oath that they would keep the peace. These specially appointed knights have been regarded as the forerunners of the later justices of the peace.[3] These three enactments form a series; one supplements and amends its predecessor as the practice of the courts revealed defects or loopholes in the machinery. They bear a close affinity to the 'articles of the eyre', the list of interrogatories with which, at least from 1194, the justices were furnished when they visited the shires.

The practice of sending royal justices into the shires to transact judicial and administrative business was already employed by the Norman kings.[4] From the Pipe Roll of 1130 (the only one which has survived from the reign of Henry I) it is evident that many of the counties were visited by the justices, and there is nothing to warrant the assumption that this was in any way exceptional. When order had been re-established after the anarchy of the reign of Stephen, we find the system again at work. At least from 1166 a year seldom passed without itinerant justices travelling the country to deal with judicial or financial business. The arrangements of these eyres, the number of justices dispatched, the grouping of the counties into circuits were still in an experimental stage and subject to frequent

---

[1] Clause 1.

[2] Hoveden, iii. 299–300.

[3] C. A. Beard, *The Office of Justice of the Peace in England*, p. 17.

[4] It has been customary in this connexion to refer to the commission sent in 1096 into Devon and Cornwall *ad investiganda regalia placita*. It has, however, been pointed out by H. P. R. Finberg (*Eng. Hist. Rev.* lix. (1944), 245–7) that this evidence is taken from a fourteenth-century cartulary and that the writer recorded a confused tradition in the language of his own day. It cannot be accepted as evidence of a judicial eyre.

change.[1] Under Richard I and John some years were allowed to elapse between one visitation and another, and after 1209 they ceased altogether, only to be revived in 1218. Henceforward the general eyre was held at long intervals of some seven years.

The coming of the justices to hold a general eyre, that is one on which they were commissioned to hear all kinds of pleas, was a big and, in later times, a much-dreaded occasion. The full county court was assembled; all who were deemed to represent the county were expected to be there.[2] Each hundred represented by an elected jury came in turn before the court to answer the questions put to them by the justices, the 'articles of the eyre'. These articles, which grew in number and detail as time went on, were not confined to judicial matters but came to include matters relating to the king's proprietary rights, his revenue, and in fact every sort of thing touching his interests.[3] The truth of the matter, Glanvill tells us, 'is examined by many and various inquiries and interrogatories'. It was a cumbersome business. The crime had already been investigated by the coroners, by the hundred, and by the county. The evidence of the hundred-jurors was checked by the local evidence of the four neighbouring townships. The story they told might conflict sharply with the record of the coroners and of the county.[4] There were other causes of impediment. A case has to be adjourned because one of the parties has failed to appear in court; he may be ill, he may be absent on crusade (a number of such excuses or 'essoins' as they were called were admitted by the law). But the reason for his absence must be investigated and another day fixed for hearing the case. By this time the justices would have passed on, and the case would be sent to another county or more probably to Westminster where there might be more adjournments and more essoining. A case might drag on from month to month, from year to year. Proceedings which seem to have arisen from the irresponsible gaiety and

---

[1] See H. G. Richardson, *Eng. Hist. Rev.* xliii (1928), 167.

[2] Unless specially exempted by charter. Thus, for instance, Henry II quit-claimed all the lands and men of Henry, bishop of Winchester, 'de tota assisa quam per justicias meas facta est per Angliam'. *Eng. Hist. Rev.* xxxv (1920), 399.

[3] The articles for the eyres of 1194 and 1198 are in Hoveden, iii. 263, iv. 61; those for the eyre of 1208 are contained in the *Liber Albus* (*Munimenta Gildhallae*, Rolls Series, i), p. 117. Cf. H. M. Cam, *Oxford Studies in Social and Legal History* (ed. Vinogradoff), vi. 17–20.

[4] *Select Pleas*, nos. 38, 62, 75.

high-handed acts of some Cornish aristocrats were begun in the hundred court of Truro in November 1212. They were continued in the hundred court of St. Austell, and then in the county court of Cornwall. There were appeals and counter-appeals; much circumstantial and conflicting evidence was produced on both sides; there was much essoining. The case was carried to Westminster where it was adjourned for one cause or another some five or six times. It was still undetermined in the summer of 1214 when the disorders of the kingdom stayed all legal proceedings.[1] If we consider the inevitable delays incidental to judicial procedure, it is astonishing to read the wealth or circumstantial detail with which a suitor would support his case. But though the injured party might well have the facts so mirrored on his mind that he could rehearse them accurately several years afterwards, this could hardly be expected of those less closely concerned, the jurors and witnesses. These infrequent eyres and adjourned hearings at Westminster placed a severe strain on their memories. Some of the chief actors might have died in the interval. Conflict of evidence was unavoidable, for the courts were generally investigating matters of ancient history.

Injured persons and juries might accuse and prosecute wrongdoers before the justices. The old rule, however, still prevailed that 'no one may be convicted of a capital charge by testimony'.[2] Proof depended not on human evidence, but on purgation or ordeal or combat, the judgement of God. We have seen that battle must be offered by an appellor, but was seldom fought. Compurgation, the method by which the defendant swore his innocence supported by oath-helpers, was still the regular procedure in the church courts, and it was jealously preserved in London and certain other privileged boroughs. In 1200, for example, a man claimed to defend an appeal of felony 'as a free citizen of Lincoln' with thirty-six compurgators, and two years later a woman at Bedford was allowed to clear herself of a charge of selling beer by a false gallon 'twelve-handed', that is to say, with the assistance of eleven others to support her oath.[3] In the criminal trials of this period, however, the normal mode

---

[1] This case which illustrates many interesting points of legal procedure is fully recorded on the *Curia Regis Rolls*, vii. 94–5, 168–73, 257. A part is printed with translation in *Select Pleas*, no. 115.

[2] *Leges Henrici*, 31, 5 (Liebermann, op. cit. i. 564).

[3] *Select Pleas*, nos. 82, 61.

of proof was, as laid down by the Assize of Clarendon, the ordeal of cold water. The trussed victim was lowered into a pool of water solemnly hallowed by the church.[1] If he sank, he was innocent; if he floated on the surface, he was guilty, for the consecrated element would not receive a sinful body. If he failed at this ordeal, he must lose one of his feet, and in this maimed condition abjure the realm. Ten years later by the Assize of Northampton it was decreed that he should lose not only his foot but his right hand as well. It is remarkable that apparently large numbers failed to surmount this primitive test. As a result of the Assizes of Clarendon (1166) and Northampton (1176) the sheriffs accounted at the exchequer for the value of 'the chattels of fugitives and of those who failed at the judgement of water'.[2] The sheriff of Middlesex accounted for the chattels 'of fugitives and of those defooted' (*expedatorum*).[3] The lists are often long. Yet even if we assume that the large majority of those whose names are subscribed were fugitives from justice, some at least must have belonged to the category of those *qui perierunt judicio aque*. We hear of few carrying the hot iron (*judicio ignis*)[4] except women who were, it seems, never subjected to the ordeal of water. This is well illustrated by a case of burglary in Cornwall heard by the justices in 1201. Five men and one woman (Matilda) were suspected. The judgement was: 'let the males purge themselves by water under the assize, and Matilda by ordeal of iron.'[5]

Clearly, however, little faith was put in these ancient modes of proof for it was further enacted by the Assize of Clarendon (cl. 14) that if the accused were men of very bad reputation, even if they succeeded in the ordeal, they must leave the country and be accounted as outlaws. This virtually put into the hands

[1] Sums of money paid to priests for blessing the pools are entered on the Pipe Rolls. In Wiltshire, for example, in 1167 'for preparing the pools for the ordeal of thieves 5s., and to the priests for blessing the same 20s.' *Pipe Roll 12 Hen. II*, p. 72. This and other instances are collected by L. F. Salzmann, *Henry II*, p. 184 n.

[2] *Pipe Roll 12 Hen. II; 22 Hen. II, passim.*

[3] *Pipe Roll 23 Hen. II*, p. 201. For other examples of persons who suffered the prescribed penalty of the loss of a foot see *Pipe Roll 25 Hen. II*, p. 83; *Curia Regis Rolls*, i. 180–1.

[4] In the lists referred to above under Hampshire *judicio ignis* is substituted for *judicio aque*. The iron was heated up after each ordeal. *Pipe Roll 21 Hen. II*, p. 131. It was clearly disliked, for Robert Fitz Brien paid as much as £20 to be quit of it. *Pipe Roll 24 Hen. II*, p. 5.

[5] *Select Pleas*, no. 12. Cf. *Curia Regis Rolls*, i. 108, where a woman appealed of sorcery successfully defended herself by ordeal of iron.

of the presenting jury the power of giving a sentence of banishment.[1] Already discredited in 1166, the system did not survive another half century. In 1215 the Fourth Lateran Council forbade the clergy to take any part in it. This was really the end. It was the sanction of the church, the superstitious and psychological force behind, that gave it any sort of effectiveness. The Lateran decree was regarded and doubtless welcomed as a strict prohibition.[2] Alternative methods of procedure were already available for those appealed of felony. From the opening years of the thirteenth century defendants could, on payment of a small sum, have their cases decided by a jury. Thus in 1202 a man appealed of wounding resulting in death on the Bedfordshire eyre offered a mark 'for having an inquest whether he is guilty or no'. The jury returned a verdict of not guilty, whereupon he was released and his accuser was 'in mercy' for a false appeal.[3] A defendant could also assert that an accusation brought against him was not a bona-fide accusation; that it was brought through malice and hate. He was not denying his guilt; he was introducing another question which, if answered in his favour, would successfully quash the appeal. It was a question which could properly be investigated and settled by a jury. He would offer the king a mark or two 'pro habenda legali inquisitione patrie utrum verum sit appellum vel athia' (hate).[4] The court would in these circumstances issue a writ *de odio et athia* directing an inquiry to be held at some future date, perhaps a fortnight or three weeks later, at which this point would be decided. The popularity of this writ is evident not only from its frequent appearance in the plea rolls, but also from the requirement in the Great Charter (cl. 36) that it was to be granted freely and not refused. Even before the abolition of the ordeal great progress had been made towards trial by jury.

Crude methods of punishment served a rough justice on wrongdoers in the early middle ages. There was a general tendency to make the punishment fit the crime; the aim was a just retribution for the wrong done. So hanging was the natural

---

[1] Thus, for example, the verdict on a man suspected of larceny in 1214 was: 'Purget se per aquam. Purgavit se et ejuravit regnum.' *Curia Regis Rolls*, vii. 241.

[2] The instruction issued to the justices on 26 January 1219 runs: 'cum prohibitum sit per ecclesiam Romanam judicium ignis et aque'. *Patent Rolls Henry III 1216–25*, p. 186.

[3] *Select Pleas*, no. 59. Cf. nos. 23, 78, 99.

[4] Ibid., no. 91. Cf. also nos. 81, 84, 86, 87, 95.

penalty for homicide, burning for arson,[1] castration for rape,[2] and the cutting out of the tongue for uttering slander or false accusation.[3] These were ancient rules and not necessarily observed after the Conquest. Capital punishment, which was abolished by William I in favour of mutilation,[4] was restored by Henry I;[5] and in 1124 as many as forty-four thieves were hanged at a single sitting of a court held by Ralph Basset acting as a royal justice at Huncote in Leicestershire.[6] Summary justice, though probably disapproved of in judicial circles, still lingered on into the thirteenth century. If a criminal was captured red-handed with the evidence of his guilt still upon him, the stolen goods, the blood-stained weapon, he could be dealt with in a very summary fashion without even formal accusation; he could not even be heard in his defence.[7] Many criminals were accounted for in this manner by lords who had the right of hanging thieves thus captured, the privilege of *infangenetheof*. The private gallows at Brimpsfield in Gloucestershire owned by the family of Giffard was, if we may believe their own story, kept actively at work hanging robbers from the Conquest to the time of Henry II.[8]

Mutilation, which was prescribed by the Assizes of Clarendon and Northampton for the more serious crimes, was certainly not the only or, at least in the later years of the twelfth century, the usual sentence given by the justices. In 1166 the sheriffs of London and Middlesex accounted at the exchequer for the cost of 34 ordeals and 14 men mutilated and 14 men hanged and 5 duels.[9] This represents the work of the justices who carried out the instructions issued at Clarendon earlier in that year. It suggests that the chances between death and mutilation were about even. In punishment as in the ordeal a differentiation was made between the sexes. Women culprits, who always

[1] William the miller, who burnt the grange of the abbot of Malmesbury, was himself burnt by the order of King John. *Pleas of the County of Gloucester*, no. 216.

[2] *Leis Willelme*, 18 (Liebermann, op. cit. i. 504). Cf. *Anglo-Saxon Chron., sub anno* 1087.

[3] *Leges Henrici*, 34. 7; 59. 13 (Liebermann, op. cit. i. 566, 579).

[4] *The Ten Articles of William I*, 10 (ibid. i. 488).

[5] Both forms of punishment were used under William II. After the rebellion of 1096 William, count of Eu, after being vanquished in a duel was emasculated and blinded while his steward, who was cognizant of the treason, was hanged. Symeon of Durham, *Historia Regum*, ii. 226.

[6] *Anglo-Saxon Chron., sub anno* 1124.

[7] Pollock and Maitland, *Hist. Eng. Law*. ii. 578–9. Assize of Northampton, cl. 3.

[8] *Rolls of the Justices in Eyre* (Selden Soc., vol. 59), no. 273. Cf. above, pp. 57–8.

[9] *Pipe Roll 12 Hen. II*, p. 131.

carried the hot iron, were, if the sentence was death, generally burnt.[1] In the king's courts, however, capital punishment was, it seems, sparingly used. There is abundant evidence that many and serious crimes were committed, yet there are relatively few convictions. Although a very large number of cases of homicide came before the justices on the Lincoln Assize of 1202, only one or possibly two criminals are recorded as having been hanged.[2] One is left with the impression that the improvements in procedure which mark the reign of Henry II worked in favour of the criminal. Often the matter is settled out of court. Often the evidence is insufficient or too conflicting to warrant a conviction. Often the guilty man has escaped, and the most that can be done is to declare him an outlaw in the county court. There was indeed a means of escape allowed by the law: he could take sanctuary in a church. Thus the jurors at Bedford in 1202 reported that a certain murderer had 'fled to church, confessed the death, and abjured the realm', and there the matter ended.[3] The whole system of detection, arrest, and procedure were inadequate to cope with the violence of the times.

The jury was no novelty in the twelfth century. As we have seen the jury of presentment, which developed into the grand jury of later times, may very possibly be found in the laws of the Anglo-Saxons.[4] In its widest aspect the jury was not limited to legal procedure, but was simply a means of obtaining information on oath. It was so employed by the later Carolingian emperors in the ninth century. From the empire it passed to the duchy of Normandy; and with the Normans it came to England where it grew and flourished as the most English of all English institutions. This is the generally accepted origin of the sworn inquest. Within a decade of the Conquest it was used for determining disputes concerning lands and rights of jurisdiction.[5] It was used also for ascertaining the requisite information for the compilation of Domesday Book. Before the death of William I it was already an established part of the machinery of administration.

If we now turn to civil jurisdiction, we notice that it is the increasing use made of the jury of recognition which is the most

[1] *Curia Regis Rolls*, vi. 306; *Select Pleas*, no. 191; *Rot. Chart.* 86b.
[2] *Linc. Ass. Rolls*, nos. 579, 722.
[3] Ibid., no. 986; *Select Pleas*, no. 48.   [4] Above, pp. 397–8.
[5] Stenton, *Anglo-Saxon England*, pp. 640–3. For the early use of the jury in Normandy see Haskins, *Norman Institutions*, ch. vi.

striking development. Men of the district who knew or were presumed to know the facts of the case were summoned to pronounce on oath the truth of the matter. Thus in a controversy over market rights between the abbey of Abingdon and the men of Wallingford in the early years of Henry II's reign the testimony of twenty-four of the older men of Berkshire, men who knew the custom in the time of the king's grandfather, was taken.[1] In the petty assizes the jury of recognition became the normal procedure.

The earliest of these assizes is that known as *utrum*, from the word in the writ that introduced the question which the jury had to decide, whether land in dispute was held by frankalmoign or by lay fee. If the former, it was a matter for the church courts. It was a preliminary action to decide the competence of courts. An action very like this was employed as early as 1138 in the reign of Stephen. The jury was called upon to declare whether five acres of land at Luton was free alms belonging to the church.[2] The procedure first clearly formulated in 1164 in the Constitutions of Clarendon (cl. ix) would seem to have conceded a large measure of jurisdiction to the ecclesiastical tribunals. But the doctrine was gradually evolved that this procedure could only be used by those who had no other remedy. Nearly all tenants in frankalmoign (religious houses for example) except rectors of parish churches could avail themselves of the same actions for the recovery of land as laymen. So the assize *utrum* became a proprietary action settling title to land of parish churches; it became the parson's remedy, the parson's writ of right.[3]

The three other petty assizes, novel disseisin, mort d'ancestor, and darrein presentment, all concern possession.[4] Their institution has rightly been regarded as among the most salutary of Henry II's legal reforms. The king's motive in establishing them may have been the laudable one of protecting the weak against the strong, or the purely selfish one of enlarging the scope of royal jurisdiction at the expense of the feudal courts and at the same time making money for the royal treasury. However this may be, their popularity is unquestioned. These assizes crowd

[1] *Chron. Monast. de Abingdon*, ii. 228.
[2] *Eng. Hist. Rev.* xxviii (1913), 727.
[3] Pollock and Maitland, i. 246–50; E. G. Kimball, *Eng. Hist. Rev.* xlvii (1932) 1; above, p. 205.
[4] As distinct from legal ownership. See below, p. 409.

the plea rolls of the reigns of Richard I and John. So highly were they valued even by the barons that a clause (18) was inserted in the Great Charter ordering that two justices should be sent into each county four times a year to take these assizes. The novel disseisin is the most important. Indeed, the authoritative history of English law claims that the ordinance establishing it was 'in the long run to prove itself one of the most important laws ever issued in England'.[1] Seisin is possession. This assize provided a speedy remedy for the man who was disseised, that is to say ejected, from his freehold unjustly and without the judgement of a court (*injuste et sine judicio*). He may obtain a writ instructing the sheriff to summon a jury of twelve men to declare before the king's justices whether he has been disseised or no. If the answer is in the affirmative, he will be put back into possession and may receive damages for the injury he has suffered. So, to take a case at random:

'An assize comes to declare whether Richard with the beard unjustly and without judgement disseised Geoffrey with the beard of his free tenement in Northborough after the king's coronation at Canterbury. The jurors say that he so disseised him. Judgement, Richard is in mercy and let Geoffrey have his seisin. Damages, nothing. Amercement half a mark.'[2]

It was a very speedy action; there is no pleading and no excuse (essoin) for the absence of the defendant is entertained. The jurors answer on the matter of fact. But they must speak from knowledge not from hearsay. A case not only failed, but the jurors were in mercy because they had not actually viewed the ground in dispute, it being at the time under flood.[3] The ejection must also have been recent (novel). From time to time a limit was set to the period within which the action could be brought. In the case cited above which was heard at Northampton in the late summer of 1202 the period of limitation was fixed at the king's coronation at Canterbury. King John wore his crown at Canterbury on 25 March 1201, some eighteen months before. This was in the early days of the assize. The period of time gradually became extended until it became meaningless.

[1] Pollock and Maitland, i. 146. The assize of novel disseisin was probably instituted by the Assize of Clarendon (1166). The earliest notice of it is in the *Pipe Roll 12 Hen. II* (1165–6), p. 65. 'Thomas de Lufham debet xx. s. pro dissaisina super Assisam Regis.'

[2] *Northants. Ass. Rolls*, no. 393.

[3] Ibid., no. 448.

In Edward I's reign a disseisin fifty years old, and in Henry VIII's reign three centuries old was still 'novel'.[1]

Although, as Bracton says, the assize of novel disseisin was contrived after many wakeful nights of labour, it is in fact simple and not strikingly original. William Rufus understood that a disseisin constituted a breach of the peace, a matter in which he himself was concerned.[2] He was not usually a respecter of the possessions of others, yet he would sometimes exercise his authority to protect the freeholds of privileged tenants such as the monks of Durham or the canons of Lincoln. Henry I ordered that the monks of Gloucester were to be put back into the possession of certain lands of which they had been 'unjustly and without judgement' disseised, and if this was not done, his agent, the bishop of St. Davids, was to take action.[3] Then at the height of the anarchy between 1139 and 1143, when it was said 'there was no king in Israel, but every man did that which was right in his own eyes' we find Stephen interesting himself on behalf of those who were 'unjustly and without judgement' disseised of their lands, and Geoffrey de Mandeville employed a jury of recognition to ascertain the facts of a disseisin.[4] The importance of Henry's assize lies in the fact that henceforth any freeman ejected from his holding, whether he were lord of a large estate or the tenant of a few acres, had the benefit of this remedy.

The assize mort d'ancestor was based on the same principle: it protected an heir from being wrongfully kept out of his inheritance. It first appears in the ordinance known as the Assize of Northampton in 1176 (cl. 4), and was directed pointedly at the practice of the lord of seizing on one pretext or another the land of his dead tenant. The heir was now furnished with a summary action. As in the novel disseisin, the jury was required to answer definite questions. Was William, the father of Miles, seised in his demesne as of fee (that is, by an hereditary and not a life tenure) of half a virgate of land in Upavon on the day on which he died? Is Miles his nearest heir? Did he die within the period of limitation? The jurors answered these questions in the affirmative. Judgement was accordingly given in favour of Miles and Hugh, who had ousted him, was in mercy.[5] The assize darrein

[1] Maitland, Collected Papers, i. 445; Hist. Eng. Law, ii. 51.
[2] Davis, Regesta Regum Anglo-Normannorum, App. nos. lxvi, lxvii.
[3] Hist. et Cartularium Mon. Glouc. i. 264.
[4] R. Howlett, introd. to Gesta Stephani (Rolls Series), pp. xxxvii–xxxviii; Round, Commune of London, pp. 114–15; Camb. Med. Hist. v. 587 n.   [5] Curia Regis Rolls, ii. 199.

presentment deals with another but none the less an important form of property—ecclesiastical benefices. It was claimed in the Constitutions of Clarendon that litigation over advowsons belonged to the lay courts. In 1179 it became a matter of urgency, for the third Lateran Council, held in that year, gave the presentation to the bishop if the benefice was not filled up within three months. A quick remedy was necessary to obviate the delays inherent in all normal proprietary actions. In the assize darrein presentment the jury was asked the simple question: who presented last? The same or his heir should present again.[1]

A heavy responsibility rested on the *legales homines* who formed these juries. If they gave a verdict which in the opinion of the justices was a wrong verdict, if they had sworn falsely, a jury of twenty-four was empanelled to attaint (*ad convincendum*) them.[2] Though often they may have got off with moderate fines, sometimes they suffered severe penalties. In 1204 the jurors in a case of novel disseisin were thrust into prison and their chattels were confiscated. It is not surprising that jury service was unpopular and that men would pay to be quit of it.[3]

The essential point in all the possessory assizes was that they provided in the king's court a rapid and effective remedy against unjust dispossession. Possession might be nine points of the law; but these assizes did not settle or even prejudice the question of ultimate right to land, the question which of two claimants had the *melius jus*, the better right in the land. The rights of ownership were determined by a slow, cumbersome, and tedious process. At every stage the case might be adjourned owing to the non-appearance of one of the parties or one of the witnesses who pleaded one of the recognized excuses. It might drag on for years. The case of Richard of Anesty is often quoted to illustrate the time and toil and heavy expense involved in pursuing itinerant courts. He had to travel all over England; he had to follow the king to Normandy and even to the south of

[1] A case concerning an advowson antecedent to the establishment of the possessory assize (probably 1156–9) was decided on the evidence of sworn recognitors. It is printed by F. M. Stenton from the Darley cartulary in *Eng. Hist. Rev.* xxxii (1917), 47–8.

[2] *Curia Regis Rolls*, iii. 134–5. Cf. Glanvill, ii. 19, and the note in Woodbine's edition pp. 204–5. In Glanvill's time juries of the grand as well as the petty assizes could be attainted. But by the time of Bracton attaint was limited to the petty assizes.

[3] See *Linc. Ass. Rolls*, no. 632, for a payment by a man of 1 mark 'that he be not placed on the jury of Holland'.

France; his representatives had to visit Rome. The adjournments were almost interminable. The costs of the suit, of which he kept a careful account, in travelling expenses, gratuities, and in extortionate interest on borrowed money (sometimes the Jews demanded 4d. a week per pound or 86⅔ per cent. per annum) were enormous. The total bill amounted to more than £330.[1] But the case was not typical. Although it began and ended in the king's court, it was turned aside into the ecclesiastical court on a question of bastardy, and it was there that most of the postponements were made; it also included appeals to Rome. It belonged to the early years of Henry II's reign (1158–63) before the legal reforms had been evolved. Nevertheless, it is doubtful whether actions for the recovery of land were carried through much more expeditiously thirty years later. Simon Grim, it was stated in 1194, had pleaded his suit 'for seven years in divers courts'.[2]

A proprietary action was recognized as properly the province of the feudal courts. The king could only intervene on the ground of failure of justice. Nevertheless, the rule, cited by Glanvill, that no man need answer for his free tenement without the king's writ was fully operative in the later part of the twelfth century and probably much earlier. Commonly it was begun by a writ of right (*breve de recto*), a command to the lord to do right to the plaintiff; and a warning was added that if he did not do so, the sheriff would deal with the matter.[3] Sometimes, however, the king would act in a more arbitrary fashion. He would issue a writ *Praecipe*, an instruction to the sheriff to order the tenant to restore the land in dispute to the plaintiff. If he does not do so, he must appear before the king or his justices to show the reason why. In effect, it transferred the suit into the king's court, ignoring the feudal court altogether. How far this should be regarded as an infringement of the judicial rights of the feudal lord and what was the precise effect of the limitation imposed by clause 34 of the Great Charter is still obscure;

[1] The text with a translation is printed by Palgrave, *English Commonwealth*, ii, pp. ix–xxvii, lxxv–lxxxvii. The costs were divided in rough figures as follows: travelling expenses £144; gratuities £142; interest on loans £43.

[2] *Rot. Curiae Regis*, i. 68, quoted *Camb. Med. Hist.* v. 588. A suitor in 1213 referred to a plea in which his father was involved in the time of Henry II which lasted for eleven years. *Curia Regis Rolls*, vii. 10.

[3] The earliest recorded reference to the writ of right occurs in a document which cannot be later than 1157. It is printed from the Spalding cartulary by F. M. Stenton in *Proceedings of the British Academy*, xiii (1927), 221–2.

probably too much importance has been attached to it from the point of view of rival jurisdictions. The writ enjoyed some popularity, and the barons appear only to have demanded that it should not be abused so as to deprive them of the cognizance of suits which they were properly qualified to determine.[1]

The form of trial in a proprietary suit was the judicial combat. The plaintiff must offer battle, not indeed, as in a criminal plea, with his own body; the fight was between hired champions, who were in theory witnesses of the truth. It was a clumsy and, to modern ideas and even to the lawyers of the twelfth century, an inequitable mode of deciding a legal dispute. In the later part of his reign, therefore, Henry II instituted the Grand Assize. This assize is twice referred to in official records as the Assize of Windsor, a fact which suggests that it originated at a great council held at Windsor, and most probably that of April 1179.[2] Glanvill speaks of it as a *regale beneficium* granted as a favour to the tenant (that is, the defendant) whereby he might decline the hazardous issue of the duel and have the case decided on the evidence of a jury. Four knights were chosen to elect twelve other knights who were required 'to declare upon oath which of the litigants has the better right to the land in dispute'.[3] The popularity of the new procedure was great. A roll of the time of Richard I records those 'who placed themselves on the Grand Assize of the lord king' since that king's coronation. It contains 135 cases.[4]

The Grand Assize was not, like the novel disseisin, a swift and summary action. It was subject to the delays and postponements incidental to all proprietary suits, and it became common for the parties to seek the licence of the court to come to an agreement, to make a 'final concord'. The fine as a method of terminating disputes about land may be traced back to the year 1163, although it did not assume its established form till perhaps a decade later.[5] Naturally the court made a charge for this licence, for it had already devoted much time and trouble to the case in the cause of justice. But it was well worth the money, for it settled the matter once and for all. The fine could conclude an action started by the writ of right or mort d'ancestor or

---

[1] See D. M. Stenton, *Pipe Roll 6 Jo.*, Introd., pp. xxx–xxxiii; N. D. Hurnard, in *Studies in Medieval History presented to F. M. Powicke*, pp. 157–79; and below, p. 475.

[2] Round, *Eng. Hist. Rev.* xxxi (1916), 268.

[3] Glanvill, ii. 7, 10.   [4] *Curia Regis Rolls*, i. 1–14.

[5] Salzmann, *Eng. Hist. Rev.* xxv (1910), 708.

darrein presentment, but it could not follow an assize of novel disseisin which involved a breach of the peace. At first the chirograph, as the document which recorded the agreement was called, was made in duplicate on the same piece of parchment, which was then cut in two and a copy given to each of the parties.[1] But in 1195 a third copy was made at the foot of the document, an addition doubtless attributable to the fertile brain of the justiciar, Hubert Walter. These 'Feet of Fines' as they came to be called were preserved in the treasury at Westminster for the purpose of record and verification.[2]

The fine also plays an important part in the history of conveyance. Land normally passed from one owner to another by enfeoffment with livery of seisin or, to use less technical language, by the delivery of possession. The donor must quit and the new tenant must be put in possession. This was generally accompanied by a symbolic transference of some material object. In Anglo-Saxon times this might be a turf of the ground to be conveyed.[3] After the Conquest, a knife was commonly used, perhaps the knife which was supposed to have cut the sod. Thus when William I gave land in England to the abbot of Sainte-Trinité du Mont at Rouen by a knife he jokingly made as though he would dash the point through the abbot's hand and exclaimed 'That is the way to give land'.[4] We hear also of rods, of boughs of trees, and of rings.[5] When this land was conveyed to a church or religious house the symbol was usually presented at the altar. The document or charter which recorded the transaction was not an essential part of the conveyance; it was a private document; it was evidence, but evidence which could be and was easily forged. The fine was very different. It was a public instrument made in a court of law, and a copy was filed among the official records. It was the safest title under which land could

---

[1] The instrument was also called an indenture because the two copies were parted by an indented cut. The genuineness of the document could be tested by placing the two copies together. If genuine, the indentations must correspond.

[2] The first fine made in triplicate is dated 15 July 1195. A facsimile of the three parts of an indenture is prefixed to vol. ii of the Final Concords of the County of Lincoln (*Linc. Rec. Soc.* xvii). See also V. H. Gàlbraith, *Studies in the Public Records*, pp. 9–13.

[3] For examples see Birch, *Cartularium Saxonicum*, nos. 107, 291, 840, 842–3. See also F. M. Stenton in *Essays in Honour of James Tait*, p. 317.

[4] Quoted in Pollock and Maitland, *Hist. Eng. Law*, ii. 87. Cf. also the grant of land at Twyning to the abbey of Winchcombe in *Landboc de Wichelcumba*, i. 212.

[5] *per baculum*, Farrer, *Yorkshire Charters*, ii, nos. 762, 845; *per ramum arboris* and *per anulum aureum* and other forms, see Madox, *Formulare*, pp. x and 54.

be held. So from the time of John it became the practice for an owner when he wished to transfer property to enter into a fictitious lawsuit with the intended recipient in order to obtain a final concord in the king's court. Towards the close of the thirteenth century nearly all the fines levied were in fact the outcome not of real disputes but of feigned litigation.[1]

From what has been said it will be evident that an ever-increasing burden of work was being thrown on the justices who sat on the bench at Westminster. Pleas both civil and criminal were heard there. Cases were adjourned there for various reasons; they might be crowded out of the eyre for lack of time; the intensity of local feeling might prevent a fair hearing in the provinces; some intricate point of law might be involved which could better be determined by the central tribunal. Many such cases were thus respited to the court which sat at Westminster. The royal court, however, had not yet been divided into separate courts each dealing with a special type of business. The justices, whether they followed the king and heard pleas *coram rege*, or visited the shires in eyre, or remained on the bench at Westminster, were the king's justices and held the king's court, since 'omnia placita que coram justiciariis de banco tenentur coram domino rege vel capitali justiciario teneri intelligantur'.[2] In 1178, we are told, Henry II chose five judges from his household who should not depart from the king's court, but should remain there to hear the complaints of the people.[3] This has generally been regarded as the origin of the court of common pleas. But it seems rash to deduce the creation of a new court from a casual statement of a chronicler writing at a time fertile in judicial experiments. There is little reason to suppose that this particular arrangement had any permanence or marked any important change. A famous clause of Magna Carta[4] ordered that common pleas should not follow the royal court, but be held in some fixed place, which came in practice to be Westminster. It would be wrong to infer from this that there was already in existence a distinct court which heard all and exclusively common pleas. The intention of the clause was to make it easier for suitors to bring their cases before the justices without the necessity of

---

[1] There is some evidence to suggest that *finis* originally stood for *finis duelli* and the object of the final concord was the avoidance of bloodshed, for a suit of ownership would end with a duel unless the defendant put himself on the Grand Assize. Cf. *Eng. Hist. Rev.* lviii (1943), 496. [2] *Curia Regis Rolls*, i. 462.

[3] *Gesta Henrici*, i. 207. [4] Cl. 17.

trailing in pursuit of the constantly moving king. It sanctioned, in fact, the prevailing practice. This chief court (*capitalis curia*) as Glanvill calls it, or great court (*magna curia*) as it is termed in some legal records of the early thirteenth century, was closely associated with the exchequer. There were judges sitting at the exchequer in almost continuous session; most of the judges were barons of the exchequer. The exchequer was the centre not only of the financial but also of the judicial administration.[1] Thus justice and finance were inextricably bound together.

Although for purposes of account sums of money were reckoned in pounds and shillings, in marks (13s. 4d.) and even gold marks (£6), the only currency throughout this period was the silver penny. The ordinary manual labourer earned one of these as his daily wage. For small change they were cut in half or in quarters. At the end of the eleventh century they were made in between fifty and sixty minting towns; but the number of towns with this privilege diminished in course of years and in the reign of John there were only perhaps a dozen in active operation. The moneyers were supplied with dies by the *cuneator* who was in general control of the mints. This post was in the hands of Otto the goldsmith (*aurifaber*) (a craftsman who was entrusted with the execution of the Conqueror's monument in the church of St. Stephen at Caen) and it remained hereditary in his house for several generations. But the coinage redounds little to the credit of the family; it is poor both in design and workmanship. Attempts at improvement were made from time to time, notably for the issue of 1180, the short-cross penny,[2] which was designed by a foreign engraver, Philip Aimer of Tours. But the improvement did not endure; deterioration is soon again evident. More serious, however, than lack of artistic merit was lack of purity of metal and of proper weight. Debasement was easy. A silver penny should weigh 22½ grains; but the average weight was generally below, and sometimes much below this standard. Evidently the trade in false coin was very rife especially in the middle years of Henry I's reign. A crisis

---

[1] Cf. D. M. Stenton in *Camb. Med. Hist.* v. 574, 585. An important contribution to the difficult question of the early history of the courts is contained in G. O. Sayles's introduction to *Select Cases in the Court of King's Bench* (Selden Soc., vol. 55), pp. xi–xxxii. For the judicial activities of the exchequer, see R. L. Poole, *The Exchequer in the Twelfth Century*, ch. viii.

[2] It is remarkable that this type continued under Richard I and John without change of name. All the coins of these kings bear the name HENRICUS.

came in 1124 when, we are told, that 'the penny was so bad that the man who had at a market a pound could by no means buy therewith twelve pennyworths'.[1] In consequence the king took strong measures: all the moneyers were summoned to Winchester at Christmas, and those who were found guilty were punished with the loss of the right hand and emasculation.[2] Nevertheless, in spite of the harsh penalties the evil of false moneying continued. The increasing volume of foreign trade under the Angevin kings made it essential to maintain a fair standard of coinage. Henry II's issue of 1180 had a good reputation on the Continent and was even copied in some German mints by the emperors Henry VI and Otto IV.[3] But before the end of the century there was clearly much bad money in circulation; the chroniclers complain of the deterioration by clipping, *per tonsuram sterlingorum*. It was largely to maintain the value of English money as a medium of foreign exchange that King John, after the loss of Normandy, undertook a drastic reform. The bad coins were called in and a new issue put in circulation which was stamped with an outer circle to guard against the practice of clipping.[4]

With coinage usually debased or clipped it was obviously impossible for the government to accept money at its face value; it had to be put to a test, a discount had to be made on the money proffered. This was done either by making a deduction of a shilling in a pound of counted pennies (payment by tale or *numero*) or a sample was tested by fire or *blanched*.

The Norman kings inherited from their Anglo-Saxon predecessors an organized financial system.[5] The ancient dues from the shires, originally rendered in kind, had mostly been commuted into fixed payments (*firma comitatus*), the system of blanching to test the purity of coin was already practised, and the treasury (which included, besides money, the king's valu-

---

[1] *Anglo-Saxon Chron.*, *sub anno* 1124.

[2] The chronicle (*sub anno* 1125) implies that all were subjected to this punishment without the semblance of a trial. But the evidence of the Pipe Roll of 1130 shows that some at least came to terms with the king and paid fines; the names of others again appear on the coinage issued after 1125. See Sir Charles Oman, *The Coinage of England*, pp. 101–3. For Henry I's charter concerning the punishment of false moneyers see *Foedera*, i. 12.

[3] Oman, op. cit., p. 136.

[4] Cf. the valuable discussion of this reform by Sidney Smith in the introduction to the Pipe Roll of 1205, pp. xxvii–xxxii.

[5] Cf. Stenton, *Anglo-Saxon England*, pp. 635–6.

ables—his crown, jewels, plate, and records) was, it seems, already located at Winchester. But the methods of accounting and audit were still very primitive; the tally, the split stick on which the sum paid in was indicated by notches of varying size, served both as a receipt and a record.

In the year 1110 Henry I addressed a writ to the barons of the exchequer (*baronibus de scaccario*) concerning the quittance of the land of St. Mary of Lincoln of the aid for the marriage of his daughter to the emperor Henry V; it is witnessed by Roger, bishop of Salisbury.[1] Both the word *scaccarium* and the name of the witness are significant. The one indicates a great advance in financial organization, the other the author of this development. The collection of the aid of 3s. on the hide for the marriage of the king's daughter was probably the first large financial operation negotiated by the reformed exchequer. *Scaccarium*, the chess board, was the chequered cloth which covered the table at which with the aid of counters the accounting was done; it was based on the principle of the abacus which, whether introduced from Laon,[2] or, as seems more likely, from Lorraine,[3] was already known in learned circles in the time of William Rufus; Robert, bishop of Hereford (1079–95), a distinguished astronomer, was certainly well acquainted with it. The lack of a zero figure in Roman numeration made simple arithmetic extremely awkward. The abacus, a rudimentary calculating machine, supplied the want, for the absence of a counter in a column assigned to tens, hundreds, or thousands meant that there was no number to be reckoned. The reckonings thus made were then entered on rolls. A Pipe Roll, as this roll is called from its cylindrical or pipe-like appearance when rolled up, exists for the 31st year of Henry I, that is for the year ending at Michaelmas 1130; from the 2nd year of Henry II there is a continuous series.

The treasury remained at Winchester till near the close of the twelfth century when Westminster became the central treasure house (*domus thesauri*);[4] but for many years afterwards Winchester continued to be a branch repository for substantial sums of money. In 1208, for instance, the servants of the treasurer

---

[1] *Registrum Antiquissimum of the Cathedral Church of Lincoln* (Lincoln Record Soc., vol. 27), i. 26. This is the earliest evidence for the existence of the exchequer and precedes by some years the evidence usually cited.

[2] R. L. Poole, *The Exchequer in the Twelfth Century*, pp. 47–56.

[3] C. H. Haskins, *Studies in the History of Mediaeval Science*, pp. 327–35.

[4] V. H. Galbraith, *Studies in the Public Records*, p. 46.

and the chamberlains were sent down there to count (*ad nume-randum*) 40,000 marks (or 6,400,000 pennies);[1] and there were several other local stores of treasure established in castles such as Nottingham, Bristol, or Marlborough so that wherever the king might be on his ceaseless travels there was always a bank at no great distance.[2] The reason for the removal of the main treasury to Westminster was obviously the convenience of proximity to the exchequer where the money was received and audited. Twice a year, at Easter and Michaelmas, special sessions of the exchequer were held at which the sheriffs and other persons responsible for the king's dues in particular localities appeared before the justiciar, chancellor, treasurer, chamberlains, and other officers to render their accounts.

The revenue of the Crown was chiefly derived directly or indirectly from the king's position as supreme landlord. It included, first, the county farms, that is the composition of the rents and rights which the king anciently had in the Crown lands within each county; these brought in a total sum slightly less than £10,000 per annum.[3] The lands held by the Crown were, however, constantly being augmented by estates which fell in by escheat; if a tenant died without heirs or was convicted of felony his land passed (escheated) to its lord. Though these escheated honors and manors were usually regranted to another tenant, they were kept in hand and farmed by the sheriff or by a specially appointed custodian for a time, often a long time, and the issues accrued to the exchequer.[4] In the same category may be reckoned the revenue from vacant churches, from bishoprics and royal abbeys; and it became the practice of the Norman and early Angevin kings to keep them vacant frequently for long periods for the sake of the income.[5]

---

[1] *Pipe Roll 10 Jo.*, p. 127.

[2] Cf. J. E. A. Jolliffe in *Studies in Medieval History presented to F. M. Powicke*, pp. 117–42. He speaks of 'the extinction of the subordinate treasure of Winchester' in 1207 (p. 129); but the evidence quoted in the text proves that it was still an important repository in 1208.

[3] The amounts of the county farms have been worked out by G. J. Turner in *Trans. R. Hist. Soc.*, N.S., xii (1898), 117–49, and his results have been tabulated by J. H. Ramsay, *Revenues of the Kings of England*, i. 192. There are also elaborate tables by W. Parow, in his *Compotus Vicecomitis* (Berlin, 1906), pp. 24–8.

[4] The very large number of escheats which resulted from the rebellion of Count John in 1194 were entered on separate rolls, see *Pipe Rolls 6, 7, 8 Ric. I*, and accounted for by two escheators, one for the northern and one for the southern counties, as was the usual practice in later times when the dividing line for this purpose, as for Forest pleas, was the river Trent.   [5] Above, pp. 170–2, 220–1.

The king was also entitled to the feudal incidents—reliefs, the regular feudal aids, and wardships and marriages, which have already been discussed;[1] to finance his wars he could take scutages or fines in lieu of military service.[2] Danegeld, the earliest direct taxation, which had been called into existence to meet an emergency in the late Anglo-Saxon period, became under the Norman kings a very frequent, if not an annual, impost;[3] it was normally assessed at 2s. on the hide, though occasionally it was as much as 4s. or even 6s. It was, however, subject to many exemptions: the demesne lands were exempted, so too were the lands of those responsible for its collection (the sheriffs) and its accounting (the barons of the exchequer); further, the tax was remitted by the king's writ in favour of certain individuals. Instead, therefore, of bringing perhaps nearly £5,000 into the exchequer, Danegeld was yielding little more than £3,000 in the early years of Henry II.[4] It was fast becoming obsolete when it was taken for the last time in 1162. It was revived again as an emergency measure by Richard I in 1194 under the name carucage and still appears to have been levied on the Domesday assessment.[5]

The taxation we have hitherto discussed fell only upon the landed interests. The urban population, whose wealth and importance was steadily increasing, were not comprehended in this scheme of finance. The king, however, claimed the right to tax his demesne tenants, which included the royal boroughs. Already in Henry I's reign we hear of these rendering 'aids' (auxilia); in his grandson's reign these aids were sometimes termed 'gifts' (dona), a euphemism which, like the benevolence of a later age, implied a compulsory contribution.[6] In 1177, when an aid was taken from the boroughs and vills, the contribution from Colchester is called a tallage.[7] This term becomes increas-

[1] Above, pp. 20–3.
[2] Above, pp. 16–17.
[3] Round, *Domesday Studies*, pp. 87 ff.; V. H. Galbraith, *Eng. Hist. Rev.* lxv (1950), 16.
[4] See the table in Ramsay, op. cit. i. 194.
[5] Cf. Maitland, *Pipe Roll Society*, xiv, pp. xxiv–v. Carucages were taken on two other occasions in this period (1198 and 1200) but they were assessed by special commissioners.
[6] e.g. 'Auxilium burgi de Bedeford' (*Pipe Roll 31 Hen. I*, p. 104); 'Donum Burgi de Bedeford' (*Pipe Roll 7 Hen. II*, p. 12.)
[7] *Pipe Roll 23 Hen. II*, p. 155. The word first appears in the rolls in connexion with the rebellion of the young king in 1173–4. Cf. ibid., p. 134, 'de tallagio facto tempore werre', and *21 Hen. II*, pp. 5, 8.

ingly used to describe the arbitrary taxation of the king's
demesne tenants; but in deference to the sensitiveness of the
boroughs (for the word tallage was associated with servitude,
with the taxation of villeins) the old words *donum* and *auxilium*
were retained at least till the end of the reign of Henry II.[1]
Similarly under colour of 'gifts' the clergy in the twelfth century
were induced under protest to furnish something to the treasury.
It became the normal practice for the king to take a tallage
whenever he took a scutage. In this way both the feudal and the
non-feudal classes were made to contribute to the expenses of
government. In 1199 an *auxilium* is said to have been exacted
de universitate Anglie.[2]

The economic prosperity prevalent at the beginning of the
thirteenth century, the vigorous development of trade and
commerce suggested a way of broadening the basis of taxation
to meet a corresponding increase in governmental expenditure,
especially expenditure on military armaments. Experiments had
already been made in taxing movable wealth—income and
chattels; but the money so collected was not for the benefit of
the government but for a definite and charitable purpose—the
crusade.[3] Thus in 1166, following the example of Louis VII of
France, Henry II ordered a levy for the relief of the Holy Land
of 2*d*. in the pound in the first year and 1*d*. in the pound in each
of the four succeeding years of all movables; everyone, both in
England and in the continental dominions, was required to
contribute. The method of assessment and collection was simple:
each man was to assess his own wealth and put his contribution
in a chest provided for the purpose in every parish.[4] His conscience was the only safeguard against dishonesty. Self-assess-
ment was again employed in the levy of a tenth of rents and
movables made in 1188 for the recovery of Jerusalem known as
the Saladin Tithe, but now a check against fraud was instituted;
if it was thought that an individual had made a false return, 'if
according to his conscience he shall have given less than he
ought to have given', a jury of local men was empanelled to
assess the right amount.[5] The money assembled at Salisbury,

---

[1] Thus in the roll of 33 Henry II under the heading 'De tallagio dominiorum
Regis &c.' the contributions of the towns and vills are almost always *de dono*.

[2] *Pipe Roll 1 Jo.*, p. 123.

[3] See W. E. Lunt, *The Valuation of Norwich*, pp. 1–9.

[4] The ordinance relating to the continental dominions has been preserved by
Gervase of Canterbury, *Opera*, i. 198–9.   [5] *Gesta Henrici II*, ii. 31.

one of the centres for collection of this tithe (and there must
have been others), was nearly £6,000.[1] Such a rich source of
revenue could hardly be long ignored by the officials at the
exchequer. From these precedents springs the modern system
of taxation. A tax on movables was raised for the king's ransom
in 1193-4 and a seventh in 1203; but the details of these taxes
are lacking. We are better informed about the thirteenth (or
more correctly 1s. on the mark) of rents and chattels levied on
the whole population, clerk and lay, in 1207;[2] it yielded over
£60,000, of which £57,421. 11s. 5d. was collected during the
fiscal year.[3] This was more than double the normal revenue
in an ordinary year. So large were the sums which had to be
accounted that they were not passed through the ordinary
machinery of the exchequer but paid into a separate exchequer.[4]
The thirteenth of 1207 is the true forerunner of the tenths and
fifteenths of later times.

In addition there were the profits of justice, which increased
proportionately with the growth of the jurisdiction of the royal
courts, amercements for breach of the Forest Laws which were
a very fruitful source of revenue, and the fines or compositions
which the king arbitrarily exacted for every conceivable irregu-
larity of conduct, real or imaginary. A man who earned the
king's displeasure would proffer a sum of money 'for having the
king's love' or that 'the king's anger might be relaxed'; similarly
if he sought a favour from the king it would be necessary to offer
some inducement in order to gain it. The whimsical character
of King John is most clearly revealed in the strange bargains he
made with his subjects. Perhaps the most curious example is the
entry of the Fine Roll which records that 'the wife of Hugh de
Neville gives the lord king 200 hens that she may lie one night
with her husband', and arrangements were made for the safe
delivery of the birds before Easter.[5] In John's time it became
more frequent to accept renders in kind rather than money in
whole or part payment of debts. Horses and hounds, hawks and
falcons for the king's sport were largely provided by fines; these
also helped to stock his larder and his cellar; Yarmouth paid in

---

[1] Cf. Round, *Eng. Hist. Rev.* xxxi (1916), 447–50.
[2] *Rot. Lit. Pat.*, p. 72b. The clergy are not mentioned in the writ, but it is clear
from other evidence that they were included.
[3] *Rot. de Finibus*, p. 459.
[4] The sums were paid *custodibus scaccarii* xiiime. Pipe Roll 9 *Jo.*, p. 63.
[5] *Rot. de Fin.*, p. 275. For other examples see A. L. Poole, *Obligations of Society*, p. 93.

herrings, Gloucester in lampreys, the king's favourite food. Pounds of pepper or cumin, and pairs of gilt spurs (generally commuted for 6*d*.) were common rents in the thirteenth century.

Sundry miscellaneous receipts swelled the royal revenue. Very substantial sums were raised from fees payable for the inspection and confirmation of charters. This practice, adopted in imitation of the episcopal chanceries, can be traced back to the reign of Stephen,[1] and was a wise and valuable precaution especially in times (such as the early years of Henry II) which followed a period of political confusion; nor was it a matter of pure formality. The document was said to have been seen *meis oculis* and touched *propriis manibus*.[2] King John refused to confirm a charter which he suspected to be a forgery.[3] But the system was liable to abuse; it was exploited for the sake of the fees. Richard I's change of seal in 1198 and his requirement that charters should be confirmed and re-sealed was nothing more than a method of extorting money, so too was John's instruction to the justices of the bench that they should disregard charters of his ancestors unless they had received his confirmation.[4] More money had to be paid for the additional security of having the charter enrolled either on the Pipe Roll or the Charter Roll. The chancery officials also took their toll. It was not for the mere dignity of the office that Henry I's chancellor Geoffrey paid £3,006. 13*s*. 4*d*. *pro sigillo* or that Walter de Gray agreed to pay as much as 5,000 marks for the chancery for his lifetime.[5] In the reign of Richard I the fees charged were exorbitant, and it was one of the first acts of King John, acting no doubt under the influence of Hubert Walter just appointed chancellor, to regulate them.[6] The county farms had not been revised since the early years of Henry II although the profits from the royal manors and the local courts had risen enormously. This profit, *proficuum*, (or part of it) which had previously accrued to the benefit of the sheriff, was now (1205) drawn into the exchequer.[7]

---

[1] V. H. Galbraith, *Eng. Hist. Rev.* lii (1937), 69–71.

[2] Cf. the confirmation of a Tavistock charter: 'quas (cartas) oculis inspeximus et propriis manibus contrectavimus' (*Eng. Hist. Rev.* lxii (1947), 364).

[3] *Rot. de Fin.*, p. 76.

[4] *Curia Regis Rolls*, i. 331.

[5] *Pipe Roll 31 Hen. I*, p. 140; *Rot. de Fin.*, p. 368.

[6] *Foedera*, i. 75.

[7] Cf. G. J. Turner in *Trans. R. Hist. Soc.*, N.S., xviii (1904), 288–90; *Pipe Roll 7 Jo.*, p. xxvi. By clause 25 of Magna Carta the county farm was to be taken 'without any increment'.

It is unquestionable that the burden of taxation was very largely increased under King John. Scutages had been increased and became almost annual imposts, the lists of amercements lengthened year by year, the county farms were subjected to an increment. John has been severely criticized for his financial extortions, and they met with violent opposition. Yet it should be recognized that prices had risen steeply in the early years of the thirteenth century; the expenses of government were very heavy. It was not unreasonable to raise a scutage of two or even three marks instead of a pound when the wages of a knight had more than doubled. It was to gain more freedom of action that more and more money was diverted from the treasury into the chamber (*camera*) where the king could more readily lay his hand on it.[1]

In spite of the great increase in taxation, the royal revenue still fell far short of the needs of the administration. It was necessary to borrow on a large scale. The Jews were under the special protection of the king who in turn could tallage them at will. Their business acumen had brought them enormous wealth which they laid out at very high rates of interest on public and private undertakings.[2] The business transactions of Aaron of Lincoln (an outstanding example) extended into twenty-five counties from Kent to Cumberland, and among his clients were counted the king of Scotland, the archbishop of Canterbury, several bishops, abbots, and earls, besides a vast number of lesser persons both lay and clerical. His capital helped to finance the building of the cathedral of Lincoln, the abbeys of Peterborough and St. Albans, and at least nine Cistercian houses. When he died about 1185 the operation of collecting up his debts (which escheated to the Crown) was so great that a special exchequer (*scaccarium Aaronis*) was set up to deal with it, and it was more than twenty years before the accounts were settled. In Richard I's reign the business transactions of the English Jewry were organized in six or seven principal towns under the supervision of two Jews and two Christians. These in turn were controlled by justices of the Jews who were established at Westminster in what came to be known as the exchequer of the Jews, which was a financial, judicial, and administrative

---

[1] Cf. J. E. A. Jolliffe, op. cit., p. 121.

[2] 43½ per cent. was a normal rate, but sometimes it was 60 per cent. or even higher. C. Roth, *History of the Jews in England*, pp. 106–7.

department like the exchequer itself, for matters in which Jews were concerned. Kings exploited the riches of the Jews mercilessly. In 1187 Henry II took a quarter of their chattels for the crusade; they were forced to contribute heavily to Richard I's ransom. King John took immense sums in fines and tallages. At the outset he sold them a confirmation of their charters for 4,000 marks; but their charters of protection were of little value, for at Bristol after his return from Ireland in 1210 he arrested and imprisoned them and imposed so crippling a tallage that many left the country in despair. It was of this tallage that the story is told of the Bristol Jew who was condemned to have a molar tooth extracted every day until he had paid the 10,000 marks demanded of him. He gave in after the seventh had been removed. The demolition of the London Jewry by the barons in 1215 and the clauses (10 and 11) of Magna Carta which limited their power of reviving their former position of affluence, left the Jews at the end of John's reign in a state of helpless confusion bordering on ruin.

The Jews, however, were not the only money-lenders and financiers in the twelfth century. In spite of the prohibition of the church, usury was practised by Christians. William Cade, a Christian of Flemish extraction who died about 1166, had financial dealings with a large number of important persons including the king himself. The roll of debts which were still owing to him at the time of his death amounted to the large sum of £5,000.[1] Though there were other Christian money-lenders none did business on anything like the same scale.[2] Already Richard I and John were borrowing extensively from foreign merchants, especially in Flanders and Italy. In 1199, for example, John borrowed 1,700 marks from Hugh Oisel of Ypres, who became a citizen of London,[3] and in the same year 2,125 marks from merchants of Piacenza.[4] The great military orders, the Templars and the Hospitallers, also performed valuable services in the field of finance. From 1185 the New

[1] See the articles by Hilary Jenkinson in *Eng. Hist. Rev.* xxviii (1913), 209–27, 522–7, 730–2; *Essays in History presented to R. L. Poole*, pp. 190–210.

[2] Gervase, a merchant of Southampton, was doing considerable business in the last years of the century. See *Pipe Roll 4 Jo.*, pp. xxi–ii. Cf. also *Introduction to the Curia Regis Rolls* (Selden Soc., vol. 62), p. 294.

[3] *Rot. Chart.*, pp. 11b, 13. Cf. G. Dept, *Revue du Nord*, xii (1926), 315–16, and *Les Influences anglaise et française dans le comté de Flandre*, pp. 71–2.

[4] *Rot. Chart.*, p. 31. Cf. *Rot. Misae 11 Jo.* (ed. Hardy), p. 148.

Temple became an important depository of royal treasure, and through their powerful international organization with their great wealth and their houses widely distributed over the Continent, the orders were in a unique position to make advances and to negotiate loans.[1]

[1] Cf. Round, *Cal. of Documents, France*, pp. 366, 382-3.

XIII

KING JOHN AND THE INTERDICT

1204–1213

KING JOHN, like so many younger sons of great families, had been destined by his parents for the life of the cloister; he had, we are told, been placed when little more than a year old as an oblate in the abbey of Fontevrault.[1] His unsuitability for this profession must, however, have become soon apparent, and by the time he was six he was brought back to be educated at his father's court. That care was taken with his education we may infer from his fondness for reading, a taste which he retained in later life. Even in the critical year 1203, when he should have been wholly absorbed in public affairs, he had his library sent across to him in Normandy.[2] We have seen how from a landless youth he became in manhood an overrichly endowed irresponsible and rebellious prince.

A malign tradition, which has its origin in the nearly contemporary church historians, especially Roger of Wendover, and his embellisher, Matthew Paris, has done much less than justice to the character of King John. This tradition, developed through the ages, received the hall-mark of critical scholarship from Bishop Stubbs.[3] Certainly the character of this tough, rather stout, energetic little man (he measured 5 feet 5 inches in height)[4] defies adequate description. Almost any epithet might appropriately be applied to him in one or other of his many and versatile moods. He was cruel and ruthless, violent and passionate, greedy and self-indulgent, genial and repellent, arbitrary and judicious, clever and capable, original and inquisitive. He is made up of inconsistencies. Nevertheless many

[1] This is stated by A. Richard, *Les Comtes de Poitou*, ii. 375, quoting a cartulary of Fontevrault (Bibl. Nat. MS. Lat. 5480).

[2] 43*s*. 10*d*. was paid 'for chests and carts for carrying the king's books beyond the sea'. *Pipe Roll 5 Jo.*, p. 139. Cf. also above, p. 243.

[3] The unreliability of Wendover and Paris has been clearly demonstrated by V. H. Galbraith in his Lecture on the David Murray Foundation (Glasgow University Publications LXI, 1944), especially pp. 35–9. Stubbs's treatment of the reign and character of King John in the introduction to vol. ii of Walter of Coventry (Rolls Series) is perhaps the only instance of the great historian's work being affected by conscious bias and preconceived ideas.

[4] Below, p. 486 n.

of these characteristics were shared in a greater or less degree by all the Angevin race. It is improper to accept the view of an eminent French historian[1] that King John was a psychological case, a cyclothymic, alternately bursting with irrepressible energy and plunged in the depths of depression and inertia. Such a diagnosis can only rest on certain fanciful passages in Wendover which, for example, describe the king in 1203 lying in bed till lunch-time and spending the rest of the day feasting with his queen while Philip Augustus was storming his castles and occupying his Norman lands.[2] He might perhaps have prosecuted the losing war more actively (though with little more prospect of success), but he was not idle. The chancery records make it abundantly clear that he attended assiduously to the business of government both at home and abroad in this fateful year 1203.[3] Though not a warrior like his brother Richard, John was no coward, and it was 'malicious backbiters and envious scoffers' who gave him the nick-name 'soft-sword' (*mollegladium*), and this softness, we are told, was in course of time turned to such hardness as none of his predecessors could equal.[4] Certainly no medieval English king before or since his time dealt more successfully with the Welsh, the Scots, or the Irish, and even his later campaigns in Poitou might have been crowned with victory had it not been for the treachery or at best the half-hearted support of the barons who followed him. Indolence was not one of John's vices. On the contrary, restless energy is a pronounced characteristic: he could not be still. Even in church he showed his impatience and would send to the preacher bidding him to conclude his sermon as he wanted his dinner.[5] Quick-tempered like all his family, he was often furious in his rage and would vent his anger on his victims with a remorseless severity. By nature suspicious, he would exact, at least in later years, an oath from members of his household that they would report anything they heard spoken against him.[6] No one

---

[1] Ch. Petit-Dutaillis, 'L'Essor des états d'occident' (*Histoire du Moyen Age*, ed. Glotz, iv, pt. 2), p. 137.

[2] Wendover (ed. Coxe), iii. 171.

[3] For the business transacted in this year see Patent Rolls and the Liberate Roll (ed. by Duffus Hardy, 1844) which is in fact the first extant Close Roll.

[4] Gervase of Canterbury, *Opera*, ii. 93. The short portion of the *Gesta Regum* dealing with the period 1199–1210 is, in the view of Stubbs, strictly contemporary. Ibid., pp. xi–xii.

[5] *Magna Vita Sancti Hugonis* (Rolls Series), pp. 292–3.

[6] *Curia Regis Rolls*, vii. 170.

knew when the king's hand would turn against him. His treatment of the wife and son of William of Braose who were starved to death in a dungeon at Windsor castle, though perhaps the best known, is only one of many examples of his wanton cruelty.[1] This side of his character is also exhibited in his morbid delight in witnessing those bloody spectacles which in a superstitious age were regarded as manifesting the judgement of God. He would often have judicial combats deferred to a time and place when it would be convenient for him to be present.[2]

From the record of his daily expenses a good deal is known of his personal tastes and habits. He was continually moving about the country, seldom spending more than a few days in one place. In this way he must have gained a very intimate knowledge of his kingdom and of his subjects. Normally his itinerary would be planned with some precision; wine and stores and the wardrobe with the whole apparatus of government were carted ahead in wagons; litigants were told to appear at a given place on a given date. John was fastidious about personal cleanliness, and arranged for a bath to be prepared for him in the towns through which he passed.[3] In contrast to the plain living which was customary at his father's court, John loved splendour and a good table. For the Christmas feast, for example, which he kept in 1206 at Winchester, he ordered 1,500 chickens, 5,000 eggs, 20 oxen, 100 pigs, and 100 sheep.[4] Evidently he proposed to

[1] This feature, however, has been particularly exaggerated by Wendover and later writers. Little credence, for instance, need be given to the story of the exchequer clerk, Geoffrey of Norwich, who, according to Wendover (iii. 229), was thrust into prison, where, starved and weighed down by a leaden cloak, he died. Taxster, in his continuation of the chronicle of Florence of Worcester (ed. Thorpe, ii. 170), improved on the story: the clerk is summoned to Nottingham where 'loaded with, or more truly clothed in iron, he died'. The fact that Wendover calls Geoffrey 'archdeacon' of Norwich illustrates the unreliability of the whole story. Geoffrey de Burgo was archdeacon of Norwich from 1200 to 1225 when he became bishop of Ely. He died comfortably in 1228. See L. Landon, *Proc. of the Suffolk Inst. of Archaeology*, xx (1948), 33–4. S. Painter suggests on good grounds that the victim was a certain Geoffrey of Norwich who was a justice of the Jews (*Speculum*, xxviii (1953), 808–13).

[2] *Curia Regis Rolls*, i. 278–9.

[3] He took, for instance, eight baths at various places in the course of his travels between 29 January and 17 June 1209, for each of which William, his bathman (*aquarius*), received a few pence in addition to his standard wage of a halfpenny a day. *Rot. Misae 11 Jo.* (ed. Hardy), pp. 115, 137. He even possessed a dressing-gown: 'Ad supertunicam domini Regis ad surgendum de nocte xxs.' Ibid., p. 151.

[4] *Rot. Lit. Claus.* i. 75. The bill for these provisions only amounted to the modest sum of £11. 16s. 6d. *Pipe Roll 9 Jo.*, p. 139.

entertain company on a large and lavish scale. Much was spent on dress and gold ornament for himself, his family, and his courtiers; and he had an immense collection of jewels.[1] Conjugal fidelity was not a characteristic of the Angevin kings, and John was no exception. He was something of a profligate.[2] He was fond of gaming, though he played with little skill, for he appears to have generally lost a few shillings to his opponent in the course of an evening.[3] In other ways, too, he was self-indulgent. He would habitually break the rules prescribed by the church, though he would readily perform the necessary penance to atone for the indiscretion. Thus he gave alms to a hundred paupers 'because he ate twice on Friday on the eve of St. Mark' or again he fed a hundred paupers 'because he went fishing at Marlborough on the feast of St. Leonard'.[4] His alms-giving was not, however, confined to atonement for sins committed.[5] He would provide food and drink for large numbers of the poor without any ulterior motive and would give liberal sick-benefit for his servants when they were ill and unable to work. He was not ungenerous, and gave freely if indiscriminately for charitable purposes. He was not wholly inattentive to the needs of the church. The foundation of Beaulieu abbey stands to his credit; he doled out small sums to religious houses, particularly to small nunneries; he made gifts of vestments and altar cloths. These facts suggest that he was not altogether out of sympathy with the church and religious life. It was not pure formality that chaplains at Chichester said masses for the soul of King John

---

[1] For an inventory of this collection, which was deposited in various religious houses, see *Rot. Chart.*, p. 134. He would add to it by including jewels in fines which he imposed. Thus from the executors of Philip, bishop of Durham, he demanded 2,000 marks and all his *jocalia*, *Pipe Roll 10 Jo.*, p. 59. Warin, son of Gerold, owes a ruby worth 20 or 21 marks, *Pipe Roll 9 Jo.*, p. 72. Monastic houses were commonly used for safe deposit, for they alone had proper receptacles for the purpose. The archives of the abbey of Jervaulx, for example, were kept in a chest with three locks. *Curia Regis Rolls*, vii. 272.

[2] The names of some of his mistresses are known. He gave a handsome present of clothes to a certain Suzanne who is described as 'domicella, amica domini Regis', *Rot. Misae 14 Jo.* (ed. Cole), p. 267. The mother of his illegitimate daughter Joan, who married Llywelyn ap Iorwerth, is said to be Clementia, *Annals of Tewkesbury, sub anno* 1236. He had a not inconsiderable family of bastards besides Joan: Geoffrey (*Curia Regis Rolls*, iii. 321), John (*Rot. Lit. Pat.*, p. 117), Oliver (Mat. Paris, iii. 41), Richard (Wendover, iv. 29), and doubtless others.

[3] *Rot. Misae 11 Jo.*, pp. 131, 139–140; ibid. *14 Jo.*, pp. 239, 249, 252–4.

[4] *Rot. Misae 11 Jo.*, p. 110: ibid *14 Jo.*, p. 246.

[5] See the examples collected in the introductions to *Pipe Rolls 6 Jo.*, pp. xxxvi–xxxvii, and 7 *Jo.*, p. xl.

'of blessed memory',[1] or that his obit was strictly observed at Worcester.

He was extortionate and wrung enormous sums from his subjects both great and small. Yet King John—and it is remarkable in a man of so unstable a character—had a genuine and even a conscientious interest in the administration of justice, perhaps inculcated by Rannulf Glanvill who at one time had been his tutor. Maintenance of the peace he regarded as among the most important of his functions, and he would strike hard those who ventured to break it, for 'our peace should be inviolably preserved, even if it were only granted to a dog'.[2] When abroad, he would often order a suit to be postponed until his return 'because we do not wish it to be heard save before us';[3] when in England he would devote much time to this side of his duties. He would frequently, for one reason or another, have a case deferred until he could attend to it personally. His opinion was sought by the judges themselves, and suitors regarded it as a valued privilege worth paying highly for to have their complaints heard in the king's presence. Though he would sometimes act arbitrarily—we hear of pleas stayed at his wish and of a plaintiff withdrawing a suit because the king did not wish him to have a jury[4]—yet generally he showed a proper sense of responsibility. We hear that he is dissatisfied with the evidence and requires more;[5] that he wishes to be fair to both parties.[6] He was at least on one occasion 'moved by compassion'.[7] He even heard a suit in October 1216 about a fortnight before his death and in the midst of a campaign.[8] He also attended at and intervened in the financial business of the exchequer.[9] It was largely to the king's personal interest and activity in judicial matters that the great development in English law during this period was due.

Widespread disturbances broke out when the news reached England that King Richard had died on 6 April 1199. A wave of crime and lawlessness swept through the country. The barons,

---

[1] *Chichester Chartulary*, no. 410 (Sussex Rec. Soc., xlvi, 1946); *Early Compotus Rolls of the Priory of Worcester*, ed. J. M. Wilson and Cosmo Gordon (Worcester Hist. Soc., 1908), p. 60: 'In pisce empto pro conventu pro obitu J. Regis.'

[2] *Rot. Lit. Pat.*, p. 33, quoted V. H. Galbraith, *Studies in the Public Records*, p. 125.

[3] *Rot. de Liberate 5 Jo.* (1203), pp. 41–2; *Curia Regis Rolls*, ii. 287.

[4] *Curia Regis Rolls*, iv. 99; v. 72, 231.

[6] Ibid. i. 392.

[8] *Rolls of the Justices in Eyre for Lincolnshire and Worcestershire* (Selden Soc., vol. 53), pp. lx–lxi.   [9] *Pipe Roll 6 Jo.*, p. 147.

in preparation for any eventuality, put their castles in a state of defence. A disputed succession was probable and a civil war more than a possibility. That peace was quickly restored was due to the prompt and effective measures taken by the justiciar, Geoffrey Fitz Peter acting with Hubert Walter and William Marshal who had been sent over from France to assist him.[1] They summoned to Northampton the barons whose conduct laid them open to suspicion, and induced them to swear fealty to John; and as a further precaution they caused the royal castles to be repaired, garrisoned, and provisioned.[2] Consequently, when John landed at Shoreham on 25 May there was no sign of opposition, and two days later, on Ascension Day,[3] he was crowned at Westminster in the presence of an imposing gathering of bishops and barons. Three weeks sufficed for ordering the affairs of his kingdom; on 20 June he returned whence he came by way of Shoreham and Dieppe; by midsummer he was once more in Rouen.

During the early years of his reign King John was chiefly occupied in fighting the losing war with Philip Augustus, described in a previous chapter. He returned to England for short periods: he was there from 27 February till the end of April in 1200, and came again in October for the coronation of his new queen, Isabel of Angoulême, and stayed on till May of the following year (1201); after this he remained on the Continent till December 1203 when Normandy was virtually lost.[4] These

---

[1] Hubert Walter resigned the justiciarship in 1198 and was succeeded by Geoffrey Fitz Peter. Immediately after the coronation Hubert Walter was made chancellor and William Marshal earl of Pembroke and Strigul.

[2] The *Memoranda Roll* of the first year of the reign (p. 12) significantly supplements the narrative sources: Reginald Basset has quittance of a debt 'propter tumultum in tempore paschali de morte R. Ricardi'. For the precautions taken see ibid., pp. 43, 68; and the instances collected in the introduction to the *Pipe Roll 1 Jo.*, pp. xiii-xv. The formal ending of the period of lawlessness is indicated in a record of a crime committed in Devonshire 'post mortem regis Ricardi et prius quam pax domini regis, qui tunc fuit dux Normannie fuit jurata'. *Curia Regis Rolls*, i. 384.

[3] It was the practice to reckon the regnal year of the king from the day of coronation. The fact that John was crowned on Ascension Day, a movable feast, has given rise to much confusion: thus 3 to 22 May 1200 and 3 to 22 May 1201 both fall into the third regnal year. A similar confusion of overlapping dates occurs in the 5th, 8th, 11th, 14th, and 16th years.

[4] Three letters on the Patent Roll of 1202, one of 14 and two of 16 May, are dated *Teste me ipso apud Rie* (Rye). There is, however, no other evidence for this rapid visit. The king was at Pont-de-l'Arche on 12, and at Arques on 17 May. It seems more likely that he dispatched these letters from Normandy, and the dating clause was added in England.

visits he employed in travelling round the country with restless activity; he but rarely slept more than three nights in one place. Business would take him to every corner of his kingdom; in November 1200 he was at Lincoln where he attended the obsequies of St. Hugh and received the homage of the king of Scotland; in February 1201 he was on the northern border, visiting Bamborough and Carlisle; in April he was at Exeter and Wells. But most of his time he spent in the midlands and especially in Wiltshire where he could conveniently combine business with the pleasures of the chase. In striking contrast to the confusion of war which during these years disturbed the duchy of Normandy and the other dominions on the Continent, England itself enjoyed a period of profound peace.[1] This was due, as a contemporary observes, to the work of the archbishop and chancellor, Hubert Walter, and the justiciar, Geoffrey Fitz Peter, whose clear-sighted efficiency can be seen in every detail of the administration. The machine ran smoothly in all its parts. Order was maintained; the judges made regular circuits through the kingdom; the large sums needed for carrying on the war were raised without serious protest; and an immense quantity of stores for provisioning the army was bought and shipped to the Continent. Nevertheless it would be wrong to suppose that the king when abroad was unconcerned with English affairs and left everything in the hands of his ministers. On the contrary, he kept in close touch with what went on, and often intervened by sending peremptory instructions regarding his wishes.

The severance of Normandy from England gave rise to a situation of extraordinary complexity. The interests of the two countries had been so interwoven that they could not be disentangled without much confusion and often serious injustice and hardship. No definite treaty of peace (until the Treaty of Paris in 1259) marks the end of the long connexion between the two countries. The kings made their own independent arrangements to deal with the social upheaval which inevitably followed. Thus Philip Augustus issued a general decree confiscating the lands of all Normans who were in England and failed to return by a given date; and John retaliated by a similar order affecting the estates of the Normans who adhered to Philip. The barons who held, as so many of them did, lands both in

[1] Gervase of Canterbury, ii. 95.

England and in Normandy had therefore to make their choice: they must sacrifice their property in one country or in the other; they must become Englishmen or Frenchmen; they could no longer well be both.[1] Difficult as such a decision may often have been, the position of the barons was easier than that of many others, the sub-tenants, the wards, and widows, whose feudal relationships might be seriously jeopardized by the defection of their overlords, guardians, or former husbands. There is reason to suppose, however, that both kings realized these difficulties and did not seek unduly to embarrass their subjects. They were, it seems, given complete freedom of choice; they might stay or go as they wished. King John, at first at least, made only provisional arrangements in dealing with the *terrae Normannorum*. The estates were carefully valued and the revenues arising from them were entered in a separate account at the exchequer.[2] Those who were deprived of their lands *occasione Normannorum* might have them restored if they should return and make their peace with the king. This in fact often happened; and the king was able to add to his income by selling pardons to those who wished to reside again in England.[3] The Norman ecclesiastics were not seriously disturbed in their English estates; their rents might be delayed or temporarily suspended; they might be required to redeem them by a fine;[4] and communication between the landlord and their alien tenantry might be dislocated. But in general things went on much as before.[5] The most outstanding consequence of the severance of the two countries was that

---

[1] William Marshal retained lands in both countries. See Powicke, *Loss of Normandy*, p. 431; and according to Bracton (f. 427*b*, quoted Powicke, op. cit., p. 434, n. 1) there were others. But there cannot have been many, and a decree of Louis IX in 1244 put an end to this slight connexion (ibid., p. 435). The private arrangement between two men in the garrison of the castle of Arques by which one agreed to keep the Norman lands of both and the other the English (*Curia Regis Rolls*, iv. 101) may illustrate how the difficulty was often overcome.

[2] 'in compoto rotuli de terris Normannorum'. *Pipe Roll 6 Jo.*, p. 186. The valuations of some estates have survived and are printed in the *Rotuli Normanniae*, ed. Hardy (Record Commission), pp. 122–43. The Pipe Rolls of the years 1204–6, which appeared in print between 1940 and 1942, do not add materially to the admirable account of the effects of the loss of Normandy in chapter x of Professor Powicke's book published in 1913.

[3] Powicke, op. cit., p. 424 and examples cited in n. 2.

[4] So, for example, in 1208 the abbot of St. Wandrille accounted for £100 and three palfreys for having the abbey's lands and possessions in England. *Pipe Roll 10 Jo.*, p. 156. For other instances see ibid., Introd., p. xi.

[5] Cf. M. Morgan, *English Lands of the Abbey of Bec* (Oxford, 1946), p. 120, and Powicke, op. cit., p. 425.

those who elected to remain in England devoted themselves to English affairs and English interests untrammelled by continental complications.

Among the more important consequences of the loss of Normandy in 1204 was the stimulus it gave to naval activity. The Anglo-Saxon kings had maintained a royal fleet;[1] but after the conquest there was no need for warships. England controlled the whole stretch of the northern and western shores of France; the counts of Flanders and Boulogne during most of this period were at least the nominal allies of England. The only serious danger to shipping came from pirates who infested the seas from secluded anchorages in islands or on the coast of Brittany; 112 pirates were beheaded in Tresco (Scilly Islands) in 1209.[2] In normal times the suppression of piracy, coastal defence, and the transport of armies could be provided for adequately by the ship-service of the Cinque Ports, 'the gates that open and shut to the perill or safety of this kingdome', as they were later described.[3] The origin of this interesting confederacy of five head towns, Hastings, Romney, Hythe, Dover, and Sandwich, to which in course of time were added the 'ancient towns' of Winchelsea and Rye, and other 'limbs' or 'members', can be carried back with reasonable probability to the time of Edward the Confessor. In return for substantial constitutional and trading privileges, the ports were required to furnish fifty-seven ships for fifteen days' service at their own cost, and for a longer period at the expense of the king. Early in Henry II's reign the 'captains or skippers' of the Kentish ports were charged with the duty of 'guarding the coast'.[4] Similarly, Maldon in Essex was under the obligation of providing one ship for forty days in the king's service.[5] It is not an insignificant indication of the rising importance of the navy owing to the loss of Normandy that the individual charters of the Cinque ports, which date back to the reign of Henry II,

[1] Stenton, *Anglo-Saxon England*, pp. 424–6.
[2] 'in crastino Ascensionis domini in insula S. Nich' de Sully decollati sunt pirate s[cilicet]cent' xii.', quoted from the Annals of Tavistock (Bodleian MS. Digby 81) by H. P. R. Finberg in *Devon and Cornwall Notes and Queries*, xxii (1945), 251.
[3] Quoted by K. M. E. Murray, *Trans. R. Hist. Soc.*, 4th ser., xviii (1935), p. 53. See also the same author's *Constitutional History of the Cinque Ports* (1935).
[4] 'In liberationem gubernatorum et sciprorum qui custodiebant marinam'. *Pipe Roll 7 Hen. II*, p. 62 (1161). The same year the five ports are mentioned for the first time. *Pipe Roll 7 Hen. II*, pp. 56, 59.
[5] Ballard, *British Borough Charters*, i. 90.

were confirmed by John in 1205, and that in the following year
the burgesses of these towns were styled 'barons', a dignity previously only enjoyed by Hastings.[1]

Besides these the king had his own royal galley or *esnecca*
(a Scandinavian word meaning a snake, a fast ship), which was
usually berthed at Southampton and kept in readiness to take
him and his friends across the Channel. It was faster and larger
than the average ship, carrying a crew of sixty compared with a
normal complement of twenty-three. £7. 10s. (the wages of the
crew at 2d. a day for 15 days) was charged against the exchequer
for each Channel passage of the *esnecca*, while an ordinary ship
could be hired for anything between 25s. and 40s.[2] In the first
part of the twelfth century the duty of furnishing this ship, the
ministerium de esnecca, was entrusted to a family probably of
Italian origin, which suggests that ship-masters with Mediterranean experience were considered the most reliable.[3] Towards
the end of the reign of Henry II this responsible post was occupied by a famous sea captain, Alan Trenchemer.[4] It was he
whom Richard I, when in captivity, sent for to bring him home
from Antwerp, and he was rewarded for his faithful service by
an estate in Surrey.

These normal naval resources were, however, quite inadequate in times of emergency; on such occasions ships were
purchased, hired, or requisitioned from the merchant marine.
A fleet of upward of a hundred vessels was needed to transport
the crusading army of Richard I and its vast equipment of
stores to Palestine, of which the Cinque Ports provided no more
than a third. For the rest, we are told,[5] the king sent his bailiffs
to search the ports of England, Normandy, and Poitou for ships
capable of carrying heavy cargoes. Henry of Cornhill, a prominent London magnate, had the spending of over £5,000 on
the purchase of ships in England and on the payment of their
crews.[6] The crusades, which brought English seamen into closer

[1] James Tait, *The Medieval English Borough*, pp. 259–60.

[2] *Pipe Roll 22 Hen. II*, pp. 199–200. The captain (*nauclerus*) of the *esnecca* had a
fixed stipend of 12d. a day paid by the exchequer (Dialogus, i. 6).

[3] Haskins, *Norman Institutions*, pp. 121–2.

[4] His name first appears in connexion with naval affairs on the Pipe Roll of
1184 (*30 Hen. II*, pp. 58, 86, 87). He died apparently in 1204 when his estates were
granted by the king to William de Braose. *Rot. Chart.*, p. 134b.

[5] Hoveden, iii. 8.

[6] *Pipe Roll 2 Ric. I*, p. 8. This account included 33 ships of the Cinque Ports, two-
thirds of which were bought for the king's use in connexion with the crusade; it

touch with the maritime enterprise of the Mediterranean, provided a great stimulus to the development of shipping, navigation, and naval warfare. Richard's fleet, however, was mustered
to serve a particular purpose, and there is nothing to suggest
that it remained in being after its purpose was accomplished. It
was only when the Channel ports fell into hostile hands that the
need of a royal fleet became imperative. It is to King John's
credit that he rose to the occasion and took immediate steps to
supply the need. Henceforth there was a regular and organized
naval establishment.

In 1205 there were 51 royal galleys stationed in 15 different
ports, 46 around the English coast from Lynn to Gloucester and
5 in Ireland, and grouped under 3 commands.[1] Two of these
commanders, Reginald of Cornhill, a brother of Henry of Cornhill who had been chiefly responsible for assembling Richard I's
crusading fleet, and William of Wrotham, archdeacon of Taunton, had already been prominent in maritime affairs; with a
certain William de Furnell, they are described as *capitales
custodes portuum* in connexion with the tax of a fifteenth on
merchandise.[2] During the following years they seem to have
been entrusted with the organization and general conduct of
the navy. William of Wrotham is often designated as 'keeper
of the king's ships'. He was charged with the duty of carrying out
the king's orders regarding the navy; he requisitioned merchant
ships to meet the abnormal demands of transport and supply
caused by a campaign on a large scale; he regulated trade;
supervised repairs, and impressed seamen into the service.[3]

Mariners received high wages. In 1207 the ordinary seaman
had 3*d.* a day and the shipmaster 6*d.*;[4] a galleyman (*galeota*)
could also earn 6*d.*; and it was customary before setting out on
a voyage to give the men an advance in pay. In addition the
seamen might expect a share, sometimes as much as a half share,
in any prize captured.[5] This, however, rested with the king, to

also included wages for 790 captains (*sturmanni*) and sailors for a year. The sailor
received 2*d.*, the captain 4*d.* a day. Cf. *Eng. Hist. Rev.* xxxvi (1921), 326–7.
  [1] *Rot. Lit. Claus.* i. 33*a*.
  [2] *Rot. Lit. Pat.*, pp. 42–3. Above, pp. 93, 96. For the importance of this document
in connexion with the office of keeper of the king's ports and galleys, see F. W. Brooks,
Eng. Hist. Rev. xl (1925), 570 ff.
  [3] Cf. his account for ships and the wages of seamen for the expedition to Poitou
in 1206, *Pipe Roll 8 Jo.*, p. 148.
  [4] *Pipe Roll 9 Jo.*, p. 168.
  [5] *Rot. Lit. Pat.* 51*a*, 52*b*.

whom all captured ships and their cargoes by right belonged to
dispose of as he pleased. A document of the year 1212, which
has chanced to survive among the records of the exchequer,[1]
supplies us with details of the disposal of 13 ships and their
cargoes (consisting of 666 tons of wine, 936 quarters of corn,
2,640 quarters of salt, and 860 salted carcases of hog) brought
into Portsmouth harbour by the galleys under the command of
Geoffrey de Lucy between 25 April and 8 September 1212.
Most of this prize, both ships and stores, was dispatched to
Wales where the king was planning a campaign. Of the remainder, some was distributed among chosen friends, some was
sold to pay off the soldiers and sailors engaged in the capture,
and some (two old and dismantled ships and ninety-eight
putrefied carcasses) were retained at Portsmouth. In 1210 £100
obtained from the sale of the cargo of a Norman ship captured
off Wales was distributed to mariners and galleymen.[2] Nevertheless, in spite of the inducement of good wages and the prospect of prize, it was found necessary to have recourse to strong
measures of impressment to obtain sufficient men. Recruiting
officers were employed on this work 'who know how to speak
wisely and cunningly to pilots and mariners in order to persuade and induce them to enter the king's service'.[3] On one
occasion in 1208 King John threatened Welsh mariners with
hanging and the loss of their chattels if they did not enter his
service at Ilfracombe.[4] Merchant ships and their crews were
often pressed into the king's service under pain of severe
penalties.[5]

These fleets were composed of ships of varying types and
capacity. The principal war vessel was the galley, introduced
into northern waters from the Mediterranean, a long, slightly
built ship, lying low in the water, and propelled by oars. For
purposes of transport, busses were used, 'strong vessels of great
capacity and wonderful agility' as they are described by the
contemporary historian Richard of Devizes,[6] and the broad-
beamed sailing-ship known as a cog. It is not easy to arrive at
any very precise idea of the size of these ships. At this time
tonnage appears to have been reckoned on the number of tun

---

[1] Printed by B. E. R. Formoy, *Eng. Hist. Rev.* xli (1926), 557.
[2] *Praestita Roll*, 1210 (ed. Hardy), p. 227.
[3] *Rot. Lit. Claus.* i. 70b.   [4] *Rot. Lit. Pat.* 79a.
[5] See the writs collected by Sir Harris Nicolas, *Hist. of Royal Navy*, i, App. vii.
[6] *Rolls Series*, ed. Howlett, p. 394.

casks of wine which could be carried. In 1214, for example, the king wrote to the sheriffs of various counties, the reeves and bailiffs of Bristol, and the barons of the Cinque Ports asking for a return of the number of ships they have capable of carrying eighty tuns of wine or more.[1] A large transport might carry several hundred men on a Channel crossing; the 'White Ship', on which Henry I's son was crossing from Normandy in 1120, is said to have capsized with 300 on board; the same number are said to have perished in a ship lost in a storm in 1177; and in one that went down in 1170 the number of passengers is given as 400.[2] Medieval estimates erred on the side of exaggeration, but certainly these would be ships of the largest capacity.

As the importance of shipping increased, there were corresponding improvements in construction and in technical devices for navigation. The galley, originally a warship propelled by oars, was fitted with mast and sail; the sailing-ship, normally used for trading, was adapted for use in naval warfare by the addition of raised platforms or castles at bow (the forecastle) and stern, from which the attackers could hurl stones, Greek fire, and other missiles upon the enemy. It was also supplied with bridges for boarding the enemy vessels. The invention of the mariner's compass, first alluded to by Alexander Neckham at the close of the twelfth century,[3] and a less primitive rudder facilitated navigation. At Dover and doubtless elsewhere there was a lighthouse;[4] and coast-guards (*awaita maris*) are mentioned in Cumberland as early as 1203.[5] The ports of the southeast coast were unsuitable for the mustering of large fleets. In consequence Southampton and Portsmouth became increasingly important, the former as a commercial,[6] the latter as a naval port. Portsmouth can have been scarcely more than a small cluster of dwellings when in 1194 'it pleased the lord king

[1] *Rot. Lit. Claus.* i. 177–8.

[2] Ordericus Vitalis, iv. 411–12; *Gesta Henrici*, i. 3–4; 195.

[3] *De Naturis Rerum* (Rolls Series, ed. Wright), p. 183. It has generally been maintained that the mariner's compass originated in Mediterranean waters, probably at Amalfi. But Heinrich Winter (*Mariner's Mirror*, xxiii (1937), 95 ff.) argues for a possible and even probable origin among the Northmen. This hypothesis receives support from the fact that in the early middle ages Norsemen were commonly used as pilots. *Esturmannus*, the usual term for pilot, is a Scandinavian word.

[4] *Phararius*, a lighthouse-keeper, is mentioned in the *Curia Regis Rolls* in 1201 (ii. 43).

[5] Ibid. ii. 274.

[6] Southampton had the largest volume of trade after London according to the return of the fifteenth on merchandize in 1204. See above, p. 96.

Richard to build the town of Portsmouth' and grant it a charter.[1] Houses for the king surrounded by ramparts were erected, and building sites were leased to new settlers; a dock (*exclusa*) was also constructed, which in 1212 was strengthened by a strong wall and furnished with warehouses for keeping marine stores.[2]

At Chinon in 1190 before embarking for the Crusade, Richard I drew up a set of rules for the discipline of the fleet, which have been described as the first 'articles of war'. The penalties prescribed were crude and severe:

'Anyone who slays a man on board ship shall be thrown into the sea lashed to the corpse; if on land he shall be buried in the ground tied to the corpse. Anyone convicted by lawful witnesses of striking another so as to draw blood shall lose his hand; but if he strikes with his hand without drawing blood he shall be dipped three times in the sea. Anyone who uses opprobrious, abusive, or blasphemous language against his fellow shall pay on each occasion one ounce of silver. A convicted thief shall be shaved like a champion, tarred and feathered, and put ashore as soon as the ship touches land.'[3]

Another disciplinary measure dated at Messina in 1190 restricted gambling during the crusade. Only kings might gamble as they pleased; knights and clergy might play, but they must not lose more than 20s. a day on pain of a fine of 100s. All others were forbidden to play at all, and disobedience was severely punished: soldiers were flogged naked on three successive days and sailors were ducked in the sea in the way of mariners (perhaps an early reference to keel-hauling) on three successive days.[4] Another ordinance, also issued from Messina, relates to wreck. Anciently, as now, wreck was a royal right. The king might claim everything that came ashore. This harsh custom was modified by Henry I who decreed that if one man escaped alive he should have everything. Richard I went farther and ordained that when there was no survivor the heirs might claim the wreckage.[5]

[1] *Curia Regis Rolls*, vi. 305. Considerable sums were expended on this work from 1194 till the end of the reign of Richard I. From 1195 a separate *compotus* for Portsmouth is entered on the Pipe Rolls. It received its charter in 1194 (*Foedera*, i. 63) which was confirmed by King John in 1200.

[2] *Rot. Lit. Claus.* i. 117. Cf. *Close Rolls, 1227-31*, p. 32.

[3] *Gesta Ric.* ii. 110. Hoveden, iii. 36. Richard was at Chinon between 2 and 7 March 1190.

[4] *Gesta Ric.* ii. 130.

[5] *Gesta Ric.* ii. 139. Cf. *Chronicon Monasterii de Bello*, p. 66. Later, in the thirteenth century, a survivor was interpreted as any live thing, such as a dog or cat; if any of these escaped, it was legally no wreck. Stat. 3 Ed. I, c. 4.

It is also generally assumed (though the authority for the assumption is not earlier than the fourteenth century) that Richard I after his return from the crusade adopted the maritime custom known as the Judgements or Laws of Oléron near La Rochelle, which was administered in the English ports and along the Atlantic coast till the end of the middle ages. The law of the sea by its very nature tended to be international and the laws of Oléron bear a close affinity to the Rhodian Sea-Law of classical antiquity and the Mediterranean codes, such as that of Amalfi, which were derived from it.[1] The laws were added to as need arose, and one such ordinance, said to have been made by King John at Hastings in the year 1200, required all ships to strike or lower their sails at the order of the commander of any of the king's ships. It was on the basis of this ordinance that Selden in the seventeenth century claimed for the English Crown dominion over the narrow seas.[2]

The months following the loss of Normandy were a period of expectancy; the country was preparing for any emergency that might arise: an attempt to recover the lost ground or to meet the threat of invasion. The precautions taken by the government suggest a condition bordering on panic. The castles, especially those along the coast, were put into a state of defence, and immense sums of money were raised by increased taxation, as though for a supreme effort. Scutage for the first time was assessed at $2\frac{1}{2}$ marks on the fee and a fifteenth on merchandise was levied at the ports. Then at a council which met at London in January 1205 the whole kingdom was organized into one gigantic commune for home defence to which all above the age of twelve were enjoined on oath to maintain. It was to be controlled by constables appointed in every hundred and borough, who at the direction of the chief constables of the county were to bring the armed forces of the local communes to do what should be necessary 'for the defence of the kingdom and the preservation of the peace against foreigners and other disturbers of the peace'. Anyone who failed in his duty was to be regarded as a public enemy.[3] Next we hear of an actual muster of

[1] The laws of Oléron are included in the *Black Book of the Admiralty*, ed. Twiss (Rolls Series), i. 88–131; the *Tabula Amalfitana*, ibid. iv. 1–51; for the Rhodian Sea-Law see the edition by W. Ashburner (1909).

[2] *Black Book of the Admiralty*, i. 128–31. Selden's *Mare Clausum* is printed in vol. ii, pt. ii of his collected works (ed. Wilkins, 1726).

[3] Gervase of Canterbury, ii. 96–7.

the forces for defence. In the writ issued on 3 April 1205 the quota system was adopted; nine knights were to equip and pay (at the rate of 2s. a day) a tenth. If, however, the foreigners (*alienigenae*) should land, all were to rush to arms. The penalties imposed on those who neglected their duty indicates the seriousness of the alarm: those with land were to be for ever disinherited; those who had no land were to be reduced to servitude (*servi fient in perpetuum*).[1]

The danger was real. Philip Augustus was free to turn his attention to England if he so wished, and the duke of Brabant and the count of Boulogne, recently English pensioners and at variance with one another, had settled their differences and were jointly planning to take steps to recover the English estates of the honor of Boulogne which they claimed by right of their wives.[2] This project, however, did not mature; and the king of France directed his attack not against England but against what still remained in English hands in Touraine and Poitou. The army, therefore, which had been destined to withstand invasion was now to be diverted to an offensive war for the recovery of the lost dominions. Preparations were made on a portentous scale. It has been reckoned that at least £5,000, about a quarter of the year's revenue, was spent on naval and military armaments.[3] As early as February instructions were issued forbidding any shipping to leave the harbours on the south and east coasts without licence. The shipyards were busy building new ships and repairing old; and the fleet, fully victualled and equipped, was mobilized at Portsmouth at Whitsuntide. At about the same time the armed forces were

---

[1] *Rot. Lit. Pat.*, p. 55.

[2] Coggeshall, pp. 148–9; Delisle, *Cat. des Actes de Philippe-Auguste*, nos. 909, 910. The following pedigree sets out the claims of the duke of Brabant and the count of Boulogne:

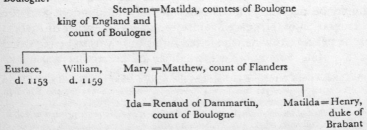

[3] See Sidney Smith's introduction to the *Pipe Roll 7 Jo.*, pp. xv–xxv.

mustered at Northampton (22 May). In popular estimation never before had so many ships been collected in one port or so large an army assembled.[1]

Yet this tremendous effort was doomed to end in a fiasco. There was little confidence between the king and his barons. At a council held at Oxford towards the end of March the latter had only agreed to render an oath of obedience if the king would first promise to maintain the rights of the kingdom inviolate. They now stubbornly resisted the projected campaign: it was too dangerous, the king of France was too strong, and it would leave the country defenceless against invasion. These were the arguments put forward by Hubert Walter and William Marshal who voiced the baronial opposition. The latter had twice visited France to treat with Philip in the spring of 1204 and again in this year, and it appears that he used the occasion to serve his own ends; for he was among the very few barons who succeeded in keeping his estates both in Normandy and in England.[2] Doubtless he had no wish to disturb this satisfactory settlement by reopening hostilities. So to the great disgust not only of the king but of the soldiers and sailors, who were eager to go and felt that they had been brought long distances on a fool's errand, the enterprise was given up.

John had not, however, abandoned the idea of doing something to relieve the situation on the Continent. He even put to sea and cruised about the Channel for a couple of days in the hope, perhaps, that the barons might change their minds and follow him. He then went to Dartmouth[3] to superintend the preparations for the dispatch of a force to Poitou. With the fall of Chinon and Loches in the summer Touraine was completely lost; but in Poitou Niort and La Rochelle were still in English hands, and could serve as bases for a campaign of reconquest. In the previous autumn small reinforcements had been sent to La Rochelle.[4] The two expeditions under the king's natural son Geoffrey and the earl of Salisbury which crossed over in the summer of 1205 were evidently on a larger scale,[5] and were

---

[1] Coggeshall, p. 154.

[2] According to the Marshal's biographer William did homage to Philip with John's permission. *Histoire de Guillaume le Maréchal*, vv. 12948–66; the question is discussed by S. Painter, *William Marshal*, pp. 138–43.

[3] Dartmouth was the port commonly used for direct communication with Poitou.   [4] See the introduction to the *Pipe Roll 7 Jo.*, p. xiii.

[5] Ibid., pp. xviii–xxi.

intended as preliminaries for the more serious campaign which John himself proposed to make in the following year. Again there was feverish activity in the ports, ships and sailors were pressed into service, a formidable army was collected, and early in June 1206 John landed at La Rochelle.

Having marched through Saintonge into Gascony, he captured, with many valuable prisoners, the strong castle of Montauban near Bourg-sur-Mer at the junction of the Dordogne and the Garonne (1 August), and thus secured himself against attack from the south.[1] He was now joined by Almeric de Thouars, one of the most powerful of the Poitevin barons,[2] and the two marched northward, crossed the Loire, and occupied Angers. This was the end of the successes. Philip had been gathering an army, and the barons refused to fight against their overlord. So at Thouars in October a truce was arranged to last for two years. The campaign, however, had not been ineffective. John had at least secured his position south of the Loire.

On 13 July 1205 the country suffered a severe loss by the death of the archbishop of Canterbury, Hubert Walter. He had been justiciar from the end of 1193 till 1198 and chancellor from 1199 till his death, and on each of his departments he has left behind him an ineffaceable mark of his administrative efficiency. The first extant plea roll dates from 1194; in the next year final concords began regularly to be preserved, and there are casual references to a 'roll of fines' (or *oblata*).[3] As chancellor he was responsible for similar bureaucratic reforms; he initiated the enrolment of chancery documents, the charter, patent, and close rolls, and he issued a 'constitution' which set out the fees which were to be paid to the chancellor and his staff for the use of the great seal and for the wax.[4] The searching character of the

---

[1] The capture of Montauban destroyed the pretensions of Castile in Gascony. Cf. *Camb. Med. Hist.* vi. 312. There are indications that Castile soon after this was moving again towards alliance with England. Queen Eleanor visited her brother in England (or at least received a safe conduct to make the visit) in the autumn of 1206. In 1208 the chancellor of Castile came to England. *Foedera*, i. 96, 100.

[2] He was brother of Guy de Thouars, count of Brittany, and in 1205 had gone over to Philip who had made him seneschal in Poitou.

[3] *Pipe Roll 7 Ric. I*, pp. 179, 225. Cf. Introd., pp. xxix-xxx. The Fine Rolls are chancery enrolments and the earliest which survive begin in John's reign during Hubert's chancellorship.

[4] *Foedera*, i. 75-6. It is dated 7 June 1199, a few days after his appointment as chancellor, and was issued 'ad instantiam . . . Huberti Cantuariensis archiepiscopi cancellarii nostri'. Evidently under Richard I exorbitant charges had been demanded.

articles of the eyre of 1194, the institution of the coroner's office, and the oath of the peace of 1195 make the period of his justiciarship memorable in local administration. Hubert Walter was a great civil servant. But like most officials of his generation he was not over-scrupulous; after his death an inquiry had to be made into numerous complaints of unjust disseisins which were laid to his charge,[1] and he died encumbered with debt.[2] He may also be criticized for neglect of his position as head of the church in England. The monks of Canterbury complained to the pope that he was too much engaged in secular business to give proper attention to the affairs of the church. Men might well look askance at an archbishop who would burn down a church in order to smoke out a popular demagogue who had taken sanctuary therein, or deliver judgements of blood in the ordinary routine of business.[3] Complaints of this nature may have led Richard to accept his resignation of the justiciarship in July 1198; but he had been out of office for less than a year when he was appointed chancellor by John about the time of his coronation; and he served John as faithfully as he had served Richard. Although the king may have resented the part his minister had played in frustrating his great plan for an attack on France in 1205, there is no reason to believe the idle gossip that he rejoiced in his death.[4]

The election of an archbishop of Canterbury generally occasioned a conflict.[5] Canonically the electors were the monks of Christ Church; but not unnaturally the bishops of the diocese

---

[1] *Curia Regis Rolls*, vi. 271.

[2] He died owing £913. 1s. *Pipe Roll 7 Jo.*, p. 116.

[3] For the story of William Fitz Osbert and his nine associates who were smoked out of the church of St. Mary-le-Bow, bound to horses' tails, and dragged to Smithfields where they were hanged in chains, see the article by J. H. Round in the *Dict. Nat. Biog.*, sub. Fitz Osbert, William.

[4] V. H. Galbraith in *Roger of Wendover and Matthew Paris* (David Murray Foundation Lecture, Glasgow, 1944) has shown that the well-known stories related by Wendover and Paris about John rejoicing at the death of his faithful minister cannot be accepted. See pp. 18, 36. Nevertheless recent events seem to justify the statement of Wendover that Hubert was suspected of being on too friendly terms with the king of France (ed. Coxe, iii. 183).

[5] The story of the Canterbury election is very confused. The account given by Stubbs in the introduction to his edition of the *Memoriale* of Walter of Coventry (Rolls Series), pp. xlix–liii, with the dramatic midnight election of the subprior Reginald before Hubert Walter was even buried, has been generally accepted. It has, however, been shown by M. D. Knowles (*Eng. Hist. Rev.* liii (1938), 211–20) to be inaccurate in many and important particulars. In what follows I have adopted Knowles's reconstruction of the events.

claimed to have a voice in the choice of their metropolitan. In practice the king's will usually prevailed. To prevent any precipitate action on the part of the monks, King John hastened to Canterbury, and two days after the archbishop's death persuaded the chapter to postpone any election for six months (till December). In the meanwhile both parties lodged appeals at Rome touching their respective rights in the matter. It appears that the king also, probably with the connivance of the bishops, sent his messengers to Rome in the hope that by diplomacy and bribery they might prevail upon Innocent III to instruct the monks to elect his nominee; doubtless he already had in mind his close friend and confidential adviser John de Gray, bishop of Norwich. It was to counteract the scheming of the agents of the king and the bishops that the monks of Christ Church, or rather a majority of them, secretly and conditionally, chose their subprior, Reginald, and dispatched him to Rome under oath not to reveal his provisional election unless the necessity of the case demanded it. On reaching Rome, however, he immediately made it known and sought papal confirmation of his appointment. Pope Innocent III was deeply interested in episcopal elections, and took up the matter of the Canterbury election with his customary energy.[1] So in deference to the protest of the bishops' proctor, he stayed proceedings pending a careful investigation of the claims of the two parties. It was not long before news of the election of the subprior reached the ears of King John, who at once went to Canterbury to ascertain the truth. The monks, intimidated by the king's unconcealed displeasure, denied having made any election, renounced their appeal, and a week later, 11 December, in the king's presence agreed to the election of the bishop of Norwich.[2] He was invested with the temporalities and even given a loan of 500 marks to defray his immediate expenses. In the following March (1206) this election was quashed by the pope as uncanonical, and a fresh delegation of fifteen monks of Christ Church and proctors of the bishops and the king having plenipotentiary authority was summoned to Rome. The final hearing was delayed till December when Reginald's election was also quashed,

[1] Cf. Powicke, *Stephen Langton*, pp. 78 ff.
[2] On 19 December 1205, 400 marks were paid to 'the bishop of Norwich elect of Canterbury' (*Rot. de Praestito* 7 *Jo.*, ed. Cole, p. 274). Another 100 marks are entered as paid to the 'elect of Canterbury' on the *Pipe Roll of* 7 *Jo.*, p. 10.

and the monks (who alone, it was decided, had the right to elect), probably on the pope's recommendation, unanimously chose Stephen Langton, an Englishman, a man with a high reputation for learning in the schools of Paris, and recently appointed cardinal priest of St. Chrysogonus, as their archbishop.

Stephen Langton was consecrated by the pope at Viterbo on 17 July 1207, and, as the king refused to confirm his appointment, he remained on the Continent for the next six years, living chiefly at the Cistercian monastery at Pontigny, which some forty years earlier had provided a refuge for Becket. About the same time the revenues of Canterbury, which amounted to £1,492. 10s.,[1] were seized into the king's hand, and the monks, all but a few who were old and infirm, were driven into exile on the Continent. A few months before the king had quarrelled with his half-brother, Geoffrey, archbishop of York, who had taken a leading part in opposing the imposition of a thirteenth of rents and movables. He excommunicated the collectors and payers of the tax, and then fled to the Continent, where he died in 1212. Like those of Canterbury, the temporalities of York were taken into the king's hand. Thus at this fateful moment in the history of the church the northern as well as the southern province was deprived of its head.

As early as August 1207 the pope had instructed his commissioners, the bishops of London, Ely, and Worcester, to threaten an interdict. It was not, however, until Sunday, 23 March 1208, that the threat was put into effect. The terms of the interdict are not precisely known; there are several versions, and they differ materially. In general it may be said that it involved a suspension of all ecclesiastical rites. The services of the church ceased to be performed. It is doubtful whether the sacrament could even be administered to the dying,[2] and, when dead, these certainly did not get decent and Christian burial, but were interred in woods or ditches by the road side without prayer or priest. Marriages were not solemnized in churches; baptisms took place behind locked doors; and churchings were

---

[1] The revenue dropped during the period of the Interdict to £986. 0s. 8d. in 1213; but it recovered remarkably quickly, for in 1214 it stood at £2,638. 1s. 3d. See the paper by R. A. L. Smith in *Eng. Hist. Rev.* lv (1940), 355, n. 2, from which these figures are taken.

[2] At Durham the viaticum was denied to the dying. See *Historiae Dunelmensis Scriptores Tres* (Surtees Soc.), p. 25.

done in the church porch. Sermons could only be preached on Sundays, frigidly in the churchyard.[1] The stringency with which the interdict was enforced may have varied in different localities, and among different religious bodies. The Cistercians, claiming the privilege of exemption, 'rang their bells, shouted their chants and celebrated the divine offices with open doors' in defiance of the interdict; but they were severely rebuked by the pope for their conduct. For the whole country it was slightly relaxed after a year. Nevertheless it may be assumed that the interdict caused grave discomfort, and that for the religiously minded life in these conditions can have been scarcely tolerable. Yet it was endured for more than six years.

Having shot their bolt, the bishops of London, Ely, and Worcester fled the country. They were followed by the bishop of Hereford; and the archbishop of York had, as we have seen, for other reasons gone into exile. But there was not, as commonly said, a general flight of bishops. The sees of Lincoln, Chichester, and Exeter were vacant with no bishops to fly; the bishop of Durham was ailing and died within a few weeks of the interdict, and the bishop of Coventry a few months later. John de Grey, bishop of Norwich, the unsuccessful candidate for Canterbury, and Peter des Roches, bishop of Winchester, were close friends of the king and active in the government throughout the period of the interdict. The bishops of Bath, Salisbury, and Rochester, also appear to have remained at their posts until the king's excommunication in October 1209 made it impossible for them to stay and serve him.[2]

John was not stubborn or regardless of consequences. Both before and after the awful pronouncement he was ready to negotiate. In January he told the pope's commissioners that he

---

[1] See T. M. Parker in *Speculum*, xi (1936), 258-60. The interpolated version of Innocent III's letter contained in the Canterbury chronicle (printed in the introduction to Gervase of Canterbury, ii, pp. xcii-iii) probably reflects most nearly the actual practice adopted in the churches. For the text in the papal register see *Selected Letters of Pope Innocent III*, ed. C. R. Cheney and W. H. Semple (Nelson's Medieval Texts, 1953), no. 36. For the condition of England during the interdict see also Cheney in *Bulletin of the John Rylands Library*, xxxi (1948), 295-317.

[2] For Jocelin, bishop of Bath, see J. Armitage Robinson, *Somerset Historical Essays*, pp. 149-55. Both the bishops of Bath and Salisbury received back their temporalities on 10 April, less than three weeks after the interdict. *Rot. Lit. Claus.* i. 111. The latter appears as present at a transaction which may be dated in 1209, *Sarum Charters and Documents*, p. 72. He and the bishop of Rochester are said to be in England in the satirical poem on the bishops during the interdict. Wright, *Political Songs*, p. 13.

was prepared to satisfy them 'saving his royal rights and liberties';[1] in February he gave a safe-conduct to Simon Langton, the archbishop's brother, to come to England to discuss the matter; on 12 March the discussion took place at Winchester where Simon, in answer to the king's reservation of royal rights, answered that he would hear of no conditions but that the king must place himself 'wholly in his mercy'. It was after receiving this uncompromising reply that John gave his answer to the impending interdict. He issued instructions for the confiscation of the property of the clergy, both monastic and secular, all, as the letter to Lincoln says, 'who are unwilling to celebrate the divine office'.[2] These sweeping orders were probably meant to be only tentative, pending a sorting out of the churches which whole-heartedly supported papal authority from those which were ready to accede to 'royal custom'. In the course of the next fortnight separate arrangements were made with the various ecclesiastical bodies. A number of bishoprics and many abbeys, among them some of the greatest like St. Edmunds, Ramsey, and Gloucester, were permitted to manage their own property, and answer for it to the king, keeping for themselves a 'reasonable maintenance' (*rationabile estuverium*). This allowance was reckoned on a generous scale, for as the Worcester annalist admits,[3] 'there was a full abundance of victuals'. The evidence of ecclesiastical records seems to indicate that churches and monasteries, apart from the cessation of church rites, carried on much as usual, farming their estates and even adding to them by the receipt of alms and gifts of property.[4] The normal royal charities continued to be deducted from the county farms. Sometimes the amounts were increased; thus on the Staffordshire account, 3 marks were paid over to the Templars, £15 to the canons of Trentham, £1 to the canons of Lanthony, and £30 to the monks of Bordesley, throughout the period of the interdict.

[1] The Margam Annals (*Ann. Mon.* i. 28) state that the discord arose because Stephen's election was 'contra profanas illas consuetudines, quas vocant avitas leges et regias libertates', which suggests that the Constitutions of Clarendon were still anything but a dead letter.

[2] The first mandate is dated 17 March 1207, nearly a week before the publication of the interdict (*Rot. Lit. Pat.*, p. 80); the mandate to Lincoln was issued on 18 March.

[3] *Ann. Mon.* iv. 397.

[4] Since this was written C. R. Cheney has made a careful investigation of the evidence. *Trans. R. Hist. Soc.*, 4th ser., xxxi (1949), 129–50. His general conclusions do not differ very materially from my own.

These are three times as great as they had been in 1206.[1] The king's policy met with the general support of the country, and he had even to restrain the zeal of his agents by issuing instructions that anyone who did or spoke evil against the religious or the secular clergy was to be hanged to the nearest oak tree.[2] During the first two years of the interdict there is little sign of extortion; the royal revenue is not abnormally swollen from ecclesiastical sources. Negotiations went on, stimulated on the king's part by the threat of excommunication. At one moment early in October 1209 it seemed that a settlement was about to be reached. Stephen Langton himself crossed the Channel and spent a week at Dover. But it came to nothing, and shortly after (November) the king's excommunication was pronounced in France.[3]

There can be little doubt that the excommunication was a more effective weapon than the interdict. The latter, though a serious inconvenience and a disturbing factor in the lives of men, could be patiently borne without injurious consequences. But no one could associate with an excommunicated king without exposing himself to the danger of excommunication. Good churchmen who, like Jocelin, bishop of Bath, had been much with the king in recent years, now withdrew from court and even from the country. John himself became more isolated, more embittered, and more violently hostile to the church. Hitherto there had been only petty plundering of the churches: he had filched 61 silver plates from Durham, melted them down, and made them into money; he had blackmailed the monks of Montacute to the extent of 60 marks by threatening to reinstate their prior whom they had deprived for misconduct.[4] But it was only after his excommunication that the king began to rob the churches on a large scale. The sums paid into the exchequer from ecclesiastical sources rose (in round numbers) from £400 in 1209 to nearly £3,700 in 1210 and £24,000 in 1211, and these figures are certainly very far from complete.[5]

---

[1] See *Staffordshire Historical Collections* (William Salt Arch. Soc.), ii (1881), 153, where the Pipe Rolls for the reign of John are printed.

[2] *Rot. Lit. Claus.* i. 111.

[3] *Ann. Mon.* iii. 32.

[4] *Rot. Misae 11 Jo.*, p. 110; *Pipe Roll 10 Jo.*, p. 110.

[5] These figures are taken from S. K. Mitchell's *Studies in Taxation under John and Henry III.* He abstracted them from the unprinted Pipe Rolls. The monastic annals agree that the heavy exactions began after the excommunication in November 1209.

The receipts, for example, from the Cistercian houses are not entered in the exchequer accounts. They suffered, however, more heavily than any other religious body, were indeed so broken by the extortion that many of the houses were dispersed; the monks fled and sought refuge in other monastic establishments. They were mulcted to the extent of £16,018. 6s. 8d. The total of these exactions from bishoprics, abbeys, and other clergy according to the reckoning in the exchequer exceeded £100,000.[1]

These large sums relieved the laity of some of the heavy financial burden incurred in the expeditions to Scotland, Ireland, and Wales which occupied the king's attention in the years 1210 to 1212. Each of these was a triumphant success. The Barnwell chronicler can justly claim that in these countries John was obeyed as none of his predecessors had been, and, he adds, he would seem to be as happy and as powerful as he could wish were it not that he was deprived of his overseas dominions and under the ban of the church.[2] The events of 1204, which were followed by no treaty of peace, he never regarded as final. The recovery of the continental lands was the determining factor in the later policy of King John.

The diplomatic history of the Norman wars is involved. It largely affected and was affected by the ebb and flow of the fortunes of Otto IV in the German civil war which raged incessantly from 1198 until it, like the continental aspirations of King John, was brought to an end by the decisive action at Bouvines in 1214. It was a contest of Angevin and Welf against Capetian and Hohenstaufen. Richard I had at once realized the enormous advantage which might accrue if his nephew Otto were firmly seated on the imperial throne; he took the matter up with his customary impetuous energy and poured out money on the enterprise. His death a year later was a serious blow to Otto's prospects. John was half-hearted in his nephew's cause, and in the treaty of Le Goulet (May 1200) he agreed to the insertion of a clause by which he promised Philip Augustus to render Otto no assistance in men or money. Consequently there was a stoppage of payments. Moreover, the handsome legacy bequeathed by Richard to his nephew was likewise withheld. His brothers, Henry the count palatine and William, came

---

[1] *Red Book of the Exchequer*, ii. 773. But cf. C. R. Cheney, *Trans. R. Hist. Soc.*, 4th ser., xxxi (1949), 129, n. 4. where it is suggested that the sum was marks not pounds.
[2] Walter of Coventry, ii. 203.

to fetch it, but they returned empty-handed.[1] The payments made since 1194 to the archbishop of Cologne also ceased.[2] But the interests of John and Otto were too similar, their dependence on each other too essential, for them to remain long estranged. How close was this interdependence may be judged from a letter written by Otto seemingly in the latter part of 1203 or the beginning of 1204 in which, after referring to the improvement of his fortunes (the pope had not long since publicly pronounced in his favour) and expressing his sorrow at the decline of his uncle's, he proposes to make a truce for a year or two with his rival, Philip of Swabia, in order that he might be free to create a diversion on the western front by attacking Philip Augustus in the region of Rheims or Cambrai.[3] Nothing came of this proposal. Indeed, hardly was it made than Otto's cause suddenly collapsed. In 1204 his own brother, the count palatine crossed to the enemy's camp, and he was followed by the archbishop of Cologne and the duke of Brabant. The Rhenish confederacy, carefully built up by Richard I in his later years, was at an end. The aspirations of both John and Otto were thus simultaneously shattered in 1204, the year of the fall of Rouen. Nevertheless, they did not abandon them; Otto fought on doggedly, and John, as we have seen, planned a campaign in 1205 and made a not unsuccessful one with a limited objective in 1206. But then another disaster occurred: Cologne, the city whose commercial interests were inextricably bound with those of England, was forced to capitulate, and Otto, deserted and friendless (even the pope had thrown him over and was negotiating with his rival), made his way by a devious route through Denmark and the North Sea to England (1207).[4]

[1] Hoveden (iv. 83) says the legacy consisted of three parts of the king's treasure and all his jewels (baubella); the Annals of Burton (Ann. Mon. i. 201) says two parts of the treasure and the jewels. The Annals of Winchester (ibid. ii. 73) puts it at 25,000 marks. Some of the jewels were handed over later: among the ludicra which Otto received were 60 cups, 4 precious stones, 8 brooches, and 18 rings. Rot. Chart., p. 133b.

[2] See A. L. Poole in Studies in Medieval History presented to F. M. Powicke, p. 92.

[3] Rot. Chart., p. 133b. It is enrolled under the 5th year of John which ran from 15 May 1203 to 2 June 1204.

[4] The isolation of Otto's position about this time is strikingly emphasized by the fact recorded in the royal chronicle of Cologne that when Archbishop Adolf seceded to the enemy and was deposed, he was replaced in 1206 by Bruno of Sayn at the pope's command; but the archbishop of Mainz could find no German bishop prepared to support him, and two English bishops had to be brought from England to assist at the consecration. Chron. Reg. Colon. (ed. Waitz), pp. 179, 223.

Though, as we have seen, King John had not hitherto given much substantial help to Otto, he had kept in close touch with him. He was a well-known figure, at least by repute, so when he arrived he was given a cordial welcome. The streets of London, according to a late authority,[1] were decorated and the people wore their best clothes. He was received in audience by the king in the chamber of Abbot Samson of Bury at Stapleford,[2] and the result of the interview was satisfactory, for he returned to Germany with 6,000 marks.[3] Otto in his turn bestowed upon John a great crown, a sceptre, and a golden rod surmounted by a dove, besides many other rich presents.[4] The significance of this visit was not merely transitory. It was the beginning of a great combined effort on the part of the two kings for the recovery of their respective dominions. A year later (21 June 1208) an unexpected stroke of fortune strengthened their hopes of success. Philip of Swabia was murdered, and Otto himself was accepted as king by a once more united Germany. Doubtless in order to ingratiate himself with the pope, Otto interceded with his uncle on behalf of Stephen Langton, and his brother, the count palatine, actually came to England in the spring of 1209 for the same purpose. Though these overtures failed in their object, as a result of his visit the count palatine was firmly bound to the English alliance by a pension of 1,000 marks a year.[5] John was no longer negotiating with a mere handful of Rhenish princes, but with the leading magnates of the whole of Germany. He was aiming at a great coalition of England and Germany directed against France. This was the object of the mission dispatched under the leadership of the earl of Salisbury and announced in a letter addressed to the princes on 24 March 1209.[6] Then, in the autumn, an express messenger arrived in

---

[1] *Flores Historiarum* (ed. Luard, Rolls Series), ii. 133–4.

[2] The place is supplied by the Annals of St. Edmund's (*Memorials of St. Edmund's Abbey*) (Rolls Series), ii. 16.

[3] The writ for these payments is given on the Close Roll, *Rot. Lit. Claus.* i. 82*b*. Otto's seneschal, Conrad of Wilra, was at the same time given a fief of 40 marks. Ibid.   [4] *Foedera*, i. 99.

[5] Ibid. i. 103. Cf. the Annals of Waverley, *Ann. Mon.* ii. 261 (under a wrong year). The order for the payment of the 1,000 marks is entered on the Patent Roll (89*b*) on 24 March 1209, 'de dono et de feodo suo'. The payment for the half year Easter to Michaelmas 1211–12 appears on the Misae Roll (ed. Cole), p. 238. When he returned to Germany he left his son, also named Henry, at the English court. Numerous items of expenditure on his account are recorded.

[6] *Foedera*, i. 103. The letter is addressed to 4 archbishops, 10 bishops, 2 abbots, 5 dukes, and 4 margraves.

England with the momentous news of Otto's imperial coronation at Rome on 4 October.[1] A little more than a couple of
months later (12 December) another report of the emperor's
activities reached England; letters *de rumoribus imperatoris Romani*
were delivered to the bishop of Winchester at Bristol.[2] We can
but guess at their contents; but it has been plausibly suggested[3]
that they revealed Otto's intention to conquer the kingdom of
south Italy and Sicily, the country which the pope above all
things was resolved to keep separate from the empire. It may
well be that this project was planned in concert with the English
government. Between England and the Norman kingdom of the
south there was much affinity and the inclusion of the latter in
the Anglo-Welf alliance would be a great addition to its strength.
In fact this enterprise led to an upheaval in Germany and the
undoing of Otto.

In November the emperor was excommunicated, and the
young Frederick of Hohenstaufen was brought into the political
arena. Philip Augustus was not slow to take advantage of the
involved situation. He was in close correspondence with the
pope, with the disaffected princes of Germany, and with some
English barons who already were chafing at the growing arbi-
trariness of King John's government. The outcome of these
overtures was the conclusion of an alliance directed against
Otto and John between himself and Frederick (Toul, 19
November 1212) who was a few days later formally elected and
crowned king of Germany.

John was equally active in the diplomatic field. Messengers
between the German and English courts were ceaselessly coming
and going. The negotiations were carried out with the strictest
secrecy; so secretly indeed that the very name of one of the
envoys could not be disclosed by the treasury clerks.[4] With a
judicious distribution of pensions, he was carefully rebuilding
the old coalition of princes in the Low Countries which Richard I
had formed and he himself in his early years had allowed to fall

[1] The news was known on 12 November at latest or 39 days after the event,
when the messenger who brought it was paid for his services. *Rot. Misae* (ed.
Hardy), p. 138. The quickest recorded time for a journey from Rome to London
was 31 days. See *Itinerary of Richard I* (Pipe Roll Soc., N.S., vol. xiii), app. B.

[2] *Rot. Misae 11 Jo.*, p. 142.

[3] See particularly K. Hampe, 'Beiträge zur Geschichte Kaiser Friedrichs II' in
Historische Vierteljahrschrift, iv (1901), 181.

[4] 'quia non ausi sumus scire nomen ejus, ideo non ponitur in hoc scripto'. *Rot.
Misae 11 Jo.*, p. 157.

apart. The chief organizer and agent in this work was Renaud of Dammartin, count of Boulogne. This remarkable, cultivated, ambitious, and versatile man, alike at home on the battlefield or in the courtly society of troubadours, had recently (1211) quarrelled with Philip Augustus, who not without good cause suspected him of having dealings with his enemies.[1] Philip seized his Norman fiefs of Mortain, Domfront, and Aumale, and then proceeded to occupy the county of Boulogne itself. The count, deprived of his possessions, thenceforward bent all his indomitable energy to the task of working the ruin of France. He first sought out his kinsman, Count Theobald of Bar, who was to become his active fellow conspirator. From Bar, on the borders of Upper Lorraine, he got into communication with the count of Flanders and the Emperor Otto; and with Otto's brother, Henry the count palatine, early in the spring of 1212 he arrived in England, where he was received by the king and on Ascension Day, 3 May, did homage and fealty. The next day by a solemn treaty in the presence of many witnesses he and the king bound themselves to make no separate peace with the king of France. 'These things', John informed the Vicomte de Thouars, 'we wished to be done publicly in London [the treaty was actually dated at Lambeth] that our friends may rejoice and our enemies be openly confounded.'[2] What store the king set upon the count's services may be judged by the reward. He received the greater part of the English fiefs which had at one time belonged to the counts of Boulogne, and in respect of further claims £1,000 a year for three years pending a settlement. These unsettled claims may refer to the honor of Eye which had been granted to his brother-in-law the duke of Brabant. He, like the count, had joined Philip Augustus in 1205, and both had then been deprived of their English fiefs. Henceforth the duke played a very shifty role. He had even allowed himself to be put forward after the murder of Philip of Swabia as a rival to Otto for the empire, and had made a compact with Philip Augustus to render no help to John.[3] This, however, was but a temporary escapade; he had more to gain from friendship with England, and by 1212 he was once again reckoned among

[1] Negotiations were conducted by Eustace the Monk between King John and the count of Boulogne as early as 1209. H. Malo, *Un grand feudataire, Renaud de Dammartin et la coalition de Bouvines*, p. 137.

[2] *Foedera*, i. 104.

[3] *Mon. Germ. Hist., Constitutiones et Acta Publica*, ii. 618.

the allies.[1] Nevertheless, this fickle and irresponsible prince was to change sides more than once before the decisive battle. Another Lorrainer, Henry, duke of Limburg, joined the coalition in the same year. He visited England, took the oath of fealty, and became a pensioner of King John.[2]

But the greatest and most important achievement which the count of Boulogne accomplished was the winning of Flanders for the coalition. He had visited Flanders before coming to England, and had prepared the way; and on 4 May 1212, the day after he himself had rendered his homage, John wrote to Ferrand, count of Flanders, requesting an alliance. He regarded the matter as one of urgency, for he told the count that he would remain near the coast and asked him to do likewise that the negotiations might be carried on the more rapidly.[3] Since the death of Baldwin IX, a captive in the hands of the Bulgarians, in 1206, the English influence in Flanders had been seriously eclipsed. The regent, Philip of Namur, who in 1206 married the daughter of Philip Augustus, was of course firmly attached to the French alliance; so too were most of the aristocracy; only the commercial interest clung to England, for they well knew that the king would open or close the ports according to their attitude; and their livelihood depended upon English trade. Philip Augustus had also secured the custody of the daughters of the late count, the elder of whom, Joanna, was married in January 1212 to Ferrand, the son of Sancho I of Portugal, who thus became count of Flanders. Received with little enthusiasm by his subjects, he was thrown naturally on the protection of the king of France, and the alliance would probably have persisted but for the action of the king's son, Louis, who, with the connivance of his father, seized the towns of St. Omer and Aire near the borders of Flanders and Artois. This act of folly at once united the aristocracy and the towns in antagonism to France and in favour of England. Count Ferrand hesitated long; he was not anxious to break completely with his overlord. But the crisis came when in April 1213 he refused to take part in the projected invasion of England unless

---

[1] His brother, Godfrey of Louvain, had settled in England and was custodian of the honor of Eye. When the duke of Brabant deserted the cause of Otto, he was ordered to deliver it to the earl of Salisbury (25 February 1205, *Rot. Lit. Pat.*, p. 50b). He was reinstated as custodian in 1208. Ibid., p. 81; *Rot. Lit. Claus.* i. 109b.

[2] Poole, in *Studies in Medieval History presented to F. M. Powicke*, p. 93.

[3] *Foedera*, i. 105.

the two towns were restored to him. Philip retaliated by over-running Flanders, and the count on the advice of his barons threw in his lot with the coalition.[1]

John seems to have contemplated making immediate use of the coalition. In May Waleran, son of the count of Limburg, and about the same time the duke of Brabant were requested to come to England 'well prepared with horse and arms'.[2] On 15 June he addressed writs to the reeves of thirty-nine towns ordering them to provide bodies of troops ready for overseas service.[3] In the same month an inquiry was made on a large scale with the object of checking the service due from the royal tenants-in-chief and of discovering what alienations had been made which might impair their capacity to render their service. The original returns of this great inquest, which were delivered to the barons of the exchequer on 25 June 1212, have survived for many counties and they throw much light on the history of feudal society in this period.[4]

These plans for a decisive action on the Continent in 1212 were frustrated. The Welsh broke into revolt; their leader Llywelyn was negotiating a treaty with Philip Augustus (August);[5] and the army mobilized for foreign service had to be diverted to Wales. Then again his plans miscarried. The army was assembled at Nottingham in September when ugly rumours of treason warned him that he could not rely on his own barons. Substance was given to these reports by the sudden flight of Robert Fitz Walter and Eustace de Vesci, the one to France, the other to Scotland. They were outlawed and their lands seized, and Robert's great fortress to the south-west of St. Paul's, Baynard's castle, was demolished.[6] A fanatical rustic, Peter of Wakefield, who lived on bread and water, alarmed the king by predicting the speedy termination of his reign; there was talk of deposition and a fresh election. These and other significant signs of a growing discontent at the king's arbitrary rule were not without

[1] For these events see Dept, op. cit., pp. 87 ff., and below, pp. 459, 461.

[2] *Foedera*, i. 106, 107.

[3] *Rot. Lit. Claus.*, p. 130b.

[4] *Book of Fees*, pp. 52–228. In his introductory remarks the editor shows the relation between these returns and the lists entered in the *Red Book of the Exchequer*. He proves that the theory expounded by J. H. Round in chapter xii of his *Commune of London* is incorrect.

[5] Delisle, *Catalogue des Actes de Philippe-Auguste*, no. 1416.

[6] It has been supposed that these two men had been personally injured by the king. For the evidence see Norgate, *John Lackland*, pp. 289–93.

effect on his character and actions; they developed in him a sense of suspicion; he always went about, we are told, armed and with an armed bodyguard; he distrusted all the ruling class but a small circle of intimates. In contrast to his attitude to the barons, he was indulgent to the proletariat. He mitigated the forest penalties, *sortem miseratus afflictorum*, and made the chief foresters promise only to enforce those customs which had been observed in his father's time; he relieved traders and foreigners of many irksome exactions imposed at the seaports; he was gracious, it is said, to widows, and solicitous for domestic peace;[1] and he came to realize the urgency of healing the breach with Rome.

Negotiations with the papacy had never entirely ceased during the years of the interdict. The king's messengers were continuously passing back and forth between England and Rome.[2] In the summer of 1211 the subdeacon Pandulf and Durand, a Templar, were sent over with proposals for the restoration of peace. They met the king at Northampton at the end of August, but their demands were deemed too high, and the discussions broke down. The next year, however, the uncomfortable situation in England and the threatening aspect abroad convinced John that he must make great sacrifices. In November 1212, therefore, he sent the abbot of Beaulieu at the head of an embassy to discuss matters at Rome. There his emissaries accepted on his behalf the terms which had been offered and declined in the previous summer. In February Innocent himself wrote to John requesting him to ratify this agreement before 1 June or take the consequences, and he took no pains to conceal what the consequences would be: deposition and ruin. The king can hardly have received this uncompromising letter before he was made acquainted with the news that Philip Augustus at a council held at Soissons early in April had resolved to invade England.[3] Faced with the double threat of deposition by the pope and of invasion by the French king, John wisely chose sub-

[1] Walter of Coventry, ii. 207.

[2] The intercourse with Rome in 1209-10 is illustrated by the payments to messengers entered on the Misae Roll (ed. Hardy), pp. 112, 141 ('quod cito venit de Roma'), 149, 151, 153, 158, 165.

[3] C. R. Cheney has finally disposed of the fiction spread abroad by the contemporary chroniclers, especially Roger of Wendover, and accepted by many modern historians, that John was actually deposed, or that Innocent III called upon Philip Augustus to execute the sentence by invading England. *Studies in Medieval History presented to F. M. Powicke*, pp. 100-16.

mission. He was in Kent, anxiously awaiting the return of his envoys when they reached Flanders on their homeward journey towards the end of April, and evidently matters were settled there by negotiation[1] before Pandulf, who accompanied them, actually met the king at Dover on 13 May; for the terms were accepted at once without further debate. John agreed to receive Stephen Langton as archbishop, to reinstate the exiled clergy, and to compensate the church in full for the losses it had sustained. Four of the chief barons, the earls of Salisbury, Warenne, and Ferrers, and the count of Boulogne, stood guarantors for the king's good faith. Two days later, on 15 May at the house of the Templars at Ewell, near Dover, John resigned the kingdoms of England and Ireland to Pope Innocent and received them back under the bond of fealty and homage in return for a tribute to the Holy See of 1,000 marks a year, 700 for England and 300 for Ireland. This momentous concession, which bound England to the Roman church for more than a century and a half, was solemnly ratified in St. Paul's cathedral in the presence of Nicholas, cardinal bishop of Tusculum, on 3 October and sealed with a golden Bull.[2] It remains in doubt whether this act was done at the pope's dictation or, as the instrument declares, by the king's 'spontaneous good will and the counsel of his barons'.[3] Certainly two years later the insurgent barons were claiming that the king in this matter was acting under compulsion by them;[4] and a contemporary writer tells us that John added this to the other conditions of peace with the church on his own account.[5] It is probable, therefore, that the idea originated not in Rome but in England. At the time it did not seem very extraordinary nor give rise to adverse comment;

[1] This is clear from the fact that one of the envoys, Brother William of Saint Ouen, was in England on 29 April and returned with the king's message to Stephen Langton and the exiled bishops (*Rot. Misae*, ed. Cole, p. 260); on 8 May Boenammus, Pandulf's messenger, was in England and returned to his master with letters (ibid., p. 263).

[2] *Foedera*, i. 111–12; the confirmation is on the Charter Roll (p. 195). John's formal release from excommunication was delayed till after the return of the archbishop in July (below, p. 461), and the interdict was not finally withdrawn by Cardinal Nicholas till a year later, after a settlement had been reached about reparations due to the church. Cf. *Foedera*, i. 122.

[3] The question is fully discussed by Miss Norgate, *John Lackland*, pp. 180–3.

[4] See the letter of Walter Mauclerc to the king in which he says that the barons declare that the latter was actuated not by his will, or duty, or indeed fear, but *per eos coactus*. *Foedera*, i. 120.

[5] Walter of Coventry, ii. 210.

ignominious, perhaps, but prudent and wise.[1] It was only later generations with bitter experience of papal control that denounced the transaction in violent language.[2] Nor can it have been regarded as very revolutionary. Henry II himself, when alarmed for the safety of his kingdom owing to the rebellion of his sons in 1173, had acknowledged in a letter to Alexander III the feudal superiority of Rome.[3] King John's more senior advisors would remember that, less than twenty years before, Richard I had acknowledged the feudal superiority of the emperor, and they were aware that Innocent III stood in the same feudal relationship to many other European countries.[4] To John and his ministers it might appear well worth while to make considerable sacrifices in order to secure the active support of the pope in the coming struggle with France; and they were not disappointed. Henceforth Innocent III abetted the king unswervingly, even in his most arbitrary conduct. So in the last phase we are presented with the paradoxical situation of the pope aiding the lately excommunicated John who was allied with the pope's bitterest enemy, the excommunicated Otto, against the pope's protégé, Frederick of Hohenstaufen, and his previous ally, the king of France.

[1] Walter of Coventry, ii. 210.

[2] e.g. Matthew Paris punctuates the account of Wendover by additions 'carta omnibus seculis detestanda' (*Hist. Ang.* ii. 135), 'carta detestabilis' (ibid. 146), and he closes his story with the words 'Et sic humiliatus est rex Johannes'.

[3] 'Vestrae jurisdictionis est regnum Angliae, et quantum ad feudatarii juris obligationem, vobis duntaxat obnoxius teneor et astringor.' England is 'patrimonium beati Petri'. *Foedera*, i. 29.

[4] Sicily, Sweden, Denmark, Aragon, and Poland. See Davis, *Normans and Angevins*, p. 368, n. 3.

XIV

KING JOHN AND THE CHARTER
1213–1216

K ING PHILIP, confident of success, had at the Soissons
Council in April 1213 drafted a scheme to govern the
relations between himself and his son Louis when the
latter should be crowned king of England.[1] All preparations
had been made: his fleet and army were in readiness at Grave-
lines just across the Flemish frontier. John's submission to the
pope was a severe blow to his plans. His expedition would now
be deprived of the character, with which he doubtless wished to
clothe it, of a Holy War against an avowed enemy of the church.
He did not, however, abandon his design, but it was first necessary to secure himself from a possible attack from the count of
Flanders who, as we have seen, had refused to take part in the
campaign. With this object he overran the county and moved
his fleet into the Zwyn estuary. It was at this critical moment
that Count Ferrand took the decisive step and made an urgent
appeal for English help.

King John had not underestimated the danger from France.
He had spent the months of spring near the coast personally
supervising offensive and defensive operations. The army was
mobilized on Barham Down between Canterbury and Dover;
his navy (and he relied, a chronicler tells us, more on destroying
his enemies at sea, drowning them in the ocean, than on defeat-
ing them on land) was at Portsmouth, where all ships capable
of carrying six or more horses had received orders to assemble
on 21 March, well manned with good and proved mariners.
Damaging raids had already been made on shipping in the
Seine and at Fécamp, and Dieppe was burnt before the main
French fleet was moved to the Flemish coast to cover the invasion of Flanders.[2] The appeal of the count of Flanders met with
instant response; his envoy arrived on 25 May; the same night

---

[1] The document is printed in *Foedera*, i. 104, under a wrong date (1212). Cf.
Delisle, *Cat. des Actes*, no. 1437.

[2] These raids, mentioned only in the Annals of Dunstable under the year 1212
(*Ann. Mon.* iii. 35), probably took place about this time, for instructions for the dis-
posal of prisoners taken at Dieppe are entered on the Close Roll under 3 June 1213.
Rot. Lit. Claus. i. 134–5.

THE LOW COUNTRIES

a conference was held at Ewell and the terms arranged. But in
his reply John could not refrain from hinting that the count
had somewhat jeopardized the situation by his unconscionable
hesitation: 'had you sent to us sooner', he wrote, 'we would have
sent you greater help'.[1] On the 28th the fleet of 500 ships with
700 English and Flemish knights besides numerous men-at-
arms under the command of William, earl of Salisbury, and the
count of Boulogne set sail. They found the French fleet anchored
off Damme, the port of Bruges, a few miles inland but connected
by a narrow channel with the Zwyn.[2] According to William
le Breton,[3] the royal chaplain, who was himself present in the
French camp, it numbered 1,700 vessels richly laden with arms,
provisions, and other stores. It was caught unawares, the French
knights having dispersed in search of plunder or being engaged
in the siege of Ghent. The mariners left on board were killed,
and many of the ships were either captured or destroyed. The
remaining ships, unable to escape to the open sea, were later
(2 June) burnt by the order of Philip Augustus. An attempt to
follow up this easy victory was beaten off with loss. Nevertheless,
it had achieved its purpose; it removed the immediate threat
of invasion and effected the evacuation of Flanders by the
French army. By good fortune perhaps rather than by good
strategy the first encounter between the maritime strength of
England and France had resulted in the total destruction of the
French fleet.

John planned to follow up this success by a double attack on
France: the count of Flanders supported by Otto was to invade
from the north-east, while John himself would operate from
Poitou. The army was assembled at Portsmouth; the fleet was in
readiness. But the barons refused to accompany him on the pretext, according to one account, that the king had not been formally released from his excommunication. Stephen Langton and
his fellow exiles only reached England in July, and a few days
later (20 July) at Winchester, in a scene where emotion, solemnity,
and rejoicing were happily blended, the king was absolved from
the ban of the church; not before, however, he had renewed the

---

[1] *Foedera*, i. 113.

[2] It ceased to be a port in the fifteenth century owing to the silting up of the
Zwyn estuary.

[3] *Gesta Philippi Augusti* (ed. Delaborde), p. 251; the estimate of the size of the
English fleet is from Wendover, iii. 257. The best recent account of the engagement
is by Cartellieri, *Philipp II August*, iv. 363 ff.

coronation oath and promised to maintain the ancient laws of the kingdom. At peace with the church John again prepared to start, but again he was frustrated. This time the opposition came from the north-country barons (*barones Northanhumbrenses*), who, since the loss of Normandy, were little interested in continental wars and now insisted that they were only bound by reason of their tenure to serve on campaigns in England. As on a somewhat similar occasion in 1205, the king showed his disgust by putting to sea with his household and cruising as far as Jersey. From this futile expedition he returned within three days to take his vengeance on the barons who had thwarted him.

Very soon after he had arrived in England, Stephen Langton assumed a position of highly respected authority not only in matters relating to the church, but in politics. When the king was intending to set out for Poitou, he had left the maintenance of the peace and the administration of the kingdom in the hands of the bishop of Winchester and the justiciar; but they were instructed to seek the counsel of the archbishop. He was present at the council held at St. Albans soon after the king's absolution where it was ordered in the king's name that the laws of Henry I should be universally observed, and he took a leading part at the assembly on 25 August at St. Paul's. There, according to one report, he produced and read aloud the charter of Henry I, and the barons present declared that they would fight for the liberties contained in it. If, then, Wendover may be trusted (and there is no serious reason to doubt it) we have here the real beginning of the struggle for the Charter.[1]

While these events were taking place, King John was marching northwards to punish the recalcitrant barons. The archbishop followed him, overtook him at Northampton, reminded him of the oath he had taken at the time of his absolution, and pleaded with him not to proceed against his opponents except by judgement of his court. But the king, as was his habit, merely lost his temper and continued on his way to Nottingham. Stephen pursued, even threatened to excommunicate all who took part against the barons, John alone excepted. Ultimately he persuaded the king to adopt peaceful and legal methods, and

---

[1] For these events, the evidence for which rests chiefly on Wendover (iii. 262-3), see Powicke, *Stephen Langton*, pp. 113-16. On the supposed representation at the council of St. Albans of four men and the reeve from the vills of the royal demesne, see D. Pasquet: *An Essay on the Origins of the House of Commons*, pp. 38-43.

the northerners were soon afterwards temporarily reconciled at Wallingford (1 November).[1]

The ill-fated expedition to Poitou, twice planned and twice cancelled, had now been postponed till the next year. Throughout the winter preparations were in progress, and the fleet received orders to be ready at Portsmouth to sail early in the new year. It is probable that the summons of armed knights and unarmed barons to meet the king at Oxford on 15 November had to do with the forthcoming campaign. The barons, as we have seen, had balked the previous attempts to invade France; their attitude had for some months been threatening; it would have been a wise precaution that they should be ordered to come without their weapons. The same writ requires the presence at the council of four discreet knights of the county to discuss the business of the kingdom—the earliest example of a summons of knights of the shire for this purpose. The king was certainly at Oxford on the appointed day, but no record of this interesting assembly, if indeed it took place, has survived.[2]

The king's diplomatic agents were busily engaged keeping in being the widely spread coalition. In the summer he was corresponding with his allies in the south, with the count of Auvergne, with his brother-in-law, Raymond of Toulouse, and with King Peter of Aragon. But before the end of the year the savage Albigensian crusade had rendered these confederates a liability rather than a source of strength. The king of Aragon was defeated and slain at the hands of Simon de Montfort in the bloody battle of Muret (12 September 1213) and the count of Toulouse, deprived of his domain save only his capital city, came to England, a fugitive seeking aid, only to be expelled as a heretic on the orders of the papal legate.[3] John, of course, still

[1] Annals of Dunstable, *Ann. Mon.* iii. 40.

[2] Many things relating to this writ, which is printed in *Foedera*, i. 117, remain obscure. Much that has been written about it is irrelevant owing to an unfortunate error in the text as printed by Stubbs in the *Select Charters*, 8th ed., p. 287, of *homines* for *milites*, such as 'the summoning of the folkmoot' &c., cf. ibid., 9th ed., p. 282. See A. E. Levett, *Eng. Hist. Rev.* xxxi (1916), 85–90. Also in the *Foedera* text the writ bears a wrong date: *XV* instead of *VII die Novemb.* A further difficulty is the shortness of time allowed to elapse between the issue of the writ (7 November) and the time of meeting eight days later. The surviving writ addressed to the sheriff of Oxford is dated from Witney, only ten miles away, and the election of the knights and their dispatch would be relatively easy. But the production of knights from Yorkshire in this short space of time would be almost impossible.

[3] King John apparently welcomed his brother-in-law and paid his expenses (*Rot. Lit. Pat.*, pp. 106*b*, 108*b*), and Coggeshall reports a rumour (p. 168) that he

kept in close touch with the emperor Otto whose agents were constantly at his court. But it was the group of princes in the Low Countries who were most essential to his plans. Since his reconciliation with England in 1212, the duke of Brabant had again changed sides; in April 1213 he was aiding and abetting Philip Augustus (whose daughter Marie, the widow of Philip of Namur, was given him in marriage) in the projected invasion of England. But the battle of Steppes (south of St. Trond) on 13 October 1213, in which the duke was utterly defeated by the bishop of Liége and the count of Loos, settled many local feuds; and nearly all the leading princes in the Low Countries—the dukes of Brabant and Limburg, the counts of Flanders, Holland, and Boulogne, were ranged on the side of England for the final round in the great encounter with France. Immense sums were poured out by the English treasury in support of these princes, and large numbers of Flemish knights were retained in the king's service by annual pensions charged on the exchequer. Soon after Christmas 1213 the count of Flanders himself came to England and at Canterbury between 8 and 10 January did homage for the estates which he claimed in England.[1] Doubtless it was at this meeting that the final plans for the joint attack were decided. It is possible that William, earl of Salisbury, who was to take command of the English contingent operating from Flanders, and William, count of Holland, who entered the alliance in the preceding March, took part in these discussions.[2]

The organization of war, finance, and supply was now in different hands, for Geoffrey Fitz Peter, who had held the office of justiciar for fifteen years, died on 14 October 1213. On the eve of sailing (1 February) the king appointed to succeed him, Peter des Roches, a man who enjoyed his complete confidence, and who had been rewarded for his services after the

returned with 10,000 marks, which is not impossible. The Annals of Dunstable (p. 39) wrongly state that he took part in the campaign to Poitou with 200 knights. Neither he nor the king of Aragon was in any sense heretical. They merely entered the war to protect the defenceless people of Languedoc from the ruthless savagery of the so-called 'Crusaders'.

[1] Coggeshall (p. 168) says the homage was *de tota Flandria*. But it is more probable that it was, as is said in the *Hist. des Ducs de Normandie*, pp. 139 ff., for the English estates only. This is suggested also by Henry III's confirmation of Ferrand's fee in 1227. *Foedera*, i. 187. Cf. Papst, *Ferrand von Portugal*, p. 95, n. 1.

[2] Cf. Annals of Waverley (*Ann. Mon.* ii), p. 280. William of Holland had done homage in return for an annual fee of 400 marks on 29 March 1213. *Foedera*, i. 110.

loss of Normandy by an estate in Bedfordshire,[1] and by the bishopric of Winchester. The appointment was unpopular with the barons who distrusted him as an alien from Poitou and as one who despised them and their pretensions, and by the church party because he had been behind the king in the period of the interdict.[2] But he was not a mere foreign adventurer. He had ability of a high order, and if he was a hard man to deal with ('hard as a rock', as the Tewkesbury annalist punningly describes him),[3] he was certainly very capable. He was a soldier and statesman besides being a clergyman. Nevertheless, his outlook was not altogether secular; he looked after the welfare of his diocese, and was liberal in the founding and endowment of monastic houses. As justiciar he was responsible for the government of the country in the king's absence, and he undoubtedly increased the baronial discontent by his ruthless efficiency.

The campaign which ended at Bouvines, a battle decisive in the fortunes of the empire and France no less than of England, requires more than a passing notice. Unlike most medieval campaigns it was not merely a haphazard series of sieges of castles interrupted by an occasional clash of arms in the open. The plans had been long and carefully conceived; the strategy was sound—a combined operation on two fronts, the main attack from the north-east with the object of destroying the enemy, and a subsidiary attack from the west with the object of creating a diversion. Had these operations been properly synchronized, it is possible that the future of the warring countries would have been very different.

On the feast of the Purification King John with his family (the queen, his infant son Richard, and his niece Eleanor of Brittany accompanied him), his household, and an army composed chiefly of knights 'of small fortune' and other mercenaries, embarked at Portsmouth. Owing to bad weather the party was delayed in the Solent for a week and only reached La Rochelle on 15 February. This port which was largely dependent for its prosperity on English trade, and therefore loyal to English rule, remained his base throughout the campaign. The record of events in the narrative sources is meagre and confused; but the

---

[1] *Rotuli Normanniae*, 131.

[2] Coggeshall, p. 168; Annals of Waverley (*Ann. Mon.* ii), p. 281; cf. also the satire in *Political Songs* (ed. Wright, Camden Soc.), p. 10.

[3] *Ann. Mon.* i. 110: *durus ut rupes fuerit.*

king's movements can be traced with precision from the orders issuing from his itinerant chancery and from an occasional dispatch in which the king reported his progress to the government at home. In the first of these addressed to the earl marshal on 8 March he reports his initial successes: 'immediately on our arrival 26 castles and fortified places were restored to us'.[1] Then moving rapidly along the valley of the Charente he passed through Saintonge, the Angoumois, and the Limousin, meeting apparently with little resistance, receiving the homage of the barons, and appointing officials. At Limoges, which he reached on 3 April, the Vicomte Guy did homage to him as his 'natural lord' because, as he informed Philip Augustus, 'I could not resist him or await your help', and, he continues, 'these things I tell you so that you may know that for the future you may not rely on me'.[2] Before returning to his headquarters, John made a detour southward as far as La Réole on the Garonne, southeast of Bordeaux. Having secured his position in Aquitaine, he marched north towards the Loire. On his way at Parthenay he achieved by force and diplomacy a great success: at the end of May he brought to terms the powerful house of Lusignan with whom he had quarrelled fifteen years before on account of his marriage with Isabel of Angoulême. The long list of Poitevin lords who witnessed the contract of marriage between John's daughter Joan and the son of Hugh the Brown, count of La Marche, significantly reveals the strength of the position John had won south of the Loire.[3] The situation was very favourable when he entered Angers on 17 June. The movements of Philip Augustus, while John was recovering control of the country south of the Loire, are obscure. Judging rightly that the danger from the north was the more serious, he did not allow himself to be drawn away into Aquitaine. Towards the end of April he was at Châteauroux where he divided his forces; with the main body he himself moved northward to watch the outcome of events from Flanders, leaving his son Louis with some 800 knights to deal with King John. It was not, however, till two months later that Louis came in contact with his enemy. John was engaged in besieging La Roche-aux-Moines, a castle recently

---

[1] Foedera, i. 118.

[2] Rot. Lit. Pat., p. 115a.

[3] Foedera, i. 125. Cf. the king's dispatch describing these events, ibid. i. 123 (from Wendover, iii. 280-1). The marriage did not take place; and the younger Hugh ultimately married not John's daughter, but his widow Isabel.

built by William des Roches, the seneschal of Anjou, on the Loire, west of Angers. He then learnt what reliance could be placed on the barons of Poitou; they refused to fight a pitched battle. Thus deserted John fled precipitately (2 July). But once back at La Rochelle his spirits revived, and he wrote to the barons in England for reinforcements, intending, it would seem, to continue the campaign: 'We are safe and sound, and, thanks to God, everything with us is prosperous and happy'. He felt bound to dissemble the magnitude of the disaster at La Roche-aux-Moines.

It was more than three weeks after this misfortune that the great coalition in the Netherlands was ready for action. Local feuds and other distractions had wasted invaluable time, and Philip Augustus could now defend the road to Paris relieved of any anxiety from the English armies south of the Loire. The opposing forces were concentrated within striking distance in Hainault: the Emperor Otto at Valenciennes, Philip at Tournai. The allies with a superiority in numbers and confident of success were attempting to cut off the French line of retreat across the river Marque near the village of Bouvines (between Tournai and Lille) when they came in touch with the enemy. The battle was fought on 27 July, a hot summer afternoon when the dust rose so thickly that the combatants could scarcely see to fight. It was a series of confused mêlées in which personal acts of prowess rather than directed manœuvres were the conspicuous feature, a type of fighting in which the French aristocracy, skilled and trained in the tournament, excelled. The Flemings on the allied left were routed after their severely wounded count was captured. In the centre both leaders, the emperor and the king of France, were unhorsed and only saved by the devoted courage of their bodyguards. Otto escaped to Valenciennes; but already the duke of Brabant, whose conduct both before and during the engagement was open to the suspicion of treason, by his flight caused panic in the allied ranks. It ended on the right flank where the English commander, the earl of Salisbury, was clubbed, felled from his horse, and captured by the bishop of Beauvais. A last, very gallant, but quite hopeless stand was made by Renaud of Boulogne until he too was captured by another warlike prelate, Guérin, the bishop-elect of Senlis.

The victory was decisive: it ended Otto IV's rule as emperor; it ended John's aspiration to recover his lost continental

dominions; it established the French monarchy. The whole of
Paris turned out to welcome their king on his triumphant
return. In this, William le Breton tells us,[1] the university
students were particularly prominent: 'indefatigably for seven
successive nights they did not stop feasting, leaping and dancing,
and singing'. King John lingered for some months in the neighbourhood of La Rochelle. On 18 September a truce was
arranged to last till Easter 1220;[2] on 15 October he was again
in England to meet a situation scarcely less gloomy than the
one he had left in France.

The struggle for the Charter had, as we have seen, already
begun before John had set out in the previous February on his
ill-fated expedition to Poitou; and after his return the refractory
element among the barons clamoured with increasing vehem-
ence, then with threats, and finally with force until they got
what they wanted on 15 June 1215. Their temper, already
rough, was further aggravated when the king issued from Poitou
a demand for scutage at three marks on the fee from those who
had neither accompanied him nor sent their service. Again it
was the northern barons who resisted the demand, and in fact
only a fraction of what was due reached the exchequer.[3] At a
conference held in London at Epiphany 1215, where the barons
again insisted on the restoration of the 'ancient and accustomed
liberties', the king succeeded in getting a decision deferred till
the following Easter, the archbishop with eight bishops and
seven leading magnates guaranteeing the security and safe conduct of the malcontents during the interval.[4] It was not unnatural in view of the recent submission that both parties should
bring the matter before the pope 'since he is lord of England'.
Of what happened there we are fully informed by a report from
the king's confidential agent, Walter Mauclerc, and from Innocent's own letters.[5] Eustace de Vesci on behalf of the barons
urged that the king at the meeting in London at Epiphany had
not only refused to grant the liberties they demanded, but had
tried to get them to promise never to raise the matter again.
Innocent III was not convinced by these representations. He
may have already known of John's intention to take the cross[6]

---

[1] *Gesta Philippi Augusti* (ed. Delaborde), p. 297.   [2] *Foedera*, i. 124-5.
[3] S. K. Mitchell, *Studies in Taxation under John*, &c., pp. 112-14.
[4] *Rot. Lit. Pat.*, p. 126b.   [5] *Foedera*, i. 120, 127.
[6] Innocent had been urging John to take the cross since the conclusion of the
truce with France in the previous September. See the pope's letter of November 1214

(he did so on Ash Wednesday, 4 March) and he gave him his full support. So, while recommending the king to treat graciously with the barons and to accede to their 'just demands', he wrote on 19 March to the barons themselves forbidding them under pain of excommunication to make conspiracies or rebellions (*conspirationes aut conjurationes*) against the king and to the archbishop and his fellow bishops ordering them to take the necessary steps to prevent them. But about the time these uncompromising letters reached England the barons were already assembling under arms at Stamford.

Speaking of this gathering the Barnwell chronicler says: 'Since the majority had come from northern parts they were hitherto (*adhuc*) called northerners (*Aquilonares*)',[1] and the other contemporary writers with remarkable unanimity endorse this statement. They are Northanhumbrenses, Norenses, Norois, Boreales.[2] We need not, therefore, question that the hostile movement originated with a body of north-country barons; these then made common cause with a group of magnates, drawn together by family ties or by private or public grievances, whose sphere of influence was chiefly centred on Essex. And so, as the movement expanded, becoming more and more widespread, the old designation 'Northerners' lost its geographical significance, and came to be applied to all who rose against the king.[3] They were for the most part young men; and it sometimes

(Cheney and Semple, *Selected Letters of Innocent III*, no. 72). Many people in England were taking the cross about this time: 300 persons of both sexes are said to have done so at Northampton on 5 February 1214. Chronicle of the Cluniac Priory of St. Andrew's, Northampton, in *Eng. Hist. Rev.* xliv (1929), 96.

[1] Walter of Coventry, p. 219; cf. p. 217.

[2] Coggeshall, pp. 167, 170; Annals of Dunstable (*Ann. Mon.* iii), p. 40; *Hist. des Ducs*, p. 145; *Foedera*, i. 120. The settlement of 1215 is described in the Annals of Southwark as made between the king and the *barones norrenses* (*Surrey Arch. Coll.* xxxvi (1925), 49). The emphasis on the eastern element, first made by J. H. Round (*Eng. Hist. Rev.* xix (1904), 707 ff.) and developed by Powicke (*Stephen Langton*, pp. 126 ff., 207 ff., and *Camb. Med. Hist.*, pp. 243 f.), has perhaps been exaggerated. It is impossible that Ralph of Coggeshall, living in Essex, could designate the insurgents as *Northanhumbrenses* if, as Sir Maurice Powicke says, 'the centre of the opposition was in reality Essex and East Anglia'. The Barnwell (Cambs.) and Dunstable (Beds.) annalists also belong to the eastern counties. An analysis of the list of barons at Stamford given by Wendover, iii. 297, and of the twenty-five barons in the security clause of the Great Charter, reveals a large proportion from the northern counties, if not north of the Humber, at least north of the Welland; for Lincolnshire barons were strongly represented.

[3] Cf. *Curia Regis Rolls*, vii. 315, where it is said of Roger de Cressi, a Norfolk baron, 'Rogerus est unus ex Norensibus qui habent pacem usque ad clausum Pasche'.

happened that the older and more experienced barons remained with the king, while their hotheaded sons joined the ranks of the insurgents. Stamford, situated on the great north road, easily accessible to the barons of north and east, and familiar to them as a recognized resort for jousting, was an obvious meeting place.

The leaders of the revolt do not inspire confidence. Eustace de Vesci, lord of Alnwick, and Robert Fitz Walter, lord of Dunmow in Essex, were not men with a good record behind them. The stories of personal wrongs, which they had suffered at the hands of the king, rest either on fabrications concocted many years later to blacken the character of John, or on evidence so confused as scarcely to deserve serious consideration.[1] Fitz Walter with Saer de Quincy, another insurgent baron, whom John in 1207 made earl of Winchester, were together responsible for the cowardly surrender of Vaudreuil in 1203 for which they became objects of ridicule and contempt both in England and France. In 1212 Eustace and Fitz Walter were guilty of treasonable designs and outlawed;[2] and while in exile they were in communication with the king's enemies, with Philip Augustus and the pope; and by the pope they were specially included with the archbishop and his fellow bishops in the peace of 1213.[3] In the autumn of 1214 Innocent remonstrated with Eustace for interfering with the king and his ministers;[4] and in the following spring he was voicing the grievances of the barons at the papal court.[5] It was Fitz Walter who in 1215 was appointed by the malcontents 'marshal of the army of the Lord and Holy Church'.[6] It is difficult to concede to these men or to many of the others (such as Fulk Fitz Warin, ex-outlaw and hero of romance) that high sense of responsibility and public duty with which they have often been credited. Not one of them rose to any position of eminence as a statesman.

During April and May 1215 events moved rapidly.[7] From Stamford the insurgents advanced to Northampton, and thence to Brackley where they 'defied' the king, that is to say, they formally renounced their homage. It was a declaration of war. They returned to Northampton, besieged the castle for a fort-

---

[1] See Norgate, *John Lackland*, pp. 289 ff.   [2] Above, p. 455.
[3] Cheney and Semple, *Selected Letters of Innocent III*, no. 45.
[4] *Foedera*, i. 126.   [5] Ibid. i. 120.   [6] Ibid. i. 133.
[7] The chronology of the events leading to the Charter is very confused and uncertain.

night, and, failing to take it, moved eastward to Bedford. On 17 May they were secretly admitted into London by a city faction, before the majority and more rational of the citizens, mindful of the exceptionally favourable charter of privileges which the king had granted them only a week before, were aware of it.[1] Both parties anticipating a hard struggle sought aid from abroad. The barons were in close touch with Philip Augustus who promised to help them as far as he could, and actually sent over to England Eustace, the renegade monk turned pirate, with siege-engines.[2] King John used continental troops, especially from Flanders and Poitou, on a large scale to garrison the royal castles which were being put into a state of defence. The presence of these foreigners was an added grievance; but the king was willing to dismiss them (some were in fact sent home), and on 27 May he issued strict orders to his mercenary captains, Falkes de Bréauté, Hugh of Boves, and Waleran the German, enjoining them to observe the truce which had been made by the archbishop between himself and the barons in order to smooth the way for a peaceful solution which he seems to have been genuinely anxious to bring about.[3] If, as seems most probable, the document usually called 'the Unknown Charter of Liberties' belongs to a stage in these negotiations, John was evidently prepared to go a long way to meet the barons. After reciting the coronation charter of Henry I, on which the Great Charter was eventually modelled, this obscure document proceeds to draft concessions designed to remedy just those feudal grievances of which they most insistently complained—arbitrary judgement, abuses of relief, wardship, and marriage, testamentary disposition, liability for service abroad, scutage, forestation, debts to the Jews, and security of life and limb for killing game. All these, with the exception of the clause restricting the obligation of service overseas to Normandy and Brittany, reappear in an amplified or modified form in the Great Charter. Soon after the king's return from Poitou in the autumn of 1214, the Barnwell chronicler relates, a dispute arose between him and the northern barons about their liability to scutage and foreign service, in the

---

[1] 'Ignorantibus qui intus erant regalibus quibusdam et civium, ut dicitur, parte majore et saniore.' Walter of Coventry, ii. 220. The charter is dated 9 May 1215. Above, p. 71.

[2] Coggeshall, p. 172.

[3] *Rot. Lit. Pat.*, p. 142.

course of which Henry I's charter was produced and a demand was made for its confirmation. This may well have been the occasion for the drafting of the 'Unknown' charter. Whether it ever reached a stage beyond a first draft we have no means of knowing.[1]

On 9 May the king proposed that the differences between himself and the barons should be submitted to a court of arbitration composed of eight members, four chosen from each party, with the pope as 'superior'.[2] Pending the findings of this committee, he formally granted what the barons deemed as the most essential of their demands—trial by due process of law in the king's court ('per legem regni nostri vel per judicium parium suorum in curia nostra').[3] The concession, indeed, is couched in almost the identical terms as the famous clause 39 of the Great Charter. To prove his sincerity, the very same day he ordered that Geoffrey de Mandeville, one of the insurgent barons, should have the judgement of his court in the matter of a debt.[4] But the barons refused the offer of arbitration, and the king in exasperation ordered the sheriffs to seize the lands and chattels of his enemies (12 May). In a letter to the pope written on 29 May he recounted the efforts he had made in the interests of peace. Though he made, perhaps, unfair capital out of his position as a crusader and was scarcely justified in accusing the barons of impeding the holy enterprise, there is no reason to doubt the main facts which he discloses: that he had offered to abolish the evil customs, that he had proposed arbitration, that he would show them full justice regarding their demands *per considerationem parium suorum*, and, finally, that he was ready to submit the whole matter to the decision of the pope.[5] The barons, no doubt, distrusted alike the impartiality of the pope and the sincerity of the king, but they could not distrust the honesty of

[1] Walter of Coventry, ii. 217-18. The text and a summary of the various views regarding the date and significance of the 'Unknown Charter' are conveniently set out by W. S. McKechnie, *Magna Carta* (2nd ed. 1914), pp. 171-5, 485-6. See also Powicke, *Stephen Langton*, pp. 112-20, and V. H. Galbraith, *Studies in the Public Records*, pp. 133-4. The document, which is preserved among the *Archives du Royaume* at Paris, is apparently written in a chancery hand and bears signs of hasty drafting. It is somewhat carelessly written on a damaged piece of parchment and is more than ordinarily abbreviated. I am indebted to Professor Robert Fawtier for kindly providing me with a photostat.

[2] *Rot. Chart.*, p. 209b.

[3] *Foedera*, i. 128; *Rot. Lit. Pat.*, p. 141. Cf. also the pope's letter of August 1215 in *Foedera*, i. 136.

[4] Galbraith, op. cit., p. 132.   [5] *Foedera*, i. 129.

Stephen Langton, whose guiding hand we can discern behind all these negotiations, indeed they much respected him.[1] He was supported by a group of men on whose advice the king acted in granting the Charter. An analysis of these counsellors, whose names are set out in the preamble of Magna Carta, shows them to be of a very different calibre from their opponents. They were not barons whose influence was chiefly confined to a particular locality—the north or the east; they were men who stood for the interests of the country as a whole; they were men who had long played their part in war, politics, or administration. This party included two archbishops and seven other bishops; it included four earls, among them the wise senior statesman, William Marshal with his nephew John, who had long served the king faithfully in Ireland. Among them also was Hubert de Burgh, an outstanding administrator who was shortly after to become justiciar, Hugh de Neville, Alan and Thomas Basset, and others, less well known, but who had for years been conspicuous in the government of King John and whose names appear in scores of royal writs and charters. Experience and political sagacity were unquestionably on the side of the Crown. It gives therefore a false picture to speak of the Charter forced on a king deserted by the nation and alone except for a mere handful of mercenary captains.

If we may assume, and it seems a warrantable assumption, that the barons could have had all they wanted at least by 10 May, how can the long delay be explained? We cannot believe that they were haggling over trifles, fish weirs on the Thames and the like. Was it mere intransigency? It seems more probable that this month was spent, not in forcing John to accept the Charter, but in persuading the insurgent barons to insert into it clauses that would benefit others than themselves. This was the task of Stephen Langton and his party, and on 15 June he had succeeded in converting a purely baronial document into the Great Charter.

The king was at Windsor and the barons at Staines. A safe-conduct had been granted to the latter for the purpose of negotiating a peace, and on Monday, 15 June, the two parties met in the meadow on the banks of the Thames called Runnymede. There the king set his seal to the draft agreement known as the Articles of the Barons. Then several days elapsed while

[1] Walter of Coventry, ii. 221.

the draft was being put into its final form, clauses were modified or amplified, and the chancery scribes were engrossing numerous copies for distribution in the counties.[1] By Friday, 19 June, this work was accomplished. The twenty-five barons who were to act as executors had been appointed; the Great Seal had been attached; and both parties had sworn to abide by the provisions of Magna Carta.

The sixty-one clauses, into which for convenience of reference the Charter has been divided in modern times, cannot be discussed in detail. Most of them have been variously interpreted at different times. It will only be possible here to attempt a brief summary. As one would expect in a feudal age, it is feudal in form and character, a statement of feudal law and custom. The council it describes (cl. 14) is a feudal council, and it controls feudal taxation—scutage and aids (cls. 12, 15); a number of clauses (2–8, 37, 43) deal specifically with abuses of the feudal incidents of relief, wardship, and marriage; others (cls. 9–11) refer to the payment of debts, a serious administrative problem in the thirteenth century since a large proportion of the upper and middle classes were in a chronic state of insolvency and therefore at the mercy of the royal bailiffs or the Jews; others again (cls. 26, 27) laid down rules governing the rights of inheritance. Although these concessions are in the main made by the king to his tenants-in-chief, these by a comprehensive clause (60) are similarly bound in their relations with their tenants. Nevertheless, Magna Carta did much more than define with precision the obligations of feudal society. To some degree all classes shared in its benefits. In the opening chapter the liberties of the church, including the recently granted right of free election, are guaranteed. The towns were not forgotten: by a general clause (13) the liberties and free customs of all cities, boroughs, towns, and ports were confirmed. The citizens of London had surrendered the city to the insurgent barons (who indeed made it their headquarters) and they sought to make capital out of their submission by the insertion of a clause restricting the king's power to tallage them at will; but in this they failed; the king was evidently not prepared to give up this valuable prerogative, which in fact was retained till 1340.[2] For

[1] All the copies bear the date of the original draft, i.e. 15 June. For the publication of the Charter see R. L. Poole, *Studies in Chronology and History*, pp. 313–18.
[2] Cf. cl. 32 of the Articles of the Barons with cl. 13 of the Charter.

the advantage of trade the charter granted to all merchants the right to come and go freely except in time of war (cls. 41–2), and in the interest of the consumer it established standard weights and measures (cl. 35). In the sphere of administration a serious attempt was made to check the abuse of power by local officials (cls. 23–5, 28–31, 38), and a beginning was made to limit the extent of the forest and to restrain the oppression of the forest officers in three clauses (44, 47, 48) which in the next reign were expanded into the separate Charter of the Forest.

The interpretation of the judicial clauses of the Charter has given rise to the sharpest divergence of view. They are certainly the most important. The weight of opinion today would allow that the great development in legal procedure which had taken place during and since the reign of Henry II was generally accepted. The possessory assizes were to be taken more frequently (cl. 18); common pleas were not to follow the court but be held in a fixed place (cl. 17);[1] the concession already made by letter patent on 10 May that no freeman should be proceeded against except by due process of law ('per legale judicium parium suorum vel per legem terrae')[2] was embodied in the Charter (cl. 39), and as a corollary was added the laudable but somewhat chimerical assertion that 'to no one will we sell, deny, or defer, right or justice' (cl. 40). Clause 34, which relates to the issue of the writ *Praecipe*, has generally been condemned as reactionary. But evidence has recently been adduced to show that its importance has been exaggerated. The barons were not, it seems, intending to put back the clock; they were not attempting to abolish the use of the writ in proprietary actions; they wished only to ensure that they did not lose their jurisdiction on some technical ground in cases with which they were ad-

---

[1] See Galbraith, op. cit., pp. 137–8.

[2] The word *pares* should not be interpreted in the narrow sense of peers meaning fellow barons, though the barons of Magna Carta were, no doubt, primarily thinking in this way. It seems to be loosely used in the sense of equals. For example in a suit between the bishop of Lincoln and the abbot of Peterborough, *c.* 1133–5, the abbot 'rectum faciat episcopo Linc' per judicium capituli sancte Marie et parium suorum abbatum'. *Eng. Hist. Rev.* xxiii (1908), 727. In view of the controversy on the interpretation of this clause (especially by Vinogradoff and Powicke in *Magna Carta Commemoration Essays*) the following entry on the *Curia Regis Rolls* in the year 1200 (i. 258) is of interest: 'Willelmus filius Oliveri . . . venit et posuit se super visnetum et super pares suos ut recongnoscatur. . . .' Here the *pares* appear to be equated with a jury of sworn recognitors.

mittedly competent to deal.[1] The severity and arbitrary character of amercements was a very real and general grievance in the
time of King John, and the Charter went a long way towards
providing a remedy. Amercements were to be proportionate to
the size of the offence, and were to be assessed by a jury of
neighbours; and no one, be he freeman, merchant, or villein,
might be so heavily amerced as to be deprived of his means of
livelihood (cl. 20).[2] The power of the king to amerce barons and
clergy was similarly regulated (cls. 21, 22).

The Great Charter was then a practical assertion of existing
law and custom and it imposed limitations on the arbitrary
power of the Crown. The king could no longer override the law.
If he did so, the twenty-five barons entrusted with the execution
of the Charter were empowered together with the community of
the whole land 'to distrain and distress him in every possible
way'. They were given a legal right of resistance (cl. 61). It was
a crude but probably the only form of sanction conceivable
at the time.[3] Nevertheless, legalized rebellion, to which it was
tantamount, was a dangerous weapon to put in the hands of
unscrupulous and reactionary barons who, seemingly, neither
desired nor had any intention of keeping the settlement. Not
one of the moderate party, who had associated themselves with
the king in granting the Charter, was appointed to the executive
committee. Consequently, for John's reign, the constitutional
importance of Magna Carta is negligible. Its importance lay in

---

[1] See N. D. Hurnard in *Studies in Medieval History presented to F. M. Powicke*,
pp. 157–79.

[2] A. L. Poole, *Obligations of Society*, &c., pp. 89–91; the following extract from the
Feodarium Prioratus Dunelmensis (Surtees Soc., 1872), p. 215, to which my attention
was drawn by Mr. Frank Barlow, illustrates how this clause was applied on episcopal manors. Its date is 1229:

'Et si aliquis de terra vel de feudo prioris in misericordiam inciderit in curia
episcopi, in praesentia ballivorum episcopi, per juramentum duorum liberorum
hominum de terra episcopi, et duorum de terra prioris, amerciabitur, secundum
quantitatem delicti, scilicet, liber homo salvo continemento suo, mercator salva
merchandia sua, rusticus salvo wannagio suo.'

[3] T. F. T. Plucknett, *Legislation of Edward I* (1949), pp. 75–6, regards this as
merely legal distraint or distress. Very possibly, but distraint so violent, involving
the seizure of the king's castles, lands, possessions, and everything else, is not very
different from rebellion and could scarcely be accomplished without war. Compare
the similar passage (probably taken from this clause of Magna Carta) in the
settlement made by Henry III, when in 1265 he was likewise in the power of a
baronial faction after the battle of Lewes. Here the expression 'to rise against us'
is used: 'liceat omnibus de regno nostro contra nos insurgere et ad gravamen
nostrum opem et operam dare'. *Foedera*, i. 452.

the future. Within half a century of his death an enthusiast for the constitution could write:

> Dicitur vulgariter 'ut rex vult, lex vadit';
> Veritas vult aliter, nam lex stat, rex cadit.[1]

It was in the three centuries that elapsed after 1215, when it was thrice reissued and many times confirmed, that Magna Carta gained its real significance.[2] It had once and for all superseded the vague laws of Edward the Confessor as the criterion of good government.

The government at once set to work to give effect to the settlement. On 19 June, the very day on which the Charter was sealed, letters were dispatched to all the sheriffs and royal officers notifying them that peace had been made between the king and the barons, ordering that the Charter be publicly read and that all should swear obedience to the twenty-five barons; they were further to choose twelve knights in each county who should inquire into evil customs, especially those of the forest.[3] Clause 52, requiring the immediate restitution of lands, castles, and franchises of which anyone had been unjustly disseised, was at once put into operation,[4] and Hugh of Boves was instructed to send home the foreign troops stationed at Dover.[5] Evidently the king was seriously trying to make the peace a reality.

Not so the barons. Once in power they revealed the pettiness and arrogance common in men placed in positions beyond their capacity or their deserts. They broke faith at once by refusing to fulfil their promise to the king that they would give him any security he wished about their observance of the peace; and this was the subject of a formal protest by the bishops.[6] It would appear that they did not intend to observe the Concord of Runnymede.[7] Some of the northerners, we are told,[8] left the

---

[1] 'Song of Lewes', ll. 871–2. *Political Songs* (ed. Wright, Camden Soc.), p. 116.

[2] The best commentary on the significance of the Charter in the later middle ages is by C. H. McIlwain, *Magna Carta Commemoration Essays*, pp. 122–79.

[3] *Foedera*, i. 133–4.

[4] During the last weeks of June numerous letters ordering these restitutions are enrolled on the Patent and Close Rolls. Cf. Walter of Coventry, ii. 221.

[5] *Foedera*, i. 134. Two clauses of Magna Carta, 50 and 51, relate to the expulsion of foreigners. The group of men from Touraine, the relatives of Gerard de Athée, who are specifically named in cl. 50 do not appear to have been banished; two of them, Engelard de Cigogné and Philip Marc, certainly remained in the country and played a conspicuous part in the administration of the country under Henry III. Cf. G. J. Turner in *Trans. of the R. Hist. Soc.*, N.S., xviii (1904), 248–55.

[6] *Foedera*, i. 134.   [7] 'Concordia de Runingemede.' *Curia Regis Rolls*, viii. 16.

[8] Walter of Coventry, p. 222.

meeting before the conclusion of the business, and under the pretext that they were not present fortified their castles, opened hostilities, and wasted the royal manors. Others impeded and even maltreated the royal officers who were trying to carry out the provisions of the Charter. As an excuse for remaining under arms they appointed tournaments. One was arranged at Stamford, but they feared to be so far from London, their headquarters (*recepticulum*), lest in their absence it should be delivered up to the king (the Tower was not in their hands, having been entrusted to Stephen Langton).[1] It was, therefore, transferred to Staines, and the prize for the winner was to be 'a bear which a certain lady will send to the tournament'. They intended war; they talked of electing a new king.[2]

In these circumstances it is not surprising that John declined to attend a conference arranged by the bishops at Oxford on 16 August on the ground that he had received nothing but ill treatment since the Charter had been granted and that it was neither safe nor prudent to trust himself among the barons and their large armed retinues.[3] Instead he again began to look for help from abroad and especially from the pope. Innocent at this time was deeply occupied in preparing the great programme of reform, which was to be initiated at the Fourth Lateran Council in November, and a great attempt to recover the Holy Land from the infidel. It is remarkable that he could give any attention to the affairs of England. Nevertheless, he was anxious to remove all impediments to the successful launching of the crusade. He therefore wrote on 18 June, at the very time that the Charter was being put into its final shape, ordering the archbishop and bishops to excommunicate the barons unless they submitted within eight days.[4] This was followed by a stronger letter dated 7 July in which he excommunicated all disturbers of the king and kingdom with their accomplices and supporters.[5] But Stephen Langton was reluctant to promulgate

[1] *Foedera*, i. 133.
[2] H. G. Richardson in two articles in the *Bulletin of John Rylands Library*, xxviii (1944), 422 ff. and xxix (1945), 184 ff., takes a more favourable view of the conduct of the twenty-five barons.
[3] Walter of Coventry, ii. 223.
[4] Printed by Adams, *Magna Carta Commemoration Essays*, pp. 43-5. This was written, of course, before Innocent had knowledge that the Charter had been granted.
[5] The Bull *Mirari cogimur*. For the text see F. M. Powicke, *Eng. Hist. Rev.* xliv (1929), 87-93, and Cheney and Semple, op. cit., no. 80.

or to give effect to these sentences, and was in consequence in September suspended by the bishop of Winchester and the pope's nuncio, Pandulf, and their action was ratified by the pope himself on 4 November.[1] Innocent, who was now fully apprised of recent events in England, wrote on 24 August condemning the whole settlement as not only vile and base, but illegal and unjust, and quashed the Charter forthwith.[2] On the same day he addressed a letter to the barons upbraiding them for their conduct;[3] and before the end of the year (16 December) thirty[4] of them were excommunicated by name. But long before this sentence was delivered, England was plunged in civil war.

The barons in taking up arms against the king were acting without right or provocation. While John and his advisers had endeavoured to carry out the provisions of the Charter, they had done everything they could to thwart them. It would seem that the demand for the Charter was a mere subterfuge; and what they really wanted was to rid themselves of King John. They had failed, and they realized that the only way by which they might achieve their object was by undisguised rebellion. But they were disunited, and some were half-hearted. They had greatly over-estimated the strength of their position, and were compelled, like the king, to look abroad for assistance. They appealed to Louis, the son of Philip Augustus, offering him the crown; but though he sent in the course of the winter two contingents which gave little relief or comfort to the barons, it was many months before he ventured to cross the sea in person.

The king spent September at Dover or Canterbury, organizing the defences and the disposition of the mercenary troops as they arrived from the Continent. The first trial of strength was at Rochester, which blocked the way for a direct attack on the capital. The castle, through the disaffection of its custodian, Reginald of Cornhill, was delivered over to the insurgents on 30 September, and placed under the command of William de Albini, one of the twenty-five barons of the Charter.[5] The king immediately occupied the city (13 October) and closely invested the castle, his soldiers sleeping, eating, drinking, and even stabling their horses within the cathedral. But in spite of unre-

---

[1] Cheney and Semple, op. cit., no. 84. [2] Ibid. no. 82. [3] Ibid. no. 83. [4] Ibid. no. 85.
[5] He is not to be confused with his contemporary William de Albini, earl of Arundel, who remained loyal to John till June 1216.

mitting efforts and the use of every device of siege warfare,[1] the castle held out for seven weeks and was only surrendered on 30 November when the small garrison was threatened with starvation. The barons had remained during the long siege helpless and inert at London. Twice they had sent pressing messages to Louis to come in person; three times they made overtures to treat with the king; only once did they make a half-hearted attempt to come to the assistance of the Rochester garrison.

Rochester was the only castle at which the king encountered serious resistance. Master of the south and west, he now prepared to subdue the north and east. Leaving part of his forces under the command of the earl of Salisbury and Falkes de Bréauté to watch events round London, he set out from St. Albans on 19 December. By Christmas he was at Nottingham, and early in the New Year at York; on 14 January he reached Berwick whence for nine days his troops harried the Lowlands of Scotland to punish Alexander II who, closely allied with the northern barons, had made a feeble incursion across the border. He returned through Lincolnshire and the eastern counties, even capturing the strong castle of Colchester which had successfully resisted the attack of Savory de Mauléon. Town after town opened its gates; castle after castle surrendered without a show of resistance.

The chroniclers record terrible ravaging, plundering, and burning during this triumphant march, scenes of atrocity such as events in the reign of Stephen alone in English history afford a parallel. An army composed largely of foreign mercenaries, accustomed to live on the land over which they fought, doubtless would be not too careful of the rights of property or of the welfare of the inhabitants. The war was an obvious excuse for

---

[1] On one occasion he used the fat of bacon pigs as fuel to burn down a tower. On 25 November he wrote to the justiciar, Hubert de Burgh, 'We order you to send to us night and day with all haste 40 bacon pigs of the fattest and those less good for eating to use for bringing fire under the tower'. *Rot. Lit. Claus.* i. 238*b*. During the siege of La Roche-aux-Moines in July of the previous year the king was preparing to use a more scientific incendiary mixture, for he writes to Hubert: 'We command you to send us immediately, upon sight of these letters, ten pounds each of sulphur, tallow, gum, and pitch, and four pounds of quicksilver; and if we stand in need of more to provide us therewith.' Ibid., p. 167*b*. At this period many experiments were made in incendiary mixtures akin to Greek Fire and many of them derived from the treatise *Liber Ignium ad comburendos hostes* of Marcus Graecus. Cf. P. E. M. Berthelot, *La Chimie au moyen âge* (1893), i. 89 ff., where the text is printed, and Lynn Thorndike, *A History of Magic and Experimental Science*, ii. 785 ff.

violent lawlessness, and many were disseised of their property
by their more powerful and unscrupulous neighbours. One
Yorkshire squire frankly admitted that he had behaved so
villainously that he dared not face a local jury.[1] The rolls of the
justices in eyre and at Westminster provide ample testimony of
the great dislocation. Case after case refers to men who have
'intruded' themselves into other men's land *tempore guerre*.[2]
Nevertheless, there are indications that some attempt was made
to preserve discipline during the war. Wrongdoing did not
always pass unpunished; one man, for example, had his hand
cut off by judgement of the marshal of the army for stealing
a cow in a churchyard.[3] Moreover, wanton destruction was not
John's method of revenging himself on rebels; he preferred to
extort money by threat of despoiling them. So the towns of York
and Beverley bought the king's goodwill at the price of £1,000,
the men of Melton Mowbray and Retford paid 100 marks for
the king's protection (*tenseria*), and those of Laxton (Notts.) and
Thirsk gave £100 and 80 marks respectively that their houses
might not be burnt. The names of numerous knights and barons
are recorded on the Fine Roll as having purchased the king's
goodwill usually for moderate sums ranging from 10 to 100
marks, sometimes with a palfrey or two in addition to the
money fine. They went free, rendering one or more hostages for
their loyalty in the future. The prisoners captured at the siege of
Rochester and elsewhere were ransomed; only in exceptional
cases were crippling fines imposed.[4] Indeed, there are indications that the king was not at this time vindictive. When three
of the leaders of the northerners, Eustace de Vesci, Robert de
Ros, and Peter de Bruis, were contemplating submission in
April, John wrote that it was not so much money that he wanted
from his opponents as good and faithful service.[5] The king
naturally deprived those who rebelled against him of their land;
but if and when they returned to their allegiance, they were
able to recover it without great difficulty. So numerous were

[1] *Rolls of the Justices in Eyre for Yorkshire* (Selden Soc., vol. 56), no. 1140.
[2] See the interesting case on the *Curia Regis Rolls* (viii. 16) which shows the king's
court dealing with such cases *post concordiam de Runningemede*.
[3] *Rolls of the Justices in Eyre for Yorkshire* (Selden Soc., vol. 56), no. 851.
[4] See *Rotuli de Finibus*, pp. 568–601. An exceptionally heavy fine was imposed on
William de Albini, the commander at Rochester, who was released on payment of
a ransom of 6,000 marks (p. 599).
[5] *Rot. Lit. Pat.* i. 176.

these claims for recovery that a common-form writ was devised by the chancery to deal with them. Many hundreds of such writs were issued in the last months of the reign of John and in the first years of his successor. The confusion in estate-ownership resulting from the civil war was evidently enormous and the process of reinstatement was inevitably slow.[1]

The political upheaval, of course, affected not only the lives and property of the people but also the administration. The machinery of government worked under severe difficulties. In an often-quoted passage Wendover tells us that after the capture of London by the barons (17 May 1215) 'pleas of the exchequer and of the shire courts ceased throughout England because there was no one who would pay dues to the king or obey him in anything'.[2] In the light of the evidence of records, however, this statement needs considerable modification. What is surprising is not that the governmental machine was thrown out of gear, but that, notwithstanding the great commotion, it worked at all. Of the activity of the courts of law we have already given some account.[3] The chancery was always busy: the clerks, despite long journeys and short rests, toiled unceasingly, issuing the king's orders with scrupulous care till within a day of his death, and the letters are methodically enrolled. Similarly, as we have seen, the fines made with the king and the conditions of payment are carefully entered on the Fine Rolls. The exchequer naturally suffered something of an eclipse when the barons gained control at Westminster. The accounts are only made up in regular form to Easter (19 April) 1215, two months before Magna Carta was sealed. Yet fragments of the accounts for the eighteenth, the last year, of John have survived to show that the financial organization was not completely in abeyance.[4] Among

[1] See the Rolls of the Justices in Eyre for Lincolnshire 1218-9 and Worcestershire 1221 (Selden Soc., vol. 53), pp. lix-lxiii.

[2] iii. 301. Quoted Stubbs, Select Charters (9th edn.), p. 274. Commenting on this passage Sir James Ramsay, The Angevin Empire, p. 473, writes: 'The sittings of the Courts at Westminster and throughout the country were suspended, and the whole administration of the country was brought to a standstill', and H. W. C. Davis, England under the Normans and Angevins, p. 376, adopts the same view: 'The secession of the capital from the King's cause gave the signal for a total suspension of government throughout the country. The Exchequer and the Curia Regis ceased to hold their sessions; the authority of the sheriffs was set at nought; the collection of the revenue became impossible.'

[3] Above, p. 481 and n.

[4] See Hilary Jenkinson in Magna Carta Commemoration Essays, p. 259, and Mabel H. Mills in Trans. R. Hist. Soc., 4th ser., viii (1925), 161-2.

these fragments, particularly significant is an entry on the Lancashire roll of the fine of 12,000 marks for the release of Gilbert Fitz Reinfred, his son, William of Lancaster, and two of his knights who were captured in Rochester castle which fell into the king's hands on 30 November 1215. The agreement for his release was made on 22 January 1216,[1] and it provides irrefutable proof that the exchequer officials were still keeping records of financial transactions.

In three months the king had totally subdued the north and east of England, the two spheres of influence of the insurgent barons. Their power was now confined to London which the king was preparing to attack. Their prospects were anything but propitious when the long-awaited arrival of Louis marked a turning-point in the fortunes of war. John had attempted to keep on friendly terms with Philip Augustus. A truce existed between their countries; as late as 28 April he wrote to 'the dictators of the truce' in France suggesting a conference; and the pope through his legate Gualo was exerting his influence in the same direction. But both the king's overtures and the legate's protests were alike unavailing, and towards the end of April the decision was taken at a council at Melun. To justify the invasion it was alleged that John had been tried by the court of France in 1203 for the murder of Arthur of Britanny and condemned to the loss of his English crown. Neither this supposed trial, which has long been shown to be fictitious,[2] nor the claim by hereditary right through his marriage with Blanche of Castile, the granddaughter of Henry II, which Louis adduced, could be taken very seriously, but they removed any scruples of conscience which the French king and his son may have entertained in breaking the truce[3] and in May the expedition set forth.

Precautions to repel the invasion had been taken, but the ships of twenty-one seaports which were mobilized at the mouth of the Thames were dispersed by a storm, and in large part destroyed. The French fleet, therefore, under the com-

[1] *Rot. de Fin.*, pp. 570–1; W. Farrer, *Lancashire Pipe Rolls and Early Charters*, pp. 252, 257–8.

[2] By Bémont in 1884. See Petit-Dutaillis, *Studies supplementary to Stubbs' Constitutional History*, i. 107–15.

[3] Louis maintained that he was no party to the truce which only concerned his father and King John. Louis's case is expounded in a letter addressed to the abbot and convent of St. Augustine's, Canterbury. The text is given in William Thorne's Chronicle, ed. Twysden, *Scriptores Decem*, pp. 1868–70; and in the translation by A. H. Davis, pp. 176–8.

mand of the pirate Eustace the Monk, was able to cross the Channel unimpeded.[1] Within a fortnight of his landing in Thanet (21 May) Louis had joined the barons at London, while the king, who had been watching events from the Kentish coast, (on the advice of William Marshal) withdrew to Winchester. The rest of the reign was a tumult of confusion and civil war. As the barons expected, the presence of the prince in the country had an immediate effect. Castles were surrendered; there were many desertions; and several of the great earls, including the king's brother, the earl of Salisbury, changed sides. Even the king of Scotland ventured across the border, captured Carlisle, and managed to make the hazardous journey to render his homage to the prince whom he found engaged in besieging Dover. Driven from Winchester the king moved westward and to the coast. There, chiefly at Corfe, he spent a month planning and organizing the defences, while the barons recovered their influence in the south-east. In this area Lincoln, Windsor, and Dover alone remained loyal. But a foreign invader, especially one anathematized by the church,[2] is never popular, and even in those districts which were brought under Louis's control there were local loyalists, like Willikin of the Weald (William of Kensham)[3] on the Kent and Sussex border, who caused much havoc among the Frenchmen. The Cinque Ports, though forced to take an oath to Louis, were in fact steadfast in their loyalty to the king throughout the civil war and effected much damage to French shipping.[4] In the late summer the king was in the

---

[1] The *Chronicon Universale Anonymi Laudunensis* (ed. Bouquet, *Recueil*, xviii. 719D) describes Eustace as from a black monk becoming a blacker demon: *de nigro monacho nigrior daemoniacus*. Cf. Matthew Paris (*Chron. Maj.* iii. 29), *piratarum magister*. He was in the service of King John from 1205, engaged in naval enterprises chiefly round the Channel Islands, till 1212 when he fled to France (Annals of Dunstable, *Ann. Mon.* iii. 34). He became the hero of a romance *Wistasse le Moine* (ed. Foerster and Trost, 1891) with an historical introduction. See the article by H. L. Cannon in *Eng. Hist. Rev.* xxvii (1912), 649-55, where all the available evidence is assembled.

[2] Louis and his adherents were excommunicated by the legate Gualo at Winchester on Whit Sunday (29 May) and their lands and the city of London were laid under interdict.

[3] Or Cassingham. Cf. G. R. Stephens in *Speculum*, xvi (1941), 216. See also John's letter of thanks dated 3 September 1216 to the men of Kent, Sussex, and Hampshire in *Foedera*, i. 142.

[4] *Rot. Lit. Pat.*, p. 196 (2 September 1216), i, cf. ibid., p. 195, a mandate of 27 August 1216 to the merchants of Poitou and Gascony ordering them to put into ports between the Isle of Wight and Bristol which are 'not in the power of our enemies'. The only indication of disaffection in the ports was in 1208 when they had to pay 1,000 marks to recover the king's goodwill. *Pipe Roll 10 Jo.*, p. 72.

west and on the Welsh border collecting reinforcements; and in September he set out on his last campaign, the object of which was the recovery of his position in the eastern counties. At his approach Gilbert de Gant abandoned Lincoln, whose castle was gallantly held for the king by Nicolaa de la Hay, its hereditary castellan and widow of Gerard de Camville.[1]

The story of the king's last days is but imperfectly known. On 9 October he crossed from Lincolnshire to King's Lynn, where, it seems, he was attacked by dysentery brought on by fatigue and over-indulgence in food and drink. But he was still capable of astonishing energy, riding long distances (he had been covering thirty, forty, and even fifty miles a day) and attending to the business of government before he slept. He decided to return into Lincolnshire, he himself and his army moving by the circuitous inland road by way of Wisbech, while his baggage train proceeded by the more direct but extremely hazardous route, possible only at low tide and with the help of local guides, across the four-and-a-half-mile-wide estuary of the Wellstream (now known as the Nene) between Cross Keys and Long Sutton.[2] This journey was never accomplished. The whole convoy, horses and wagons loaded with stores and equipment, with the king's treasure and wardrobe, with his chapel and relics, and with all the paraphernalia which accompanied a medieval king on his travels, either swept away by the incoming tide or swallowed up in the treacherous quicksands, was lost in its entirety. Not a man, it is said, survived to tell the tale.[3] On the evening of the disaster (the news of which is said to have aggravated his fever) the king reached the Cistercian abbey of Swineshead (12 October) and after short rests he pushed on again through Sleaford to Newark (16 October). On the last stage he was too ill to ride and had to be borne on a litter. There in the castle, attended upon for his spiritual and physical wants by the abbot

---

[1] She was also sheriff of the county. Selden Soc., vol. 53, p. 233.

[2] This estuary, which stretched nearly to Wisbech, is now by silting, embankment, and drainage, filled up, and tolerably firm ground.

[3] The story has been skilfully reconstructed by W. H. St. John Hope in *Archaeologia*, lx (1907), pp. 93–110. Gordon Fowler (*Proc. of Cambridge Antiq. Soc.* xlvi (1952), 4–20), minimizes the episode, and concludes (p. 19) 'only part of king John's baggage train was overwhelmed by an abnormally early-flowing tidal surge when crossing a ford over the now extinct Wellstream river between Walsoken and Wisbech. Little of value was lost that could not have been recovered by local people at low water the following day'.

of Croxton[1] (who was accredited by Matthew Paris to be a skilful physician), he died on 18 October. Though worn out in body, he remained lucid in his mind till the end, dealing with the business of the day and planning for the safety of his kingdom and his heir after his death. In a short and dignified will he committed the disposal of his property to the legate Gualo, the bishops of Winchester, Chichester, and Worcester, the earls of Pembroke, Chester, and Derby, and certain others who had served him faithfully through the last stormy years. He was buried, as he had desired, near the shrine of his favourite, his patron saint St. Wulfstan, at Worcester where his memory was kept fresh by the observance of an annual fast.[2] In some circles at least his name was remembered with respect.

[1] This Premonstratensian house in Leicestershire profited by the good offices of its abbot, for not only did it receive the king's heart, but also 100 shillings' worth of land in Finedon (Northants.), *Cal. Pat. Rolls, 1216–25*, p. 41. Cf. *Rot. Lit. Claus.* i. 381: 'pro anima domini Johannis Regis patris nostri cujus cor ibi sepultum est.'

[2] Above, p. 429. In 1797 his tomb was opened. The following eye-witness's account is preserved among the Gough MSS. (Gen. Top. 24, f. 339). I am indebted to Mr. H. M. Colvin who discovered it and provided me with a transcript.

24 July 97. King John.

The venerable Shrine of this Monarch was opened on Monday last in consequence of a general reparation of the Cathedral Church at Worcester. The remains of the Illustrious Personage appears entire, his robes, in which he was interred, they are undecayed, but the colour through length of time is indiscernible; on one side of him lay a sword, the bones of his left arm lying on his breast, his teeth quite perfect, his feet stood erect, the coffin which is of stone, lay even to the surface of the floor of the Church; his remains measured five Feet, five Inches being his stature when living.

An account of the opening of the tomb was also printed by Valentine Green in 1797 in which further details and measurements are given. The robe was crimson damask and he wore a monk's cowl. Cf. also *Monthly Magazine and British Register*, iv (1797), 79.

BIBLIOGRAPHY

Note. The following list of authorities is not intended to be in any sense complete. Articles and books on special points referred to in the footnotes are generally not included.

1. Bibliographies and Books of Reference.
2. Charters, Records, and Other Documents.
3. Narrative Sources.
4. General, Political, and Ecclesiastical History.
5. Constitutional History.
6. Social and Economic.
7. Military and Naval.
8. Scotland.
9. Wales.
10. Ireland.
11. Learning, Literature, and Art.

1. BIBLIOGRAPHIES AND BOOKS OF REFERENCE

The Sources and Literature of English History by C. Gross (2nd ed., London, 1915) is a comprehensive and critical guide; a new edition to include medieval historical literature, published since 1915, has been planned and is much needed. To fill the gap it is necessary to consult the *Annual Bulletins of Historical Literature* published by the Historical Association till 1939. M. S. Giuseppi's *Guide to the Manuscripts preserved in the Public Record Office* (Stationery Office, 1923–4) is the authoritative account of the record material; a new edition by the Deputy Keeper is in process of publication. A handy list of Record Publications (formerly known as List Q) is published by the Stationery Office from time to time (last edition 1949). *An Introduction to the Use of the Public Records* by V. H. Galbraith (Oxford, 1934) will be found very helpful. For the manuscripts of literary sources T. Duffus Hardy's *Descriptive Catalogue of Materials relating to the History of Great Britain and Ireland* (Rolls Series, 1862–71) is important; the appendix to part ii of vol. i contains a list of the printed sources. Owing to the close connexion between England and France during this period, the sources of history of the two countries largely overlap; the critical bibliography by A. Molinier, *Les Sources de l'histoire de France* (Paris, 1901–6), is therefore valuable also for English history. For manuscripts and editions of the narrative sources, the comprehensive work by A. Potthast, *Bibliotheca Historica Medii Aevi* (2nd ed., Berlin, 1896), is also useful. The excellent chapters on English history contained in vols. v and vi of the *Cambridge Medieval History* are supplied with full lists of authorities.

The *Dictionary of National Biography* is an indispensable work of reference, and contains lives of all the more important persons and a summary of the biographical material written by some of the best scholars of the time, including J. H. Round, R. L. Poole, K. Norgate, and W. Hunt. The *Victoria History of the Counties of England*, begun in 1900 and still in progress, besides general chapters on the political, ecclesiastical, and economic history of each county, contains a translation of the relative portion of Domesday Book with valuable commentaries and the history of each parish in the county. The *Complete Peerage* by G. E. Cokayne, of which a new edition was begun in 1910 and nears completion, gives the most accurate account of the descent of noble families. Among the many books on chronology, the two volumes published by the Royal Historical Society, *Handbook of British Chronology* (ed. F. M. Powicke, 1939) and *Handbook of Dates* (ed. C. R. Cheney, 1945,) will be found most convenient. The former contains lists of kings, bishops, peers, and officers of state, the latter contains calendars, regnal years, &c. Complete lists of dignitaries of the church are given in J. le Neve's *Fasti Ecclesiae Anglicanae* (ed. T. Duffus Hardy, Oxford, 1854). For the pedigrees of reigning houses the *Genealogical Tables* by H. B. George (6th ed. by J. R. H. Weaver, Oxford, 1930) should be consulted. *L'Art de vérifier les dates*, 18 vols. (Paris, 1818–19), which gives brief accounts of kings, dukes, counts, &c., in all countries, is still invaluable. Pending the completion of the county volumes published by the English Place-Name Society, the authoritative *Oxford Dictionary of English Place-Names* by E. Ekwall (Oxford, 1936) is indispensable. The third and index volume of the *Book of Fees* contains the most comprehensive list of the different forms of medieval personal and place-names. Some useful articles with short bibliographies on English medieval institutions (many of them, such as that on 'Justiciar', by D. M. Stenton) are contained in *Chambers's Encyclopaedia*, 1950.

Medieval England, new edition and rewritten, ed. A. L. Poole (Oxford, in the press) contains useful chapters on various topics such as architecture, heraldry, costume, &c.

2. CHARTERS, RECORDS, AND OTHER DOCUMENTS

The Charters of Liberties (of which Magna Carta was the last and the greatest) are printed in vol. i of *Statutes of the Realm* (1810) and in a convenient form with notes by C. Bémont, *Chartes des libertés anglaises* (Collection de Textes, 1892). The *Regesta Regum Anglo-Normannorum*, vol. i (ed. H. W. C. Davis, Oxford, 1913), contains a calendar of William II's charters, forty-seven of which are printed in full in an appendix; for corrections and criticisms of this volume see J. H. Round, *Eng. Hist. Rev.* xxix (1914), 347–56. The completion of vol. ii of this series dealing with the charters of Henry I (begun by Davis) edited by C. Johnson and H. A. Cronne is in the press, and the work is being continued for the reign of Stephen under the editorship of H. A. Cronne and R. H. C. Davis. Over 700 charters and documents of the reign of Henry I have been briefly described by William Farrer in *An Outline Itinerary of King Henry the First*, published in *Eng. Hist. Rev.* xxxiv (1919) and separately. There is no collection or even calendar of the charters of King Stephen and the Empress Matilda nor of the English Charters of Henry II, though many of these are briefly noticed by R. W. Eyton in *Court, Household, and Itinerary of King Henry II* (London, 1878). The charters and documents relating to the continental dominions and the affairs of France have been superbly edited by Leopold Delisle and E. Berger, *Recueil des Actes de Henri II* (Paris, 1909–27). The introductory volume by Delisle is the best account of the chancery of Henry II. There is a list of the charters of Richard I by L. Landon in *The Itinerary of King Richard I* (Pipe Roll Society, New Series, vol. xiii).

Facsimiles of Royal and Other Charters in the British Museum, vol. i, William I–Richard I (ed. G. F. Warner and H. J. Ellis, London, 1903), contains a number of original charters selected in order to illustrate points of historical interest as well as handwriting and the forms of documents. Rymer's *Foedera*, vol. i (Record Commission, 1816), contains a valuable collection of documents, especially treaties and correspondence with foreign powers. A *Syllabus* (in English) of the documents contained in this collection was published with an index by T. Duffus Hardy (3 vols., London, 1869–85). The *Calendar of Documents preserved in France, 918–1206* (ed. J. H. Round, 1899), contains full abstracts of grants, &c., chiefly to religious houses. Among other miscellaneous collections of charters may be mentioned T. Madox, *Formulare*, and J. H. Round, *Ancient Charters* (Pipe Roll Society, vol. x). Important collections of charters relating to the possessions of a church, an honor, or a region have been published by local and learned societies. Especially valuable both for their contents and their fine editorship are the following: *Registrum Antiquissimum of the Cathedral Church of Lincoln*, ed. C. W. Foster and Kathleen Major, Lincoln Record Society, 1931– (continuing); *Early Yorkshire Charters*, ed. W. Farrer, 3 vols., 1913–16 (Index vol., 1942), continued by C. T. Clay for the Yorkshire Archaeological Society, 1935–52; *Documents illustrative of the Social and Economic History of the Danelaw* (cited Danelaw Charters), ed. F. M. Stenton, 1920, and *Feudal Documents from the Abbey of Bury St. Edmunds*, ed. D. C. Douglas, 1932, both published for the British Academy in *Records of the Social and Economic History of England and Wales; Facsimiles of Early Charters from Northamptonshire Collections*, ed. F. M. Stenton for the Northamptonshire Record Society, 1930; *Transcripts of Charters relating to Gilbertine Houses*, ed. F. M. Stenton for the Lincoln Record Society, vol. 18, 1922; *Facsimiles of Early Charters in Oxford Muniment Rooms*, ed. H. E. Salter, Oxford, 1929; and *Sir Christopher Hatton's Book of Seals*, ed. L. C. Loyd and D. M. Stenton, Oxford, 1950. A large number of charters relating to religious houses are included in Dugdale's *Monasticon Anglicanum* (ed. Caley, Ellis, and Bandinel, London, 1849). *English Historical Documents 1042–1189*, ed. with introductions and notes by D. C. Douglas and G. W. Greenaway (London, 1953) contains a large number of charters, narratives, and other sources illustrative of the history of the period.

CHANCERY. With the beginning of enrolment in the first year of John, record material becomes more plentiful and more accessible. Though there are gaps in the rolls, those of the reign of John which have survived have been printed in full by T. Duffus Hardy for the Record Commission: *Rotuli Chartarum* (1837), *Rotuli Litterarum Patentium* (1835), *Rotuli Litterarum Clausarum* (1833); included in the introduction to the Patent Rolls there is a valuable itinerary of King John. A large number of royal charters relating to this period have been preserved in later charters of *Inspeximus*; they are printed or calendared in *Calendar of Charter Rolls*, 1903–27. *Liberate Rolls* (orders for making payments out of the treasury) exist for the second to the fifth year of John (ed. T. Duffus Hardy for Record Commission, 1844). Some further fragments of the *Liberate Roll* of 2 John together with fragments of other early rolls have been printed by the Pipe Roll Society (vol. xxi). After 1204 for the remainder of the period such writs are entered on the close roll. The fine rolls (*Rotuli de Oblatis et Finibus*, ed. T. Duffus Hardy, Record Commission, 1835) contain the proffers in money or kind made to obtain royal favours and have survived with some gaps for the whole reign. The *Norman Rolls* which contain various documents issued from the chancery relating to Normandy, are extant for the years 1200–5 (ed. T. Duffus Hardy for Record Commission, 1835). A number of miscellaneous charters were enrolled in a series known as *Cartae Antiquae*; the first ten rolls have been edited by L. Landon for the Pipe Roll Society, New Series, vol. xvii.

EXCHEQUER. The great rolls of the exchequer, known as the *Pipe Rolls*, are of the first importance not only for the royal revenue but also for the constitutional and political history of this period. One roll exists for the thirty-first year of Henry I; from 2 Henry II the series is continuous. The rolls for 31 Henry I, 2–4 Henry II, and 1 Richard I have been edited by J. Hunter for the Record Commission, 1833, 1844. The remainder down to the year 1211 have been published by the Pipe Roll Society. Some of the original series (which extends to the end of the reign of Henry II) and all the new series are furnished with introductions of very great value by J. H. Round, D. M. Stenton, and others. A portion of a *Receipt Roll* (which records payments into the treasury) exists for Michaelmas term, 1185, and has been published with facsimiles by Hubert Hall (London School of Economics, 1899); a small fragment of the roll of 7 Richard I also survives and has been printed by the Pipe Roll Society, New Series, vol. vi. Memoranda Rolls for 1 and 10 John are extant; the former is published with an introduction by H. G. Richardson, ibid., vol. xxi. *Praestita Rolls* (on which are entered advances made on account of wages, &c.) for 7 and 12 John and *Misae Rolls* (recording the daily expenses of the king's court) for 11 and 14 John are extant. These four rolls have been printed by T. Duffus Hardy (*Rotuli de Liberate ac de Misis et Praestitis*) and H. Cole (*Documents illustrative of English History in the Thirteenth and Fourteenth Centuries*), both for the Record Commission, 1844. There are rolls or portions of rolls of the Norman exchequer for the years 1180, 1184, 1195, 1198, and 1201–3 (*Magni Rotuli Scaccarii Normanniae*, ed. with valuable introductions by T. Stapleton, 1840–4); some further fragments relating to the years 1199–1204 have been edited by S. R. Packard in *Smith College Studies in History* (Northampton, Mass., 1926–7). The *Dialogus de Scaccario* by the treasurer Richard Fitz Nigel (ed. with translation by C. Johnson, in Nelson's Medieval Texts, 1950) is an invaluable contemporary account of the working of the exchequer.

LEGAL. The definitive edition of the law books compiled in the twelfth and early thirteenth century is *Die Gesetze der Angelsachsen*, by F. Liebermann (Halle, 1903–16): cf. F. M. Stenton, *Anglo-Saxon England*, p. 692. There is also a handy edition of the earlier compilations with a translation by A. J. Robertson, *The Laws of the Kings of England from Edmund to Henry I* (Cambridge, 1925). The treatise *De Legibus et Consuetudinibus Regni Angliae* attributed to Rannulf Glanvill has been edited by G. E. Woodbine (Oxford, 1932). The earliest plea rolls were published by Maitland for the Pipe Roll Society, vol. xiv (1891), and others by F. Palgrave (*Rotuli Curiae Regis*) for the Record Commission, 1835. The remainder down to the end of the period have been published by the Record Office, 1922–35. The editor of this important series, C. T. Flower, has written a valuable introduction for the Selden Society (vol. lxii). Useful 'Notes on Thirteenth-Century Judicial Procedure' drawn from a study of the Curia Regis Rolls by Charles Johnson are contained in *Eng. Hist. Rev.* lxii (1947). *The Earliest Lincolnshire Assize Rolls, 1202–9*, and *The Earliest Northamptonshire Assize Rolls, 1202–3*, have been edited with valuable introductions by D. M. Stenton for the respective county Record Societies (1926, 1930). A useful selection of the plea rolls was published by F. W. Maitland, *Select Pleas of the Crown*, for the Selden Society (vol. i, 1888). M. M. Bigelow's *Placita Anglo-Normannica* contains a miscellaneous collection of records of litigation. The printing of the Final Concords arranged under counties was begun by J. Hunter for the Record Commission in 1835, but the work was only completed for Beds., Berks., Bucks., Cambs., Cornwall, Cumberland, Derbyshire,

Devon, and Dorset. The work of publishing the early fines was then undertaken by the Pipe Roll Society and all the fines down to 10 Richard I have now been printed (Pipe Roll Society, vols. xvii, xx, xxiii, xxiv). The fines of many counties have also been either published in full or calendared by local societies.

The legislation of ecclesiastical councils is contained in vol. i of *Concilia Magnae Britanniae et Hiberniae* (ed. D. Wilkins, London, 1737). A much-needed new edition of this work is in the course of preparation.

Selected Letters of Pope Innocent III have been well edited with a translation by C. R. Cheney and W. H. Semple (Nelson's Medieval Texts, 1953).

3. NARRATIVE SOURCES

Most of the more important narratives have been published in *Chronicles and Memorials of Great Britain and Ireland during the Middle Ages published under the direction of the Master of the Rolls*, commonly referred to as the *Rolls Series*. Except when otherwise stated, the chronicles and annals mentioned in this section are the volumes included in this series. The editing of these is uneven; some, such as those by Stubbs, are excellent and contain valuable historical introductions.

The *Anglo-Saxon Chronicle* (ed. B. Thorpe with translation, 1861) was continued at Peterborough to the year 1154, the earlier portion (to 1121) being copied from a manuscript probably compiled at St. Augustine's, Canterbury (cf. Stenton, *Anglo-Saxon England*, p. 681). It is valuable as showing the native attitude to events in the years following the Conquest. William of Malmesbury, who set himself the task of filling the gap between Bede and his own day, is the most literary and scholarly of the writers of the time. His *Historia Regum* and *Historia Novella* (ed. W. Stubbs, 1887–9) extend to 1142, and the part relating to the reign of Henry I and the early years of Stephen is a strictly contemporary authority. His *Gesta Pontificum* (ed. N. E. S. A. Hamilton, 1870), though mainly concerned with the Anglo-Saxon period, contains useful notices of the bishops of his time. The *Historia Ecclesiastica* of Ordericus Vitalis (ed. A. Le Prévost, Société de l'histoire de France, 1838–55) contains the fullest account of events down to 1141. The author, though born in England, spent most of his life in the monastery of St. Évroul in Normandy, and is well informed especially on the wars and the personalities of the reigns of William II and Henry I. His history, however, is rather confused and badly arranged. The *Historia Novorum* and the *Vita Sancti Anselmi* by Eadmer, a monk of Christ Church, Canterbury, who became chaplain to Archbishop Anselm (ed. M. Rule, 1884), are indispensable for the history of the church to 1122. The letters of Anselm as archbishop are also valuable. They are printed in *S. Anselmi Opera Omnia*, 6 vols., ed. F. S. Schmitt, O.S.B. (Edinburgh, 1946–55), and also in Migne, *Patrologia Latina*, vol. 159. The *Chronicon ex Chronicis* attributed to Florence, a monk of Worcester (ed. B. Thorpe, English Historical Society, 1848–9), is based on the chronicle of Marianus Scotus (an Irish monk who wrote at Mainz) which ends in 1082. It has little independent value as the matter relating to England is chiefly derived from the Anglo-Saxon Chronicle and other known sources and for the later years till Florence's death in 1118, from Eadmer. It was continued to 1140 by John, another Worcester monk (ed. J. H. Weaver, *Anecdota Oxoniensia*, 1908), who was a witness of much that he relates. The later continuations made at Bury St. Edmunds are of little value. The *Historia Anglorum* of Henry, archdeacon of Huntingdon (ed. T. Arnold, 1879), becomes a more independent source from about 1121 and is carried down to the coronation of Henry II in 1154. The writer is liable to draw too much on his imagination to be an altogether reliable authority.

Simeon, a monk of Durham, who wrote a history of his church (*Historia Dunelmensis Ecclesiae*) to 1096 with continuations to 1154, also wrote a general history, *Historia Regum*, which is useful especially for the affairs of the north and is an original work from 1119 to 1129; it was continued by John of Hexham to 1154 (*Symeonis monachi opera omnia*, ed. T. Arnold, 1882–5). For the years of the anarchy the *Gesta Stephani* is the principal authority. It was edited by R. Howlett in *Chronicles of the Reigns of Stephen, Henry II, and Richard I*, vol. iii, 1886, from an incomplete manuscript which breaks off in the middle of a sentence in 1147. Professor R. A. B. Mynors has discovered a manuscript containing the lost ending which brings the story to the end of the reign. The complete text will be published in Nelson's Medieval Texts (edited by K. R. Potter).[1] The writer,

[1] Through the courtesy of the editors I have had access to the proofs, and references in the text are given to the pages of this edition.

a partisan of the king and possibly a chaplain of Henry, bishop of Winchester, is well informed and an eyewitness of many of the events he recounts. For the war with Scotland, Richard of Hexham's *Historia de gestis regis Stephani et de Bello Standardi* and Ailred of Rievaulx's *Relatio de Standardo* (both ed. R. Howlett in *Chronicles of Stephen*, &c., vol. iii) are valuable first-hand accounts. *The Life of Ailred of Rievaulx by Walter Daniel*, with translation and notes has been edited by F. M. Powicke in Nelson's Medieval Texts, 1950. The *Historia Pontificalis* of John of Salisbury (ed. R. L. Poole, Oxford, 1927), though, as the title suggests, mainly concerned with the affairs of Rome, throws considerable light on the ecclesiastical history of the reign of Stephen, particularly the years 1148–52.

There are no adequate contemporary sources for the early years of the reign of Henry II. The *Chronica* of Robert of Torigni, successively prior of Bec in 1149 and abbot of Mont-Saint-Michel in 1154 (ed. R. Howlett in vol. iv of *Chronicles of Stephen*, &c., 1889), an independent source from about 1150 to its conclusion in 1186, is very valuable for the foreign relations of Henry II, but is only incidentally concerned with the internal affairs of England which the author twice visited in 1157 and 1175. The long rambling poem *Draco Normannicus* ascribed to Étienne of Rouen (ed. R. Howlett in *Chronicles of Stephen*, &c., vol. ii, 1885) only occasionally adds new facts for the period 1153–69. The ecclesiastical history is largely covered by the collection of *Materials for the History of Thomas Becket* (ed. J. C. Robertson, 1875–85). Vols. i–iv contain the *Lives* of Becket; vols. v–vii the correspondence of the leading actors in the great struggle. The contemporary metrical *Vie de Saint Thomas* by Guernes de Pont-Saint-Maxence (ed. E. Walberg, Lund, 1922) is also valuable and the later Icelandic *Thomas Saga Erkibyskups* (ed. with English translation by Eirikr Magnusson, Rolls Series, 1875–83) also contains some matter not found elsewhere. Complete collections of the letters of John of Salisbury and Gilbert Foliot are still only available in the unsatisfactory editions of J. A. Giles (*Patres Ecclesiae Anglicanae*, 1845, 1848) but a critical edition of John of Salisbury's letters, edited by W. J. Millor, H. E. Butler, and C. N. L. Brooke (Nelson's Medieval Texts), is now in the press. The letters of Arnulf of Lisieux have been well edited by F. Barlow in the Camden Series, 3rd series, vol. lxi (1939).

There are again good literary sources from about the year 1170. Of primary importance are the *Gesta Henrici Secundi* and the *Gesta Ricardi* (1170–92), ascribed wrongly to Benedict of Peterborough (ed. W. Stubbs, 1867); the author almost certainly was Roger of Hoveden who revised and continued them to 1201 in the *Chronica* which bears his name (ed. W. Stubbs, 1868–71). The identification is proved by D. M. Stenton, *Eng. Hist. Rev.* lxviii (1953), 574–82. The value of these works is greatly enhanced by the inclusion in them of many official documents. The *Chronique de la guerre entre les Anglois et les Ecossois*, an Anglo-Norman poem by Jordan Fantosme (ed. R. Howlett in vol. iii of *Chronicles of the Reigns of Stephen*, &c., 1886), is a valuable and in part an eye-witness's account of the rebellion of 1173–4. The author was probably chancellor of the diocese of Winchester. Though the *Historia rerum Anglicarum* of William of Newburgh (ed. R. Howlett in vols. i–ii of *Chronicles of the Reigns of Stephen*, &c., 1884–5) was only composed about the end of the century, it is of great value for the period it covers owing to the literary merit and discriminating judgement of the writer. The *Imagines Historiarum* of Ralph de Diceto (ed. W. Stubbs, 1876) is a good contemporary authority from 1180, when Ralph became dean of St. Paul's, to its close in 1202. The *Historical Works* of Gervase of Canterbury, who was not perhaps an historian of the first rank, are useful, especially for ecclesiastical affairs (ed. W. Stubbs, 1879–80). He became a monk of Christ Church in 1163 and his work extends till about the middle of the reign of John when it was continued by other hands. Two works, the *Chronica* of Ralph Niger (ed. R. Anstruther, Caxton Society, 1851) and the *De Principis Instructione* of Giraldus Cambrensis (ed. G. F. Warner, *Opera*, vol. viii) are chiefly interesting on account of their violent hostility and criticism of Henry II. The *De Nugis Curialium* of Walter Map (ed. T. Wright, Camden Society, 1850) contains a lively description of the court in the time of Henry II. There is a good translation by M. R. James in Cymmrodorion Record Series, no. ix, 1923. An important and independent account of the events in England between 1189 and 1192 is provided by the *De rebus gestis Ricardi Primi* of the Winchester monk, Richard of Devizes (ed. R. Howlett in vol. iii of *Chronicles of the Reigns of Stephen*, &c., 1886). The best account of the crusade of Richard I has survived in two versions: (*a*) *Itinerarium Perigrinorum et Gesta*

Regis Ricardi (ed. W. Stubbs, 1864); (*b*) *L'Estoire de la Guerre Sainte* by Ambroise (ed. Gaston Paris, in Collection de documents inédits sur l'histoire de France, 1897). On the relation between these texts see J. G. Edwards in *Historical Essays in Honour of James Tait*, pp. 59–77. The principal narrative sources for the reign of John are the *Chronicon Anglicanum* of Ralph of Coggeshall (ed. J. Stevenson, 1875) and the *Memoriale* of Walter of Coventry (ed. W. Stubbs, 1873) which is derived from annals compiled at the monastery of Barnwell. The *Flores Historiarum* of Roger of Wendover (ed. H. O. Coxe, English Historical Society, 1841–4, which was copied and embellished by Matthew Paris, has usually been freely used as an authoritative source, but the unreliability of this writer has been demonstrated by V. H. Galbraith (*Roger Wendover and Matthew Paris*, David Murray Lecture, Glasgow, 1944). The portion of the *Histoire des ducs de Normandie et des rois d'Angleterre* (ed. Francisque Michel, Société de l'histoire de France, 1840) which relates to the reign of John, appears to be the work of an eyewitness. The Norman-French metrical *Histoire de Guillaume le Maréchal* (ed. Paul Meyer for the Société de l'histoire de France, 1891–1901) is very valuable both for political history and for the history of manners in the age of chivalry. Many continental chronicles supplement the English sources for the foreign policy of the period. Among the more important are Suger's *Vie de Louis le Gros* (ed. A. Molinier, Collection de Textes, 1887); the Angevin sources in *Recueil d'Annales Angevines et Vendômoises* (ed. L. Halphen, Collection de Textes, 1903) and *Chroniques des Comtes d'Anjou* (ed. L. Halphen and R. Poupardin, Collection de Textes, 1913); and the two contemporary histories of Philip Augustus, the *Gesta Philippi Augusti* by Rigord and William le Breton, and the latter's verse biography, the *Philippide* (both ed. H. F. Delaborde for the Société de l'histoire de France, 1882–5).

The *Annales Monastici*, compiled at Margan, Tewkesbury, Burton, Winchester, Waverley, Dunstable, Bermondsey, Oseney (Oxford), and Worcester (ed. H. R. Luard, 1864–9), very brief for the early part of this period, become fuller and useful, particularly for ecclesiastical affairs, in the early years of the thirteenth century. Some other short monastic annals have also been published by F. Liebermann in *Ungedruckte Anglo-Normannische Geschichtsquellen* (Strassburg, 1879). For monastic history the *Chronica* of Jocelin of Brakelond (latest edition in Nelson's

Medieval Texts with translation by H. E. Butler, 1949) and the *Chronicon* of Battle Abbey (ed. J. S. Brewer, Anglia Christiana Society, 1846) are particularly valuable for the government and internal affairs of the monasteries. The works contained in vols. i–iv of the *Opera* of Giraldus Cambrensis (ed. J. S. Brewer), especially the *Gemma Ecclesiastica* and the *Speculum Ecclesiae*, though characterized by violent invective, throw much light on the condition of the church. The *Epistolae Cantuarienses* (ed. W. Stubbs, 1865) contain an interesting collection of letters composed by the convent of Christ Church relating to disputes in which it was involved. Vols. ii and iii of *Historians of the Church of York* (ed. J. Raine, 1879–94) contain lives of archbishops and important letters and documents relating to the northern province.

4. GENERAL, POLITICAL, AND ECCLESIASTICAL HISTORY

The most detailed account of the period is given by J. H. Ramsay in *The Foundations of England*, vol. ii (1066–1154), and *The Angevin Empire* (1154–1216) (Oxford, 1898 and 1903). The period is also covered by G. B. Adams in *The Political History of England*, vol. ii (London, 1905), and by H. W. C. Davis in *England under the Normans and Angevins* (first published, London, 1905). *The Reign of William Rufus* by E. A. Freeman (2 vols., Oxford, 1882), in spite of its serious defects (it takes little account of any aspect of history except the purely political), is still of considerable value for the careful narrative compiled from the literary sources. The works of Kate Norgate, *England under the Angevin Kings* (2 vols., London, 1887), *Richard the Lion Heart* (London, 1924), and *John Lackland* (London, 1902) cover very fully the period from the accession of Henry I to the death of John. Though, especially in her early work, she was too much influenced both in style and treatment by her master, J. R. Green, her books are scholarly and important. Of all the volumes produced by J. H. Round, his *Geoffrey de Mandeville* (London, 1892) alone is a sustained history; it is an admirable and very important study of the anarchy in the time of Stephen, and is supplemented by numerous appendixes in which points of detail are discussed. O. Rössler, *Kaiserin Mathilde* (Berlin, 1897), is a scholarly and valuable biography written with a bias in favour of the empress, and on some points challenges the views of Round. There is a good biography of *Henry II* by L. F. Salzman

(London, 1917). S. Painter has published *The Reign of King John* (Johns Hopkins Press, Baltimore, 1949), which treats the subject in detail in the political and administrative aspects.

FOREIGN POLICY. *The Normans in European History* by C. H. Haskins (London, 1919) provides a useful introductory sketch. F. M. Powicke's *Loss of Normandy* (Manchester, 1913) is a full and very valuable study of the Angevin Empire, particularly, of course, its last phase. The wars in Normandy at the opening of the period are well treated by C. W. David in *Robert Curthose* (Harvard Hist. Studies, 1920). The standard biographies of the kings of France: *Philippe Ier* by A. Fliche (Paris, 1912), *Louis VI le Gros* by A. Luchaire (Paris, 1890), *Philipp II August* by A. Cartellieri (4 vols., Leipzig, 1899–1921), and *Louis VIII* by C. Petit-Dutaillis (Paris, 1894) are valuable, and also those of *Renaud de Dammartin* by H. Malo (Paris, 1898) and of *Henri I Duc de Brabant* by G. Smets (Brussels, 1908), on account of the active part played by these princes in English politics in the reign of King John. Two monographs are particularly important for the study of foreign policy: W. Kienast, *Die Deutschen Fürsten im Dienste der Westmächte* (Utrecht, 1924), and G. G. Dept, *Les Influences anglaise et française dans le comté de Flandre* (Ghent, 1928). F. Hardegen's *Imperialpolitik König Heinrichs II von England* (Heidelberg, 1905) is an interesting, if slightly exaggerated, discussion of the king's imperial ambitions. *Le Comté d'Anjou sous Henri Plantagenet et ses fils*, by J. Boussard (Paris, 1938), gives the best account of the history and administration of Anjou. A. Richard, *Histoire des comtes de Poitou* (2 vols., Paris, 1903), is very detailed on the reign of Eleanor of Provence.

ECCLESIASTICAL. There is a useful survey of the history of *The English Church, 1066–1272*, by W. R. W. Stephens (London, 1901). H. Böhmer's *Kirche und Staat* (Leipzig, 1899) is a pioneer work of great value for the conflicts between church and state down to 1154. It is based on much new material, especially the Anonymous of York, some of whose writings are printed in an appendix. The most important contribution to ecclesiastical history in recent years is *The English Church and the Papacy* by Z. N. Brooke (Cambridge, 1931). It emphasizes particularly the importance of the growth of the Canon Law. On the relations with Rome, H. Tillmann's *Die päpstlichen Legaten in England bis zur Beendigung der Legation Gualas, 1218* (Bonn, 1926) is useful. For the Becket conflict, Maitland's essay on 'Henry II and the

Criminous Clerks' in his *Roman Canon Law in the Church of England* (London, 1898) and R. Génestal's *Le Privilegium Fori en France* (Paris, 1924) are valuable. The recent elaborate study by R. Foreville, *L'Église et la Royauté en Angleterre sous Henri II Plantagenet* (Paris, 1942), though very full and learned, is marred by bias and lack of judgement. There are biographies of the leading churchmen of varying quality: *Lanfranc* by A. J. Macdonald (Oxford, 1926); *The Life and Times of Anselm* by M. Rule (2 vols., London, 1883) is thorough but suffers from a strong bias in favour of the papacy; *St. Anselm* by R. W. Church (London, 1870) in spite of its age can still be read with profit; L. B. Radford's *Thomas of London* (Cambridge, 1894) is useful for the early years of Becket; the best study of his character is by M. D. Knowles (British Academy, 1949) who has also published his important Ford lectures on *The Episcopal Colleagues of Archbishop Thomas Becket* (Cambridge, 1951); there is a good life of *Bartholomew of Exeter* by Adrian Morey (Cambridge, 1937); F. M. Powicke has finely treated the life and work of *Stephen Langton* (Oxford, 1928): see also his *Christian Life in the Middle Ages* (Oxford, 1935). F. Makower's *Constitutional History and Constitution of the Church of England* (London, 1895) is a useful reference book. *The Monastic Order in England* by M. D. Knowles (Cambridge, 1940) is the authoritative work. This fine book supersedes what had been previously written on the history of monasticism in this period. *Religious Houses of Medieval England* 2nd edition (London, 1953) by the same author in collaboration with R. N. Hadcock contains convenient lists of the religious houses of the different orders with dates of foundation. An excellent *Map of Monastic Britain* has been published by the Ordnance Survey, 1950. More detailed accounts of the development of the several orders are: A. M. Cooke, 'The Settlement of the Cistercians in England' (*Eng. Hist. Rev.* viii [1893], 625), J. C. Dickinson, *The Origins of the Austin Canons* (London, 1950), and H. M. Colvin, *The White Canons in England* (Oxford, 1951), R. Graham, *St. Gilbert of Sempringham and the Gilbertines* (London, 1901); the same author's work on Cluny has been collected in her *English Ecclesiastical Studies* (London, 1929). *Canterbury Cathedral Priory* by R. A. L. Smith (Cambridge, 1943) is an important study in monastic administration. C. R. Cheney's *English Bishops' Chanceries 1100–1250* (Manchester, 1950) is useful for the organization of the bishop's household.

5. CONSTITUTIONAL HISTORY

The classical *Constitutional History of England* by W. Stubbs (Oxford, 1874–8) remains, in spite of its date, the best and most authoritative starting-point for a detailed study of medieval institutions. Unfortunately later editions were not subjected to serious revision. A number of points on which later research has proved Stubbs to be wrong have been corrected in a series of studies appended to the French edition of this work by C. Petit-Dutaillis. These have been collected and translated in *Studies Supplementary to Stubbs' Constitutional History*, 3 vols. (Manchester, 1908–29). Stubbs's *Select Charters and Other Illustrations of English Constitutional History* (Oxford, 1870; 9th edition revised by H. W. C. Davis, Oxford, 1921) contains a very valuable selection of the more important documents. As a new edition of this indispensable work of reference thoroughly revised by J. G. Edwards is shortly to appear, it has been thought best not to give references to the existing edition in the text. The *Constitutional History of Medieval England* (London, 1937) by J. E. A. Jolliffe is very suggestive and original, but the plan of the work makes it difficult to use as a text-book on the subject.

The *History of English Law* by F. Pollock and F. W. Maitland (2nd ed., Cambridge, 1911) is the authoritative book on the legal history of the middle ages. The author—it is substantially the work of Maitland—has a remarkable gift of bringing lucidity to the most complex and technical legal problems. The book is unlikely to be superseded. Maitland's *Constitutional History of England* (ed. H. A. L. Fisher, Cambridge, 1908) contains early courses of lectures by Maitland and was printed posthumously. The lectures were not subjected to systematic revision and cannot be regarded as the author's final and authoritative opinions. The great *History of English Law* by Sir William Holdsworth, 9 vols. (London, 1922–6), though valuable, is less good on the medieval than on the later periods of English history.

G. B. Adams's *Origin of the English Constitution* and *Council and Courts in Anglo-Norman England* (Yale Univ. Press, 1912 and 1926) are based on a number of articles contributed to learned periodicals. They are original contributions to our knowledge of English institutions and always emphasize the feudal background.

The following monographs on particular institutions may be

profitably consulted: W. A. Morris, *The Frankpledge System* (Harvard Historical Studies, 1910), and, by the same author, *The Medieval English Sheriff to 1300* (Manchester, 1927) and *The Early English County Court* (University of California Press, 1926); *Serjeanty Tenure in Medieval England* by E. G. Kimball (Yale Univ. Press, 1936). The same author has contributed two important articles on frankalmoign, *Eng. Hist. Rev.* xliii (1928), xlvii (1932). W. S. McKechnie's *Magna Carta* (2nd ed., Glasgow, 1914), in spite of the author's strong reactionary views, is still the most detailed and best study of the subject; *Magna Carta Commemoration Essays* (edited by H. E. Malden for the Royal Historical Society, 1917) contains some valuable essays by various authors on particular problems. The authoritative work on the parallel development of Norman constitutional history is C. H. Haskins' *Norman Institutions* (Harvard Univ. Press, 1918). Vol. i of T. F. Tout's *Chapters in the Administrative History of Medieval England* (Manchester, 1920) contains the best account of the early administrative system. A good survey of this subject is contained in S. B. Chrimes's *Introduction to the Administrative History of Medieval England* (Oxford, 1952).

FINANCE. The *History of the Exchequer* by T. Madox (London, 1711, index 1741) is the first scholarly treatment of the problems of the English financial system of the middle ages and is still an indispensable authority. The introduction to the *Dialogus de Scaccario* by Charles Johnson (London, 1950), R. L. Poole's *Exchequer in the Twelfth Century* (Oxford, 1912), and the essay by J. H. Round on the 'Origin of the Exchequer' in *The Commune of London* (Westminster, 1899) are the most important studies of this institution. The *Revenues of the Kings of England, 1066–1399*, by J. H. Ramsay (Oxford, 1925) contains useful tables. S. K. Mitchell's *Studies in Taxation under John and Henry III* (Yale Univ. Press, 1914) based on the Pipe Rolls, many of which are unprinted, are valuable. The same author's *Taxation in Medieval England* (Yale Univ. Press, 1951) contains much useful material, but it was printed posthumously without adequate revision. The best books on the history of the Jews, who played such an important part in finance in this period, are by Cecil Roth, *The History of the Jews in England* (Oxford, 1941) and Joseph Jacob, *The Jews of Angevin England* (London, 1893). There is also a valuable paper, 'The Records of Exchequer Receipts from the English Jewry', by H. Jenkinson in the *Jewish Historical Society*

Transactions, vol. viii. The history of the coinage may be studied in the *Coinage of England* by Charles Oman (Oxford, 1931) and G. C. Brooke, *English Coins* (London, 1932). For more detailed study the British Museum Catalogues should be consulted: 'The Norman Kings' by G. C. Brooke (1916); 'The Cross-and-Crosslets (Tealby) type of Henry II' by D. F. Allen (1951).

6. SOCIAL AND ECONOMIC

FEUDAL SOCIETY. Domesday Book was a book of reference in the twelfth century and remains so (for historians) today. For this and its 'satellites' and the literature relating to them see F. M. Stenton, *Anglo-Saxon England*, pp. 693–5. For purposes of reference in the exchequer it was abridged and copies relating to particular counties were made in the twelfth and thirteenth centuries, cf. V. H. Galbraith, *The Herefordshire Domesday* (Pipe Roll Society, New Series, vol. xxv). The *Red Book of the Exchequer* or *Liber Rubeus* (ed. Hubert Hall, Rolls Series, 1896) and the *Black Book* or *Liber Niger Parvus* (ed. T. Hearne, 1774), compiled probably by Alexander of Swereford about 1230 for the use of the exchequer officials, contain inquisitions, charters, and other documents relating to feudal tenures. Both volumes contain the *Constitutio Domus Regis* and the *Cartae* of 1166. Hall's edition of the *Red Book* was severely criticized by J. H. Round in *Studies on the Red Book of the Exchequer* (printed for private circulation). The *Book of Fees* (Stationery Office, London, 1920–31), which is referred to by historians writing before the Record Office published this edition as the *Testa de Nevill*, contains returns of inquisitions, lists of fees, &c. The unique *Rotuli de Dominabus et Pueris et Puellis*, 1185 (Pipe Roll Society, vol. xxxv), which provide information about widows and wards and their estates when in the hands of the Crown, are of great value for feudal history.

The best detailed commentaries on Domesday society are F. W. Maitland, *Domesday Book and Beyond* (Cambridge, 1907) and P. Vinogradoff, *English Society in the Eleventh Century* (Oxford, 1908). J. H. Round's *Feudal England* (London, 1895) is of fundamental importance, especially his essay on the introduction of Knight Service into England. This service as it affected the ecclesiastical tenants is well treated by H. M. Chew, *The English Ecclesiastical Tenants-in-Chief and Knight Service* (Oxford, 1932). The best and most recent study of the organization of society in the age following the Conquest is *The First Century of English Feudalism* by F. M. Stenton (Oxford, 1932). The burdens to which the various classes were subjected under the feudal system are discussed by A. L. Poole in *Obligations of Society in the XII and XIII Centuries* (Oxford, 1946). The intricate history of certain individual fees has been traced by W. Farrer in his remarkable volumes on *Honors and Knights' Fees* (London, 1923–4, and Manchester, 1925). R. S. Hoyt, *The Royal Demesne in English Constitutional History, 1066–1272* (Cornell Univ. Press, 1950), makes an important and original contribution to a hitherto little investigated subject. Much of the work of J. H. Round was devoted to investigating the origin and descent of feudal families; these are contained in his *Peerage and Family History* (Westminster, 1901), *Peerage and Pedigree* (London, 1910), and *Family Origins and Other Studies* (published posthumously by W. Page, London, 1930). In these studies Round often took as his starting-point Dugdale's *Baronage of England* (London, 1675), and this work is still of considerable value.

THE FOREST. The *Select Pleas of the Forest*, ed. with an excellent introduction by G. J. Turner (Selden Society, vol. xiii, 1899), contains a selection of pleas of the forest eyre of 1209. M. L. Bazeley's essay on 'The Extent of the English Forest in the Thirteenth Century' in *Trans. R. Hist. Soc.*, 4th ser., vol. iv (1921), and the chapters of C. Petit-Dutaillis in *Studies and Notes supplementary to Stubbs' Constitutional History*, vol. ii (1914), are both valuable for the organization of the forest. H. A. Cronne gives a detailed account of 'The Royal Forest in the reign of Henry I' in *Essays in British and Irish History in Honour of J. E. Todd*, ed. Cronne, Moody and Quinn, (London, 1949).

RURAL SOCIETY. The most important material for the study of rural conditions is to be found in the surveys of great ecclesiastical estates: *The Burton Abbey Twelfth Century Surveys* (ed. C. G. O. Bridgeman for the William Salt Archaeological Society, 1916); the *Liber Niger* of the abbey of Peterborough (ed. T. Stapleton in his edition of the *Chronicon Petroburgense*, Camden Society, 1849); the *Liber Henrici de Soliaco abbatis Glastoniensis* of 1189 (ed. J. E. Jackson, Roxburghe Club, 1882); the *Cartularium Monasterii de Rameseia* (ed. W. H. Hart and P. A. Lyons, Rolls Series, 1884–93); the *Bolden Book* of the bishopric of Durham, 1183 (printed in vol. iv. of *Domesday Book*); the *Domesday of St. Paul's*, 1222 (ed. W. H. Hale, Camden Society, 1858); and the

Records of the Templars in England, the Inquest of 1185 (ed. B. A. Lees for the British Academy, 1935). The *Shaftesbury Cartulary* and the *Cartulary of the Abbey of Holy Trinity at Caen* are not available in print, but have been used by M. Postan in his valuable paper on the 'Chronology of Labour Services' in *Trans. R. Hist. Soc.*, 4th ser., vol. xx (1937), 169–93. *The Pipe Roll of the Bishopric of Winchester, 1207–8* (ed. Hubert Hall for the London School of Economics and Political Science, 1903), giving detailed accounts of receipts and expenditure and an inventory of stock on all the manors of the bishop of Winchester, is an invaluable record of the working of the farms on these estates. The series of treatises on estate management published under the title *Walter of Henley's Husbandry* (ed. E. Lamond, London, 1890), though written some years after the close of this period, describe methods and systems probably little different from those in use at the opening of the thirteenth century.

The best and most recent survey of the agricultural conditions of Europe is contained in vol. i of the *Cambridge Economic History*: *The Agrarian Life of the Middle Ages*, ed. J. H. Clapham and Eileen Power (Cambridge, 1941). P. Vinogradoff's *Villainage in England* (Oxford, 1892) gives the fullest discussion of the conditions of the English peasant population. His other works, *The Growth of the Manor* (London, 1911) and *English Society in the Eleventh Century* (Oxford, 1908), chiefly relate to an earlier period, but they provide a good background for the study of twelfth-century society. The essay on 'Agricultural Services' in his *Collected Papers*, vol. i, is also important. An interesting and well-written account of *Life on the English Manor* is given by H. S. Bennett (Cambridge, 1937). H. L. Gray's *English Field Systems* (Harvard Univ. Press, 1915), though mainly based on later evidence, is valuable as a comparative study of the systems in use in different parts of England. For particular areas, F. M. Stenton's *Types of Manorial Structure in the Northern Danelaw* and D. C. Douglas's *The Social Structure of Medieval East Anglia* (vols. ii and ix of *Oxford Studies in Social and Legal History*, ed. P. Vinogradoff), F. W. Maitland, 'Northumbrian Tenures' (*Eng. Hist. Rev.* v [1890], 625), and J. E. A. Jolliffe, 'Northumbrian Institutions' (ibid. xli [1926], 1) should be consulted. The brilliant book on *The Open Fields* (Oxford, 1938) by C. S. and C. S. Orwin, though primarily based on a study of the conditions at Laxton in Nottinghamshire, is of general application and rendered particularly valuable as being written by scholars with an expert practical knowledge of agriculture. On particular aspects of rural conditions the following are useful: N. Neilson, *Customary Rents* in *Oxford Studies in Social and Legal History*, vol. ii; E. A. Kosminsky, 'Services and Money Rents in the Thirteenth Century' in *Econ. Hist. Rev.* v (1935).

TOWNS. The earlier literature on this subject is fully set out in the *Bibliography of Municipal History* by C. Gross (Harvard Historical Studies, 1897), and the more recent work is noted in the bibliography prefixed to J. Tait's *The Medieval English Borough* (Manchester Univ. Press, 1936). This work, though rather confused in arrangement, is the most authoritative discussion of this difficult subject. He criticizes, however, with undue severity, the interesting views expressed by C. Stephenson in *Borough and Town* (Cambridge, Mass., 1933). The town charters have been analysed by A. Ballard in *British Borough Charters* (Cambridge, 1913). The value of the other writings of this author is seriously impaired by the tenacity with which he maintained Maitland's untenable 'garrison' theory of the origin of boroughs. Maitland's *Township and Borough* (Cambridge, 1898) is important as emphasizing the agrarian background of urban life. The archaic custom to which the boroughs clung is amply illustrated by Mary Bateson in *Borough Customs* (Selden Society, 1904–6). The same author's articles on the laws of Breteuil in *Eng. Hist. Rev.* xv and xvi (1900–1) are also important. M. de W. Hemmeon's *Burgage Tenure in Medieval England* (Harvard Univ. Press, 1914) is a useful study of this aspect. M. Weinbaum's *Verfassungsgeschichte Londons 1066–1268* (Stuttgart, 1929) and F. M. Stenton's concise essay on *Norman London* (Hist. Assoc. Leaflets, [1934], nos. 93, 94) are important; the latter contains a translation of Fitz Stephen's description and a plan of the city as it was in the twelfth century. There are separate monographs on most of the principal towns; among them may be mentioned: M. Bateson, *Records of the Borough of Leicester*, vol. i, with a valuable historical introduction (Cambridge, 1899); J. Tait, *Mediaeval Manchester* (Manchester, 1904); H. E. Salter, *Medieval Oxford* (Oxford Hist. Society, 1936); M. D. Lobel, *The Borough of Bury St. Edmund's* (Oxford, 1935). C. Gross, *The Gild Merchant* remains the standard work; but his conclusions on the relation between the gild merchant and the government of the borough have been modified by Tait (*Medieval English Borough*, ch. ix). Eileen Power's lectures on

The Medieval English Wool Trade (Oxford, 1941) is a brilliant exposition of this important subject; unfortunately it lacks documentation. Industry and commerce are comprehensively treated in vol. ii of the *Cambridge Economic History of Europe*, ed. M. Postan and E. E. Rich (Cambridge, 1952). L. F. Salzman's *English Industries of the Middle Ages* (Oxford, 1923), and *English Trade in the Middle Ages* (Oxford, 1931) should also be consulted.

7. MILITARY AND NAVAL

The standard work on the *History of the Art of War in the Middle Ages* by Charles Oman (2nd ed., 2 vols., London, 1924) is a good synthesis of the subject, but it is inaccurate in detail and does not make use of record material. H. Delbrück, *Geschichte der Kriegskunst*, Pt. III, *Das Mittelalter* (Berlin, 1907), is also unsatisfactory. Harris Nicolas's *History of the Royal Navy* (2 vols., London, 1847), based as it is on a thorough knowledge of the record material, is still valuable. The most recent and detailed work is by F. W. Brooks, *The English Naval Forces, 1199–1272* (London, 1933). The same author's article on William de Wrotham in *Eng. Hist. Rev.* xl (1925) is important for early naval administration. On *Medieval Military Architecture* the work by G. T. Clark (2 vols., London, 1884) is still valuable for details and plans, but owing to the author's erroneous views on the Norman *motte* it must be read with J. H. Round's 'Castles of the Conquest' (*Archaeologia*, 1902) and E. Armitage, *The Early Norman Castles of the British Isles* (London, 1912). The best recent account is A. Hamilton Thompson's *Military Architecture in England during the Middle Ages* (Oxford, 1912), which contains a useful bibliography, and F. M. Stenton's sketch of the *Development of the Castle in England and Wales* (Historical Association Leaflet, no. 22, 1938).

8. SCOTLAND

The Scottish records which existed at the death of Alexander III in 1286 and which were handed over by Edward I to John Balliol practically all disappeared in the disturbances of the following years. There are only two contemporary chronicles: the fragmentary *Chronicon Anglo-Scoticum* or *Chronicle of Holyrood* and the much fuller and more valuable *Chronicle of Melrose*. Both have been printed for the Bannatyne Club (Edinburgh, 1828, 1835). The history of Scotland during this period is therefore mainly dependent on English sources. The materials bearing on Scottish history in the Public Record Office have been calendared by J. Bain, *Calendar of Documents relating to Scotland*, vol. i (*1108–1272*), 1881. Many of the important charters and other material for this period have been printed with excellent notes by A. Lawrie in two volumes: *Early Scottish Charters prior to 1153* (Glasgow, 1905), and *Annals of the Reigns of Malcolm and William (1153–1214)* (Glasgow, 1910). The same scholar collected a great number of charters relating to the period 1153–1249, and his transcripts bound in fifteen volumes are now accessible in the National Library; for notes on this collection see the *Scottish Hist. Rev.* xix, 241 ff. A convenient collection of passages (in translation) from English narrative sources has been made by A. O. Anderson, *Scottish Annals from English Chroniclers* (London, 1908) and more fully in *Early Sources of Scottish History, 500–1286* (2 vols., London, 1922). Vol. ii of Haddan and Stubbs, *Councils and Ecclesiastical Documents* (Oxford, 1873), relates to the church of Scotland.

The most recent and important study of Scottish history is *The Normans in Scotland* (Edinburgh Univ. Press, 1954) by R. L. Graeme Ritchie. There are textbooks by P. Hume Brown (Cambridge, 1899) and by Andrew Lang (4 vols., Edinburgh, 1900–7), but neither of these authors was primarily interested in the history of medieval Scotland. More detailed accounts may be read in W. F. Skene's *Celtic Scotland* (3 vols., 2nd ed., Edinburgh, 1886–7) (especially valuable for the native history), and E. W. Robertson, *Scotland under her Early Kings* (2 vols., Edinburgh, 1862). The introduction and early chapters of R. S. Rait's *Relations between England and Scotland* (London, 1901) and H. Maxwell's *Early Chronicles relating to Scotland* (Glasgow, 1912), though admittedly sketches, are often suggestive. M. Morgan, 'The Organization of the Scottish Church in the Twelfth Century' (*Trans. R. Hist. Soc.* xxix [1947], 135–50), is important for the development of the parochial system. Valuable articles on controversial questions of Scottish history are contained in the *Scottish Historical Review*, 25 vols., 1904 to 1928, in which year it became defunct; it was revived in 1947.

9. WALES

The English narrative sources deal fairly fully with the political history of Wales. The most important Welsh chronicle is the *Brut y Twysogion*, a contemporary narrative compiled possibly at Strata Florida. It has been poorly edited with a translation by J. Williams ab Ithel (Rolls Series, 1860). There is a well-edited Welsh text by J. Rhys and J. G. Evans in the *Red Book of Hergest* (Oxford, 1890) and a good translation by T. Jones (Cardiff, 1952). The *Itinerarium Kambriae*, a narrative of Archbishop Baldwin's tour through Wales in 1188 to preach the crusade, and the *Descriptio Kambriae*, both by Giraldus Cambrensis (*Opera*, vol. vi, ed. J. F. Dimock, Rolls Series, 1868), give a valuable picture of Welsh manners and customs in this period. The autobiography of Giraldus, *De Rebus a se Gestis* (*Opera*, vol. i, ed. J. S. Brewer, Rolls Series, 1861), is also valuable. There is a spirited translation of this work by H. E. Butler (London, 1937). *Episcopal Acts and Cognate Documents relating to Welsh Dioceses, 1066–1272*, ed. J. Conway Davies, 2 vols., 1946–8, is valuable.

Vol. ii of the excellent *History of Wales from the Earliest Times to the Edwardian Conquest* by J. E. Lloyd (2 vols., London, 1911) is a standard and authoritative book.

10. IRELAND

Two contemporary narratives form the basis for the history of the English conquest: (1) Giraldus Cambrensis, *Expugnatio Hibernica* written about 1188 after he had completed his *Topographia Hibernica* (both in *Opera*, vol. v, ed. J. F. Dimock, Rolls Series, 1867). Several of Gerald's relatives took part in the conquest and he himself visited Ireland on two occasions. (2) *The Song of Dermot and the Earl*, an old French poem, probably based on a lost chronicle composed by Morice Regan, interpreter or 'latimer' of Dermot McMurrough. It is printed with a translation and notes by G. H. Orpen (Oxford, 1892). These can be supplemented from the Irish side by numerous native annals of varying quality. The most valuable is that of *The Four Masters* (ed. O'Donovan, Dublin, 1851). Others are the *Annals of Loch Cé* (ed. W. M. Hennessy, Rolls Series, 1871), *The Annals of Ulster* (4 vols., ed. W. M. Hennessy, Dublin, 1887–1901), *The Annals of Clonmacnoise* (R. Soc. of Antiq. of Ireland, 1896), the continuation of the *Annals of Tigernach* (ed. Whitley Stokes in *Rev. Celtique*, xvii, 1897), and the *Annals of Ireland* (printed with the *Cartularies of St. Mary's Abbey, Dublin*, Rolls Series, 1884, vol. ii). There is a *Calendar of the Documents relating to Ireland* preserved in the Public Record Office, 1171–1251 (ed. Sweetman, 1875). *Historic and Municipal Documents of Ireland, 1172–1320* (ed. J. T. Gilbert, Rolls Series, 1870), contains important documents relating to Dublin. *Irish Historical Documents, 1172–1922*, edited by E. Curtis and R. B. Dowell (London, 1943), contains some of the more important documents for the period of the conquest.

There are two good recent histories of medieval Ireland: (1) G. H. Orpen, *Ireland under the Normans, 1169–1216* (2 vols., Oxford, 1911). This is a very careful account of the Anglo-Norman conquest. (2) The *History of Medieval Ireland* by E. Curtis (2nd ed., London, 1938) is written more from the point of view of the native Irish. From these two books the account in the text is mainly compiled. The medieval section of the *History of the Church of Ireland from the Earliest Times to the Present Day*, ed. W. Alison Phillips (3 vols., London, 1933–4), contributed by G. H. Orpen is a valuable sketch. The two essays by J. H. Round on 'The Conquest of Ireland' and 'The Pope and the Conquest of Ireland', printed in *The Commune of London* (Westminster, 1899), and the article by E. Curtis on 'The English and the Ostmen in Ireland' in *Eng. Hist. Rev.* xxiii (1908), 209, are also valuable. Orpen has given special attention to the castles of the conquest in articles in *Eng. Hist. Rev.* xxi, xxii (1906–7) and in the *Proceedings of the R. Soc. of Antiq. of Ireland*, xxxvii (1907).

11. LEARNING, LITERATURE, AND ART

The best general surveys of the intellectual movement of the twelfth century are R. L. Poole's *Illustrations of Medieval Thought* (London, 1884, 2nd ed. revised, London, 1920) and C. H. Haskins's *The Renaissance of the Twelfth Century* (Harvard Univ. Press, 1927). The latter author's *Studies in the History of Medieval Science* (Harvard Univ. Press, 1924) and *Studies in Medieval Culture* (Oxford, 1929) contain valuable contributions on particular aspects. The best general *History of Classical Scholarship* is by J. E. Sandys (3 vols., Cambridge, 1903–8). The philosophical works of John of Salisbury, the *Policraticus* (2 vols., Oxford, 1909) and the *Metalogicon* (Oxford, 1929), have been finely edited by C. C. J. Webb who has also written a good popular life of *John of Salisbury* (London, 1932). *Mediaeval Humanism in the Life and Writings of John of Salisbury* by Hans Liebeschütz (London, Warburg Institute, 1950) is an important commentary. The essays on John of Salisbury by R. L. Poole contained in *Studies in Chronology and History* (Oxford, 1934) should also be consulted. There is only an uncritical edition of John of Salisbury's *Entheticus de Dogmate Philosophorum*, by C. Petersen (Hamburg, 1843). The *History of Magic and Experimental Science* by Lynn Thorndike (2 vols., New York, 1923) and *Augustine to Galileo, the History of Science, A.D. 400–1650* (London, 1952), by A. C. Crombie are valuable and comprehensive histories of scientific development. The new and revised edition of H. Rashdall's *The Universities of Europe in the Middle Ages* by F. M. Powicke and A. B. Emden (3 vols., Oxford, 1936), particularly vol. iii which deals with the English universities, is the standard work on this subject. *The Rise of the Universities* by C. H. Haskins gives in a course of lectures an excellent sketch.

The *Wandering Scholars* by Helen Waddell (6th ed. revised, London, 1926) contains a brilliant account of student life which may be read with her *Medieval Latin Lyrics*, an anthology with good English versions. The most important works on medieval poetry are those by F. J. E. Raby, *The History of Christian Latin Poetry* (Oxford, 1927) and *A History of Secular Latin Poetry* (2 vols., Oxford, 1934). Collections of contemporary Latin poems are contained in: *Satirical Poets of the Twelfth Century* (ed. T. Wright, 2 vols., Rolls Series, 1872); *Latin Poems attributed to Walter Mapes* (ed. T. Wright, Camden Society, 1841); *Political Songs of England* (ed. T. Wright, Camden Society, 1839); and *Carmina Burana* (ed. J. A. Schmeller, Stuttgart, 1847). *The Catalogue of Romances in the Department of Manuscripts in the British Museum* (vols. i and ii ed. H. L. D. Ward, vol. iii by J. A. Herbert; London, 1883–1910) is a great quarry of information about the literature of the middle ages.

The first volume of the *Cambridge History of English Literature* (Cambridge, 1907) contains some good chapters both on language and literature. The famous lectures by W. Stubbs on 'Learning and Literature at the Court of Henry II' printed in *Seventeen Lectures on the Study of Medieval and Modern History* (3rd ed., Oxford, 1900) and V. H. Galbraith's 'The Literacy of the Medieval English Kings' (*Proceedings of the British Academy*, xxi, 1935) give a good account of the state of learning in the twelfth century. W. P. Ker's *English Literature: Medieval* (Home University Library) is an admirable sketch. Among other books on the early English language and literature may be mentioned the following: R. W. Chambers, *On the Continuity of English Prose from Alfred to More and his School* (published for the Early English Text Society, London, 1932); J. Hall, *Early Middle English, 1130-1250* (Oxford, 1920); and the papers by R. M. Wilson, 'English and French in England, 1100-1300' in *History*, xxviii (1943) and 'Lost Literature in Old and Middle English' in *Leeds Studies in English and Kindred Languages* (vol. ii, 1933). There is an immense literature on the Arthurian legend on which E. K. Chambers's *Arthur of Britain* (London, 1927) is a useful guide. E. K. Chambers's *The Medieval Stage* (2 vols., Oxford, 1905) is the best book on the early history of the drama.

ART. Of the very large literature about the art of the period, only a few of the more important books can here be mentioned. The best work on the whole subject is *English Art 1100-1216* by T. S. R. Boase (Oxford, 1953). On architecture *English Romanesque Architecture after the Conquest* by A. W. Clapham (Oxford, 1934) is the standard work of high quality. *English Art in the Middle Ages* by O. E. Saunders (Oxford, 1932) is a useful general textbook. The finely illustrated *British Art and the Mediterranean* by E. Saxl and R. Wittcower (Oxford, 1948) is an interesting comparative study. *English Illuminated Manuscripts from the Xth to the XIIIth Century* by E. G. Millar (Paris–Bruxelles, 1926) is the best book on the subject of illumination. F. Wormald's papers on 'The Development of English Illumination in the Twelfth Century' (*Journal of British Arch. Assoc.*, 3rd ser., viii, 1943) and 'The Survival of the Anglo-Saxon Illumination after the Norman Conquest' (*Proceedings of the British Academy*, xxx, 1944) should also be consulted. E. S. Prior and A. Gardiner, *An Account of Medieval Figure Sculpture in England* (Cambridge, 1913) is the best book on early sculpture. This was abridged and revised by Gardner in 1935 under the title *Handbook of English Medieval Sculpture*, and a new and revised edition with additional plates appeared in 1951. *Later English Romanesque Sculpture, 1140-1210*, by G. Zarnecki (1953) is also valuable. For wall painting, *English Medieval Wall Painting: The Twelfth Century* by E. W. Tristram (The Courtauld Institute of Art, 1944), which contains a large number of plates, is the standard work. For the Sicilian–Byzantine influence on English art Otto Demus's *Mosaics of Norman Sicily* (London, 1950), pp. 448–53, should be consulted. Domestic architecture in the twelfth century is treated by M. Wood in *Arch. Journal*, xcii (1935), 167–242.

INDEX

OXFORD

MORE OXFORD PAPERBACKS

This book is just one of nearly 1000 Oxford Paper-
backs currently in print. If you would like details of
other Oxford Paperbacks, including titles in the
World's Classics, Oxford Reference, Oxford
Books, OPUS, Past Masters, Oxford Authors, and
Oxford Shakespeare series, please write to:

UK and Europe: Oxford Paperbacks Publicity Man-
ager, Arts and Reference Publicity Department,
Oxford University Press, Walton Street, Oxford
OX2 6DP.

Customers in UK and Europe will find Oxford
Paperbacks available in all good bookshops. But in
case of difficulty please send orders to the Cash-
with-Order Department, Oxford University Press
Distribution Services, Saxon Way West, Corby,
Northants NN18 9ES. Tel: 0536 741519; Fax:
0536 746337. Please send a cheque for the total cost
of the books, plus £1.75 postage and packing for
orders under £20; £2.75 for orders over £20. Customers outside the UK should add 10% of the cost
of the books for postage and packing.

USA: Oxford Paperbacks Marketing Manager,
Oxford University Press, Inc., 200 Madison Av-
enue, New York, N.Y. 10016.

Canada: Trade Department, Oxford University
Press, 70 Wynford Drive, Don Mills, Ontario M3C
1J9.

Australia: Trade Marketing Manager, Oxford University Press, G.P.O. Box 2784Y, Melbourne 3001,
Victoria.

South Africa: Oxford University Press, P.O. Box
1141, Cape Town 8000.

ILLUSTRATED HISTORIES IN OXFORD PAPERBACKS

THE OXFORD ILLUSTRATED HISTORY OF ENGLISH LITERATURE

Edited by Pat Rogers

Britain possesses a literary heritage which is almost unrivalled in the Western world. In this volume, the richness, diversity, and continuity of that tradition are explored by a group of Britain's foremost literary scholars.

Chapter by chapter the authors trace the history of English literature, from its first stirrings in Anglo-Saxon poetry to the present day. At its heart towers the figure of Shakespeare, who is accorded a special chapter to himself. Other major figures such as Chaucer, Milton, Donne, Wordsworth, Dickens, Eliot, and Auden are treated in depth, and the story is brought up to date with discussion of living authors such as Seamus Heaney and Edward Bond.

'[a] lovely volume . . . put in your thumb and pull out plums' Michael Foot

'scholarly and enthusiastic people have written inspiring essays that induce an eagerness in their readers to return to the writers they admire' *Economist*